Internet Law for the Business Lawyer

Editors
David Reiter
Elizabeth Blumenfeld
Mark Boulding

Section of Business Law
American Bar Association

Defending Liberty
Pursuing Justice

The materials contained herein represent the opinions of the authors and editors and should not be construed to be the action of the American Bar Association or the Section of Business Law unless adopted pursuant to the bylaws of the Association.

Nothing contained in this book is to be considered as the rendering of legal advice for specific cases, and readers are responsible for obtaining such advice from their own legal counsel. This book is intended for educational and informational purposes only.

Library of Congress Cataloging-in-Publication Data

Internet law for the business lawyer / David Reiter, Elizabeth Blumenfeld, Mark Boulding, editors.
    p.cm.
  Includes bibliographical references.
  ISBN 1-57073-989-7 (softcover)
    1. Interactive multimedia—Law and legislation—United States. I. Reiter, David, 1967–
II. Blumenfeld, Elizabeth. III. Boulding, Mark.

  KF390.5.C6 I569 2001
  343.7309′944—dc21   2001046062

Cover design by Catherine Zaccarine

Discounts are available for books ordered in bulk. Special consideration is given to state and local bars, CLE programs, and other bar-related organizations. Inquire at Book Publishing, American Bar Association, 750 North Lake Shore Drive, Chicago, Illinois 60611

05 04 03 02 01   5 4 3 2 1

Summary of Contents

Contents

Chapter 4   Third-Party Content Liability

Chapter 8   Jurisdiction
By Margaret Stewart

Acknowledgments

A book on a new subject often takes a long time to write, leaving its editors with many to thank. Foremost among those in this case is the original editorial team of Amy Boss and David Phillips. Without their early vision, this volume would never have been produced. Coming in at a close second are Jeffrey Ritter and Tom Vartanian, the past and present chairs, respectively, of the ABA Business Law Section's Cyberspace Law Committee, whose enthusiasm for a project that at times looked like it would never finish was untiring. In addition to Jeffrey and Tom, Cyberspace Law Committee members who played supportive roles include Mike Dunne, Lenny Nuara, Scot Graydon, the entire membership of the Internet Law Subcommittee (the true parent of this book) and many others who we do not have the space to name. The editors particularly wish to thank those individuals on the Internet Law Subcommittee who volunteered for related efforts that were merged into this book, especially those who spent their valuable time and energy working on a never-published update to this book's predecessor volume, *Web Linking Agreements: Contracting Strategies and Model Provisions.* Of course, we also want to thank all of the authors of this book for giving so much of themselves. Without all of their hard work, this paragraph and everything that follows would not have been possible.

Finally, as editors and authors, we wish to acknowledge the support of our family and friends, as well as the various law firms, companies and other entities who employed us during the time we worked on this project. These people and organizations had the patience and consideration to allow each of us to work on a project that, at times, must have seemed very unrelated to our job descriptions or to putting bread on the table.

—*David Reiter, Elizabeth deGrazia Blumenfeld and Mark Boulding*

Foreword

In 1994 the Internet was not far removed from amateur radio in terms of the number and characteristics of the users and the technological hurdles that one faced to make use of it. Access to the Internet was most often accomplished through shell accounts that required the mastery of obscure Unix-based commands and the use of spartan software like the elm and pine newsreaders and e-mail clients. Even in the Internet's primitive era, it was clear that it had the potential to dramatically alter almost every facet of modern life. The Internet gave an ordinary user the ability to deliver views and opinions to thousands (who could even foretell millions) of people around the world. Someone in a small town in the American Midwest could access information from libraries in Prague and Tokyo and could peruse the collections of the Louvre (although doing so at 9600 baud required a comfortable chair and real endurance).

In only a few years, the Internet burst into the popular consciousness. Suddenly, everyone had an e-mail address, and dot-com became the suffix of choice. Many lawyers quickly realized that the unique attributes of the Internet would require new paradigms of legal thought, but the path was not well marked. In 1996, specially convened three-judge panels in New York and Philadelphia had to consider the constitutionality of the Communications Decency Act and, more importantly, gain an understanding of the medium the Act was meant to regulate. When the Supreme Court issued its opinions in *ACLU v. Reno* and *Shea v. Reno*, it invalidated the indecency provision of the Communications Decency Act. More significantly, the Court recognized that the Internet was a fascinating, new medium that gave ordinary users extraordinary powers to communicate with others and access information and was, thus, deserving of the highest levels of constitutional protections.

The rapid adoption of the Internet by consumers as a way to communicate, travel, shop and learn was not only forcing people to rethink their methods of doing business, but it was also forcing serious consideration of many novel legal issues. The effort to frame the correct legal paradigm for the Internet in those early days often involved the search for an appropriate analogy or metaphor. Was the Internet more like a library or a broadcast network? Were e-mail servers more like a gated community or a quasi-public shopping mall? Was the Internet more like a huge multi-lane interstate highway (I still wince when I hear people talk of the "information superhighway")?

Many early Internet lawyers would regularly fall back on the often-used but never proved bromide that the "old rules" did not apply to this new technology and suggested that the rules needed to be completely re-written. Providing false or misleading information to investors, however, is still a violation of the securities laws whether it is accomplished by whispers in the corridor or postings on a Yahoo! message board. It is just as illegal to e-mail child pornography as it is to use the U.S. mail to distribute it, and making untrue statements about someone online is as good a way to get sued for defamation as publishing those same comments in a magazine or newspaper. The real issue was the way that existing law and precedent should apply to this new medium, not whether it ought to.

The famous case of *Zeran v. America Online* is often cited as an inappropriate immunity from the defamation laws for Internet service providers. That misguided criticism ignores the central lesson of *Zeran*: that, in the age of the Internet, the defamation laws should be enforced against speakers, not from the ISPs who simply provided the technological tools for the speech. What is unique about the Internet and what has been expressed in *Zeran* and the line of cases that followed is that, unlike traditional media, there is a distinction between the speaker and the conduit. Speech over the Internet is not created in a centralized fashion and then disseminated to a broader audience (the broadcast or publication model); instead, it is created by users and disseminated to other users with no effective opportunity for pre-screening.

In 2001, more than 100 million Americans use the Internet every day, and they are joined by tens of millions more across the globe. The Internet has become a part of everyday life and a fixture in modern business. What has emerged is not a radical new set of rules to govern the Internet but sensible interpretations of existing principles that take account of the technological realities of the medium. The ancient tort of trespass to chattels has been updated to include the misuse of e-mail servers on the Internet. What drives the need to constantly re-interpret the legal paradigm is the relentless pace of technological innovation. Five years ago we pondered the application of the copyright laws to postings on message boards and newsgroups; now we try and decide how the copyright laws should treat peer-to-peer networks. Although much has been accomplished and settled, there is much that remains to be done and many questions that have yet to be asked, much less answered. There are many who think that we stand not at the end of the Internet era, but simply at the end of the first chapter. If that is true, the effort to adjust, revise and understand the legal framework of the Internet has also just begun.

Randall J. Boe
Executive Vice President and General Counsel
America Online, Inc.

Introduction

Growth of the Internet and Corresponding Changes in the Law

The Internet and electronic commerce have the potential to transform the world economy. Since its early inception in concept by the Defense Advanced Research Projects Agency (DARPA) in 1962, use of the Internet has steadily progressed over the past three decades. This growth has been particularly pronounced during the past decade, largely as a result of the development of the world wide web.[1] From 1996 through September 2000 alone, the estimated number of worldwide users increased from less than 40 million to approximately 380 million.[2]

The growth rates are even more promising for the future. Most of the growth in the late 1990s occurred in the United States. By 2003, Forrester Research predicts that 40 million households will be shopping online, spending more than $108 billion while there.[3] As Internet access charges continue to drop outside the U.S., the number of users is likely to grow even more quickly outside of the U.S. and worldwide. Already, there are more users outside of the U.S. than within it.[4] The number of users is also likely to explode as more and more wireless users begin to access the web with broadband and wireless technologies.

This unprecedented growth brings with it an increase in legal issues and challenges. The advent of more commercial applications and of internationalization of the Internet has made this increase even more pronounced. The new

---

1. *NUA Internet Surveys, cited in* U.S. DEPARTMENT OF COMMERCE, THE EMERGING DIGITAL ECONOMY 2 n. 4 (April 1998) <http://www.esa.doc.gov>; NUA, *How Many Online?* (Sept. 2000) <http://www.nua.net/surveys/how_many_online/index.html>.
2. *Id.*
3. *Forrester Research, cited in* ACTIVEMEDIA RESEARCH, Mar. 12, 1999, <http://www.activemediareserch.com/magic/t_top100list.html>.
4. Press Release, EMarketer, eMarketer Releases the eGlobal March 2000 Report, <http://www.emarketer.com/aboutus/press/032800_global.html>.

communication medium that the Internet represents has pushed application of existing law to its limits, created the need to review issues never considered, and forced compromise among jurisdictions with dramatically different philosophies on certain legal issues. Each of these trends will become quite clear to the reader of this book.

Another point that this book highlights is that the law, as it is applied in an online environment, is only just developing. In fact, certain jurisdictions have not even pushed off the starting blocks. For example, with the exception of children online, there is essentially no U.S. federal law for Internet privacy at this point. However, various members of Congress have continued to press the Internet privacy issue by presenting numerous online privacy bills over the last several years. With the change in administration, whether or not there will be privacy legislation passed in the next Congress is anybody's guess. Another example highlighting the infancy of Internet law is that that most jurisdictions worldwide have not yet determined how to tax transactions occurring on the Internet. Although there are many reasons for this slow development in key areas of the law, it is important to note that this law will develop over the next decade. Moreover, in order to effectively counsel clients on the law applicable to the Internet, it is important to understand the current state of the law, its philosophical basis, and the forces that are likely to mold future laws.

Purpose of This Book

We had several purposes in mind when preparing this book. First and foremost, this book is intended as a tool for the general business practitioner. In each chapter the reader will find that the author provides a thorough, but concise, update of the law in his or her topic area. The chapters not only provide a review of the law but also a tremendous amount of practical advice, ranging from compliance plan recommendations for recent changes in the law to advice on how to construct online transaction provisions.

Because this book focuses on the general practitioner, we have avoided use of technical jargon and legal affectations. Additionally, this book is not intended as a treatise in a particular area being discussed. Throughout this book you will find that authors cite additional sources that provide a greater level of analysis, and we encourage those interested in more granular detail to use the bibliography at the end of the book. We have also provided a glossary near the end of the book to provide an explanation of terms with which you may be unfamiliar.

This book covers a broad range of topics. In fact, we have tried to address all major legal topic areas that a general practitioner might face when supporting a client doing business on the Internet. We have also highlighted areas of inevitable change, such as privacy self-regulation, in anticipation of changes in the law, even where they do not currently exist.

The book largely has a domestic focus, although there are certain topic areas where the jurisdictional focus is much broader. With that said, we have provided foreign analysis where we believed it was critical to the understanding of a particular topic area, such as where there have been international agreements that impact domestic practices. Privacy is an excellent example of this type of topic area, where the "Safe Harbor" provisions developed jointly by the U.S. and the European Union will have a substantial impact on certain U.S. companies. We also have taken this approach with the chapters on Taxation and Jurisdiction. We would have liked to provide a global review in all topic areas, but space limitations simply would simply not permit us this luxury.

Because of the importance of this publication to a broad audience of readers, we have made every effort to recruit the leading authorities in their respective areas to write in their area of expertise. In addition, we asked our authors to update their chapters several times to ensure that all analysis considered the most recent changes in the laws at the time of publication. Beyond the authors, the acknowledgments section at the beginning of this book also identifies the many individuals who were critical in assuring that this publication is of a very high quality. We are confident that you will find the level of analysis and guidance extremely useful to your practice. We anticipate providing supplements and, as such, welcome feedback on chapters. Please contact one of us if you would like to make suggestions.

Summary of Chapters

The eight chapters to this book focus on the most relevant Internet legal topics currently facing the general practitioner. A brief description of each chapter is provided below. You will also find a more detailed content description at the beginning of each chapter.

Chapter 1.   The Online Landscape addresses the history of the Internet, exploring its conceptual underpinnings. It also evaluates where the Internet is likely to head in coming years. This chapter is an excellent means of gaining a general understanding of the current state of the online environment and its future direction.

Chapter 2.   Intellectual Property addresses the fundamental principles of patents, copyrights, trademarks and trade secrets as they relate to the Internet. Statutory and case law developments are evaluated to advise the reader on the current and likely future state of the law. Practical advice is provided to the reader on how to protect these intellectual property rights and how to avoid infringement.

Chapter 3.   Web Transactions addresses transactions involving the Internet. This chapter covers a wide variety of substantive areas, so it will be useful to the reader to understand how it has been organized. There are five substantive areas that are addressed: licensing transactions, development/linking agreements, joint ventures, advertising transactions and electronic transactions.

Chapter 4.   Third-Party Content Liability addresses how liability arises as a result of the distribution of content online. A multitude of issues are explored in this chapter ranging from defamation to obscenity to infringement claims. U.S. and European treatment of this subjected matter is evaluated separately. Practical advice is provided to the reader on how to mitigate the risk of claims arising in this area.

Chapter 5.   Regulation addresses regulation of the Internet, including both criminal and noncriminal behavior. This chapter focuses primarily on U.S. law. Given the scope and depth of applicable U.S. regulations, we believe that this analysis is more likely to be useful to our audience. The reader should be aware that many foreign jurisdictions either apply existing law or have developed new regulations applicable to an online context.

Chapter 6.   Taxation addresses how taxes are incurred in transactions occurring online. The focus is on U.S. federal, state and local developments in this area. A summary is also provided of the state of several international jurisdictions, including the European Union and key Asia and Pacific countries. Fundamental differences in the treatment of taxation as it applies to the Internet among the various jurisdictions will become apparent to the reader.

Chapter 7.   Information Practices addresses information practices as they relate to the Internet. Three primary topics are discussed. The first section focuses on the state of U.S. law as it relates to privacy. The second segment of this chapter evaluates European treatment of privacy, including the European philosophy toward privacy and how it dramatically differs from U.S. approaches. The final segment of this chapter focuses on anonymity and encryption, and how each can be used as tools to obtain the desired security and privacy online.

Chapter 8.   Jurisdiction addresses how jurisdiction and venue are established in an online environment. This chapter evaluates the application of existing principles of establishing jurisdiction and how they are applied in the context of the Internet. Particular attention is paid to U.S. and European Union treatment of this subject matter.

Bibliography.   For those seeking a more detailed treatment of a particular topic area, you will find a topical bibliography at the end of the book.

Glossary.   The book contains a short glossary that lists key terms, italicized in text, used in this publication.

Topical Index.   This book also provides a topical index for quick and easy reference to any particular topic area of interest.

About the Authors.   Please see this section to read about the backgrounds and expertise of the authors of each chapter.

The Online Landscape

Contents

By Elliot E. Maxwell, Patricia A. Buckley, Sabrina L. Montes
and Amanda J. Mills

The Online Landscape*

The excitement generated by the Internet reflects the immense power of this latest step in network development. The Internet was conceived and developed with the same spirit of collaboration and cooperation that it now fosters. This network of networks stands in stark contrast to the public telecommunication networks that had slowly developed under central control and to private telecommunication networks that served limited groups of users. The Internet as it has emerged is fundamentally decentralized and open. It offers a communications medium to people all over the globe, from all walks of life, using all kinds of devices, uniform only in its enabling protocols.

As the technologies underlying the Internet evolve, the possibilities continue to expand. Anyone with Internet access can now obtain more information than was available to the most powerful potentate of the past. Anyone with Internet access can invent a new application and make that innovation available to all 400 million users within moments, without notifying or seeking permission from a controlling authority. Anyone with Internet access can create a work of art and immediately have the world as a potential audience.

Even with the incredible advances of the past few years, we continue to be surprised on an almost daily basis by new applications and functionality. And there is no reason to believe that the Internet's ability to evolve is nearing its limit. On the contrary, the rapid rate at which technology continues to advance—feeding a process of relentless innovation—increases the likelihood that we are only at the beginning stages of the process.

This chapter, authored by Elliot E. Maxwell, Patricia A. Buckley, Sabrina L. Montes and Amanda J. Mills, discusses the beginnings and future course of the Internet. Section 1.1 explains the development of the Internet, Section 1.2 discusses some of the technological advances that have facilitated the growth of the Internet, and Sections 1.3 and 1.4 observe the possibilities attending Internet use in the future.

§ 1.1 Foundations: Origins of the Internet

The Internet, because of its open architecture, digital format and unifying protocols, has emerged as *the* platform to support increased connectivity and in-

---

* The views expressed in this chapter are those of the authors and do not necessarily reflect the view of any other employee or entity of the U.S. government.

teraction among disparate networks.[1] Since its inception, it has been a platform upon which users could develop and share innovative applications as long as the applications used the basic Internet protocols. In its openness and digital foundation, and in the capabilities that it offered to users at the network's edge, it was a radical departure from previous communications networks. Nobody controlled it, in the sense of a central authority determining how the bandwidth was allocated, who could connect to it, the kinds of devices that could be attached to it or the applications that could run on it.

The concept that developed into the Internet was proposed in 1962 as a project of the U.S. Defense Advanced Research Projects Agency (DARPA) to develop an interconnected network of computers. Work began in 1966 on the network that became known as ARPANET. One goal of the original project was a network that was resilient to the breakdown or destruction of portions of the network. The architecture developed to meet this challenge was based upon packet switching. Data were divided into small, individually addressed "packets" and routed separately through the network (and around problems) to be reassembled at the specified destination.[2]

By 1969, computers at the Los Angeles and Santa Barbara campuses of the University of California, Stanford Research Institute and the University of Utah were connected to one another via ARPANET. Additional computers (hosts) were connected to the network over the next few years until the ARPANET went global with the addition of European hosts.

By the early 1970s, the advantages of being able to interconnect other networks with the ARPANET became evident. In 1972, while working at DARPA, Bob Kahn established the four ground rules that still define the open-architecture networking environment of the Internet:

- Each distinct network would have to stand on its own and no internal changes could be required to connect it to the Internet.
- Communications would be on a best-effort basis without any guarantee of completion. If a packet did not make it to the final destination, it would shortly be retransmitted from the source.
- Black boxes would be used to connect the networks. There would be no information retained by the gateways about the individual flows of packets

---

1. Computers and computer storage use digital formats, and the networks in which they operate are digital networks. This is an important distinction between present and past technologies, as well as an underlying reason for the seemingly sudden interoperability of formerly distinct technologies. Because images, sound, text and video can all be digitized, boundaries between formerly distinct networks are fading and opportunities for interoperability are increasing. Telephone, cable and broadcast radio and television networks were created to transmit specific types of information, but as these networks migrate to digital formats, there are fewer technological reasons for differing public policy treatment of the networks based solely upon the type of media—text, images, video or voice—transmitted over them. Digital networks—whether the underlying medium is twisted-pair copper wire, coaxial cable, optical fiber strands, terrestrial wireless (mobile or fixed), satellite or some combination—make no a priori distinction about whether the bits and bytes of data traveling over them are text, voice or images. To a digital network, a bit is a bit.
2. An added benefit is that packet switching is much more efficient for transmitting data than circuit switching.

passing through them, thereby keeping them simple and avoiding complicated adaptation and recovery from various failure modes.
• There would be no global control at the operations level.[3]

The following year, Bob Kahn and Vint Cerf developed a communications protocol based upon these ground rules, which would support the needs of open-architecture networking—the Transmission Control Protocol/Internet Protocol (TCP/IP).[4] The ARPANET adopted this protocol, as did many new networks. It was this voluntary adoption of a common communications protocol that allowed various computer networks to connect with each other, leading to the "creation" of the Internet.[5] The creation process was formalized when the National Science Foundation (NSF) created NSFNET to serve as a nationwide backbone for the Internet in 1986.

As the number of hosts connected to the Internet rose, it became necessary to devise an addressing system. In the early days of ARPANET, when the number of hosts was still small, names were assigned to each host so that users did not need to remember the underlying numeric addresses. When maintaining a single list of assigned host names became too unwieldy, a hierarchical system—the Domain Name System (DNS)—was created to link host names to their underlying numerical Internet addresses.[6]

When it established NSFNET, NSF limited use to noncommercial activity. In 1991, NSF lifted these restrictions, and an association of commercial Internet providers was formed to help organize the flow of traffic on the network. By 1995, when NSFNET ended its sponsorship of the Internet backbone, commercial backbone networks were extensive enough to enable network users to route online traffic from one commercial site to another.[7]

Applications developed by the early users were quickly disseminated over the Internet. Two of these in particular, the World Wide Web and web browsers, had a profound impact on the development of the Internet and played key roles in expanding its reach beyond its initial user base of academics and government researchers.

The Web—released in 1991 by Tim Berners-Lee, a researcher at the Center for European Nuclear Research (Centre Europen le Recherche Nucleaire, CERN) in Geneva, Switzerland—facilitated access to information over a TCP/IP network using hypertext, a database system that enables objects such as text, graphics and

---

3. Barry M. Leiner et al., *A Brief History of the Internet*, Version 3.31 (revised Apr. 14, 2000) <http://www.isoc.org/internet/history/brief.html>.

4. *Id.*

5. Although we often speak of "the Internet" as if it were a single network, it is not. It is a network of networks that have been "internetworked"—thus the name, "Internet."

6. The Domain Name System was created by Paul Mockapetris. *See* Leiner et al., *supra* note 3.

7. In 1979, CompuServe began offering the first dial-up access to the Internet, and in the early 1980s, commercial and educational entities developed other networks such as BITNET and CSNET to provide networking services to those researchers and scientists without access to ARPANET. In 1985, Quantum Computer Services (which became America Online) introduced its first dial-up service, Q-Link, for Commodore Business Machines.

programs to be linked to one another. In creating the Web, Berners-Lee developed the Hypertext Markup Language (HTML), which is still the primary authoring language used to create documents for the Web. The creation of the Web gave the Internet vast new capabilities as a medium for publishing and retrieving information and reduced the cost of developing client-server software for these purposes.

In 1993, the National Center for Supercomputing Applications (NCSA) introduced a web browser—Mosaic—that provided a graphical front-end for the World Wide Web. By enabling users to navigate through the network by clicking on graphics and "links," rather than typing complex text commands to move between web pages, Mosaic made the Internet far easier for nontechnical people to use.

Complementing these technological advances was the increase in the number of firms offering local-dial Internet access. Competition among these firms led to reduced costs and spurred the availability of flat-rate pricing schemes.[8]

The number of home and business Internet users began to grow rapidly as the Internet became easier to access and cheaper to use. This growth accelerated increases in the value that accrued to Internet users from *network effects*—the increase in the value of the network to all its users, which occurs as the number of network participants increases.[9] Having the ability to send e-mail is not of much use if those you wish to contact are not reachable on the network. On the other hand, the more people you can reach, the more valuable the network becomes.

In addition to these network effects, the growing Internet offered a second advantage. As David Reed has noted,

> Group forming is . . . the technical feature that most distinguishes the Internet's capabilities from all other communications media before it. Beyond either the hub-and-spokes broadcast networks of print, television, and radio, or the peer transactional networks of telegraph, telephone, and online financial transactions, the Internet's architecture also supports group-forming networks whose members can assemble and maintain persistent communicating groups.[10]

This allows a dramatic increase in communities of interest. Networks provide a space and means, according to John Seely Brown, for "the cross-fertilization of people in different types of research centers, universities, companies, factory

---

8. These users relied heavily upon telephone-based dial-up connections where state-of-the-art connection speed was 14.4 kilobytes per second (kb/sec). Even today, the vast majority of users connect to the Internet with dial-up modems limited to 56 kb/sec.

9. The growth of value of the network as related to the growth in its number of users is known as Metcalfe's Law. Metcalfe's Law suggests that the value of the network increases roughly with the square of the number of participants (at the rate of n^2-n, when n is the number of participants). CARL SHAPIRO & HAL VARIAN, INFORMATION RULES: A STRATEGIC GUIDE TO THE NETWORK ECONOMY 183–84 (1998).

10. Reed's Law—An Interview, J. OF HYPERLINKED ORGANIZATIONS, (Jan. 19, 2001), <http://www.hyperorg.com/backissues/joho-jan19-01.html>.

floors—anywhere things are getting discovered," allowing them to aggregate into communities of interest and collaborate.[11]

The growth of the Internet is the best evidence of the value it offers its users. On a worldwide basis, the estimated number of users increased from fewer than 40 million in 1996 to approximately 400 million as of November 2000.[12] As of January 2001, there were almost 110 million hosts on the Internet, up from 56 million in July 1999[13] (and up from the original four in 1969). Inktomi, a software applications company, estimates that the number of unique web pages had surpassed 1 billion in early 2000; other analysts claim that the Web is much larger and is growing at a rate of 2 to 7 million web pages per day.[14]

Until recently, much of the growth took place in North America, which has low Internet access costs compared with most of the rest of the world. Not only does this make it possible for more individuals and organizations in the United States to have Internet access, but it also encourages others to locate servers and hosting facilities here. Although the flow of traffic over the Internet does not matter to most users (users are usually unaware of the paths their communications travel), it has raised issues surrounding the commercial arrangements that are made for carrying Internet traffic.

The Web is becoming more global. The United States no longer accounts for the majority of individuals online. Similarly, although English remains the predominant language of the Web, there has been a dramatic increase in the use of other languages.

§ 1.2 Advancing Technological Capabilities

The development of the Internet did not occur in a vacuum. As it was emerging, the technologies underlying it—technologies for data processing, storage and

11. Michael Schrage, *John Seely Brown*, WIRED, Aug. 2000, at 204 <http://www.wired.com/wired/archive/8.08/brown.html>.

12. *NUA Internet Surveys, cited in* U.S. DEP'T OF COMMERCE, THE EMERGING DIGITAL ECONOMY 2 n.4 (Apr. 1998) <http://www.esa.doc.gov>; NUA, *How Many Online?* (November 2000) <http://www.nua.net/surveys/how_many_online/index.html>.

13. Internet Software Consortium, *Internet Domain Survey* (July 1999) <http://www.isc.org/ds/WWW-9907/report.html>; Internet Software Consortium, *Internet Domain Survey* (January 2001) <http://www.isc.org/ds/WWW-200101/index.html>.

14. Inktomi, *Inktomi WebMap* (Jan. 2000) (press release) <http://www.inktomi.com/webmap>; David Lake, *The Web: Growing by 2 Million Pages a Day*, THE INDUSTRY STANDARD, Feb. 28, 2000, <http://www.thestandard.com/research/metrics/display/0,2799,12329,00.html>. In a July 2000 study, Cyveillance estimated there were 2 billion web pages, and that same month BrightPlanet released a report stating there were 550 billion web pages. *See* Cyveillance, *Internet Exceeds 2 Billion Pages* (July 10, 2000) (press release) <http://www.cyveilance.com/newsroom/pressr/000710.asp>; BrightPlanet, *The Deep Web: Surfacing Hidden Value* (July 2000) <http://www.completeplanet.com/Tutorials/DeepWeb/index.asp>.

transport—were undergoing cycles of rapid improvement. These advances continue and will offer users a range of new technology-enabled capabilities in the future.

1. Advances in Communications

As the U.S. telecommunications market has become more competitive, and the demand for faster connections to the Internet has grown, the cost of data transport has fallen and the availability of broadband communications has risen. Deployed bandwidth has tripled every year since 1995, and industry experts estimate that this pace will continue until 2020.[15]

The deployment of fiber optics further into the network and, over the longer term, the deployment of a broadband wireless infrastructure, are likely to provide dramatic increases in end-to-end bandwidth. The carrying capacity, for example, of fiber-optic cable—which was first employed in high-volume long-distance transport links—is doubling every twelve months, reducing the cost per bit of throughput.[16] Optical networks have become more efficient and, rather than carrying a single wavelength, are able to carry multiple wavelengths, thereby greatly increasing capacity.

Although fiber is already used throughout the long-distance infrastructure, it has not yet been used extensively for the "last-mile" connection to homes, due to its relatively high installation and component costs. But even with its high cost, fiber deployment continues its expansion from the backbone toward the edges of the network. It is being implemented in wide-area networks in many metropolitan areas. In some cases (mostly new installations), providers deliver residential broadband services directly into the home via fiber. In other cases, known as *fiber-to-the-curb*, service is provided to a neighborhood connection point or node by fiber optics; homes are then connected to the node with copper wire or coaxial cable. Because of the now-shortened distance between the residence and the point of interconnection, copper and coaxial cable can deliver high-speed data. In addition, in response to greater competition, and to satisfy growing demand for faster Internet access, some providers are upgrading their existing infrastructures, such as copper-wire telephone networks and cable television networks, to deliver interactive broadband service.

Increasing broadband connectivity is only one way that the capabilities of the communications infrastructure are expanding. Important new technologies, such as optical switches, are currently under development. Optical switches,

---

15. Jim Gray & Prashant Shenoy, *Rules of Thumb in Data Engineering, Microsoft Research Technical Report* (Dec. 1999, revised Mar. 2000) <http://www.research.microsoft.com/~gray>.

16. David Clark, senior research scientist at MIT's Laboratory for Computer Science, *cited in* Jeff Hecht, *Wavelength Division Multiplexing*, Tech. Rev., Mar./Apr. 1999, at 72 <http://www.techreview.com/magazine/ma99/hecht.htm>.

when deployed, will enable optical networks to achieve increased network throughput because they can handle thousands of wavelengths, eliminate optical-electric connections and automate the process of configuring the wavelengths on the network.[17]

2. Advances in Processing Power and Storage

Rapid advances in processing power and data storage are also driving the Internet's expansion. The ability to process digital information has grown at an astounding rate and processor performance continues to double approximately every eighteen months, following *Moore's Law*.[18] This extraordinary advance in processing power has come at even lower costs. Prices have fallen at an average annual rate of twenty-four percent in the computer industry and twenty-nine percent in the semiconductor industry.[19]

Less widely known is that the ability to store information has more than kept pace with the ability to process it. "Today disk capacities are doubling every nine months, fast outpacing advances in computer chips. . . ."[20] These advances have also come at decreasing costs. "[T]he average price per megabyte for hard-disk drives fell from $11.54 in 1988 to $0.04 in 1998, and an estimated $0.02 in 1999. Industry analysts forecast that it will be as low as $0.003 per megabyte by 2003."[21]

Even as processing power and storage density continue to increase dramatically amid steeply falling costs, there are physical limits to the present technology. The rising cost of the continued scaling down of microelectronics and the skyrocketing cost of fabrication facilities may limit the additional amount of processing power that can be cost effectively squeezed onto today's silicon chip.[22] Similar difficulties are expected to occur in the current storage technologies such as magnetic hard-disk storage technology.

But we are likely to continue to make progress in all these areas through the accumulation of many small improvements in current technologies. We are also

---

17. Peter Heywood, *Optical Networking in Five Easy Pieces*, Bus. Comm. Rev., May 2000, at 54 <http://www.bcr.com/bcrmag/2000/05/p54.asp>.

18. Gordon Moore, *The Continuing Silicon Technology Evolution inside the PC Platform*, 2 Platform Solutions (Oct. 15, 1997) <http://developer.intel.com/update/archive/issue2/feature.htm>.

19. U.S. Dep't of Commerce, Digital Economy 2000 25 (June 2000) <http://www.esa.doc.gov>.

20. Jon William Toigo, *Avoiding a Data Crunch*, Sci. Am., May 2000, at 58 <http://www.sciam.com/2000/0500issue/0500toig.html>.

21. *Id.*

22. Intel estimates that the company will reach the physical limitations of wafer fabrication technology in 2017. *See* Moore, *supra* note 18. As more transistors are packed onto a chip, phenomena such as stray signals, the need to dissipate the heat and the difficulty of creating the devices in the first place will halt or severely slow progress. Experts predict that around 2015, a fabrication facility will cost nearly $200 billion, which will put an end to the advances in the processing power of computer chips based upon current technologies. *See* Mark A. Reed & James M. Tour, *Computing with Molecules*, Sci. Am., June 2000, at 86 <http://www.scientificamerican.com/2000/0600issue/0600reed.html>.

likely to see the substitution of new technologies that may outpace even the extraordinary advances we have seen so far. Nanotechnology, the field of research focusing on building structures at a molecular level, is anticipated to enable the fabrication of a new generation of computer hardware that is cleaner, stronger, lighter and more precise.[23] For example, it may soon be possible to store the contents of a digital videodisc in a space smaller than a conventional semiconductor chip.[24] With circuits built on a molecular scale, nanotechnology holds the potential to decrease the size of devices dramatically—allowing what some call smart dust.[25]

3. Software Developments Driving New Capabilites

Software is playing an important role in employing the enhanced capabilities of processing, storage and communications technologies. A new environment is emerging that will increase interactivity among various computing devices and applications.

i. Distributed Computing

Software development has made possible massively *distributed computing*, sometimes known as *community computing*. In distributed computing, computers are linked together to work on shared projects when they are not engaged in local tasks. This approach provides a cost-effective way to tackle large processing projects because it allows many computers—networked via the Internet—to work simultaneously on different parts of a single processing project.

Community-computing projects have rapidly solved computation problems that some observers estimated would take years. In 1997, for example, RSA Security, a leading encryption software vendor, issued an open challenge to test

---

23. Ralph C. Merkle, *Nanotechnology Web Site* (visited Mar. 23, 2000) <http://www.zyvx.com>.

24. John Markoff, *Computer Scientists Are Poised for Revolution on a Tiny Scale*, N.Y. TIMES, Nov. 1, 1999, at C1 <http://www.nytimes.com/library/tech/99/11/biztech/articles/01nano.html>.

25. Nanotechnology was envisioned decades ago and thought to have the potential for commercial applications later in the twenty-first century, but recently—far outpacing the most optimistic forecasts—the research has progressed to where there is potential for near-term commercial developments. Two separate teams of researchers have announced the successful development of rudimentary molecular logic gates—the fundamental component of an electronic device. Mark Reed and James Tour, writing for *Scientific American*, put the scale of potential nanotechnology computer hardware into perspective by noting that, if the conventional transistor were scaled up so that it occupied a page of *Scientific American*, a molecular device would be the period at the end of a sentence. They predict that "[e]ven in a dozen years when industry projections suggest that silicon transistors will have shrunk to about 120 nanometers in length, they will still be more than 60,000 times larger in area than molecular electronic devices." *See* Leander Kahney, *Quantum Leap in Computing*, WIRED NEWS, Mar. 23, 2000 <http://www.wired.com/news/technology/0,1282,35121,00.html>; Markoff, *supra* note 24; Reed & Tour, *supra* note 22.

its state-of-the-art 56-bit encryption technology. In March 1997, a group established distributed.net and began recruiting volunteers to begin testing the 72,057,594,037,927,936 possible keys. By October, the key had been found by the distributed.net community, which had grown to 4,000 active teams of volunteers using a "combined computing power equivalent to more than 26,000 high-end personal computers."[26] It may not be long before commercial projects are developed to take advantage of the 70% of the typical workstation's capacity that presently sits idle.[27] In fact a coalition including the National Foundation for Cancer Research and Oxford University has begun recruiting volunteer machines to compare molecules to targeted proteins, searching for possible anti-cancer drugs.

ii. Peer-to-Peer Networking

The potential to link computers and take advantage of improved processing, storage and transport can also be seen in recent developments in peer-to-peer (P2P) networking, which extends and develops one of the earliest Internet applications—data file transfer.[28] These programs are different from client-server-based web sites that provide for downloading of digital files (a many-to-one model), in that the files are not stored centrally on servers; instead the files of interest are located on the hard drives of the individual computers that are participating in the network (a many-to-many model). The content available to the network participants depends upon which participant computers are logged on the network.

Some have speculated that peer-to-peer computing will be the next Internet revolution.[29] The most prominent of the programs that enable peer-to-peer networking is Napster (which is distributed by a company of the same name).

26. Distributed.net, *Press Kit* (Nov. 26, 1999) <http://www.distributed.net/pressroom/presskit.html>; Distributed.net, *Secure Encryption Challenged by Internet-Linked Computers* (Oct. 22, 1997) (press release and background sheet) <http://www.distributed.net/pressroom/56-PR.html>. Another example of distributed computing is the SETI@home project, an offshoot of the Search for Extraterrestrial Intelligence (SETI). It is the largest cooperative computing effort underway today. It links about 2 million computers worldwide in an effort to analyze the 50 gigabytes of data collected by SETI's radio telescopes each day. Each computer in the SETI@home project is given part of the intercepted radio signals to analyze when it is not otherwise occupied. *See* Howard Rheingold, *You Got the Power*, WIRED, Aug. 2000, at 176 <http://www.wired.com/ wired/>.

27. Patrick P. Gelsinger, Peer to Peer—The Next Computing Frontier, Keynote Address at the Intel Developer Forum (Aug. 24, 2000) <http://www.intel.com/pressroom/archive/speeches/pg082400.htm>.

28. Professor Lawrence Lessig, Expert Report Pursuant to Federal Rule of Civil Procedure 26(a)(2)(B), at 7–8, in A&M Records, Inc. v. Napster Inc., Jerry Leiber v. Napster, Inc., Nos. C 99–5183 MHP (ADR), C 00–0074 MHP (ADR) (June 2000).

29. For example, officials at Intel's Fall 2000 Developers' Forum described peer-to-peer networking as revolutionary, with important implications for business use. Intel, *Peer-to-Peer Technology: Backgrounder* (Aug. 2000) (Intel Developers' Forum virtual press kit) <http://www.intel.com/pressroom/kits/events/ idf_fall_2000/#backgrounders>. *See also* John Borland et al., *The P2P Myth* (Oct. 26, 2000) <http:// news.cnet.com/news/0–1005–201–3248711–0.html>.

Napster was developed to enable users to contribute to, and retrieve from, a centralized directory of available MP3 files (a compressed-file format popular for storing digital music). However, after being sued by intellectual property rights holders, Napster has been forced to change its free online service.

Napster, however, was not a "pure" peer-to-peer networking program, as it relied upon a central registry of available song titles. Other types of music-swapping software, such as Gnutella and Freenet, have no centralized directories and have no directly associated companies to distribute the software. The Freenet software even provides complete anonymity for those posting and transferring files.[30] Peer-to-peer systems are not limited to exchanging MP3 music files; they allow for the transfer of other types of data files, including text and video. Because peer-to-peer networking requires the ability to search other computers on a network remotely, it has sparked privacy and security concerns in addition to the well-publicized intellectual property rights issues.

Although peer-to-peer technology is most commonly used for trading music files, it could potentially challenge search engines, portals and other technologies that are aimed at helping Internet users find information. The technology also enables project participants to create a network for a specific project and rapidly dissolve it when the project ends. This type of networking also could have important businesses uses allowing enterprises to share information, processing cycles and storage, particularly within an organization's private, firewall-protected network. Numerous issues—including access to bandwidth, developing common protocols, interoperability, scalability, security, privacy and ease of use—must be resolved.

iii. The Rise of Untethered Computing

Industry analysts estimate that the number of mobile-phone customers will reach 500 million worldwide by 2003 and that 75% of those phones will be Internet-enabled.[31] Some suggest that by 2004 more people will access the Internet from a wireless device than from a wired one[32] and that by 2005, 50% of wireless traffic will be data rather than voice traffic.[33] Increasingly, therefore, PCs will share the Internet with web-enabled mobile phones, handheld computers, personal digital assistants and cars that have IP addresses and wireless

---

30. Freenet was created by Ian Clark, a strong advocate for freedom of expression, who developed the software to allow for dissemination of material without government censorship. *See* Adam Cohen & Chris Taylor, *The Infoanarchist*, TIME, June 26, 2000, at 46.

31. WAP Forum, *Momentum for Wireless Application Protocol Continues to Surge* (Feb. 2000) (press release) <http://www.wapforum.org/news/200020969MOM.htm>.

32. Motorola, *cited in* MERRILL LYNCH, A DAY IN THE FUTURE: THE FUTURE OF WIRELESS DATA 6 (Apr. 4, 2000).

33. Lucent, *cited in* MERRILL LYNCH, A DAY IN THE FUTURE: THE FUTURE OF WIRELESS DATA 6 (Apr. 4, 2000).

access to the Internet. The increased use of mobile Internet devices is likely to change the way we use the Internet in ways that are not easily foreseen in today's PC-centric networking environment.

Today's mobile Internet is most advanced in Europe and Japan where telecommunications companies are developing and deploying wireless Internet based upon two different models—the Wireless Application Protocol (WAP) model in Europe and the Japanese i-mode model. WAP is a protocol developed by a consortium of companies (which includes most of the leading firms in the global communications technology sector) to enable mobile Internet applications developers, carriers and content providers to have a uniform programming model and language (wireless markup language or WML) for the development of mobile Internet applications.[34] I-mode is a service offered by NTT DoCoMo, the wireless subsidiary of NTT, Japan's dominant and partially government-owned telecommunications company. I-mode is a proprietary product based upon HTML, the present language of today's web pages.

Mobile Internet may converge upon a single protocol, or develop via multiple noncompatible networks to be bridged by multimode devices—a tradeoff between reaching agreement on a standard and allowing technology to achieve the same practical result. Although some make strong arguments for the development of a single technical standard, there are many instances in which multiple technical standards coexist and compete.[35] Multimode phones, for example, although more expensive than single-mode phones, provide a bridge between the differing second-generation standards. Companies even now are developing multimode phones compatible with the underlying technologies of both WAP and i-mode.[36]

Early WAP and i-mode users made heavy use of entertainment-oriented applications, such as peer-to-peer short-message services (a wireless application similar to PC-based instant messaging) widely used by teenagers to communicate with each other. The growth of mobile Internet access and "always-on" connections, however, is encouraging developers to focus on new applications, such as location-based services. Now that entire Global Positioning System (GPS) systems are available on a single chip, they will likely become ubiquitous in mobile devices. Services that combine mobility and location (enabling a user to find the nearest location of a store or enabling a store to deliver promotions to nearby wireless users) are forecasted to be popular, but they also raise substantial privacy concerns, as a user's location can always be determined.

---

34. WAP Forum, *supra* note 31.

35. Many believe the development of a single protocol will speed the deployment of wireless Internet access by reducing the risks and cost for manufacturers and service providers. But achieving a cooperative standard—as can be seen in the development of second-generation wireless systems around the world—is a difficult process because of the large financial stakes and the aggressive competition among players with differing approaches. Some analysts believe that the absence of a standard slowed the development of wireless networks in the United States. Others believe that choice in wireless technology led to the development of a better technological standard—Code Division Multiple Access (CDMA).

36. David Pringle, *NTT's i-mode Mobile Web a Hit in Japan, Will Take on Rival WAP in Europe*, WALL ST. J., June 5, 2000, at A13.

Mobile commerce will likely dramatically expand and increase in importance. But the types of Internet transactions that can readily be accomplished
using mobile devices are constrained by the limitations of the devices and the
characteristics of the mobile environment. Mobile Internet access devices are
currently subject to technical constraints such as limited battery life, relatively
small visual displays, low data rates and the accompanying need for simplicity
(mobile users are unlikely to tolerate complex menus and multiple clicks to get
to needed information) and problems with maintaining connectivity in a mobile environment (which is technically more challenging than in a fixed or hard-
wired environment).[37]

At present, wireless Internet access, both mobile and fixed, is constrained
by the bandwidth limitations of existing wireless networks. This constraint is
likely to ease significantly in coming years as wireless broadband—also called
third-generation wireless (3G) and Universal Mobile Telecommunications Systems (UMTS)—is developed and deployed. Most existing mobile networks
have slow data download speeds of only 9.6 to 14.4 kilobits per second, which
translates into the ability to download only a few lines of text per second. The
broadband wireless networks under development may enable data rates of 384
kilobits per second or more, essentially enabling the delivery of video to a
wireless device in real time with an always-on connection.[38]

The governments of various countries have begun distributing licenses for
the 2-gigahertz band radio frequency spectrum used to deliver broadband wireless service, even as companies have begun experimenting with broadband wireless in unlicensed bands. The prices paid for these licenses greatly outstripped
projections.[39] There has been debate about whether the high cost of the licenses
will delay the rollout (as companies rethink their business plans to accommodate the greater-than-anticipated license costs) or accelerate it (as companies
come under enormous pressure to obtain quick returns on their 3G license
investments), but it is clear that major players have been prepared to invest
billions of dollars to obtain the licenses and are facing even more billions to
deploy the requisite networks. These investments are premised upon the economics of as-yet-to-be-defined services—services that obviously will have to
be superior to today's income-generating services that do not require broadband. In the meanwhile, much cheaper transitional technologies (termed 2.5G)
are being developed and deployed. Critical issues associated with the availability
and cost of spectrum for 3G globally, including whether similar bands will be
designated around the world, now rest with government policymakers.

---

37. WAP Forum, *WAP White Paper: Wireless Application Protocol, Wireless Internet Today* (Oct. 1999)
<http://www.wapforum.org/what/WAP_white_pages.pdf>.

38. David Pringle, *Cheaper Mobile Technologies May Hurt UMTS Revenues*, (June 18, 2000) <http://
www.wsj.com>.

39. In April 2000, five applicants bid a total of $35.4 billion for United Kingdom licenses, seven times
the amount the government predicted. In August 2000, bidders for German licenses paid over $46 billion.
Jonathan Miller, *Europe Packs a Wireless Wallop: Will the Quaint Continent Leave the U.S. in the Digital Dust?*
(MSNBC television broadcast, May 5, 2000).

iv. Pervasive Computing

Although much attention has been focused on mobile Internet access, the potential of wireless is far broader. It may well be that in the future almost every device that connects to the Internet will have the capability of making that connection wirelessly, even if the device itself is not designed for mobility. And the 4 billion Internet addresses now available are unlikely to be sufficient for all these devices. This will require a migration to IPv6, a new version of the Internet addressing system which vastly expands the number of unique addresses available (3.4×10^{38} under Ipv6 versus 4 billion using the current IPv4).[40]

Wireless access already encompasses connecting machines to one another and letting them interact in new ways. A group of prominent companies is developing a standard for short-range wireless connections (Bluetooth), which will enable short-range wireless communications among a variety of electronic devices—from laptops and cell phones to microwaves and blenders.[41] Bluetooth will allow devices to transmit information to each other seamlessly—enabling a phone to ring when a computer receives an e-mail or when a meal in the oven is ready. Bluetooth is not the only option in this space. For example, 802.11b is a competing protocol that is becoming more popular.[42]

Wireless connectivity can also be seen as part of a larger and more important trend—the trend toward a world of pervasive computing. Pervasive computing envisions the integration of computer processors and networking capabilities in devices found throughout our business and personal environments. This is a world where "smart" devices are everywhere—in our pockets, in the walls of our homes, in our furniture and appliances and in our vehicles. These devices will be seamlessly linked using both wireline and wireless networks. In the future all electric devices are likely to contain installed network software, allowing easy connections to other electrical devices and the Internet.[43] Before pervasive computing becomes a reality, however, software that allows for seamless interactions among devices—a world that every PC user knows is not yet in existence—must be developed.[44]

Pervasive computing will create a far different networking environment than we have today. Devices may be capable of detecting, recognizing and using the

---

40. John Shantz, *Addressing the Shortage*, Wireless Review, Mar. 15, 2001, at 50–56.

41. These companies include, for example, Telefon AB L.M. Ericsson, 3Com Corp., International Business Machines Corp., Motorola and Toshiba Corp. Nicole Harris, *Motorola to Release Products That Use Bluetooth Technology*, Wall St. J., June 12, 2000, at B20.

42. Bluetooth and 802.11b coexist in the same unlicensed spectrum and there have been reports of interference between them, raising issues of how they will develop in the future.

43. Bill Joy, *Design for the Digital Revolution*, Fortune, Mar. 6, 2000, at 10 <http://www.fortune.com/fortune/2000/03/06/hnd2.html>.

44. Software languages such Jini (Sun Microsystems), Universal Plug and Play (Microsoft) and Home Linking Technology are currently under development. Jini, for example, is designed to be a lingua franca among devices that will "provide an overarching, universal platform—a distributed operating system, in effect, on which devices of every description can meet." *See* Jura Knocius & Maryann Haggerty, *That's No Refrigerator, It's a Command Center; Alliances Speed Appliance Net Links*, Wash. Post, Jan. 18, 2000, at A1.

components of networks other than the ones to which they were originally linked. A cell phone might automatically detect and make use of the speakers in a car, so the driver can carry on a phone conversation while keeping her hands on the wheel.[45] Similarly, calls could be routed to whichever device is in use—the desktop, the palm-top or the web-enabled phone—based upon linked addresses and previously agreed-upon protocols. Users will be able to communicate whenever and wherever they are to whatever devices are their intended recipients rather than encountering the incompatibility of present-day devices.

One implication of advances in pervasive computing will be even more rapid growth in the amount of data being transmitted over networks. Perhaps the only thing that can match the probable growth of pervasive computing is the associated growth in concerns about privacy, interoperability, security and reliability.

v. The Semantic Web

The full development of machine-to-machine Internet communications requires that devices recognize and use data that are generated by other machines. This capability is associated with the *Semantic Web*, a term coined by Tim Berners-Lee, which describes a "Web of data with meaning in the sense that a computer program can learn enough about the data to process it."[46]

To understand this concept, it is necessary to understand the limitations of the languages currently used on the Web, specifically HTML, and what could be done if web pages were written in a language that had broader capabilities. HTML tells a browser how it should display text and images.[47] Information encoded in HTML cannot automatically be used *in context* by another computer. For instance, although a doctor may access a web page that lists a patient's drug allergies, she could not automatically import these data into the hospital database because HTML does not enable programmers to distinguish the data elements from the other elements (such as graphics) on the page. If data elements could be given standardized labels that indicated they were specific types of information, such as "patient's name," "price" or "stock number," then PCs and other web-enabled devices could process those data.

The software language Extensible Markup Language (XML) will likely bring many of these capabilities to computer networking. XML is a metalanguage— that is, a language used to standardize software-to-software data exchanges by

---

45. Joy, *supra* note 43.

46. Tim Berners-Lee, Weaving the Web: The Original Design and Ultimate Destiny of the World Wide Web by its Inventor 217 (1999).

47. Jon Bosak & Tim Bray, *XML and the Second-Generation Web*, Sci. Am., May 1999, at 89 <http://www.sciam.com/1999/0599issue/0599bosak.html>.

defining elements of other Internet languages.[48] Use of XML depends upon the development of tags that have common meanings. These can be either global (recognized by machines across the Internet) or local (recognized by members of a limited group, such as members of the medical profession who develop a "local" markup language for encoding medical records).[49]

The development of a Semantic Web has broad implications for increasing the cross-language communications and search capabilities of the Internet. XML relies upon Unicode, a character-encoding system that supports intermingling of text in all the worlds' major languages.[50] This has the potential to help automate the translation of communications in the various languages of the world. XML tags may also provide common-language search engines, enabling more targeted searching.

Tagging may also speed the development of intelligent agents—software programs that are designed to act on behalf of a user. The functions of intelligent-agent software range from shopping (for example, a more advanced form of the "bot" that can accumulate comparative price data and negotiate purchases on a user's behalf) to managing information flows. An intelligent-agent might act as an executive secretary—managing the flow of voice, mail, e-mail, appointment requests and Internet information.[51] Statistical probability and decision theory techniques embedded in the program enable the software to "learn" a user's preferences based upon his past actions.

As these technologies have developed, futurists envision a return to a time of a barter economy given the potential for constant auctions and automated price negotiations across all goods in the economy. As a thirsty shopper walks through a mall, her intelligent agent will be able to scan nearby soda prices and negotiate with vendors' programs to get the best deal, given her preset conditions of brand, size or maximum price per ounce.[52] These agents may also foster larger more sophisticated barter-based markets because today's technologies can keep track of all the complex information needed to conduct trade in such a market.[53] But in a world where people rely upon agents, the rules of liability will need to encompass the actions of millions of cyber-servants.

---

48. Bob Metcalfe, *Web Father Berners-Lee Shares Next-Generation Vision of the Semantic Web*, Info-World, May 24, 1999, at 110 <http://archive.infoworld.com/cgi-bin/displayArchive.pl?/99/21/o14–21. 110.htm>.

49. Bosak & Bray, *supra* note 47. Other related languages build on XML, promising even broader capabilities. The extensible style language (XSL) will offer users control over how their computers display XML files—letting the user determine font, text size and line spacing. SOAP, an XML standard, promises to ease computer-to-computer communications, enabling, for example, a web page (such as a news story) to update itself continuously based upon changing data from other Internet sources (economic statistics or sports scores, for example). VoiceXML has the potential for better voice recognition by computers. *See* Bill Barnes, *The XML Men: Saving the World from Evil Mutant Data!*, Slate, Aug. 23, 2000 <http://www.slate. msn.com/webhead/00–08–22/webhead.asp>.

50. Bosak & Bray, *supra* note 47.

51. John Markoff, *Microsoft Sees Software "Agent" as Way to Avoid Distractions*, N.Y. Times, July 17, 2000, at C1.

52. David Brooks, *The Mall: Where Every Price Is Negotiable*, N.Y. Times Mag., June 11, 2000, at 66.

53. Chip Bayers, *Capitalist E-Construction*, Wired, Mar. 2000, at 210 <http://www.wired.com/wired/archive/8.03/markets.html>.

Tagging information may also provide a vehicle for improving the efficiency of transmission. Different types of traffic have different transmission requirements. A "bit is a bit" to the network, which is indifferent to whether the bit represents part of a video image or a balance sheet, but specific services have differing transmission and delivery requirements. Streaming video, for example, requires a large amount of bandwidth for the duration of the transmission; otherwise, the motion of the images appears jerky. Online banking transactions may have fewer bits and require less bandwidth than streaming video, but they require absolute accuracy; there can be no information lost due to dropped data packets. And some users want their communications to have the highest priority—something not obtainable on the current "best-effort" Internet—and are willing to pay extra to ensure it.

In the past, in a largely analog world, we created dedicated networks with specific capabilities optimized for particular services—voice telephony and home video delivery are obvious examples. We are now learning how to accommodate differences in service requirements (creating different quality of service, or QOS) by providing either more bandwidth or more intelligence within the network. But providing different levels of QOS across networks is still a considerable challenge.[54]

§ 1.3 The Internet Enabling Change

In all of the planning, there was no notion of what the network would really be used for except to improve e-mail that was then unreliable and taking many hours to transmit. The supercomputer users wanted to transfer large files. None of us foresaw the Web. It was pure serendipity, coming from increased bandwidth that decreased response time that made interactive computing across the Net possible. . . . —Gordon Bell[55]

The capabilities inherent in the Internet are enabling change throughout the economy. In the relatively few years since the Internet became widely accessible, the uses that people and businesses have found for it have evolved and expanded. Old things are being done in new ways and completely innovative activities are emerging. Many of these new activities are pushing at the boundaries of our social, economic and legal norms. The changes revolve around enabling better communications among individuals and among other economic

---

54. For an interesting vision of a network that can respond to the needs of the data, see David Isenberg, *The Rise of the Stupid Network*, COMPUTER TELEPHONY, Aug. 1997, at 16 <http://www.isen.com>.
55. Gordon Bell, *The Next Killer App: An Extended Conversation with Gordon Bell*, IMP MAG., June 2000 <http://www.cisp.org/imp/june_2000/bell/06_00bell.htm>.

actors, such as businesses and governments. And, because the Internet is a global network, individuals and businesses from across the world have the potential to join in these online communications and to conduct online transactions.

Access to the enabling technologies is a necessary precondition for the diffusion of innovations like e-commerce. Such access is limited in many countries by inadequate communications infrastructure or by relatively high user costs. The benefits of e-commerce are limited where there is, at best, a single telephone for an entire village. In these locations, however, even very limited access to the Web could offer important benefits by providing health information or data on prices available at different local markets for commodities.

Even in places where a robust communications infrastructure is available, the costs of access to the Internet, computers or other access devices, and/or other services needed for e-commerce (such as access to credit), may create barriers to e-commerce. For example, per-minute charges for local phone calls make it expensive for those using dial-up services to stay online for any length of time, and high private-line telecommunication costs may limit connectivity.

1. E-mail and Online Conversations

E-mail remains the single most common reason people go online, with over eighty-five percent of Internet users sending and receiving e-mail.[56] U.S. web users sent 132 billion e-mail messages in 1999, according to one estimate.[57] These communications capabilities at first were tied to the desktop, but communicating as well as accessing online information no longer requires a personal computer. E-mail, web surfing and other Internet activities can be done via a widening variety of devices, from personal digital assistants (PDAs) and cell phones to systems embedded in automobiles themselves.

Online communications are not limited to interaction between people who are specifically trying to contact each other. Computer networking allows for the creation of online spaces or chat rooms where strangers can meet and participate in real-time, or near real-time, discussions on topics of interest, covering everything from gardening tips to stock tips, from parenting advice to alternative medical remedies. Individuals and groups also use online spaces to play games.

The online environment can offer anonymity (or the perception of anonymity), allowing for greater freedom of expression to those engaging in online

---

56. ACNielsen, *ACNielsen Survey Finds Nearly Two-Thirds of U.S. Population Age 12 or Older Are Online* (May 8, 2000) (ACNielsen news release) <http://www.acnielsen.com/news/american/us/2000/20000508.htm>.

57. Jupiter Communications, *cited in* David Lake, *Message in a Packet, The Industry Standard Metrics Report* (July 2000) <http://www.thestandard.com>.

conversation (chat rooms or discussion lists), playing online games or organizing political activities. This same anonymity, however, facilitates a variety of deceptions and abuses that range from predatory criminals trolling Internet spaces for victims to online businesses engaging in tax evasion.

Although a variety of technologies can make electronic communications anonymous (for example, re-mailers or services like Anonymizer), many e-mail or online conversations are neither anonymous nor as ephemeral as they seem. Electronic communications typically have a higher degree of permanence than do voice conversations. E-mail can be recovered even after the recipient thinks it has been deleted and, depending upon how a chat room is set up, online conversations may be posted and stored in newsgroups. Electronic comments made to a friend years ago (in anger, jest, frustration or drunken rage) can be retrieved and published to the world at large. For example, in February 2001, Google (an online search service) bought from "the failed information site Deja.com an archive of more than 650 million messages posted on electronic bulletin boards, known as Usenet newsgroups, that dates to 1995."[58]

Although some protection from unauthorized viewing and publishing can be obtained through encryption, in general, people must operate under the assumption that "e-mail is forever."[59] Courts are already wrestling with balancing claims for anonymity with competing claims from victims of alleged libel and harassment. Some corporations have turned to the courts in an attempt to stifle anonymous criticism, leading some observers to fear a chilling effect on open information exchange.

There is also the potential for interception and alteration of messages between sender and recipient, which raises issues of authentication and security for online communications and transactions. Authentication refers to assuring that a file or document has not been altered since its creation and that it comes from whomever or whatever is identified as the sender. These concerns are particularly important for legal records, such as contracts, or in situations where control of duplication can be the key to profits, such as limiting distribution of digitized copyrighted materials. Related to authentication issues are security concerns. When data are transferred across a computer network, interception and tampering are always possibilities. Even if the data are not tampered with (that is, the original message is still authentic), unauthorized access can be damaging. Perhaps the greatest concern of individuals making purchases over the Internet is the security of their credit card numbers and other personal information while they are in transit or stored in someone else's database.

---

58. Susan Stellin, *New Economy: Privacy Concerns for Google Archive*, N.Y. Times, May 7, 2001, at C4.
59. Even with the higher degree of permanence of information posted on the Internet, electronic media can also be less durable or reliable than previous formats. Links that exist one day are gone the next. Hard drives can be damaged and the information they contained may be prohibitively expensive to retrieve or permanently lost. The fact that some information may be stored in a way that makes it device- or software-specific may also limit the ability to retrieve it in the future. For example, digital art is impermanent and nonarchival because it can be viewed only with a certain generation of software.

Authentication and security concerns can be addressed through a number of technologies, including encryption. The use of strong encryption, however, produces a different set of issues that pit the privacy and security concerns of users against the needs of law enforcement and intelligence officials. In the Internet environment, it is difficult to ensure that individuals and businesses can conduct their lawful activities in a confidential manner without also affording the same degree of protection to criminal or antisocial activities. And the downside of increased connectivity, exemplified in pervasive computing, are increased privacy and security concerns.

2. Web Publishing and Broadcasting

Many employers use intranets, extranets and the Internet extensively for the publication of organizational information.[60] In many organizations, employees can obtain daily valuations of their 401(k) plans, change beneficiaries, evaluate their health plan options during open season and file expense reports online. These activities raise questions about the organization's right to—and responsibilities for—monitoring those communications. These questions affect virtually all areas of employment law, including, for example, what constitutes adequate notification about a change in a retirement plan, what an employee's expectation of privacy should be, what constitutes adequate accommodation under the Americans with Disabilities Act, what constitutes a hostile work environment and what records must be retained under the Electronic Signatures in Global and National Commerce Act.

The fact that anyone can establish a web site makes it difficult for web users to determine the "bona fides" of the publisher of any specific site, complicating efforts to find accurate, reliable information on the Internet. In addition, many web sites have similar-sounding names but very different content. For example, www.cybergrrl.com is an information technology-oriented portal for women and girls, whereas www.cybergirl.com is a pornographic web site.

The amount of information online makes finding a web site or a specific fact a challenge, even for experienced web users. The various search engines use differing criteria to respond to a user's search request. Even the most sophisticated of the search engines cover only a relatively small proportion of the total number of sites.[61] Some engines search using full text comparisons, whereas others search on key words or links (provided by the site originator or selected by the search engine company). Still others provide responses to

---

60. Many companies use Internet protocols to create Internet-like networks for company-only use (intranets) or for use by the company and its business partners (extranets). Intranets and extranets that are connected to the public Internet are typically protected from unauthorized access by security programs known as firewalls.

61. Inktomi, *supra* note 14.

searches based upon popularity; that is, the number of "hits" that a site receives or the number of other sites linked to it. In addition to the stated criteria, some search results are affected by financial arrangements between the site hosting the search engine and other sites that pay to be featured prominently in search results.

Even with the difficulties of sorting through so much information, some of which is of questionable quality, there is no doubt that the availability of information online is changing personal and business behavior. For example, physicians face patients who arrive at their offices armed with treatment information, and some car dealerships refer to the Internet-informed potential buyers who appear at their showrooms as the "armed unfriendlies."

Because anyone can establish a web site, the Internet also makes it easy for anyone to publish or broadcast creative efforts, ranging from creative writing or reporting to digital movies. The cost structure of making creative content has also been fundamentally altered with the availability of low-cost devices such as digital cameras and editing software.[62]

The increasing capacity to publish and broadcast over the Internet is blurring the lines that have traditionally distinguished professionals from others. For example, there are shield laws that protect professional reporters, but it is unclear how they will apply when anyone with a web page can be a reporter and/or publisher.

3. Online Commerce

Although it was conceived as a communications and information-sharing network, the Internet has become firmly entrenched as a commercial medium. It is having the kind of transforming effect on commerce that one might equate with the effect of reliable roads or the construction of railway systems. The Internet provides a new way for organizations to engage in existing activities and enables the creation of new products and services.

i. Customization and Web User Information

Internet technologies allow businesses to know more about their customers, which enables them to target products and prices with a specificity that would

---

62. For example, with a digital video camera, digital videocassettes and editing software, anyone can create a digital movie and post it to the Web for only about $10,000. According to one estimate, this one-time investment that could be used to create an unlimited number of movies is about $30,000 less than it would cost for equipment and editing to make a single twenty-minute short on celluloid. *See* Rob Kenner, *My Hollywood! So You Wanna Be in Pictures? Pick up Your Tools and Shoot*, WIRED, Oct. 1999, at 214 <http://www.wired.com/wired/archive/7.10/microcinema_pr.html>.

not be possible without the Internet. In some cases, consumers knowingly provide detailed information about themselves. At BizRate.com, for example, customers are invited to rate their online shopping experiences and that information is aggregated and made available to other shoppers. BizRate.com also sells aggregate information back to the online shopkeepers.

In other cases, however, people may provide information about themselves without even realizing it, as "cookies" track their online browsing behavior. These tracking systems can provide an immense amount of data that, combined with personal information gathered from other sources, creates a vivid picture of a web surfer. Although allowing sellers to tailor their offerings to individual shoppers, these capabilities create a tension between the benefits of obtaining a customized product and the privacy of an individual's online activities.

ii. Pricing in an Online Environment

There is little doubt that the existence of online sales channels is having an impact on "real-world" pricing policies, despite online retail sales accounting for less than one percent of total retail trade. Even if users choose not to make purchases online, the Internet makes it easier for consumers to comparison shop. Potential buyers (or their digital agents) can check the price and availability of products from a variety of sites in far less time than it would take to conduct store-to-store comparisons in the world of bricks and mortar. In addition to obtaining price information, online shoppers can avail themselves of third-party reviews and ratings to assist them in buying decisions, whether or not the sale itself occurs online.

Internet technology is also permitting the development of various dynamic pricing mechanisms. In the brick-and-mortar economy, a single-price model holds for most consumer goods and services. Most offline sellers do not have sufficient information to vary their prices from customer to customer, and physically changing the price of individually tagged items is expensive. In the online world, not only is it inexpensive and easy to change prices, it is possible to sift through data about a particular customer, discern her price sensitivity and offer customized pricing. With individual-level price discrimination now a reality, questions arise about how the law will respond.[63]

Online auctions are one type of dynamic pricing that is growing in popularity, particularly in business-to-business transactions. The Internet provides a relatively low-cost and convenient way of bringing buyers and sellers together, and the use of auction sites has grown rapidly. Variations on the

---

63. In September 2000, Amazon.com experimented with dynamic pricing of digital videodiscs. *See* David Streitfeld, *On the Web, Price Tags Blur; What You Pay Could Depend on Who You Are*, Wash. Post, Sept. 27, 2000, at A1.

standard auctions are also gaining popularity. In the reverse auction format, the consumer names the price and the seller decides whether to accept it. In an aggregation format, the number of people that want to buy a product determines its price—the greater the number of buyers, the lower the price.

One would expect that this ability to gather information on prices and product characteristics so easily and cheaply would force Internet retailers to charge the same low price—one that would approach their cost—on the same or comparable products. One might also expect these lower online prices to influence prices charged in physical stores. Thus far, the evidence on the price effects is mixed. (It does appear, however, that attributes other than price, such as reputation, play important roles in purchasers' decisions.)[64] The same technologies that enable potential buyers to comparison shop also enable firms to track the prices being charged by their competitors, potentially leading to higher prices.[65] In the past, such activities have led to explicit or implicit collusion. It is possible to see how tacit price collusion and market-sharing arrangements could arise if the collection of buyers and/or collection of sellers in a particular market had instantaneous notification of price movements. The Justice Department, the Federal Trade Commission and the European Union are giving careful consideration to the potential for anticompetitive behavior based upon the availability of pricing data, particularly in the new online marketplaces where industry leaders may collectively own the site while simultaneously competing with other site participants and each other.[66]

iii. Electronic Money

The ability to make purchases online has generated interest in the development of new electronic payment mechanisms. Though credit cards may be suitable

---

64. A recent study of books and CDs sold by Internet and conventional retail outlets found that Internet prices were between nine and sixteen percent lower than prices in conventional outlets, depending upon whether taxes, shipping costs and shopping costs were included in the price. Another study of book prices, however, found that prices online and in physical bookstores were the same. This suggests that certain web sites have sufficiently differentiated themselves through factors other than price (such as convenience and product reviews) that they can attract sales even when they are not the lowest-price seller. *See* Karen Clay et al., Retail Strategies on the Web: Price and Non-price Competition in the Online Book Industry (Dec. 1, 1999) (unpublished manuscript, available on the Heinz School of Public Policy and Management, Carnegie Mellon University web page) <http://dnet.heinz.cmu.edu/dcsrg/books/papers/paper1.pdf>. Some market research studies find that differentiating factors include site brand name awareness, ease of navigation while on the site and a reputation for reliability. *See* Cyber Dialogue, *Online Shoppers Embrace Free Shipping* (Feb. 28, 2000) (Cyber Dialogue press release) <http://www.cyberdialogue.com/resource/press/releases/2000/02-28-ic-free_shipping.html>.

65. Hal Varian, *When Commerce Moves Online, Competition Can Work in Strange Ways*, N.Y. TIMES, Aug. 24, 2000, at C2.

66. The Federal Trade Commission recently held a workshop to examine the available evidence on business-to-business marketplaces and the potential implications on the competitiveness of markets. Documents related to the workshop can be found on the Federal Trade Commission web site <http://www.ftc.gov/bc/b2b/index.htm>.

for many purchases, they are not suitable for all purchases. Credit card payments are not convenient for consumer-to-consumer transactions (such as in online auctions), for sales by very small companies and for very small-value transactions, when the price of the good or service (say reproduction rights priced at a penny a page) can be less than the cost of the credit card transaction. Although escrow-type systems can be arranged, they raise costs and may raise regulatory issues based upon regulations applied to escrow services in the physical world.

Alternatives are being developed, including cards that would allow funds to be transferred over a network from a buyer's card to the seller's card, electronic wallets or prepaid cards. In Europe, smart-card-equipped mobile phones are used for purchasing. The smart card is linked to a bank account and the user, paying with the mobile phone, draws down that account. In other instances, mobile commerce transactions are billed through the user's mobile phone bill.

If new forms of electronic payment gain broad acceptance in the marketplace, they will raise new questions. How will these payment mechanisms relate to existing financial instruments? Will companies that offer digital money be subject to the same regulatory standards imposed upon firms in the financial-services sector? In addition, the potential for anonymity online raises questions about the impact of electronic payment mechanisms on illegal activities, such as money laundering.

iv. Digital Delivery

One can order, pay for and arrange delivery of almost any physical good or service over the Internet. Some products and services, such as professional services, software, music or video, can be digitized and delivered directly over the Internet. Digital delivery can have many benefits to a firm—packaging, shipping and handling costs, as well as delivery time, can be dramatically reduced. Digital delivery, however, can present businesses with considerable challenges because once an image, sound or video is digitized, an infinite number of copies can be made and distributed at virtually no cost and with virtually no degradation in quality. Industries whose business models depend upon being able to control the distribution of copyrighted digitized information (such as the publishing, television, radio, music and motion picture industries) potentially lose their ability to control duplication of their material.

Members of the music industry have been forced to face this issue directly because of a dramatic increase in the exchange of music over the Internet. This resulted from the confluence of related technological developments, including the development of file compression formats for music (MP3, for example), the creation of portable devices capable of playing MP3 files and inexpensive read/writeable CD-ROM drives (both of which made it possible to use the content of the files away from the desktop) and the popularity of peer-to-peer software designed for sharing music files (such as Napster and Gnutella) in communities with access to broadband connections to the Internet, such as in colleges and universities.

Although Napster had been required by the courts to change its free online swapping service, the existence of this type of technology will continue to impact industries whose product can be digitally delivered.[67] The movie and television industries have been somewhat protected (for the time being) because bandwidth constraints limit the ability to transfer large video files. These business models, however, will face the same challenges as the book and music industries as access to broadband connectivity increases and compression technology improves.[68]

Although developments in the electronic marketplace raise many challenges to protecting digitized copyrighted products, advances in related technologies offer businesses new tools for dealing with these issues. As Lawrence Lessig has written, "[t]echnologies for watermarking copyrighted material are proliferating; technologies for tagging copyrighted material are common; technologies for making copyrighted material uncopiable [or to limit the number of copies] are emerging."[69]

There is a great deal of uncertainty regarding how the tension between digital delivery capabilities and intellectual property rights protection will be resolved. Hal Varian has written that "the current business model for music distribution is unlikely to survive. But this doesn't mean there will be no music; it just means the business will have to change."[70] Varian's insight may well apply broadly to any industry whose product can be digitized, including education, medical and financial services. Some companies are already stepping into the fray and attempting to develop a business model that will enable secure digital delivery and a means by which copyright owners can charge for their materials.[71] These new models will eventually require definitions of the boundary between the copyright holders' interests and the rights of the purchasers of goods who have previously been allowed to make copies for their personal use and to transport and share them. The law has also been called upon to resolve the tension between claims made by intellectual property rights holders and a long

---

67. Matt Bailey, *Napster Use in Sharp Descent: Song-Screening Preceded Dramatic Drop*, The Arizona Republic, May 3, 2001, at A7.

68. Bandwidth is a critical factor in this equation. It takes hours to download video and audio files over the 28–56 kb/per-second modem connection that most people use today to connect to the Internet. These same files can be downloaded in minutes or seconds with a broadband connection.

69. Lessig, *supra* note 28. For example, three mathematicians at Brown University recently patented an encryption code that would make it possible to encrypt every second of a music file with a different encryption key. This encryption method could be employed so that *only* the purchaser of the music could play the downloaded music. *See* Sabra Chartrand, *New Encryption System Would Protect Digital Music*, N.Y. Times, July 3, 2000, at C8.

70. Hal Varian, *The Internet Carries Profound Implications for Providers of Information*, N.Y. Times, July 27, 2000, at C2.

71. David Streitfeld, *The Web's Next Step: Unraveling Itself*, Wash. Post, July 18, 2000, at A1.

standing tradition of "fair use" that had allowed non-rights holders to utilize portions of protected works.[72]

Copyright and intellectual property rights are not the only concerns. The electronic delivery of digital products and services also raises new tariff and taxation issues, such as determining whether the digitally delivered items are products or services, how a digital transaction should be characterized and where (in geographic terms) a digital transaction occurs. Determining the responsible parties in a transaction will be made even more complex with the potential development of intelligent agents capable of engaging in online transactions on behalf of individuals, firms or other entities.

v. Changing the Structures of Organizations and Industries

Across the economy, organizations and firms are rethinking how to provide value to their customers as business processes—including transactions like product delivery—move online. Some find that their old business models do not work anymore. For example, travel agents are seeing strong competition from web-based services (such as Expedia and Travelocity).[73]

The Internet also allows for goods and services that, until now, have been offered in bundled form, to be provided separately. Philip Evans and Thomas Wurster in *Blown to Bits* illustrate how information technologies are dismantling and reformulating current business structures.[74] One example is the newspaper: in the past, economies of scale in printing made it more efficient to bundle news, classifieds, stock quotes and cartoons, even though every reader was not interested in every feature. Technologies like the Internet, however, make that model of cross-subsidization unravel because the individual products (such as articles or cartoons) can be provided over the Internet to people who want them.

Although in some industries the Internet is forcing reassessment of business models, in others the ability to share complicated information over networks is broadening the availability of business practices that increase efficiency in design and production. The idea of using computer networks and direct digital communication to facilitate business transactions between firms is not new. For

---

72. One judge recently suggested that "fair use" may not require access to the most technologically advanced version of the work.

73. For example, since 1997, the number of travel agencies selling airline tickets has fallen by more than 2,500, or 8%. *See* Mark Albright, *Slashed Commissions, Internet Spark Travel Business Revolution; Fewer Agencies Book Flights as Relationship Grows Adversarial with Airlines*, COM. APPEAL, June 18, 2000, at F6.

74. PHILIP EVANS & THOMAS S. WURSTER, BLOWN TO BITS: HOW THE NEW ECONOMICS OF INFORMATION TRANSFORMS STRATEGY (1999).

well over twenty years, suppliers have engaged in e-commerce with large-volume customers through electronic data interchange (EDI) systems over value-added networks (VANs) to reduce the costs of interbusiness transactions. EDI allows companies to automate the routine paperwork surrounding business transactions (such as invoices and confirmations), to manage arrangements (such as automatic inventory replenishments) and to place orders according to preestablished terms, all over secured networks. Much of what is currently counted as business-to-business e-commerce is this type of transaction. Until recently, the use of EDI was limited to large-volume supplier/customer relationships because it is expensive to deploy, requiring special computer terminals, proprietary software and leased space on VANs. The Internet provides a secure, low-cost platform to spread these types of efficiencies to businesses of all sizes.

Internet-based EDI, however, operates under many of the same constraints as VAN-based EDI: it requires a preexisting relationship where details concerning the transaction are set in advance. One of the significant advantages of the Internet is that it provides a forum for parties to establish new relationships. Online auction sites, for instance, bring together online buyers and sellers who otherwise might never have completed a sale because of the physical distance between them. Others aggregate sales, arrange logistics and in many ways redefine the role of all types of intermediaries—wholesalers, freight forwarders and financial agents.

Networking technologies also greatly increase the number of concurrent activities (design and engineering, for example) that can occur and increase the amount of subcontracting that can take place, as complex information can be shared almost instantaneously. Manufacturers, for example, have been moving toward purchasing components or subassemblies rather than individual parts from their suppliers. The ability to share design and manufacturing information online greatly increases the efficiency of such activities.

Technology-enabled organizational changes are not confined to specific industries or sectors of the economy. The potential to use these technologies to achieve new efficiencies through reengineering organizational structures is broad in its scale. The changes that are sweeping through the private sector are affecting the public sector as well. Governments use the Internet to provide information to citizens (trash pickup days or county library hours, for example), to make purchases or sales and to carry out other consumer-to-government transactions (such as accepting tax filings, license applications or payment of fees and fines). Using these technologies will likely lead to reexamination of organizational structures presently in place and spur organizational changes as misalignments are identified. Although governments do not face the imperatives of "fear and greed" that force change in the private sector, they are now more exposed to comparisons with the private sector in how efficiently they conduct the business of government.

The same forces that encourage a rethinking of organizational structures are creating new dynamics in the workforce. The Internet facilitates project teams that come together for limited periods of time and purpose, such as those involved in the film or construction industries. The possibility of a new class of employees—e-lancers—raises important questions about employment security and pension policies, among others.[75]

Businesses that do not understand these new technologies will be at a competitive disadvantage. This holds true across large, medium and small firms. Larger firms may outsource noncore functions and concentrate on those areas in which they have a sustainable competitive advantage and that directly affect their success. This would expand opportunities for smaller niche players, provided they had the ability to interact digitally with their larger customers. Smaller firms may also find it easier to compete for business from geographically distant potential customers. Conversely, smaller players lacking the ability to digitally connect or failing to meet the entry standards set for a given online marketplace may find that their opportunities are rapidly shrinking. As Andy Grove, chairman of Intel, put it in May 1999, as "much as we talk about Internet companies today, in five years' time there won't be any Internet companies. All companies will be Internet companies or they will be dead."[76]

§ 1.4 Some Observations on the Future

The technological developments occurring today offer a vision of the future marked by dramatic new capabilities in processing speed, transport and storage. The constraining influence of bandwidth is beginning to diminish as communications technologies continue to improve. With robust competition between telephone, cable and wireless companies, as well as improvements in transmission media—optical fiber, twisted-pair copper wire, coaxial cable and various wireless technologies—we can move data more efficiently across communications networks. We may reach the point where anything that can be digitized can be delivered efficiently to an ever-growing number of users and where the marginal cost of transport approaches zero.

A far wider variety of data is being stored and made available electronically—locally or, increasingly, on the Internet itself. These data are also increasingly carrying descriptive tags. These *metadata* enable machines to attach mean-

---

75. Thomas W. Malone & Robert J. Laubacher, *The Dawn of the E-Lance Economy*, Harv. Bus. Rev., Sept.–Oct. 1998, at 145.

76. Andrew S. Grove, Address at the *Los Angeles Times* Third Annual Investment Strategies Conference (May 22, 1999) (transcript available at <http://www.intel.com/pressroom/archive/speeches/cn052499.htm>).

ing to individual data elements, making it possible for computers to conduct more data exchanges with less human mediation.

Network technology is being used for an ever-growing number of tasks as we shift away from today's PC-based model. The desktop computer is becoming only one among many platforms for accessing networks such as the Internet. There will be small, lighter devices optimized for basic activities—such as e-mail, text communications and simple graphics sharing—and larger, more sophisticated devices or collections of devices for more complex activities.

Applications running on these devices are becoming "smarter" as a result of the increasingly robust capabilities of the languages used to develop them. These advances enable content developed for one environment to be used easily in another. Computer and communications equipment—laptops, cell phones, printers and so forth—communicate with each other and move in and out of the many networks of the infrastructure. Software applications act on behalf of users—connecting to local networks, managing the flow of information and negotiating with other applications to achieve the tasks that we, the users, ask of them.

We can see these possibilities in current trends. But, given the accelerated rate of technological change, it would be foolhardy to try to predict what will be possible in the long term.[77] Therefore, instead of *predictions*, following are some observations about the future and the changes that we will encounter.

Innovation is not linear. Technological developments do not lead inexorably to a single result. There are too many discontinuities where a technology invented to solve a problem in one context is picked up and used to solve problems in completely different fields. This can be seen in the past—the steam engine used to generate the electricity that in turn fueled the Industrial Revolution was based upon an eighteenth-century pump developed to remove water from flooded mines.[78] It can also be seen today—a standard technology used in ink-jet printers is the foundation of recent developments in optical switching, a technology that when perfected and commercialized will dramatically increase the efficiency of communications backbones.[79] The Internet, by linking diverse communities, can only increase the number of these cross-over innovations.

The laws of economics have not been repealed and demand will continue to drive innovation. The rapid changes in technological capabilities that we

77. For examples of the wide range that predictions can take, see Bryon Spice, *Experts Divided over Future Benefits of Computer Technology*, Seattle Post-Intelligencer, Oct. 23, 2000, at D8.

78. Nathan Rosenberg, *The Impact of Technological Innovation: A Historical View, in* The Positive Sum Strategy: Harnessing Technology for Economic Growth 17–32 (Ralph Landau and Nathan Rosenberg eds., 1986).

79. Peter Fairley, *The Microphotonics Revolution*, Tech. Rev., July/Aug. 2000, at 38 <http://www.techreview.com/articles/july00/fairley.htm>.

have seen in the past few decades, however, are altering the supply-and-demand equation. The relative costs of the components of a system drive its design regardless of whether the system is a computer network or a business process. When data storage is relatively cheaper than data transport, computer engineers build systems that can store frequently used data locally rather than continually transporting it to and from a remote server. When there is a shortage of skilled workers, processes are automated and capital is invested in training to increase workforce productivity.

The technological changes that are taking place in processing, data storage and communications are changing the relative costs of many systems. This in turn has the potential to change the products and services that are available. An example is the development of packet switching, fundamental to the development of the Internet, which can be seen as substituting relatively cheap processing at the network's edge for relatively expensive circuit-switched transport.

If present trends continue, the marginal cost of processing, storing and transporting a bit will approach zero. In such circumstances we can imagine, for example, today's long-distance communications being offered for "free" when purchased bundled with other products. Even if not offered without additional charge, voice services offered utilizing the Internet protocols have changed the marketplace for international communications and are likely to play an ever increasing role in the domestic marketplace. But as the cost of moving a bit approaches zero, we will still need to find sustainable business models to justify not only the lumpy, large-scale investment in the networks that underlie the Internet but also the complementary investment in areas such as marketing, billing and servicing that still have to be undertaken.

Heterogeneity is likely to be the rule. Information technologies and their applications are today characterized by heterogeneity. People access the Internet by using a wide variety of devices that range from high-performance workstations to handheld appliances. The underlying technologies that enable connection to the Internet are highly diverse—twisted-copper wires, coaxial cable, fiber optics, fixed and mobile wireless, satellite and so forth. Heterogeneity will continue with innovation occurring across a wide range of technologies.

Enormous investments have been made in computer systems and in mobile devices, as well as in twisted-pair copper wire, coaxial cable networks and satellite systems. Market participants seek to leverage, rather than write off, their existing investments and to compete by enhancing their own technology. This competition should stimulate even greater innovation by incumbent firms and by new firms providing "disruptive technologies."[80] And, because differences in the technologies and their deployment patterns provide differing advantages to one or another player, we are unlikely to see one player "sweep the board."

---

80. Clayton M. Christensen, *The Innovator's Dilemma: When New Technologies Cause Great Firms to Fail*, HARPERS BUS., May 2000.

There may be situations, however, where winner-take-all results will ensue. Such examples are perhaps more likely in a world where first movers gain enough users to obtain strong network effects and thus discourage competition. Such markets provide strong financial incentives to be *the* winner.

One of the fundamental checks on monopolistic behavior is rapid technological change. The forces of technological change can be seen even in the market for operating systems—in the Internet-enabled development of open-source competitors (such as Linux) and in the prominence of firms other than Microsoft in developing operating systems for handheld computers (such as Palm). Government competition policies will continue to have major roles in dealing with the winner-take-all situation, not the least of which will be to ensure that technology development is encouraged, not thwarted.

The competitive and heterogeneous marketplace increases the importance of the role of standards. The unifying nature of the TCP/IP protocol has been critical to the Internet's success. Given the increasing importance of information technology and telecommunications, the role of standards will become even more crucial and contentious in the future. In particular, for a world of pervasive computing to succeed, we must have standards to ensure interoperability. Without them, the Tower of Babel becomes a reality.

Such standards will not be easy to achieve. The hope of achieving monetary and reputational gains from having a proprietary standard established as an industry standard is enticing. But experience with the Internet and the growing benefits of open-source software and open standards achieved through open processes means that there is an alternative to proprietary standards that deserves our close attention. The most successful standards in the Internet age have been market driven. Although governments can exert significant pressure in their roles as large purchasers, they are more likely to be successful in fostering openness and competition than in formulating specific standards.

Public policy is likely to have a substantial impact upon technological developments and the resulting applications. Public policy has already had an important impact upon the development of the Internet—it may even claim paternity based upon the ARPANET. At the same time, many argue that the phenomenal growth of the Internet is due to the absence of government interference—particularly of the public-utility regulation type. Whatever the merits of these claims, the impact of public policy is likely to grow as the Internet becomes an essential element of our economic and social lives.

Some of the impact will be direct. Already, we see how federal research funds affect the technological underpinnings of the next-generation Internet. But other policy decisions may inadvertently influence the development of new products and services. For example, a Federal Communications Commission regulation enacted in 1996 required wireless carriers to create an emergency "911-type" system that would, by 2001, allow carriers to know the location of users within 125 meters so they could provide emergency services. This requirement spurred the development of new location-based e-commerce services, but it also raised new privacy issues by making the location of the mobile user available to law enforcement officials.

Conversely, policy concerns have led to new technological tools to enhance privacy, such as the Platform for Privacy Preferences (P3P) of the World Wide Web Consortium. These tools allow individuals to specify their privacy preferences and utilize intelligent agents to ensure they interact only with those web sites whose privacy policies satisfy them. Other public policy imperatives, such as the need to authenticate electronic contracts, develop efficient and equitable taxation collection programs, establish simple and cost-effective online mechanisms for dispute resolution of international consumer complaints and protect intellectual property from unauthorized dissemination are likely to stimulate technological development and new applications.

In the future, thoughtful policymakers will look to technology as part of the solution to difficult policy questions. Technological solutions can adapt to change more readily than can laws or regulations. They can be made to reflect our values and can be adopted globally without the arduous process of harmonizing incompatible laws. In areas such as taxation or intellectual property protection, technological solutions have the potential to make interoperable vastly different rules that, if applied strictly, could balkanize the Internet and impede the growth of electronic commerce.

The Internet's openness has fostered competition at every level—including network, access and application—and with it, ever-increasing innovation. Developments that threaten that openness are already in view and are likely to continue to propagate. Openness is a key issue in almost every technology, policy and business debate involving computers and communications. The strongly resisted obligations of incumbent telecommunications providers to offer access to their facilities and provide nondiscriminatory access to independent Internet service providers (ISPs) has contributed to the vibrancy of the market for Internet access. The applicability of such obligations to cable television companies has dominated policy discussions as the cable industry moves toward providing interactive telecommunications and Internet services. And such questions have arisen in connection with providing wireless Internet access because mobile subscribers are now limited to using their mobile companies' affiliated ISPs.

Similar questions have arisen regarding access to Internet content. The Internet allows any user to reach any publicly posted web site. Concerns have been raised about the vertical integration of facilities-based access providers (such as cable companies) with content providers due to concerns that the access providers have an incentive to provide technically superior access to their own content rather than that of their competitors. These concerns echo those raised nearly twenty years ago about the ability of incumbent telecommunications providers to discriminate against competitive information service providers if they were allowed to enter the information services market—concerns that were addressed by requiring nondiscriminatory treatment of their information service competitors as they provided them with necessary telecommunications services.

There are other less dramatic examples of the threat to the openness that allows anyone to connect with anyone and anything. The present difficulties in interconnecting today's instant-messaging systems raise this issue. The menu of affiliated providers on DoCoMo's i-mode phones is being paralleled by the growth of "walled gardens" of web sites economically affiliated with the access provider, which may not offer the same access to the whole disorderly field of wildflowers now blooming on the Web. Recent judicial decisions restricting linking between sites (such as auction sites) raise similar questions. And France's attempt to force Yahoo.com to restrict French citizens from accessing certain sites raises a vision of state-enforced balkanization of the Web where an individual country, or even a locality within a country, would set parameters for the content that could be made available to its citizens.

Inherent in each of these examples is a debate about choice. Predictability and ease of use for end users are attractive elements of the "walled garden" networking environment. Countries arguably have an interest in protecting their citizens from particular content, but each country may have a different view of what content is harmful. Each time we slice away at the fundamental openness of the Internet, however, we weaken it as a vehicle for communication, innovation and progress. If countries aggressively pursue attempts to control content and conduct beyond their borders, we may substantially inhibit the growth of the Internet and unravel the World Wide Web, which could lead to an uneasy federation of national nets.

§ 1.5 Conclusion

Much of this chapter focuses on technological developments as enabling change. But these technologies will not determine the future of the Internet—that will be determined by individuals and organizations that find new uses for the technologies and policies that either encourage or discourage certain activities. Existing and proposed uses raise important issues in the areas of electronic contracts, authentication, taxation, jurisdiction, intellectual property protection, privacy, consumer protection, security, reliability, competition policy and standards, among others. Although the future is impossible to predict, it seems highly likely that the exciting possibilities that we can envision based upon technological progress will continue to raise new issues and demand creative policy responses.

Intellectual Property

Contents

By Jeff Dodd and Ray Nimmer

Intellectual Property

Chapter 2, authored by Jeff Dodd and Ray Nimmer, deals with intellectual property issues affecting Internet commerce. It focuses on three primary intellectual property regimes at work in this environment—patent, copyright and trademark law. The goal is to provide a broad outline of the law and issues, not to delve deeply into the myriad of issues that arise, or into competition and other factors that shape the development of intellectual property law in this context.[1]

Along with contract law and potential regulation by states and countries, the law of intellectual property is one of the major influences that will determine the contours of Internet commerce and competition in informational assets and other more tangible assets. Yet, it is also true that digital systems and Internet commerce are rapidly reshaping the traditional fields of intellectual property law. There is an important and still-developing feedback loop here, the eventual product of which cannot be completely predicted. Law, including intellectual property law, shapes competition, while competition and its demands shape the law. The best we can do in this chapter is to paint a broad picture of the status of these fields and their roles in commerce at a given point in time.

Section 2.1 discusses the nature of IP law, and Sections 2.2, 2.3 and 2.4 focus on the three primary intellectual property regimes: patent, copyright and trademark law, respectively.

§ 2.1 Nature of Intellectual Property Law

To begin, it is important to understand the nature of intellectual property law, many characteristics of which are foreign to commercial lawyers.

A property right is a legally recognized right that gives the person holding it the ability to control actions by others in connection with a stated subject matter, even absent a contract or other relationship.[2] In intellectual property law, the subject matter—or at least its primary value—is intangible. Thus, for example, copyright law establishes certain exclusive rights regarding a work of

---

1. For a more extensive discussion of the issues, see RAYMOND T. NIMMER, THE LAW OF COMPUTER TECHNOLOGY (3d ed. 1998).

2. *See, e.g.*, Raymond T. Nimmer & Patricia A. Krauthaus, *Information as Property: Databases and Commercial Property*, 1 OXFORD J. INFO. L. & COMP. TECH. 2 (1993).

authorship. These rights focus upon the expressive work and handling it, and only indirectly affect the handling or distribution of the tangible property upon which the work is represented. Patent law creates "preclusive" rights in patented inventions, but those rights are independent of any particular, physical manifestation of the invention.

Intellectual property law entails a link between preconditions and protected rights. This is true in both patent and copyright law, where fulfilling certain preconditions establishes stated, limited rights in the subject matter. The precondition for establishing property rights in copyright law is that the work entail copyrightable expression and be fixed in some media from which it can be perceived. The images, sounds or text cannot be entirely transitory.[3] In patent law, the invention must meet the entry conditions for being patentable subject matter and qualifying for a patent, and it must have received an issued patent from the relevant governmental office. In each case, meeting the preconditions gives the owner certain rights to control the subject matter of the property, but in both cases, the rights are neither universal nor comprehensive.

All three traditional areas of intellectual property discussed here have undergone significant changes during the past ten years. In varying degrees, the changes relate to the demands of the new, online and digital commerce systems. This is not a stable or fixed legal regime, such as that pertaining to goods and real estate, where fundamental property rights have been established over the years and rapid change does not occur.

In large part, the changes in intellectual property law involve an expansion of the idea of property and its application, coupled with frequent adjustments preserving limited regions for competition and free discourse unencumbered by property rights.[4] The changes also involve an increasingly direct relationship between the laws of the United States and other countries, especially the European Union. The lead—at least in terms of shaping the direction of law—has frequently fallen to European or international venues, rather than to the United States, even in connection with law within the United States. A lawyer involved in intellectual property law must truly be an international lawyer, at least to the extent of understanding the scope and direction of foreign law.

These developments underscore the reality that the law of property responds to the economic thrust of a society—in this case, a rapid thrust toward increasing economic dominance of information assets, online commerce and international trade in information and services. There are offsetting interests,

---

3. *See* Lewis Galoob Toys, Inc. v. Nintendo of Am., 964 F.2d 965 (9th Cir. 1992) (enhancement kit that did not alter underlying computer game program, but merely enhanced images on screen, did not create derivative work; screen images were transitory).

4. A recent illustration of the relationship between competition and intellectual property policy is in the Ninth Circuit Court of Appeals decision in *Sony Computer Entertainment, Inc. v. Connectix Corp.*, 203 F.3d 596 (9th Cir. 2000). In that case, the court held that copies made in a process of reverse engineering of a Sony encoding device were fair use because they were needed to obtain an interoperable system. Although this resulted in significant harm to Sony's competitive position in reference to a video game player market, the court observed simply that copyright law was not intended to protect that competitive position and that this type of harm did not weigh against a finding of fair use.

however, and the proper answer to each question involving economically valuable assets is not always to recognize in law a right to exclusivity, even in part, in connection with those rights.

Besides feeling the effect of a rapid thrust toward expansion and change, property laws dealing with intangible property have different underlying features than property laws pertaining to real estate and goods. The most important of these is the relative unimportance the law attaches to possession or control of tangible things. In real estate and goods law, one can generally presume that a person in visible possession or control of the tangible item has rights in it. Although that presumption does not fully apply to property governed by registration or recording systems, historically it led to the concept of good-faith purchase, in which a buyer might obtain more than its seller owned, even if the sale was not authorized by the person from whom those greater rights were taken. This concept, which focuses upon tangible items, does *not* govern in intellectual property law. Unless there is an *authorized* sale of a copy, the buyer takes the copy subject to (and perhaps in violation of) the intellectual property rights of a remote party.[5] Even in an authorized sale, many of the owner's property rights remain intact. For example, 17 U.S.C. § 106 grants the owner of copyright in a computer program the exclusive right to rent its work, and this right is not cut off by a first sale.[6] This has direct consequences for handling information assets in the Internet, both in terms of referring to them or handling them for or on behalf of others.

§ 2.2 Patent Law

1. General Nature of the Law

Patent law is perceived as the most powerful of the intellectual property rights regimes. It is, however, the one area of intellectual property law whose impact on the Internet and other fields of digital commerce has been the least extensive.

In the United States, patent rights are established exclusively by federal law. Section 101 of the Patent Act provides that "[w]hoever invents or discovers any new and useful process, machine, manufacture, or composition of matter, or any new or useful improvement thereof, may obtain a patent therefore, subject to the conditions and requirements of this title."[7] This refers to obtaining a

---

5. *See, e.g.,* Adobe Sys., Inc. v. One Stop Micro, Inc., 84 F. Supp. 2d 1086 (N.D. Cal. 2000); Microsoft Corp. v. Harmony Computers & Elecs., Inc., 846 F. Supp. 208 (E.D.N.Y. 1994).

6. *See* Central Point Software, Inc. v. Global Software & Accessories, Inc., 880 F. Supp. 957 (E.D.N.Y. 1995) (applies to any "act or practice in the nature of rental, lease or lending").

7. 35 U.S.C. § 101 (1998).

patent; the U.S. patent system entails a process of stating and pursuing ("prosecuting") a claim for a patent through a patent application. The U.S. Patent and Trademark Office reviews and either approves or rejects the application. If issued, the patent applies solely to the approved claims. The patent may still be contested in court and, in practice, courts hold many patents invalid.[8]

An issued patent does *not* give the patent holder the right to use or "practice" its invention. Instead, the owner receives what amounts to a negative right: the right to prevent anyone else from making, selling, offering for sale, or using the patented invention.[9] This is equivalent to saying the owner of real estate can prevent anyone from entering that real estate, but the owner does not have a right to enter its own real estate or build a house on it. This peculiar result in patent law stems from the fact that in many cases actual use of an invention requires rights under several patents; one valid patent may effectively block use of the other patented invention.

Under current U.S. patent law, an owner's rights are limited to a period of twenty years from the date of filing. The owner controls only the following rights for the patented invention:[10]

- Right to use
- Right to make
- Right to sell
- Right to offer for sale

Actions outside the scope of the limited rights are outside the scope of the patent and are not controlled by the patent owner through the patent. Patent case law further holds that, for a patented item sold at an authorized sale, these rights may be exhausted (that is, used up) for that item, while remaining in effect for that patent as a whole.[11]

Importantly, patent rights are not limited to preventing or seeking a remedy for knowingly copying an invention.[12] A third party who independently develops a process or item covered by the patent infringes that patent, even if that person is not aware that the patent exists. As a consequence, in commercial or technological fields dominated by patent law rights, it is common to conduct patent searches (an analysis of the Patent Office records to determine if an issued patent governs the proposed process) before commercialization. To the extent that Internet commerce becomes a field for patent law development and

---

8. *See, e.g.,* Michael O. Sutton, Patent Case Law Update (July 11, 2000) (paper presented at Texas State Bar Annual Meeting) (of those patents contested at Federal Circuit Court of Appeals during one year, only thirteen percent held valid and infringed, while another thirty-six percent held valid but not infringed; nineteen percent held invalid by appellate court).

9. *See* 35 U.S.C. § 105 (1998).

10. *Id.*

11. *See, e.g.,* Intel Corp. v. United States Int'l Trade Comm'n, 946 F.2d 821 (Fed. Cir. 1991) (doctrine applies to product manufactured pursuant to "foundry" license; producer free to resell).

12. 35 U.S.C. § 271 (1998).

for the application of preclusive patent rights, that same research process may become necessary.

There are significant limits on issuing a patent for a particular claimed invention. Not every new process or product that is commercially successful or, in relative terms, "inventive," will qualify for a patent. To qualify, the patent claim must satisfy various disclosure rules, as well as the following substantive rules (each standard has been subject to extensive litigation in various technological fields over the years; a thorough discussion is well beyond the scope of this chapter):

- It must be within the subject matter scope of patent law.
- It must be useful in the sense that it meets concepts of utility.
- It must not have been on sale for more than one year before the patent application.
- It must have been non-obvious to persons schooled in the art to which it applies.
- It must be novel and not have been anticipated by a prior patent or publication.

Beyond questions about patentable subject matter, the most significant of these limitations is the concept of non-obviousness. This awkward term comes from section 103 of the Patent Act, which states as follows:

> A patent may not be obtained . . . if the difference between the subject matter sought to be patented and the prior art are such that the subject matter as a would have been obvious at the time the invention was made to a person having ordinary skill in the art to which said subject matter pertains.[13]

This rule limits the application of patent law and patent rights to inventions that differ from ordinary expectations in the relevant technological or other field to which the patent pertains. Predictably, there is massive case law on this rule.[14] Just as predictably, its application ultimately hinges upon resolving often-difficult issues of fact about the current state and direction of technological art at the time of the invention. In a nascent world where the idea of patents on Internet business methods now exists, the doctrine of non-obviousness is likely to be the most contested substantive standard applied in determining the extent to which Internet businesses will be involved in property rights of this type.

When applying "obviousness" and other standards, however, the focus is upon the patent claim itself, as defined by its own terms. Thus, for example, as a matter of patent law, one would react differently to a claim for a "word processing program" than a claim for a "data correction routine for use within

---

13. *Id.* at § 103.
14. *See, e.g.,* Graham v. John Deere Co., 383 U.S. 1 (1966); In re Hayes Microcomputer Prods., Inc., 982 F.2d 1527 (Fed. Cir. 1992) (invention using escape codes in modem not obvious); Constant v. Advanced Micro-Devices, Inc., 848 F.2d 1560 (Fed. Cir. 1988).

a word processing program." The standards applied in law would be the same, but the likelihood of the claimed invention being satisfactory under these standards would differ greatly.

2. Subject Matter: Internet Hardware Systems

The application of patent law to the hardware underpinning of Internet systems has been clear for years. The number of reported decisions dealing with hardware patents—including microprocessor and similar systems—is legion.[15]

3. Subject Matter: Computer Software

Patent law also applies to software inventions.

This simple statement represents the culmination of long-term and ongoing disputes in the patent law system about the scope of patent subject matter. Initially, the disputes primarily involved a series of Supreme Court rulings occurring between 1972 and 1981. In the earliest of these cases, *Gottshalk v. Benson*,[16] the Court held that patent law did not apply to a claim for a mathematical method of converting numbers from one numerical base to another because all that was involved in the claim was a "mathematical algorithm" unconnected to anything else. The Court viewed this as a claim to a patent on a natural law or an idea, which is not allowed under patent law. *Benson* produced a wealth of litigation, centering largely upon the extent to which a particular claim adequately connected the software or other application to a tangible or practical result, thereby eliminating the risk that the claimed patentable subject matter was simply the idea or mathematical process.

The simple statement that patent law applies—in terms of subject matter—to computer software inventions is based upon a series of decisions by the Court of Appeals for the Federal Circuit during the late 1990s, which stripped away a large number of arcane and complex distinctions that had come to govern the law. In *State Street Bank & Trust Co. v. Signature Financial Group, Inc.*, the court held that a claim for a process of calculating—through software—the value of

---

15. *See, e.g.*, U.S. Phillips Corp. v. National Micronetics, 550 F.2d 716 (Fed. Cir. 1977).

16. Gottshalk v. Benson, 409 U.S. 63 (1972). *See also* Parker v. Flook, 437 U.S. 584 (1978) (claim for use of program to establish "alarm limit" in process of catalytic conversion not within patent subject matter; "conventional or obvious" activity after formula is solved and produces number does not in itself create patent subject matter); Diamond v. Diehr, 450 U.S. 175 (1982) (process for curing rubber, which involved continuous monitoring of data and automatic opening of curing door when appropriate number reached, was within patent subject matter).

various mutual investment funds from a shared pool of assets was within the subject matter of patent law:

> Unpatentable mathematical algorithms are identifiable by showing they are merely abstract ideas constituting disembodied concepts or truths that are not "useful." From a practical standpoint, this means that to be patentable an algorithm must be applied in a "useful" way. . . . Today, we hold that the transformation of data, representing discrete dollar amounts, by a machine through a series of mathematical calculations into a final share price, constitutes a practical application.[17]

Transformation of data, representing discrete dollar amounts, by a machine through a series of mathematical calculations into a final share price, for purpose of managing mutual fund investment structure, was practical application of a mathematical algorithm and thus within the scope of patent subject matter. The question in any case now becomes simply whether *what* the program is doing (as claimed in the patent claim) has a *practical meaning*, rather than merely computing abstract numbers. Of course, most software qualifies under this standard *for purposes of subject matter coverage.*

The general lawyer should understand several important facts in reference to this doctrine, which do not require the depth of knowledge about patent law that few of us will ever achieve. First, either the process the computer code implements or the machine it creates when combined with hardware is what is being patented, not the computer code itself. The computer code is in the domain of abstract language and, even more pertinent, the domain of copyright law. Thus, it is not a defense to a patent infringement claim to prove that different code was used to achieve the same result or process, as it is the result or process that is patented. On the other hand, it is not infringement to use similar code to achieve an entirely different process.

Furthermore, the court's holding in *State Street* addressed whether the process is capable of being patented as a matter of subject matter coverage. The court did not say anything about whether the process achieves patent protection in light of other standards, such as non-obviousness. The issue cuts both ways: Obviousness entails questions about the state of the "prior art" at the time of the invention. In fields that have long been under patent law protection, Patent Office records and other standard resources provide a good indication of prior art at any given time. That is not true in the software world or in the business world. As a result, there is a likelihood of overzealous issuance of patents and complex litigation regarding whether, in fact, the particular claim would have been obvious at the time.

---

17. State Street Bank & Trust Co. v. Signature Fin. Group, Inc., 149 F.3d 1368, 1373 (Fed. Cir. 1998).

4. Subject Matter: Business Methods

Traditionally, patent law has not applied to claimed inventions that were mere "methods of doing business." This exception to patent subject matter was historically based upon a variety of theories, largely associated with the idea that abstract ideas cannot be patented (for example, the idea of how to run a business).[18] It also may have reflected a judgment that patent law should focus upon the world of technology and leave the world of business to its own devices and other incentives for innovation.

In *State Street Bank & Trust Co. v. Signature Financial Group, Inc.*,[19] that world changed. The Court of Appeals for the Federal Circuit expressly repudiated the exemption for business methods, opening a new area for patent law that has great significance, especially in Internet businesses where the connection between methods of doing business and their technological implementation is quite close. *State Street* involved a method of allocating value among groups of mutual funds whose assets were in a single pool. This was patentable, according to the court, because it achieved a practical result even though it involved nothing more than manipulating numbers. The practical result resided in the fact that the numbers represented the value of investments. The court said, "We take this opportunity to lay this ill-conceived exception to rest. Since its inception, the 'business method' exception has merely represented the application of some general, but no longer applicable" exclusions.[20]

State Street was followed by *AT&T Corp. v. Excel Communications, Inc.*, in which the court held that patent law applied to a process for allocating a number identifying a telephone user's primary service carrier as a data field in a record using Boolean algebra principles to produce a useful number for billing purposes: "Because the claimed process applies . . . to produce a useful, concrete, tangible result without preempting other uses of the mathematical principle, on its face the claimed process comfortably falls within the scope of section 101."[21]

Where these decisions leave the law is not entirely clear. The court has never been presented with a wholly nontechnical method-of-doing-business claim, but it is signaling that how one transacts business is potentially a matter of patent law consideration. This represents an expansion of the role of patent law into the world of business and raises issues involving both defensive and offensive considerations. Offensively, it seems that any Internet business should at least consider the value of seeking a patent to establish claims over the methods involved. Defensively, of course, there is now the risk that an innovative business method, especially one implemented in the automated work of the Internet,

---

18. *See, e.g.,* RAYMOND T. NIMMER, THE LAW OF COMPUTER TECHNOLOGY ¶ 2.06[2] (3d ed. 1998).
19. State Street Bank & Trust Co. v. Signature Fin. Group, Inc., 149 F.3d 1368 (Fed. Cir. 1998).
20. *Id.* at 1375.
21. AT&T Corp. v. Excel Communications, Inc., 172 F.3d 1352, 1358 (Fed. Cir. 1999).

may entail patent law issues about infringement. Indeed, that litigation has already begun.[22]

In 1999, the Patent Act was amended to provide for a limited prior-use defense in a new section 273.[23] The defense is available to defendants charged with infringing "a method in a patent" if the defendant reduced the infringing subject matter to practice one year before the "effective filing date" of the patent and commercially used that subject matter in the United States before the effective filing date. The section defines a "method" as "a method of doing or conducting business." The revision, therefore, relates to the expanded availability of patent protections for methods of doing business. The legislative history indicates that the "method" status of an invention is not determined by the "technical form of the patent claims" but by the invention's underlying nature. The method that is the subject matter of the defense may be an internal method for doing business, such as an internal human resources management process, or a method for conducting business, such as a preliminary or intermediate manufacturing procedure, which contributes to the effectiveness of the business by producing a useful end result for the internal operation of the business or for external sale.

§ 2.3 Copyright Law

1. General Nature of the Law

In some respects, federal copyright law is the opposite of patent law in what it protects and how.

Copyright grants an author certain exclusive rights in a *work of authorship.* Under copyright law, a work of authorship applies to a wide range of works, including computer programs, databases and other digital works.[24] It refers to works that contain original expression of the author that is fixed in a tangible medium of expression. But copyright law expressly excludes any copyright protection for ideas, discoveries, or processes (methods of operation).[25] Indeed, if

---

22. *See* Amazon.com, Inc. v. Barnesandnoble.com, Inc., 239 F.3d 1343 (Fed. Cir. 2000) (question of obviousness regarding one-click method of Internet ordering); Mediacom Corp. v. Rates Technology, Inc., 4 F. Supp. 2d 17 (D. Mass. 1998) (product did not infringe patent claiming device for automatically routing telephone calls to carrier offering least expensive rates for each call, and patent claiming method for automatically updating database of calling rates used by such call rating device).

23. 35 U.S.C. § 273 (1999).

24. 17 U.S.C. § 101 (1999).

25. *Id.* § 102.

expression cannot be protected without protecting a process (as might be true when the two have merged), there is no protection for the expression.[26] In contrast, a primary focus of patent protection is upon processes.

The exclusive rights granted to a copyright owner are the following:[27]

- Right to reproduce the work in copies;
- Right to distribute the work;
- Right to prepare derivative works from the work;
- Right to publicly perform the work; and
- Right to publicly display the work.

Under copyright law, these rights attach immediately upon the creation of the expressive work and do not require a copyright notice, an approved application for copyright or registration of a copyright.[28]

Unlike rights under patent law, the rights in copyright are *exclusive*. The rights themselves, however, exclude copyright protection for allegedly infringing works that are independently developed or created. Thus, although a patent owner may successfully pursue a claim against a third party who independently created the patented process, a copyright owner must show that the allegedly infringing work has some connection to the copyright owner's work of authorship. This typically involves proof that the infringing work was copied from the original.[29] The complaining party need not prove that the defendant intended to infringe but merely that there was copying involved; as a general matter, it is not a defense to an infringement claim that the defendant was an innocent party with no wrongful intent or knowledge.[30]

Although the statute refers to protecting works of authorship, the focus of protection is upon the expression contained in a work of authorship. For example, if I examine your work of authorship and extract and copy into my own work nonexpressive (unprotected) factual material from your work, I have not infringed your copyright. The proof of infringement resides in showing that copyright elements have been reproduced, although those elements may often reside in the structure and organization of the work rather than simply in the specific language used.[31]

---

26. *See, e.g.,* Baker v. Seldon, 101 U.S. 99 (1879); Lotus Dev. Corp. v. Borland Int'l, Inc., 49 F.3d 982 (1st Cir. 1998).

27. 17 U.S.C. § 106 (1999).

28. Registration is required, however, to bring a court action for infringement. *See, e.g.,* Raquel v. Education Management Corp., 196 F.3d 171 (3d Cir. 1999) (copyright registration of work as "audiovisual work" was insufficient to support infringement action based upon song contained in that work; mischaracterization of work not immaterial but related to nature of work itself; also no evidence that misstatement inadvertent).

29. *See, e.g.,* Streetwise Maps, Inc. v. Vandjam, Inc., 159 F.3d 739 (2d Cir. 1998) (no copying shown; although competitor had access to publisher's maps, maps left viewer with sufficiently different impressions, notwithstanding fact that both maps used clarified street grids and color purple to depict water).

30. Such a situation, however, may affect the application of statutory damages for infringement.

31. *See, e.g.,* Mitek Holdings, Inc. v. Arce Eng'g Co., Inc., 89 F.3d 1548 (11th Cir. 1996); Engineering Dynamics, Inc. v. Structural Software, Inc., 26 F.3d 1335 (5th Cir. 1994); Brown Bag Software v. Symantec, 960 F.2d 1465 (9th Cir. 1992).

There are several exceptions to the exclusivity of copyrights. For example, if there is an authorized sale of a work, the buyer at the first sale does not infringe the copyright if it subsequently resells the copy.[32] This *first-sale rule* is paralleled in section 117 for computer programs, where the statute provides that the owner of a computer program can make copies and adaptations essential for its use of the program, an archival copy, and transfer the copy so long as it transfers all copies and destroys any adaptations.[33]

These exemptions refer to what would otherwise be rights exclusively within the copyright owner's control. Importantly, however, and especially for digital works, courts have held that the rights of the first transferee do not include first-sale rights if the transfer entailed an enforceable license under which the licensee's use was restricted in a manner inconsistent with ownership of the copy of the work.[34] The net result, when dealing with digital works (Internet or otherwise), is that one cannot assume mere possession of a copy gives the party with that copy any right to make other copies available to another person or, indeed, any right to have made the copy it already made.[35] The rights issues and rights clearance issues in digital environments, though perhaps commonplace for lawyers who have cleared rights in the motion picture and similar industries, provides far greater challenges for the commercial lawyer than the world of goods to which she is accustomed.

A second significant limitation on the exclusive rights of the copyright owner lies in the doctrine of *fair use*. Fair use is a defense to a claim of infringement. This doctrine, which originated in equity-based case law, is codified in the Copyright Act.[36] It has been accurately described as one of the most troublesome doctrines in copyright law.[37] The core of the concept is that there are some uses of copyrighted material whose minor effect on the copyright owner are far outweighed by general benefits for society in the use of published material. The statute lists four nonexclusive factors to consider in an analysis of whether a particular use is a fair use:[38]

- The purpose and character of the use, including whether it is for commercial or nonprofit purposes;
- The nature of the copyrighted work;
- The amount or proportion of the original work that is used; and
- The effect of the use on the potential market for, or value of, the copyrighted work.

---

32. 17 U.S.C. § 109 (1999).

33. 17 U.S.C. § 117 (1999).

34. *See, e.g.,* DSC Communications Corp. v. Pulse Communications, Inc., 170 F.3d 1354 (Fed. Cir. 1999); Adobe Sys. Inc. v. One Stop Micro, Inc., 84 F. Supp. 2d 1086 (N.D. Cal. 2000).

35. *See* Tasini v. New York Times, Inc., 192 F.3d 356 (2d Cir. 1999) (fact that publisher owned copyright in magazine and similar works that compiled separate works of authorship did not allow it to create online version of compilation without permission of individual authors).

36. 17 U.S.C. § 107 (1999).

37. Dollar v. Samuel Goldwin, Inc., 104 F.2d 662 (2d Cir. 1939).

38. 17 U.S.C. § 107 (1999).

Not surprisingly, the fair-use defense is a subject of extensive litigation and, given that it is a several-factor balancing test, the outcome of litigation is often unpredictable.[39]

Although this chapter does not survey the case law on fair use, two important features should be noted. The first is that the doctrine has a competition law theme. This is explicit in the factor that refers to the effect on the original author's market for, or value of, the work. In some cases, explicitly or implicitly, a court deciding a fair-use case determines the nature of the permitted marketplace. Thus, for example, the Ninth Circuit held that use in comparative advertising of photographs of particular screens of a copyright video game was fair use, even thought the advertising might have a significant adverse impact on the copyright owner's market.[40] The advertising was for a product that enabled the user to show the games on an ordinary computer, rather than solely on the system sold by the plaintiff. Although there might be a reduction in the original author's market share, the court concluded this effect was offset by the benefits to the consuming public and that copyright law was not intended to protect the marketplace for video game hardware.

The second feature involves so-called *transformative use*. This term was first used by the Supreme Court in holding that a parody of a popular song was fair use, even though it was for commercial purposes.[41] The transformation refers to use of the expression of the original to create a new work that does not compete with the original but may reference it in innovative ways. This theme is important in copyright litigation and has great significance for digital materials.

2. Copying into and within a Computer

One reason copyright law has become a major factor in the modern information age, especially in digital systems, lies in the nature of the systems and how they operate. In a word, most digital technology involves the frequent making and transferring of copies. This engages the copyright owner's exclusive right to reproduce its work.

Courts have consistently held that loading a copyrighted work into a computer makes a copy of that work.[42] If that copy is not protected by fair use or first sale, the copy is an infringement. For works loaded into the Internet, merely

---

39. *See generally* David Nimmer & Melville Nimmer, Nimmer on Copyright (1990).
40. Sony Computer Entertainment Am., Inc. v. Bleem, LLC, 54 U.S.P.Q.2d 1753 (9th Cir. 2000).
41. Campbell v. Acuff-Rose Music, Inc., 510 U.S. 569 (1994).
42. *See, e.g.*, Vault Corp. v. Quaid Software, Ltd., 847 F.2d 255, 260 (5th Cir. 1988) ("loading a program from a medium of storage into a computer's memory creates a copy of the program"); Apple Computer, Inc. v. Formula Int'l, Inc., 594 F. Supp. 617 (C.D. Cal. 1984); Bly v. Banbury Books, 638 F. Supp. 983 (E.D. Pa. 1986).

making the work available in a form different from its prior form is not fair use. One court held that loading musical works into an Internet site for later retrieval by alleged copy owners was not fair use; the court emphasized that whether to exploit this Internet market for its work was reserved to the copyright owner under copyright law.[43] Even if the owner decided not to enter this market, the unauthorized acts of the defendant had a significant impact on a potential market for the copyrighted work.

The courts' treatment of what constitutes making a copy is both correct and inevitable. Yet, when coupled with the fact that copyright attaches to any work without a requirement of notice or registration, it creates a difficult framework for author's rights in the Internet—one that restricts commercial providers of information. Most written or otherwise even marginally expressive works carry with them, when brought into the Internet, an important residue of copyright protection.

A further extension of this concept comes in the view that moving a work within a computer also makes a copy of the work, so long as movement from one part of memory to another or from one part of a network to another has sufficient permanence to satisfy the copyright rule that a copy must be in tangible form. This occurs when a computer program is copied into another part of the computer memory when the computer is turned on.[44] Operating a program within a computer, for its intended purposes, also may result in copying it within the machine.[45]

These conclusions flow from the nature of copyright law's focus on copying and the nature of digital systems. For example, when I send an e-mail to you, the end result is that both you and I have copies of the e-mail. When I forward an e-mail from you to another person in my network, all three of us have copies. E-mails, of course, are copyrighted if they contain sufficient original expression. Communications on the Internet thus typically involve making repetitive copies of various portions of material at various places in the system. Many of these copies are ephemeral in nature and insignificant for copyright purposes, but others are stored. In the view of some, the Internet is simply a giant copying machine.

This does not result in a world that calls for express copyright licenses (waivers) from uncounted people simply to do business. It does indicate, however, that the copyright dimension of information exchange on the Internet cannot be ignored. Concepts of implied authorization and fair use will work overtime in this environment.

---

43. UMG Recordings, Inc. v. MP3.com, Inc., 92 F. Supp. 2d 349 (S.D.N.Y. 2000); *see also* A&M Records, Inc. v. Napster, Inc., 239 F.3d 1004 (9th Cir. 2001).

44. MAI Sys. Corp. v. Peak Computer, Inc., 991 F.2d 511 (9th Cir. 1993) (moving program into RAM is copying); Advanced Computer Servs. of Mich., Inc. v. MAI Sys. Corp., 845 F. Supp. 356 (E.D. Va. 1994).

45. Stenograph L.L.C. v. Bossard Assocs., Inc., 144 F.3d 96 (D.C. Cir. 1998).

3. Independent Service Providers and Bulletin Boards

Some entities provide intermediary or conduit functions for the Internet, either as service providers who enable sending and gaining access to messages across Internet, or bulletin board or similar providers who make available a resource for exchange of information among participants. To see the problem of copyright liability, one need only recognize that transit across, or residence in, a system can create a copy that may be an infringement if not authorized by the copyright owner.

Courts initially dealing with this problem concluded that there were copies but that liability questions should most often center on the role of the intermediary—its intent and control of the transit or storage on the system. Thus, one early decision held that an Internet access provider might be liable for infringement committed by a subscriber, but this could not be direct infringement because the automated system precluded the operator from taking affirmative steps to cause copies of particular works from being made.[46] The relevant liability issue was contributory infringement; the operators could be liable if they knew about the infringing acts but took no steps to stop them from being distributed. The circumstance of bulletin board operators is more precarious. In reality, some operators actively engage in promoting and, perhaps, benefiting from infringing activity.[47] Additionally, these operators face questions about whether making the copies available online infringes the copyright owner's distribution or public display rights.[48]

In 1998, Congress enacted the Digital Millennium Copyright Act, which, among other things, contains specific provisions for Internet service providers, limiting their liability for the conduct of others that creates infringing copies.[49] Viewed from a commercial law perspective, these rules provide guidance on how an online resource of the type involved here should be structured to minimize the risk of liability. Section 512 covers a "provider of online services or network access, or the operator of facilities therefor."[50] For this category, there are liability rules for system caching, information residing on a system put there

---

46. Religious Tech. Ctr. v. Netcom On-Line Communication Servs., Inc., 907 F. Supp. 1361 (N.D. Cal. 1995).

47. *See, e.g.*, Sega Enters., Ltd. v. MAPHIA, 948 F. Supp. 923 (N.D. Cal. 1996) (operator of electronic bulletin board liable for contributory infringement; users were able to upload copyrighted video games to, and download games from, bulletin board—users who copied games directly infringed; operator knew that his users were copying games, provided facilities for infringing conduct, actively solicited users to upload unauthorized games, and provided road map on bulletin board for easy identification of games available for downloading); Playboy Enters., Inc. v. Webworld, Inc., 968 F. Supp. 1171 (N.D. Tex. 1997) (individuals who received share of site's income vicariously liable for infringement).

48. Playboy Enters., Inc. v. Russ Hardenburgh, Inc., 982 F. Supp. 503 (N.D. Ohio 1998) (operators of bulletin board system liable to publisher for direct copyright infringement; operators "distributed" and "displayed" copies of publisher's photographs in derogation of publisher's copyrights).

49. 17 U.S.C. § 512 (1999).

50. *Id.* § 512(k). Only the first definition applies to limitations created under subsection (a), while both definitions apply to all other parts of section 512.

by others, linking and nonprofit organizations.[51] It also deals with transmitting entities.

i. Transmitting Entities

Section 512(a) of the Digital Millennium Copyright Act provides that an "entity offering the transmission, routing, or providing of connections for digital online communications, between or among points specified by a user, of material of the user's choosing, without modification to the content of the material as sent or received," is not liable for monetary damages and is subject to limited exposure to injunctive relief by virtue of its activities, if the entity comes within the terms of subsection (a), which include the following:[52]

- the transmission is initiated by, or at the direction of, another party;
- the transmission is carried out through an automatic technical process without selection of the material by the provider;
- the provider does not select recipients, except as an automatic response to the request of another person;
- no copy of the material is maintained on the system or network in a manner ordinarily accessible to one other than the anticipated recipient and, as to such copies, is not maintained for a longer period than is reasonably necessary for the protected act; and
- the material is transmitted without modification of its content.

This subsection thus grants protection for automated passive carriers or service providers who have no role in selecting, shaping, directing or retaining the material.

ii. Information Placed on a System by Users

Section 512 addresses situations where copyright material is placed on a service provider's site, such as a bulletin board system. Section 512(c) provides not only a safe harbor for cases involving such systems but also a procedure through which copyright owners can assert and arguably enforce their rights without necessarily resorting to litigation.[53]

The basic structure of the law uses standards consistent with copyright case law on contributory and vicarious infringement. The service provider (for

---

51. *Id.* §§ 512(b)–(e).
52. *Id.* § 512(a).
53. *Id.* § 512(c).

example, the site operator) can avoid liability for the storage of infringing material on its system if stored at the direction of a user (for example, material posted by users). The system operator must not have actual knowledge of the infringement and may not be aware of "facts or circumstances from which infringing activity is apparent."[54] If the system provider obtains knowledge, it is protected only if it acts "expeditiously" to remove or disable access to the infringing material. This does not create a duty to monitor the site, but does create a duty to act quickly in the event infringement is discovered.[55] Section 512(g) provides that there is no liability "for any claim" resulting from good-faith removal of—or disabling access to—the material, regardless of whether it proves to be infringing, if the provider complies with a statutory notice requirement.[56] In addition, to avoid liability, the service provider must not receive a financial benefit "directly attributable" to the infringing activity. The service provider retains the exemption only if, on notification consistent with procedures outlined in the statute, it responds expeditiously to remove or disable access to the infringing activity. To implement the exemption generally and the notification procedure in particular, the service provider must designate an agent to receive notification.[57]

4. Modifying and Using Digital Images

Images in digital form are given copyright protection under the same standards as those for more traditional photographs and paintings.[58] The difference between the two lies in the fact that digital images, whether on or entered into the Internet, are more susceptible to creative manipulation and alteration than their paper counterparts. If the image is copyrighted, the right to make modi-

---

54. *Id.* § 512(c)(1). A similar baseline existed under general law. *See, e.g.,* Sega Enters., Ltd. v. MAPHIA, 948 F. Supp. 923 (N.D. Cal. 1996) (operator of electronic bulletin board liable for contributory infringement; users were able to upload copyrighted video games to, and download games from, bulletin board—operator did not directly infringe, but users who copied games directly infringed; operator knew his users were copying games, and provided facilities for infringing conduct).

55. *See* Religious Tech. Ctr. v. Netcom On-Line Communication Servs., Inc., 907 F. Supp. 1361 (N.D. Cal. 1995) (operator of computer bulletin board service and Internet access provider could be liable for copyright infringement committed by subscribers, but under contributory infringement analysis, operators liable if they knew of infringing postings but took no steps to stop subscriber from distributing postings; because of First Amendment concerns and notice not received until postings occurred, court denied preliminary injunction).

56. 17 U.S.C. § 512(g) (1999).

57. *Id.* § 512(c)(2).

58. Not all photographs or similar images are protected under copyright law. Especially when the sole purpose is to reproduce an original work of art faithfully, in photographic form, the slavish reproduction—if done well—may add no new expression and thus not be independently copyrightable. The issue is especially significant when the underlying work being photographed is not copyrighted. *See, e.g.,* Bridgeman Art Library, Ltd. v. Corel Corp., __ F. Supp. 2d __ (S.D.N.Y. 1998) (under British law, insufficient originality for copyright protection in photographic reproductions of famous works of art; therefore not infringement for software company to duplicate works of art in its digital clip-art products). *Cf.* Tiffany Design, Inc. v. Reno-Tahoe Specialty, Inc., 55 F. Supp. 2d 1113 (D. Nev. 1999) (copyrighted aerial photograph of Las Vegas).

fications lies with the copyright owner; it is encompassed within the exclusive right to make derivative works based upon the original work and, often, in the parallel right to make copies of the original.

This being said, in some cases the nature of the digital manipulation may constitute fair use, and these cases may begin to define the nature of Internet images as a fair source of secondary, commercial exploitation. In *Leibovitz v. Paramount Pictures Corp.*,[59] for example, the court held that an advertising image showing the body of a pregnant woman and the face of a male actor was a fair-use parody of the plaintiff's then-famous photograph of a nude pregnant woman. The advertisement image was transformative in nature and did not interfere with any potential market for the original photograph or other derivative works based upon it. The court emphasized that in the context of parody, the amount of copying is not the standard. To do a parody, an author must capture the heart of the original. Here the manipulated image was a fair parody.[60]

The court in *Kelly v. Arriba Soft Corp.*[61] held that there was a fair-use defense when the operator of a visual search engine web site acquired images from the Internet without authorization and used the images to create thumbnail references for its search engine. If the user desired to view the full image or acquire it, the image was displayed by opening a link to its originating web page. The lawsuit was brought by a photographer whose photographs were included in this system without his authorization. The court concluded that the thumbnail reproductions were a transformative use that did not affect the market for the copyrighted works: "Where, as here, a new use and new technology are evolving, the broad transformative purpose of the use weighs more heavily than the inevitable flaws in its early stages of development."[62]

Decisions such as *Arriba Soft* can be seen simply as applying copyright doctrine to a new setting in the Internet. Although they do that, they also serve an important function in beginning to define the nature and range of competition and business opportunity available on the Internet, consistent with existing property rights. In effect, they are beginning to outline the nature of the information market on the Internet.

It is important, however, to not read a decision like that in *Arriba Soft* as holding there exists a broad copyright exemption for taking images and other expressive work from Internet sites and using them commercially, or for distributing them over the Internet without permission.[63] It is quite clear that merely posting work on the Internet does not waive copyright protection for that work; thus, as in *Arriba Soft*, a fair use or similar defense is necessary to avoid infringement liability, if that liability can be avoided at all. Similarly,

---

59. Leibovitz v. Paramount Pictures Corp., 137 F.3d 109 (2d Cir. 1998).

60. *See also* Sony Computer Entertainment Am., Inc. v. Bleem, LLC, 54 U.S.P.Q.2d 1753 (9th Cir. 2000) (use of screen shots of video game in comparative advertising).

61. Kelly v. Arriba Soft Corp., 77 F. Supp. 2d 1116 (C.D. Cal. 1999).

62. *Id.* at 1121.

63. *See, e.g.*, Michaels v. Internet Entertainment Group, Inc., 1998 WL 211257 (C.D. Cal. 1998) (Internet distribution of film clip would not be fair use).

courts have held that merely posting copyrighted works on the Internet for free downloading and distribution does not waive copyright by the author in connection with downloading and distribution for commercial purposes.[64] Although cases of waiver, implied authorization and fair use may be found, the norm remains that a copyrighted work retains copyright protection for the expression that it contains.

5. Linking and Copyright Issues

Arriba Soft partly involved the use of linking technology to create a commercial site borrowing access to—or availability of—sites owned by third parties. The format is unique to the Internet. Although one could draw some parallels to ordinary indexing or reference services, the power and effect of this technology is a world of a different process and different product. The question in the context of copyright law is when, or whether, the creation of links without authorization by the other party exposes the site operator to liability for copyright infringement.[65]

In *Ticketmaster Corp. v. Tickets.com*,[66] the court rather summarily held that deep linking was not a copyright infringement. In this case, Ticketmaster operated a web site at which customers purchased tickets to events. Tickets.com operated a similar site but also provided customers with links to Ticketmaster to purchase tickets that could not be purchased on Tickets.com. The links conveyed the user directly to an interior location in the other site, from which the ticket was purchased. To obtain the relevant information for establishing these links, Tickets.com copied the Ticketmaster pages and extracted the relevant information. The court concluded this latter activity adequately alleged copying that might constitute infringement. The copying was not in extracting the facts from the site, but in making copies of the pages, as the facts themselves were not protected under copyright law. Regarding linking, the court said as follows:

> [H]yperlinking does not itself involve a violation of the Copyright Act (whatever it may do for other claims) since no copying is involved. The customer is automatically transferred to the particular genuine web page of the original author.

---

64. *See* Micro Star v. Formgen Inc., 154 F.3d 1107 (9th Cir. 1998) (court notes that enforceability of license not relevant; if not enforceable, acts unauthorized; if enforceable, acts exceeded license); Storm Impact, Inc. v. Software of Month Club, 13 F. Supp. 2d 782 (N.D. Ill. 1998).

65. There are other bases on which liability might rest, of course. One of the most likely to find play in the future concerns the simple right of the other party to control access to its own computer system. Thus, the law of most states and the federal government proscribes unauthorized access to a person's computer. One court conceives of acting in a manner that ignores this limiting right as a form of trespass. *See, e.g.,* eBay, Inc. v. Bidder's Edge, Inc.,—F. Supp. 2d—, 5 ILR (Pike & Fisher) 3059 (N.D. Cal. 2000); Hotmail Corp. v. Van$ Money Pie, Inc., 47 U.S.P.Q.2d 1020 (N.D. Cal. 1998); America Online, Inc. v. Ims, 48 U.S.P.Q.2d 1857 (E.D. Va. 1998).

66. Ticketmaster Corp. v. Tickets.com, 54 U.S.P.Q.2d 1344 (C.D. Cal. 2000).

There is no deception in what is happening. This is analogous to using a library's card index to get reference to particular items, albeit faster and more efficiently.[67]

In *Ticketmaster*, there was no proven, enforceable contract to buttress the claims against linking. More generally, it is clear that such an analysis will not preclude claims based upon indirect infringement, given that the system user is—more likely than not—making a copy of the linked work, even if the link supplier is not.

The Digital Millennium Copyright Act also addresses infringement liability for linking.[68] It gives a limited exemption from liability in a manner consistent with copyright law doctrine concerning contributory and vicarious infringement. The service provider (for example, the site operator) avoids liability if it lacks knowledge or awareness that the linked material is infringing. The subsection also provides that if the system provider obtains knowledge or awareness, it is protected by the exemption only if it acts "expeditiously" to remove or disable access to the infringing material. In addition, to avoid liability, the service provider must not receive a financial benefit from the infringing activity. The statute specifies standards under which the adequacy of a notice of infringement is to be measured for purposes of this exemption.[69]

Under copyright law, at least, there may be situations in which unauthorized links can be established and used as part of a commercial product. The freedom to do so, however, is clearly not absolute. Thus, for example, an operator who uses linking technology to enable and encourage infringing activity is not protected under the Digital Millennium Copyright Act or under case law dealing with contributory infringement.[70] Also, in some cases, links may violate rights unrelated to copyright law.

§ 2.4 Trademark Issues

1. General Nature of the Law

Unlike patent and copyright laws, which are entirely federal law systems, trademark laws consist of both federal and state law regimes.

---

67. *Id.* at 1350.
68. 17 U.S.C. § 512(d) (1999). *See infra* Section 3.2.B.(4) and Chapter 4 for more details on the DMCA.
69. *Id.* § 512(d)(3).
70. *See, e.g.,* Intellectual Reserve, Inc. v. Utah Lighthouse Ministry, Inc., 75 F. Supp. 2d 1290 (D. Utah 1999) (browsers of copyright infringing web sites themselves committed infringement when they viewed copyrighted text, and thus web site operators who actively directed users to those infringing sites could be held liable for contributory infringement).

In both federal and state law, the focus is on the marketplace, rather than on questions of protecting inventiveness or expressive creation. Generally, in trademark law, the mark owner is given a right to enforce exclusive rights in the use of the mark as a means to prevent confusion in the consumer marketplace.[71]

In a sense, then, although a trademark is properly considered a form of property, the rights of the mark owner are derivative in nature. It is not primarily the qualitative or inventive work of the mark owner that is protected; it is the risk of confusion about the source in the marketplace that serves as the basis for enforceable rights. The standard for proving infringement of a mark is to show that the competing (infringing) use created a likelihood of customer confusion.

2. Domain Name Registration

The most active area of litigation, legislative activity and administrative action involving trademarks on the Internet has centered on the relationship between trademarks (more accurately, trade names) and the registration or use of Internet domain names. The core issue focuses upon the idea of *branding* or identifying a product, service or company. From a commercial standpoint, this is especially important for the Internet where, by virtue of the nature of the system, contact with a product or web site often depends upon accessing it by an identifying name (such as the relevant trademark).

In the law, the issues ultimately deal with deciding who has the right to control identifying names on the Internet and under what conditions names that read on registered trademarks should be held solely within the control of the registered mark owner.

The initial focus centers upon the administrative structure through which domain names are issued by the numerous registries that exist around the world. Beginning in late 1998, the registration system was moved to a nonprofit, umbrella organization (ICANN), and other domain name registries had been created in addition to those in existence before the restructuring. In late 1999, ICANN approved a Uniform Dispute Resolution Policy (UDRP) establishing an arbitration procedure for domain name disputes. Several arbitration providers have been named. This is an expedited procedure that includes electronic filing and disposition. The dispute criteria and procedures are described in the ICANN web site at <http://www.icann.org/udrp>. Since the first decision was rendered in January 2000, there have been several hundred reported arbitration rulings.

---

71. *See generally* J. Thomas McCarthy, McCarthy on Trademarks (1999).

3. Domain Name Litigation

According to a number of reported decisions, a domain name may be an infringing use of a registered trademark. Depending upon the nature of the mark and the nature of the name that allegedly infringes it, however, ordinary trademark standards on infringement apply. Under these standards, in some cases, a mere name should not be treated as an enforceable trademark or as infringing a mark.[72]

This being said, a domain name may—and in fact has been held to—infringe by creating a likelihood of confusion with a valid trademark.[73] Of course, there are many cases where the facts indicate no infringement.[74]

The infringement standard focuses upon the likelihood of confusion in the market. The details of the tests used to make that determination vary somewhat from circuit to circuit, but in all cases entail a multifactor analysis that includes a review of these factors: similarity to the protected mark, the extent to which the business activities are similar or distinct, and the strength and descriptive capability of the mark.[75]

4. Cybersquatter Prevention

Shortly after the Internet became popular, a number of individuals with modern entrepreneurial spirit sought to capitalize on the domain name system and

---

72. *See, e.g.,* Data Concepts, Inc. v. Digital Consulting, Inc., __ F.3d __ (6th Cir. 1998); Green Prods. Co. v. Independence Corn By-products Co., 992 F. Supp. 1070 (N.D. Iowa 1998) ("ICBP's argument basically boils down to the idea that the [c]ourt should view the domain names as mere addresses which—along with the web sites attached to each name—are products in and of themselves. The [c]ourt disagrees. There is a close competitive proximity between the products that the two companies sell, and there is also a close competitive proximity between the domain name 'greenproducts.com' and the trademark 'Green Products.' The domain name . . . identifies the Internet site to those who reach it, much like a person's name identifies a particular person, or, more relevant to trademark disputes, a company's name identifies a specific company. Because customers who do not know what a company's domain name is will often guess that the domain name is the same as the company's name, a domain name mirroring a corporate name may be a valuable corporate asset, as it facilitates communication with a customer base.").

73. *See, e.g.,* Playboy Enters. Int'l, Inc. v. Global Site Designs, Inc., 1999 WL 311707 (S.D. Fla. 1999) ("plaintiff PEII is likely to succeed on the merits in proving trademark infringement, in [d]efendants' use of the domain names Playboyonline.net and Playmatesearch.net and use of the term 'welcome to Playboyonline.net' as the title of [d]efendant web sites so that trademark is accessible to individuals or Internet search engines"); Playboy Enters., Inc. v. Universal Tel-a-Talk, Inc., 1998 WL 767440 (E.D. Pa. 1998).

74. *See, e.g.,* Hasbro, Inc. v. Clue Computing, Inc., 66 F. Supp. 2d 117 (D. Mass. 1999) (game manufacturer's "Clue" mark not infringed by Internet consulting company's clue.com domain name; manufacturer's game not similar to company's computer consulting service, and little evidence of actual consumer confusion); CCBN.com v. C-Call.com, Inc., 73 F. Supp. 2d 106, 1999 WL 1075371 (D. Mass. 1999) (no proof of likelihood of infringement in use of StreetFusion.com in connection with mark StreetEvents.com between two competing companies that provide online stock market information; mark weak because of word "street" and not sufficient likelihood of confusion in this context when two companies essentially the only competitors in market).

75. *See, e.g.,* Polaroid Corp. v. Polarad Elecs. Corp., 287 F.2d 492 (2d Cir. 1995) (eight-factor test). *See also* GOTO.com, Inc. v. Walt Disney Co., 202 F.3d 1199 (9th Cir. 2000) (in case dealing with logo online, court noted the three most important factors in determining trademark infringement on Internet: similarity of marks, relatedness of goods or services, and simultaneous use of Web as marketing channel).

search methods by registering large groups of domain names, selecting names that coincided with the names of companies. Often (though not always), these were offered for sale to the companies whose names they resembled or duplicated. This activity and its impact on large, successful companies led to legislative action.

In 1999, Congress enacted the Anticybersquatting Consumer Protection Act (ACPA).[76] ACPA creates a cause of action against one who—with a bad-faith intention to profit—registers, traffics in or uses a domain name that:

1. is identical or confusingly similar to a mark that was distinctive when the domain name was registered;
2. is identical or confusingly similar to or dilutive of a mark that was famous when the domain name was registered; or
3. is protected under 18 U.S.C. § 706.

The statute sets forth various factors to consider when determining whether actions involve bad faith, including whether the mark is the registrant's legal name, whether the registrant intended to divert consumers and whether the registrant has offered to sell the domain to the mark owner and was warehousing multiple domain names that track marks of others. The statute provides for injunctive relief and actual or statutory damages (ranging from $1,000–$100,000 per name). The statute allows in rem jurisdiction for actions taken against the name itself. Of course, in the absence of personal jurisdiction, exercising this type of jurisdiction limits the remedy available to the complaining party.

Before the ink was dry on this statute, the Ninth Circuit, in *Sporty's Farm, LLC v. Sportsman's Market, Inc.*,[77] held that it could be applied retroactively and that, in this case, ACPA supported an injunction against continued use of the domain name. The court held that the "sporty's" trademark as used in connection with the company's catalog of merchandise and advertising was *distinctive* within the meaning of ACPA. According to the court, this result does not depend upon whether the mark was also famous. Rather, distinctiveness hinges on inherent qualities of a mark. A mark may be distinctive before it has been used, whereas even a famous mark may be so ordinary as to be notable for its lack of distinctiveness.

The next question is whether the domain name sportys.com is "identical or confusingly similar to" the sporty's mark. As we noted above, apostrophes cannot be used in domain names. As a result, the secondary domain name in this

---

76. 15 U.S.C. § 1125(d) (1999).

77. Sporty's Farm, LLC v. Sportsman's Mkt., Inc., 202 F.3d 489 (2d Cir. 2000). *See also* Spear, Leeds & Kellogg v. Rosado, 2000 WL 310355 (S.D.N.Y. 2000) (court granted permanent injunction against use of domain name associated with SLK's well-known REDIBOOK trademark under trademark law and under ACPA).

case (sportys) is indistinguishable from the Sportsman's trademark (sporty's). We therefore conclude that . . . it is certainly "confusingly similar" to the protected mark.[78]

Finally, there was adequate evidence of bad faith to profit. The defendant's companies had no intellectual property rights in sportys.com when the defendant registered the name. Indeed, the user company was not formed until nine months after the name was registered, and it did not begin operations until after the lawsuit was filed.[79]

5. General Issues of Infringement: Metatags and Search Engines

Although domain name disputes are the most common topics of Internet trademark litigation, they are not the only trademark issues that will continue to arise. Generally, many of these other issues do not differ materially from trademark issues in nontechnological settings. If an Internet site uses—without authorization—the mark of another person, that use is infringement if there is a likelihood of confusion under the same standards by which that issue is determined in other contexts. Some courts, however, suggest that the Internet alters the analysis, at least to an extent. In *GOTO.com, Inc. v. Walt Disney Co.,*[80] for example, the court affirmed a preliminary injunction against Disney based upon the conclusion that Disney was infringing a logo similar to a logo used on plaintiff's "GoTo" web site. The infringing use involved the Disney "Go Network" logo. According to the court, the three most important factors in determining trademark infringement in Internet cases are (1) the similarity of the marks, (2) the relatedness of the goods or services and (3) the simultaneous use of the Web as a marketing channel. Here, there were strong similarities and the two companies were involved in providing search engines. The court also indicated a willingness to look more broadly for confusing uses on the Internet than in other contexts:

> With respect to Internet services, even services that are not identical are capable of confusing the public. Although even Web tyros can distinguish between a

---

78. *Sporty's Farm,* 202 F.3d at 497.
79. *See also* Morrison & Foerster, LLP v. Wick, __ F. Supp. 2d __ (D. Colo. 2000) (Morrison & Foerster mark is distinctive and/or famous and therefore entitled to ACPA's protection; there was bad-faith intent for profit; "Mr. Wick argues that he uses the domain names merely to display 'parody' web pages, making fun of Morrison & Foerster and the practice of law in general. He contends this is a bona fide noncommercial use of the mark. However, I conclude that use of Morrison & Foerster's trademark in this domain name would confuse the public and disparage the firm. I further conclude that this is not bona fide parody."); Shields v. Zuccarini, 89 F. Supp. 2d 634 (E.D. Pa. 2000) (mark "Joe Cartoon" both distinctive and famous for purposes of ACPA; thus, defendant's use of joescartoon.com, joecarton.com, joescartons.com, joescartoons.com, and cartoonjoe.com. domain names were confusingly similar to plaintiff's joecartoon.com mark, within meaning of ACPA).
80. GOTO.com, Inc. v. Walt Disney Co., 202 F.3d 1199 (9th Cir. 2000).

web site that, for example, provides discounted travel tickets and one that provides free Web-based e-mail, a user would almost certainly assume a common sponsorship if the sites' trademarks were the same. The Yahoo.com web site is just one example of web genies that coordinate a bevy of distinct services under a common banner. . . . Whereas in the world of bricks and mortar, one may be able to distinguish easily between an expensive restaurant in New York and a mediocre one in Los Angeles, the Web is a very different world. Our ever-growing dependence on the Web may force us eventually to evolve into increasingly sophisticated users of the medium, but, for now, we can safely conclude that the use of remarkably similar trademarks on different web sites creates a likelihood of confusion amongst web users.[81]

Beyond this, some Internet contexts are clearly different from those associated with non-Internet commerce. One illustration involves use of trademark names in *metatags*. These are, essentially, identifiers that can influence Internet search engines to select a particular site given a particular search request.[82] It is quite clear that, in appropriate circumstances, unauthorized use of trademarks in metatags that attract searchers to a particular site may constitute infringement and create a likelihood of confusion, even though the tags themselves are not seen by the customer.[83] The Ninth Circuit Court of Appeals, in *Brookfield Communications, Inc. v. West Coast Entertainment Corp.*,[84] explained this result in terms of "initial interest confusion." The plaintiff's trademark in a metatag would have the effect of steering consumers who were using the Internet to that web site that was infringement. There was wrongful use of the plaintiff's trademark to capture initial customer attention, even though the consumer did not purchase products from the defendant under the mistaken impression that he was purchasing the plaintiff's products.

As litigation increasingly centers on the confusing effect of words used alone, there is an increasing risk that complaints will overstep the bounds and propose too heavy a restraint on free speech. For example, should an Internet search engine be prevented from associating certain types of advertising with situations where a user of the engine selects words such as "playboy" or "Playmate"? One court held that this steps too far:

---

81. *Id.* at 1206.

82. *See* Playboy Enters., Inc. v. Welles, 7 F. Supp. 2d 1098, 1104 (S.D. Cal. 1998) ("[M]etatags are not visible to the web surfer although some search engines rely on these tags to help web surfers find certain web sites. Much like the subject index of a card catalog, the metatags give the web surfer using a search engine a clearer indication of the content of a web site.").

83. Brookfield Communications, Inc. v. West Coast Entertainment Corp., 174 F.3d 1036 (9th Cir.1999); SNA, Inc. v. Array, 51 F. Supp. 2d 554 (E.D. Pa. 1999); New York State Soc'y of Certified Pub. Accountants v. Eric Louis Assoc., Inc., 1999 WL 1084220 (S.D.N.Y. 1999). *Cf.* Playboy Enters., Inc. v. Welles, 7 F. Supp. 2d 1098 (S.D. Cal. 1998).

84. Brookfield Communications, Inc. v. West Coast Entertainment Corp., 174 F.3d 1036 (9th Cir. 1999). *See also* New York State Soc'y of Certified Pub. Accountants v. Eric Louis Assoc., Inc., 1999 WL 1084220 (S.D.N.Y. 1999).

Parties may not leverage their rights in certain intellectual property to infringe the First Amendment rights of others. . . . Here, PEI is seeking . . . a monopoly on the words "playboy" and "playmate." Indeed, by seeking a prohibition on all advertisements that appear in response to the search words . . . PEI would effectively monopolize the use of these words on the Internet. This violates the First Amendment rights of (a) [the alleged infringers]; (b) other trademark holders of "playboy" and "playmate"; as well as (c) members of the public who conduct Internet searches.[85]

6. Trademark Dilution

A final area related to trademark law that has some currency in Internet environments involves the issue of trademark dilution. There are a number of state law dilution statutes, but the major legislation is a federal law adopted in 1995. The federal dilution statute defines *dilution* as a lessening of the capacity of a famous mark to identify and distinguish goods or services.[86] Importantly, the act does not require that there be competition, likelihood of confusion, or deception to state a cause of action. Fair use, noncommercial use and news reporting are exempt.

The statute recites a number of factors to consider when determining whether the affected mark is famous, such as the distinctiveness of the mark, the duration and extent of use, the extent of advertising and publicity, the geographical area of use, the degree of recognition of the mark, any use of similar marks by third persons and whether the mark is registered. Although this seemingly points toward requiring some significant level of fame, the cases are not consistent on this issue. The leading case involves an Internet-related context. In *Avery Denison Corp. v. Sumpton*,[87] the defendant obtained a variety of surname registrations, planning to license use of those registrations as a form of vanity e-mail address. Two of the names, Avery and Denison, were registered trademarks of Avery Denison. The trademark holder sued for trademark dilution under federal law and California law. The appellate court held that there was insufficient proof of either famousness of the marks or of commercial use by the defendant.

For a claim of dilution, the mark must be famous. This requires more than a distinctive mark. The mark must be truly prominent and renowned.[88] The court emphasized that the policy decision in dilution law is to limit the cause of action to:

---

85. 15 U.S.C. § 1125(c).

86. Playboy Enterprises, Inc. v. Netscape Communications Corp., 55 F. Supp. 2d 1070, 1085 (C.D. Cal. 1999).

87. Avery Denison Corp. v. Sumpton, 189 F.3d 868 (9th Cir. 1999).

88. *See* I.P. Lund Trading ApS v. Kohler Co., 163 F.3d 27 (1st Cir. 1998).

[a] select class of marks—those marks with such powerful consumer associations that even non-competing uses can impinge on their value. In the infringement and unfair competition scenario, where the less famous a trademark, the less the chance that consumers will be confused as to origin, a carefully crafted balance exists between protecting a trademark and permitting non-infringing uses. In the dilution context, likelihood of confusion is irrelevant. If dilution protection were accorded to trademarks based only on a showing of inherent or acquired distinctiveness, we would upset the balance in favor of over-protecting trademarks, at the expense of potential non-infringing uses.[89]

The concept of dilution has special relevance to the Internet because the holder of a prominent mark is effectively able to assert a monopoly position over that mark. For example, no web site could ever use the mark "Coca-Cola" for any purpose without risking an infringement action. The monopoly power conferred by a prominent mark creates a strong incentive for companies to argue that their marks are prominent, when in fact they may not be.

§ 2.5 Summary

It is difficult, if not impossible, to summarize a chapter that covers so much material in such a small space. In many cases, we left out the nuances of the law in these dynamic fields as they pertain to commerce on the Internet. Our goal has been to capture and portray the broad patterns and dynamic nature of traditional intellectual property law as it pertains to this new field of electronic commercial activity.

One pattern is clear to us. The developments in these areas of law and in other areas that create rights in information (such as privacy, trade secret and database protection law) will shape the competitive framework of the Internet, especially as it relates to informational assets and services. That competitive framework is emergent, rather than stable. The task for lawyers—both for themselves and on behalf of their clients—is to deal with the law not only as it is, but as it will be. The one certainty in this context is the certainty of change.

---

89. *Id.* at 876.

CHAPTER **3**

Web Transactions

Contents

Web Transactions

Chapter 3 addresses transactions involving the Internet. This chapter covers a wide variety of substantive areas, so it may be useful to understand how it has been organized. Five substantive areas are addressed: licensing transactions, web development and linking agreements, joint ventures, advertising deals and electronic transactions.

The first of these substantive areas, Section 3.1, complements the analysis in Chapter 2 by focusing upon the licensing of intellectual property, as opposed to how ownership rights are created through online technology. In the first segment, William F. Swiggart discusses the licensing of trademarks, trade secrets and copyrights arising in an online environment. The second segment, written by John G. Flaim, Truiken J. Heydn and William D. McSpadden, considers patent licensing and its application to Internet technology. In the third segment, David Daggett, Mary L. Williamson and Mark H. Wittow consider software and data licensing that has developed as a result of the Internet, and discuss the Uniform Computer Information Transaction Act. The final segment, written by Warren E. Agin, closes this substantive analysis with a discussion of how bankruptcy affects licensing transactions involving intellectual property.

Section 3.2 addresses web development and linking agreements. The first segment, authored by Mark Grossman and Joann Nesta Burnett, involves a discussion of web development agreements. The writers evaluate the key provisions of web development agreements and other considerations that arise in negotiations for this type of transaction. In the second segment, Andrew R. Basile and Michael W. Hauptman cover web linking agreements. They discuss the structure of these agreements and the current state of the law regarding their enforcement.

Section 3.3 involves a discussion of joint venture transactions related to the Internet. This segment is authored by Jeffrey D. Neuburger and Robert E. Freeman. They address traditional forms of joint ventures in the context of online deals, and provide guidance on structuring specific terms of these transactions, such as those related to exclusivity, promotion, intellectual property ownership and termination. The authors also provide model language.

Section 3.4 covers advertising deals. Lawrence M. Hertz describes the different types of advertising agreements available and the key provisions that typically arise. As part of his analysis, Hertz makes specific recommendations about how parties can mitigate risks that are often created by these relationships.

The final area of Chapter 3, Section 3.5, involves electronic transactions. Thomas J. Smedinghoff discusses the current state of the law regarding electronic transactions at the state, federal and international levels. He makes recommendations about how to ensure enforceability of electronic contracts and how to comply with specific requirements of recently passed legislation.

§ 3.1 Licensing Transactions

1. Licensing of Copyrights, Trade Secrets, Trademarks and Domain Names

i. License versus Linking Agreement

What is a license? A license is, literally, any granting of permission.[1] Because permission requires ownership, a license of intellectual property—such as a copyrighted work or a trademark—must be a grant of something short of full ownership to a third party; that is, permitting the licensee to use the property, but restricting the nature, geography or time—or any combination—of the use. A license thus allows multiple parties to share use of the same piece of intellectual property.

Internet domains, on the other hand, may not be shared per se[2] and their reach is, with some exceptions,[3] global. Therefore, unless a domain owner allows a third party the complete use of his domain for a limited period of time, a license per se is not possible. Many varieties of shared use of domain names, however, are achieved over the Internet through the use of linking agreements, which are compared and contrasted with licenses in different parts of this chapter. (A detailed discussion of linking agreements appears in Section 3.2.2 of this chapter.)

ii. Copyright Law and License Provisions

A. What Is a Copyright?[4]

The U.S. Copyright Act[5] protects—for a term of more than seventy years from their creation[6]—nearly all *works of authorship* that have been reduced to

---

1. BLACK'S LAW DICTIONARY 1067 (4th ed. 1968) ("authority or liberty given to do or forbear any act"); Monsour v. City of Shreveport, 194 So. 569, 571 (La. 1940) (leave to do thing that licensor could prevent); Western Elec. Co. v. Pacent Reproducer Corp., 42 F.2d 116, 118 (2d Cir. 1930).

2. *See* Section 3.1.1.v of this chapter.

3. *See* LICRA et UEJF contre Yahoo! Inc. et Yahoo France, Superior Court of Paris, Jean-Jacques Gomez, J., Nov. 20, 2000 (English translated text available at *Webliography on the Yahoo Case*, <http://www.lapres.net/html/yahweb.html>) (U.S.-domiciled company ordered by French court to employ technical means to restrict access by French citizens to auctions that sell Nazi memorabilia on its site).

4. For more information on copyrights, see *supra* Chapter 2, Intellectual Property.

5. 17 U.S.C. §§ 101–1332 (1999).

6. The Sonny Bono Copyright Protection Act, signed into law on October 27, 1998, added another twenty years to the already significantly extended copyright term of the life of the author, plus fifty years retroactively to all works that had not yet entered the public domain.

any tangible form of expression.[7] Subject only to the right of *fair use*,[8] copyright law prevents any person other than the author from copying, making a derivative work from, or displaying or performing publicly a copyrighted work without the author's permission.[9]

B. Copyright License Provisions

Unlike trade secret and trademark licenses, copyright permission may be licensed freely, and a license need not include certain restrictions in order to avoid jeopardizing the licensed property. Most computer software is primarily protected through license restrictions on use, and prohibitions against the development of derivative works and against reverse engineering, whereby a version of the software is derived without violating its copyright per se (for example, through use of a *clean room* whereby engineers without direct exposure to the program are asked to duplicate its functions).

Largely at the behest of the recording and movie industries, the Digital Millennium Copyright Act (DMCA), signed into law without fanfare in 1998,[10] criminalized the development or use of any device to circumvent technological measures intended to prevent decoding of copyright protected material.[11] The constitutionality of such a broad prohibition is still open to question.[12] If DMCA's anticircumvention provisions continue to be upheld, one may argue that license restrictions against reverse engineering are no longer needed in software licenses as long as underlying code is protected by copyright law, because DMCA could be construed to prohibit reverse engineering as circumvention. Meanwhile, it is probably advisable to take a "belt-and-suspenders approach" and continue to include such restrictions.

---

7. 17 U.S.C. § 102 (1999).

8. *Id.* § 104.

9. *Id.* § 106.

10. *Id.* § 1201. For more information on the DMCA, see *infra* Chapter 4, Content Liability.

11. (1)(A) No person shall circumvent a technological measure that effectively controls access to a work protected under this title.

    . . .

    (2) As used in this subsection—

    (A) to "circumvent protection afforded by a technological measure" means avoiding, bypassing, removing, deactivating, or otherwise impairing a technological measure; and copyright owner under this title" if the measure, in the ordinary course of its operation, prevents, restricts, or under this title.

Id.

12. *See* Pamela Samuelson, *Intellectual Property and the Digital Economy: Why Anti-Circumvention Regulations Need to Be Revised*, 14 Berkeley Tech. L.J. 519 (1999); John H. Mutchler, *Circumvention of Copyright Protection Systems*, 10 Intell. Prop. Today 12 (2000).

iii. Trade Secret Law and License Provisions

A. What Is a Trade Secret?[13]

Trade secret law, though subject to state regulation only, is fairly consistent state by state, and generally protects any formula, device, pattern or compilation of information that affords a business an advantage over its competitors and that is kept secret through consistent vigilance by the business.[14]

Computer software without Hypertext Markup Language (HTML) and other copyrighted works, such as movie and sound recordings, rely upon the protection of their underlying software code through trade secrets. DVD recordings, for example, contain secret codes that degrade the quality of recordings when copies are made.

B. Trade Secret License Provisions

Because a trade secret loses legal protection once it is revealed with the owner's permission, each and every trade secret license requires the licensee to maintain the same efforts to protect the secrecy of the process as the owner does. The absence of such a provision in a single license can cause complete loss of the trade secret that is the subject of the license.

iv. Trademark Law and License Provisions

A. What Is a Trademark?

Trademarks are often thought of as brand names, which identify a product or service as coming from a particular company. *Branding* is simply increasing marketplace recognition of a trademark. A trademark thus carries no value apart from the manner in which it is used and perceived in the marketplace. This distinguishes trademarks from other forms of intellectual property that carry inherent value, such as the originality of expression protected by copyright, the uniqueness of a patented invention or the usefulness of a secret process protected by trade secret law.

---

13. For more information on trade secrets, see *supra* Chapter 2, Intellectual Property.
14. *See* Restatement of Torts § 759 (1939).

B. Can a Trademark Be Licensed?

A trademark may be licensed, though with some caveats. In the early twentieth century, courts viewed any attempt at licensing a trademark apart from the goods or services that were sold under the mark as deceptive; therefore, the law prohibited any such licensing.[15] Courts later recognized that the public's perception of a mark may follow it to its licensee without deception, and therefore began to uphold licenses when the licensor retained quality control.[16] This change was codified into the federal Lanham Act.[17] Conversely, a *naked license* without control over trademark quality still may be found deceptive,[18] or to constitute actual abandonment by the owner of the mark.[19]

Thus, each trademark license must still include the right of the licensor to control the manner in which the trademark is displayed, and the nature and quality of the goods or services associated with the mark.

C. Trademark License Provisions

Most intellectual property licenses that include trademarks ought to include the following in addition to the more general provisions stated above:

- *Registration, Date of First Use*: The parties should specify whether and where the mark is registered. It may also be useful for the licensee to know the date of first use, to guard against conflicting users.
- *Building the Mark's Strength*: The party selling the license ought to ensure that the trademark is used in a manner that builds the distinctiveness of the mark; that is, (a) that the mark is marketed and advertised appropriately, (b) that the mark is used for goods or services that are consistent

---

15. *See* MacMahan Pharm. Co. v. Denver Chem. Mfg. Co., 113 F. 468, 474–75 (8th Cir. 1901) (invalidating trademark that had been assigned apart from its underlying business).

16. *See* 3 J. Thomas McCarthy, McCarthy on Trademarks and Unfair Competition § 18:39 at 18–62 (3d ed. 1996).

17. The Lanham Act defines a trademark to include:
> any word, name, symbol, or device, or any combination thereof—
> (1) used by a person, or
> (2) which a person has a bona fide intention to use in commerce and applies to register on the principal register established by this chapter, to identify and distinguish his or her goods, including a unique product, from those manufactured or sold by others and to indicate the source of the goods, even if that source is unknown.

15 U.S.C. § 1127 (1999). The Lanham Act also states that a trademark may be used by a "related company" (*id.* § 1055), defined as "any person whose use of a mark is controlled by the owner of the mark with respect to the nature and quality of the goods or services on or in connection with which the mark is used." *Id.* § 1127.

18. *See* Societé Comptoir de L'Industrie Contenniere Etablissements Boussac v. Alexander's Dep't Stores, Inc., 299 F.2d 33, 35–36 (2d Cir. 1962).

19. *See* E.I. DuPont de Nemours & Co. v. Celanese Corp. of Am., 167 F.2d 484, 487–88 (C.C.P.A. 1948).

with or that expand the existing use of the mark, (c) that the licensee display no other mark in conjunction with the licensed mark in a way that confuses the public about its owner and (d) that the licensee avoid the use or adoption of any confusingly similar mark.

- *Quality Control*: The parties must specify standards for quality control, to maintain the strength of any licensed mark. This especially becomes an issue in any value-added-reseller (VAR) negotiation, in which it is essential to require that any products being sold in conjunction with the mark are consistent with the quality of the licensor's products and services.
- *Accrual of Goodwill*: The parties should state that all goodwill from the mark's use accrues to the licensor. Accrual of goodwill is necessary to ensure the continued ownership of, and growth in, the value of the mark.
- *Responsibility for Registration*: It is also useful to allocate responsibility for maintenance of any registration(s) of the mark within the licensee's sales territory. If the owner of a mark has engaged distributors or VARs on a nonexclusive basis or within the same trademark jurisdiction, the licensor would be the obvious choice of a party to register or maintain the registration of the mark, and the parties may not need to determine who must file to register or maintain the mark in the relevant jurisdictions.

However, if the licensee accepts a lion's share—or the exclusive use—of the mark's value within a trademark jurisdiction, it may make the most sense for the licensee to accept responsibility for maintaining and perhaps expanding upon the mark's registration. It is important that the parties address this concern clearly in any license agreement. Any eagerness on the part of the licensor to push to the licensee the responsibility to maintain the registration of a mark within a foreign jurisdiction should be tempered by the concern to ensure that ownership of the registration is retained in the event the licensor wishes to cancel or substantially reduce the scope of the distributorship.

v. Domain Name Law and Linking

A. What Is a Domain Name?

The Virginia Supreme Court recently went a long way toward establishing a legal definition of the domain name.[20] Each computer server on the Internet displays a numerical Internet Protocol (IP) address enabling it to communicate with other Internet computers.[21] A *domain name* is a unique string of letters

---

20. *See* Network Solutions, Inc. v. Umbro Int'l Inc. et al., 259 Va. 759, 529 S.E.2d 80 (Va. 2000).
21. *Id.* at 764.

that the domain registrar agrees—on a first come, first-served basis—to associate with a given IP address for a given length of time, thus enabling other participants on the Internet to find certain files that the operator of the server associates with the domain name.[22]

The court refused garnishment under state statute by a creditor of the registrant of thirty-eight domain names on the grounds that a domain name is a contractual right that does not fit within the statute's definition of property. A domain name is therefore strictly "the product of a contract for services between the registrar and registrant."[23] For any transfer of ownership of a domain name, the registrars require only that the transferor agree to a registrant name change agreement.[24]

B. Domain Names Compared with Other Intellectual Property

Domain names resemble trademarks closely, as either can be strings of characters used to sell goods or services. In other ways, they are completely different: though any trademark can be identical to another trademark as long there is no likelihood of confusion,[25] no two parties may share a domain name within a given top-level domain.[26] Thus, no holder of a domain name may license it per se and retain its concurrent use, as can be done with any trademark.[27] Though domain names also resemble other forms of intellectual property— such as copyrights, patents and trade secrets—in their uniqueness and inherent value, those forms may be freely licensed, while domains cannot.

This does not mean that a domain name that resembles another trademark or domain name cannot infringe that trademark, or the trademark represented by the domain. The holder of a domain that is an obvious variant of a registered trademark may be found to have registered the domain in bad faith, in violation of the Anticybersquatting Consumer Protection Act of 1999 (ACPA)[28] or in violation of the Uniform Dispute Resolution Policy (UDRP) of the Internet

---

22. *Id.* at 769.

23. *Id.* (citing Dorer v. Arel, 60 F. Supp. 2d 558, 561 (E.D. Va. 1999). *See also* Electronic Funds & Data Corp. v. Zlobec, No. 99–26830 (N.Y. Sup. Ct., Suffolk Cty., June 27, 2000) (agreeing with *Umbro* that Internet domain name registration not "property," but "writing that is only an 'evidentiary manifestation' of a right" to contractual performance by domain name registrar). *Cf.* Online Partners.com Inc. v. Atlanticnet Media Corp, No. C98–4146 SI ENE (N.D. Cal. Jan. 20, 2000), No. 5ECLR 217 (N.D. Cal. Mar. 1, 2000) (ordering attachment under theory of "constructive trust" against domain name used to display homosexual pornography, whose owner had not responded to complaint).

24. *See, e.g.,* <http://www.networksolutions.com/makechanges/rnca/agreement.html>.

25. 15 U.S.C. § 1052 (1999).

26. The registrars, as coordinated by the Internet Corporation for Assigned Names and Numbers (ICANN), will not allow the registration of more than one unique character string. *See* Network Solutions, Inc. v. Umbro Int'l Inc. et al., 259 Va. 759, 767 (2000).

27. *See, e.g.,* Pueblo Int'l Inc. v. Pueblo Online, Nat'l Arbitration Forum No. FA00700095250 (Aug. 24, 2000) (full text available at National Arbitration Forum's web site, <http://www.arbforum.com/domains/>) (panelist decision under Uniform Dispute Resolution Policy that commercial grocery store chain with ".com" site lacked rights to identical domain name in ".org" top-level domain).

28. Codified within Lanham Act at 15 U.S.C. § 1125(d) (1999).

Corporation for Assigned Names and Numbers (ICANN) for domain names.[29] Using a domain name that resembles a registered trademark can also constitute straightforward trademark infringement if the plaintiff can show that the domain name was used in commerce.[30]

Thus, any party wishing to register and use a domain that contains—or at all resembles—a strong, registered trademark would be well advised to license the right to do so from its owner or face losing registration in a UDRP arbitration or court case under ACPA or the Lanham Act.[31]

vi. Interactive Media License/Linking Provisions

A. Web Linking Agreements: Quasi-Licenses in Interactive Media

Web linking agreements are covered later in this chapter, but one point is worth making here: All commercial links must include a license, whether explicit or implied, to use the copyright protected content and trademarks of the linked party. Even an internal link may run afoul of this requirement. In a recent New York case, for example, the owner of a domain name that did not infringe an identical, domestic trademark was nonetheless held in contempt of an earlier order simply for including within its own, noninfringing U.S. sites a link to its foreign domain.[32] It is thus advisable to be vigilant about the need to seek and obtain any licenses that may be required for a link.

Interactive media licenses/linking agreements tend to fall into the categories discussed below.

---

29. <http://www.networksolutions.com/legal/dispute-policy.html>; Yahoo! Inc. v. Zively a/k/a Names Oz, World Intellectual Property Organization (WIPO), Case No. D2000–0273 (June 14, 2000) <http://arbiter.wipo.int/domains/decision/html/d2000–0273.html> (arbitrator's holding under UDRP that thirty-seven confusingly similar variants of yahoo.com were registered in bad faith, and should be transferred to Yahoo! Inc.); *but see* Lifeplan v. Life Plan, Nat'l Arbitration Forum Claim No. FA00005000094826 (July 13, 2000) <http://www.arbforum.com/domains/> (no bad faith found under UDRP when complainant was diet and weight loss company that registered U.S. trademark LIFEPLAN in 1994 and respondent registered domain name lifeplan.com in 1995 in connection with "non-financial lifetime goal setting services").

30. In a recent New York case, for example, the court found federal trademark infringement and federal trademark dilution by the defendant's www.buffalonews.com because, although the defendant claimed his site was just a parody of the plaintiff *Buffalo News*, a daily newspaper whose name had been registered as a trademark since 1980, the site offered a link to the web site of the defendant's competing newspaper, *Apartment Spotlight Magazine*, thus satisfying the Lanham Act's "use in commerce" requirement. OBH Inc. v. Spotlight Magazine Inc., No. 99-CV-746A (W.D.N.Y. February 28, 2000); *cf.* Northland Ins. Cos. v. Blaylock, No. 00–308 DSD/JMM (D. Minn. Sept. 25, 2000) (First Amendment right of operator of www.northlandinsurance.com to criticize insurance company outweighed whatever initial confusion was experienced by consumers looking for information about plaintiff company; no Lanham Act violation because plaintiff did not use domain commercially, and no ACPA violation because domain not used in bad faith).

31. *See, e.g.* Porsche Cars N. Am. Inc. v. Spencer, No. Civ. S-00–471 GEB PA (E.D. Cal. May 18, 2000) (registrant enjoined against use of porschesource.com in likely violation of ACPA; "registration of a domain name in no way trumps federal trademark law"); Banco Inverlat v. www.Inverlat.com, No. 00–640-A (E.D. Va. Sept. 8, 2000) (suit by Mexican financial services corporation against apparent cybersquatter).

32. Jeri-Jo Knitwear Inc. v. Club Italia Inc., No. 98 CV 4270 RO (S.D.N.Y. Apr. 18, 2000) (defendant ordered to remove all links to www.energie.it from its own ".com" sites).

B. End User Licenses versus Terms of Service

End user licenses cover articles of software that are protected by copyright and, in the case of non-HTML software, also trade secret.[33] A freestanding software program might be licensed with a *shrink-wrap*[34] or *click-through* agreement.

The end user's right to use an Internet or web site, on the other hand, may take the form of a linked page on the site entitled, "Terms of Service." Web site terms of service must be displayed prominently to be binding.[35] Some form of click-though arrangement is preferable, as virtually all click-through licenses for software have been upheld when challenged.[36] In the case of subscription news services or databases, the equivalent of an end user license would be the subscription or access agreement.

C. Distribution Licenses versus Outsourcing Links

Reseller—or value-added-reseller (VAR)—licenses are entered into by the manufacturer of software and some type of distributor. A reseller is a company that brings the product unadorned to a retail or catalog customer, while a VAR incorporates the software into another product or bundle of related products.[37] Such licenses include agreements to use the copyrights inherent in the product, and the trademarks associated with it. On the theory that a reseller has better knowledge of, and control over, a product's end users than the manufacturer, a distribution agreement often binds the reseller with affirmative covenants to notify the manufacturer of any infringement of the manufacturer's intellectual property of which the reseller becomes aware, and possibly to take action against the infringer.

The interactive media equivalent of such a reseller license is a linking agreement, whereby a VAR buys an outsourcing link to third party services that enable the VAR to offer a more complete Internet site.

---

33. HTML source code is transparent to any user using the "Source" command under the "View" tool of either Netscape Navigator or Microsoft Explorer, and therefore can never be a protectable trade secret, unlike most non-HTML code.

34. The leading case upholding the enforceability of shrink-wrap agreements remains *ProCD Inc. v. Zeidenberg*, 86 F.2d 1447 (7th Cir. 1996).

35. In the only published decision so far concerning a web site's terms of service, the court held in a suit for trespass and copyright violation that the plaintiff's terms of service barring "deep linking" to pages other than its homepage were nonbinding on the defendant linker, because they were not displayed prominently. Ticketmaster v. Tickets.com, Inc., 2000 U.S. Dist. LFNEXIS 4553 (C.D. Cal. 2000).

36. Lieschke v. RealNetworks Inc., No. 99 C 7380 (N.D. Ill. Feb. 10, 2000) (online accept-or-reject agreement that must be assented to before installation of software package held enforceable in connection with arbitration clause); Caspi v. The Microsoft Network, L.L.C., No. A-2182–97&5 (N.J. Super. Ct. App. Div. July 2, 1999) (same holding in connection with subscriber agreement for Microsoft Network); *see also* ProCD, Inc. v. Zeidenberg, 86 F.2d 1447, 1452 (7th Cir. 1996) (court noted that buyer of software had to know about terms of agreement "because the software splashed the license on the screen and would not let him proceed without indicating acceptance").

37. *See, e.g.*, Adobe Sys. Inc. v. One Stop Micro Inc., 84 F. Supp. 2d 1086 (N.D. Cal. 2000).

Affirmative covenants are often not necessary in outsourcing linking agreements, unless the linker is in a better position to know how the link is being used than its provider. Such a covenant may make sense for a database provider, because the provider may need the cooperation of its distributors to keep the distributors' end user customers from downloading the provider's non-copyright-protected data in bulk.

D. Development Licenses

Licenses for the development of software, including web sites, tend to be provided on either a time-and-materials or a fixed-price basis. Fixed-price service providers generally rely upon the reuse of previously developed, proprietary subroutines, so they fall under the agreed upon budget. Fixed-price development contracts therefore are more likely to involve only a partial assignment of ownership to the customer, with the service provider retaining ownership of its subroutines, and a nonexclusive license thereof going back to the customer (often made contingent upon the full payment of the development fee) so the customer can operate the portion of its program that it owns in full.

A time-and-materials contract is more likely to grant the customer full ownership of the software, both because it provides compensation for having assumed more of the development risk and because the developer is likely to own less code in the first place. Ownership of non-HTML software is nearly always an issue for extensive discussion and careful negotiation.

HTML software development agreements, on the other hand, usually do not address the issue of ownership of subroutines. Because of the openness of HTML code, any rival may view the source display of any of the developer's special techniques and methods at any time, and there is no reason to protect it. This openness has been a major factor in the rapid growth of the Internet.

E. Licenses Made in Connection with the Sale of a Business versus Link Referral Agreements

Although the sale of a business often involves complete assignments of all the intellectual property of the business, a seller may sometimes wish to retain limited use of its software, through either an assignment and license back to the buyer, or a straight retention of ownership and license back of more limited rights. The sale of an Internet business, because of the nonshareability of domain names, is more likely to involve the full transfer of the entire site to a different domain.

If the seller wishes to sell only its site and retain its domain, the parties may agree to refer Internet surfers from the seller's domain to that of the buyer. If the domain carries intrinsic value (for example, drugstore.com), the parties may agree to set a time limit on referrals, or the seller may simply agree to offer a link to the buyer's site from a new site at the old location.

vii. Some Common License Provisions

Many license provisions are shared among all license types regardless of the nature of the intellectual property being licensed, though their extent and specific terms may still vary according to the nature of the property being licensed.

A. Extent of Use; Right of Sublicense

End user licenses are by definition limited to personal use by the user. End user licenses carry no right of sublicense, and often restrict use to the specific "purchaser"—which sometimes, absurdly, prevents transfer of ownership of a given single program to another individual, but allows free use throughout any corporation that may have purchased the license.

Unless a distributor simply passes the vendor's shrink-wrap license along to the end user, distributor licenses must always specify a right of sublicense, so the licensee may carry out the purposes of the license.[38] VAR licenses may restrict any sublicensing to within the product or software bundle offered by the VAR.[39]

The equivalent of a restriction on sublicensing in a linking agreement might be when the link provider wants to restrict third parties such as competitors from linking to the linked site. Another roughly comparable restriction might be a prohibition against the linking site allowing the linked services to be used for illegal or immoral purposes, such as furthering the Web's thriving pornography industry.

B. Exclusivity; Territory

It is important to state whether a license conveys exclusive or nonexclusive rights to the property. Most licenses—other than those for custom, time-and-materials built software—are nonexclusive, and in those cases it often makes more sense to assign ownership than effect a license.

---

38. Generally, a license agreement conveys no right of sublicense unless specified. *See* Council of Better Bus. Bureaus, Inc. v. Better Bus. Bureau, Inc., 200 U.S.P.Q. (BNA) 282 (S.D. Fla. 1978).

39. As an example of the loose language sometimes employed in software licenses, Adobe Software recently brought suit for a third party's pirating of software that the defendant obtained from an Adobe reseller under a license that referred to the licensed software as having been "sold," a common misnomer in the software industry for "licensed." Fortunately for Adobe, the judge applied industry usage and held for the plaintiff. Adobe Sys. Inc. *supra* note 37.

Although most shrink-wrap licenses contain no geographic restrictions, companywide or "site" licenses may restrict usage of the software to company sites. Territorial restrictions must be specified in any distributorship or VAR arrangement. If there are only a limited number of large customers, it may make more sense for several distributors to divide the customers, rather than restricting their efforts to a particular geographic territory.

Territorial limitations in linking agreements might consist of limiting the use of trademarks and domain names to certain country domains.[40]

C. Duration

All licenses must specify a duration. Software licenses often state they are perpetual because the current copyright term of seventy-plus years seems an eternity in the context of rapid technological development. In reality, even a "perpetual" license expires at the end of the copyright term when the product enters the public domain. Trademark licenses, tied as they are to goodwill, and usually made in the context of some form of distributorship, are more likely to be renewable annually, and are often terminable upon short notice from the licensor.

Most linking agreements contain a limited term, contingent upon an end user's payment of a subscription fee or, in the case of an outsourcing agreement, either for a limited time period or contingent upon the linked site owner's continued satisfaction with revenues from the linking site.

D. Fees

Licensee fees should be specified in detail for all licenses, and especially for licensing arrangements involving more than an end user's one-time, fixed fee. For VAR licenses, the parties should negotiate whether the licensee should pay a one-time "access" fee to reflect overhead costs, including costs of sale. Similarly, in linking agreements, a "development" fee may be paid by the company accessing the linked services as a means of sharing the costs of initiating the site as well as sales overhead.

Royalty issues for discussion in copyright and trademark licenses should include the following:

1. A decision should be made about whether minimum royalties will be payable over given periods, and whether any minima for a given period

---

40. *See* Jeri-Jo Knitwear Inc. v. Club Italia Inc., No. 98 CV 4270 RO (S.D.N.Y. Apr. 18, 2000).

will be creditable against future royalty payments in periods when the minimum is exceeded.

2. The base amount from which the royalty is to be drawn should be defined. Licensors are usually better off taking a percentage of gross, to avoid encouraging the licensee to inflate overhead costs to reduce the royalty.

3. Audit provisions may serve to warn licensees to hew to the straight and narrow, even though such provisions are rarely exercised in practice.

Any minimum royalties payable in linking agreements may reflect hosting, as well as other ongoing expenses of the linked site. Audit provisions are often unnecessary in linking agreements because surfers' clicks may be continuously monitored by the licensor. Determining the party to collect credit card revenues is also an issue for discussion, as it may sometimes be just as easy for the licensor to do so as the licensee.

2. Patent Licensing and Internet Commerce

i. Introduction

The licensing value of an invention is determined by a variety of factors, including the economic value that the invention will create for the licensee and the ability of the licensee to exclude competitors from the marketplace. When entering into a license agreement, the parties should therefore assess the likelihood that a patent will be issued on the invention. This assessment will often be an important factor in the royalty negotiations. A licensee will certainly not be ready to pay high royalties for an invention of which the patentability is questionable. But even if a patent has issued on the licensed invention, questions may remain as to whether it could be invalidated later. Accordingly, unique provisions should be included in license agreements to deal with the Internet-related patents.

This section 3.1.2 will provide guidance to potential licensees and licensors when preparing license agreements for Internet-related patents. First, this section will provide a brief background on the patentability of Internet-related inventions. Because a general overview of the requirements for patentability is provided in Section 3.1.1, this section will focus on issues specific to Internet-related inventions. Second, this section will provide examples of existing Internet-related patents to illustrate the current trends in patentability of Internet-related inventions. This section also provides a brief overview of recent cases in which the validity of Internet-related patents has been litigated. Third, this section will provide a list of issues which should be considered by the parties when negotiating licenses on Internet-related patents.

ii. Patentability of Internet-Related Inventions

An invention can be patented only if it relates to patentable subject matter and fulfills further requirements of novelty, non-obviousness and usefulness.[41]

Internet-related patents often pertain to business methods. As mentioned in Chapter 2, the *State Street* decision held that the business method exception no longer applies under U.S. patent law.[42] The *State Street* court ruled that a software patent should claim a "useful, concrete and tangible result."[43] For instance, software that produces a binding sales contract with a customer probably fulfills the requirement of a "useful, concrete and tangible result," as the contract results in mutual obligations that generate revenue for the operator of the web site.

Under U.S. patent law, the threshold for proving utility is very low. Anything that has the potential of fulfilling an existing demand or creating a new demand (which is true for most Internet-related patents) would be considered "useful" under 35 U.S.C. § 101. Indeed, the utility requirement will be considered to be met irrespective of whether the invention is accepted by the market or not.

The requirement of novelty under 35 U.S.C. § 102, however, has become a particular challenge for the Patent and Trademark Office (PTO) whenever an Internet-related patent is involved. Section 102 requires, inter alia, that the invention must not have been (1) known or used by others in the United States before the applicant's invention or (2) patented, published or publicly used or on sale in the United States more than one year before the patent application date. Whereas it is virtually impossible for PTO to determine whether an invention has been known or used by someone else in the United States, it can search existing patents and publications to determine if the invention has been patented or published before the critical date. Therefore, the database of prior art patents and publications at the PTO provides a critical database for evaluating the novelty of the invention.

The database of existing patents and publications at the PTO related to Internet-related inventions is limited because the patentability of these inventions did not become clear until the *State Street* decision in 1998. Because the patentability of these inventions was uncertain prior to this time, most inventors chose to protect their Internet and computer-related inventions as trade secrets, thus limiting the body of publicly available prior art. In addition, the PTO generally will not research the Internet for existing concepts to determine if an Internet-related invention is already in public use. As a result, every Internet-related patent, despite its being approved and issued by the PTO, bears a considerable risk of being anticipated by prior art and therefore invalidated. It is,

---

41. *See* United States v. Adams, 383 U.S. 39 (1966); Radio Steel & Mfg. Co. v. MTD Prods., Inc., 566 F. Supp. 609 (D.C. Ohio 1983).
42. State Street Bank & Trust Co. v. Signature Fin. Group, Inc., 149 F.3d 1368 (Fed. Cir. 1998).
43. *Id.* at 1375.

consequently, strongly advisable to perform thorough prior art research when investigating the novelty of Internet-related inventions.

The so-called on-sale bar to patentability is particularly important for Internet-related patents. The term "on sale" under 35 U.S.C. § 102 means any offer to sell, irrespective of whether the offer disclosed the invention, whether the offer was confidential, or whether a sale was ever actually consummated. In any of these cases, a patent application must be filed within one year from the first offer for sale, otherwise patentability is barred. Internet applications, as software products in general, are often offered for sale before their development is completed. Accordingly, a thorough investigation of sales activities must be conducted.

It remains unclear how closely prior art must be related to the subject matter of the invention to render a patent invalid for lack of novelty. A concept may be new to the realm of the Internet, yet be part of prior art in the "real world." This raises a question about whether implementation of a prior-art concept in the Internet should be considered as new, or whether existing prior art outside the Internet renders such concept unpatentable. For instance, the idea of community shopping is by no means new. For many years mail-order businesses have offered discounts for large orders, which results in collective orders by consumer groups. When community shopping was first offered via the Internet, it was certainly new to Internet commerce, but not new to commerce in general. Although community shopping through the Internet brings additional benefits when compared to the mail-order system, questions remain about whether these benefits are inherent in any interconnected system such as the Internet, and whether the implementation of a known concept into a new environment, which results in additional benefits should be patentable.

A patent may not be issued if the subject matter would have been obvious to a person having ordinary skill in the art to which the subject matter pertains.[44] To determine non-obviousness of an Internet-related patent, both the prior art in the "real world" and the prior art in the virtual reality of the Internet must be considered. As already mentioned, PTO generally does not search for prior art systems in use on the Internet, so it may well issue a patent for an invention that is, in fact, obvious.

Because prior art from within and outside the Internet should be taken into consideration, this raises the question about whether the mere implementation of a well-known business concept (such as community shopping or reverse auction) into the Internet environment is generally obvious. Business concepts that already exist in the real world are clearly prior art. The concept of the Internet, a worldwide network of interconnected computers, is also within the prior art. The mere combination of those two elements of prior art may well be within the level of ordinary skill of someone from the Internet industry or someone from the industry that uses such a business concept. In other words,

---

44. 35 U.S.C. § 103(a) (2001).

it does not necessarily require extraordinary skill to do something over the Internet, which so far has been done only outside the Internet. The mere combination of an existing business method with the Internet is, therefore, not usually sufficient to establish non-obviousness. The invention must have an additional element that exceeds the level of mere application of ordinary skill. This additional element is difficult, if not impossible, to cover by an abstract definition—its existence must be decided on a case-by-case basis.

iii. Examples of Internet-Related Inventions and Recent Cases

Following are practical examples of Internet-related patents issued by PTO.

A. Priceline.com, Inc.—U.S. Patent Nos. 5,794,207; 5,797,127 and 5,897,620

Priceline.com, Inc. has obtained several patents for specific methods of selling goods and services over the Internet, such as the reverse auction.

According to the Priceline.com patents, the customer places a conditional purchase offer; that is, a binding offer containing one or more conditions for the purchase of an item, such as airline travel at a customer-defined price. Upon the server's receipt of a conditional purchase offer, the server accesses a database containing seller-defined rules (including prices) to determine if the offer matches any of the rules. Depending upon whether the conditional purchase offer matches the seller's rules, the offer is accepted, rejected or countered; a counteroffer must be accepted by the customer. Upon acceptance of an offer, the system orders the item (for example, books the flight).

Priceline.com filed suit against Microsoft and one of its subsidiaries, Expedia, Inc., alleging that Expedia.com's hotel price matching service infringed Priceline's U.S. Patent No. 5,794,207. The alleged infringing process utilized a reverse auction to sell hotel rooms. In January 2001, the parties settled the lawsuit and Microsoft and Expedia.com became licensees under the '207 patent. Microsoft and Expedia joined other reported licensees Alliance Mortgage Company, Budget Rent-a-Car and WebHouse Club in paying royalties to Priceline.com.

B. Amazon.com: Method and System for Placing Purchase Orders—U.S. Patent No. 5,960,411

Amazon.com, Inc. obtained a patent for a method for placing orders online that requires only one step (i.e., one mouse click[45]). When shopping online at Amazon.com, the customer can place an order for a specified item by one single mouse click. One-click shopping, however, works only if the customer has prer-egistered with Amazon.com so that the system can identify the customer's computer. After a customer pre-registers for one-click shopping, a button for the one-click order is displayed on each web page which contains information about a specified item. By utilizing this button, the customer does not need to follow the multistep check-out procedure that the so-called shopping-cart model provides. During the height of the 1999 Christmas shopping season, Amazon.com filed a patent infringement lawsuit against Barnes & Noble alleging that their website's Express Lane shopping feature infringed Amazon.com's one-click shopping patent. On December 1, 1999, the U.S. District Court for the Western District of Washington issued a preliminary injunction against Barnes & Noble restraining the latter from infringing Amazon's one-click patent. The court, however, allowed Barnes & Noble to continue to offer an Express Lane feature if it was modified to avoid infringement of Amazon's patent, such as by requiring one or two more additional actions from the user.

Although Amazon.com won a significant victory against its competitor during an important holiday shopping season, Amazon.com also attracted harsh criticism from others in the Internet industry and from the public in general. In fact, Jeff Bezos, the President and CEO of Amazon.com, published an open letter in March of 2000 which advocated reform of the patent system to deal with the difficulties of Internet patents.[46] In February of 2001, the Federal Circuit overturned the preliminary injunction against Barnes & Noble citing substantial questions of validity of the one-click shopping patent.

C. British Telecommunications—U.S. Patent No. 4,873,662

In June 2000, the seventeen largest U.S. Internet providers received a demand letter from British Telecom offering a license. British Telecom claimed that eleven years ago, it patented the well-known hypertext link—an essential feature of the Internet. If British Telecom were successful in claiming a license fee for each hyperlink, the revenue would be astronomical, considering the billions of hyperlinks that exist in the Internet. In December 2000, British Te-

---

45. The first company that licensed Amazon's one-click patent was Apple. *See* Troy Wolverton, *Apple Licenses Amazon's 1-Click*, CNET News.com, Sept. 18, 2000, at <http://news.cnet.com/news/0–1007–200–2811079.html?tag=st.ne.1007.saslnk.saseml>.

46. Jeff Bezos, *An Open Letter from Jeff Bezos on the Subject of Patents*, Mar. 9, 2000, <http://www.amazon.com/exec/obidos/subst/misc/patents.html/002–3274153–0297620>.

lecom filed suit against Prodigy, one of the seventeen Internet providers, in New York alleging infringement of its patent. Substantial questions have arisen, however, with respect to the validity of the patent. In particular, many individuals following this lawsuit have identified numerous computer conference papers dated from the early 1970s that describe the concept of hyperlinks for computer systems.

The cases discussed illustrate that Internet-related patents involve a substantial risk of litigation, and that patentees must always defend themselves against the argument of invalidity of the patents. Although many of these cases have not yet been decided, one can predict that the validity of Internet-related patents is more likely to be challenged than other patents. Licensing an Internet-related invention requires a sound assessment of the patentability of the invention and of the likelihood that the patent, once issued, might be later invalidated. Apart from the invalidity issue, there are other aspects of Internet-related patents that call for specific provisions in license agreements. These aspects are outlined below.

iv. Patent Licensing Concerns

A. Subject of the License

There are three different licensing subjects for Internet-related inventions: disclosures, patent applications and patents. Of course, a license agreement must specify the subject of the license. In addition, if the license pertains to a disclosure or a patent application, the license agreement should contain a provision about whether a future patent or patent application is covered by the license agreement.

When defining the subject of the license, possible future improvements and further developments of the invention should be taken into account. As with software in general, Internet-related inventions are subject to rapid development and can become quickly outdated. A licensee, of course, wants future improvements included in the license. The licensor, however, may not want to include improvements without additional charge. For instance, the licensor may want the licensee to sign a separate software maintenance agreement that provides for the delivery of updates against an additional fee, while also establishing a licensor's positive obligation to improve the invention continually and to eliminate possible software defects.

B. Ownership of Changes and Combined Technology

If, under the terms of a license agreement, the licensee is entitled to change the software or to combine it with other software (as in a VAR agreement), ownership in the changed or combined product must be agreed upon in the license agreement. When defining the ownership of the technology, ownership of both copyright and patent rights should be explicitly recited in the agreement. This is because the default rules of ownership for these intellectual property rights often produce opposite results. For example, in the absence of an agreement, an employee who develops software code will be the owner of any patent rights that arise from the code. On the other hand, the employer will own any copyrights that arise from the same code. This can produce a situation in which the respective ownership rights of the parties are nearly insoluble. Accordingly, an agreement that clearly defines ownership of *all* intellectual property rights will avoid any ambiguity.

C. Confidentiality Concerns and Source Code

Confidentiality concerns must be considered in connection with the subject of the license, particularly the extent to which a licensor must make disclosures. Internet-related patents consist mainly in software, which raises the question of protecting the source code. A license agreement can prohibit decompiling and reverse engineering of the software, or it can provide the contrary, such as an obligation of the licensor to disclose the source code. Although the licensor has an interest in keeping the source code secret, the licensee wants the source code, so it can obtain control over the software and continue using it after the licensor has gone bankrupt or otherwise ceased doing business. Depending upon the purpose of the license, disclosure of the source code may be appropriate, particularly if the licensee is to modify the licensed software. A licensee's concerns that relate only to bankruptcy or dissolution of the licensor can be satisfied by an escrow agreement.

These issues and suggestions apply only to the source code of the computer programs that run in the background of an Internet application. There is no point in establishing a confidentiality clause for web page source code, as it can be viewed by any Internet browser. To avoid confusion, the scope of the non-disclosure clause should be clarified by providing a precise definition of source code.

D. Provision for the Case of Invalidity

The fact that a patent has been issued does not firmly establish the novelty and non-obviousness of the patent. This raises a question about whether specific provisions regarding possible invalidity should be included in Internet-related patent license agreements. Standard patent license agreements rarely contain such express provisions, because both parties rely upon the validity of the patent and because the conventional patent license agreement is based upon the parties' mutual desire to enter an amicable business relationship.

With Internet-related patents, however, the situation may be different. As stated above, Internet-related patents may be more likely to be attacked on invalidity grounds. Accordingly, the license agreements should expressly state whether the agreement is based solely on the patent rights associated with the technology, or whether the license also covers other intellectual property rights such as copyrights, trade secrets and know-how. A well crafted license agreement describing other intellectual property rights may therefore survive even if the underlying patents are invalidated.

(1) Termination Right and Refund of Royalties

In a situation where a patent license is entered into under the threat of litigation by the patentee, it may be worthwhile for the license agreement to provide for the possibility of the patent proving invalid. Whereas a patent owner may be determined to initiate litigation unless the infringing party signs a license agreement, the prospective licensee may not want to litigate the case itself, but instead would prefer to benefit the patent is invalidated at some time in the future. This clause may contain anything from a mere right of the licensee to terminate the license agreement without observing a notice period, up to refund of part or all of the royalties paid by the licensee.

(2) Warranty

A licensee may request that the licensor warrant the validity of a patent, which, in the event of invalidity, would result in claims for breach of warranty. A licensor's warranty, however, is most likely to be limited to a statement that the licensor, at the time of signing the agreement, does not know and has no reason to believe that the patent is invalid. Claims for breach of the warranty would then require that the licensee furnish proof of substantial facts regarding the licensor's knowledge of invalidity.

(3) Validity of the Patent as a Condition for Validity of the License Agreement

As an alternative, validity of the licensed patent may be stipulated as a condition—precedent or subsequent—for the validity of the license agreement. In the former case, the licensor would be obliged to return all royalties to the licensee, whereas in the latter case the license agreement would terminate automatically without any refund of royalties.

(4) Invention as Subject of the License

If the licensee has an interest in the license notwithstanding the invalidity of the patent, the subject of the license may be defined as the invention plus the respective patent, along with a provision that invalidation of the patent will not affect the license of the underlying invention. The licensee will have such an interest if it invested considerably in the Internet application and cannot afford to shut down the web site. By extending the license to both the patent and the underlying invention, the licensee's and licensor's rights under the agreement will be safeguarded even if the patent is invalidated.

(5) No-Challenge Clauses

One potential problem facing licensors is the situation where a licensee enters into a license agreement to obtain the technology, and later challenges the validity of the patent and refuses to pay royalties while continuing to use the technology. From the licensor's perspective, there may thus be a need to include in the license agreement some protection against the licensee challenging the patent.

This could be achieved by a *no-challenge clause* whereby the licensee agrees to refrain from challenging the validity of the patent. As an alternative, the agreement could include a *no-challenge termination clause* that would authorize the licensor to terminate the license if the licensee challenged the validity of the patent.

There is, however, a considerable risk that such clauses are unenforceable. Although no court has ruled directly on no-challenge termination clauses, similar clauses were considered unenforceable in the early seventies.[47] This was based on a 1969 decision by the U.S. Supreme Court in *Lear, Inc. v. Adkins*.[48] The Court held that licensees cannot be stopped from challenging the validity of licensed patents. The subject of the license in *Lear* was a patent application for improvement of an existing product. The license agreement allowed the licensee to terminate the agreement if the licensor's patent application was unsuccessful or if a court declared the patent invalid. The licensee began withholding royalties after PTO rejected the application and then terminated the agreement after a second rejection by PTO. When the patent was finally granted, the licensee still refused to pay the royalties based upon an argument that the patent was invalid. The licensor subsequently sued the licensee for the unpaid royalty payments. On appeal, the Supreme Court held that the licensee was entitled to avoid payment of the royalties accruing after the patent issued if the licensee could prove invalidity of the patent. In addition, the Court held that there is often no person better suited to challenge a questionable patent than a licensee and that it is in the public interest to invalidate questionable patents.

During the 1980s, the Federal Circuit held that a Licensee that entered into a settlement agreement requiring it to pay royalties to the patentee regardless of whether the licensed patents may later be held invalid and/or unenforceable is bound by the agreement and could not later challenge the validity of the patent.[49] In 1991, the Federal Circuit rendered a similar decision regarding consent decrees.[50] Although these more recent decisions hold that a licensee

---

47. Bendix Corp. v. Balax, Inc., 421 F.2d 809 (7th Cir. 1970); Panther Pumps & Equip. Co. v. Hydrocraft, Inc., 468 F.2d 225 (7th Cir. 1972).
48. Lear, Inc. v. Adkins, 395 U.S. 653 (1969).
49. Hemstreet v. Spiegel, Inc., 851 F.2d 348 (Fed. Cir. 1988).
50. Foster v. Hallco Mfg. Co., 947 F.2d 469 (Fed. Cir. 1991).

can be restrained from challenging a patent in the future when litigation is to be concluded, they do not give a clear indication about the enforceability of no-challenge clauses that have been incorporated in license agreements that were entered without the pressure of pending litigation.

Because the question of enforceability of no-challenge clauses and no-challenge termination clauses remains open, the use of such provisions requires in-depth analysis of their advantages and disadvantages; whether they should be used depends upon the facts and circumstances of each situation. It is, therefore, particularly important to obtain the advice of a specialist when licensing Internet-related patents.

E. Royalty Terms

Case law has identified royalty terms as a means to protect invalid patents. In the *Lear* case, the Supreme Court noted that competition should not be repressed by worthless patents.[51] It concluded that a licensee may cease paying the agreed-upon royalties if the licensed patent proves invalid. Although pursuant to *Lear* a contractual obligation to pay royalties for invalid patents is not enforceable, an obligation to pay royalties for a patent application is not per se unenforceable.

Due to its strong position, a licensor can often force a licensee to accept royalty terms that effectively protect worthless inventions, by shifting a considerable part of the royalty payments to the beginning of the license term. Typically, the real value of an invention can only be determined later, when PTO reaches a decision on the patent application and the commercial success of the invention can be assessed; hence the licensor has quite a risk. This risk can, however, be shifted to the licensee. The software industry, for instance, has been quite successful in using business-to-business license agreements that provide for initial royalties that are large and nonrefundable. In most cases the initial royalty is credited against the incurred per-unit royalties, but the risk of being able to sell enough units to pay off the initial royalty lies with the licensee. When it becomes apparent that the licensed invention has little value, the licensor may—due to the initial, nonrefundable royalty—already have received value from the licensee that far exceeds the value of the invention.

The quick, technical development of the Internet adds to this effect. Licensors can quickly generate large amounts in royalties by licensing inventions that are outdated by the time the patent is invalidated or PTO rejects a patent application. It remains to be seen whether the courts will take this into consideration, and whether they will question the legality of nonrefundable initial royalties on this basis.

---

51. Lear, Inc. v. Adkins, 395 U.S. 653 (1969).

F. Field-of-Use Restrictions

When an invention that is to be licensed can be used in more than one area, a question arises about *field-of-use restrictions*. Internet-related inventions—which often consist of business methods—frequently have more than one field of use. Field-of-use restrictions enable a licensor to maximize the amount of royalties, because the licensor can arrange lower royalties for low-demand fields and higher royalties for high-demand fields. In addition, a field-of-use restriction enables the licensor to participate in the expansion of the licensees. For instance, if the object of the license is a computer program that implements a specific method of selling goods or services over the Internet, the license to a seller of books may be restricted to the sale of books. Once the licensee expands its business and begins to sell videos, the parties must amend the license agreement to cover the sale of videos, possibly at a higher royalty.

G. Exhaustion

The question of patent exhaustion has been discussed in connection with cases involving parties who did not have licenses for patented goods they wished to sell, and who solved this problem by having the goods manufactured by licensees.[52] Because Internet-related patents usually involve software, the license agreement must be clear that the licensee is not entitled to sell the software to someone else. The licensor otherwise runs the risk that the licensee will distribute copies of the software to third parties who may then, based upon the patent-exhaustion doctrine, resell those copies.

H. Indemnity

A licensee naturally has an interest in fighting patent infringements by third parties. Particularly when a sole and exclusive license is granted (that is, a license that excludes everyone but the licensee from making use of the patent in a certain territory), the licensee is often the only party pursuing infringements by third parties, because the licensee is the only party that suffers and seeks compensation for damages. With the greater risk of invalidity of Internet-related patents, a licensee may be concerned about expenses if it pursues a seeming infringement and it becomes apparent later that the patent is invalid. The licensee will have to bear attorney fees and possibly pay damages if the patent is found to be invalid.

---

52. Intel Corp. v. United States Int'l Trade Comm'n, 946 F.2d 821 (Fed. Cir. 1991); Intel Corp. v. ULSI Sys. Tech., Inc., 995 F.2d 1566 (Fed. Cir. 1993).

Whereas standard patent license agreements often stipulate that all expenses in connection with pursuing infringements must be borne by the party that initiated the action, the uncertain situation about the validity of Internet-related patents calls for indemnity clauses that shift the risk of invalidity from the licensee to the licensor. Through such a clause, the licensor agrees to indemnify the licensee for costs, expenses and losses caused by the invalidity of the licensed patent.

Of course, the indemnity clause should provide for appropriate notification as a precondition for indemnity, as well as obligations of both parties to support each other in patent infringement lawsuits. The indemnity clause should cover not only patent infringement, but any infringement of intellectual property rights, including copyright and trademark infringements.

The license may, however, cover more than one particular invention. The licensor may deliver to the licensee a software product that combines the licensor's invention with other software products that were developed and licensed to the licensor by a third party. In such a case of combined technology, it is important to exclude indemnity because the costs incurred in connection with a patent infringement lawsuit refer to the combined technology and were not solely caused by the component, the patent for which has been found to be invalid.

I. Acquisition of the Licensee

Many e-commerce companies are start-ups financed by venture capital, and they are often bought by larger companies at a later stage of development. This raises a question about whether the license agreement should include a change-in-ownership provision. The licensor may not want to be confronted with a large company or competitor on the same conditions as the agreement with the small start-up. Accordingly, an Internet patent license agreement should address a possible change in ownership of the licensee.

The licensor's continuity interest can be safeguarded in several ways. The license agreement can give the licensor the right to terminate if ownership in the licensee changes. Of course, "change of ownership" must be defined precisely in the agreement. For instance, it may be defined as a transfer of 50% or more of the shares in the licensee. (It should be made clear that two or more subsequent transfers of less than 50% of the shares constitute a change of ownership as soon as 50% or more of the original shareholders have been replaced.) Alternatively, the license agreement could provide that any (or a certain) transfer of shares requires the consent of the licensor, in which case the license agreement should specify the reasons such consent may be denied. To avoid excessive use of the license after the licensee has been acquired, the license can be limited to a certain product line, a certain number of sold items or a certain term.

J. Multijurisdictional Issues

Due to the global nature of the Internet, all Internet applications, once they go online, can be used in—and thus become subject to the laws of—each jurisdiction that has Internet access. Although a U.S. patent provides protection against use of the invention only in the United States, a licensee indemnification agreement should be limited to infringement that takes place only in the United States. Otherwise the licensor may be forced to bear costs that were incurred by patent infringement litigation all over the world.[53]

v. Conclusion

The Federal circuit's *State Street* decision has been criticized by groups other than lawyers. Software patents in general, and Internet-related patents in particular, are heavily disputed and fought against by associations such as the Free Software Foundation. It may well be that the pressure of the public will lead to a different approach by courts, legislatures or PTO.

At the moment, however, the trend seems to be moving in the opposite direction. This is the case even in Europe, where—until now—software patents were issued under very limited circumstances. Indeed, the German Federal Supreme Court (Bundesgerichtshof) issued a decision on May 11, 2000, in which it held that a computer system that analyzes human language meets the requirement of "technical character" required under German patent law.

Accordingly, practioners should proceed with caution when preparing license agreements covering Internet-related patents. In particular, attention must be paid to the evolving standards for patentability of Internet-related inventions, as these could dramatically affect the value of such licenses.

3. Software and Data Licensing and UCITA

Vendors engaged in software and data transactions must address several issues over and above those faced by vendors of physical goods. Generally, vendors of such "information products" must address unauthorized copying and redistribution of their products and define the scope of rights they intend to grant to legitimate customers. As high-speed Internet access becomes more prevalent, the Internet not only increasingly facilitates transactions between information vendors and consumers, but also provides the means of distribution of such vendors' products. At the same time, the high-speed distribution capabilities of

---

53. For more information on jurisdictional issues generally, see *infra* Chapter 8, Jurisdiction.

the Internet constitute a significant risk for vendors of information, because absent protective technologies, digital and digitized products can be perfectly and inexpensively copied and redistributed.

Typically, information vendors have sought to protect their products and control usage by contracting with their customers to establish the rights that the customers have. Such a contract, or license, between the information vendor and its customer is, in fact, what defines the "product" that is the core of the transaction. In this regard, Professor Raymond Nimmer has stated as follows:

> Consider the following contract term:
>
> "A right to publicly perform *James Bond 1998* in Houston from June 1 through July 1."
>
> There is no doubt that the contract term defines and describes the product being transferred. While the tangible subject matter of the contract is most likely to involve delivery of a copy of the motion picture *James Bond 1998*, the product is not the copy, but the rights granted in use of the content contained on the copy. If that point is not clear, compare the value of the contract term stated above to the value of the product in a contract in which the contract term provides the transferee with "exclusive rights throughout the United States" to publicly perform or display *James Bond 1998*. Yet, both contracts are satisfied by delivery of the same copy of the motion picture. The contract, not merely the copy, is the product.[54]

The right to perform a particular motion picture in one city is certainly of less value than the exclusive right to perform the same motion picture nationwide. Similarly, the right to use a particular software product on one workstation within General Motors is certainly of less value than the right to use that software product on all workstations throughout General Motors, yet the underlying obligation on the vendor's part can, in both cases, be satisfied by delivery of the same CD-ROM.

The vendor may wish to employ technological means to try to limit unauthorized access to software or other information content, and the license is the vehicle whereby the vendor clarifies that introduction of such technical limitations is permissible. The license is also where the vendor clarifies that the information provided is for use on one workstation or for thousands of workstations throughout a commercial enterprise. Thus, structuring the license transaction is a critical step in the information vendor's effort to monetize its products optimally and safely.

Section 3.1.3 first offers some observations about the nature of software, and how this affects software licensing. Then, and presuming a basic under-

---

54. Raymond T. Nimmer, *Breaking Barriers; The Relation between Contract and Intellectual Property Law*, 13 BERKELEY TECH. L.J. 827, 842 (1998).

standing of the legal issues generally involved in drafting licenses, it describes several issues of concern for software licenses. Last, it touches on use of a new commercial code available for adoption by U.S. states—the Uniform Computer Information Transactions Act—as a guide for navigating the waters of software licensing.

i. Overview of Software and Software Licensing

A. Software

The term *software*, which generally refers to a set of instructions and procedures guiding the operation of a computing system or computing functions, is imprecise. There are three formulations of software typically subject to license—source code, object code and executable code. *Source code* refers to the various high-level languages in which computer programmers write.[55] *Object code* technically refers to the interim by-product of running source code through a translation program called a *compiler*.[56] *Executable code* refers to the machine language that a computer platform can read, which is produced by running object code through a program called a linker, assembler or loader.[57] For some—but not all—computer languages and compilers, object code may be similar or identical to executable code.[58] This imprecision can be mitigated in licenses where the distinction between object and executable code is irrelevant by employing the term "object code" and defining it to include executable or machine code. Software licenses often address issues relevant to software documentation and specifications as well.

(1) Copying

In most cases, software is very easily copied and redistributed. Processes exist and are widely accessible to make, in a matter of moments, perfect digital copies of software that may have taken hundreds of thousands of person-hours to create.[59] The ease with which software may be copied raises an obvious issue. To the extent the licensed software contains trade secrets or other confidential information (which typically is a concern of source code licensors), the license must account for the gravity of harm arising out of unauthorized copying and disclosure. This also affects legal treatment of software. For example, a European

---

55. *See* <http://webopedia.internet.com/TERM/s/source_code.html>.
56. *See* <http://webopedia.internet.com/TERM/o/object_code.html>.
57. *Id.*
58. *Id.*
59. The speed with which perfect copies can be made and redistributed cannot be underestimated. A perfect copy of the CD containing Windows 2000 Professional can be made in less than ten minutes, using equipment that is now standard on many high-end personal computers. The entire set of source code for the Netscape Communicator program can be downloaded via the Internet in less than eight minutes.

Union directive regarding consumer contracts that are not made in a face-to-face encounter grants the consumer a right to return goods—no questions asked—but excepts from that right returns of unsealed software. The obvious concern is that the customer will copy the software and then return it.

(2) Programming Practices

Like lawyers drafting new agreements from prior forms, many programmers work from *toolkits* of prewritten (by the developer or others who have licensed the developer to use the code) source code, and will often add code to such a toolkit. Some programmers, however, may be careless regarding ownership, choosing to add code that was downloaded or copied without authorization from the Internet or that, while personally authored, was written while the programmer was employed elsewhere or under a contract assigning ownership to another party. For example, a programmer may have included so-called *Open Source* code in a toolkit. Many programmers see Open Source as an ideal for decentralized, broad-based development of intellectual property. The problem, however, is that Open Source licenses often purport to assimilate all of a work in which any Open Source code is included into the body of available Open Source.[60] In short, the heredity of code is a common concern for licensees who do not want to use a product that comes with an infringement issue. Accordingly, the licensee should seek to be indemnified against claims of intellectual property infringement arising out of the developer's incomplete authority to use the code provided to the licensee.

B. Licensing

Software is generally licensed rather than sold.[61] Licensing allows the licensor to create multiple products, by distributing essentially identical products with rights tailored to the needs of disparate customers and markets.[62] Licensing also allows software and other publishers of information to avoid the one-size-fits-all approach created when the federal *first-sale doctrine* applies.[63] A good ex-

---

60. *See, e.g.,* <http://www.opensource.org/licenses/gpl-license.html>.

61. There are, of course, exceptions. One obvious example would be the sale of the assets of a software developer in the context of an acquisition.

62. For example, the "Enterprise," "Site," "Personal," and "Academic" versions of a given product may be identical, from the perspective of bits and bytes on the program CD. Each will likely be subject to a market-specific grant of rights, however, and marketed at a different price. *See also* Robert Merges, *The End of Friction? Property Rights and Contract in the 'Newtonian' World of On-Line Commerce,* 12 BERKELEY TECH. L.J. 115, 117 (1997).

63. *See* Quality King Distribs., Inc. v. L'anza Research Intern., 523 U.S. 135, 141 (1998) (citing 17 U.S.C. § 109(a) and noting that under first-sale doctrine of copyright law, owner of particular copy is entitled, without authority of copyright owner, to sell or otherwise dispose of possession of that copy); Glass Equip. Dev., Inc. v. Besten, Inc., 174 F.3d 1337, 1342 n.1 (Fed. Cir. 1999) (noting that first-sale doctrine stands for proposition that, absent unusual circumstances, courts infer that patent owner has given up right to prevent resale of particular patented article that owner sells).

ample of the problems that doctrine can create is illustrated by *Adobe Systems Inc. v. One Stop Micro, Inc.*[64] Adobe, a software publisher, made software available at a deep discount to teachers and students in an "educational" distribution channel. The software was distributed to an education "reseller" who agreed to redistribute to educational users only. One Stop obtained the educational software and proceeded to do this:

> One Stop admits that it adulterated approximately one-half of the Adobe educational versions it acquired in 1996 and 1997 by doing the following: (1) cutting open and removing Adobe's shrink wrap; (2) peeling off and destroying the "EDUCATION VERSION—Academic ID Required" stickers, as well as the UPC bar code label and the serial number label which further identify the packages as educational versions; and, (3) re-shrink-wrapping the boxes.[65]

One Stop then distributed the adulterated versions in the commercial market. One Stop claimed it was entitled to do this because the agreement between Adobe and the educational reseller was a "sale" instead of a "license," and thus the copyright first-sale doctrine allowed One Stop, as the owner of copies, to ignore all restrictions and sell its copies without restriction. The court disagreed. It noted that the first-sale doctrine is only triggered by an actual sale and that Adobe did not forfeit its right of distribution by entering a licensing agreement. As explained by one of the expert witnesses in the case:

> In my experience, no software company ever sells its software, with the occasional exception of some CD-ROMs which are included as an ancillary feature with books. . . . [S]oftware companies license because they need the control that licensing affords. The rate of change of technology is orders of magnitude greater than the ability of intellectual property laws to keep up. The industry must be able to license its products in order create and protect innovation.[66]

There are other reasons why publishers license—rather than sell—software, and this creates benefits for customers as well as publishers.[67]

(1) Intellectual Property Covered[68]

Software typically includes copyrights, patents and trade secrets (and software licenses often cover these types of intellectual property and may also address know-how and other proprietary rights). These rights are primarily in source, object and executable code, but may also be in related materials such as designs, logic diagrams, documentation, manuals, flowcharts and marketing

---

64. Adobe Sys. Inc. v. One Stop Micro, Inc., 84 F. Supp. 2d 1086 (N.D. Cal. 2000).
65. *Id.* at 1088.
66. *Id.* at 1092.
67. *See* Robert W. Gomulkiewicz & Mary L. Williamson, *A Brief Defense of Mass Market License Agreements*, 22 RUTGERS COMPUTER & TECH. L.J. 335 (1996).
68. For more information intellectual property generally, see *supra* Chapter 2, Intellectual Property.

materials. In addition, a software license applicable to a marketing or distribution transaction may include grants of limited rights in connection with trademarks.

For a copyright license, the licensor generally controls the right to (1) reproduce and prepare derivative works based upon the copyrighted work, (2) distribute copies to the public by sale or other transfer of ownership, or by rental, lease or lending, (3) perform and display the copyrighted work publicly and (4) perform the copyrighted work publicly by means of a digital audio transmission.[69] If the licensor grants the right to make derivative works, the licensee's ability to use, distribute or transfer the derivative works may be limited by the terms of the license. These rights vary in part based upon the subject matter and nature of the work.[70] For a patent license, the licensor generally controls the right to make, use, sell and import the subject matter of the patent.[71]

(2) Rights in Data

It is difficult to protect data through "property rights" under U.S. law. Pursuant to U.S. copyright law, a work of authorship must contain a requisite degree of originality to be copyrightable. Facts are not copyrightable, nor is a database comprising facts such as names and addresses.[72] Aspects of a database, however, such as data selection and database structure, may be sufficiently original as to be copyrightable.[73]

Some factual data are protectable as trade secrets, if not widely known and subject to reasonable efforts to maintain secrecy,[74] which occurs only in limited circumstances.[75] A licensor may attempt to require the licensee to acknowledge

---

69. *See* 17 U.S.C. § 106 (2000). *See also supra* Chapter 2, Intellectual Property.

70. *Id.*

71. *See* Sears, Roebuck & Co. v. Stiffel Co., 376 U.S. 225, 230 (1964) (citing 35 U.S.C. § 271).

72. *See* Feist Publications, Inc. v. Rural Tel. Serv. Co., Inc., 499 U.S. 340, 344–45 (1991).

73. *See id.* at 348 (noting that choices regarding selection and arrangement, if made independently by compiler and entail minimal degree of creativity, are sufficiently original as to be copyrightable). *See also supra* Chapter 2, Intellectual Property.

74. *See* Uniform Trade Secrets Act (UTSA) § 1(4) (1999). *See also supra* Chapter 2, Intellectual Property.

75. For example, if a program is designed to display to the general public the facts contained in a database, without restriction, the licensor cannot likely claim such contents are a trade secret. If, however, the database contained information such as arguably proprietary multipliers, and the program merely accessed such multipliers in an invisible way to perform calculations, the results of which were displayed to the general public, the licensor could reasonably claim, if all other requisites of a trade secret were present, that the contents were a trade secret. The practitioner should be aware that databases may be subject to protection pursuant to law of the European Union, if such law is relevant to the deal. *See* <http://www.europa.eu.int/eur-lex/en/lif/dat/1996/en_396L0009.html>. Furthermore, there are various legislative movements afoot in the United States to establish similar protection for factual content of databases. *See* <http://thomas.loc.gov/cgi-bin/query/D?r106:1:./temp/~r106rox0KL:e0:> (detailing comments of Senator Orin Hatch regarding proposed Database Antipiracy Legislation); *see also* <http://fairuse.stanford.edu/database/index.html> (collecting various sources regarding database protection). The practitioner should also review state unfair competition law for possible application expressly or by analogy to database piracy.

that the data, data structures, data organization and other aspects of the data are original to the licensor.[76]

There are other practical means for protecting data, such as through contract or intellectual property laws. For example, a financial data aggregator may license its product for public display on web sites. The underlying data is not copyrightable. The licensor can, however, proactively structure its data to make data selection and organization copyrightable, and can design its site so that only a de minimis amount of data is displayed at any one time, to discourage copying by third parties. If the value of the data is maintained only by regular updates, the license can prohibit bulk data transfers, require implementation of technology to prevent data mining, and require removal of the data if data mining cannot be prevented, which should also discourage copying and limit the value of any copied data. Also, or in the alternative, the licensor and licensee may make a contract regarding use of the noncopyrightable information. Whether such contracts are enforceable was the subject of *ProCD, Inc. v. Zeidenberg*, where the court concluded that as arrangements between contracting parties, such contracts are enforceable.[77]

(3) Variable Licenses

Technology may provide opportunities for creative, variable licenses. For example, a licensor can produce one CD or executable file that contains all possible permutations of its software program or suite. Then, by controlling which of several "unlock" or "activation" keys are distributed to the end user, the licensor can control the rights granted to the licensee. As an alternative to a more traditional licensing model allowing unlimited usage within the scope of rights granted, software can be licensed on a per use or subscription basis, using the Web to verify compliance.[78] Also, metering technology can be used to report relevant information to the licensor for creation of an invoice. In the United States, such models are assisted by chapter 12 of the Copyright Act, which generally prohibits persons from circumventing a technological measure that controls access to a copyrightable work (that is, if in the example, the licensor uses technology to control access to the portion of the work that is

---

76. Such language may not ultimately survive judicial scrutiny. However, in conjunction with terms confessing that violation of the data license will cause irreparable harm and allowing an injunction without the need for posting a bond, such an approach may assist in obtaining at least short-term relief.

77. ProCD, Inc. v. Zeidenberg, 86 F.3d 1447 (7th Cir. 1996). For an example of a contract regarding a fact that is not copyrightable, see the contract used by Consumers Union for Access to Consumer Reports Online. The contract, which can be viewed at <http://www.consumerreports.org/Subscribe/subtos.html>, provides at No. 5: "Neither the Ratings nor the reports nor any other information, nor the name of Consumers Union or any of its publications, may be used in advertising or for any other commercial purpose, including any use on the Internet. . . ." *See also* Nimmer, *supra* note 54 (discussion of long-standing symbiotic relationship between contract and property law); Maureen A. O'Rourke, *Copyright Preemption after the ProCD Case: A Market-Based Approach*, 12 Berkeley Tech. L.J. 53 (1997) (explaining in Part III-A the competing views of copyright and contract law; that is, view that Copyright Act is series of default rules that may be changed by contract and that act balances competing rights through series of immutable rules).

78. *See Microsoft Sketches .Net Plan*, at <http://www.zdnet.com/eweek/stories/general/0,11011,2599008,00.html> (July 10, 2000) (discussing Microsoft.Net initiative).

supposed to stay "locked" until an activation key is purchased, federal law prevents tampering with that technological measure).

ii. Key License Issues

A. Applicable Law—U.C.C. Article 2 and UCITA

The Uniform Commercial Code (U.C.C.) is the only source of uniform commercial contract law in the United States. Although the *Restatement (Second) of Contracts* is also an influential source, its principles have not been accepted on a uniform basis—it reflects the common law, which is variable among states and industries. Thus, any search for uniform contract law will ultimately lead to the U.C.C. Once reached, however, the U.C.C. has nothing to offer those who search for laws reflecting the unique attributes of computer information, the driving force in the U.S. economy.

This is no surprise, given that Article 2 of the U.C.C. was written before software and other computer information even existed. Many courts have treated some software delivered on a plastic diskette as a "good" under Article 2.[79] Any thorough review of those decisions, however, cannot lead to a comfortable conclusion that those courts got that issue right.[80] Also, interpreting Article 2 to treat software as a good is not consistent with the trend in state law, which is to clarify laws written for goods to acknowledge that computer information is not a good.[81] For example, recent revisions to U.C.C. Article 9,

---

79. Article 2 applies to transactions in goods. U.C.C. § 2–102. Goods are all things movable at the time identified to the contract. *Id.* § 2–105(1). Article 2 is phrased in terms of sales. *See, e.g., id.* § 2–314(1). Courts are split regarding whether software is a "good." *Compare* Data Processing Servs., Inc. v. L.H. Smith Oil Corp., 492 N.E.2d 314, 317–19 (Ind. 1986) (finding customer software to be a service), *with* Advent Sys. Ltd. v. Unisys Corp., 925 F.2d 670, 675–76 (3d Cir. 1991). The rule in many states, however, is that prepackaged software is a "good" for purposes of the applicability of Article 2. *See, e.g.,* Micro Data Base Sys., Inc. v. Dharma Sys., Inc., 148 F.3d 649, 654 (7th Cir. 1998); Mortenson v. Timberline, 998 P.2d 305, 310 (Wash. 2000).

80. *See, e.g.,* Lorin Brennan, *Why Article 2 Cannot Apply to Software Transactions,* 38 DUQ. L. REV. 459 (2000) (noting errors made by courts that have concluded Article 2 applies to software, explaining that in many cases litigants or courts simply assumed coverage of Article 2 or effectively opted into coverage, and explaining that use of Article 2 as comprehensive code for software is virtually impossible given number of contrary rules in federal copyright law). *See also* Raymond T. Nimmer, *Images and Contract Law: What Law Applies to Transactions in Information,* 36 HOUS. L. REV. 1 (1999); United States v. Stafford, 136 F.3d 1109, 1111, 1114–15 (7th Cir.) (illustrating distinction between information, here codes for obtaining money transfers, and goods, and demonstrating difficulty of predicting when and if laws written for goods apply in any given circumstance), *cert. denied,* 525 U.S. 849 (1998).

81. Proposed revisions to Article 2 clarify that it should not be applied to software. *See* U.C.C. § 2 (Proposed Draft July 28–Aug. 4, 2000; preliminary comment to § 2–103 cmt. 2) (copy available at <http://www.law.upenn.edu/bll/ulc/ulc_frame.htm>) ("Current Article 2's scope provision refers simply to 'transactions in goods.' It does not address whether computer information falls within the definition of goods. The Study Report that preceded the drafting project identified this as an area that required change given that many courts have applied Article 2's rules to computer information transactions, either directly or by analogy, in ways that lead to inappropriate results.").

the article governing secured financing, clarify that software is a "general intangible" and not a good.[82]

Accordingly, a practitioner looking for the state contract law that applies to software and other computer information should not make any assumptions— depending upon what state law applies to the contract and depending upon the type of software involved, U.C.C. Article 2 might apply, the common law might apply or the Uniform Computer Information Transactions Act might apply (see below). And even in states where Article 2 applies, we are not aware of any decision applying Article 2 to software that has no tangibility, such as software that is downloaded from the Internet. In addition, of course, federal intellectual property law acts as an overlay to state contract law and can preempt state contract law.[83]

Given this chaos, about ten years ago, the National Conference of Commissioners on Uniform State Laws (NCCUSL) started drafting the Uniform Computer Information Transactions Act (UCITA) to create a uniform commercial code for computer information transactions.[84] Released in 1999 and adopted in Virginia and Maryland thus far,[85] UCITA is designed to codify and facilitate commercial contracting practices while reflecting intellectual property principles, industry practices and the unique attributes of software and other computer information. Commercial legislation has been described as "legislation which is designed to clarify the law about business transactions rather than to change the habits of the business community" while the principal objects of the drafters of commercial legislation "are to be accurate and not to be original."[86] UCITA largely takes the same approach by seeking to clarify or resolve confusion and establish "default" or "fallback" rules that apply if parties do not otherwise contract. Accordingly, UCITA provides a guide that, depending upon what law applies to the contract, can or must be used directly or by analogy when determining how to draft licenses for computer information, including software.

---

82. *See* U.C.C. § 9–102(42) (2000) (revised Article 9: " 'General intangible' means any personal property ... other than ... goods. . . . The term includes payment intangibles and software."). The definition of "goods" states that it does not include "general intangibles." *Id.* § 9–102(44).

83. *See* Brennan, *supra* note 80 (discussion of sections of U.C.C. Article 2 that may be preempted by federal law).

84. A copy of UCITA can be obtained from <http://www.law.upenn.edu/bll/ulc/ulc_frame.htm>.

85. Delaware, Hawaii, Illinois, Iowa, New Jersey, Oklahoma and the District of Columbia have all introduced bills pertaining to the adoption of UCITA. It may be a while before UCITA is widely adopted, if the adoption of U.C.C. Article 2 is any guide. Article 2 was officially introduced in 1949 and Pennsylvania was the first to adopt it in 1954; Massachusetts followed in 1958, while the remaining states delayed adoption until the 1960s. *See* Ingrid Michelsen Hillinger, *The Article 2 Merchant Rules: Karl Llewellyn's Attempt to Achieve The Good, The True, The Beautiful in Commercial Law*, 73 Geo. L.J. 1141, 1148–49 (1985). UCITA also has become the subject of opposition that has little to do with traditional commercial codes. *See, e.g.,* Washington State Bar Association, Report of Law of Commerce in Cyberspace, at <http://www.wsba.org/sections/biz/lcc/report/2000Ucita.htm> (June 28, 2000) (which report is part of recommendation of Business Section of Washington State Bar Association's recommendation for adoption of UCITA in Washington state).

86. Grant Gilmore, *On the Difficulties of Codifying Commercial Law*, 57 Yale L.J. 1341 (1948).

B. License Grant

A license grant can specify all the following information: what rights are being granted, in what subject matter, to whom, for how long, for use where, in what way, and subject to what limitations. The granting language should reflect the language of the applicable statute (for example, the Copyright Act of 1976). The license may also expressly address the specific purpose for which the software is being licensed and reflect business models of the relevant industry, such as "Licensor grants Licensee the right to make derivative works of the Software, including without limitation the right to incorporate the Software, in object code form only, in New Product and to distribute New Product under the terms of the end user license set forth below."

Commercial license grants typically reflect the complex nature of commercial transactions. The following is a sample grant between software developers:

> Subject to the provisions of this Agreement, Licensor hereby grants to Licensee and Licensee hereby accepts a nonexclusive, worldwide, except where prohibited by law, revocable license and right to do the following during the Term as defined below: (1) modify and create derivative works of the Database Engine in Source Code and Object Code form, but solely for purposes of integrating the Database Engine with the New Product and for bug fixes and minor enhancements; (2) manufacture, reproduce, distribute, publish and transmit the Database Engine in Object Code form only, and only within the New Product; (3) sublicense the rights to reproduce, distribute and transmit the Database Engine, in Object Code form only, and only within the New Product; and (4) evaluate and use the Database Engine for the sole purpose of developing the New Product.

The license should expressly set forth what is allowed, along with any exclusions or limitations. The purpose of the granting clause is to specify the intellectual property rights of the licensor that may be exercised by the licensee without fear of infringement. Thus, the licensor should clearly define the boundaries of rights it intends to share, and the licensee should obtain a grant that covers all its possible uses of the software.

Although no language is generally applicable to all licenses, issues such as the following should be examined for possible applicability, particularly in commercial transactions:

- the purpose for which the software is used;
- the manner in which the software is handled;
- the personnel who may access the software;
- reverse engineering;[87]

---

87. *Compare* Sony v. Connectix, 203 F.3d 596, 602–03 (9th Cir. 2000) (citing Sega Enters. Ltd. v. Accolade, Inc., 977 F.2d 1510 (9th Cir. 1993) (amended opinion) for proposition that disassembly of copy-

- assignment of rights;
- redistribution and sublicensing (including conditions, such as the subset of rights that may be sublicensed, the license agreement applicable to such redistribution, and the form and content of redistribution);
- modifications;
- prohibition against removal of copyright and other notices; and
- prohibition against disabling functionality or making modifications other than those expressly set forth in the license.

C. Laws Other Than Basic Contract Law

In addition to state contract law such as U.C.C. Article 2, the common law or UCITA, other state and federal statutes and regulations may affect a particular transaction. An incomplete list of these include the Uniform Electronic Transactions Act,[88] the Electronic Signatures in Global and National Commerce Act (E-SIGN),[89] state and federal consumer protection statutes,[90] import and export restrictions,[91] antitrust and unfair and deceptive acts and practices acts, the Uniform Trade Secret Act and trademark laws. Some of these statutes apply only to goods and thus may not apply to software or other information. For example, the Magnuson-Moss Warranty Act applies only to tangible consumer products that are sold, and the Federal Trade Commission (FTC) has solicited comments on whether that act should be amended or construed as applying to software or other information. Though a discussion of all such law is beyond the scope of this chapter, the practitioner must be sufficiently aware of the general application and requirements of these bodies of law to craft licenses in a way that accounts for them.

---

righted software is fair use under Copyright Act, to extent necessary to gain access to functional elements of software itself), *with* Alcatel USA, Inc. v. DGI Techs., Inc., 166 F.3d 772, 792 (5th Cir. 1999) (discussing copyright misuse as defense to infringement when copyright holder attempts to secure exclusive right or limited monopoly not granted by Copyright Office and which it is contrary to public policy to grant).

88. See <http://www.law.upenn.edu/bll/ulc/uecicta/eta1299.htm> for a copy of the Uniform Electronic Transactions Act (UETA). UETA has been enacted in Arizona, California, Delaware, Florida, Hawaii, Idaho, Indiana, Iowa, Kansas, Kentucky, Minnesota, Nebraska, North Carolina, Ohio, Oklahoma, Pennsylvania, Rhode Island, South Dakota, Utah and Virginia, and there is legislation currently pending in several other states. Some commentators have recommended against adoption of UETA, due to concerns that it creates problems for electronic commerce. *See, e.g.,* Washington State Bar Association, Uniform Electronic Transactions Act, Report of Law of Commerce in Cyberspace Committee <http://www.wsba.org/sections/biz/lccc/report/1999.htm> (Nov. 6, 1999).

89. *See* S. 761, 106th Cong. 2d Sess. (2000). Section 102(a) of E-SIGN defers to UETA if it is adopted by states exactly in the form issued by NCCUSL. Most states that have adopted UETA have amended it and thus should not come within this deference provision.

90. UCITA section 105(c), for example, expressly preserves substantive state consumer protection statutes. For federal consumer protection statutes, the FTC web site, <http://www.ftc.gov/>, provides general information.

91. *See* 50 U.S.C.A. app. § 2401 *et seq.* (2000) (Export Administration Act of 1979); 15 C.F.R. § 700 *et seq.* (2000). *See also* <http://www.bxa.doc.gov/>.

D. Technical Support and Maintenance

Providing for technical support and maintenance is often an important aspect of a software license. *Technical support* refers to the licensor's postformation willingness or obligation to answer technical questions regarding the licensed software and its use. *Maintenance* refers to the licensor's postformation willingness or obligation to provide subsequent modifications or new releases of the licensed software.[92] The license should specify the nature and quantity of support and maintenance included in the license transaction. The license should also clarify whether such topic is covered by a separate agreement or necessitates payment of a separate fee. UCITA covers service contracts for the creation or modification of computer information (that is, software development contracts) and also covers support contracts, to a small extent.[93]

There are no mandatory rules regarding support and maintenance, so the parties may structure a broad range of arrangements. Support and maintenance options vary from free and unlimited (which is uncommon), to a given quantity without charge, to a fee-based regimen.[94] Licensors often provide a short period of technical support and access to at least minor maintenance releases without charge. There is much confusion in this area and UCITA supplies some helpful default rules that illustrate the issues parties ought to consider (see UCITA section 612).

E. Prerelease or Beta Code

Software vendors often provide prerelease or *beta software* to selected licensees or any licensee that requests access. Given the complexity of software code, sometimes beta testing is the only or best way to locate problems with the product before it is released. To the extent a license contemplates delivery of beta code, it should clarify the parties' understanding that the code does not have the quality of a released product and that, if applicable, the licensor has no obligation to provide a finished version. A license that includes beta code, even if the code is executable, often provides that such code is confidential and subject to significant restrictions on use and disclosure, so the testing can fulfill its purpose.[95] The license may also require bug reporting by the licensee to prevent termination of the grant.

---

92. The provision of fee-based maintenance arguably implies a duty on the part of the licensor to continue to develop, or at least debug, the applicable source code.

93. UCITA covers only "computer information transactions," generally defined in UCITA section 102(11) as an agreement to create, modify, transfer or license computer information or informational rights in it, including a support contract to the extent covered in UCITA section 612.

94. Support pricing models are limited only by the licensor's creativity, and commonly vary by method of delivery (web site, e-mail or telephone, for example) and quantity (per incident, per telephone call, per month or per year, for example).

95. Because these kinds of restrictions restrict speech, they sometimes generate questions or controversy about enforceability. UCITA is the only statute that attempts to deal with the issue. Section 105(b) allows

F. Warranty/Disclaimers

All software has bugs.[96] This is not a consequence of lazy programmers or licensor negligence. Further, a *bug* is not a synonym for a defect—for example, some bugs are design decisions intended to avoid a problem that would be worse than the perceived bug, and some bugs result from the fact that the software was designed before the design of other software or hardware with which it later runs. Software is expected to run in virtually infinite permutations of hardware and other software,[97] some or all of which may interact negatively with the program.[98] Even if a licensor could fully debug a program, this would certify only that the software was without bugs on the platform on which debugging occurred—it is likely impossible to create a completely bug-free program. In any case, software licensors generally disclaim any implied warranties, such as the implied warranty of merchantability that exists under U.C.C. Article 2 and UCITA; in most states implied warranties are not created by the common law but, as noted, which law applies to software is unclear. Thus, the usual concerns regarding the efficacy of warranty disclaimers in contracts are also relevant to disclaimers in software licenses, at least where U.C.C. Article 2 or UCITA applies; if the common law applies, the efficacy of disclaiming any common law duties must be considered. If the forum would construe the license pursuant to U.C.C. Article 2 or UCITA, a disclaimer in a record should be conspicuous,[99] appropriate verbiage should be used[100] and the disclaimer will be ineffective if prohibited.[101]

Warranties are clarified and extended by UCITA.[102] Under UCITA, a licensor of computer information generally makes warranties of noninfringement and

---

courts to refuse to enforce a contract term that violates a fundamental public policy, after balancing competing public policies such as any contract or free-speech rights. Under that test, terms restricting disclosure in a beta contract should be enforceable, but that would not necessarily be the case for such restrictions in other contracts, such as licenses for finished products.

96. Micro Data Base Sys., Inc., v. Dharma Sys., Inc., 148 F.3d 649, 656 (7th Cir. 1998).

97. The modern personal computer generally has a hard drive, a motherboard, one or more microprocessors, RAM, a video controller card, an audio controller card, a modem, a diskette drive and a CD-ROM. Each of these pieces of hardware has one or more software drivers that allow the hardware to function and be recognized by the operating system. Moreover, thousands of software programs are marketed in one form or another. If there were only one possible hardware combination, one set of software drivers, one operating system, and only thirty possible programs, there would be at least 1,073,741,823 possible unique configurations in which any of these thirty programs could be expected to run.

98. Some of this interaction is theoretically mitigated by modern programming techniques, such as addressing all system resources through the operating system rather than directly, designing the operating system to run certain processes in separate memory spaces, and implementing driver certification programs. Though these technologies may enhance stability, they do not eliminate the problem.

99. U.C.C. § 2–316(2) (1999); UCITA § 406(b)(1) (2000).

100. U.C.C. § 2–316(3) (1999); UCITA §§ 406(b)(2), (b)(3) (2000).

101. For example, if the Magnuson-Moss Warranty Act were amended or construed to apply to software licenses, then for software viewed as a consumer product, the implied warranty of merchantability could not be disclaimed if the licensor provided an express written warranty or a service contract. *See* 15 U.S.C. § 2308 (2000).

102. UCITA contains detailed provisions on warranties, which should be reviewed if UCITA applies to the transaction. *See* UCITA §§ 401–09 (2000).

quiet enjoyment unless these are disclaimed using appropriate verbiage.[103] A licensor of a computer program makes an implied warranty of merchantability to its licensee (and end user or distributor, depending upon with whom the licensor is in privity of contract).[104] Importantly, UCITA codifies common law concepts that reflect the First Amendment by stating that merchantability warranties do not apply to public information (called *published informational content*); that is, a newspaper seller or licensor does not warrant that its articles (whether they appear on paper or as computer information) are merchantable. UCITA does, however, create an implied warranty regarding the accuracy of informational content when there is a special relationship of reliance—this too reflects common law principles.[105] UCITA also contains an implied warranty of fitness for the licensee's purpose and a new implied warranty that components of an integrated system will function correctly together as a system.[106] As in U.C.C. Article 2, these implied warranties can be disclaimed.[107]

G. Fee Models

Fee structures for software and data licenses are infinitely variable, yet generally all fee models can be placed in two basic classes—those requiring a one-time payment and those requiring a recurring payment. The one-time payment model is fairly straightforward—the licensee pays a fee and is entitled to the grant of rights set forth in the license, subject to termination for breach. This is typical of many mass-market licenses,[108] but may also be found in a commercial context.

There are limitless ways to structure a recurring-revenue license. Most of these models have several common threads, however. The simplest model involves software licensed for a fixed duration, with perpetual rights to renewal absent default and subject to payment of a fee. With this model, the licensor merely needs to keep accurate records and collect its periodic fee. When the fee is periodic, this should be made clear in the license so no misunderstandings occur (that is, so the licensee does not believe that only a one-time fee is contemplated).

Other recurring-revenue models are based upon use.[109] For a license granting the right to copy and sublicense copies, a royalty may be assessed on a per-

---

103. *Id.* § 401.

104. *Id.* § 403, cmt. 3(a) (noting that presence of minor errors in software is fully within common expectation).

105. *See* UCITA § 404 and the comments thereto—this is a new implied warranty.

106. UCITA § 405 (2000). The fitness warranty has parallels in U.C.C. Article 2, but the system integration warranty does not. The latter is a new implied warranty.

107. *See* UCITA §§ 401, 406(b), 406(c) (2000).

108. A one-time fee would not apply, for instance, to a mass-market transaction involving an Application Service Provider. *See* Section 3.1.3.iii of this chapter.

109. Such a license, if the licensee is not the ultimate consumer of the software or data, will often be accompanied by minimum revenue guarantees.

copy basis. Using metering technology, fees may be based upon functions accessed, duration of use or other commercially acceptable bases. Recurring license fees can also be based upon a subscription model, which allows for marketing of high-end software at a low entry cost to the licensee.

Another popular recurring-revenue model involves a revenue share. This model is often found in licenses for software or data to be incorporated in a product for third-party licensees.[110] The licensor's justification for seeking a revenue share is that the licensed software or data causes—directly or indirectly—the third-party licensees to use or acquire the product. The percentage to which the licensor is entitled is based upon the perceived value of the licensor's software or data. In these structures, it is important to ensure that the content or other aspect of the transaction does not invoke an "anti-kickback" or similar statute that would prohibit revenue sharing.

H. Ancillary Revenue Issues

(1) Revenue Recognition

The timing of a licensor's ability to recognize revenue arising out of, or related to, a software or information license will likely turn on the manner in which the license transaction is structured. Guidance in this area is provided in Statement on Position (SOP) 97–2 of the American Institute of Certified Public Accountants.[111]

(2) Audit and Reporting

If a license provides for royalty-based redistribution of some or all of the licensed software, and in many other recurring-fee models, the licensor should provide for periodic reporting by the licensee to enable the licensor to verify royalties due and owing. In addition, the license should provide the licensor the right to audit the licensee's books, records and possibly facilities to the extent necessary to verify such royalty information and other aspects of the licensee's compliance with the agreement.

iii. Other License Terms

A. Indemnity

A licensor in a commercial license often agrees to indemnify the licensee for liability arising out of claims that the licensee's use of the software infringes

---

110. A typical example is a web portal. Providers of particularly attractive content, for example, may be able to negotiate for a share of revenue (such as advertising revenue) derived from web pages in which such content is featured.

111. *See* <http://www.aicpa.org/pubs/cpaltr/nov97/softrecg.htm>.

the proprietary rights of third parties. This approach is most justified when the licensor has control over the source code and programmers and is in a position to avert infringement; that is not always the case and even when it is, the price of the software affects the willingness of the licensor to provide an indemnity. A more complex situation is presented in a development deal in which a software developer licenses a given module, such as a database engine, for inclusion in the licensee's end product. In such a case, the licensee may logically demand indemnification from the licensor for claims that the database engine infringes third-party proprietary rights. The licensor, however, also has reasonable cause to demand indemnification from the licensee for claims that the database engine, as combined with other software or modified by the licensee, infringes third-party proprietary rights as a consequence of such combination or modification.

In addition to either a reciprocal or nonreciprocal indemnity provision, the indemnity section may provide the indemnitee a right to employ separate counsel and/or a right to withhold consent to settlement, provide for repayment of costs incurred by the indemnified party and obligate the indemnitor to provide substitute code in case of infringement. Software licenses may also contain indemnity provisions related to product liability and the actions of each party in the course of performance (for example, to address issues posed by on-site maintenance of software).

B. Confidentiality

If the licensed software contains confidential source code[112] or other confidential materials, robust confidentiality language is essential. Given the speed with which source code can be copied and redistributed online, the licensor should insist on confidentiality terms commensurate with the value of the confidentiality of the source code to the licensor.[113] Generally, confidentiality language must specify (1) what is deemed confidential, (2) how such confidential information must be handled and the scope of its permitted use, (3) how long such measures apply and (4) any exceptions. Thus, for example, the parties may specify that licensed source code and anything else designated in writing by the licensor is confidential and may be used only for specified purposes and only by certain designated employees of the licensee during the term of the agreement. The parties may also agree that confidential information remains confidential for a period of years after termination.

Depending upon the needs of the parties, the confidentiality terms may also provide (1) that certain information is "strictly confidential" and subject to

---

112. Not all source code is confidential. For example, open source code, and source code included as part of a commercially available Software Development Kit (SDK), are not confidential.
113. The practitioner should be aware that for a high-end software developer, source code is analogous to the recipe for Classic Coke. Licensors quite reasonably require broad protection of source code.

more exacting standards of protection, (2) that disclosure of confidential formation may be enjoined and (3) that the retention of confidential information in the unaided minds of those with rightful access to it, and the subsequent use of it, does not constitute a breach of confidentiality.

C. Limitation of Liability and Disclaimer of Damages

The concept of limiting liability is not unique to software licensing transactions. There are, however, three issues worth mentioning. First, given the value of source code to the extent it is kept secret, and the relative ease with which source code may be redistributed, damages arising from breaches of terms regarding source code, as well as other breaches of confidentiality, are often excluded from any limitation on liability.[114] Second, and to the extent that the license excludes liability for certain types of damages, the parties may wish to specify that such exclusion does not apply to indemnity obligations. Third, though limitations of liability and remedy in commercial contracts are generally enforceable,[115] there should be some minimum adequate remedy, to avoid claims of unconscionability under U.C.C. Article 2,[116] UCITA or the common law (in some states), and avoid claims that the contract is unilateral or that there is a failure of consideration.[117]

D. Delivery

Mass-market software has traditionally been delivered via diskette or CD accompanying the mass-market license agreement. With the advent of ubiquitous web access, relatively small software packages are often delivered to the licensee by downloading a compressed install file from a web site of the licensor or a third-party host.[118]

Mass-market software is typically designed to be loaded on either the end user's workstation or a local area network server, and to run within the random access memory of such end user's workstation.[119] Over time, client-server and

---

114. Excluding breaches of the license grant from the limitation of liability is typical if the subject matter of the grant is particularly sensitive, such as confidential source code. If the subject matter is less sensitive, breaches of the grant may be subject to the limitation, at least to the extent that such breach does not lead to claims for which the breaching party is obligated to indemnify the other.

115. *See* U.C.C. § 2–719(3) (1999); UCITA § 804 (2000). *See also* Mortenson v. Timberline, 998 P.2d 305 (Wash. 2000).

116. See U.C.C. § 2–719(2) (1999).

117. *See, e.g.,* CogniTest Corp. v. Riverside Pub. Co., 107 F.3d 493, 496 (7th Cir. 1997) (noting that U.C.C. permits limitation of remedies for breach, if at least minimum adequate remedy available).

118. *See, e.g.,* <http://www.digitalriver.com>.

119. Technically, what this means is that the executable code—whether installed on the end user's local hard drive or on the local area network hard drive—must be copied into the random access memory of the end user's computer before instructions in such executable code are executed.

server-based applications have evolved. With client-server applications, some of the executable code is run on the end user's workstation and some is run on the applicable server platform, which is a computer or computers that may be owned in common with the client computer(s) or may be owned and controlled by a third party. With server applications, all the executable code is run on the applicable server platform.

As high-speed web access becomes more prevalent, software functionality may be increasingly available via the Application Service Provider (ASP) model.[120] The ASP approach takes server-based applications to the next level, by making software available for remote use on a web server.[121] Thus, rather than delivering the core application executable code to end users, a licensor can provide access to the functions of software as a fully functional application that runs from a server on the Web. This approach lends itself to a variety of revenue models, including a "one-time fee, unlimited future access" model, a monthly or other subscription model, and a "fee for services" model, whereby the end user is metered and billed on the basis of connect time, features accessed or a myriad of other factors.

As the ASP model evolves, it will provide interesting licensing and intellectual property issues. What from the end user's perspective appears to be a simple access contract to a fully functional suite of applications, requiring one license between the ASP and end user, may overlay a multitude of underlying licenses among the ASP, independent software publishers and infrastructure providers. For example, the ASP cannot simply obtain a single-user license for a software application and then offer access to that application to myriad customers of the ASP—that would infringe the publisher's copyright. Other concerns not typically inherent in traditional software distribution must be resolved, such as the confidentiality and privacy of end user data that, even if residing on a local storage device, may be accessible by the ASP and possibly the underlying software vendor when processing is occurring. Thus, structuring the service and licensing arrangement for an ASP could be a complex endeavor.

E. Insurance

As in all industries, the practical worth of a judgment for breach of contract, including a software license, may be the insurance coverage available in satisfaction thereof. Similarly, the practical value of indemnity is limited by the assets available to satisfy a judgment against the indemnitor. A party concerned about

---

120. *See* <http://www.aspnews.com/>.
121. The application software generally is not loaded on the end user's workstation under this model, as with a true server-based application, although for technical reasons, an ASP-delivered application may require some processing on the end user's workstation and other processing at the ASP level, as with a client-server application.

the financial means of the other may wish to require the other party to maintain commercially reasonable insurance applicable to satisfy such judgments.[122]

F. Export

If the licensee may export the software, the licensor must include language putting the licensee on notice that export to certain countries violates export laws. The licensor may also require the licensee to indemnify the licensor for liability arising out of unauthorized export.[123]

G. Source Escrow

Language providing for the escrow of source code may be appropriate in a commercial context if the licensed software is, or is included in, a mission-critical application of the licensee, and the licensor may become unable or unwilling to maintain or support the licensed software. The escrow language should provide for storage of the source code, the conditions upon which it will be released, and a license upon such release to use the source code as contemplated by the parties (for example, for debugging and maintaining the licensed software).[124] Releasing source code represents a significant risk for the licensor. Therefore, source escrow clauses are typically found only when the number of licensees is relatively small[125] and the licensee's relative bargaining power is significant, such as in the marketing of software in a small vertical market.

H. Consistency

As with all contracts for products that are described in product literature, the practitioner drafting a license should be certain that the license terms are

---

122. The requesting party may also ask to be expressly named as an additional insured on the insurance policy. As a named insured, the requesting party will have greater rights vis-à-vis the insurer upon the occurrence of a covered event.

123. All commodities, technology or software subject to the licensing authority of the Bureau of Export Administration of the U.S. Department of Commerce are included in the Commerce Control List (CCL), which is found in Supplement 1 to Part 774 of the Export Administration Regulations. *See* <http://www.bxa.doc.gov/Default.htm>.

124. Information regarding source code escrow, including sample clauses, may be found at <http://www.dsiescrow.com/index.html>.

125. With a large installed base of licensees, the value of fees for continuing maintenance will likely provide sufficient incentive to maintain the source code, and thus the licensor can reasonably resist an escrow clause.

not contradicted by marketing material, language in the product manual or language on the box describing functionality of the software. Notwithstanding a merger clause, such loose language can invite a court to find ambiguity in the agreement and subject the agreement to construction based upon external sources. It can also invite a finding of express warranty under U.C.C. Article 2 or UCITA if it becomes part of the basis of the bargain and is not "puffing."

I. Survival

Generally, the concept of posttermination survival is fairly straightforward—if the license terminates, the grant of rights regarding the software also terminates. This is an oversimplification that will not work in all circumstances. Depending upon the terms of the deal, part of the grant terminates when the agreement terminates, but other parts may stay in effect. For example, in a deal between software developers, the license may provide the right to use the Licensor's Database Engine in the development of New Product and to incorporate the Database Engine, in object code form only, within New Product for subsequent distribution to end users, but only in conjunction with the license of New Product to such end users. The license may further provide that Licensee has the right to use the Database Engine for such development solely during a fixed term, such as two years. Though the right to use the Database Engine in developing New Product may terminate, Licensee may be able to bargain to retain two rights in relation to the Database Engine—the right to continue distribution of the Database Engine, but solely to the extent already incorporated in New Product as of termination, and the right to fix bugs in New Product. To the extent these terms would survive, other terms related to the handling of the Database Engine (such as confidentiality) should also be stated as surviving.

iv. Conclusion

Software licensing can be fairly complex, particularly if the practitioner is unfamiliar with the applicable nomenclature and usage of trade, and does not possess a working understanding of the technology to be licensed. Other facts exacerbate all problems—U.C.C. Article 2 was written for a manufactured-goods economy instead of an information economy, the common law is not uniform, and there is no clarity regarding which contract law applies to software, although UCITA provides a way out of that thicket. In addition to working closely with the technical personnel on the client side, lawyers may want to review other licenses for similar technology by referring to some web-based repositories for such documents.[126]

4. Bankruptcy

Practitioners counseling clients doing business online are often called upon to provide legal advice on both the inbound and outbound licensing of technology. The bankruptcy process[127] potentially affects any commercial deal, including technology licensing. When one party has financial problems, the impact on the other parties to a license can be very serious. A poorly drafted license agreement creates pitfalls when a party goes bankrupt. A well-crafted license agreement protects against possible unanticipated treatment of the license if a party files a bankruptcy petition.

i. The Concept of Executory Contract

Almost all license agreements will be *executory contracts* for bankruptcy purposes.[128] The Bankruptcy Code does not define executory contract, but in general it can be described as a contract for which "performance remains due to some extent on both sides."[129] Most courts use the *Countryman definition* to determine whether a contract is executory.[130] Under this standard, also described by some courts as the *material-breach test*, an executory contract is:

> a contract under which the obligations of both the bankrupt and the other party to the contract are so far unperformed that the failure of either to complete performance would constitute a material breach excusing the performance of the other.[131]

Some courts use an alternative test, referred to as the *functional analysis approach*, to determine whether a contract is executory.[132] This approach is more flexible than the Countryman definition, and looks to the nature of the parties and goals of reorganization, as well as whether acceptance or rejection will benefit the bankruptcy estate.

---

126. *See* <http://techdeals.findlaw.com/> (collecting technology agreements); *see also* <http://cyber.findlaw.com/ip/> (collecting background information); <http://www.sec.gov/edgarhp.htm> (collecting material from public entities).

127. In this context, a filing under Title 11 of the United States Code.

128. 11 U.S.C. § 365 (1994).

129. NLRB v. Bildisco & Bildisco, 465 U.S. 513, 522 n.6 (1984) (interpreting legislative intent regarding meaning of term "executory contract").

130. WARREN E. AGIN, BANKRUPTCY AND SECURED LENDING IN CYBERSPACE § 10.02[a] (2000).

131. Vern Countryman, *Executory Contracts in Bankruptcy, Part I*, 57 MINN. L. REV. 439 (1973).

132. AGIN, *supra* note 130.

Software licenses with ongoing payment obligations are executory because the software licensor and software user typically have continuing obligations under the license. For example, the licensor might agree to indemnify and defend the licensee from infringement claims.[133] Other covenants found within technology-related licenses that can make the license executory include payment obligations, indemnities and warranties, training and support obligations, and confidentiality provisions.[134]

ii. Assuming and Assigning Licenses

What happens to a software license in a bankruptcy case? In bankruptcy, assuming the license is an executory contract, the debtor has a choice between keeping the license in effect, called *assuming* the license, and terminating or *rejecting* the license.[135] To assume a license, the licensee must (1) cure—or provide adequate assurance that it will promptly cure—any default, (2) compensate any third party for any pecuniary loss caused by a default and (3) provide adequate assurance of future performance.[136] By rejecting, the debtor loses the license's benefit, but leaves the other party with a prepetition unsecured claim.[137] When the debtor wants to sell its business, or believes its interest in the license has value, it may try to *assign* its interest in the license to a third party. Understanding how this process works when either the licensee or licensor files bankruptcy can help guide the initial drafting process.

A. The Licensee's Bankruptcy

When a licensee files bankruptcy, the licensor's primary concern is payment. Making the license executory forces the licensee to assume the license if it wants to continue using the licensed content. Because assumption requires that the licensee cure any monetary breach, the licensor is paid in full. The licensee's alternative is rejecting the license and giving up the benefit of the license. The licensee must choose between foregoing the licensed rights and performing under the terms of the license.

In some cases, the licensor is also concerned with controlling the licensed technology. For instance, the debtor might want to transfer the license interest to a competitor or potential customer of the licensor. In bankruptcy, a licensee

---

133. In re Qintex Entertainment, Inc., 950 F.2d 1492, 1496 (9th Cir. 1991).
134. Andrew M. Kaufman, *Technology Transfers and Insolvency—Some Practical Considerations*, 10 COM-PUTER LAW. 21, 23 (Sept. 1993).
135. 11 U.S.C. § 365(a) (1994).
136. *Id.* § 365(b)(1).
137. *Id.* § 365(g)(1).

may assign a license interest in this manner even though prohibited by the license terms,[138] but this right is not absolute.

Rather than define the specific instances when a license may not be assigned, the Bankruptcy Code restricts assignment when nonbankruptcy laws (but not contractual terms) excuse the nondebtor party to the contract from accepting performance from an assignee.[139] Thus, the Code looks to other law, either statutory or judicial, to determine when forced assignment of contract rights should not be allowed.

This principle affects primarily a licensee's interest in nonexclusive patent licenses, which courts have almost uniformly held is not assignable in a bankruptcy case absent the licensor's express consent.[140] The relevant applicable law is the federal common law principle that nonexclusive patent licenses are personal in nature and contain an implied term restricting assignment.[141] The principle may also apply to copyright licenses, which are considered personal in nature, from an intellectual property perspective.[142]

Potentially, Bankruptcy Code section 365(c)(1) prevents not only assignment of patent and copyright license rights, but mere assumption by a reorganizing debtor. The provision uses the language, "the trustee may not assume or assign any executory contract . . . of the debtor. . . ."[143] Some courts have said the use of the word "or" means a patent licensee may not assume the patent in a bankruptcy case.[144] This position is not universal, however, and there may be instances when assignment is enforceable. For example, a debtor might be able to assign a licensee's interest in a patent license indirectly, by selling its stock to a third party.[145]

B. The Licensor's Bankruptcy

When a software licensor files bankruptcy, the licensee may have a problem, especially if the license agreement is not executory. The licensor in that case can breach the license agreement, by either failing to provide support or technology, or relicensing the subject matter of the license in contravention of the license terms. If the license is executory, the licensor might reject the license, ending the licensee's rights to use the licensed technology. The licensee, perhaps

---

138. *Id.* § 365(f)(1).

139. *Id.* § 365(c)(1)(A).

140. Everex Sys., Inc. v. Cadtrak Corp., 89 F.3d 673, 679–80 (9th Cir. 1996).

141. *See, e.g.,* Commissioner v. Sunnen, 333 U.S. 591, 609 (1948).

142. Emmylou Harris v. Emus Records Corp., 734 F.2d 1329 (9th Cir. 1994); In re Patient Educ. Media, Inc., 210 B.R. 237 (Bankr. S.D.N.Y. 1997); Sony Corp. of Am. v. Universal City Studios, Inc., 464 U.S. 417, 429 (1984).

143. 11 U.S.C. § 365(c) (1994).

144. In re Catapult Entertainment, 165 F.3d 747 (9th Cir. 1999); In re Access Beyond Techs., Inc., 237 B.R. 32 (Bankr. D. Del. 1999).

145. Institut Pasteur v. Cambridge Biotech Corp., 104 F.3d 489 (1st Cir.), *cert. denied,* 521 U.S. 1120 (1997).

deprived of an essential technology, is left only with a damage claim against the licensor's bankruptcy estate. The Bankruptcy Code fortunately provides technology licensees with some protection. Bankruptcy Code section 365(n) allows certain licensees to retain their rights in intellectual property despite the licensor rejecting the license agreement.[146]

Section 365(n), however, applies only to executory contracts under which the debtor is a licensor of a right to intellectual property.[147] The term "intellectual property" has a special meaning under the Bankruptcy Code and is limited to trade secrets, U.S. patents and patent applications, U.S. copyrights and U.S. mask works.[148] Section 365(n) does not protect licenses for the use of a trademark, licenses of technology or content that are not protected by federal copyright or patent law,[149] or licenses for the use of some database compilations.[150]

When a debtor rejects a technology license, the licensee has two options. First, the licensee can treat the contract as terminated.[151] The licensee then loses its ability to use the content provided under the license, but has a damage claim against the debtor—essentially the same treatment obtained upon breach of a regular executory contract.

Second, the licensee can elect to retain its rights under the license to the intellectual property as such rights existed immediately before the bankruptcy filing.[152] In that case, the licensee can continue using the licensed technology or information, with certain restrictions. A licensee electing to retain rights does not retain all its rights as described in the license, but a specific bundle of rights provided by the Bankruptcy Code. These rights include the right to enforce any exclusivity provision of the license,[153] the right to the intellectual property as such rights existed immediately before the case commenced for the duration of the contract,[154] and access to and protection of confidential information or rights under any supplementary agreement held in escrow by a third party.[155] The licensee will also have the right, if provided under the license or any supplementary agreement, to the surrender of intellectual property related to the license.[156] In return for these rights, the licensee must make all royalty payments due under the license for the duration of the license,[157] and must waive its rights of setoff and all administrative claims against the bankruptcy estate arising from the performance of the license.[158]

---

146. 11 U.S.C. § 365(n) (1999).
147. *Id.* § 365(n)(1).
148. *Id.* § 101(35A).
149. 35 U.S.C. §§ 1 *et seq.* (2000); 17 U.S.C. §§ 101 *et seq.* (2000).
150. *See* Feist Publications, Inc. v. Rural Tele. Serv. Co., 499 U.S. 340 (1991).
151. 11 U.S.C. § 365(n)(1)(A) (1994).
152. *Id.* § 365(n)(1)(B).
153. *Id.*
154. *Id.*
155. *Survey: The Treatment of Intellectual Property Interests in Bankruptcy*, 4 J. BANKR. L. PRAC. 437 n.383.1 (May/June 1995).
156. 11 U.S.C. § 365(n)(3)(A) (1994); AGIN, *supra* note 130, §§ 10.03, 11.04.
157. 11 U.S.C. § 365(n)(2)(B) (1994).
158. *Id.* § 365(n)(2)(C).

iii. Drafting Techniques

Properly drafting the original license agreement can help provide for consistent treatment of the license in a bankruptcy case, and eliminate some of the danger presented when a party to the agreement files a bankruptcy petition.

Because Bankruptcy Code section 365(n) provides significant additional benefits to the intellectual property licensee, licensees should ensure the license explicitly refers to the statute. To apply, the statute requires certain key terms. The license should describe the intellectual property in terms that satisfy the Bankruptcy Code definition of intellectual property and state that the contract is subject to the provisions of section 365(n) when the licensor files a bankruptcy petition. To ensure courts treat the license as an executory contract, the license should state that each parties' failure to perform continuing obligations constitutes a material breach of the contract, excusing performance by the licensee.

The license should clearly provide that the licensor, in case of the licensor's bankruptcy, will—upon written request—provide to the licensee any intellectual property and any embodiment of that intellectual property held by the licensor. The license should also describe the intellectual property and embodiments of intellectual property that must be turned over.

If the licensor rejects the license, the licensee may need to hire third-party vendors to perform support, maintenance or development tasks previously performed by the licensor. The license should allow the licensee to provide intellectual property to such third parties without violating nondisclosure or exclusivity provisions.

Section 365 requires a licensee that elects to continue using intellectual property under a rejected license to continue making royalty payments to the licensor. This obligation continues for the duration of the contract and any extension period available to the licensee.[159] The term "royalty payments" is defined broadly for bankruptcy purposes, regardless of the terminology used in the agreement to describe the payments.[160] The licensee can be forced to make all future payments under the license while the licensor eliminates continuing license obligations, such as continuing development obligations, maintenance and support obligations, obligations to provide updates, or obligations to defend against or prosecute infringement actions. The license should separate royalty payments made for the use of the intellectual property itself from the payments made for other services, in effect creating two executory contracts. Another option is to include a clause reducing royalty payments in case of the licensor's nonperformance of its obligations. A license of trademark rights should include a provision reducing royalty payments if trademark license rights are terminated or lost. Any such provision must be triggered by nonperfor-

---

159. *Id.* § 365(n)(2)(B).
160. In re Prize Frize, Inc., 32 F.3d 426, 429 (9th Cir. 1994).

mance, rather than a bankruptcy or insolvency case. Penalties triggered by bankruptcy or insolvency are generally unenforceable under the Bankruptcy Code.[161]

The license should clearly define the events the parties consider to be material breaches of the contract. This will help courts employing the Countryman standard to determine whether—and at what point—the contract is no longer executory. In some cases, the licensor or licensee may want to draft around the executory nature of the contract so that section 365 does not apply. This can be attempted by deemphasizing the parties' continuing obligations.

Several additional points regarding drafting techniques favor the licensor, while others favor the licensee.

A licensee can further protect itself by requiring technology escrows and drafting the license to allow recovery of the escrowed materials during a bankruptcy case. In a technology escrow, the parties entrust essential information and data, such as source code, with a trusted third party.[162]

A licensor might protect itself against a licensee rejecting the license by including special early termination fees, or by including liquidated damage provisions accelerating payment of future royalties upon termination. Such provisions may help increase the licensor's unsecured claim and thus its recovery in a bankruptcy case.

The licensor typically wants to guard against the licensee assigning its interest in the license to a third party. The Bankruptcy Code allows such assignment, notwithstanding assignment restrictions in the contract. The sole qualification is that the assignee provide adequate assurance of future performance,[163] a term the Bankruptcy Code does not define.

License provisions can attempt to define what constitutes adequate assurance of future performance in case of an assignment to a third party, allowing the licensor more control over the assignment process. For example, the assignee may be required to affirmatively assume the assignor's obligations under the license, or the license may require certain net worth or capital requirements for assignees. To eliminate the risk that a license is assigned to the licensor's competitor, the original parties should incorporate noncompete clauses in the license. The license should clearly describe the scope of the license granted, to eliminate the risk that the assignment conflicts with exclusive licensing arrangements with third parties. To limit the risk that the assignee of a development license or VAR license lacks the skill or resources necessary to generate value for the licensor, the license should include benchmarks—financial or otherwise—that the licensee must meet. Such provisions should be carefully drafted to apply to the original licensee, not just assignees, as the Bankruptcy Code recognizes neither provisions that prohibit, restrict or condition assignment,[164] nor provisions that terminate or modify a license on account of assignment.[165]

---

161. 11 U.S.C. §§ 365(e)(1), 541(c)(1) (1994).
162. AGIN, *supra* note 130, Chapter 11.
163. 11 U.S.C. § 365(f) (1994).
164. *Id.* § 365(f)(1).
165. *Id.* § 365(f)(3).

To address case law prohibiting assumption of patent licenses, the licensee will want the license to allow assumption or retention in a bankruptcy proceeding, even when the license prohibits or restricts assignment. The licensor might limit a *consent to assumption* provision to situations that do not involve a change of control over the licensee.

Both licensees and licensors can protect against bankruptcy filings by obtaining security interests in the licensed intellectual property, and other related assets. This technique is not widely used, but can provide substantial protection for both the licensor and licensee in various situations. For the licensor, retaining a security interest in embodiments of intellectual property held by the licensee assists the licensor in recovering the intellectual property in case of a bankruptcy. For the licensee, obtaining a security interest against intellectual property held by the licensor will assist it in recovering additional materials necessary to use the intellectual property retained. For example, a VAR that uses technology under license and also licenses the right to use a patent holder's trademark may want to obtain a security interest in the trademark. This technique complements the protections provided by section 365(n), which do not extend to trademark licenses. For both licensees and licensors, obtaining a security interest in assets will turn a general unsecured claim against the bankruptcy estate into a secured claim, improving any monetary recovery on the claim.[166]

§ 3.2 Development/Linking Agreements

1. Web Development Agreements

i. Introduction

Developing a homepage or web site on the Internet's World Wide Web has become a key strategy for any business or organization hoping to capitalize on the increasing range of commercial activity taking place online.[167] For instance, through a web site, a company can advertise its products and services, allow Internet users to order its products, conduct transactions, provide customer service and facilitate communication between geographically dispersed Internet users.[168]

---

166. *Id.* § 506(a).
167. Richard Raysman & Peter Brown, Computer Law: Drafting and Negotiating Forms and Agreements ch. 8, § 8.15A (1992).
168. *Id.*

Proponents of e-commerce point to low operational costs, convenience, customization and the chance to access a global marketplace as the chief reasons behind the inevitable rise of e-commerce.[169] To compete in this market successfully, a company must have an extraordinary web site that attracts Internet users.

This presents the first question concerning an e-commerce web site. How does a company go about developing a unique and sophisticated web site? The company (here referred to as the customer or client) must first determine its objectives and goals, and then choose the developer or designer (referred to as the vendor, designer or creator) to build the site.[170]

The company in search of a web site developer may want to consider including fundamental terms and conditions in the *Request for Proposal* provided to potential vendors or designers.[171] Web site development agreements usually require that attention be given to definitions, to avoid likely areas of dispute.[172] By beginning with a proposed form of agreement, customers may avoid negotiations that are based upon a vendor's form contract.[173]

Once the agreement's foundation is drafted and a designer is chosen, the parties should enter a development contract or work-for-hire contract for the creation or development of the web site.[174] This contract is essentially an agreement between the customer and the chosen web site designer, in which the designer agrees to develop the web site and provide programming services for the customer.[175]

Despite the astonishing number of existing web sites, the development and design of web sites is a contemporary phenomenon. Similarly, contracts for the development and design of e-commerce web sites are creatures of contemporary commerce. The law governing the issues raised by these contracts, therefore, is

---

169. *Id.*

170. Brian T. Nash & Diane L. Liskowski, *Law and the Internet: Crafting Contracts for Your Web Site*, 19 Oct. Pa. B. Ass'n 21 (Sept.–Oct. 1997).

171. Julian S. Millstein et al., Doing Business on the Internet: Forms and Analysis § 2.04[1] (1999).

172. J.T. Westermeier, *Representing the New Media Company 1999: Web Developments and Web Hosting Agreements*, 545 PLI/PAT 477, 481 (Jan. 1999).

173. Millstein et al., *supra* note 171.

174. Raysman & Brown, *supra* note 167. *See also* Eric Goldman, *eCommerce: Strategies for Success in the Digital Economy: A Fresh Look at Web Development and Hosting Agreements*, 570 PLI/PAT 91 (Aug./Sept. 1999). Web development can include, but is not limited to, the following:
  - File Conversion: This is the most basic service. It involves manipulation such as converting non-HTML documents into HTML, scanning photos or graphics and saving such files into GIF or JPEG.
  - Web Design: This involves designing the "look and feel" of the web site, including logos and banners, navigation bars or tools, page layout and object placement.
  - Code Development: This involves coding HTML pages, cgi scripts, Java applets or other applications.
  - System Integration—Web Site Only: This involves integrating the web site with one or more third-party applications, such as chat engines, search engines, electronic commerce store fronts and so on.
  - System Integration—Web Site and Back-end Systems: This involves integrating the web site with one or more existing customer applications, such as legacy systems.
Id. at 93–94.

175. G. Gervaise Davis, III, *Multimedia 1997: Protecting Your Client's Legal and Business Interests, Website and Multimedia Development Agreements*, 467 PLI/PAT 299 (Jan. 1997).

considerably embryonic, providing the legal drafter with little or no guidance on judicial interpretations concerning these agreements, the validity of certain clauses and many other important issues. These concerns, coupled with the fact that technology and/or computer lawyers are expensive and sparse commodities, explain the existence of poorly drafted development or work-for-hire agreements.

Many development or work-for-hire contracts fail to address the most important issues concerning web site development, such as intellectual property issues and the parties' fundamental responsibilities. These inadequacies are due, in part, to lawyers' lack of necessary experience in drafting technology or computer contracts—they often approach these contracts as though they were drafting standard contracts for services.

ii. Initial Considerations Associated with Drafting a Development or Work-for-Hire Agreement

To draft even the most rudimentary development or work-for-hire agreement, the drafter must consider and address several issues.

The initial formation of an Internet-related agreement for web site services involves a Request for Proposal (RFP). The customer can use the RFP to gather information that describes the desired services and to present such information to prospective vendors. A well-drafted and researched RFP is also important for vendors, as it provides the vendor with a better understanding of the customer's needs and forms the basis for the vendor's well-informed proposal.[176]

An artfully drafted RFP includes a complete and realistic definition of the services the customer expects to receive.[177] This may require the customer to perform an analysis of the many different types of existing web sites and then compare those sites with the customer's intended objectives for its own site. If a thorough analysis is not accomplished before the time the RFP is drafted, or at least by the time the contract is drafted, the customer may be disappointed with the end product.[178] To further eliminate confusion and unwarranted expectations, and to communicate needs and desires, the customer should—at a minimum—become familiar with the basic terminology associated with the creation and/or development of a web site.

To ensure that the customer receives the desired product, the customer should insist on "clearly defined commitments" from the designer.[179] These include a detailed design specification, a general functional description and a

---

176. MILLSTEIN ET AL., *supra* note 171, § 2.04[2].
177. RAYSMAN & BROWN, *supra* note 167, § 8.02.
178. *Id.*
179. *Id.*

commitment from the designer that once the customer begins using the system for the processing of live daily transactions, the system will run without significant errors for a defined period of time.[180] The specifications should include (1) the source materials to be provided by the customer, (2) the overall layout, content and functionality of the web site, including data processing, capacity and security requirements and (3) browser compatibility requirements.[181] A description of the parties' commitments or "General Specifications" provides the designer with precise specifications to follow in developing the web site. Should the designer be unable to provide any of these services, he would recognize the impossibility long before execution of the contract. Obviously, this would decrease the necessity for litigation arising out of a breach of the contract.

These specifications should clearly address the responsibilities of each party. For example, who is to provide the content for the site? Who will license any needed third-party software? How will credit cards be handled? Who is responsible for obtaining required intellectual property releases or consents? Who will write and provide the terms and conditions of web site use? Who will be responsible for necessary disclaimers? Who will provide for hosting of the site? Who will develop the basic "look and feel" of the site?

Obviously, the more detailed the commitments and specifications, the less likely mistakes and ambiguities will arise. Of course, these specifications cannot completely describe the final product. A good agreement will provide broad outlines of the web site's look and function, but the agreement cannot address every aspect of the web site's development.

The RFP is an important document for defining the final software development agreement.[182] It acts as the customer's representations regarding its business functions and expectations for the final system.[183] If the vendor relies upon the RFP in developing pricing, program deliverables, and implementation schedules, and the customer subsequently changes the requirements, the designer has some measure of future protection.[184] It may also be helpful to include a definition section within the RFP, which can be either incorporated into the contract or added to the contract as its own section. By defining various terms, the contract becomes less ambiguous and each party understands and can appreciate the nature of the bargain.

Once drafted, the RFP is distributed to any number of designers who may be interested in bidding on the development project.[185] The designer submits a response or proposal explaining her theories for accomplishing the project's goals[186] and detailing the project's development plan.[187] The designer also describes how the software will operate, the expected final results of the devel-

---

180. *Id.*
181. Nash & Liskowski, *supra* note 170, at 21–22.
182. RAYSMAN & BROWN, *supra* note 167, § 8.05.
183. *Id.*
184. *Id.*
185. *Id.* § 8.06[1].
186. *Id.*
187. *Id.*

opment effort and the hardware configuration necessary to run the completed software.[188]

The designer's response to the RFP acts as its representations regarding concepts of the development project.[189] The customer relies upon the promises contained in the designer's proposal, particularly regarding delivery and performance. If the proposal is substantially correct, the customer may have some protection if the software project fails, particularly if the proposal was made part of the final contract with the vendor.[190]

Once the designer agrees to undertake development of the web site pursuant to the terms and conditions contained in the RFP, and the customer selects the designer as the most suitable one for the job, the parties are prepared to enter the contract negotiation phase of the project.[191]

iii. Contract Negotiation

After the customer submits its RFP and accepts one of the designer's proposals, the parties must begin drafting the final contract. This contract is the most critical document of the transaction, because it governs each and every aspect of the project. For that reason, it is imperative that the parties commit as much as possible to writing. If the contract specifically and unambiguously addresses an issue, the risk of future litigation is substantially decreased. Any and all topics capable of debate should be contemplated by the contract. These topics are likely to include how and when payment for services will occur, who owns the web site, the costs associated in developing the web site and many other potential pitfalls. Before determining the payment schedule, it may be helpful to recognize and appreciate the cost of developing a web site.

A. Cost of Developing a Web Site

How much does the creation of a web site cost? A web site can cost as little as one hundred dollars for the development of an electronic flyer on a generic template.[192] On the other hand, the creation of a web site can cost several million dollars for a more complex site, such as those with a large sales presence over the Web.[193] The design specifications and goals of the web site will drive its development cost and timetable.[194]

---

188. *Id.*

189. *Id.*

190. *Id.* For that reason, the contract drafter may wish to incorporate the RFP and the designer's proposal into the final contract.

191. *Id.*

192. Rinaldo Del Gallo, III, *Who Owns the Web Site? The Ultimate Question When a Hiring Party Has a Falling-Out with the Web Site Designer*, 16 J. Marshall J. Computer Info. L. 857, 862 (Summer 1998).

193. *Id.*

194. Matthew M. Neumeier et al., *Ecommerce: Strategies for Success in the Digital Economy 2000, E-commerce "Storefront" Development & Hosting*, 588 PLI/PAT 237, 239 (Jan. 2000).

Typically, the cost of a web site is directly proportional to costs associated with traditional graphic design.[195] Unlike graphic design, however, the price of a web design is usually determined by the complexity of the design rather than the length of the document.[196] Costs of a site can be based upon a price-per-page basis or certain prearranged package deals.[197] To put this in perspective, a five-page site usually costs between $1,000 and $5,000 dollars to create.[198]

B. Payment Schedule

One of the most important issues for the web site designer concerns when he will be paid for the development of the web site. Although this issue may appear to favor the designer, that is not necessarily the case.

By including a realistic and practical payment schedule in the contract, the customer protects itself, as well as the designer.[199] Payments should be dependent upon completion of specific milestones.[200] For example, if the parties provide that the designer will receive X number of dollars upon completion of a prototype that substantially complies with the design specifications contained in the contract, then the customer has created a safeguard, in that the designer does not receive payment if the prototype is not in substantial compliance. If, on the other hand, the contract provided for the designer to receive payment upon completion of the project, or was silent about the issue, then the customer may be in breach of the contract for failing to make payment upon receipt of the noncompliant prototype.

It is paramount that the contract specifically address the amount and time of payment. If the parties agree upon a one-time, flat-rate fee (which is not recommended, for the reasons stated above), the contract should state the exact amount and date of payment. If the parties contemplate that periodic payments will be made based upon the achievement of milestones, the payment schedule should clearly define the milestones and the amount of payment for reaching each milestone. If the parties decide that payment will be based upon an hourly rate, that rate should be set forth with an estimate of the time needed to complete the project. In this instance, the agreement should require regular or periodic updates revealing the amount of time spent to date, so the customer is not devastated when it receives a shockingly large bill at the end of the process. No matter what type of payment plan is chosen, payment schedules benefit all the parties to the agreement, and therefore should be included.

---

195. RAYSMAN & BROWN, *supra* note 167.
196. Del Gallo, *supra* note 192, at 862.
197. *Id.*
198. *Id.*
199. RAYSMAN & BROWN, *supra* note 167, § 8.10[1].
200. *Id.*

iv. Penalty Provisions for Delay or Failure

The agreement should also deal with remedies for delay or failure to perform. Realizing that both parties are capable of causing delay, the parties should be careful when crafting such a provision and the remedies associated with it.

Many times the customer is the culprit in causing delay, when it fails to provide the designer with certain required items, such as the text, logos or graphics to be included in the web site. Other times the designer is at fault, because it accepted too much work or failed to staff the projects adequately.

For these reasons, the agreement should state the dates upon which certain items will be accomplished. In other words, the agreement should identify milestones and the dates they are to be reached. Additionally, the agreement should provide detailed remedies for the failure of either party to comply with its duties and responsibilities.

These remedies often include a monetary penalty. For example, if the designer fails to comply with a certain task, the overall price is reduced by an amount commensurate with the delay or failure. If the customer fails to comply, the designer is often allowed an extension of time to complete the project, equal to the length of the customer's delay.

A. Conditioning Acceptance and Final Payment on Testing

In addition to a payment clause, a provision on acceptance testing is one of the most essential clauses in a development contract.[201] A customer is well advised to condition final acceptance and payment of the web site design on the initial installation, testing and approval of the web site on the Internet service provider's server under actual operating conditions.[202]

Typical clauses provide that the customer is permitted a limited period of time to conduct acceptance testing and to report any areas in which the web site fails to conform to specifications or otherwise operate properly.[203] The designer is then given a certain period of time to bring the project into compliance. The customer should be given an additional testing and approval period, followed by subsequent periods of time for the designer to correct any deficiencies or errors. A schedule of these time periods should be included in the acceptance-testing clause, and should be realistic—it should not provide for an infinite number of testing and correction sessions, and should have an outside completion date for the final project. A final completion date protects the customer by ensuring that the designer will have completed the project by a specific date or breached the contract.

---

201. Nash & Liskowski, *supra* note 170, at 22.
202. *Id.*
203. *Id.*

The customer should be in constant contact with the designer during the entire development process, and not view the project for the first time during the final stages of completion. The process should be collaborative, where the customer provides the designer with constant feedback about the way the project is unfolding and the customer's preferences. This permits the developer to remedy portions of the project without the need for litigation. Modifications and corrections can be performed throughout the development process rather than at the conclusion, when they may be much more difficult, or impossible, to rectify.

In addition, because the original specifications cannot completely describe the final product, the contract should address the necessity of midcourse corrections and change orders. The designer may encounter unanticipated problems that require deviations from the original contract specifications. The customer and designer must anticipate these types of problems and be flexible regarding the need to execute change orders. For instance, the agreement might call for weekly status updates, a password-protected area where the customer can view the site as it is developing, and a procedure for the customer to authorize discrete parts of the development process before it continues. Following is a sample change order provision:

> Changes in this Agreement or in any of the Specifications or Deliverables under this Agreement shall become effective only when a written change request is executed by [Customer], and by Developer's Contract Coordinator, on behalf of Developer. Change requests that do not substantially affect the nature of Deliverables, their performance or functionality, and that do not cumulatively extend the due date of the Deliverables by more than five (5) days or cumulatively increase the dollar amount of the Agreement by more than 5% may be requested and/or accepted by the parties' Contract Coordinators if in writing. Developer may not decline to accept any change requests that reduce the cost of performance, provided that an equitable adjustment in compensation is made for the out-of-pocket costs of any performance or preparation already undertaken. Developer further may not decline any change requests that increase the cost or magnitude of performance, provided that the changes are reasonable in scope and a commensurate increase in compensation (as measured by the initial prices set in Developer's Response and in this [agreement]) is fixed.[204]

---

204. The web site of King & Spalding states that this is the contract between King & Spalding and CyberNet Communications Corp. for the development of King & Spalding's World Wide Web site. King & Spalding has dedicated this contract to the public domain. It disclaims all warranties, whether express or implied, regarding this contract. See its web site at <http://www.kslaw.com/menu/agr.htm> for further information. The author of this Section 3.2.1 strongly suggests that this not be used as a form, but only as a starting point for original work.

B. Continuing Obligations

The customer's need for the designer to perform additional maintenance and updating of the web site is almost as important as the creation of the web site.[205] As a general rule, there is a strong correlation between a web site's popularity and the frequency of updating the site; therefore, the development agreement should establish a means for periodically updating the site's content.[206] This should include updating information as it becomes outdated or incorrect, as well as updating new technological advancements so the site can evolve and change as needed to continue attracting web viewers.[207]

Many times the parties fail to address this issue in the initial agreement and the customer's site becomes outdated very quickly. Viewers may spend a lot of time searching the Web for a specific answer to a question or for a certain product, only to find that the site containing the answer or product had not been updated in six months. This lack of current information leaves the searcher with little confidence in the web site owner, and with little or no need to access the site because it is likely incorrect or outdated. This becomes extremely important to a web site owner with a routinely changing or expanding base of available products.

v. Intellectual Property Issues[208]

Internet development and work-for-hire contracts implicate several areas of law that may not arise under standard contracts, with intellectual property having the greatest impact. Many issues can arise: Who owns the newly created web site? What rights in the project does each party own? Can the designer subsequently create an identical web site for another customer? The answers to these questions should never be left to chance. Such questions, in fact, can generate the most litigation related to these contracts.

Moreover, not only must the parties contemplate their own intellectual property rights, the designer must be attentive to other legal risks that can result from the design and execution of a web site.[209] Such risks can include (1) copyright infringement arising from copying or adaptation of third-party copyrighted works, including copyrighted images, screens or audio-visual effects, (2) trademark infringement and similar causes of action arising from the use or display (including via linking) of third-party marks, logos or insignias, or

---

205. Nash & Liskowski, *supra* note 170, at 22.

206. *Id.*

207. Del Gallo, *supra* note 192, at 862.

208. For more information on intellectual property issues generally, see *supra* Chapter 2, Intellectual Property.

209. Clarence H. Ridley et al., Computer Software Agreements: Forms and Commentary § 19–2 (3d ed. 1999).

false impressions regarding the association between one business and another, (3) violation of individual rights of permission and (4) various forms of unfair competition or disparagement.[210]

The categories of intellectual property that may be implicated in the development and operation of a web site include the following:

1. preexisting source materials to be furnished by the web site owner/customer, such as text, graphics (including trademarks and logos), audio and video,
2. preexisting formats, applets, routines and other software developed by the web site developer,
3. custom software to be developed during the performance of the web site development agreement,
4. third-party software for which the web site will require a runtime license and
5. information generated during the use and operation of the web site (such as customer registration and customer orders).[211]

The first category, referring to preexisting materials furnished by the web site owner/customer, poses the least threat of dispute because the owner/customer should be able to demonstrate that it holds the intellectual property rights to those materials.

The second category, referring to preexisting software developed by the designer, requires the designer to assign the rights in those materials to the customer or obtain authority from the owner to use the materials. A sample provision concerning preexisting works follows:

In the event any portion of any Deliverable (including the entirety thereof) constitutes a preexisting work for which Developer cannot grant to [Customer all intellectual property rights] Developer shall specify . . . (1) the nature of such preexisting work; (2) its owner; (3) any restrictions or royalty terms applicable to Developer's or [Customer's] use of such preexisting work or Sponsor's exploitation of the Deliverable as a Derivative Work thereof; and (4) the source of Developer's authority to employ the preexisting work in the preparation of the Deliverable. . . . [insert list here]. The works set forth above will be referred to as "Preexisting Works." The only preexisting works that may be used in the construction of any Deliverable are the Preexisting Works specified above and any Preexisting Works that may be approved in writing by [Customer] prior to their use. Further, before initiating the preparation of any Deliverable that contains one or more such Preexisting Works, Developer shall, at Developer's sole expense, cause [Customer], its successors and assigns, to have and obtain the

---

210. *Id.*
211. Nash & Liskowski, *supra* note 170, at 22.

perpetual, irrevocable, nonexclusive, worldwide, royalty-free right and license to (1) use, execute, reproduce, display, perform, distribute internally or externally, sell copies of, and prepare Derivative Works based upon all Preexisting Works and Derivative Works thereof and (2) authorize or sublicense others from time to time to do any or all of the foregoing.

The term "Deliverables" is defined within the contract as . . .

all Code, Documentation, reports, and other materials developed by Developer in the course of its performance under this Agreement, and any other items necessary for the operation of Customer's Web Site (other than third-party operating system software, third-party networking software, Web browsers, and hardware) including all Enhancements thereto.[212]

The third category refers to software developed during the course of the development of the web site, and requires either an assignment of all intellectual property rights or performance pursuant to a work-for-hire agreement.

The fourth category refers to third-party software that is necessary for the operation of the web site. This requires the developer to obtain a license enabling the customer to use the software without fear of infringing on the third party's rights.

The final category refers to information generated during the creation of the web site. As a general rule, the creator of a work owns the intellectual property rights in the work unless otherwise specified. If the customer is to own the intellectual property rights in the information without fear of infringement or future litigation with the developer, the developer must either assign those rights to the customer or perform its services pursuant to a work-for-hire agreement, which by its very nature vests in the hiring party ownership of—and rights in—the product.

A. Copyright Issues[213]

The most critical question posed by a development agreement is determining who owns the site. Like all ownership questions, the most logical approach is to first determine the original owner and then determine which rights, or ownership interests, have been transferred to other parties.[214] Consider the thoughts of an expert on the topic:

The law couldn't be clearer. The copyright owner of "a[n] . . . audiovisual work" has the exclusive right to copy, distribute or display the copyrighted work publicly. To display the work publicly means to transmit or otherwise communicate

---

212. *See supra* note 204.
213. For more information on copyright issues generally, see *supra* Chapter 2, Intellectual Property.
214. Del Gallo, *supra* note 192, at 870.

a performance or display of the work . . . to the public, by means of any device or process, whether the members of the public capable of receiving the performance or display receive it in the same place or in separate places and at the same or at different times. It is almost as if this definition was written with the Internet in mind. Simply put, to use a web site, one must effectively either own the copyright in it or have permission to use it.[215]

Based upon that analysis, and absent an agreement to the contrary, the copyright in a work is initially vested in the author/designer.[216] The following hypothetical demonstrates the importance of this issue to the customer.

Assume that Customer enters an agreement with Designer for the development of a web site that incorporates a specialized system for processing orders by credit card. Also assume that the agreement is silent about the owner of the web site or any intellectual property rights regarding the web site. The web site is completed and Customer is pleased with the outcome. Customer uses the site for a substantial period of time. At some point, Designer is contacted by a potential customer who asks Designer to create a web site that is identical to Customer's and that includes the specialized system for processing orders by credit card. Designer does so. What rights does Customer have to prevent Designer from creating an identical system and to prohibit the potential customer from using this specialized system?

Under these circumstances, the customer is usually without a remedy (or at least an inexpensive remedy) to prevent either the designer from creating an identical system, or a potential customer from using the identical credit card processing system. The law states that the author/designer is the owner of the intellectual property rights (in this case, the copyright) to the specialized system, as well as the web site itself. If the designer chooses to create an identical system, the customer may have no recourse. Even more disturbing is the fact that the designer could prevent the customer from continuing to use the web site. Clearly, the question of who owns the web site—and the intellectual property rights contained in it—is of utmost importance.

Other than by designing the web site, there are two additional methods of obtaining author status, along with the rights associated with being the original author: being the hiring party in a work-for-hire agreement or being a joint author.[217]

If the web site is created pursuant to a work-for-hire agreement, the hiring party is the sole author and owner, assuming there are no agreements to the contrary.[218] For this reason, it is critical to the customer that the agreement used for development of the web site be a work-for hire agreement, or contain a provision stating that the customer is the owner of the of the web site and all

---

215. *Id.*
216. *Id.*
217. *Id.*
218. *Id.* at 870–71.

intellectual property rights contained therein.[219] A typical provision contained in such a contract might be the following:

> Except as described elsewhere in this agreement, all elements of all Deliverables shall be exclusively owned by Customer and shall be considered works made for hire by Developer and Customer. Except as set forth elsewhere in this agreement, Customer shall exclusively own all United States and international copyrights and all other intellectual property rights in the Deliverables. Developer agrees to assign, and upon creation of each element of each Deliverable automatically assigns, to customer, its successors and assigns, ownership of all United States and international copyrights and all other intellectual property rights in each element of each Deliverable. This assignment is undertaken in part as a contingency against the possibility that any such element, by operation of law, may not be considered a work made for hire by Developer for Customer. From time to time upon Customer's request, Developer and/or its personnel shall confirm such assignments by execution and delivery of such assignments, confirmations, of assignments, or other written instruments as Customer may request. Customer, its successors and assigns, shall have the right to obtain and hold the in its own name all copyright registrations and other evidence of rights that may be available for the Deliverables and any portion(s) thereof.

> The term "Deliverables" is defined within the contract as . . . all Code, Documentation, reports, and other materials developed by Developer in the course of its performance under this Agreement, and any other items necessary for the operation of Customer's Web Site (other than third-party operating system software, third-party networking software, Web browsers, and hardware) including all Enhancements thereto.[220]

B. Indemnification Provisions

Due to the number of intellectual property issues involved with the creation and operation of a web site, the parties should provide a means for determining who is liable for errors in the materials prepared and the system used to host the web pages, as well as other inevitable problems that will arise over time.[221] Further, some of the content may prove to be infringing or otherwise unacceptable to third parties, so provisions must be made for determining who is liable for damages and defense of claims of third parties, and how and when to take the offending materials down from the host system to mitigate damages.[222] An example of an indemnification provision contained in a development or work-for-hire agreement is as follows:

---

219. *Id.* at 870.
220. *See supra* note 204.
221. Davis, *supra* note 175, at 306.
222. *Id.* at 306–07.

In performing services under this Agreement, Developer agrees not to design, develop, or provide to [Customer] any items that infringe one or more patents, copyrights, trademarks, or other intellectual property rights (including trade secrets), privacy or other rights of any person or entity. If Developer becomes aware of any such possible infringement in the course of performing any work hereunder, Developer shall immediately so notify [Customer] in writing. Developer agrees to indemnify, defend, and hold [Customer], its partners, employees, representatives, agents, and the like harmless for any such alleged or actual infringement and for any liability, debt, or other obligation arising out of or as a result of or relating to (a) the Agreement, (b) the performance of the Agreement, (c) the Deliverables. This indemnification shall include attorneys' fees and expenses, unless Developer defends against the allegations using counsel reasonably acceptable to [Customer].[223]

The failure to include an indemnification provision within the agreement will almost ensure that the parties will wind up in court, not only to defend the infringement claims brought against them, but also to determine which party committed the infringement. By including an indemnification provision, the customer is assured that it will be indemnified in actions involving these types of claims. Inclusion of the provision may also prove to be an incentive for the developer to ensure that no portion of the web site violates the intellectual property rights of any third party.

vi. Confidentiality and Competition Provisions

Consideration must be given to questions of confidentiality of proprietary methods regarding development and coding, as well as protecting the source of the contents, which might have competitive value to others.[224] As with any other aspect of a company's confidential information, the customer may wish to have an "exclusive" on certain types of presentations, and may require the designer to refrain from creating similar work for others, or prevent the designer from working for competitors.[225]

A well-drafted agreement will most likely grant the customer the rights to the final product, though the developer may wish to draft the confidentiality provision in such a way that permits it to retain the rights to use any experience or know-how gained during the creation of the project, provided that in exercising these rights, the developer does not disclose the web site owner's/customer's confidential information.[226] An example of such a provision follows:

---

223. *See supra* note 204.
224. Davis, *supra* note 175, at 307.
225. *Id.*
226. MILLSTEIN ET AL., *supra* note 171, § 8.15A[3].

Developer acknowledges that it and its employees or agents may, in the course of performing its responsibilities under this Agreement, be exposed to or acquire information which is proprietary to or confidential to [Customer] or its affiliated companies or their clients. Any and all information of any form obtained by Developer or its employees or agents in the performance of this Agreement shall be deemed to be confidential and proprietary information of [Customer]. Developer agrees to hold such information in strict confidence and not to copy, reproduce, sell, assign, license, market, transfer or otherwise dispose of, give or disclose such information to third parties or to use such information for any purposes whatsoever other than the provision of Services to [Customer] hereunder and to advise each of its employees and agents of their obligations to keep such information confidential. . . . Developer shall advise [Customer] immediately in the event developer learns or has reason to believe that any person who has had access to Confidential Information has violated or intends to violate the terms of this Agreement and Developer will at its expense cooperate with [Customer] in seeking injunctive relief in the name of [Customer] or Developer against any such person.[227]

This type of provision is especially important when the developer is exposed to the customer's confidential information—such as sales practices, business practices and other related topics—during the course of developing the web site.[228] Accordingly, the agreement should carefully and clearly define any and all confidential information and require that the developer and its employees use reasonable measures to prevent disclosure of that information.[229] One such measure may be to require the developer and its employees to sign nondisclosure or noncompetition agreements that are either incorporated into, or included within, the development agreement.[230] An example of a noncompetition agreement follows:

Developer shall be free during and after the development of [Customer's] Web Site to develop Web Sites for any other client. Developer shall not, however, design a Web Site for one of its other clients that "looks and feels" peculiarly like [Customer's] Web Site.[231]

Generally speaking, the developer should be required to use similar or the same measures it would use to protect its own confidential information or trade secrets.[232]

---

227. *Id.* § 8.22. The author of this Section 3.2.1 strongly suggests that this not be used as a form, but only as a starting point for original work.
228. *Id.* § 8.15A[3].
229. *Id.*
230. *Id.*
231. *See supra* note 204.
232. MILLSTEIN ET AL., *supra* note 171, § 8.15A[3].

vii. Warranties

Each party to the agreement makes certain representations and warranties concerning the responsibilities it will undertake. One such warranty, often overlooked, is that the party has the "power and authority" to enter such an agreement.[233] The developer should warrant that its work will be performed in a workmanlike manner and that it shall "substantially conform" to the description of services set forth in the agreement for a specific period of time.[234] The developer should be careful not to warrant the work's compliance with the exact specifications of the contract, because of the strong possibility that change orders or other alterations will be necessary that were not contemplated by the contract.

Moreover, the "developer must warrant that the materials it creates, or incorporates into the product, do not and will not infringe on the rights of third parties, to the extent the customer has not altered the product."[235] The customer must warrant that the materials and content it provides do not and will not infringe on the rights of third parties and that it has obtained the necessary releases, consents, or licenses to use the materials.[236]

The following are examples of warranty provisions for both the developer and customer:

Developer's Warranties

Developer represents and warrants that (a) Developer has the power and authority to enter into and perform its obligations under this Agreement, and (b) Developer's Services under this Agreement shall be performed in a workmanlike manner. Developer further represents and warrants that, for a period of (____) days after [Customer's] Acceptance of the Web Site, the Web Site will operate substantially in accordance with the Specifications. Developer further warrants to [Customer] that, to the best of Developer's knowledge, the Developer Materials do not and will not infringe, or be misappropriations of, the property rights of third parties, provided, however, that Developer shall not be deemed to have breached such warranty to the extent that [Customer] or its agent(s) have modified the Web Site in any manner or if the Web Site incorporates unauthorized third-party materials, through framing or otherwise.

Customer's Warranties

[Customer] represents and warrants that (a) [Customer] has the power and authority to enter into and perform its obligations under this Agreement, (b) [Customer] Content does not and shall not contain any content, materials,

---

233. *Id.* § 2.05.
234. *Id.*
235. *Id.*
236. *Id.*

advertising or services that are inaccurate or that infringe on or violate any applicable law, regulation or right of a third party, including, without limitation, export laws, or any proprietary, contract, moral, or privacy right or any other third party right, and that [Customer] owns the [Customer] Content or otherwise has the right to place the [Customer] Content on the Web Site, and (c) [Customer] has obtained any authorization(s) necessary for hypertext links from the Web Site to other third-party Web Sites.[237]

viii. Termination Provision

As discussed earlier, the issue of "who owns the web site" is a complicated one. For that reason, it is suggested that the agreement contain an assignment clause in which the developer agrees to assign any and all of its rights in the product to the customer and to create a work-for-hire agreement that governs the development of the product. What happens, however, if after the parties enter the agreement, and after substantial work has been performed by the developer, the parties decide to terminate the contract? Who owns the partially completed product?

To protect the developer and customer should their relationship deteriorate, the agreement should address the early termination of the contract.[238] Without such a provision, either party can claim ownership rights in the partially completed product and spend hundreds of thousands of dollars in court attempting to resolve the issue. Unfortunately for all concerned, there is no case law that specifically states who will be the ultimate winner in such a battle.[239] Accordingly, the safest and easiest way to predict the outcome is to include a termination provision in the agreement, which designates the ownership rights in the partially completed product should the relationship between the parties disintegrate. An example of a termination provision for a development or work-for-hire agreement is as follows:

> This Agreement shall be effective as of the Effective Date and shall remain in force for a period of 99 years, unless otherwise terminated as provided herein. [Customer] may, at its sole option, terminate any or all work outstanding, or any portion thereof, immediately upon written notice. Upon receipt of notice of such termination, Developer shall inform [Customer] of the extent to which performance has been completed through such date, and collect and deliver to [Customer] whatever work product and Deliverables then exist, in a manner prescribed by [Customer]. Developer shall be paid for all work performed

---

237. *Id.* The author of this Section 3.2.1 strongly suggests that this not be used as a form, but only as a starting point for original work.

238. Del Gallo, *supra* note 192, at 868–69.

239. *Id.*

through the date of receipt of notice of termination as specified in [this Agreement]. Developer may not terminate any work under this Agreement without the prior written consent of [Customer], which consent may be withheld for any reason or for no reason at all.[240]

Early termination presents another issue concerning how the developer is to be paid. The agreement should provide that the developer will be paid for services rendered until notification of the termination.[241] This provision should correspond to the method of payment contained in the original agreement. An example follows:

> If this Agreement is terminated for any reason, Developer shall be entitled to payment for work done up to the date of termination that conforms to specifications (the total of all payments to developer under this Agreement shall not, however, exceed _____), and Developer shall and hereby does grant to [Customer] in that event all right, title, and interest, including all United States and international copyrights and all other intellectual property rights in the Deliverables in the form in which they exist on the date of termination, which form shall not materially differ from the status described in the invoices and reports that Developer has submitted to [Customer].[242]

ix. Additional Standard Clauses

As with any standard contract, several other provisions can be added to clarify or address certain issues.[243] For example, the parties should explain that a particular state's laws govern the contract. Additionally, the agreement should provide for consent to a specific venue and jurisdiction. An entirety clause should be included, stating that the agreement (and any attachments, addenda or documents incorporated by reference) is the final agreement between the parties and supercedes any and all other prior or contemporaneous agreements, whether written or oral.

x. Conclusion

The creation or development of web sites is a novel practice. Those who call themselves experts often have only two or three years of experience, at the most.

---

240. *See supra* note 204.
241. Del Gallo, *supra* note 192, at 868–69.
242. *See supra* note 204.
243. Del Gallo, *supra* note 192, at 868–69.

The law concerning the development or creation of web sites is almost non-existent. For these reasons, the parties must be prepared to create not only a web site, but also the governing contract. A properly drafted agreement, by someone with a solid grasp of the terminology and an understanding of the concepts, is necessary. Although Section 3.2.1 discusses several areas that can cause conflict between the parties and should, therefore, be addressed in the agreement, many other areas related to the unique aspects of a development relationship will also need attention.

2. Web Linking Agreements

Section 3.2.2 reviews the technical, business and legal aspects of linking on the World Wide Web and explains the essential elements of agreements between web site operators to permit linking.

i. Technical Aspects of Linking

The Internet's most prominent feature is the World Wide Web, often simply referred to as the Web. The Web consists of files or pages specially formatted using Hypertext Markup Language (HTML) and made available to the public via computers known as web *servers*. Users accessing the Internet can view web pages using software known as a *browser*. The browser interprets each web page's HTML code to display the page as a screen of formatted text and graphics.

Each web page has its own unique address or Uniform Resource Locator (URL). To access a particular page, the user may enter that page's URL into the user's browser. The browser then contacts the server on which the desired page is resident, which is then downloaded via the Internet into the user's computer and displayed by the browser.

A *link* is a URL that is embedded in a web page. When the web page is displayed on a user's screen, the URL is presented as specially highlighted text. If the user clicks on that text, the user's browser automatically loads the web page located at the underlying URL. In this manner, a user can move (or *navigate*) from web page to web page by clicking on links. The site that contains the link is known as the *linking page*. The site to which a link leads is known as the *linked-to page* or the *target page*.

Links make referencing and retrieving information on the Web faster and easier than using most traditional printed documents. Users can navigate without following a linear hierarchy—that is, they can jump among pages on the Web in no particular order. Without links, the Web as we know it would not function.

Web links may be either local or remote links. *Local links* are links in one web page that refer to a document stored at the same *web site* (that is, the integrated collection of web pages posted on one server under the same domain name) as the originating page. These links are used to navigate internally within a single web site. *Remote links* are those that refer to a web page that is stored at a web site other than the site where the linking document resides. These links connect the pages of independent (usually third-party) sites. When a remote link is activated, the remote web page is loaded directly by the user's browser. The remote page is not transferred through the web site that contains the link.

Web links usually have one of two primary attributes: either invoke-to-load or auto-load. *Invoke-to-load links* are the typical links with which most web users are familiar. These may appear either as highlighted text or an image. When the user clicks on the link, the user's browser loads the target page. Thus, the user must invoke the link before the link's target page is displayed. An *auto-load link* (or *in-line link*) is invoked automatically by the viewer's web browser when the linking page is displayed in the viewer's browser. In-line links do not necessarily load an entire target web page. Rather, they may load only a single image located on another page and display that image as part of the linking page. The user viewing the linked image is often unaware that the linked image originates from another page.

ii. Business Aspects of Linking

A. Traffic

Many web sites exist to sell goods, promote companies or advertise products. Each of these purposes is furthered by heavy *traffic*—that is, the number of people who visit the site. Links to a site generate traffic and are therefore considered beneficial by some site operators. Links may also be desirable, in some cases, from a market-positioning standpoint because search engines may rank the popularity of a site based upon the number of links that lead to the site. For these reasons, many web site operators do not object to links directed to their sites and, in fact, actively encourage—even pay for—such links. Of course, in some circumstances, a link may be seen as undesirable, even if it generates traffic.

B. Deep Linking

Deep links are links to a remote page that is not the *homepage* of the target site, but rather a *subpage* within the interior of that site. For example, a newspaper might operate a web site with a homepage at URL www.newspaper.com.

To view a particular article posted on the newspaper's site, a user would first go to the homepage (where he would see the newspaper's branding and advertising) and then drill down through several links to reach a subpage containing the article. A link from a third-party page directly to the page containing the article is a deep link.

Site operators use deep links because they more expediently direct users to the desired resources. For example, a web site promoting movies might offer users links to reviews of the movies that are posted at newspaper.com. It is possible for the movie site to include a link to the homepage of newspaper.com. This would, however, require movie.com's users to spend time and effort navigating the newspaper.com site to locate the desired article. It would be far easier for users if the movie site were to deep link directly to the target article within the newspaper site.

Despite its utility, deep linking raises business issues for the target site because it directs traffic around the target site's homepage, disrupting or defeating the target site's business model. For example, suppose newspaper.com generates revenue through the advertisements placed on its homepage. Deep links to the movie reviews allow users to read those reviews without viewing the homepage advertising. Deep linking may also permit users to bypass the target owner's terms of service and proprietary information notices (such as disclaimers and copyright notices). The recognition of a target site's trademark may be diminished if users bypass the homepage and the prominent trademarks displayed there. In some instances, users may not realize they have been transported to a new site, and may have the impression that the target material is the work product of the linking site. Thus, though web site operators generally encourage linking to their homepages, many object to deep linking.

C. Framing

Framing is a particular type of linking in which the linking page includes commands that cause the user's browser to divide the screen display into separate windows or frames. A different web page (or pieces of different web pages) may be displayed in each frame. Using framing technology, a web designer can create a link to the target page, with the linked information appearing in one or more of the windows on the framing page while surrounded by a frame displaying the linking page.

Framing is used to create a border around the target page information. As the viewer invoke links to the target page, the static frame continues to display images, navigational buttons and the *branding* of the framing site. In other words, framing allows a web page operator to maintain a display of its web page even after a user has linked to a third party's page. Depending upon how the linking site is designed, the user may not even realize she is viewing a third-party site.

Framing raises several business issues. First, a frame may undermine the target site's business model because the frame may conceal or obscure branding or advertising on the framed target page.

Second, framing may juxtapose the trademark of the linking site with the trademark of the linked-to site and imply a potentially unwarranted and unwanted association between the marks. The presence of the linking site's mark may also cause users to mistakenly believe that materials on the target site originate from the linking site.

Third, framing may allow the linking site to "piggyback"—perhaps unfairly—on the content and other facilities contained in the target site. This concern is especially acute when framing is combined with deep linking. For example, consider two newspapers that operate competing web sites at times.com and post.com. Rather than bother with writing its own articles, times.com could simply deep link from its site to the articles provided at post.com. By using frames, times.com could keep its branding, advertising and navigational buttons displayed on the user's screen, effectively using the post.com articles while keeping advertising and other revenue for itself.

iii. Linking Causes of Action

At least two legal doctrines—trademark and copyright—may provide a legal basis for challenging a link. Note that each cause of action may be asserted by two classes of plaintiffs—plaintiffs who own the target sites and third-party plaintiffs who own trademarks or copyrighted materials on the linking or linked-to sites.

A. Trademark Actions

A trademark is any word, name or symbol, or any combination thereof, adopted and used by a manufacturer or merchant to identify and distinguish its goods or services from those of others. Federal trademark law is codified in the Lanham Act.[244] Under the Lanham Act and general state law trademark principles, a trademark owner has three potential causes of action against a web site operator who uses the trademark as a link or who links to the trademark owner's site: infringement, unfair competition and dilution.

(1) Trademark Infringement

Generally speaking, trademark infringement is the use of a mark by the defendant in a manner that is likely to cause confusion, mistake or deception

---

244. 15 U.S.C. §§ 1501 *et seq.* (2000).

in connection with another party's mark. For example, suppose ACME is a registered trademark for toothpaste held by Acme Inc. If defendant Beta Co. uses the mark ACME on toothpaste without permission of Acme Inc., consumers may be confused about the source of the toothpaste (mistakenly believing it to come from Acme Inc., the trademark owner).

A key factor in determining whether a likelihood of confusion exists is the similarity of the defendant's and plaintiff's marks, and whether their respective goods are "related" in the sense that consumers are apt to believe that the goods are of the type supplied by the same company.

To illustrate these points, suppose defendant Beta Co. used the mark ACME on dental floss, a product Acme Inc. does not sell. Acme Inc. may still be able to establish infringement, if toothpaste and dental floss are found to be related goods. In contrast, if Beta Co. used the mark ACME for a line of bread-baking equipment, Acme Inc. might have a very difficult time establishing confusion, because toothpaste and bread-baking equipment are probably not related goods.

In the context of linking, claims for trademark infringement might arise when a plaintiff's trademark (especially a graphic logo) is used as a link. For example, if Beta Co., the toothpaste seller, were to place ACME at the top of its web site as a link, users seeing the web site could mistakenly believe that the site is sponsored by or affiliated with Acme Inc. The potential for confusion may be higher if the defendant uses the graphic ACME logo as the link. Obviously, the outcome of each case is highly fact-specific.

Even when the defendant does have a limited right to use a particular mark (such as in a specific market), links may give rise to trademark claims if they cause the defendant's use of a mark to exceed that limited right. For example, let us assume that the ACME bread-baking site by itself raises no issue of trademark infringement relative to the ACME mark for toothpaste. Suppose, however, that the bread-baking site includes links to other target sites and that the bread-baking site maintains a frame around those target sites. If one of those target sites happens to display pictures of toothpaste, then an infringement issue may arise because the mark ACME for bread making (located in the frame) would be juxtaposed with pictures of toothpaste in a manner that may cause confusion with the mark ACME for toothpaste.[245]

---

245. The potential for this type of claim is illustrated in *Hard Rock Cafe International Inc. v. Morton*, 1999 U.S. Dist. LFNEXIS 13760 (S.D.N.Y. 1999). In that case, the defendant had a license to use the mark HARD ROCK. The license included certain territorial limitations in connection with merchandise. The defendant operated a web site, which was used to frame a third-party target web site featuring music CDs. The frame included the licensed HARD ROCK mark. The plaintiff trademark owner sued, alleging that the framed juxtaposition of the HARD ROCK mark and the CDs constituted a use of the mark on merchandise outside the licensed territory (the Internet is accessible worldwide). The district court held that the presentation of the mark in the frame was, for trademark purposes, a use in connection with the advertising and promotion of the CDs featured on the target site and, as such, exceeded the scope of the defendant's license.

(2) Unfair Competition

The law of unfair competition has been called an umbrella for statutory and nonstatutory causes of action arising out of business conduct that is contrary to honest practice in commercial matters.[246] It has been applied to cases involving trademark infringement, false advertising and the practice of "palming off" goods by unauthorized substitution of one brand for the brand ordered. Unfair competition is a matter of both state and federal law. Section 43(a) of the Lanham Act provides a remedy in federal court for infringement of unregistered marks and many types of false advertising and false designation. Under section 43(a), a use of a word or symbol is actionable if it is likely to cause confusion, mistake or deception regarding the affiliation, connection or association of the defendant with another person, or regarding the origin, sponsorship or approval of his or her goods, services or commercial activities, or, in commercial advertising, if such use misrepresents the nature or geographic origin of the defendant's or another person's goods, services or commercial activities.[247]

With linking, unfair competition claims may arise in many situations, including when a link is presented in a manner suggesting that the products or facilities of the target site are provided by the linking site. For example, suppose the defendant web site included the text "Click here to see our products." If the result of clicking the link were to load a web page bearing the plaintiff's products, then the plaintiff may have a claim for unfair competition. With framing and deep linking, opportunities for unfair competition and false advertising claims increase as the presentation of marks and goods can be intermingled on a user's screen in a potentially confusing or misleading manner.

(3) Dilution

Dilution is a cause of action under section 43(c) of the Lanham Act and state law that protects owners of "famous marks" against commercial uses that cause dilution of the distinctive quality of a mark.[248] Dilution claims are based principally on two theories: blurring and tarnishment. Blurring occurs when the defendant uses the plaintiff's famous mark to identify its own goods or services. Tarnishment may occur when the famous mark suffers negative association through defendant's use.

Dilution claims were raised in a settled linking case, *Washington Post Co. v. TotalNEWS Inc.*[249] There, defendant TotalNEWS operated a web site that linked to content from various news sources. This content was displayed using frames that contained the TotalNEWS logo and advertisements. In February 1997, a number of these target web sites sued TotalNEWS alleging, among other things, a violation of section 43(c) of the Lanham Act. The owners of the framed sites,

---

246. American Heritage Life Ins. Co. v. Heritage Life Ins. Co., 494 F.2d 3 (5th Cir. 1974).
247. 15 U.S.C. § 1125(a) (2000).
248. *Id.* § 1125(c).
249. *See* Washington Post Co. v. TotalNEWS Inc., 97 Civ. 190 (PLK) (S.D.N.Y. filed Feb. 20, 1997).

including the Washington Post, Time and CNN, contended that their marks were famous and that these marks were diluted by being shown within the TotalNEWS frame. The TotalNEWS case settled before trial on terms reportedly favorable to the plaintiffs.

B. Copyright Actions

A web page containing text or graphics is protected under the Copyright Act, codified at 17 U.S.C. § 101. Under Section 106 of the act, the owner of copyright has the exclusive right, among other things, to reproduce copyrighted materials and to create derivative works of the materials. Under Section 103 of the Digital Millennium Copyright Act of 1998,[250] copyright owners also have rights regarding the presentation of copyright management information. These rights may raise implications for linking.

(1) Copying

Section 106(1) of the Copyright Act gives the owner of a copyright the exclusive right to reproduce the copyrighted work in copies. When a user clicks on a link, the user's browser requests a copy of the web page located at the URL underlying the link. This copy is transmitted from the server hosting the target page to the user, and is stored in the user's computer's *random access memory* (RAM). In *MAI Systems Corp. v. Peak Computer*, the Ninth Circuit held that the copying of information into RAM could constitute a potentially infringing reproduction.[251] Under *MAI Systems*, then, a person browsing the Web makes a potentially infringing copy of each web page that she views.

In practice, mere web browsing does not spark infringement claims because most web sites include an express license grant in their posted terms of use that allows users to make copies inherent in browsing. For the sake of discussion, however, assume a situation in which a user has no express or implied license to view a plaintiff's copyrighted web page. What happens when a third-party web page operator includes on its page a link to the copyrighted page? A technical analysis of linking suggests that a mere link should not constitute direct copyright infringement by the operator of the linking site because the linking site copies only the target page's URL, not the material contained on the target page. When a user activates a link, it is the user—not the linking site—who accesses and copies the target page.

This reasoning was followed in *Ticketmaster Corp. v. Tickets.com, Inc.*, where plaintiff Ticketmaster alleged that deep linking by Tickets.com infringed Ticketmaster's copyright in the linked-to pages.[252] The District Court for the Central

---

250. 17 U.S.C. § 1201 *et seq.*, Pub. L. 105–304, 112 Stat. 2860 (Oct. 28, 1998).
251. MAI Sys. Corp. v. Peak Computer, 991 F.2d 511 (9th Cir. 1993).
252. *See* Ticketmaster Corp. v. Tickets.com Inc., No. CV-99–7654, 2000 U.S. Dist. LFNEXIS 4553 (C.D. Cal. Minute Order filed Mar 27, 2000).

District of California found that deep linking was not itself a violation of the Copyright Act because no copying is involved. The court analogized the use of hyperlinks to the use of a library index card to get reference to particular items in a library.

(2) Derivative Works

As explained above, section 106(2) of the Copyright Act also provides a cause of action for the unauthorized creation of derivative works of the copy-righted work.[253] Some web site operators have claimed that unauthorized framing constitutes the creation—on the user's computer screen—of an un-authorized derivative work of the targeted (that is, framed) web page.

Proponents of this argument have cited for support an offline case involving derivative works, *Mirage Editions, Inc. v. Albuquerque*.[254] There, the defendant removed prints from pages of a book and then individually framed (in the offline context) those pages for sale. The Ninth Circuit found that the defendant violated the copyright owners' exclusive right to create derivative works. To date, however, courts have not applied *Mirage Editions* to cases involving online frames.[255]

(3) Contributory Infringement

Even when a copyright owner cannot establish that the operator of a linking web page committed direct copyright infringement, circumstances may arise where the link nonetheless constitutes contributory copyright infringement. A party may be liable as a contributory infringer if it has knowledge of an infring-ing activity, and induces, causes, or materially contributes to the infringing conduct of another.[256] Underlying the contributory infringement claim is the direct infringement (by the third party) of the copyright owner's exclusive rights.

In the linking context, a plaintiff alleging contributory infringement by a linking party must show that the end user's access to, or viewing of, the target web site constituted a copyright violation. To understand when the end user may be violating a copyright, two separate circumstances must be considered: when the copyright is owned or licensed by the operator of the target site, and when the copyright is owned by an unrelated third party (the owner of the target site being merely another infringer).

---

253. 17 U.S.C.A. § 106(2) (2000).

254. Mirage Editions, Inc. v. Albuquerque, 856 F.2d 1341 (9th Cir. 1988). *See also* Munoz v. Albuquerque A.R.T. Co., 829 F. Supp. 309 (D. Alaska 1993), *aff'd*, 38 F.3d 1218 (9th Cir. 1994); The Greenwich Workshop, Inc. v. Timber Creations, Inc., 932 F. Supp. 1210 (C.D. Cal. 1996).

255. *See, e.g.,* Futuredontics, Inc. v. Applied Anagramics, Inc., 45 U.S.P.Q.2d (BNA) 2005 (C.D. Cal. 1998).

256. Gershwin Publ'g Corp. v. Columbia Artists Mgmt., Inc., 443 F.2d 1159, 1162 (2d Cir. 1971). *See also* Lewis Galoob Toys, Inc. v. Nintendo of Am., Inc., 964 F.2d 965, 970 (9th Cir. 1992).

Copyright holder owns target site. Turning to the first circumstance (the copyright holder owns the target site), the linking site operator's obvious defense to a claim of contributory infringement is that the plaintiff copyright owner has, by operation of the target site, expressly or by implication, licensed the user to access the target site. Though this may be true in many cases, there are circumstances where the user's access to the target site—via the link—may be impermissible.

For example, the target site may argue that any end user license is limited to viewing the web page in the manner intended by the site operator. In the case of in-line linking, pieces of the target page are selectively extracted for viewing in a manner not intended by the target site. If this use were found to exceed the scope of any end user license, the end user's browsing might be infringing and the placement of the in-line link might be deemed to contribute to that infringement.[257]

A web site operator who intends to prohibit deep linking in its terms of service should ensure that users are actually bound by those terms. This may require users to affirmatively indicate their acceptance. In *Ticketmaster Corp. v. Tickets.com, Inc.*, for example, the court dismissed a breach of contract claim by plaintiff Ticketmaster that the defendant's deep linking to plaintiff's site violated the express terms of service for that site. The court found that the terms of service did not constitute a binding contract because the terms were inconspicuously posted at the bottom of the target page and Ticketmaster provided no vehicle (such as clicking an "I accept" icon) whereby users would be made aware of the contract and given an mechanism for indicating their acceptance. According to the court, "it cannot be said that merely putting the terms and conditions in this fashion [at the bottom of the homepage, and without a requirement of affirmative acceptance] necessarily creates a contract with anyone using the Web site."[258]

Copyright holder is third party. The contributory infringement analysis differs when the complaining copyright owner is not the operator of the target web site but rather an unrelated third party. In that case, the target web site operator is itself an infringer and has no authority to grant an express or implied license. When a user visits the infringing target site, she creates yet another infringing copy on her computer. Presumably, the target web site operator has contributed to the end user's infringement. The question for purposes of linking is whether the operator of a web site that links to the target page also contributes to the end user's infringement. In some cases, the answer may be yes, if the plaintiff can show that the defendant had knowledge that the end user's access

---

257. *See* Kara Beal, *The Potential Liability of Linking on the Internet: An Examination*, 2 BYU L. Rev. 703–39 (1998). The operator of the Dilbert Hack Page has chronicled the history of the page at <http://www.cs.rice.edu/dwallach/dilbert/>.

258. Ticketmaster Corp. v. Tickets.com, Inc., No. CV-99–7654, 2000 U.S. Dist. LFNEXIS 4553 (C.D. Cal. 2000).

of the target web site constitutes an infringement and the defendant induced, caused or materially contributed to the infringing activity.

A fairly recent case, *Intellectual Reserve Inc. v. Utah Lighthouse Ministry*,[259] demonstrates the level of knowledge and encouragement that may be required for liability to attach in such cases. Plaintiff Intellectual Reserve Inc. alleged that defendant Utah Lighthouse Ministry posted substantial portions of a work in which plaintiff held the copyright. The district court granted a temporary restraining order requiring the defendant to remove the copyrighted material. The defendant removed the copyrighted work from its web site, but subsequently placed a notice on its site that the copyrighted work was available on three other web sites, and provided links to these sites. The defendant's web site also encouraged users to visit the sites, download the information, print it and send it to others. Moreover, the site featured responses to e-mails that included instructions to a user who could not access one of the sites containing the copyrighted material.

The district court in *Intellectual Reserve*, citing *MAI Systems*, found direct infringement of the plaintiff's copyright when users visited the target site and viewed the information by downloading it into their browsers, resulting in a reproduction in the user's RAM. It was also established that the defendant had knowledge of the infringing activity. The remaining question—whether the defendant had induced, caused or materially contributed to the user's infringing activity by providing the links to the sites containing the copyrighted information—was answered affirmatively. The court found that the defendant actively encouraged the infringing activity by directing users to the copyrighted materials on the other sites. The court ordered the defendant to remove the links.

(4) Digital Millennium Copyright Act[260]

The Digital Millennium Copyright Act of 1998 (DMCA) amended the Copyright Act in a number of ways that affect linking, most significantly in the adoption of a safe harbor on liability for linking and in the imposition of new rights to prohibit the removal of copyright management information.

Section 512 safe harbors. DMCA added section 512 to the Copyright Act to create four new limitations on liability for copyright infringement by online service providers. One of the limitations, codified at section 512(d), limits liability for the acts of referring or hypertext linking users to a target site that contains infringing material. To take advantage of this limitation, a web site operator must:

1. have no knowledge that the material is infringing,
2. not receive a financial benefit directly attributable to the activity if the provider has the right and ability to control the infringing activity and

---

259. Intellectual Reserve Inc. v. Utah Lighthouse Ministry, No. 2:99-CV-808C (D. Utah Dec. 6, 1999).
260. *See infra* Chapter 4, Content Liability.

3. expeditiously take down or block access to the material upon receiving proper notification of a claimed infringement.

Other conditions and limitations apply, so web site operators relying upon the safe harbors of section 512 should carefully study DMCA.

Section 1202 protection for copyright management information. DMCA added section 1202 to the Copyright Act, which bars the intentional removal or alteration of copyright management information. *Copyright management information* is defined as the title, copyright notice, name of the author and other specified information. Civil remedies and criminal penalties are provided for violation.

In the linking context, a case under section 1202 arose in *Kelly v. Arriba Soft Corp.*[261] The defendant operated a visual search engine that generated images of web sites in lieu of descriptive text. The images were reduced-size "thumbnail" pictures of the sites. By clicking on a desired thumbnail, a user could view the address of the web site where the image originated. The plaintiff, a photographer whose web site was included in the defendant's engine, sued, claiming that the thumbnail images not only violated the plaintiff's copyright but that the removal of the plaintiff's copyright notice (lost in the process of creating the thumbnail image) violated section 1202. The court granted the defendant's motion to dismiss, holding that the use of the images was a permissible fair use and that the defendant lacked the requisite intent required to establish a violation under section 1202.

iv. Agreements to Permit Linking

A. What Is a Linking Agreement?

A linking agreement is an understanding in which the operator of a target web site grants another party permission to link to the target web sites. The permission can be unilateral or mutual and can be given for free or for a fee. The principal issues to be addressed in a linking agreement are set forth in this section.

In many linking agreements, the target site actually pays the linking site to place the link. The target site's motivation in these deals is to encourage links, which in turn generate traffic. For example, in an *affiliate agreement*, the target site allows other sites to link to it and pays linking sites a referral fee based upon customers who arrive at—and conduct business on—the target site. In an *advertising agreement*, the target site pays another site a fee to place a link (in the form of an advertisement) to the target site. Fees may be based upon the number of times the ad is displayed (*impressions*).

---

261. Kelly v. Arriba Soft Corp., 77 F. Supp. 2d 1116 (C.D. Cal. 1996).

More complex relationships are often referred to as *co-branding agreements.* These may vary widely, but the classic structure is when one site (branded site) commissions another site (provider site) to create a co-branded web page bearing both the branded site's brand (as the dominant brand) and the provider site's brand (as the lesser brand). Often, the provider's brand is displayed as a legend, such as "Powered by Excite."

Though all these relationships involve linking, more complex agreements, such as affiliate and co-branding agreements, raise additional issues that are addressed in the section of this chapter dedicated to advertising deals (Section 4.4). This section focuses upon the most basic transaction, in which the target site grants permission to a linking site to place a link.

B. Why Enter a Web Linking Agreement?

The Web has billions of links, the overwhelming majority of which are not subject to linking agreements. When should clients go to the trouble of preparing a linking agreement? The answer depends upon whether the client is the linking site or the target site.

From the perspective of the linking site, a linking agreement is appropriate when the proposed link would raise some risk of a claim by the target site. This risk is addressed by obtaining the target site's permission—in the form of a linking agreement—to place the link. Of course, in those relatively rare circumstances when the linking party is paying for the right to post the link, it will also be appropriate to document the parties' understanding in a contract.

Drawing from the analysis of the preceding section, situations in which links may raise risks (and, therefore, justify a linking agreement) include the following:

- when the link employs framing;
- when the link is to specific content provided by a media outlet;
- when the linking site employs deep linking, especially between two commercial web sites;
- when the target site includes terms of use that limit, condition or prohibit linking;
- when there is any in-line linking to a third-party target site;
- when there is any possibility that users may become confused about the source or sponsorship or affiliation of the web pages or the products offered on them;
- when the link constitutes a trademark, particularly a logo or stylized word mark; and
- when the material on the target site raises known copyright infringement risks.

From the perspective of the target site, a linking agreement may be appropriate when links are desired but only if maintained in a particular way. The target site might also aspire to derive revenue for the grant of permission. Of course, in many transactions, the target site is willing to pay for the link. In our rubric, these transactions enter the realm of affiliate or advertising agreements and go beyond the scope of the basic linking agreement.

For example, a site that reviews restaurants may wish to link to a site that provides maps so that visitors to the linking site will find it convenient to locate the restaurants that are reviewed. The owners of the restaurant site may want to enter an agreement to make clear they have permission to create deep links to—or frames around—the supplemental site, and to avoid the uncertainty regarding the deep link or frame. The owner of the map site may approve of links to its site because such links will boost traffic to the site and the overall advertising revenue of the site. At the same time, however, the map site owner wants to be paid a modest fee by the restaurant site for the privilege of linking, and wants to ensure that links to the site are displayed in a certain manner or that the proprietary information and advertising on the site are displayed properly when users visit the site via the agreed-upon links.

These objectives can be achieved through a properly drafted linking agreement.

C. Grant of Permission

The very essence of a linking agreement is the target site's grant of permission to the linking site for the linking site to include a link to the target site. The grant of permission should recite:

1. whether the permitted link is an invoke-to-load link or an in-line link,
2. what URL may be linked to and
3. on what URL or domain the link may be placed.

As with an IP license, the grant of right should be conditioned upon the grantee's compliance with its obligations under the agreement (such as payment). In many actual transactions, the grant of permission is reciprocal, although for simplicity all the examples in this section assume a one-way grant.

If deep linking will be used, the linking site should procure a clause specifically permitting that practice. Target sites that permit deep linking should ensure that the target page to which the link is directed includes appropriate disclaimers, links to terms of use, links to privacy statements, and proprietary rights notices. (The example below prohibits deep linking.)

Example:

Subject to the terms and conditions of this Agreement, Linking Site may, during the term of this Agreement, display an invoke-to-load link (Link) on the Linking Site [*defined with reference to a URL*] to the homepage (but no other page) of the Target Site at URL [*specify*]. The foregoing permission is contingent upon Linking Site's ongoing fulfillment of its obligations under this Agreement.

D. Link Placement and Appearance

The target site may want to control the placement and appearance of the link as it appears on the linking site. Otherwise, the linking site should consider inserting a clause in the agreement leaving the placement and appearance of the link to its sole discretion.

The degree to which the target site will insist upon controlling placement and appearance depends upon whether the link includes a reference to the target site's trademark, the nature of the linking site and whether the target site is paying a fee for the placement of the link. (Agreements in which the target site pays a fee for the link, including affiliate agreements, advertising agreements and the like, are discussed separately in Section 3.4 of this chapter.)

Provisions addressing appearance and placement may include link size, which may be stated in terms of numbers of pixels on a given browser and at a specific monitor resolution. Agreements may also require that links appear on the linking site's homepage or on a page that can be accessed in "one click" from the homepage. With a given page, agreements can specify that the link be "above the fold," meaning that the link will be visible when the page is loaded, without requiring users to scroll down or sideways.

Linking agreements may—and often do—require the linking site to post a link using an image file provided by the target site. This allows the target site to exert great control over the appearance of the link.

E. Framing

A web agreement should contain a clause expressly permitting or prohibiting framing, as the parties decide. If framing is permitted, the target site operator should specify whether the frame may contain third-party brands or advertising. If these are permitted, it may in some cases be appropriate for the linking site to share with the target site revenue derived from such third-party advertisement (see discussion of payment below). The following clause permits framing but prohibits third-party ads. It also leaves to the target the right to approve the appearance of the frame and the portions of the target page that will be obscured by the frame.

Example:

Linking Site may frame any or all Web Pages of the Target Site within a frame containing the Listing Site's trademark but otherwise containing no third-party branding or advertisements (the Frame). The format, presentation, content, size and placement of the Frame are subject to Target Site's prior written approval, which approval may be withheld for any reason or for no reason.

F. Trademark and Content Licenses

The linking agreement should also include provisions regarding licenses to use trademarks and copyrights.

(1) Trademarks

If the target site's trademarks are to be used by the linking site, this use should be expressly licensed. This protects both the linking site (from claims of infringement) and the target site (from third-party claims that the mark has been abandoned through uncontrolled licensing).

(2) Content

Content provided by one party to the other may be contained in the link itself, provided by the target site for posting on the linking site in connection with the link or (in the case of in-line linking) displayed as part of the linking site. Such content should be expressly licensed. Note that when the content includes sound recordings or audiovisual clips, potentially complex licensing issues may arise that are outside the scope of this section. The grant of license related to content should expressly include the rights to "publicly display and publicly perform" by means of digital audio transmission or otherwise.

(3) End Users

For drafters who aspire to tie down every lose end, it may be appropriate when representing the linking site to insist upon an acknowledgement by the target site that end user viewing of the target site is permitted, notwithstanding any provision in the target site's standard terms of access to the contrary. This concern may arise when deep linking or in-line linking is used. The purpose of such an acknowledgement is to preclude the possibility that individual end users are committing copyright infringement when accessing the target site via the agreed-upon link. Consideration should be given to whether end users should be third-party beneficiaries.

Example:

Subject to the terms and conditions of this Agreement, Target Site hereby grants to Linking Site, and Linking Site hereby accepts, a nonexclusive, non-transferable, nonsublicenseable, royalty-free, worldwide license under Target Site's Intellectual Property to (a) display the Target Site Marks on the Linking Site for the sole purpose of providing the Links from the Linking Site to the Target Site, (b) reproduce, distribute, publicly display and publicly perform by means of a digital audio transmission or otherwise the Content [*defined term depending upon the transaction*] but only as incorporated in or invoked by the Link. Notwithstanding any provision to the contrary in Target Site's standard terms of access, Target Site agrees to allow end users accessing Target Site via the Link to view the Target Site for such end user's own personal, noncommercial purposes.

G. Proprietary Rights Notices

A party licensing its copyrights or trademarks to the other party should insist upon a requirement that the licensed subject matter will include proprietary rights notices such as the ® or © symbols. In connection with content, however, the licensor may need to be flexible, particularly when the licensed subject matter is an image displayed via an in-line link. It may not be practical for such images to be accompanied by a copyright notice placed next to the image. One option is to place the notice in the linking site's "Legal Notices" or other comparable page. Linking sites that intend to display in-line content without copyright notices and other copyright management information could secure consent from the target site to preclude any claim under section 1202 of the Copyright Act.

H. End User Data

Information is often collected from individuals browsing the Web, including information affirmatively provided by the user (such as through a registration form) and information generated through mere use of sites (such as which pages are viewed and for how long). This information is commercially valuable to the parties that collect it. In a linking agreement, parties may wish to agree about whether they will share end user data, and which party will own the data.

The collection of end user data also raises sensitive privacy issues that may be of both legal and public relations concerns. Many web site operators post a privacy policy to explain to the public how end user information is collected and used. In the context of linking, a user may flow seamlessly from one party's web site to another party's web site, which may lead to misunderstanding about which party's privacy policy governs the data collected from that user. If privacy concerns arise, the parties to a linking agreement may wish to have a mutual covenant that each will abide by its respective privacy policy and any applicable law or regulation regarding collection, use and dissemination of end user data. The parties may wish to agree upon minimum standards for privacy. Finally, the parties may also agree upon a procedure for advising users that, upon leaving the linking site, they are subject to a different privacy policy. Privacy issues are covered extensively in Chapter 7 of this book.

Example:

Each party will retain ownership of (and is under no obligation to disclose to the other) any data that it collects on its respective site from end users or their use of the site, either directly through the end user's affirmative submission of data or otherwise (User Data). Each party will comply with its respective privacy policy and all applicable laws and regulations regarding collection and handling of User Data. Linking Site will provide programming so that, upon activation of the Link, a legend will be displayed to the user informing the user that he or she is leaving the Linking Site and entering the Target Site and that user's activity on the Target Site is not subject to the Linking Site's terms of use or privacy policy.

I. Editorial Content

In some situations, the parties may choose to restrict the editorial content of the target or linking site. For example, the target site may not want a link (particularly one referring to it by name) on a site that contains indecent, obscene or otherwise offensive content. A linking site may similarly wish to avoid linking its users to sites that contain inappropriate content. Contractually, parties can attempt to regulate editorial content of each other's sites by providing certain minimum standards (such as "no material that is obscene, indecent, deceptive or that otherwise violates any law or the rights of any third party").

More detailed controls may include specifications regarding the layout and features of pages, and limitations regarding the types of other links that may be included on the linking site. A common type of restriction is a *no-competitive-links provision*, which prevents the linking site from posting links of business entities that compete with the target site. These competitors may be explicitly enumerated or defined by class or industry segment. The owner of the target site may also wish to control the total number of links that appear on the linking page or the total amount of space, measured in pixels, that other links occupy on the page. A provision stating that the agreed-upon link will be "no less prominent" than other links on the page is often useful. These types of broader controls are typically appropriate in agreements where the target site is paying a fee for the link, such as advertising agreements. Such provisions help ensure that the link is not lost in a sea of other advertising links.

J. Service Levels

Service levels are agreed-upon standards for the performance of a web site. As a practical matter, service level understandings will not be part of a simple linking agreement in which the linking site has merely obtained approval to link to the target site. When the linking site is paying for the privilege of including its link, however, it should insist that the target site provide at least a minimum service level. Most commonly, the specified service levels relate to uptime (for example, "24x7 except for scheduled maintenance occurring between 2:00 a.m. and 5:00 a.m. EST"), response time and other metrics used in the online services industry to measure performance.

K. Warranty

Many simple linking agreements are made without substantive warranties and with broad, mutual disclaimers of liability. As a general practice, both parties should disclaim all warranties not expressly granted. Typical warranties include the following:

- a warranty that the party granting a license to trademarks or content has the right to grant such licenses;
- a warranty that exercise of the license rights by the licensee will not violate any third-party rights; and
- a warranty that both parties will comply with all applicable laws and regulations.

More elaborate warranties are appropriate when monetary consideration is exchanged, particularly in affiliate and advertising agreements.

L. Indemnity and Liability

A fundamental reason for a linking site to enter a linking agreement with the target site is to avoid the risk that the target site will assert a claim against the linking site based upon the link. By procuring the target site's permission, this type of claim is precluded. Suppose, however, that a claim is lodged not by the target site but by a third party alleging that both the target site and the linking site are infringing intellectual property rights. To manage that type of risk, the linking site should seek an indemnification obligation in the linking agreement, which would require the target to defend against the third party claim.

Similarly, targets may be concerned that activities by the linking site expose them to third-party claims. They, too, may want indemnity against such claims to the extent the claims are "based upon the operations of the Linking Site or its breach of its warranties and obligations under this Agreement."

As a practical matter, a target site may be reluctant to indemnify a linking site when the target is providing gratuitous permission for a link.

Most parties will want to include standard exclusions of consequential and incidental damages, as typically found in commercial agreements.

M. Term

Given the fluid nature of the Internet, most simple linking agreements should have a short but renewable term. In many agreements where money is not changing hands, both parties have the right to terminate the agreement for any reason on a few days' or weeks' notice.

At a minimum, the linking party will want rights to remove a link as necessary to qualify for, and comply with, the liability limitation provided in section 512(d) by DMCA. That limitation exonerates linking parties from certain copyright claims if they expeditiously take down or block access to the link upon receiving proper notification of a claimed infringement. In the agreement, therefore, the linking party should insist that, upon its receipt of a bona fide claim of infringement, it can remove the link. Target sites may even wish to insist that the link be removed when a claim is lodged.

A linking site or target site that has paid money to establish a link should resist a clause that allows the other party to terminate unilaterally, and should insist upon a reasonable cure period (such as ten to thirty days) to cure any breach that would otherwise give the other party a termination right.

N. Payment

Many simple linking agreements do not involve payment. There may be circumstances, however, when the linking site is willing to pay the target site for the right to post a link to the target. In these arrangements, payment may be structured in a variety of ways. Note that affiliate and advertising agreements—where the target site pays the linking site—are discussed in Section 3.4 of this chapter.

The simplest payment provisions are based upon flat initial or recurring fees. These may be appropriate when the linking site incorporates material from the target site via an in-line link (such as a graphic). Payment by the linking site may also be based upon impressions—that is, the number of times the in-line link is displayed to unique visitors. This arrangement is the reverse of an advertising deal, in which the target site pays the linking site for each impression. When the link is an invoke-to-load link, other payment metrics may be used that depend upon the users "clicking through" the link. For example, the linking site could pay a few pennies each time a user accesses the target site through the link. From the linking site's perspective, it may be important to limit payment to the number of unique visitors, so that if the same user accesses a link several times in a given session, only one "click-through" would be counted.

Compensation paid by the linking site could also be calculated as a percentage of the revenue that the linking site generates from selling advertising space to third parties on the page where the link appears. This may be especially appropriate when the linking site sells advertising space on frames that surround content from the target site.

A target site that is anticipating payment based upon the linking site's revenues or impressions should insist upon an auditing procedure to verify this information. The linking site must have a reliable method of tracking impressions if that is the relevant metric. Use of an impartial third-party auditing service may be appropriate.

v. Stopping Undesired Linking

Web site operators can determine which sites are linking to them by various means, including conducting a search of the site's URL using a search engine. Once links are identified, the site operator can determine whether they are beneficial or detrimental. In some cases, detrimental links can be stopped by contacting the linking site and requesting desired changes (for example, eliminating a deep link). In such situations, it may be appropriate for the target site to suggest that the parties enter a linking agreement. If the linking site is not cooperative, the target operator can resort to technological measures to stop linking.

These technological measures are generally quicker and may be more cost-effective than legal action. Some technological fixes are quite simple. A web site may periodically change the internal URLs of its web site, while updating all the site's internal links. By changing all the site's internal web addresses, the existing external links to those pages become outdated. Linking web sites are forced to update their web pages constantly, or to link to the homepage of the target site. This solution may be cumbersome to administer, however, and may make it difficult to maintain deep links that the target site desires to keep intact.

One of the most effective means of limiting unauthorized use of a site is to require users to enter a user name and password each time they enter the site. By keeping out visitors who have not entered this information, web sites may be able to prevent unauthorized linking, or, at the least, ensure that users have manifested agreement to the site's terms of access. Many sites are reluctant to adopt such measures, however, because they are believed to reduce site traffic. Many visitors to a site will simply turn away when faced with such a procedural hurdle. If site traffic is lowered, the site's advertising value diminishes, and this may outweigh the benefits gained from the password protection.

§ 3.3 Joint Ventures

1. Introduction

Most e-commerce business plans—including both business-to-consumer and business-to-business[262]—involve the aggregation and collective exploitation of various assets, including content, technology, contractual relationships, data, distribution infrastructure and, of course, money. As most entities do not have all the necessary elements for a sophisticated e-commerce venture under one roof, e-commerce joint ventures have become the vehicle of choice to exploit the opportunities presented by new technologies.[263]

Joint ventures in the e-commerce arena are important for a number of unique reasons. Rapid technological advances force business ventures to take advantage of, and have access to, available best-of-breed technology. Products and services must be brought to market on accelerated Internet-time schedules.[264] E-businesses, moreover, bring together varied areas of expertise, and joint ventures are a particularly convenient means of marrying that expertise.

2. Form of Joint Venture

i. Introduction

A joint venture is often implemented in the form of a separate, unique entity. Generally, separate-entity joint ventures take three forms: a corporation, a partnership (either general or limited) or a limited liability company (LLC). Each of these forms, if structured properly, can achieve insulation for the participants

---

262. The Internet industry divides e-commerce into two primary categories: business-to-business and business-to-consumer. Business-to-business implies the selling of products and services between companies and the automation of systems via integration. By 2003, Forrester Research Inc. estimates that business-to-business commerce will balloon to $1.3 trillion. Jupiter Communications estimates this figure to be $6 trillion by 2005. By 2006, business-to-business commerce could represent 40% of all business conducted in the United States. In contrast, business-to-consumer commerce involves interaction and transactions between a company and its consumers. Companies such as Amazon and eBay use a business-to-consumer e-commerce model.

263. For purposes of this discussion, we have made a distinction between a joint venture and a strategic alliance, which we define as a relationship that may be implemented as a contractual arrangement or as a series of interdependent contractual agreements without the creation of a separate entity.

264. Not surprisingly, high-tech companies are entering joint ventures in larger numbers than other companies.

from legal and financial liability related to joint venture activities. When determining the form and structure the joint venture should take, participants should consider—among other things—the following:

- Tax issues
- Liability issues
- Fiduciary obligations
- Required regulatory filings and approvals
- Assignment rights
- Voting rights
- Financing issues and expected return on investment
- Asset contributions
- Profit participation
- Management issues
- Restrictions on competition
- Circumstances triggering termination or dissolution of the joint venture
- Governing law
- Related agreements
- Formation and maintenance costs

ii. Corporation

A. Introduction

The corporation is the classic structure for providing personal-liability protection to the owners of a business, including a joint venture. Although a corporate joint venture is relatively easy to organize, it is not always the best choice. If, however, a public offering or venture capital financing is realistically contemplated, a corporation—despite some of its limitations—may still be the most advantageous form.[265]

B. Regulatory and Reporting Requirements

In a corporation, each of the participants is a shareholder. The shareholders must agree upon the purpose of the venture as well as the structure to be achieved. Running a corporation requires adherence to strict rules, which in-

---

265. Although entities can convert from one form to another, due to tax, timing and financial reasons, choosing the initial vehicle is an important decision.

clude requirements for meetings, regular meetings of the board of directors and shareholders, documentation of those proceedings with specificity and periodic filings with a central filing office in the state of incorporation. The reporting and documentation requirements for a corporation are stricter than those for any other entity.

C. Governing Documents

If joint venture participants decide to form a corporation, the first step is to create the articles of incorporation, the shareholders agreement, the corporation's charter and the bylaws. The articles of incorporation must include a brief description of the purpose for which the corporation was formed. Bylaws are usually created after the articles of incorporation are filed with the secretary of state. The bylaws contain provisions for governance, meetings, removal and designation of directors and officers, duties of officers and reports to the shareholders.

D. Creation

Creating a corporation is only slightly less expensive than organizing a partnership. While a partnership's initial expenses lie primarily in the extensive drafting process required to create the partnership agreement, the bulk of a corporation's initial expenses are in the filing and tax fees associated with the creation of a corporation. The assistance of legal counsel in the drafting of a corporation's bylaws, articles and other governing documents is advisable, and will lead to certain expenses. Continuing maintenance costs of a corporation are generally higher than those for other forms of joint ventures.

E. Taxation

One of the biggest disadvantages to choosing a corporation as the form of joint venture is double taxation. Both the corporation and the shareholders are taxed; corporations are taxed on their income at the corporate level and then, if the corporation pays dividends to its shareholders, the dividends are taxed again at the shareholder level.

F. Management

Management of a corporation is centralized. A board of directors is first elected by the shareholders. The board of directors then elect or appoint the officers who will run the day-to-day operations under the direction of the board of directors, the bylaws, and as state statutes require. In general, shareholder approval is required for major changes in corporate charter documentation and for major transactions outside the corporation's regular course of business. In a joint venture, a major transaction may include expanding the purpose of the venture as a result of market trends.

iii. Partnership

A. Introduction

For a joint venture, there are two types of partnership forms to consider: the general partnership and the limited liability partnership (LLP). Participants in a joint venture who are contemplating the formation of a partnership should consider the issues discussed below.

B. Taxation

In contrast to corporations, both forms of partnerships are taxed only once.

C. Creation

Unlike general partnerships, LLPs require a formal creation process in which a certificate of limited partnership is filed with the state. Such a certificate usually contains the rights and duties of the partners.

D. Management

One of the most distinctive characteristics of a general partnership is its decentralized management. Partners in a general partnership have complete managerial control, unless restricted by contractual agreements. All partners are co-owners even if contributions or shares in profits and losses are unequal. Neither management nor control is specified by law. If a general partnership is structured like a corporation, it may become difficult to manage if there are too many partners. In such a case, an LLC or a corporation may be the better form for the joint venture. In an LLP, one general partner is designated with full managerial control and full liability, while limited partners have less managerial control and limited liability.

E. Liability

Unlike a general partnership, in which each party is subject to unlimited liability, an LLP benefits from the same protection from liability as a corporation; that is, the partners are not personally liable for the obligations of the business. Instead, liability is limited to the amount of each limited partner's capital contribution to the partnership.[266] The general partner in an LLP, however, has the same liabilities as partners in a general partnership. General partners may be jointly and severally liable for all tortious acts of their copartners acting within the scope of the partnership business.

F. Partnership Agreement

The partnership agreement usually addresses all issues important to the partners, and functions as a guide for relationships involving the partners, the partnership and third parties dealing with the partnership. Participants in an e-commerce joint venture may use the partnership agreement to enumerate each party's rights and obligations, to avoid later disputes. Venturers may also delineate the management responsibilities, based upon the expertise of the parties to the venture. For example, a software and infrastructure provider might manage technical operations, while another participant manages corporate operations. The partnership agreement should also address matters such as voting or consent rights, distribution to partners, buy/sell agreements and other matters not addressed by the Uniform Partnership Act.[267]

G. Reporting Obligations

General partnerships are usually not subject to the reporting and record-keeping requirements of corporations and LLPs. Rights and obligations for LLPs are set forth in the certificate of limited partnership.

H. Formation Costs

Formation costs for general partnerships are higher than those for corporations, because general partnership agreements are less standardized and often require greater legal input.

I. Term of Existence

Unlike a corporation, which has a perpetual existence, a partnership exists only until the end of the term stated in the partnership agreement.

---

266. The exception to this rule is if a limited partner's name appears improperly in the partnership name or if a limited partner takes control of the partnership.

267. *See, e.g.,* DEL. CODE ANN. tit. 6, §§ 101–1210 (2000); N.Y. PARTNERSHIP LAW §§ 1 *et seq.* (Consol. 2001); CAL. CORP. CODE §§ 15006 *et seq.* (Deering 2001); CAL. CORP. CODE §§ 16100 *et seq.* (Deering 2001); 805 ILL. COMP. STAT. 205/1 *et seq.* (2001).

iv. Limited Liability Companies

A. Introduction

LLCs are the creation of state statutes. The concept of an LLC arose out of an effort to combine the benefits of a corporation with the tax treatment of a general partnership. As a consequence, an LLC has attributes of a sole proprietorship, a general partnership and a corporation. Most significantly, an LLC insulates participants from liability to the same extent as shareholders of a corporation, thereby avoiding a significant disadvantage of the partnership form. At the same time, for tax purposes, an LLC is treated as a partnership and, as a nontaxpaying entity, avoids double taxation.

B. Management

An LLC has members rather than shareholders. Management may be vested in the members or in a manager or managers.

C. Operating Agreement

Essentially, an LLC is a business entity created by contract between the members, much the same as a general partnership. This contract is called an operating agreement. In general, the operating agreement for an LLC should describe the principles of management, the distribution of profits and losses, and the rights and obligations of membership in the LLC.

D. Formation

To be legally recognized, an LLC must file articles of organization with the department of state, in the state in which it is formed.

E. Liability

Members of an LLC are protected from personal liability for the acts of the LLC, much like shareholders of a corporation. Unlike an S corporation, an LLC is not restricted in the number or types of individuals or entities that may become members. An LLC also differs from a limited partnership, in that it does not impose personal liability on members who participate in the management of the LLC.

F. Fiduciary Obligations

Managers have a duty of care and a duty of loyalty. These duties can be limited in the articles of organization, however.

G. Advantages over Other Forms

For e-commerce joint ventures, the LLC can provide a number of benefits over both the corporate and partnership forms. Like a corporation, an LLC can offer joint venture participants the protection of limited liability. Unlike corporate income, income generated by the LLC is taxed only once. An S corporation also avoids double taxation, but to maintain S corporation status, the Tax Code imposes a number of restrictions that minimize flexibility and therefore the utility such a form has for joint ventures. General partnerships also have favorable tax treatment and avoid many of the structural limitations of S corporations, but raise the possibility of unlimited liability. LLPs offer protection from liability but only at the cost of sacrificing management rights.

3. Contributions

i. Introduction

Typically, the creation of an e-commerce joint venture involves the contribution of important assets by each of the participants to the venture. Participants may contribute, among other things, money, management, technical and industry-related expertise, software and other technology, content and contractual relationships. As a threshold matter, the value of each party's contribution must be considered and evaluated. The contributions are unlikely to be of equal value and the contractual agreements used to form the joint venture should address valuation and resulting equity participation issues.

ii. Form of Contributions

The form of effecting the contribution to the venture varies depending upon the circumstances. For example, if a party to a venture "contributes" an existing web site, it may make sense for that party to transfer and convey to the venture certain software that it owns. It may also make sense, however, for the party to license—on an exclusive basis—the right to use the URL. Licensing may be appropriate for a number of reasons, such as related trademark issues or foreign sites. An exclusive, perpetual license of the right to use the URL is a valid contribution to the venture, and is valued as such for purposes of evaluating equity participation. Similarly, one or more of the participants to the venture may lease tangible property to the venture rather than make an outright capital contribution. Such an arrangement can be a contribution as well, and the associated value depends upon the terms of the lease.

iii. Intellectual Property

Obviously, intellectual property is often at the heart of an e-commerce joint venture. A participant in a venture frequently contributes intellectual property as part or all of that participant's contribution. Such contribution can be in the form of an outright transfer (that is, an assignment) or a license. Again, the value of a contribution in the form of a license depends upon the rights granted to the venture. Issues to consider include whether the license is exclusive, whether it is perpetual, whether there are any conditions upon which it can be revoked, and whether the licensor retains any rights to the licensed technology or any new versions or derivatives of that technology.

iv. Contractual Relationships

If a participant brings certain contractual relationships to the venture, part or all of that venturer's contribution is often an assignment of those relationships to the venture. Those relationships should be reviewed as part of the due diligence process, to ensure they are assignable and, if certain procedures are required (such as notice or consent), that such procedures are followed. Participants should also consider whether the assignment has any impact on pricing or other material terms. To the extent the contributor needs to retain any portion of the benefits under the agreement(s) being assigned for endeavors independent of the venture, creative thought must be used to determine how best to "split the baby."

v. Other Assets

Other assets that can be contributed to a joint venture include cash, services, equipment or facilities, subject matter expertise, administrative and management services, supply arrangements, web infrastructure (including both web site design and hosting infrastructure) and agreements for distribution, marketing, advertising, leases or licenses.

4. Intellectual Property Licensing[268]

Participants in the venture often provide software or other technology that enables the e-commerce business to operate. In some cases, the software or other technology is contributed to the venture. More often, however, there is a software license agreement between the venture and the participant, which grants to the venture certain rights. This agreement presents a common—but somewhat precarious—situation, where the venture is based upon technology provided by one of its participants on a somewhat encumbered basis. (Section 4.1 of this chapter discusses intellectual property licensing more extensively.)

5. Confidentiality

Confidential information is often exchanged by and between joint venture participants. For example, financial information—including revenue, profits, royalties or net income—may be shared. The participants may also share technical materials (such as software, technical specifications or source code), business plans, research, customer lists and contractual arrangements.

To maintain the confidentiality of such information, a joint venture agreement should include a confidentiality provision. It should define confidential information in a way that covers all information provided by the disclosing party to a receiving party, subject to certain standard exclusions, such as information that (1) is in the public domain, (2) enters the public domain after disclosure (but not due to disclosure by the receiving party), (3) the receiving party obtains from a third party not under a confidentiality obligation to the disclosing party and (4) is not independently created by the receiving party.

Confidentiality provisions should also describe each party's obligations regarding its treatment of confidential information. For example, a receiving party might be allowed to disclose the information only to the extent necessary to carry out the business of the venture.

Sample Form Language:

Safeguarding: The Members and their Affiliates shall each act to safeguard the secrecy and confidentiality of, and any proprietary rights to, any nonpublic information relating to the Company and its business, except to the extent such information is required to be disclosed by law or reasonably necessary to be disclosed to carry out the business of NewCo. NewCo may, from time to time, provide the Members written notice of its nonpublic information that is subject to this section.

---

268. For details on intellectual property licensing, see *supra* Chapter 2, Intellectual Property.

6. Management and Employees

i. Personnel

Proper staffing of an e-commerce joint venture is critical to its success. A joint venture may be staffed with existing personnel from the venture participants, with new employees hired specifically by the joint venture, or with some combination thereof. Human resources issues—such as ERISA, pension plans and the like—must also be considered. In addition to identifying the role each participant will play in the joint venture, the joint venture agreement should identify the personnel, if any, who will be committed to operating the joint venture. Specifically, if there are key personnel essential to the overall success of the joint venture, the agreement should identify those individuals. Furthermore, the agreement should address what effect, if any, the resignation of such personnel will have on the joint venture.

> *Form Language—Sample 1:*
>
> ABC, Company A and Company B shall make available for employment by NewCo the persons identified on Schedule [___] annexed hereto and such other persons as ABC, Company A and Company B shall mutually agree, each of whom shall be offered employment by NewCo on reasonable terms. If the location of the Principal Office is more than fifty miles from any such employee's current principal residence, NewCo shall be responsible for any customary costs of relocating such employee.
>
> *Form Language—Sample 2:*
>
> Specified employees of ABC will be reassigned to NewCo and will receive salaries and benefits substantially equivalent to those they received from their former employer. NewCo will also hire new employees.

ii. Nonsolicitation of Employees

The joint venture agreement should address the issue of solicitation of personnel attached to the joint venture. More specifically, parties to a joint venture should consider placing limits on the ability of each participant to solicit employees of the joint venture.

iii. Equity Options for Management and Employees

Like most business ventures, the success of an e-commerce joint venture is largely dependent upon the talents of its management team. As a consequence, participants should pay close attention to creating a compensation structure that adequately compensates key members of the management team, as well as other employees.

Equity options can serve as an effective means to motivate management and other employees to work for the long-term success of the joint venture. Furthermore, this incentive method often enables the venture to attract and retain talented key managers and other employees, while helping to limit cash expenditures.

The joint venture agreement should describe any equity incentive plans (such as stock purchase plans or stock option plans) to be offered to management and other employees of the joint venture. The agreement should also specify which individuals have authority to implement such plans (for example, the Board of Directors).

To maintain flexibility, the joint venture agreement can be drafted in a way that does not limit available equity options to one or two types. Alternatively, the agreement can specify the type of incentive compensation plan that will be offered—such as a stock purchase plan or a stock option plan. A stock purchase plan allows an employee to purchase a direct equity stake in the joint venture, often at either a discounted value or with financing assistance from the venture itself. Stock option plans are often attractive to joint ventures, because they provide a method of compensation that does not further deplete valuable cash reserves and because such plans are often preferred by employees.

Sample Form Language:

The Board of Managers has the power to establish a plan for granting equity interests or options to employees of the Company and may grant equity options to employees of the Company in accordance with any such plan; provided, however, that the total amount of equity that may be subject to such options or other incentives shall not at any given time exceed ten percent of the total equity of the Company, as calculated on the date on which a given option or other incentive is granted, unless a Supermajority of the Members decides to increase or decrease such amount.

7. Finances

The joint venture agreement should set forth the method of distribution to the shareholders, for both net profits and any revenue that may be generated from the sale of assets owned by the joint venture. Generally, and unless otherwise agreed, participants in a venture share in all distributions in proportion to the value of their respective capital contributions. The joint venture agreement may provide specific terms regarding the timing of distributions and any priorities that might exist between the participants, in the event the amounts available for distribution are less than originally contemplated. Furthermore, the agreement may specify the method by which cash will be allocated for reinvestment in the activities of the business.

8. Services Agreements

Participants may provide certain services to the separate entity, including technical or managerial services, which are often set forth in separate services agreements. A service agreement must address the scope of services the venturer agrees to render; these provisions typically reference schedules or exhibits that describe in detail the specifics of the arrangement. Whether, and to what extent, the venture should contract with a venture participant—rather than an outside third party—to build the means to engage in electronic commerce is a crucial decision.

9. Noncompete and Exclusivity Issues

i. Noncompetition Agreements

Participants in an e-commerce joint venture should assess the extent to which either the venture itself or the other participants could pose significant competitive threats during and after the term of the venture. There are two issues to consider: (1) whether the venturers can choose to compete with the venture and (2) whether the venture can choose to compete with any of its owners.

A joint venture agreement may contain an absolute ban on competition:

Form Language—Sample 1:

Neither party or its affiliates shall, without the prior written consent of the other, directly or indirectly own, operate, manage, be employed by, be an agent of, act as a consultant for, financially support or have a proprietary interest in any enterprise or business that provides services in the relevant market.

Alternatively, a joint venture agreement may not enact any limitations at all:

Form Language—Sample 2:

Each Member shall be free to engage in, or possess an interest in, any other business of any type, including any business in direct competition with NewCo, and to avail itself of any business opportunity available to it without offering NewCo or any Member the opportunity to participate in such business.

ii. Exclusivity Agreements

Sometimes, joint venture agreements embody some form of exclusive rights. For a specific technology or content, the greatest benefit of exclusivity is that it solidifies a competitive advantage to the venture against unlicensed third parties. Moreover, exclusivity ensures that the licensor/venturer cannot use the licensed technology to compete against the venture. The exclusivity is often limited to a specific period of time, to make it more acceptable and to comply with potential antitrust and anticompetition issues.

10. Transfers of Interest

i. Introduction

Not surprisingly, venture participants are often concerned that their co-venturers remain committed to a venture, if not perpetually, then at least for a specific period of time. To ensure this, appropriate limitations can be placed upon the right of the participants to transfer equity interests in the venture. Of course, each participant should consider the likelihood that he may want to exit the venture at some future time or upon some event.

ii. Restrictions

In some cases, the joint venture partners agree to a strict prohibition on any sale or transfer of equity interest in the venture for a specific period of time; this includes not only outright sales, but any pledge or encumbrance of the equity interest. Often in such cases, an exception is made when the equity interest is transferred to a successor corporation or a subsidiary of the party, particularly when the transferor remains obligated for any failure of the transferee to perform its duties under the joint venture agreement.

Alternatively, participants sometimes choose to set limits on the right to transfer, rather than imposing an absolute ban. For example, a limitation may be placed upon transferring equity to an individual or entity that competes directly with the venture or with any of the participants.

Even when restrictions are placed upon the participants' rights to transfer their equity interests, the participants generally agree to a date certain when such prohibitions will cease. Often, after such a restrictive period ends, participants have a *right of first offer*, a *right of first refusal* or certain *buy/sell rights*.

A. Right of First Offer

If the joint venture agreement provides for a right of first offer, each participant is obligated to offer its co-venturers the first opportunity to purchase its equity interest. If the co-venturers do not choose to purchase the equity interest, the seller is then able to offer the equity interest to outsiders.

B. Right of First Refusal

A right of first refusal is similar to a right of first offer, except that it involves an offer being made by an outside party before the transferring party becomes obligated to offer the equity to its co-venturers. The transferring party must give its co-venturers the opportunity to acquire its equity interest on the same terms as the offer it has received from the outside party.

C. Buy/Sell

If a joint venture agreement includes a buy/sell provision, each venturer has the right—after a date certain—to set a price at which it would be willing to buy the other party's interest in the venture. If this right is exercised, the offering venturer names the price at which it would be willing to buy the other party's equity interest. The responding venturer then has the right to decide if it would rather sell its interest or buy the offering venturer's interest at the specified price. Because the responding venturer has the right to decide whether it will buy the other party's interest or sell its interest to the other party, the offering venturer has every incentive to set a fair price.

11. Promotion

Joint venture agreements often include promotional obligations for the participants. For example, the agreement could indicate the extent to which the participants will publicize the formation of the joint venture in conventional print publications and on the Internet. In addition, separate linking agreements may be entered between the venture and each of the individual participants.

Links, or *hyperlinks*, are points in web documents through which viewers may branch outward from a central text to other bodies of information, often third-party web sites. Instead of manually typing the URL of the desired location, viewers are often invited to click on an icon or piece of text that will establish a new connection with the new linked site. Linking encourages open, easy and seamless access from one web site to another—in this respect it can be seen as one of the Internet's most distinguishing and valuable features. E-commerce joint venturers may take advantage of this feature by using it to cross-promote each other and the venture itself. (Web linking relationships are discussed in Section 3.2.2 of this chapter.)

12. Antitrust

Entities and individuals considering participation in an e-commerce joint venture must be cognizant of U.S. antitrust laws and should seek the advice of antitrust counsel before proceeding. This is particularly true when competitors are involved in the proposed venture. During the planning and negotiating stages of a joint venture, the parties should assess whether they need to make filings with antitrust regulators, detailing current activities and the proposed business of the joint venture.[269]

In general, joint ventures are undertaken to pool resources, share talents and minimize risks among firms. Recently, the purpose of many e-commerce joint ventures has been to develop the business-to-business Internet marketplace. Because joint ventures frequently produce new players in the marketplace, antitrust regulators often view them more favorably than mergers. Still, such ventures can run afoul of antitrust laws. For both Sherman and Clayton Act purposes, the primary question to ask is the following: Is this combination, viewed objectively, procompetitive or anticompetitive?

Business-to-business marketplaces connect suppliers, distributors, e-commerce service providers, infrastructure providers and customers for the purpose of communicating and effecting transactions. Entrepreneurs who perceived a business opportunity in establishing online intermediaries through which buyers and sellers could transact business on a fee-for-service basis—thereby replacing traditional brokers in many industries—formed the original business-to-business marketplaces. More recently, however, the business-to-business marketplaces that have emerged are organized by either buyers or sellers within a particular industry who seek to eliminate the "middle person" and use the joint venture as the format for rapid development. Though such joint ventures hold great promise for achieving substantial cost savings and efficiencies, they also raise antitrust concerns, particularly when the joint venture is organized and managed by competing buyers or sellers within an industry.

Recognizing the significant efficiencies that business-to-business marketplaces can achieve, but also wary of the antitrust issues that may be implicated, federal agencies have begun reviewing a number of these marketplaces for po-

---

269. *See generally* U.S. FED. TRADE COMM'N & U.S. DEP'T JUSTICE, ANTITRUST GUIDELINES FOR COLLABORATIONS AMONG COMPETITORS (Apr. 2000).

tential antitrust concerns. Although the nature of government investigations is confidential, the enforcement agencies have articulated in several speeches that their primary concerns are these: price transparency, the possibility that anticompetitive effects might result from dominant marketplaces, and the effects of various marketplaces rules and restrictions.

i. Price Transparency

The government's primary concern appears to be that an online marketplace may create a setting for anticompetitive coordination among competitors that could lead to reduced price competition and higher market prices. Many business-to-business marketplaces contemplate the online display of real-time price information, either quotes or transaction prices. Increased price transparency can be procompetitive because it often leads to better-informed and more efficient decision making. The regulatory agencies, however, appear to be concerned that access to competitors' bid and ask or execution prices could also facilitate coordinated activity among companies. In evaluating a proposed marketplace, the agencies will likely consider the extent to which the parties have taken steps to minimize the online sharing of pricing and transaction data among the competitors through technological and behavioral firewalls.

The antitrust enforcement agencies have also expressed concerns about off-line information sharing, as well as online information exchanges. Accordingly, antitrust regulators may consider the extent to which business-to-business marketplace collaboration will lead to other forms of information sharing among competitors, particularly when competitors are involved in the management of the marketplace. Safeguards to prevent "spillover" of competitively sensitive information may take the form of detailed restrictions on competitors' participation in discussions and decision-making activities.

ii. Size of the Business-to-Business Marketplace

Antitrust enforcement agencies have expressed concerns that marketplaces that are too large may create adverse consequences for the marketplace. Antitrust enforcers may take the position that conduct undertaken by entities with market power is subject to greater scrutiny under the antitrust laws than similar conduct undertaken by smaller companies.

It may be important to consider the potential size of a marketplace when establishing marketplace membership criteria and marketplace rules. Though parties are generally free to make unilateral decisions concerning those with whom they will transact business, the government may contend that competitor-controlled networks may not exclude competitors if the particular site has such a significant presence that access to the facility is critical to competing and denial of access would become a problem.

Federal agencies have also expressed concerns about exclusivity provisions under certain circumstances. Membership rules at times require that members use that marketplace exclusively to transact business. Under most circumstances, exclusivity should not raise concerns and may further the important goal of enabling the marketplace to build sufficient volume to achieve its procompetitive potential. Enforcement agencies may take the position that exclusivity restrictions may reduce the likelihood that competing exchanges will develop. Antitrust enforcement authorities have expressed a preference that there be competing exchanges—rather than a single dominant exchange—within an industry. The likely competitive effects of exclusivity provisions are highly fact sensitive, but should be considered within the context of access rules and the characteristics of the particular market.

iii. Marketplace Rules

Business-to-business marketplaces set rules for conducting their auctions or other matching functions. Generally, the specifics of auction functionality do not create antitrust concerns, but antitrust enforcement agencies have cautioned that standardization of transaction terms and conditions could be anticompetitive. In *Catalano, Inc. v. Target Sales, Inc.,*[270] the U.S. Supreme Court held that a conspiracy among competing wholesalers to standardize credit terms offered to a purchaser was per se illegal. And, several years ago, the Department of Justice levied severe sanctions upon a large group of Nasdaq market-makers who allegedly adhered to a quoting convention by which they would bid only in even-eighth increments. The government charged that the effect of adhering to the quoting convention was to inflate the "inside spread" of certain stocks quoted on Nasdaq, increasing the prices to consumers and the profits to market-makers.

It may be efficient for exchanges to standardize the number of factors that might otherwise be open to negotiation—such as terms governing delivery, credit or risk of loss—or to regulate factors such as bidding increments. Standardizing terms of trade in connection with achieving the bona fide goals of streamlining the procurement process is unlikely to be deemed per se illegal. The government may nevertheless scrutinize marketplace transaction rules to determine if the effect of any rule is to limit competition.

---

270. Catalano, Inc. v. Target Sales, Inc., 446 U.S. 643 (1980) (per curiam).

13. Termination

A joint venture agreement should address how the venture may be terminated, and the implications of termination. Typically, the participants can wind up the venture on mutual agreement. If there is not mutual agreement, various other exit strategy mechanisms may be triggered. In the event the venture terminates, one of the most complicated issues is the question of what happens to the venture's assets. Unlike a brick-and-mortar business, where there are hard assets that can be divided or liquidated, an e-commerce venture's assets may be, in large part, in cyberspace. For example, a URL, a new brand or an online marketplace may be the most valuable part of the business. How do you divide those types of assets?

Typically, a joint venture agreement provides for a series of transitions in the event of termination, whereby those cyberspace assets are used to direct customers to the particular participants, when appropriate. Often these transitions are phased in over time, to appear relatively seamless to the customer. As a result, venturers often find themselves working together during a transition period, even after the venture terminates. This can result in many other problems and issues, particularly if the venture terminates as the result of a dispute between any of the participants.

14. E-Commerce Joint Venture Checklist

By way of summary, following is a checklist of items to consider when developing a joint venture:

- Business Plan
    - Purpose of venture
    - Funding
    - Markets
    - Competitors
    - Marketing/sales plan
    - Revenue projections/targets
- Form of Joint Venture
    - LLC
    - Corporation
    - Partnership
- Contributions, Valuation and Intellectual Property
    - Cash
    - Technology
        Software
        E-commerce technology infrastructure
        Databases

- Content
- Contractual relationships
- Contribution versus license
- Trademarks/copyrights/patents/trade secrets
- Jointly developed works
- Dissolution
- Excluded Assets
- Confidentiality
- Management and Employees
- Finances
  - Profit allocation
  - Dividends/distributions
- Services Agreements
- Noncompete and Exclusivity
- Transfer Rights
  - Restrictions
  - Right of first offer
  - Right of first refusal
  - Buy/sell
- Marketing/Promotion
- Antitrust
- Dispute Resolution
- Termination/Withdrawal/Dissolution

15. E-Commerce Joint Venture Memorandum of Understanding—ABC, Inc.

[Date]

COMPANY D
[Address]

COMPANY E
[Address]

Ladies and Gentlemen:

This memorandum of understanding (Memorandum of Understanding) sets forth the terms and conditions pursuant to which ABC, INC. (ABC) proposes to form a joint venture with COMPANY D and COMPANY E to fund and otherwise contribute to the development, production, marketing and distribution of a World Wide Web portal serving the widget industry, which will include [news, editorial content (e.g., feature articles), procurement sourcing information and e-commerce applications regarding certain segments of the widget industry], [as set forth in the business plan (the Business Plan) attached hereto as **Exhibit A**] (the Transaction).

1. Closing Date. It is the intention of ABC, COMPANY D and COMPANY E (each, a party, and collectively, the parties) that definitive agreements evidencing the Transaction (the Transaction Documents) be executed by _____, [2000] (the Closing). If the parties do not enter the Transaction Documents by _____, [2000], this Memorandum of Understanding shall terminate in accordance with its terms unless the parties agree in writing to extend the term of this Memorandum of Understanding.

2. Conditions of the Transaction. The Closing of the Transaction shall be contingent upon the following conditions:

A. Transaction Documents. The parties shall endeavor in good faith to negotiate and execute the Transaction Documents and reach mutual agreement regarding the other legal documents necessary to complete the Transaction, substantially in accordance with the terms and conditions set forth in the Summary of Terms and Conditions (the Term Sheet) attached hereto as **Exhibit B**. The Transaction Documents shall be mutually satisfactory to the parties thereto and shall be in a form customary for transactions of this kind and will, among other things, (i) contain customary representations, warranties, and covenants and (ii) provide for indemnification against losses, claims or liabilities related to any infringement, misrepresentation, breach of warranty or nonfulfillment of any agreement, subject to qualifications and limitations to be mutually agreed upon by the parties.

B. Approvals. All necessary approvals and consents for consummation of the Transaction, as provided in the Transaction Documents, including contractual and governmental consents and corporate authorizations, shall have been received.

C. Liability. Except as expressly provided herein, neither party shall have any liability or obligation in connection with the Transaction until, and the Transaction shall in all respects be subject to, execution and delivery of all Transaction Documents.

3. Financial Information; Books; Due Diligence. To facilitate preparation of the Transaction Documents and accomplish the other matters covered hereby, each party hereto shall furnish to the other party such financial information, contracts, books, records and other relevant information and shall provide such access to assets or properties constituting part of or pertaining directly to the Transaction, as may be material to and reasonably applicable to the Transaction.

4. Confidentiality. In connection with the Transaction, the parties have disclosed and will disclose to each other certain confidential and proprietary information of each of them. The parties acknowledge that the confidential information, and any work product derived from the confidential information, is proprietary to and a valuable trade secret of the owner thereof. Each party agrees to hold in confidence any and all confidential information disclosed to it, directly or indirectly, and agrees not to disclose such information, without the prior written consent of the other parties, other than (i) to those affiliates, parents, subsidiaries, directors, officers, employees, agents and advisors, including, without limitation, attorneys, accountants, consultants, bankers and financial advisors (collectively, Representatives) who need to know such information to complete the Transaction and (ii) as required by law or governmental or judicial proceeding or arbitration. The parties further agree not to utilize the confidential information of the other parties for any purpose other than in connection with the Transaction, to take all reasonable precautions to safeguard such information and to return such information, including all copies and records thereof, to the other parties upon receipt of a written request therefor. Each party's Representatives shall be bound by the above obligations of such party. The terms "confidential and proprietary information" and "confidential information," as used herein, shall not include any information relating to a party which the party receiving such information can show (i) to have been in its possession before its receipt from another party hereto, (ii) to be now or to later become generally available to the public through no fault of the receiving party, (iii) to have been available to the public at the time of its receipt by the receiving party, (iv) to have been received separately by the receiving party in an unrestricted manner from a person entitled to disclose such information or (v) to have been developed independently by the receiving party without regard to any information received in connection with this Transaction.

5. Broker and Finder's Fees. The parties hereto represent that they have not dealt with any broker or finder in connection with this Transaction. If any brokerage commission or finder's fee is payable due to agreements or arrangements entered by either party in connection with this Memorandum of Understanding or the Transaction, it shall be paid solely by the party having entered such agreements or arrangements.

6. Publicity. The parties shall not make any public disclosure regarding this Memorandum of Understanding or the Transaction contemplated hereby without the prior written consent of the other parties.

7. Term Sheet. The Term Sheet outlines the proposed terms and conditions relating to the Transaction. The Term Sheet constitutes an integral part of this Memorandum of Understanding and is incorporated herein by reference.

8. Termination. This Memorandum of Understanding is a nonbinding expression of intent only and is not a definitive agreement. No legally binding obligation shall be created by this Memorandum of Understanding except for Paragraphs 4, 5, 6, 9, 10, 12, 13 and 14 hereof, which paragraphs shall survive the termination of this Memorandum of Understanding. This Memorandum of Understanding shall terminate on the earlier of (i) the mutual execution by the parties hereto of the Transaction Documents or (ii) _____ [2000] (unless extended by agreement of both parties in accordance with Paragraph 1 hereof).

9. Equitable Relief. The parties acknowledge and agree that, in the event any party shall violate or threaten to violate any of the restrictions of Paragraphs 4 or 6 hereof, the aggrieved party will be without an adequate remedy at law and will therefore be entitled to enforce such restrictions by temporary or permanent injunctive or mandatory relief in any court of competent jurisdiction without the necessity of proving damages and without prejudice to any other remedies that it may have at law or in equity.

10. Expenses. The parties shall separately bear their own expenses incurred in connection with this Memorandum of Understanding and all matters relating to the Closing of the Transaction.

11. Authorization. The execution and delivery of this Memorandum of Understanding by the parties hereto has been duly authorized and approved by all necessary action of the relevant parties. The parties acknowledge that additional authorization will be necessary before the execution and delivery of the Transaction Documents.

12. Damages. No party shall make a claim against, or be liable to, any other party or any such other party's affiliates or agents for any damages, including, without limitation, lost profits or injury to business or reputation, resulting from the continuation or abandonment of negotiations and the consequences thereof, except for actual damages (excluding consequential damages) to the extent that such damages arise out of a breach of a party's obligations under Paragraphs 4 or 6 hereof.

13. Governing Law. This Memorandum of Understanding shall be construed in accordance with, and governed by, the laws of the State of [New York] applicable to contracts made and to be performed within such state excluding choice-of-law principles thereof.

14. Entire Agreement. This Memorandum of Understanding sets forth the entire understanding of the parties regarding the subject matter hereof and can be modified only by a writing executed by the party sought to be charged.

Please indicate your acceptance of the proposal set forth herein by signing this Memorandum of Understanding where indicated below and returning it to the undersigned.

Sincerely yours,
ABC, INC.

By: _____

    Name:
    Title:

The terms of the foregoing Memorandum of Understanding
are hereby agreed to and accepted by the
undersigned as of this ___ day of [insert date]

COMPANY D

By: _____
Name:
Title:

COMPANY E

By: _____

Name:

Title:

i. Attachments to E-Commerce Joint Venture Memorandum of Understanding

Exhibit A—Business Plan; Exhibit B—Summary of Terms and Conditions; Appendices A–D.

A. Exhibit A—Business Plan

(The Business Plan will be situation-specific.)

B. Exhibit B—Summary of Terms and Conditions

ABC, INC. (ABC), COMPANY D and COMPANY E (collectively the Members) have entered negotiations regarding a proposed joint venture (the Joint Venture) relating to the funding, development, production, marketing and distribution of a World Wide Web portal serving the widget industry (the Web Site), which will include [news, editorial content (e.g., feature articles), procurement sourcing information and e-commerce applications regarding certain segments of the widget industry] (the Transaction). In furtherance of such discussions, and not intending to create any legal or binding obligation or commitment on the part of ABC, COMPANY D and COMPANY E, set forth below are certain terms and conditions that serve as a basis upon which the parties could enter definitive agreements on the closing date (the Closing Date) in connection with the formation and operation of the Joint Venture.

I. DEFINITIVE AGREEMENTS

To form the Joint Venture and consummate the other transactions contemplated hereby, the parties would, among other things, enter—or their appropriate affiliates would enter—the following definitive agreements: (i) a certificate of formation, an operating agreement and other usual and customary documents (collectively, the Organizational Documents) required to establish a limited liability company (NewCo), setting forth the terms and conditions applicable to the formation, governance, ownership, funding and other organizational affairs of NewCo, (ii) certain licensing and assignment agreements required to contribute or license assets to NewCo, including, without limitation, rights regarding the [identify assets and IP to be contributed: electronic content, software, databases, trademarks, etc.], all as more particularly described in Section V, (iii) service agreements between NewCo and each of the Members to provide support for contributed assets and ongoing operations of NewCo, (iv) [print and electronic media advertising commitments by NewCo to (enter Member name, if applicable)] and (v) such other agreements and documents as may be reasonably required to effectuate the Transaction (the agreements described in clauses (ii), (iii) and (iv), together with the Organizational Documents, are collectively referred to as the Transaction Documents).

II. FORMATION OF JOINT VENTURE COMPANY

1. Joint Venture Company. The Members would jointly form NewCo as a limited liability company under the laws of the State of [Delaware], with the understanding that the Members may convert NewCo to a Delaware corporation at any time, but in any event before a Public Offering (as hereinafter defined in Section VI.6 below).

2. Purpose of Venture. The purpose of NewCo would be to develop, produce, market and distribute the Web Site [in accordance with the Business Plan], enabling users to [learn about products, identify sources of supply, and buy products and services relevant to their businesses] [, and otherwise to effectuate the objectives described in the Business Plan].

3. Membership Interests. ABC would initially hold 80% of the membership interests (Units) in NewCo. COMPANY D and COMPANY E would each initially hold 10% of the Units of NewCo. It is the intent of ABC to subsequently divest up to 25% of its Units (20% of the total Units) to an original equipment manufacturer serving the widget industry, and to subsequently divest up to 25% of its Units (20% of the total Units) to an alliance of customers served by NewCo in the widget industry.

III. MANAGEMENT

1. Board of Managers. NewCo would have an initial Board of Managers which would consist of [12] persons, [8] of whom would be appointed by ABC, [1] of whom would be appointed by COMPANY D and [1] of whom would be appointed by COMPANY E. The Chief Executive Officer/President (the Chief Executive Officer) and next most senior officer of NewCo would be appointed as the remaining 2 members of the Board of Managers. [In addition, 2 nonvoting advisory persons who are knowledgeable in the field would be appointed to the Board of Managers by unanimous consent of the Members.] Except as otherwise specifically provided herein, the vote of a majority of the voting members of the Board of Managers shall control. Except as otherwise specifically provided herein, the Board of Managers would be vested with the authority customarily or by statute reserved for the Board of Directors of a public company. The Board of Managers would meet periodically to review NewCo's operations and performance.

The Chairperson of the Board of Managers shall initially be a person designated by ABC and, [thereafter, the position of Chairperson shall rotate annually between a person designated by ABC, a person designated by COMPANY D and a person designated by COMPANY E]. The Chairperson shall hold office for a term of 1 year.

2. Officers. The Members shall jointly appoint the Chief Executive Officer and Chief Financial Officer. The Board of Managers shall appoint a

Secretary, a Treasurer and such other officers of NewCo as the Board of Managers shall determine (collectively, the Officers).

3. Responsibilities of Officers. Subject to the control of the Board of Managers, the Officers would have complete control and responsibility for, and would manage all aspects of, the day-to-day operations of NewCo, including, without limitation, administration, finance, operations, information systems, sales, customer service, account management and creative control, and control over the development, production and distribution of the Web Site, in material accordance with the Operating Plan and Budget (as hereinafter defined).

The Officers would cause NewCo to establish and maintain full, true and accurate books, accounts and records of NewCo, which would be available for review by the Board of Managers and any Member.

Within limits to be established by the Board of Managers, NewCo's officers would have the authority to engage third parties, including, without limitation, editorial staff, to perform services for NewCo.

Within limits to be established by the Board of Managers, NewCo's officers would be responsible for appointing the persons who will fill key management positions for NewCo, hiring and dismissing employees for NewCo, and determining the compensation of such employees.

4. Actions Requiring Supermajority Approval. In addition to any Member approvals required by law, the following actions (Material Actions) can be put into effect with, and only with, the approval of Member(s) holding at least [two-thirds (2/3rds)] of the outstanding Units:

(i)   approving any Operating Plan and Budget,

(ii)   making material changes to any Operating Plan and Budget,

(iii)   engaging in any material transactions or activities not in the ordinary course of NewCo's business,

(iv)   selling all or substantially all of the assets of NewCo,

(v)   merging or consolidating NewCo,

(vi)   amending the Organizational Documents,

(vii)   dissolving NewCo (except that either party may elect to dissolve NewCo [if there is not a Public Offering of NewCo's shares within 24 months of the Closing Date, or] if there is a rejection of a Material Action within 24 months following the Closing Date),

(viii) the incurrence of any liens, security interests or encumbrances on, or the pledging of, any of the assets of NewCo, or granting any guarantees, indemnities or letters of comfort, other than noncapital leases entered in the ordinary course of business and other than in accordance with the current Operating Plan and Budget,

(ix)   the incurrence of debt (including guarantees, leases and assumption of liabilities) other than trade payables in the ordinary course of business of NewCo and other than in accordance with the then current Operating Plan and Budget,

(x)   the establishment of any plan for the granting of equity options to employees of NewCo (Equity Options), and the granting of Equity Options under any such plan,

(xi)   the sale or issuance of additional equity securities (including options, warrants or other convertible interests) by or contribution of additional capital to, NewCo, other than in connection with the exercise of an Equity Option or the exercise of a funding commitment,

(xii)   a Public Offering,

(xiii) the acquisition of a business or the assets comprising a business or

(xiv)   entering or amending any agreement between NewCo and a Member or its Affiliates (as defined in Section IV.6).

   5. Dispute Resolution. Each Member shall appoint a senior executive of such Member as its NewCo representative to assist in resolving disputes among the Board of Managers or disputes among the Members regarding Material Actions in situations in which 1 Member does not own at least [two-thirds (2/3rds)] of the outstanding Units. Such representative shall not be a member of the Board of Managers. If a dispute arises regarding any matter that cannot be resolved by the Board of Managers, then the representative of each of the Members would have 30 days from the date the matter was referred to them by the Board of Managers to resolve the issue. If such issue is not resolved at the expiration of such 30-day period, then (a) if the matter is not a Material Action, the matter shall be deemed rejected by the Board of Managers, (b) if the matter is a Material Action and occurs more than 24 months from the Closing Date, (i) the matter shall be deemed rejected by the Members and (ii) either Member may immediately elect to exercise its buy/sell right in accordance with Section VI.3 of this Term Sheet, and (c), if the matter is a Material Action and occurs within 24 months from the Closing Date, (i) the matter shall be deemed rejected by the Members and (ii) any Member may elect to dissolve NewCo.

   6. Books and Records. NewCo would provide each Member with reports of its operations in the form and for the period reported in accordance with NewCo's regular business practices, but in any event no less frequently than quarterly. Each Member shall have access to the books and records of NewCo in accordance with applicable Delaware law and shall also have the right, at such Member's own expense, to audit NewCo's books and records no more frequently than once each calendar year.

IV. BUSINESS AND OPERATIONS

   1. Operating Plans and Budgets. NewCo would conduct its operations materially in accordance with an operating plan, an operating budget and a capital budget (collectively, the Operating Plan and Budget). The initial Operating Plan and Budget agreed to by ABC, COMPANY D and COMPANY E shall be based upon the Business Plan and will be attached to the Transaction Documents.

The initial Operating Plan and Budget (which shall include the Members' funding commitments) shall cover (i) the period beginning on the Closing Date and ending on [December 31, 2000] and (ii) each of the subsequent 2 calendar years.

At least 90 days before the end of each calendar year, the Chief Executive Officer would prepare and submit to the Board of Managers a revised Operating Plan and Budget for the following 3 calendar years. Such proposed Operating Plan and Budget would become effective upon, and only upon, approval by Member(s) holding at least [two-thirds (2/3rds)] of the outstanding Units. If the proposed budget and funding commitments are not so approved, then the then-current Operating Plan and Budget would remain in effect and, if a revised Operating Plan and Budget were not approved before the expiration of the 3-year period covered by such Operating Plan and Budget, the most recent calendar year of the last approved Operating Plan and Budget would be carried over as the operating budget for the next operating year, provided that (i) expenses governed by contract would be adjusted to the then-current contractual amounts and (ii) the capital requirements of NewCo would be adjusted accordingly, provided that neither party will be required to contribute in excess of the aggregate commitment of each party to contribute cash to NewCo set forth on **Appendix A** attached hereto (the Initial Funding Commitment).

Debt financing would be permitted within limits established by, and only by, Member(s) holding at least [two-thirds (2/3rds)] of the outstanding Units. Debt financing in excess of preestablished limits would again require the approval of [two-thirds (2/3rds)] of the members of the Board of Managers.

2. [Intergration to _____ Customer Desktops]. [_____ and _____ will use commercially reasonable efforts to link the NewCo Web Site and e-commerce service to _____'s customers' desktops. Linking shall include, at a minimum, a prominent button on the _____ client software.]

3. NewCo Databases. NewCo would maintain and own certain databases developed in connection with the operation of the Web Site (e.g., user information). ABC, COMPANY D and COMPANY E would each have the right to use such databases in accordance with terms and conditions to be agreed upon by ABC, COMPANY D, COMPANY E and NewCo and subject to applicable laws.

4. [Advertising]. [NewCo shall commit to purchase a minimum dollar amount of print advertising from [_____].

5. Location of Office. NewCo shall establish and maintain a principal office in the city of _____ (the Principal Office) and may establish and maintain offices at such other locations as the Board of Managers may determine.

In the event that NewCo shares office space with ABC, COMPANY D or COMPANY E, NewCo shall pay ABC, COMPANY D or COMPANY E, as the case may be, rental for such space and reimbursement for related expenses consistent with Section VIII.2 hereof.

6. Exclusivity and Noncompetition. For purposes hereof, the term Affiliate shall mean, in connection with a person, any person that is in control of, under common control with or controlled by such person, whether directly or indirectly, through equity ownership or when such control can be exercised by reason of a contractual relationship.

Under a limited noncompete in the license agreements, property licensed to NewCo by any Member or Affiliate may not be licensed to any person set forth on **Appendix D** hereto.

[A Member or its Affiliates may conduct any operation that competes with the Web Site business or any segment thereof (e.g., operating an informational e-commerce engine for a single segment of the widget market), provided that a Member or its Affiliates may not compete with the Web Site business or any segment thereof directly or indirectly through a joint venture or other business relationship (whether in partnership, as a shareholder, through a contractual arrangement or otherwise), with any person listed in **Appendix D** (or such person's Affiliates).]

The foregoing noncompete restrictions would remain in effect until the earlier of (i) a Public Offering and (ii) 24 months following the Closing Date. There will be no additional noncompete restrictions unless mutually acceptable to the Members.

NewCo will never be permitted to compete with ABC's Core Business, COMAPNY D's Core Business or COMPANY E's Core Business. [**Such Core Businesses to be defined.**] In addition, without the consent of the Members, at any time before 12 months following an initial public offering of NewCo's securities, NewCo would not be permitted to solicit or hire any employee (excluding administrative staff and clerical employees) employed by any of the Members at any time within the preceding 24 months.

7. Company Overhead and Services. Each Member will provide certain maintenance, company overhead and administrative services to NewCo consistent with the Business Plan. NewCo shall be charged fees for such services equal to the fair market value of such service, or, if such amount is disputed by the Members, the actual cost of providing such services plus 15%.

V. FUNDING AND CONTRIBUTIONS

1. Funding Commitments. At the closing of the Transaction each Member would enter a subscription agreement with NewCo pursuant to which each Member would subscribe for Units of NewCo in exchange for an immediate transfer or license of property as described on **Appendix A** hereto and its agreement to contribute cash in the amount of its Initial Funding Commitment. The value of the property contributed by the Members shall be agreed to by the Members, and the cash contributions of the Members adjusted accordingly, to result in a 80/20/20 aggregate contribution by the

Members. The timing of all contributions (property and cash) shall be based upon the Business Plan. A Member shall not be required to make any contribution (or loan) to NewCo in excess of its Initial Funding Commitment without its specific consent. Any Additional Contribution (defined below), if authorized as set forth in Section III.4 and this Section V.1, shall be funded as herein provided.

The Members will fund their Initial Funding Commitments in accordance with the then-applicable Operating Plan and Budget. The timing of the funding commitments set forth in the then-applicable Operating Plan and Budget may be accelerated only upon the approval of [two-thirds (2/3rds)] of the members of the Board of Managers. If a Member fails to fund any portion of its Initial Funding Commitment (the Shortfall), the other Members will have the right to either (i) make additional pro rata capital contributions to NewCo to fund the Shortfall in exchange for an additional number of Units equal to (a) 125% of the Shortfall, divided by (b) the number of Units outstanding immediately before such funding divided by the aggregate amount funded by the Members before the then-current funding; (ii) fund pro rata the other Member's Shortfall, with such funding to be treated as a loan to the defaulting Member to be repaid over 36 months with interest rate of prime plus 10% and secured by such Member's NewCo Units; or (iii) contribute its pro rata portion of the Shortfall and purchase its pro rata portion of the defaulting Member's interest in NewCo for 80% of the fair market value of such interest (to be determined by an appraisal process) without regard to any control premium.

If the Initial Funding Commitment or any subsequent funding commitment agreed to by the parties contained in the then-applicable Operating Plan and Budget for any quarterly period is not called by NewCo, the uncalled balance will be carried over to the following quarterly period so that such uncontributed funds will increase the maximum commitment by the Members for such following quarterly period.

If, and only if, Member(s) holding at least [two-thirds (2/3rds)] of the outstanding Units determine that capital in excess of the Initial Funding Commitment is required, the Board of Managers shall notify the Members of the amount of additional capital required (the Additional Contribution), and each Member shall then have the right to contribute its proportionate share of the Additional Contribution and maintain its proportionate share of equity ownership.

If a Member elects not to contribute its share of the Additional Contribution, the other Members shall have the right to contribute and/or loan their pro rata portion of the underfunded amount. Any loan made pursuant to this provision will bear interest at the prime rate plus 4%. Any contribution made in connection with the deficiency shall be in exchange for additional Units issued to the contributing Members pursuant to the formula set forth in the first paragraph in this Section V.1, but substituting 100% for 125%.

If a Member makes a contribution to fund a Shortfall or the another Member's portion of an Additional Contribution or as a result of another party's decision not to participate in additional contributions, then [insert mechanism for reapportioning board seats].

2. [_____ **Content**]. [____ would grant to NewCo a worldwide, non-transferable, nonexclusive license (subject to the limited noncompete restrictions set forth in Section IV.6 above), to exploit through the Web Site, as implemented on the Internet, Intranets, Extranets, Wide Area Networks, Local Area Networks, and virtual public networks, its Content excerpted from the _____ set forth on **Appendix A** annexed hereto (collectively, the _____ Content), subject to any necessary third-party consents or restrictions on the use of such assets and _____ editorial control and integrity. _____ shall reserve the right to sell, transfer, modify or cease the operations of any publication without encumbrance by the license. _____ shall reserve the right to modify the nature of any of the Content in any of the publications. The foregoing license would be in effect for so long as ____ maintains an equity interest in NewCo, plus [3] years thereafter; provided, however, that such licenses shall be terminable by ____ if (a) ____ no longer holds any equity position in NewCo and (b) a person listed by ____ on **Appendix D** acquires more than a 30% equity interest in NewCo (unless such person acquires the equity interest from ____).

In exchange for the foregoing license of the _____ Content, NewCo would pay ____ a royalty in an initial amount to be agreed upon by the parties, with such royalty rate to be adjusted every 2 years to the then current market rate.]

3. [_____ **Databases**]. [_____ would (i) grant to NewCo a worldwide, nonexclusive, royalty-free, nontransferable license (subject to the limited noncompete restrictions set forth in Section IV.6 above) to exploit through the Web Site, as implemented on the Internet, Intranets, Extranets, Wide Area Networks, Local Area Networks and virtual public networks, all of its _____ databases (and all related software) now or hereafter owned or licensed set forth on **Appendix A**, including, without limitation, its _____-related database collection (collectively, the _____ Databases), (ii) use its best efforts to develop databases described on the road map described in **Appendix A**, which databases will be subject to the foregoing licenses and included in the term "_____ Databases", and (iii) use its best efforts to cause the licensors of any Content contained in the _____ Databases to modify existing license agreements or enter into new license agreements with _____ and NewCo, to provide, at no cost to NewCo, that NewCo and _____ shall both be deemed licensees of such Content thereunder. The foregoing licenses would be in effect for as long as NewCo remains in existence; provided, however, that such licenses shall be terminable by _____ if (a) _____ no longer holds any equity position in NewCo and (b) a person listed by _____ on **Appendix D** acquires more than a 30% equity interest in NewCo (unless such person acquires the equity interest from _____).

During the term of the license thereof, _____ would be responsible for creating, upgrading, updating, supporting and maintaining the _____ Databases, at no cost to NewCo. To the extent that the _____ Databases include any software, the Members shall negotiate a mechanism to allow NewCo to have access to the technical resources or tools for such software, if specified events occur, to modify and maintain such software as required. _____ shall implement and customize its software for NewCo as requested by NewCo; provided that any such implementation or customization of _____'s software will be paid for by NewCo.]

4. [Web Site Content and Related Assets]. [_____ would grant to NewCo, at no cost to NewCo, a worldwide, nontransferable, exclusive license to exploit through the Web Site, as implemented on the Internet, Intranets, Extranets, Wide Area Networks, Local Area Networks and virtual public networks, the trademarks, trade names, domain names and any other intellectual property owned or controlled by _____ and set forth on **Appendix A** (other than the _____ Content), subject to any necessary third-party consents or restrictions on the use of such assets.

The term of all of the foregoing licenses or other grants of rights would continue for as long as NewCo remains in existence.]

5. [_____ Software]. [_____ would grant to NewCo a worldwide, nonexclusive, royalty-free, nontransferable license to use, distribute and copy its _____ software and all successors thereto as set forth on **Appendix A** (_____) through the Web Site, as implemented on the Internet, Intranets, Extranets, Wide Area Networks, Local Area Networks and virtual public networks. The foregoing license would be in effect for as long as NewCo remains in existence; provided, however, that such license shall terminate if (a) _____ no longer holds any equity position in NewCo and (b) a person listed by _____ on **Appendix D** acquires more than a 30% equity interest in NewCo (unless such person acquires the equity interest from _____).

Pursuant to the foregoing license, _____ would be responsible, at no cost to NewCo, for upgrading, updating, supporting and maintaining _____ and all successors thereto, as reasonably required by NewCo, and for providing any training reasonably required in connection therewith. _____ shall implement and customize _____ for NewCo as requested by NewCo; provided that any such implementation or customization of _____ will be paid for by NewCo.

The Members shall negotiate a mechanism to allow NewCo to have access to the source code for _____ if specified events occur.]

6. Ownership of Intellectual Property. _____ would retain exclusive ownership (as among ABC, COMPANY D, COMPANY E and NewCo) of all the following, including all derivative works thereof, subject to any license rights granted to NewCo: (i) all the intellectual property currently located at the existing _____ web site, including, without limitation, all of the rights licensed by ____ in connection with the _____ web site and the rights to any domain names associated therewith, (ii) all the _____ Content and

(iii) all other Content licensed by _____ to NewCo. would retain exclusive ownership (as among ABC, COMPANY D, COMPANY E and NewCo) of all of the following, including all derivative works thereof, subject to any license rights granted to NewCo: (i) the _____ Databases, (ii) _____ and related tools and (iii) all other Content or software licensed by _____ to NewCo.

NewCo would own all intellectual property rights (as among ABC, COMPANY D, COMPANY E and NewCo) in and to any work product created independently by or for NewCo and, subject to the ownership rights of _____ and _____ set forth above, all derivative works thereof.

7. Valuations of Contributions in Kind. Contributions of property in kind (e.g., licenses, content, employee and other agreements) by each Member would be valued at the fair market value of such property on the date of contribution as determined by the mutual agreement of the Members.

8. _____ Employees. _____ shall make available for employment by NewCo the persons identified on **Appendix B** annexed hereto and such other persons as ABC, COMPANY D and COMPANY E shall mutually agree, each of whom shall be offered employment by NewCo on reasonable terms.

If the location of the Principal Office is more than 50 miles from any such employee's current principal residence, NewCo shall be responsible for any customary costs of relocating such employee.

9. _____ Employees. _____ shall make available for employment by NewCo the persons identified on **Appendix C** annexed hereto and such other persons as ____ and _____ shall mutually agree, each of whom shall be offered employment by NewCo on reasonable terms.

If the location of the Principal Office is more than 50 miles from any such employee's current principal residence, NewCo shall be responsible for any customary costs of relocating such employee.

10. Dividends. Dividend distributions shall be made upon, and only upon, the approval of Member(s) holding at least [two-thirds (2/3rds)] of the outstanding Units.

VI. TRANSFERS; RIGHT OF FIRST OFFER; BUY/SELL

1. Transfers. Except in connection with a Public Offering, merger or consolidation of stock, or sale by a Member of all or substantially all of its assets, each Member would agree not to transfer, pledge, assign or encumber, in whole or in part, its NewCo Units to any person except to an affiliate (to be defined) of such Member for a period of 2 years from the closing of the Transaction (such period, the Initial Period). No permitted transfer would relieve a Member of any of its obligations under the Organizational Documents or any related agreements between the Members.

On the closing of the Transaction, each Member may provide to NewCo and the other Member a list of not more than [5] persons or entities to whom Units in NewCo may not be transferred (any such person, a Prohibited Transferee). Such list of Prohibited Transferees may be updated from time to time as will be provided in the Transaction Documents.

Following the Initial Period, each Member may, subject to compliance with the Right of First Offer, transfer all or a portion of its respective Units in NewCo to any person, other than a Prohibited Transferee.

2. Right of First Offer. At any time following the Initial Period, any Member (the Selling Member) may offer its NewCo Units to the other Members (the Receiving Members), at a price and on the terms specified in the notice (the Offer Notice) to the Receiving Members. The Receiving Members may, within 30 days of receipt of the Offer Notice, notify the Selling Member whether they wish to purchase their pro rata portion of the Selling Member's interest in NewCo at such price and on such terms (such notice, the Exercise Notice), which purchase shall be completed within 90 days of receipt by the Receiving Member of the Offer Notice.

If the Receiving Members do not deliver an Exercise Notice or consummate the purchase within the period specified in the preceding sentence (other than by reason of a failure of the Selling Member to consummate such sale), the Selling Member may offer its NewCo Units to one or more third parties (other than a Prohibited Transferee) at a price and on terms no more favorable than those contained in the Offer Notice. Any such sale to a third party must be completed within 90 days of receipt by the Receiving Members of the Offer Notice. If any proposed sale to a third party is not completed within such 90-day period, the Selling Member shall be required to deliver a further Offer Notice to the Receiving Members.

The foregoing right of first offer shall not apply to any transfer permitted pursuant to Section VI.1 hereof.

3. Buy/Sell. If, within 30 days after the date of a referral of a Material Action, as referred to in Section III.5, which occurs more than 24 months after the Closing Date, the Members' respective upper management cannot agree upon or resolve the difference pertaining to a Material Action, any Member may, but is not obligated to, deliver to the other Members (the Buy/Sell Notice Recipients) a notice (a Buy/Sell Notice) stating the price at which it is willing to sell all its interests in NewCo or purchase all the Buy/Sell Notice Recipients' interests in NewCo, which price shall be payable in cash and shall be the same price per Unit. The Buy/Sell Notice Recipients may, within 30 days of receipt of the Buy/Sell, notify the Member who delivered such notice (the Buy/Sell Notice Giver) whether they wish to purchase their pro rata portion of the Selling Member's interests in NewCo or sell all their interests in NewCo (such notice, the Buy/Sell Exercise Notice) on the same terms, which purchase or sale shall be completed within 90 days of receipt of the Buy/Sell Notice.

If the Buy/Sell Notice Recipients do not deliver a Buy/Sell Exercise Notice within the period specified in the preceding sentence, the Buy/Sell Notice Recipients shall be deemed to have elected to sell all of their interests in NewCo to the Buy/Sell Notice Giver, which sale shall be completed within 90 days of receipt of the Buy/Sell Notice.

4. Continuing Obligations. Notwithstanding any transfer by a Member of some or all of its interests in NewCo, whether to another Member or otherwise, the license agreements to which such transferring Member is a party shall remain in full force and effect in accordance with their respective terms.

5. Equity Options. The Board of Managers may grant Equity Options or similar incentive compensation to employees of NewCo; provided, however, that the total amount of equity which may be subject to such options or other incentives shall not exceed more than [20%] of the total equity of NewCo, with approximately [10%] of such equity intended for senior management.

6. [Public Offering]. [ABC, COMPANY D and COMPANY E intend that NewCo enter a public offering of NewCo's stock (a Public Offering), to monetize their investment in NewCo. The timing of the Public Offering, the amount of stock to be offered, and the price at which such stock would be offered, will be determined by, and only by, the Member(s) holding at least [two-thirds (2/3rds)] of the outstanding Units, and will be dependent upon market conditions.

Unless objected to by the underwriter, each Member will have tag-along rights in connection with any Public Offering by NewCo, such rights to be pro rata between them based upon their then-current interests in NewCo and to be customary for similar public offerings.

Twenty-four months following the Public Offering, each Member shall have the right, regarding any of their stock in NewCo that is not the subject of the Public Offering, to have such stock registered, such rights to be customary for similar offerings.

The then-current Members shall execute agreements in connection with any Public Offering containing representations and warranties, indemnifications and other covenants and conditions as are customary in similar public offerings.]

7. Insolvency Protections. The Members shall agree that a violation by any Member of certain financial covenants to be established (e.g., specified debt/equity or quick asset ratios) would trigger a "call" right, at fair market value, on the part of the other Member.

VII. DISSOLUTION/LIQUIDATION

NewCo would be dissolved upon the occurrence of any of the following events:

(i)   the vote of those Members holding at least [two-thirds (2/3rds)] of the outstanding Units,

(ii)   the vote of the Members upon notice from the Board of Managers following the sale of all or substantially all the assets of NewCo,

(iii)   the conversion of NewCo into another entity,

(iv)   judicial dissolution under [Delaware] law,

(v)   [at the election of any Member if there is not a public offering of NewCo's shares within 24 months of the Closing Date] or

(vi)   at the election of either Member if there is a rejection of a Material Action within 24 months following the Closing Date.

During a reasonable period following the dissolution of NewCo, in accordance with [Delaware] law, the Board of Managers would liquidate and wind up the operations of NewCo. Upon dissolution the licenses granted to NewCo by each Member would expire.

VIII. MISCELLANEOUS

1. International Web Sites. The Members would agree to negotiate in good faith regarding the terms and conditions for establishing international web sites related or substantially similar to the Web Site.

2. Contracts with Affiliates. NewCo would be permitted to engage the services of the Members or affiliates of the Members, provided that the cost of such services to NewCo are comparable to those applicable to third parties in arm's-length transactions.

3. Governing Law. The Transaction Documents shall be governed by the laws of the State of [Delaware].

4. Additional Definitions. "Content" means all materials created in the past or in the future, including but not limited to any images, photographs, illustrations, graphics, audio clips, video clips or text, and each and every element thereof, in whole or in part, and in each case in any and all media whatsoever whether now known or hereafter devised.

5. Promotions. Each Member shall be entitled to broad recognition and promotion (e.g., hypertext links, etc.) in connection with those elements of the Web Site contributed by such Member to NewCo.

6. Other Provisions. The definitive agreements would include representations and warranties (including, without limitation, Y2K warranties), indemnifications, and other covenants and conditions contained customarily in documents memorializing the type of transactions contemplated by the parties.

(1) Appendix A

Contributions
Cash
Content
Databases
Web Site
Trademarks
Software
Patents

(2) Appendix B

__ Employees to Be Contributed [to be provided]

(3) Appendix C

__ Employees to Be Contributed [to be provided]

(4) Appendix D

Competing Persons [to be provided]

§ 3.4 Advertising Transactions

1. Introduction

Internet advertising began in October 1994 when the first banner advertisement appeared on HotWired.com.[271] Despite a recent overall slowdown in ad revenue across all media, total online ad revenue reportedly reached $ 8.2 billion in the United States for the year 2000.[272] Although nearly half of such revenue is still generated by the banner ad, the remainder comes from various other types of advertisements including, among others, online sponsorships, classified advertisements, interstitial or pop-up advertisements, e-mail advertisements and advertisements tied to keyword searches conducted at search engine sites.[273]

Internet advertising typically requires one or more of three principal types of advertising agreements. The first is the *common advertising agreement* executed directly between the advertiser and the host site that will display its advertisements. Such an agreement sets forth specific requirements regarding the advertisements to be delivered, the method or methods for calculating the advertising fee earned and various representations, warranties, disclaimers, indemnities, termination rights and other rights and obligations of the parties. The second is the *advertising network agreement*, also referred to as a *sales representative agreement*, pursuant to which an ad network agrees with each member to negotiate with advertisers to place advertisements at the sites of categories or groups of members of the network. The last is the *ad broker agreement*, wherein a third party broker is retained by a site owner to design a strategic media plan for the site and negotiate for the purchase of advertising space at appropriate web sites. The principal provisions of each type of agreement are discussed below.

---

271. *Why Internet Advertising?*, <http://www.iab.net/iab_banner_standards/bannersource.html> (last visited June 1, 2001).

272. *Interactive Advertising Bureau (IAB) Reports $8.2 Billion Online Ad Revenue In The United States For Year 2000 Fourth Quarter Totals $2.2 Billion Gain Over Q3 2000 Slows To 9 Per Cent* (April 23, 2001), <http://www.iab.net/news/newssource.html> (last visited June 1, 2001).

273. *Id.*

2. Common Advertising Agreement

The first type of agreement is the basic advertising agreement between an advertiser desiring to advertise a particular product or service through advertisements placed at a host web site; ideally the host web site is either a heavily-trafficked web site, such as a portal site or search engine, or a site with desirable demographics. While some provisions will need to be tailored to a particular agreement, there are several standard provisions that should be addressed in all advertising relationships.

i. Type, Style and Dimensions of Advertisement

Although it is common to describe ads in terms of *banners* or *buttons*, variations in styles and sizes of each have proliferated. The style of banner or button desired, and dimensions in *pixels*, must be clearly established. The Internet Advertising Bureau, an advertising industry trade association, has identified eight different styles and sizes of banners and buttons as the most commonly accepted: (i) full banners that are 468 pixels in width and 60 pixels in height; (ii) full banners with vertical navigation bar that are 392 pixels in width and 72 pixels in height; (iii) vertical banners that are 120 pixels in width and 240 pixels in height; (iv) half banners that are 234 pixels in width and 60 pixels in height; (v) square buttons that are 125 pixels by 125 pixels; (vi) buttons that are 120 pixels in width and 90 pixels in height; (vii) buttons that are 120 pixels in width and 60 pixels in height; and (viii) microbuttons that are 88 pixels in width and 31 pixels in height.[274]

Two other types of commonly used advertisements are the *interstitial* or *pop-up* advertisement (which appears while the page requested by the user is loading), and the *text link*. As with banners and buttons, the size and shape of the pop-up ad, and the number of characters in the text link (including spaces and punctuation), must be clearly specified.

On February 26, 2001, the Interactive Advertising Bureau unveiled its recommendation for seven additional standardized online advertising formats. These new formats, termed Interactive Marketing Units ("IMU's"), are distinguished by their larger size and their interactive nature enabling the user to "click-within" the advertisement to access additional information rather than "clicking-through" to a completely separate site.[275] Within a month after their

---

274. *IAB/CASIE Proposal for Voluntary Model Banner Sizes,* <http://www.iab.net/advertise/content/adstandards.html> (last visited June 1, 2001).

275. *New Ad Units Focus on Branding* (Feb. 27, 2001), <http://www.business2.com/marketing/2001/02/27101.htm> (last visited June 1, 2001).

introduction, these new advertising units were already being offered to advertisers at a significant number of major websites and portals including AOL Time Warner, Microsoft Network, Terra Lycos, Yahoo!!, Snowball, Salon.com, CNET, Yahoo!!, Excite@Home and DoubleClick.[276]

The new IMU's consist of two vertical units and five large rectangular units with the following dimensions: (i) IMU Skyscrapers that are 120 pixels in width and 600 pixels in height; (ii) IMU Wide Skyscrapers that are 160 pixels in width and 600 pixels in height; (iii) IMU Rectangles that are 180 pixels in width and 150 pixels in height; (iv) IMU Medium Rectangles that are 300 pixels in width and 250 pixels in height; (v) IMU Large Rectangles that are 336 pixels in width and 280 pixels in height; (vi) IMU Vertical Rectangles that are 240 pixels in width and 400 pixels in height; and (vii) IMU Square Pop-ups that are 250 pixels by 250 pixels.[277]

Sample Form Language:

Minimum Advertisement Delivery Obligation: Company agrees to use commercially reasonable efforts to deliver the following during each month of the Term: (1) 62,500 Click-throughs on Text Links and (2) 175,000 Banner Impressions. Text Link shall mean a textual reference on the Company Web Site to Advertiser Products containing up to twenty characters of underlined text (including spaces and punctuation). Banner shall mean an advertisement for Advertiser Products that appears at the top of a web page on the Company Web Site and is at least 468 x 60 pixels in size.

ii. Type of Display

Advertisements may appear as (i) a static display, where the advertisement is displayed at a single location at the host site without rotation with advertisements from other sources; (ii) a random rotation display, where the advertisement is randomly rotated with advertisements from other sources; (iii) a scrolling display, where the advertisement scrolls down the page as the user scrolls down the page; (iv) a targeted results display, where the advertisement appears on the search results page produced when users perform searches on designated keywords; and (v) a targeted page display, where the advertisement appears on specified pages at the host site.

---

276. *Id.; Internet Advertising Bureau (IAB) Finds Growing Usage Of Larger Ad Units* (April 3, 2001), <http://www.iab.net/news/newssource.html> (last visited June 1, 2001).

277. *Internet Advertising Bureau (IAB) Issues Voluntary Guidelines For New Interactive Marketing Units* (Feb. 26, 2001), <http://www.iab.net/iab_banner_standards/bannersource.html> (last visited June 1, 2001).

iii. Placement of Display

Advertisers generally view the most desirable placement for their advertisements as locations that are *above the fold* on a user's computer screen. An advertisement qualifies as "above the fold" if it loads onto a user's computer screen (that is viewed at 800 by 600 resolution) without the need to scroll in any direction. Placement in this location guarantees viewing of the advertisement regardless of whether the user opts to scroll down the screen to view the entire page or click onto another page. Alternatively, for a relatively lower price, the advertiser will permit placement of the advertisement within the *first two scrolls* on a web page (i.e., within the top 1200 pixels of a user's computer screen). Advertisers who negotiate any such placement requirement should not be obligated to pay for advertisements that appear elsewhere.

iv. Type of Advertisement Fees

Advertising fees can be based upon impressions, page views, click-throughs, user actions, actual product sales or a combination of the foregoing.

An advertisement *impression* is generally understood to mean access by a single Internet user of a data file containing an advertisement. Impressions are generally charged on a cost per thousand ("CPM") basis. Impressions may be delivered either on an untargeted basis or targeted to users meeting identified criteria. Targeted impressions generally cost significantly more than untargeted impressions. Host sites frequently will attempt to negotiate deals that require payment based upon impressions since they can completely control the number of impressions delivered and therefore the fee earned. Advertisers do not prefer the impression as the basis for determining compensation since there is no user response or other objective indication of whether the impression has actually been noticed by the user. A common compromise is for the parties to agree on a hybrid deal containing both impression-based and non-impression-based fee components, with a cap on the total fee that can be generated by impressions.

Page views are similar to impressions in all respects except that the advertiser is obligated to pay only where the full page containing the advertisement is fully loaded onto the user's computer. This method enables the advertiser to avoid paying for impressions loaded onto a user's machine where the user clicks away from the page before the page has fully loaded. In this latter scenario, a user not interested in the page is likely not to notice the advertisement.

Click-throughs or *clicks* represent the number of times that users click through the hyperlink connecting the advertisement to the advertiser's site. Click-throughs indicate an interest by the user in the advertiser's products or services, and are therefore more valuable to advertisers. Advertisers frequently will attempt to negotiate deals that require payment for click-throughs rather than impressions (or page views); host sites, however, strongly resist such deals since they force the host site to share the risk that the advertisement is not creative enough to catch the user's eye and the risk that the products or services simply are not desirable. A common compromise is for the parties to agree on a hybrid deal containing both impression-based and click-through fee components.

User action transactions refer to transactions where the host site receives fixed payments for users who take a specified action such as completing a survey, requesting product information, or opening a customer account. As with click-through fees, user action fees generally are seen as a single component of a hybrid pricing deal.

User purchase transactions refer to transactions where the host site receives a percentage of the gross sales revenue realized by the advertiser (net of taxes, duties, shipping, handling and insurance costs and actual returns) when users click-through an advertisement and purchase products or services at the advertiser's site. Although advertising management software is used to record the *referring site* for purchases, one major risk to the host site is that it receives no compensation if the user delays the purchase until a return visit to the site. User purchase fees are also generally part of hybrid transactions.

Advertising agreements that compute fees based upon any method other than user purchases should include provisions that exclude from the official count of impressions, page views, click-throughs, etc., any units that have been generated artificially through mechanical, computerized or other means that could falsely inflate the number of impressions, page views, or click-throughs at the site. Obviously, the host site should not be permitted to satisfy its delivery obligations, or inflate the fee earned, by including units generated by an employee or machine programmed to repeatedly access the site since it is not generating potential purchasers for the advertiser in the process.

Finally, advertising agreements can include additional fees for setting up and changing the content of the advertisement.

Sample Form Language:

Consideration.

a. CPM Fee. Advertiser shall pay to Company a fee of one dollar and sixty-seven cents ($1.67) per thousand Advertisement Impressions delivered, subject to an aggregate maximum payment of $250,000 for delivery of Impressions during the Term. Advertiser shall pay such amounts within thirty (30) days after receipt of Company's monthly invoice therefor.

b. Commissions. Advertiser shall pay to Company a commission of seven percent (7%) of the Net Sales Price of each Qualifying Purchase of Advertiser Product made during the Term. Advertiser shall pay such commissions within ten (10) days following the end of the month in which payment is received. A purchase is a Qualifying Purchase if an Advertiser Product is sold through the Advertiser Web Site to a user of the Company Web Site who connected to the Advertiser Web Site through a Link, provided that payment in full has been made for such product. Net Sales Price equals the aggregate amount actually paid to Advertiser excluding amounts collected for sales taxes, duties, shipping, handling, and similar charges, amounts due to credit card fraud and bad debt, and credits for returned product.

v. Reports

Reports summarizing the number of impressions, page views, click throughs, and/or click-through rates (i.e., number of click-throughs divided by the number of impressions or page views) actually provided are necessary for two reasons.

First, such reports will verify compliance by the host site with its advertisement delivery obligations (and therefore the fee earned) and enable the parties to calculate the extent of any adjustments necessary in the event of any failure to satisfy such delivery obligations. For this reason, advertisers typically will negotiate rights to audit the records of the host site used to prepare the reports.

Second, reports also will determine the effectiveness of the placement and content of particular ads and enable the advertiser to make adjustments to the ad content, position and allocation among various types of advertisements to optimize the performance of its ad campaign. For this reason the advertiser should negotiate for the right to receive performance reports for each advertisement provided and each search term to which an advertisement is linked, and such reports should be made available as frequently as possible (i.e., on a weekly basis). Where advertisers negotiate the right to make changes in the allocation and/or content of their advertisements, the host site typically will impose change frequency limitations and limitations based upon lead time and space availability requirements. Host sites generally will retain the absolute right to determine advertisement positioning (except for targeted page displays).

In the event that both parties plan to generate their own reports, provisions must be added to the advertising agreement to resolve discrepancies. Frequently, the parties agree that invoices will be generated based upon host site reports but, where discrepancies exceed an agreed upon percentage, an average of units reported by each party will be used to adjust the fee due.

Sample Form Language:

Reports: The Company shall prepare and provide to Advertiser, on a monthly basis, reports containing daily, weekly, monthly, quarterly and cumulative totals of the following information: (a) the number of Impressions and Click-throughs by individual Advertisement; and (b) the number of Impressions and Click-throughs by inventory category (i.e. Banner Ad, Button, etc.). The Company shall deliver such reports to Advertiser within ten (10) days following the end of each month of the Term.

vi. Confidentiality

Host sites generally will require the terms of the advertising agreement to be kept confidential and not be disclosed without the prior written consent of the host. Hosts generally will agree to permit disclosure of the existence of the agreement along with a description of the nature of any category of exclusivity granted to the advertiser. Hosts, however, will need to protect any information that could enable other advertisers to derive advertisement rate information that could be used to their advantage in future negotiations.

vii. Limitation of Remedies and Liability and Disclaimers

Host sites generally will require the advertiser to agree that in the event that the host fails to deliver any guaranteed number of impressions, click-throughs, etc. during the term, its sole remedy shall be limited to the right to require a brief extension of time to enable the shortfall to be delivered.

It is also typical for host sites to cap their liability for errors in displaying the advertisements or for failing to fully perform their obligations under the advertisement agreement at the amount of the advertising fees actually received during the term or during the twelve months preceding the date the cause of action arose, whichever is shorter.

Host sites also will disclaim liability for incidental and consequential damages arising from their breach of the agreement (primarily the failure to deliver any promised numbers of impressions, click-throughs, etc.).

Sample Form Language:

Makegood: In the event that the Company fails to satisfy the Minimum Advertisement Delivery Obligation in a given calendar month, the sole remedy of Advertiser shall be to require Company to use commercially reasonable efforts to implement a makegood delivery of Impressions and/or Click-throughs (using reasonable response rate projections mutually agreed upon by the parties), as the case may be, during the sixty-day period immediately following the end of the month in which such failure occurred.

viii. Representations, Warranties and Indemnities

Host sites generally require advertisers to warrant that their advertisements will be truthful, not violate any applicable laws or regulations and not misappropriate, infringe or otherwise violate any third-party copyright, patent, trademark, trade secret, right of privacy or publicity, or any other industrial or intellectual property right. They generally also require advertisers to warrant that the advertisements will not contain materials that are hateful, obscene, threatening or defamatory. Host sites usually require the advertiser to provide a full indemnification for damages resulting from breach of any of these representations and warranties.

Many advertisers will require host sites to make similar representations and warranties regarding the content posted at the host site. Host sites should be careful to narrow the scope of such representations to exclude postings by third parties at the site.

Host sites generally disclaims all implied warranties under Article 2 of the Uniform Commercial Code.

ix. Rights to Reject Advertisements and Terminate Agreement

Host sites commonly retain the right to reject proposed advertisements in the event that they (i) are not submitted in the required format; (ii) breach any of the representations and warranties described above; (iii) violate any applicable laws, statutes, ordinances, rules, and regulations; or (iv) are deemed by the host to be unsuitable to appear on, or be linked to, the host site. Such rejections frequently trigger termination rights on the part of the host site.

Finally, both parties will require termination rights in the event of material breaches by the other that are not cured within a specified cure period and in the event of various bankruptcy, insolvency or other similar proceedings affecting the other party.

3. Advertising Network or Sales Representative Agreement

Owners of web sites that find it difficult to sell their entire inventory of ad space directly have an additional opportunity to sell ad space by joining ad networks such as Doubleclick or Burst! Ad networks offer advertisers the ability to purchase ad space at reduced rates across groups or categories of similarly situated host sites (organized, for example, by geographic location, industry, demographic audience, etc.) and thereby target their message. In the process, ad networks offer hosts the opportunity to gain access to ad revenues that otherwise would not have been available.

The Advertising Sales Representative Agreements that govern these relationships contain terms similar to those of the direct advertising agreement described above but do not offer the opportunity for much substantive negotiation.

i. Eligibility Requirements

The ad network typically imposes a variety of eligibility requirements on those seeking to participate. For example, the site typically will need to be in English and satisfy minimum user traffic requirements. Most networks will not accept sites established on free services. Content restrictions will exclude sites that are adult-oriented or that contain nudity or profanity or that promote illegal substances or activities. Advertisements will not be permitted to appear in areas of the web site where the site owner is not completely in control of the content, such as bulletin boards, e-mail or chat services. Site owners also are prohibited from using *automatic refresh* or other devices that effectuate a timed rotation of advertisements or otherwise could falsely inflate the number of impressions or page views at the site. Finally, sites desiring to accept advertising will be required to post privacy policies at the site (describing the information collected, the intended use of such information, and whether or not such information will be shared with third parties[278]) since most large advertisers have voluntarily agreed not to advertise at sites that have not adopted such policies.

ii. Network Requirements for Ad Space

Sites owners will need to adopt certain conventions with respect to the advertising space made available to the network. Typically the network will require ad banners and buttons to be of a size endorsed by the Internet Advertising Bureau, and appear above the fold and above all other ads of a similar size that appear on a web page.

iii. Fee, Term and Exclusivity

The fee deductible by the network for arranging the advertisements will vary based upon the length of the term of the sales representation agreement and whether the representative has been designated as the exclusive representative for the web site. Fees generally are quite high, ranging from thirty percent for

---

278. For information on privacy, see *infra* Chapter 7, Information Practices.

a three-year exclusive deal to fifty percent for a month-to-month nonexclusive deal. Even in an exclusive deal, however, host sites should negotiate to retain the right to arrange for additional advertising directly (i.e., not through another ad network) and to accept advertisements with disclosed advertisers with which they enjoy pre-existing relationships. Regardless of the agreed upon fee, early terminations will trigger a rate readjustment based upon the length of the period prior to the effective date of termination.

iv. Right to Reject Advertising

Site owners should retain the right to reject any objectionable advertisements but the network generally will require that such objections be received within twenty-four hours of notification since the networks themselves only require receipt of the proposed advertisement twenty-four hours prior to the effective start date of the ad campaign.

v. Payment

Revenue earned by the host site will be calculated based solely upon the reports of the network's central server from which the ads are served. Fees are generally paid monthly and the network should be required to retain the risk of collection and guaranty payment regardless of whether or when it receives payment from the advertiser.

vi. Limitation of Liability and Disclaimers by the Network

Ad networks generally can be expected to disclaim liability for the content of any advertisements or for viruses transmitted along with the advertisement. They also will disclaim liability for failure of the ad server to operate or to properly deliver ad impressions. Lastly, networks typically can be expected to disclaim liability for consequential damages and to limit total liability to the amounts actually received by the networks under such agreements.

vii. Other Typical Provisions

Ad networks will require standard representations and warranties regarding the nature of the content at the host site (e.g., no proprietary rights violations, defamatory content, etc.), and indemnification for breach of such warranties and will impose strict confidentiality obligations regarding the fees actually paid by advertisers.

4. Ad Broker Agreement

The last major type of advertising agreement is the advertising broker agreement pursuant to which an independent broker is hired by the advertiser to select and purchase advertising space, at the best available price, at web sites that are appropriate for the advertiser's messages and goals.

i. Ad Broker Services

Ad brokers should be required to (1) familiarize themselves with the advertiser's business, products, services and customers, (2) consult with the advertiser on strategic marketing and positioning of the advertiser's message to consumers and (3) develop an appropriate media plan. Following approval of the plan, the broker then will negotiate with host sites the terms of insertion orders that will set forth the type of advertisement, positioning, pricing, etc. Advertisers should negotiate the right to continue to directly place advertisements with disclosed web sites with which they enjoy pre-existing relationships and should take care to retain the right to review and reject the terms of any insertion order that the broker proposes to execute with host sites.

ii. Fees and Costs

Brokers typically will negotiate a fee equal to a percentage (approximately ten to fifteen percent) of the fees payable for the advertisements. Travel, hotel and meal charges incurred in connection with negotiating the insertion orders are additional.

iii. Exclusivity

Brokers frequently require that they be appointed the exclusive agency of record during the term of the broker agreement.

iv. Representations, Warranties and Indemnities

Brokers will require standard representations and warranties regarding the nature of the content of the advertisements to be provided by the advertiser (e.g., no proprietary rights violations, defamatory content, etc.), and indemnification for breach of such warranties.

v. Replacement Advertising Sites

Advertisers may wish to include a provision granting them the right to receive a refund of brokers' fees paid with respect to insertion orders that cannot be completed by a host site. Brokers, however, generally will negotiate to include a provision permitting the broker to retain the broker fee and requiring the advertiser to accept, or at least consider in good faith, replacement insertion orders presented by the broker.

vi. Limitation of Liability and Disclaimers

Brokers will disclaim any warranty as to the level of web site traffic or sales that can be generated from any insertion order executed on the advertiser's behalf. Brokers also will disclaim liability for any delays in delivery or non-delivery of advertisements due to events beyond their control. It is typical for both parties to disclaim liability for consequential damages.

§ 3.5 Electronic Transactions

What is required to do transactions on the Internet? In a commercial environment, parties enter an endless variety of transactions. These include contracts governing the purchase and sale of goods, lease agreements, negotiable instruments, agreements for the creation of security interests, loan agreements and promissory notes, filings with government agencies, assignments of rights or title, license agreements, insurance contracts, proxy agreements and the like. As commerce moves to the Internet, there is an ever-increasing desire to conduct these transactions in that electronic medium. This section addresses the legal issues raised by the process of entering a transaction using electronic means. It focuses primarily upon U.S. law, although the issues are generally the same worldwide.

Like all transactions, electronic transactions involve documents (usually referred to as *records* or *electronic records*)[280] and signatures (usually referred to as *electronic signatures*)[281] that are created, communicated and stored in *electronic form*.[282] They may be created through the manual efforts of an individual (such as by typing an e-mail message), through the automated processing of computers (via electronic agents, for example) or through a combination of human interaction with a computer agent (such as when an individual accesses a web site and enters into a purchase agreement). They are communicated via an electronic medium, such as the Internet or a private value-added network, and they are typically stored on a computer-readable medium, such as a disk, tape, CD-ROM or DVD-ROM. Typically, evidence of electronic transactions never exists on paper, unless there is a need to provide a copy or to introduce evidence to a court or other fact finder.

1. Key Issues for Electronic Transactions

For anyone desiring to conduct business transactions online, the goal, of course, is to ensure that each electronic transaction is legally valid, binding and enforceable. This requires consideration of three fundamental legal issues:

1. *Is the transaction enforceable in electronic form?* That is, under applicable law, can the transaction (such as a contract, security interest or negotiable instrument) be done in electronic form and, if so, has the transaction been properly effected, to ensure that it is legally enforceable?
2. *Do the parties trust the transaction?* Are the parties to the transaction sufficiently comfortable with the authenticity and integrity of the electronic documents that they are willing to ship their products, transfer funds, provide services, change their positions or otherwise act in reliance upon electronic records communicated over the Internet, especially when

---

280. *Record* is typically defined as "information that is inscribed on a tangible medium or that is stored in an electronic or other medium and is retrievable in perceivable form." Electronic Signatures in Global and National Commerce Act (E-SIGN), 15 U.S.C. § 7006(9) (2000); Uniform Electronic Transactions Act (UETA) § 2(13) (1999). *Electronic record* means a "record created, generated, sent, communicated, received, or stored by electronic means." 15 U.S.C. § 7006(4) (2000); UETA § 2(7).

281. *Electronic signature* means "an electronic sound, symbol, or process, attached to or logically associated with a contract or other record and executed or adopted by a person with the intent to sign the record." 15 U.S.C. § 7006(5); UETA § 2(8).

282. *Electronic form* means "relating to technology having electrical, digital, magnetic, wireless, optical, electromagnetic, or similar capabilities." 15 U.S.C. § 7006(2) (2000); UETA § 2(5). *See also* 5 ILL. COMP. STAT. 175/5–105 (1998).

asked to do so in a real-time environment? In many respects, this boils down to the question of whether the details of the transaction are ultimately provable and enforceable in a court of law.[283]

3. *Which rules apply to conducting the transaction in electronic form?* What are the rules that govern the conduct of the parties when doing a transaction in electronic form, including rules regarding the time a message is sent, the time a message is received, the place of sending and receiving the message, incorporation by reference, and record keeping relating to the transaction? Do rules for paper-based transactions apply to the same transactions in electronic form, or do new and/or different rules apply?

Section 3.5 examines these three fundamental questions about transactions in the online environment.

2. Is the Transaction Enforceable in Electronic Form?

For every business, commercial and governmental transaction—whether a contract for the sale or lease of goods, a license of intellectual property, the granting of a security interest in collateral, the filing of a document required by statute or regulation, or any other transaction—a basic question must be addressed: Is the transaction legally valid and enforceable if done in electronic form? The answer focuses upon requirements that arise solely because of the electronic nature of the transaction, and assumes that basic legal elements are otherwise present and satisfied. For example, if the transaction involves entering a contract, we assume that the basic requirements of a contract—such as offer, acceptance and consideration—are present, and focus only upon the additional requirements for enforceability that arise because of the electronic nature of the transaction.

i. What Law Governs Enforceability?

The enforceability of electronic transactions has been the subject of extensive legislative efforts. All fifty states, the U.S. federal government and the governments of at least fifty-seven other countries have enacted, or are currently

---

283. There are, of course, other issues relating to trust, including the creditworthiness of the other party, confidence in the other party's ability to perform, and so forth. These issues remain the same regardless of whether the transaction takes place via paper or electronically, however, and are not addressed here. Here, we focus upon trust as it relates to the authenticity and integrity of the electronic records that form the basis of the transaction.

considering, some form of legislation governing the enforceability and conduct of electronic transactions.[284] In the United States, the enforceability of electronic transactions is primarily governed by the Electronic Signatures in Global and National Commerce Act (E-SIGN),[285] which was enacted by Congress in 2000 and largely preempts inconsistent state law, and the Uniform Electronic Transactions Act (UETA),[286] which was finalized by the National Conference of Commissioners on Uniform State Laws (NCCUSL) in 1999 and has now been adopted by thirty-six states.[287] Also, the European Union adopted a Directive on a Common Framework for Electronic Signatures for the European Union in 1999,[288] and the United Nations Commission on International Trade Law (UNCITRAL) Working Group on Electronic Commerce[289] completed work on its Model Law on Electronic Commerce[290] in 1996, and finalized its Model Law on Electronic Signatures in 2001.[291]

Based upon current legislation being proposed and enacted in the United States and internationally, the question of enforceability requires that the parties address the following questions:

- *Authorization*: Does the law allow this type of transaction to be conducted in electronic form?
- *Consent*: Have the parties consented to conduct this transaction in electronic form?
- *Signature*: Have the signature formalities required for this transaction (when applicable) been satisfied with a legally recognized form of electronic signature?
- *Record accessibility*: Are copies of the transaction records available to all parties?

---

284. *See, e.g.,* the Baker & McKenzie Global E-Commerce Law web site, <http://www.bakernet.com/ecommerce>, which provides a regularly updated summary of all enacted and pending e-commerce legislation.

285. 15 U.S.C. §§ 7001 *et seq.* (2000) (signed by President Clinton on June 30, 2000, and effective October 1, 2000).

286. UETA was approved by the National Conference of Commissioners on Uniform State Laws (NCCUSL) on July 23, 1999. A copy of this act is available at <http://www.law.upenn.edu/bll/ulc/fnact99/1990s/ueta99.htm>. As of July 2001, thirty-six states had enacted the UETA. For an updated list of those states that have enacted the UETA, see www.bakernet.com/ecommerce/uetacomp.htm.

287. See <http://www.bakernet.com/ecommerce/uetacomp.htm> for an up-to-date list of states that have adopted UETA.

288. Directive 199/93/EC of 13 December 1999 on a Community Framework for Electronic Signatures, *available at* <http://www.europa.eu.int/comm/internal_market/en/media/sign/index.htm>.

289. UNCITRAL is the body within the United Nations primarily charged with oversight of international commercial law. It was created in 1966 by General Assembly Resolution 2205 (XXI) to enable the United Nations to play a more active role in reducing or removing legal obstacles to the flow of international trade. A list of its completed projects and their current status may be found at UNCITRAL's homepage, <http://www.un.or.at/uncitral>. *See* Amelia H. Boss, *Electronic Commerce and the Symbiotic Relationship between International and Domestic Law Reform,* 72 Tul. L. Rev. 1932 n.3 (1998).

290. *See* United Nations, UNCITRAL Model Law on Electronic Commerce with Guide to Enactment 1996 (visited July 17, 2001) <http://www.un.or.at/uncitral/english/texts/electcom/ml-ec.htm>.

291. *See* United Nations, UNCITRAL Draft Guide to Enactment of the Model Law on Electronic Signatures (A/CN. 9/WG.IV/WP.88) <http://www.uncitral.org/english/sessions/wg_ec/wp-88e.pdf>.

- *Record keeping:* Will the electronic records of this transaction satisfy applicable legal requirements?

ii. Authorization

As a result of E-SIGN and UETA, most transactions in the United States can now be done in electronic form. E-SIGN essentially authorizes "any transaction in or affecting interstate or foreign commerce" to be conducted in electronic form, using electronic signatures.[292] It effectively sweeps away a myriad of inconsistent state and federal law requirements for paper-and-ink documents and signatures, as well as multiple inconsistent state requirements for enforceable electronic transactions,[293] and permits electronic commerce to proceed on a substantially uniform legal basis nationwide. E-SIGN preempts all inconsistent state legislation, other than state enactments of UETA in the form promulgated by NCCUSL. UETA achieves essentially the same result, authorizing the use of "electronic records and electronic signatures relating to a transaction."[294]

The "authorization" provided by E-SIGN and UETA is stated in the negative. E-SIGN provides that, notwithstanding any other rule of law, "a signature, contract, or other record relating to [a] transaction [in or affecting interstate or foreign commerce] may not be denied legal effect, validity, or enforceability solely because it is in electronic form."[295] Likewise, UETA provides that "a record or signature may not be denied legal effect or enforceability solely because it is in electronic form."[296] UETA also goes somewhat further, affirmatively stating that "if a law requires a record to be in writing, an electronic record satisfies the law," and "if a law requires a signature, an electronic signature satisfies the law."[297] Nonetheless, the effect of these statutes is important (at least for covered transactions) because it prohibits a holding that such transactions are unenforceable solely because they are conducted in electronic form.

---

292. 15 U.S.C. § 7001(a) (2000). *Transaction* is defined in E-SIGN as "an action or set of actions relating to the conduct of business, consumer, or commercial affairs between two or more persons, including any of the following types of conduct: (A) the sale, lease, exchange, licensing, or other disposition of (i) personal property, including goods and intangibles, (ii) services, and (iii) any combination thereof; and (B) the sale, lease, exchange, or other disposition of any interest in real property, or any combination thereof." *Id.* § 7006(3).

293. *See* Thomas J. Smedinghoff & Ruth Hill Bro, *Moving with Change: Electronic Signature Legislation as a Vehicle for Advancing E-Commerce*, 17 J. MARSHALL J. COMPUTER & INFO. L. 723 (Spring 1999). A copy of this article is also available at <http://www.bakernet.com/ecommerce>.

294. UETA § 3(a). UETA section 2(16) defines transaction as "an action or set of actions occurring between two or more persons relating to the conduct of business, commercial, or governmental affairs."

295. 15 U.S.C. § 7001(a)(1) (2000).

296. UETA § 7(a).

297. *Id.* §§ 7(c), 7(d).

Although both of these acts cover electronic records and signatures that are used in business, commercial (including consumer) or governmental transactions, their operative provisions relate to requirements for writings and signatures under other laws. They do not, however, affect *all* other laws that require writings and signatures. Both E-SIGN and UETA contain a variety of exceptions to the scope of transactions they authorize in electronic form.

E-SIGN does not apply to transactions governed by the following laws, or to the electronic use of the following documents:[298]

- all articles of the U.C.C., other than sections 1–107 and 1–206, and Articles 2 and 2A;
- laws governing the creation and execution of wills, codicils or testamentary trusts;
- laws governing family law matters such as adoption or divorce;
- court orders or notices and other official court documents required to be executed in connection with court proceedings;
- notices of cancellation or termination of utility services;
- notices of default, acceleration, repossession, foreclosure or eviction, or of the right to cure, under a mortgage or rental agreement for the primary residence of an individual;
- notices of the cancellation of health insurance or benefits, or life insurance benefits (excluding annuities);
- notices of the recall of a product, or material failure of a product that risks endangering health or safety; and
- any document required to accompany the transportation or handling of hazardous materials, pesticides or other toxic or dangerous materials.

Likewise, UETA does not apply to transactions governed by the following laws:[299]

- all articles of the U.C.C., other than sections 1–107 and 1–206, and Articles 2 and 2A;
- laws governing the creation and execution of wills, codicils or testamentary trusts;
- the Uniform Computer Information Transactions Act (UCITA); and
- other laws specified by the enacting state.

It is also worth noting, however, that neither E-SIGN nor UETA prohibit conducting—in electronic form—any of the transactions excluded from their scope. Rather, the enforceability of those types of transactions is left to other law, and is unaffected by these acts.

---

298. 15 U.S.C. § 7003 (2000).
299. UETA § 3(b).

iii. Consent

A. Requirements for All Transactions

Although both E-SIGN and UETA prohibit finding most transactions unenforceable solely because they are in electronic form, they also make clear that a party to a transaction cannot be *required* to conduct that transaction in electronic form.[300] This preserves the right of a party[301] to refuse to enter any transaction in electronic form. Thus, the parties to a transaction retain the right to establish their own requirements regarding the method of communication they will accept. The law does not limit or prohibit parties from engaging in traditional forms of communication and commerce, or from requiring that their transactions be conducted in such manner.

But UETA goes even further, and provides that the benefits of the statute will not apply unless the parties have "agreed to conduct transactions by electronic means."[302] In other words, UETA is intended as a voluntary statute that preserves the greatest possible party autonomy to refuse electronic transactions. Whether the parties agreed to conduct a transaction by electronic means is determined from the context and surrounding circumstances, including the parties' conduct.[303] This requirement can be satisfied with absolute certainty by obtaining an explicit agreement to do business electronically before relying upon electronic transactions, but such an explicit agreement should not be necessary before a party feels safe in conducting transactions electronically. The requisite agreement, express or implied, may be determined from all available circumstances and evidence.[304] Several examples are referenced in the comments to UETA. Thus, for example, if one party establishes a web site that is capable of accepting electronic communications, and another party goes to that web site and enters a transaction with the first party, it can arguably be inferred that both have impliedly agreed to conduct the transaction in electronic form.

It is unclear how this consent requirement will work in practice. Note that UETA also provides that, notwithstanding the fact that a party has given consent to conduct one transaction by electronic means, it may refuse to conduct other transactions by electronic means; moreover, the provision requiring consent may not be waived by agreement.[305] This, of course, can have significant implications for a long-term business relationship involving multiple transactions. Presumably, either party has the right, at any time, to refuse to continue con-

---

300. 15 U.S.C. § 7001(b)(2) (2000); UETA §§ 5(a), 5(c).
301. Other than governmental agencies. *See* 15 U.S.C. § 7001(b)(2) (2000).
302. UETA § 5(b). E-SIGN also has consent provisions, but they are limited to consent to receive records in electronic form in consumer transactions where a rule of law requires that information relating to the transaction be provided or made available to the consumer in writing. *See* 15 U.S.C. § 7001(b)(2) (2000).
303. UETA § 5(b).
304. *Id.* § 5 cmt. 3.
305. *Id.* § 5(c).

ducting transactions in electronic form, and to require the other party to revert to a paper-based model.

Statutory provisions requiring consent of the parties before electronic transactions will be considered enforceable, as well as statutory provisions making clear that the parties cannot be required to engage in electronic transactions, suggest the advisability of including a provision within the applicable electronic contract whereby each party authorizes and consents to doing the transaction in electronic form.

B. Requirements for Consumer Transactions

In some cases, special rules have been adopted for consumers entering into online transactions. Specifically, E-SIGN contains an extensive consumer disclosure and consent provision that applies whenever a statute, regulation or other rule of law requires that information relating to a transaction be provided or made available to a consumer in writing.[306] In such a case, the use of an electronic record to provide the relevant information to a consumer is acceptable only if the consumer affirmatively consents to the use of an electronic record in lieu of a paper record, and provides such consent electronically, and in a manner that reasonably demonstrates that he or she can access the electronic information in the form that will be used.[307]

Prior to consenting, the consumer must be provided with a clear and conspicuous notice that does the following:

- Informs the consumer of his/her option to have the record provided on paper;
- Informs the consumer of his/her option to withdraw such consent;
- Informs the consumer of the conditions, consequences and fees of withdrawing such consent;
- Informs the consumer of whether the consent applies only to the particular transaction giving rise to the obligation to provide the information or to identified categories of records that may be made available during the course of the parties' relationship;
- Describes the procedures the consumer must use to withdraw consent;
- Describes the procedures the consumer must use to update information needed to contact the consumer electronically;
- Informs the consumer how, after consent, he/she may obtain a paper copy of the electronic record, and the fee therefore; and
- Informs the consumer of the hardware and software requirements for access and retention of the electronic records.[308]

---

306. E-SIGN § 101(c).
307. E-SIGN §§ 101(c)(1)(A), (ii).
308. E-SIGN § 101(c)(1)(B).

In addition, the consumer's consent must be given or confirmed in a manner that reasonably demonstrates that the consumer can access the information in the electronic form that will be used.[309]

iv. Signature

Perhaps the biggest issue regarding the enforceability of electronic transactions has been the satisfaction of applicable legal formalities. Specifically, in many cases, for an agreement to be enforceable, the law requires that a transaction be documented in "writing"[310] and "signed" by the person who is to be held bound. The Statute of Frauds is, of course, the best example of such a law.[311] In addition, thousands of federal, state, and local statutes and regulations require other types of transactions to be documented by a writing and a signature. In Illinois, for example, over 3,000 statutory sections contain such requirements; Georgia has over 5,500 and Ohio has over 8,000 of such statutory sections.[312]

Statutes and regulations that require transactions to be "in writing" and "signed" have generally been perceived to constitute barriers to e-commerce—barriers that must be removed if e-commerce is to flourish. The concern is that an electronic record might not satisfy legal writing requirements, and an electronic signature might not satisfy legal signature requirements. In other words, the concern is that writing and signature requirements are satisfied only by ink on paper. In the United States, that concern has been largely removed by the enactment of E-SIGN and UETA. That does not, however, end the inquiry—rather, it is only the beginning.

---

309. E-SIGN § 101(c).

310. Requirements that agreements be "in writing" serve a variety of purposes, including (1) providing tangible evidence of the existence and nature of the intent of the parties to bind themselves, (2) alerting parties to the consequences of entering a contract, (3) providing a document that is legible to all, including strangers to the transaction, (4) providing a permanent record of the transaction that remains unaltered over time, (5) allowing the reproduction of a document so that each party can have a copy, (6) allowing for the authentication of the data by means of a signature, (7) providing a document that is in a form acceptable to public authorities and courts, (8) finalizing the intent of the author of the writing and providing a record of that intent, (9) allowing easy storage of data in tangible form, (10) facilitating control and subsequent audit for accounting, tax or regulatory purposes and (11) bringing legal rights and obligations into existence in those cases where a "writing" is required for validity purposes. *See* United Nations, UNCITRAL Model Law on Electronic Commerce with Guide to Enactment 1996, at par. 48, *available at* <http://www.un.or.at/uncitral/english/texts/electcom/ml-ec.htm>; ILL. COMM'N ELEC. COMMERCE & CRIME, FINAL REPORT OF THE COMMISSION ON ELECTRONIC COMMERCE AND CRIME (May 26, 1998), *available at* <http://www.bakernet.com/ecommerce>.

311. *See* U.C.C. § 2–201(1) (1998) (for Statute of Frauds and contracts involving sale of goods). *See also id.* § 1–206 (limited enforcement of unsigned, unwritten contracts for sale of securities for $5,000 or more); RESTATEMENT(SECOND) OF CONTRACTS § 110 statutory note, at 284–85 (1982) (for state-by-state listing of state Statutes of Frauds).

312. *See* Report of the National Conference of Commissioners on Uniform State Laws (NCCUSL), Uniform Electronic Transactions Act, Task Force on State Law Exclusions (Sept. 21, 1998) <http://www.webcom.com/legaled/ETAForum/docs/report4.html>.

A. Why Do You Sign Electronic Documents?

To understand the importance of a signature to an electronic transaction, consider why a signature might be necessary. Essentially, there are four reasons why an electronic signature might be appropriate for use in connection with an electronic transaction: expression of intent, legal requirements, identity and integrity.

(1) Expression of Intent

First and foremost, we sign a document to evidence our intent to authenticate it. The nature of the signer's intent varies with the transaction, and in most cases can be determined only by looking at the context in which the signature is made. A signature may, for example, signify an intent to be bound to the terms of a contract, the approval of a subordinate's request for the funding of a project, confirmation that a signer has read and reviewed the contents of a memo, an indication that the signer was the author of a document or merely that the contents of a document have been shown to the signer and that she has had an opportunity to review them.

(2) Legal Requirement

Second, we sign a document because there is some law or regulation that requires the presence of a signature before the document will be considered legally effective. The Statute of Frauds (which requires contracts for the sale of goods in excess of $500 to be "signed") is, of course, the best example of such a law. In addition, thousands of federal, state and local statutes and regulations require certain types of transactions to be documented by a writing and a signature.

(3) Identity

Third, with paper transactions, signatures are sometimes used to identify the person agreeing to be bound by the document, although this is not normally true. (For example, you sign a check to authenticate it, but not necessarily to identify yourself, as your name is typically printed on the check.) In the electronic environment, however, where the parties are remote and often not otherwise known to each other, a signature frequently serves the purpose of identifying the signer.

(4) Integrity

Fourth, a signature can be used to ensure document integrity—that is, to ensure that the document has not been altered since it was signed. It is for this reason, for example, that parties to a multipage contract sometimes initial each page of the contract. On a ten-page paper document, however, a signature on the tenth page does not verify the integrity of the first nine pages. In the electronic environment, by contrast, certain types of signatures (such as digital signatures) can play an important role in verifying the integrity of the entire document.

For electronic transactions, these secondary functions of identity and integrity can be key. When transactions are automated, and conducted over significant distances using easily altered digital technology, the need for a way to ensure the identity of the sender and the integrity of the document becomes pivotal. Thus, electronic signatures are often used even when not otherwise required by law.

Unlike the world of paper-based commerce—where the requirement of a signed writing most frequently serves the function of showing that an already identified person made a particular promise—in the e-commerce world, a requirement of a signed electronic message serves not only this function, but the more fundamental function of identifying the person making the promise contained in the message in the first place. This additional function is often critical in e-commerce because there are few other methods of establishing the source of an electronic message.[313]

B. What Is an Electronic Signature, and How Can You Sign an Electronic Record?

Traditionally, a signature is any symbol that is made with the *intent* to sign a document. Thus, for example, the definition of "signed" in the U.C.C. includes "any symbol" as long as it is "executed or adopted by a party with present intention to authenticate a writing."[314] The primary focus is on the "intention to authenticate" a document, which distinguishes a signature from an autograph.

Both E-SIGN and UETA take a similar approach to the concept of an electronic signature. Generally, to be enforceable under U.S. law, an electronic signature must possess three elements:[315]

1. a sound, symbol or process;
2. attached to, or logically associated with, an electronic record; and
3. made with the intent to sign the electronic record.

Electronic signatures that meet these requirements are considered legally enforceable as substitutes for handwritten signatures, for most transactions in the United States.[316]

---

313. R. J. Robertson, Jr., *Electronic Commerce on the Internet and the Statute of Frauds*, 49 S.C. L. Rev. 813 (1998).
314. U.C.C. § 1–201(39) (1999).
315. 15 U.S.C. § 7006(5) (2000); UETA § 2(8) (definitions of electronic signature).
316. *See* 15 U.S.C. §§ 7001(a)(2) (2000); UETA §§ 2(8), 7(d).

The foregoing definition of an electronic signature is a generic, technology-neutral definition, which recognizes one can "sign" an electronic record by many different methods. In all cases, electronic signatures are represented digitally (that is, as a series of ones and zeroes), but they can take many forms and can be created by many different technologies. Examples of electronic signatures include the following:

- a name typed at the end of an e-mail message by the sender;
- a digitized image of a handwritten signature that is attached to an electronic document (sometimes created via a biometrics-based technology called *signature dynamics*);[317]
- a secret code, password or PIN that identifies the sender to the recipient (such as that used with ATM cards and credit cards);
- a unique biometrics-based identifier, such as a fingerprint, voice print or retinal scan;
- a mouse click (such as on an "I accept" button);[318]
- a sound (for example, the sound created by pressing 9 on the phone to indicate agreement); and
- a digital signature (created through use of public key cryptography).

Note that a *digital signature* is simply a term for one technology-specific type of electronic signature.[319] It involves the use of public key cryptography[320] to "sign" an electronic record.[321]

This, of course, is not an exhaustive list of methods by which one can electronically sign a document. There are other ways, and presumably many more will be developed in the future. All forms of electronic signature, however, must satisfy the three requirements outlined above. And for online transactions, each of these requirements raises issues worthy of note.

---

317. Under the California Digital Signature Regulations, " 'Signature Dynamics' means measuring the way a person writes his or her signature by hand on a flat surface and binding the measurements to a message through the use of cryptographic techniques." CAL. CODE REGS. tit. 2, § 22003(b)(1)(D) (1998).

318. By including the term "process" as part of the definition of an electronic signature, both E-SIGN and UETA make clear that the "process" of clicking a mouse can qualify as a signature if the other applicable requirements are also present. As noted in the Reporter's notes to UETA, "this definition includes as an electronic signature the standard Webpage click-through process. For example, when a person orders goods or services through a vendor's web site, the person will be required to provide information as part of a process which will result in receipt of the goods or services. When the customer ultimately gets to the last step and clicks 'I agree,' the person has adopted the process and has done so with the intent to associate the person with all the record of that process." UETA § 2, cmt. 7.

319. For an overview of this technology and the process by which digital signatures are created, see Information Security Committee, Electronic Commerce Division, ABA Section of Science & Technology Law, Digital Signature Guidelines, August, 1996, *available at* <http://www.abanet.org/scitech/ec/isc/dsgfree.html>; ONLINE LAW chs. 3, 4, 31 (Thomas J. Smedinghoff ed., 1996); WARWICK FORD & MICHAEL BAUM, SECURE ELECTRONIC COMMERCE (1997).

320. Public key cryptography employs an algorithm using two different, but mathematically related, cryptographic keys: one key for creating a digital signature or transforming data into a seemingly unintelligible form, and the other key for verifying a digital signature or returning the message to its original form.

321. In more technical terms, a digital signature is the sequence of bits that is created by running an electronic message through a one-way hash function to create a unique digest (or *fingerprint*) of the message and then using public key encryption to encrypt the resulting message digest with the sender's private key.

First, though the requirement that an electronic signature include any "sound, symbol or process" allows for the use of virtually any type of electronic signature, many forms can be inherently insecure. For example, anyone can type someone else's name, and anyone can click on an "I accept" button. The key is to authenticate the person who applied the symbol or executed the process—that is, to know (and be able to prove) who typed the name or who clicked on the "I accept" button. This is similar to accepting an "X" as a signature on a paper contract—while a mark such as an "X" may be a legally valid signature, it may not be very trustworthy.

Second, the requirement that the signature be "attached to or logically associated with" the record being signed requires that the parties to the electronic transaction implement an electronic record-keeping process that, in the future, can provide evidence that a specific signature was applied to, or used in connection with, a specific document. The easiest way to do this, of course, is to have the signature incorporated as part of the electronic record that is stored. An alternative is to establish a demonstrably reliable and provable process whereby the signature (or evidence of the completion of a process) is stored separately from the electronic record being signed, but in a manner that allows the two to be correlated in the event it is necessary for evidentiary purposes.

Third, the signature must be executed or adopted with the "intent to sign the record." Thus, the signature must relate to a specific document, and evidence the signer's intent regarding that document. The signer's intent, as with any transaction, is determined by the contents of the document and/or surrounding facts and circumstances.

v. Ability to Retain Documents

Another key requirement for the enforceability of electronic transactions is that the documents be communicated in a form that can be retained and accurately reproduced by the receiving party. Specifically, E-SIGN provides that the legal effect, validity or enforceability of an electronic record "may be denied if such electronic record is not in a form that is capable of being retained and accurately reproduced for later reference by all parties or persons who are entitled to retain the contract or other record."[322] Likewise, UETA provides that "if a sender inhibits the ability of a recipient to store or print an electronic record, the electronic record is not enforceable against the recipient."[323]

This requirement does not, of course, limit electronic transactions to those parties that possess the technical capability for downloading or printing documents. Rather, the focus is upon the form of the document as communicated

---

322. 15 U.S.C. § 7001(e) (2000).
323. UETA § 8(c).

by the sender, and essentially requires that the sender do nothing to inhibit the ability of the recipient to download, store or print the applicable record. The fact that the recipient chooses to use a device without such capabilities (such as a handheld device without a print capability) should not affect the enforceability of the transaction. On the other hand, such provisions clearly call into question the form of *click-wrap agreement* typically used on many web sites, in which the agreement is displayed in a separate window, from which it cannot be downloaded or printed.

vi. Record Retention Requirements

An essential element for the enforceability of all electronic transactions is record keeping. In the event of a dispute, it is necessary to produce reliable evidence documenting the terms of the transaction and the agreement of the parties. Similar requirements exist, for example, to satisfy regulatory requirements (such as insurance, securities or banking regulations), as well as the requirements of government agencies, such as the Internal Revenue Service. For electronic transactions, the issue is whether keeping electronic records will satisfy applicable statutes, regulations or evidentiary rules, and, if so, the requirements that must be met for acceptable electronic records.

Both E-SIGN and UETA address this issue directly, and impose similar requirements. Essentially, an electronic record satisfies legal record retention requirements under UETA if the electronic record:

1. accurately reflects the information set forth in the record after it was first generated in its final form as an electronic record or otherwise, and
2. remains accessible for later reference.[324]

E-SIGN imposes a similar rule. That is, record retention requirements are met by retaining an electronic record of the information that:

1. accurately reflects the information set forth in the contract or other record, and
2. remains accessible to all persons who are entitled to access by statute, regulation or rule of law, for the period required by such statute, regulation or rule of law, in a form that is capable of being accurately reproduced for later reference, whether by transmission, printing or otherwise.[325]

---

324. *Id.* § 12(a).
325. 15 U.S.C. § 7001(d) (2000).

Both E-SIGN and UETA make clear that record retention requirements do not extend to information whose sole purpose is to enable the contract or other record to be sent, communicated or received.[326]

3. Do the Parties Trust the Transaction?[327]

Beyond the threshold issue of legal enforceability, the second concern of parties to an electronic transaction is the pivotal question of trust.[328] To say that an electronic transaction is enforceable (assuming it can be proven to the trier of fact) is one thing. To have a sufficient degree of trust in an electronic message that one is willing to ship product, transfer funds or enter a binding contractual commitment in real time is something else. Trust is essential to electronic commerce, and it varies from transaction to transaction, largely depending upon how high the stakes are. For example, the level of trust required for an online merchant to ship $200,000 worth of tires is much higher than that required for an online bookstore to ship a $20 book. That's because there is a lot more riding on those tires. A bank would require even greater assurances before making a real-time transfer of millions of dollars in reliance on an electronic message.

The importance of trust for the success of e-commerce is widely recognized. The Commission of the European Communities had this to say:

> The first objective is to build trust and confidence. For e-commerce to develop, both consumers and businesses must be confident that their transaction will not be intercepted or modified, that the seller and the buyer are who they say they are, and that transaction mechanisms are available, legal, and secure. Building such trust and confidence is the prerequisite to win over businesses and consumers to e-commerce.[329]

Trust, of course, plays a role in all commercial transactions. Regardless of whether the deal is struck in cyberspace or in the more traditional paper-based world, transacting parties must trust the messages that form the basis for the bargain. Trusting a message, from a legal perspective, requires consideration of the authenticity and integrity of the message, as well as an assessment of whether the message is nonrepudiable by the sender in the event of a dispute.

---

326. *Id.* § 7001(d)(2); UETA § 12(b).
327. For a different perspective on the issue of online trust, see *infra* Chapter 6, Regulation.
328. Adapted from *Online Law*, Chapter 3, by Lorijean G. Oei (Thomas J. Smedinghoff ed., 1996).
329. Commission of the European Communities, A European Initiative in Electronic Commerce, COM(97)157 final (Apr. 16, 1997) <http://www.cordis.lu/esprit/src/ecomcom.htm>.

i. Authenticity—Who Sent the Message?

Authenticity concerns the source or origin of a communication.[330] Who sent the message? Is it genuine or a forgery?

A party entering an online transaction in reliance upon an electronic message must be confident of the source of that message. For example, when a bank receives an electronic payment order from a customer directing that money be paid to a third party, the bank must be able to verify the source of the request and ensure that it is not dealing with an impostor.[331]

Likewise, a party must be able to establish the authenticity of its electronic transactions should a dispute arise. The party must retain records of all relevant communications pertaining to the transaction and keep those records in such a way that it can show the records are authentic. For example, if one party to a contract later disputes the nature of its obligations, the other party may need to prove the terms of the contract to a court. A court, however, will first require that the party establish the authenticity of the retained record of that communication before considering it as evidence.[332]

ii. Integrity—Has the Message Been Altered?

Integrity concerns the accuracy and completeness of the communication. Is the document the recipient received the same as the document the sender sent? Is it complete? Has the document been altered either in transmission or storage?

The recipient of an electronic message must be confident of a communication's integrity before the recipient relies and acts upon the message. Integrity is critical to e-commerce when it comes to negotiating and forming contracts online, licensing digital content, and making electronic payments, as well as proving these transactions using electronic records at a later date. For example, consider the case of a building contractor who wants to solicit bids from subcontractors and submit a proposal to the government online. The building contractor must be able to verify that the messages containing the bids upon

---

330. *See* Fed. R. Evid. 901(a).

331. *See* U.C.C. §§ 4A-202, 4A-203 & cmt. (1998). Section 4A-202 solves this problem for a bank and its customer who has agreed to transact its banking electronically and to be subject to Article 4A. If the bank verifies the payment order by using a commercially reasonable security procedure, the customer will be bound even if it did not in fact authorize the payment order. *Id.* § 4A-202(b). If, however, the customer can prove that the person sending the fraudulent payment order did not obtain the information necessary to send such an order from an agent or a source controlled by the customer, the loss is shifted back to the bank. *Id.* § 4A-203(a)(2). If the bank does not follow the security procedure and the order is fraudulent, the bank generally must cover the loss. *Id.* § 4A-202(a).

332. *See, e.g.*, United States v. Eisenberg, 807 F.2d 1446 (8th Cir. 1986) (disputing authenticity of letter); United States v. Grande, 620 F.2d 1026 (4th Cir.) (disputing authenticity of invoice), *cert. denied*, 449 U.S. 830, 919 (1980).

which it will rely in formulating its proposal have not been altered. Likewise, if the contractor ever needs to prove the amount of the subcontractor's bid, a court will first require that the contractor establish the integrity of the retained record of that communication before considering it as evidence.[333]

iii. Nonrepudiation—Can the Message Be Proved in Court?

Nonrepudiation concerns the ability to hold a sender to his communication in the event of a dispute.[334] A party's willingness to rely upon a communication, contract or funds transfer request is typically contingent upon having some level of comfort that the party can prevent the sender from denying that he sent the communication (if, in fact, he did send it), or from claiming that the contents of the communication as received are not the same as what the sender sent (if, in fact, they are what was sent). For example, a stockbroker who accepts buy/sell orders over the Internet would not want her client to be able to place an order for a volatile commodity, such as a pork bellies futures contract, and then be able to confirm the order if the market goes up and repudiate the order if the market goes south.[335]

With paper-based transactions, a party can rely upon numerous indicators of trust to determine whether the signature is authentic and whether the document has been altered. These include using paper (sometimes with watermarks, color backgrounds or other indicia of reliability) to which the message is affixed and not easily altered, letterhead, handwritten ink signatures, sealed envelopes for delivery via a trusted third party (such as the U.S. Postal Service), personal contact between the parties and the like. With electronic communications, however, none of these indicators of trust are present. All that can be communicated are bits (zeroes and ones) that are in all respects identical and can be easily copied and modified.

This has two important consequences. First, in many cases it is difficult to know when one can rely upon the integrity and authenticity of an electronic message. This, of course, makes difficult those decisions that involve entering contracts, shipping products, making payments or otherwise changing one's position in reliance upon an electronic message. Second, this lack of reliability can make proving one's case in court virtually impossible. For example, while

---

333. *See, e.g.,* Victory Med. Hosp. v. Rice, 493 N.E.2d 117 (Ill. App. Ct. 1986).

334. *See* Information Security Committee, *supra* note 319. One definition of nonrepudiation is "[s]trong and substantial evidence of the identity of the signer of a message and of message integrity, sufficient to prevent a party from successfully denying the origin, submission or delivery of the message and the integrity of its contents." *Id.* § 1.20.

335. *See generally* John Browning, *Follow the Money—A New Stock Market Arises on the Internet,* Sci. Am., July 1995, at 31.

a typewritten name appended at the end of an e-mail message may qualify as a signature under applicable law, that name could have been typed by anyone, and if the defendant denies the "signature" in a lawsuit, it may be impossible for the plaintiff to prove the authenticity of that signature. As a result, nonrepudiation is by no means assured in such a case, and parties thus may choose to forego e-commerce in significant transactions where the risk of repudiation is too great.

In many respects, trust is a key element of the measurement of risk. And the need for trust can vary significantly, depending upon the risk involved. Selling books on the Internet, for example, may not require a high level of trust in each transaction, especially when a credit card number is provided and the risk of loss from fraud is relatively low (for example, a $20 book). On the other hand, entering long-term, high-dollar contracts electronically may require a much higher level of trust. At a minimum, the risk of a fraudulent message must be acceptable, given the nature and size of the transaction.

Thus, when the amount involved is relatively small or the risk is otherwise low, trust in an electronic message's authenticity and integrity may not be a critical issue. If e-commerce is to reach its full potential, however, parties must trust electronic communications for a wide range of transactions, particularly when the size of the transaction is substantial or the nature of the transaction is of higher risk. In such cases, a party relying upon an electronic communication must know, at the time of reliance, whether the message is authentic, whether the integrity of its contents is intact, and, equally important, whether the relying party can establish both of those facts in court if a dispute arises (that is, nonrepudiation).

iv. Establishing Trust through Security Procedures

Establishing trust in an electronic transaction typically involves the use of a security procedure. A security procedure is "a procedure employed for the purpose of verifying that an electronic signature, record, or performance is that of a specific person or for detecting changes or errors in the information in an electronic record. The term includes a procedure that requires the use of algorithms or other codes, identifying words or numbers, encryption, or callback or other acknowledgement procedures."[336] Because they are designed to either verify the identity of the sender of an electronic record, or to detect error in—or alteration of—an electronic record, security procedures can also have a legal effect.

A number of security procedures can help establish trust for electronic communications. They include the following:

---

336. UETA § 2(14).

- digital signature
- replies and acknowledgments
- repeat-back acknowledgments
- process or system that produces a demonstrably trustworthy document[337]
- date/time stamping
- trusted third parties
- encryption

A. Digital Signature

A handwritten signature on a paper document purporting to originate from an identified source can authenticate a communication if that signature is shown to be genuine. Of course, an electronic communication cannot bear a traditional handwritten signature, but it may bear a digital signature or other digital equivalent. If a digital signature can be verified using a public key that is reliably associated with the sender, the recipient can obtain a high degree of assurance that the communication must have come from the sender.[338] Only the sender's public key can decrypt a digital signature encrypted by using the sender's private key. Furthermore, assuming the sender's key has not been lost or compromised, the sender cannot deny having sent it. Thus a digital signature can provide a means of identifying the source of a communication and preventing a sender from repudiating that communication. Also, if the recipient can verify the sender's digital signature, the integrity of the communication has been shown.

B. Replies and Acknowledgments

Computer systems are particularly well suited for screening an incoming communication and sending a return acknowledgment to the purported sender. A log showing the following helps to authenticate the source of a communication: (1) what was received, (2) the identified sender and (3) the fact that an acknowledgment was sent to the sender and not rebuked. Sending and retaining records of acknowledgments, as well as any responses repudiating those acknowledgments, can also enhance the authenticity of communications.

A reply to an earlier communication tends to authenticate that reply. For example, if a buyer offers in a letter to purchase 500 gross of #3 widgets from the seller for $1,500, and the seller counteroffers in a letter saying it will sell the #3 widgets for $1,775, the authenticity of the seller's letter is supported. By

---

337. FED. R. EVID. 901(b)(9).
338. *See generally* FORD & BAUM, *supra* note 319.

preserving a record of the course of the correspondence, each of the documents can be authenticated. This technique works equally well for paper-based and electronic communications.

C. Repeat-Back Acknowledgments

The technique of sending an acknowledgment to establish an electronic communication's authenticity can be taken one step further to establish the integrity of a communication. With electronic communications, it is simple to not only send an acknowledgment, but to repeat the entire contents of the communication back to the purported sender. If the repeat-back acknowledgment differs from the original communication, the sender can alert the recipient. The sender should create and retain a record of the communication as received, the repeat-back acknowledgment and any repudiation of the repeat-back acknowledgment (or a notation that none was received).

D. Process or System

Because electronic communications do not always have the same identifying characteristics as paper communications, it is helpful to resort to other techniques for establishing authenticity that are especially suited to electronic communications. These techniques all involve the use of a computer system to perform automated record-keeping functions.[339] For example, a company can help establish that its communication records are genuine by configuring its computers to automatically archive electronic record copies of the communications it creates and receives. Adopting system security controls that limit access to archival copies can further ensure the authenticity of such archival record copies. The use of such system security measures can help a company demonstrate the integrity of its records.

Another technique is to configure the user's computers to create a log of all incoming and outgoing communications and to cross-reference this log information to archived records. Log information showing the source of the record and the time of its creation or receipt provides further proof of its authenticity.

E. Date/Time Stamping

A digital date/time stamp is another way to verify that a communication has not been changed. A date/time stamp is issued for a message digest of the communication. This fixes the content of the message digest as of a certain

---

339. *See* Fed. R. Evid. 901(b)(9).

date. To later verify the integrity of the communication, another message digest is created for the communication. If it matches the date/time stamped message digest, the communication has not been changed.

F. Trusted Third Parties

A party can establish the integrity of a communication by sending and receiving all its electronic communications through a neutral third party that can retain a copy of each communication. Assuming this third party is trustworthy, each party can then rely upon the third party if the integrity of a record of a communication is questioned.

G. Encryption

If a sender wants to send an electronic communication to a recipient and keep it confidential, the sender can encrypt the communication.

The security measures that can be taken to help ensure that electronic communications and records are trustworthy may not yet be readily accepted, but their legal effectiveness is already being recognized. The first formal recognition of the legal effect of security procedures occurred in 1989 with the approval of Article 4A of the U.C.C.[340]

Article 4A addresses the electronic transfer of funds by wire.[341] A person who wishes to transfer funds electronically does so by transmitting an electronic message—called a payment order—to his bank. Because that message cannot bear a traditional ink signature or other paper-based security measure, security procedures must be used instead. The U.C.C. recognized this and the reality that a bank receiving a payment order needs something objective upon which it can rely in determining whether it may safely act upon that order.[342] Article 4A modernized the law by providing that a bank could rely upon security procedures as a substitute for the traditional time-tested requirement of a signature. Under Article 4A, an electronic message instructing a bank to transfer funds to a payee is considered valid, and the bank is authorized to transfer the funds in accordance with the order if (1) the bank's customer actually authorized the order or (2) the authenticity and integrity of the order is "verified" pursuant to a "commercially reasonable" security procedure, regardless of whether the order was actually authorized by that person.[343] The bottom line is that Article 4A adopts security procedures rather than signatures as the basis for verifying transactions and apportioning liability.

---

340. *See* U.C.C. § 4A (1989) (Funds Transfers). Article 4A has been adopted in forty-seven states.
341. *Id.* § 4A, pref. note.
342. *Id.* § 4A-203, off. cmt.
343. *Id.* § 4A.

v. The Law and Trust in E-Commerce

Most electronic signature statutes simply do not address the issue of trust at all. This includes both E-SIGN and UETA. The statutes that do address the issue take two different approaches.

Under the first approach, a trustworthy electronic signature is a precondition to enforceability as a signature. Statutes adopting this approach typically require that an electronic signature be (1) unique to the person using it, (2) capable of verification, (3) under the sole control of the person using it and (4) linked to the data in such a manner that if the data are changed, the signature is invalidated.[344] If all these requirements are met, the electronic signature is deemed a signature for purposes of that state's various statutory and regulatory signature requirements within the scope of the statute—that is, the electronic signature is enforceable. In the United States, statutes adopting this approach are likely preempted by E-SIGN.[345]

A number of other statutes adopt a second approach. They provide that almost any form of electronic signature can be enforceable and meet legal signature requirements, yet recognize that some electronic signatures are more trustworthy than others.[346] To encourage the use of those electronic signatures deemed more trustworthy, and to provide message recipients with an enhanced level of assurance regarding the authenticity and integrity of messages using such signatures, these statutes typically provide a legal benefit in the form of an evidentiary presumption regarding the sender's identity and/or the integrity of the document. Yet, there is an argument that these statutes also are preempted by E-SIGN.

Some of these statutes take a technology-neutral approach to identifying the class of trustworthy electronic signatures that qualify for such a legal benefit.

---

344. *See* Alaska Stat. § 09.25.510 (Michie 1999) (applying generally to all communications); Cal. Gov't Code § 16.5 (West, 1999) (limiting application to communications with public entities); Ga. Code Ann. § 10–12–4 (Michie 1998) (applying generally to all communications); Idaho Code § 67–2357 (Michie 1998) (limiting application to filing and issuing of documents by and with state and local agencies); 15 Ill. Comp. Stat. 405/14.01 (1997) (limiting application to communications between state agency and comptroller); 205 Ill. Comp. Stat. 705/5 (1998) (limiting application to communications between financial institutions and their customers); Iowa Code Ann. § 1555A.27 (West 1999) (limiting application to prescriptions); Kan. Stat. Ann. § 60–2616 (1997) (applying generally to all communications); Ky. Rev. Stat. Ann. § 369.020 (Banks-Baldwin 1999) (applying generally to all kinds of communications); Md. Code. Ann. State Gov't § 8–504 (1998) (limiting application to any communications among governmental entities); Neb. Rev. Stat. § 86–1701 (1998) (applying generally to all communications); N.H. Rev. Stat. Ann. § 294-D:4 (1999) (limiting application to communications between state and any agency or instrumentality of state); N.C. Gen. Stat. § 66–58.1 (1999) (limiting application to filings with public agencies); Okla. Stat. Ann. tit. 15, § 965 (West 1999) (applying generally to all communications); R.I. Gen. Laws § 42–127–4 (1998) (limiting application to transactions between public agencies).

345. 15 U.S.C. § 7002 (2000).

346. Electronic signatures, like traditional signatures of ink on paper, come with varying degrees of security. A handwritten signature, for example, is more trustworthy than an X mark, and a notarized signature is more trustworthy than both. Just as the law provides certain benefits to more trustworthy forms (*see, e.g.,* Fed. R. Evid. 901(a) (confirming that notarized signatures considered self-authenticating)), these electronic signature statutes seek to define the characteristics required for a trustworthy (or secure) signature.

For example, the Illinois Electronic Commerce Security Act creates a class of trustworthy signatures called "secure electronic signatures."[347] An electronic signature that qualifies as a secure electronic signature enjoys a rebuttable presumption that the signature is that of the person to whom it correlates.[348] Similar types of presumptions for a technology-neutral class of secure records and secure signatures appear in legislation that has been enacted in Iowa.[349] Other technology-neutral electronic signature legislation incorporating rebuttable presumptions—although limited to certain types of transactions—has been enacted in Alabama (limited to certain tax-related usage)[350] and Ohio (limited to certain health care usage).[351]

Technology-specific statutes that confer similar legal presumptions have been enacted in Minnesota, Missouri, Utah and Washington, and all such statutes focus solely upon digital signature technology.[352] To ensure that the digital signature possesses a level of trust sufficient to warrant enhanced legal recognition, these statutes impose a regulatory structure on certification authorities who voluntarily elect to be licensed by the state.[353] Based upon the apparent assumptions that all certificates issued by licensed certification authorities are trustworthy, and that a digital signature created by using the private key corresponding to the public key listed in such a certificate is a trustworthy signature, the legislation has bestowed attributes of trust to messages verifiable by such certificates.[354]

For electronic transactions, presumptions of the signer's identity and the message's integrity can help provide necessary assurances to relying parties, thereby enabling them to engage in online commercial activities with confidence that their transactions will be easier to enforce in court, if that should become necessary. Such presumptions can provide the predictability and trust necessary to rely upon a message, and act accordingly, in real time. Such presumptions are based upon the trustworthiness of the security procedure used to create the electronic signature, and the fact that the purported sender is more

---

347. 5 Ill. Comp. Stat. 175/10–110 (1998). This act also defines a class of secure electronic records. *Id.* at 175/10–110. *See generally* Ill. Comm'n Elec. Commerce & Crime, *supra* note 310.

348. 5 Ill. Comp. Stat. 175/10–120 (1998).

349. *See* 1999 Iowa H.B. 624, 78th Leg., 1st Spec. Sess. (Iowa, 1999).

350. Ala. Code § 40–30–5 *et seq.* (1999).

351. Ohio Rev. Code Ann. § 3701.75 (West 1999).

352. *See* Minn. Stat. Ann. § 325K.20 (West 1998); Mo. Ann. Stat. § 28.677 (West 1998); Utah Code Ann. § 46–3–101 (1998); Wash. Rev. Code § 19/34/900 (1998).

353. *See, e.g.,* Minn. Stat. Ann. § 325K.20 (West 1998); Mo. Ann. Stat. § 28.677 (West 1998); Utah Code Ann. § 46–3–101 (1998); Wash. Rev. Code § 19/34/100 (1998). The digital signature legislation enacted in Germany, Italy and Malaysia contains a similar approach.

354. *See, e.g.,* Utah Code Ann. § 406(3) (1998). The Utah Digital Signature Act provides that if a digital signature is verified by the public key listed in a valid certificate issued by a licensed certification authority, then a Utah court "shall presume that" (a) the digital signature is the digital signature of the subscriber listed in that certificate and (b) the digital signature was affixed by that subscriber with the intention of signing the message. *Id.*

likely than the recipient to possess the information necessary to prove or dis-
prove the validity of the signature.

Yet, the use of presumptions in electronic signature legislation has generated
rather extensive controversy. Criticism centers on concerns that consumers and
small businesses that lack an understanding of the sophisticated technologies
used to create the secure electronic signature may unwittingly find themselves
in a situation where their failure to protect the security of their signature devices
(for example, their private keys) exposes them to substantial liability for unauthorized transactions made by persons who unlawfully obtain access to their
signature devices.[355]

Moreover, there is an argument that such presumptions are preempted by
E-SIGN on the ground that they "accord greater legal status or effect to the
implementation or application of a specific technology or technical specification
for performing the functions of creating, storing, generating, receiving, communicating, or authenticating electronic records or electronic signatures."[356]

4. Which Rules Apply to Conducting the Transaction in Electronic Form?

To engage in any electronic transaction, one must know the rules governing the
use of the electronic medium of communication and storage. And these rules
can differ significantly from those that govern transactions documented on
paper. For example, when laws or regulations require that documents be "written," delivered by "first-class mail" or in a certain form (such as on 8½-x-11-
inch paper), how do those requirements translate to the e-commerce world?
Likewise, what are the rules regarding the time and place of sending and receiving electronic documents? How can an electronic document be notarized
or acknowledged? What is the effect of errors introduced into the communication process? What new provisions are required to protect consumers in an
electronic environment? Are click-wrap agreements enforceable? Can they incorporate by reference lengthy documents accessible by a hyperlink? Engaging
in electronic transactions requires an understanding of these rules.

Unfortunately, most electronic transaction statutes say nothing about the
rules governing the conduct of parties using electronic records and signatures.
However, UETA—and, to a lesser extent, E-SIGN—offer guidance regarding
some of the rules that govern electronic transactions.

---

355. *See also* Reporter to the Uniform Electronic Transactions Act Drafting Committee, Memorandum
(Sept. 18, 1998) <http://www.law.upenn.edu/library/ulc/uecicta/eta1098m.html> (discussing reasons for favoring and disfavoring use of presumptions in electronic signature legislation).
356. 15 U.S.C. § 7002(a)(2)(A)(ii) (2000).

i. Timing Rules

When is an electronic record considered sent? When is it considered to have been received? These issues of timing can be important for resolving a variety of issues, such as whether a binding contract has been created (particularly when a contract offer sets a deadline for acceptance), whether a document has been filed with the applicable government agency on time, when a trade was consummated and so forth. In one case, a fax transmission was not effective notice—though it was started before the deadline passed, it was not completed until afterwards.[357] Electronic transmissions may pose similar problems, especially because there can be a delay between sending and receipt.

Under UETA, an electronic record is considered *sent* when it "enters an information processing system outside the control of the sender" (when a message is sent from one computer system to another), or "enters a region of the information processing system designated or used by the recipient which is under the control of the recipient" (when a message is sent from one person to another on the same system, such as America Online).[358] An electronic record is considered sent as of that time, provided it is addressed properly to an information processing system that the recipient has designated or uses for the purpose of receiving electronic records and from which the recipient can retrieve the electronic record, and provided further that it is in a form capable of being processed by that system.[359]

Conversely, under UETA, an electronic record is considered *received* by the intended recipient when it enters an information processing system that the recipient has designated or uses for the purpose of receiving electronic records of the type sent and from which the recipient is able to retrieve the electronic record, and is in a form capable of being processed by that system.[360] Note that an electronic record is considered received even if no individual is aware of its receipt. That is, as with first-class mail, once the message is delivered, it makes no difference whether the addressee actually opens it.

ii. Venue Rules

From *where* is a message considered sent? And *where* is the message considered received? The answers may have a bearing on determining which law applies

---

357. Bomen Inc., Comp. Gen. B-234652, 3 C. Gen. (CCH) ¶ 103,198 (May 17, 1989) (twenty-three-page fax started, but not completed, before deadline).

358. UETA § 15(3).

359. *Id.* §§ 15(a)(1), 15(a)(2).

360. *Id.* § 15(b).

to a transaction. E-SIGN does not address this issue. UETA provides, as a default rule, that an electronic record is deemed sent from the sender's place of business, and received at the recipient's place of business.[361] If the sender or recipient has more than one place of business, the relevant place of business is considered to be the one that has the closest relationship to the underlying transaction. If the sender or the recipient does not have a place of business, then the place of business is considered to be the sender's or recipient's residence.[362]

iii. Requirements for Creation of Electronic Contracts

A contract may be made in any manner sufficient to show agreement (including offer and acceptance), or by conduct that recognizes the existence of a contract.[363] In theory, the same rule should apply to electronic contracts.

A variety of procedures are available for forming electronic contracts. They include the following:

- *E-mail*: Offers and acceptances may be exchanged entirely by e-mail, or can be combined with paper documents, faxes and oral discussions.
- *Web site forms*: In many cases, a web site operator offers goods or services for sale, which the customer orders by completing and transmitting an order form displayed on the screen.
- *Click-through agreements*: A merchant may offer products, data, software or digital content online, subject to a form agreement accepted by clicking on an "I accept" button. The user's conduct of downloading the content may constitute acceptance of the form agreement.
- *Electronic data interchange (EDI)*: EDI involves the direct electronic exchange of information between computers; the data is formatted using standard protocols so that it can be interpreted and implemented directly by the receiving computer. EDI is often used to transmit standard purchase orders, acceptances, invoices and other records, thus reducing paperwork and the potential for human error.
- *Electronic agents*: An electronic agent is software that is used independently to initiate an action or respond to electronic messages or performances without intervention by an individual at the time of the action, response or performance.[364]

Contract offers may be made orally, in writing or by conduct. There is no reason why an electronically transmitted offer should be any less effective than

---

361. *Id.* § 15(d).
362. *Id.*
363. U.C.C. § 2–204 (1999).
364. *See* UETA § 14.

an oral or written one.[365] To be valid, an offer must communicate to the person receiving it that once the offer is accepted, a contract is created.

An offer may be accepted "in any manner and by any medium reasonable in the circumstances."[366] Typical offline acceptances include written and oral communications, as well as acceptance by conduct. Their online counterparts include acceptance by e-mail or other form of electronic message, by electronic agent and by conduct such as clicking on a button or downloading content.

Thus, if an offer is made by e-mail, one should be able to accept it by the same means.[367] But what if the offer was made by some other method, such as letter or fax? An acceptance need not be sent the same way as the offer.[368] UETA, however, provides that an electronic record is considered received only when it enters a computer system "that the recipient has designated or uses for the purpose of receiving electronic records of the type sent."[369] Thus, if the parties have regularly corresponded in the past by e-mail, an e-mail acceptance sent to the offeror's e-mail address is presumably effective. Many people have multiple e-mail addresses that are used for different purposes, however, and some of these e-mail addresses may be rarely used or monitored. Thus, the purpose of the foregoing requirement is to assure that recipients can designate the e-mail address or system to be used in a particular transaction.

iv. Automated Transactions—Rules for Electronic Agents

Can the act of a computer (without human involvement) create a contract? The answer should be yes, depending upon the circumstances.

A computer can generate an offer. For example, an inventory system can calculate when supplies are low, and automatically generate an electronic purchase order to the vendor. Would such an order be a binding offer? Though there are not yet any cases directly on point, the court in one analogous case upheld the validity of a computer-generated insurance renewal.[370] The court, reasoning that the computer operates only in accordance with the information and directions supplied by its programmers, held the insurance company was bound by the computer-generated renewal notice.

---

365. Of course, as already discussed, there can be questions about the reliability of electronic communications, which may make it more difficult to introduce evidence in court.

366. U.C.C. § 2–206(1)(a) (1999). Also see the Uniform Computer Information Transactions Act, section 203(1), which was approved for enactment on July 29, 1999, is available at <http://www.law.upenn.edu/library/ulc/ulc.htm>, and restates the general rule that an offer to make a contract invites acceptance in any manner and by any medium reasonable under the circumstances.

367. It is well established that an acceptance may properly be sent by the same means as the offer, unless the offer says otherwise. *See* RESTATEMENT (SECOND) OF CONTRACTS § 65 (1981).

368. *See, e.g.,* Market Dev. Corp. v. Flame-Glo Ltd., 1990 WL 116319 (E.D. Pa. Aug. 8, 1990) (mailed offer may be accepted by fax).

369. UETA § 15(b)(1).

370. State Farm Mut. Auto. Ins. Co. v. Brockhurst, 453 F.2d 533 (10th Cir. 1972).

A computer can also generate acceptances. The issue, however, is likely to be whether a responsive message is an acceptance or merely an acknowledgment of receipt. In most cases it will depend upon the nature of response. For example, in one case involving a computer order entry system, orders were placed by touch-tone phone, and the system automatically generated a tracking number for each order. When the seller refused to fill the buyer's order, the buyer sued. The court held that no contract had been created, because the tracking number was merely for administrative convenience, and did not constitute a clear acceptance.[371]

This issue will certainly arise in EDI transactions, where a computer can automatically acknowledge receipt of an electronic purchase order. Usually, however, this type of acknowledgment means only that the computer received the message in a form it could read.[372] It does not necessarily mean the order was accepted. Other types of EDI messages, such as purchase order acknowledgments, would be proper acceptances. UETA also provides that receipt of an electronic acknowledgement from a computer establishes that a record was received by the computer, but does not, by itself, establish that the content sent corresponds to the consent received.[373]

A related question concerns the enforceability of contracts formed via electronic agents. An electronic agent is a computer program or other automated means used to initiate an action or respond to electronic records or performances, in whole or in part without review or action by an individual at the time of the action or response.[374]

Both E-SIGN and UETA specifically recognize the validity of contracts formed by electronic agents. E-SIGN provides that a contract or other record relating to a transaction may not be denied legal effect, validity or enforceability solely because its formation, creation or delivery involved the action of one or more electronic agents, as long as the action of any such electronic agent is legally attributable to the person to be bound.[375] Likewise, UETA recognizes the enforceability of contracts formed through the interaction of electronic agents. First, UETA recognizes that a contract may be formed by the interaction of electronic agents of the parties, even if no individual reviewed or was aware of the electronic agent's actions or the resulting terms and agreements.[376] In addition, UETA recognizes that a contract may be formed by the interaction of an electronic agent and an individual.[377]

---

371. Corinthian Pharm. Sys. v. Lederle Labs, 724 F. Supp. 605 (S.D. Ind. 1989) (seller's other correspondence stated that orders were not effective unless accepted by seller).

372. An EDI *functional acknowledgment* confirms the message was functionally complete—that is, all fields in the form were completed with recognizable codes. It does not reflect acceptance of the substantive terms.

373. UETA § 15(f).

374. *See* 15 U.S.C. § 7006(3) (2000); UETA § 2(6).

375. 15 U.S.C. § 7001(h) (2000).

376. UETA § 14(1).

377. *Id.* § 14(2).

v. Errors in Transmission

Another key concern for electronic transactions is the problem of changes or errors that may be introduced into an electronic record, either because of system or transmission problems, or intentional alteration.

E-SIGN does not address this issue, and UETA contains a limited provision. As a general rule, UETA provides that if the parties agree to use a security procedure to detect changes or errors in electronic records, and one party conforms to the procedure but the other does not, then if an error or change occurs that could have been detected by the nonconforming party had that party conformed to the procedure, the conforming party may avoid the effect of the changed or erroneous record.[378] Also, in the case of an automated transaction, an individual may avoid the effect of a record that resulted from an error made by the individual if the electronic agent of the other party did not provide an opportunity for the prevention or correction of the error, and the individual promptly notifies the other person of the error, takes reasonable steps to return or destroy the consideration received as a result of the erroneous record, and has not used or received any benefit or value from the consideration received.[379]

vi. Notarization or Witness Requirements

In many cases, a law requires that a signature or document be notarized, acknowledged, verified or made under oath. Both UETA and E-SIGN recognize that this requirement can be satisfied for electronic transactions, as long as the electronic signature of the person authorized to perform these acts—together with all other information required by applicable law—is attached to, or logically associated with, the signature or record.[380] It is important to note, however, that this provision does not eliminate any other requirements of notarial laws (such as use of a stamp or seal). It simply allows the signing of the document to be accomplished in an electronic medium. Some states, such as Florida, have already passed electronic notary statutes, designed to address how the other requirements of a notary can be accomplished in an electronic medium. For states that have not, the value of this provision may be limited.

---

378. *Id.* § 10(1).
379. *Id.* § 10(2).
380. 15 U.S.C. § 7001(g) (2000); UETA § 11.

vii. Party Autonomy

With the law in a state of flux, one common approach for parties engaged in e-commerce is simply to enter their own contract regarding the rules of their e-commerce transactions. This concept of party autonomy—that is, the right of the parties to agree between themselves about the rules governing their conduct—is a core premise of the U.S. international position regarding electronic commerce. In the Framework for Electronic Commerce (released by the Clinton administration on July 1, 1997), the U.S. position is stated as follows: "[P]arties should be free to order the contractual relationship between themselves as they see fit."[381]

Consistent with this view, UETA expressly provides that subject to certain exceptions, the effect of any UETA provision may be varied by agreement.[382] E-SIGN, however, like most other legislation, is simply silent on the subject of party autonomy. And some legislation, like consumer protection legislation, actually prohibits variation by agreement. Moreover, the common law is not always clear on this point.

Generally, under the common law, courts look more favorably upon parties' agreements regarding evidentiary matters that are entered after litigation has commenced than on prelitigation contracts.[383] Courts nevertheless uphold many prelitigation contract provisions that affect later litigation matters. For example, courts uniformly enforce arbitration clauses in contracts, even though such provisions withdraw a court's power to decide disputes.[384] Likewise, forum selection clauses are enforceable if reasonable,[385] although they cannot override exclusive federal court jurisdiction pursuant to federal statutory law.[386] Courts also enforce integration and merger clauses in contracts, which prohibit the court from considering oral evidence to alter the terms of a written contract.[387]

---

381. *See* <http://www.ecommerce.gov/framewrk.htm>.

382. UETA § 5(d).

383. *See* United States v. Mezzanatto, 513 U.S. 196, 203 n.3 (1995) ("[I]t is true that extrajudicial contracts made prior to litigation trigger closer judicial scrutiny than stipulations made within the context of litigation."). Courts have approved stipulations that waive hearsay objections (*Sac and Fox Indians of Mississippi in Oklahoma*, 220 U.S. 481, 488–89 (1911)), have held that stipulations about the admissibility of documents precludes subsequent objections regarding authenticity (*Tupman Thurlow Co. v. S.S. Cap Castillo*, 490 F.2d 302, 309 (2d Cir. 1974); *United States v. Wing*, 450 F.2d 806, 911 (9th Cir. 1971)) and have held that a stipulation to admissibility precludes a hearsay objection at trial (*United States v. Bonnet*, 877 F.2d 1450, 1458–59 (10th Cir. 1989)). Courts have also approved stipulations to waive the best evidence rule (*Finch, Van Slyk & McConville v. Le Sueur County Co-op Co.*, 150 N.W. 226 (Minn. 1914); *Skibsaktieselskapet Bestum III v. Duke*, 230 P. 650 (Wash. 1924)) and to waive the qualifications of an expert witness (*Brinck v. Bradbury*, 176 P. 690 (Cal. 1919)).

384. *See* Note, *Contracts to Alter the Rules of Evidence*, 46 Harv. L. Rev. 138, 139 (1933).

385. *See, e.g.*, M/S Bremen v. Zapata Off-Shore Co., 407 U.S. 1 (1972).

386. *See* United States for Use of B&D Mech. Contractors, Inc. v. St. Paul Ins. Co., 70 F.2d 1115 (10th Cir. 1995) (parties cannot place claim under Miller Act in state court, when act provides for exclusive federal court jurisdiction), *cert. denied*, 517 U.S. 1167 (1996).

387. Franklin v. White, 493 N.E.2d 161 (Ind. 1986). *See also* 7 Williston, Williston on Contracts § 15.13, 272–73 (4th ed. 1997).

Thus, it appears that parties may enter a contract regarding evidentiary matters before litigation, as long as those matters do not infringe upon the fact-finding and discretionary powers of the trial court. The U.S. Supreme Court stated that "[a]bsent some 'overriding procedural consideration that prevents enforcement of the contract,' courts have held that agreements to waive evidentiary rules are generally enforceable even over a party's subsequent objections."[388] The Court also stated, however, that "there may be some evidentiary provisions that are so fundamental to the reliability of the fact-finding process that they may never be waived without irreparably discrediting the . . . courts."[389]

Courts have upheld the waiver of the physician-patient privilege in an application for insurance,[390] as well as provisions in insurance policies that preclude liability for death or injury caused by a firearm unless the accidental cause is first established by the testimony of an eyewitness other than the insured or claimant.[391] Some courts have upheld provisions in insurance policies that alter the presumption of death after a seven-year absence, although many other courts refuse to enforce such agreements.[392] In one case, the parties agreed that in settlement of litigation they would abide by the results of a polygraph test, and if the witness was not truthful, there would be no claim to the monies allegedly owed; when a claim was filed but the witness refused to take a polygraph test, the court enforced the parties' agreement and dismissed the action.[393]

On the other hand, other provisions in prelitigation contracts have been held unenforceable. In one case, the court refused to enforce an agreement that only certain types of appraisals were admissible, on the ground that such a provision "purported to totally preempt the court from its consideration of legally competent evidence."[394] In another case, the court held that a licensee could dispute a contractual recital that trademark infringement was conclusive evidence of irreparable injury.[395] And in another case, the court stated that "[i]t is at best highly doubtful that parties may, by contract, allocate burdens of proof, establish standards of proof, or, in other respects, control judicial fact-finding procedures in actions arising out of their contracts."[396] Finally, the Michigan Supreme Court has held that the parties could not by contract change the required procedures for arbitration under Michigan law.[397]

---

388. *Mezzanatto*, 513 U.S. at 202 (citing 21 C. WRIGHT & K. GRAHAM, FEDERAL PRACTICE AND PROCEDURE § 5039, 207–08 (1977)).
389. *Id.* at 204.
390. *See* Adreveno v. Mutual Reserve Fund Life Ass'n, 34 F. 870 (E.D. Mo. 1888); Lincoln Nat'l Life Ins. Co. of Fort Wayne v. Hammer, 41 F.2d 12 (8th Cir. 1930); Wirthlin v. Mutual Life Ins. Co., 56 F.2d 137 (10th Cir. 1932).
391. *See, e.g.*, Schumacher v. National Travelers Benefit Ass'n, 235 P. 84 (Kan. 1925).
392. *See* WILLISTON, *supra* note 387, § 15.13, 274–75.
393. Omni Inv. Corp. v. Cordon Int'l Corp., 603 F.2d 81 (9th Cir. 1979).
394. Cronk v. State, 420 N.Y.S.2d 113 (N.Y. Ct. Cl. 1979).
395. Oleg Cassini, Inc. v. Couture Coordinates, Inc., 297 F. Supp. 821, 833 (S.D.N.Y. 1969).
396. Transamerica Ins. Co. v. Bloomfield, 637 P.2d 176, 180 (Or. Ct. App. 1981).
397. Bruker v. McKinlay Transp., Inc., 557 N.W.2d 536 (Mich. 1997).

Unfortunately, the case law regarding prelitigation contracts provides little guidance in deciding whether agreements regarding electronic signatures or attribution procedures are enforceable. To the extent those cases establish any general principal at all, it appears to be that courts are fairly amenable to enforcing agreements that affect matters of procedure or evidence, but will not enforce agreements that ignore or change substantive law or restrict the court's authority to apply the substantive law of contracts.

Third-Party Content Liability

Contents

Third-Party Content Liability

Unlike content on traditional media such as television, radio and newspapers, which typically flows from a single, centralized "publisher," information and content on the Internet and interactive computer services originate from millions of different content providers, ranging from private individuals to news organizations to specialized information clearinghouses. Providers of interactive computer services—including online services such as America Online, Inc. and Prodigy, Internet service providers, web page hosts and online portals such as Yahoo!, Inc.—function as conduits through which any individual can both instantaneously receive information from these myriad sources and publish information accessible to millions of others around the world.

This explosive democratization of the capability to publish raises fundamental questions about who bears responsibility for harmful content. Although there seems little doubt that a party who originates unlawful content may be held legally responsible, the more difficult question is whether the other actors involved in electronically disseminating such content—entities such as Internet service providers, online portals, web page hosts and other interactive computer services—should also be liable for such content and, if so, under what circumstances. Of course, courts and legislatures have confronted structurally similar questions such as whether a bookstore can be liable for selling obscene material created by others or whether a telephone company can be legally responsible for content transmitted over its network by a caller. Yet, because each of the analogies seems distinguishable (for example, content available through a public Internet web site is published to the world in a way that a remark during a telephone conversation is not), the answers in the online context are not immediately clear.

Chapter 4 examines the issue of third-party content liability in both the United States and in Europe, and covers tortious, criminal and intellectual property content principles. Section 4.1, authored by Patrick J. Carome and Samir Jain, covers third-party content liability in the United States. Alexander Duisberg and Valerio Salce, in Section 4.2, discuss third-party content liability in Europe.

§ 4.1 Third-Party Content Liability in the United States

In the United States, both courts and Congress have begun providing answers to the questions of whether and when *interactive service providers* and similar entities can be liable for third-party content available on or through their systems. In February 1996, reacting in part to two earlier court decisions, Congress enacted 47 U.S.C. § 230, a statute that, as construed by the courts, grants providers and users of interactive computer services broad-ranging immunity from liability for third-party content. This immunity is not, however, absolute; for example, it does not reach federal criminal violations or infringement of intellectual property rights. In the realm of federal criminal liability, the legal responsibility of interactive service providers for third-party content is governed by statutory and First Amendment principles that, generally speaking, insulate providers from criminal liability unless they knew (or, in some cases, should have known) of the illegal content. Congress has also stepped in on the intellectual property side with a detailed statutory scheme in the Digital Millennium Copyright Act, which governs service providers' responsibilities in connection with third-party content that allegedly infringes someone else's copyright. Section 5.2 explores the principles that govern each of these three areas.

1. Civil Liability for Third-Party Content—47 U.S.C. § 230

Before 1996, interactive service providers in the United States faced significant uncertainty concerning their potential liability for illegal or otherwise harmful third-party content available through their services. At least one court found that a provider could be liable for tortious third-party content, at least if it purported to exercise some editorial control over third-party content available on its service.[1] Because monitoring and screening the vast amounts of third-party content available online was not possible as a practical matter, service providers faced the possibility of potentially significant civil liability for content they did not originate or control, or the alternative of drastically limiting the amount of material available through their systems, which would defeat one of the great benefits of the online medium.

Congress recognized that this was not a tenable situation. As a result, it stepped into the breach by enacting 47 U.S.C. § 230, one of the few provisions of the Communications Decency Act of 1996 (CDA) that survived the U.S.

---

1. Stratton Oakmont, Inc. v. Prodigy Servs. Co., 1995 WL 323710 (N.Y. Sup. Ct. May 24, 1995).

Supreme Court's decision in *Reno v. ACLU*.[2] Section 230 establishes that providers of interactive computer services are generally immune from liability for harms resulting from the dissemination of defamatory or otherwise harmful information that other persons or entities create and make available through such services.

Every court that has construed section 230 has confirmed the broad immunity conferred by the statute. In *Zeran v. America Online, Inc.*, for example, the U.S. Court of Appeals for the Fourth Circuit held that "[s]ection 230 . . . plainly immunizes computer service providers like AOL from liability for information that originates with third parties."[3] Similarly, the U.S. Court of Appeals for the Tenth Circuit found that section 230 "creates a federal immunity to any state law cause of action that would hold computer service providers liable for information originating with a third party."[4] The U.S. District Court for the District of Columbia likewise concluded in the case of *Blumenthal v. Drudge* that, in section 230, Congress "made the legislative judgment to effectively immunize providers of interactive computer services from civil liability in tort with respect to material disseminated by them but created by others."[5]

---

2. Reno v. ACLU, 521 U.S. 844 (1997). In *Reno*, the Supreme Court struck down—on First Amendment grounds—two provisions of CDA, namely most of 47 U.S.C. § 223(a) and all of 47 U.S.C. § 223(d), which had criminalized certain online transmissions of "indecent" or "patently offensive" material. *Id.* The invalidation of these other CDA sections did not affect the operation of section 230. *See* 47 U.S.C. § 608 (1996) ("If any provision of this [act] . . . is held invalid, the remainder of the [act] . . . shall not be affected thereby."); *Reno*, 521 U.S. at 882–83 (applying severability clause to hold that portion of section 223 not implicated by First Amendment ruling remains intact).

3. Zeran v. America Online, Inc., 129 F.3d 327, 328 (4th Cir. 1997), *cert. denied*, 524 U.S. 937 (1998).

4. Ben Ezra, Weinstein & Co. v. America Online, Inc., 206 F.3d 980, 984–85 (10th Cir.), *cert. denied*, 531 U.S. 824 (2000).

5. Blumenthal v. Drudge, 992 F. Supp. 44, 49 (D.D.C. 1998); *see also* Morrison v. America Online, Inc., No. 3:00-CV-0723RM, slip op. at 4 (N.D. Ind. Mar. 14, 2001) ("Even under its most narrow construction, § 230 protects AOL from sharing liability with its subscribers who choose to use their e-mail accounts to defame."); Marczeski v. Law, 122 F. Supp. 2d 315, 327 (D. Conn. 2000) (Section 230 bars defamation claim against host of chat room based on allegedly defamatory statements made by others); Green v. America Online, Inc., Civ. No. 00–3367 (D.N.J. Dec. 20, 2000) (Section 230 bars tort claims against AOL based on allegedly defamatory chat room messages made by AOL subscribers); Does 1–30 v. Franco Prod., No. 99 C 7885, 2000 WL 816779 at *4 (N.D. Ill. June 22, 2000) (Section 230 "creates federal immunity against any state law cause of action that would hold computer service providers liable for information originating from a third party"); Truelove v. Mensa Int'l, Ltd., No. 97–3463 (D. Md. June 15, 1999) (both interactive computer service and users of interactive computer service immune from liability for allegedly defamatory postings by third party); Doe v. America Online, Inc., No. SC94355, 2001 WL 228446 (Fla. 2001) (affirming dismissal of plaintiff's claims on ground that Section 230 barred suit against AOL for injuries stemming from allegedly harmful chat room messages originated by subscriber); Kathleen R. v. City of Livermore, 104 Cal. Rptr. 2d 772, 776–79 (Ct. App. 2001) (Section 230 immunizes library from state law claims based on its provision of Internet access); Stoner v. eBay, 56 U.S.P.Q.2d 1852, 2000 WL 1705637 (Cal. Super. Nov. 1, 2000) (Section 230 immunizes provider of online auction services from liability stemming from the sale of material by third party users of its service); Jane Doe One v. Oliver, 755 A.2d 1000, 1003 (Conn. Super. Ct. 2000) (Section 230 bars tort claims against AOL based upon e-mail messages sent by one of its subscribers) (appeal pending); Kempf v. Time, No. BC-184799 (Cal. Super. Ct. June 11, 1998) (sustaining demurrers to plaintiff's cause of action against AOL and other Internet service providers on the basis of Section 230); Aquino v. Electriciti Inc., 26 Media L. Rep. (BNA) 1032, 1032 (Cal. Super. Ct. Sept. 23, 1997) (sustaining demurrer in action against Internet service provider for negligence, breach of contract, infliction of emotional distress and other claims on ground that section 230 bars such claims).

i. The Law before Enactment of Section 230

Before passage of section 230, interactive and online service providers faced great uncertainty about their potential liability for harm caused by third-party content. Two lower-court cases, *Cubby, Inc. v. CompuServe, Inc.*[6] and *Stratton Oakmont, Inc. v. Prodigy Services Co.*,[7] had addressed the issue, and they adopted different analyses and liability schemes. Because the online medium was so new, the courts struggled to find some appropriate analogy to more conventional media in an attempt to determine how to assess liability for third-party content. Unfortunately, the attempt to apply conventional media constructs to this new media resulted in great confusion and uncertainty in the law.

The plaintiff in *Cubby* sought to hold the interactive service provider CompuServe liable in tort for allegedly false information posted on its service by a third party with which CompuServe had contracted to provide "an electronic library of news publications."[8] The federal district court in New York analogized CompuServe to a distributor of information such as a library or news vendor.[9] Relying upon cases establishing heightened First Amendment protection for such distributors, the court concluded that CompuServe could not be liable unless it "knew or should have known" of the tortious information at the time it appeared on the CompuServe service.[10] On the facts of the case, the court found no evidence that CompuServe had the requisite knowledge and granted summary judgment.[11]

By contrast, in *Stratton Oakmont*, a New York state trial court concluded that the interactive service provider Prodigy could be liable for an allegedly defamatory message that an unidentified Prodigy user posted on a Prodigy bulletin board. While accepting the *Cubby* court's ruling that "distributors" may not be held liable unless they had notice of the allegedly tortious content, the court found that Prodigy was not equivalent to a distributor, but instead operated as a publisher such as a newspaper.[12] In particular, the court decided that Prodigy was not entitled to the special protection enjoyed by distributors because Prodigy held itself out to the public as a family-oriented service and attempted to exercise editorial control over third-party content by, for example, employing software to screen for objectionable content.[13] Accordingly, the court

---

6. Cubby, Inc. v. CompuServe, Inc. 776 F. Supp. 135 (S.D.N.Y. 1991).

7. Stratton Oakmont, Inc. v. Prodigy Servs. Co., 1995 WL 323710 (N.Y. Sup. Ct. May 24, 1995).

8. In particular, CompuServe contracted with a third party (CCI) to provide content, and CCI had a contractual relationship with another party (DFA) that actually provided the allegedly tortious content available over CompuServe's service. *Cubby*, 776 F. Supp. at 143. The court rejected the plaintiff's argument that CCI and/or DFA were CompuServe's agents. *Id.*

9. *Id.* at 139–40.

10. *Id.*

11. *Id.* at 141–42.

12. *See Stratton Oakmont*, 1995 WL 323710, at *2–*4.

13. *See id.*

held that Prodigy "opened [itself] up to greater liability than CompuServe and other computer networks" that engage in little or no editorial control.[14]

The two cases served only to confuse service providers about the applicable liability rules. *Stratton Oakmont* in particular seemed to create perverse incentives.[15] The court's reasoning appeared to increase the risk of liability to the extent that service providers engaged in *any* kind of editing or screening, even if just to remove clearly objectionable or illegal content. That increased legal risk discouraged service providers from engaging in any self-regulation, just when filtering programs were being developed to screen out or segregate objectionable content. This potential liability for third-party content threatened to smother the development of the medium as a forum for numerous types and vast quantities of content.

Courts themselves may have eventually reached the same conclusion. The Court of Appeals of New York has since effectively overruled *Stratton Oakmont*, holding that under New York common law, Prodigy could not be "compel[led] . . . to guarantee the content of those myriad messages" on its electronic bulletin boards and that "Prodigy was not a publisher" of such messages.[16] In any event, motivated in part by the uncertainty created by the *Stratton Oakmont* decision, Congress enacted section 230 as part of CDA in 1996. With some exceptions, section 230 is now the touchstone for determining a service provider's liability for third-party content. In an extensive preamble enacted as part of the statute, Congress made clear that it intended section 230 both to promote the continued development of the online medium unfettered by government regulation and to eliminate disincentives to self-regulation.

ii. The Language and Purposes of Section 230

Section 230 contains three key provisions. The most significant part of the statute, section 230(c)(1), states as follows:

> No provider or user of an interactive computer service shall be treated as the publisher or speaker of any information provided by another information content provider.[17]

This section generally immunizes service providers from liability for third-party content.

---

14. *Id.* at *5.

15. Indeed, the *Stratton Oakmont* case itself ended on a rather uncertain note. After the trial court decision, the two parties reached a settlement and, as a condition of the settlement, agreed to move jointly to have the initial decision vacated. The court, however, refused, leaving the decision intact despite the settlement.

16. Lunney v. Prodigy Servs. Co., 701 N.Y.S.2d 684, 687 (1999), *cert. denied*, 529 U.S. 1098 (2000).

17. 47 U.S.C. § 230(c)(1) (2000).

Another provision of the statute, section 230(c)(2), provides additional explicit protection for "Good Samaritan" actions by service providers, such as those at issue in *Stratton Oakmont*:

> No provider ... of an interactive computer service shall be held liable on account of ... any action voluntarily taken in good faith to restrict access to or availability of material that the provider ... considers to be obscene, lewd, lascivious, filthy, excessively violent, harassing, or otherwise objectionable. . . .[18]

This provision makes clear that a service provider may not be held liable for engaging in any good-faith action or program to exclude unlawful or objectionable content from its service or to limit access to such content.

Finally, section 230(e)(3) makes clear that any state-law causes of action inconsistent with the statute are barred:

> Nothing in this section shall be construed to prevent any State from enforcing any State law that is consistent with this section. No cause of action may be brought and no liability may be imposed under any State or local law that is inconsistent with this section.[19]

Section 230 also contains several exceptions from its reach. Most significantly, the statute does not immunize service providers from liability for content that they create and develop by themselves.[20] Moreover, even for third-party content, the immunity conferred by the statute does not "impair the enforcement" of any federal criminal statute,[21] does not "limit or expand" intellectual property law,[22] and does not "limit the application" of the Electronic Communications Privacy Act (as amended) or any similar state statute.[23]

The preamble and legislative history of the statute both demonstrate that Congress enacted section 230 to foster robust discourse about interactive computer services by ensuring that the intermediaries of such discourse—service providers such as AOL—are not held liable for harm caused by third-party content.

Section 230's preamble announces a congressional finding that "interactive computer services offer a forum for a true diversity of political discourse, unique opportunities for cultural development, and myriad avenues for intellectual

---

18. *Id.* § 230(c)(2).

19. *Id.* § 230(e)(3).

20. *See* Sabbato v. Hardy, No. 2000CA00136, 2000 Ohio App. Lexis 6154 (Ct. App. Dec. 18, 2000) (holding that, although web site operator was immune to the extent it was acting merely as a "distributing party" of third party content, it was not entitled to dismissal on immunity grounds where "it [was] alleged that [the operator] participated in the libelous remarks").

21. Federal criminal liability issues for third-party content are discussed in Section 4.1.2 of this chapter.

22. *See e.g.*, Gucci America, Inc. v. Hall & Assoc., No. 00-549, 2001 WL 253255 (S.D.N.Y. Mar. 14, 2001) (Section 230 immunity does not apply to claim of trademark infringement). Issues concerning service provider liability for third-party material that infringes upon another's copyright are addressed in Section 4.1.3 of this chapter.

23. 47 U.S.C. § 230(e) (2000).

activity," and that these services have "flourished, to the benefit of all Americans, *with a minimum of government regulation.*"[24] The preamble also declares that it is "the policy of the United States . . . to preserve the vibrant and competitive free market that presently exists for the Internet and other interactive computer services, *unfettered by Federal or State regulation.*"[25] As the Fourth Circuit Court of Appeals explained in *Zeran*:

> The imposition of tort liability on service providers for the communications of others represented, for Congress, simply another form of intrusive government regulation of speech. Section 230 was enacted, in part, to maintain the robust nature of Internet communication and, accordingly, to keep government interference in the medium to a minimum.[26]

Congress in particular expressed the desire to ensure that the Internet and interactive computer services remained "for a true diversity of political discourse, unique opportunities for cultural development, and myriad avenues for intellectual activity."[27] As the *Zeran* court noted, Congress sought to promote "freedom of speech in the new and burgeoning Internet medium" by eliminating the "threat [of] tort-based lawsuits" against interactive services for injury caused by "the communications of others."[28] The court explained that:

> [t]he amount of information communicated via interactive computer services is . . . staggering. The specter of tort liability in an area of such prolific speech would have an obvious chilling effect. It would be impossible for service providers to screen each of their millions of postings for possible problems. Faced with potential liability for each message republished by their services, interactive computer service providers might choose to severely restrict the number and type of messages posted. Congress considered the weight of the speech interests implicated and chose to immunize service providers to avoid any such restrictive effect.[29]

Thus, Congress determined that a legal regime under which interactive computer service providers could face tort liability for dissemination of content produced by others inevitably would hurt the development of this emerging communications medium.

At the same time, section 230's preamble reflects that Congress recognized the need to deter and punish truly harmful online speech, and chose to do so by relying upon enforcement of federal criminal laws against the actual wrongdoers who originate such speech, rather than the mere conduits of the infor-

---

24. *Id.* §§ 230(a)(3), 230(a)(4) (emphasis added).
25. *Id.* § 230(b)(2) (emphasis added).
26. *Zeran*, 129 F.3d at 330.
27. 47 U.S.C. § 230(a)(3) (2000).
28. *Zeran*, 129 F.3d at 330; *see also Ben Ezra*, 206 F.3d at 985 n.3.
29. *Zeran*, 129 F.3d at 331.

mation. The preamble declares that it is the "policy of the United States . . . to ensure vigorous enforcement of Federal criminal laws to deter and punish trafficking in obscenity, stalking, and harassment by means of computer."[30] Thus, the preamble appears to indicate that Congress made the policy decision to deter tortious online speech not by punishing the intermediary, but by strengthening the enforcement of legal remedies against the culpable source of the unlawful content.[31]

The legislative history of section 230 further confirms Congress's intent to immunize interactive computer services from liability for dissemination of third parties' tortious online speech. The CDA's conference report states that one of the purposes of section 230 was to overrule *Stratton Oakmont*:

> One of the specific purposes of [section 230] is to overrule *Stratton Oakmont v. Prodigy* and any other similar decisions which have treated such providers and users as publishers or speakers of content that is not their own because they have restricted access to objectionable material. The conferees believe that such decisions create serious obstacles to the important federal policy of empowering parents to determine the content of communications their children receive through interactive computer services.[32]

Ultimately, then, section 230 represents a policy decision by Congress to immunize interactive service providers from liability for harmful third-party content, not only to promote and preserve the development of the new electronic medium, but also to eliminate disincentives to self-regulation of third-party content by service providers.[33] Congress believed that if self-regulatory activities such as attempting to screen objectionable content were permitted to be a basis for finding service providers responsible (and therefore liable) for third-party content, "service providers would likely eschew any attempts at self-regulation."[34] Section 230 was instead designed to give interactive service pro-

---

30. 47 U.S.C. § 230(b)(5) (2000).

31. *See Doe*, 718 So. 2d at 387.

32. H.R. Conf. Rep. No. 104-458, at 194 (1996). Debate on the bill on the House floor also revealed a congressional understanding that interactive service providers should not be responsible for harmful third-party content because the nature of the medium makes it impossible for them to review and edit third-party content in any kind of systematic or comprehensive manner:

> There is no way that any of those entities, like Prodigy, can take the responsibility to edit out information that is going to be coming in to them from all manner of sources onto their bulletin board. We are talking about something that is far larger than our daily newspaper. We are talking about something that is going to be thousands of pages of information every day, and to have that imposition imposed on them is wrong. [Section 230] will cure that problem. . . .

141 Cong. Rec. 22,047 (1995).

33. *See Zeran*, 129 F.3d at 331; *see also Ben Ezra*, 206 F.3d at 986 ("Congress clearly enacted [section] 230 to forbid the imposition of publisher liability on a service provider for the exercise of its editorial and self-regulatory functions.").

34. *Zeran*, 129 F.3d at 333; *see also id.* ("[N]otice-based liability would deter service providers from regulating the dissemination of offensive material over their own services. Any efforts by a service provider to investigate and screen material posted on its service would only lead to notice of potentially defamatory material more frequently and thereby create a stronger basis for liability.").

viders "a reasonable way to . . . help them *self-regulate . . . without penalty of law*."[35]

iii. Requirements for Application of Section 230(c)(1) Immunity

Immunity under section 230(c)(1) requires the existence of three elements:

1. that the defendant be a "provider or user of an interactive computer service,"
2. that holding the provider liable would "treat [the provider] as the publisher or speaker" of the information at issue and
3. that the information be "provided by another information content provider."[36]

The plain meaning of the statutory language and the cases to date establish the basic thrust of these elements, although courts have not yet resolved the precise scope of each.

A. "Provider or User of an Interactive Computer Service"

As an initial matter, section 230 immunity is potentially available to any "provider or user of an interactive computer service." The statute defines "interactive computer service" as encompassing any information service, system or access software provider that provides or enables computer access by multiple users to a computer server, including specifically a service or system that provides access to the Internet and such systems operated or services offered by libraries or educational institutions.[37]

Clearly, section 230 applies to providers and users of services such as AOL and Prodigy, which provide or enable computer access by multiple users to a computer server. More generally, Internet service providers such as Earthlink and PSINet (and their users) fall within the protected category, particularly given the specific mention of services or systems that provide access to the Internet. In addition, section 230 applies to portals, operators or hosts of web pages, or other entities that, although have no role in enabling a user to access

---

35. 141 Cong. Rec. 22,046 (1995) (emphasis added); *see also Zeran*, 129 F.3d at 331 (Section 230 was designed "to encourage service providers to self-regulate the dissemination of offensive material over their services.").
36. 47 U.S.C. § 230(c)(1) (2000).
37. *Id.* § 230(f)(2).

the Internet, do run chat rooms, message boards or discussion forums because they enable computer access by multiple users to a computer server, namely the one on which the web pages (or message boards) reside.[38]

At least one court has applied section 230 to immunize defendants that contracted with an interactive computer service to host a news group on the ground that those defendants were "users" of an interactive computer service.[39] Yet the scope of section 230 immunity for "users" of interactive computer services remains relatively unexplored. The terms of the statute suggest that this protection is far reaching. For example, a user who electronically forwards to other people tortious content that was created or published by someone else arguably should be entitled to immunity.

B. Treatment of the Interactive Service as the "Publisher or Speaker" of Third-Party Content

The second requirement for application of section 230 immunity is that holding the service provider liable for someone else's tortious content would "treat [it] as the publisher or speaker" of that content. This issue arose most directly in the *Zeran* case, in which an unidentified person or persons used AOL's service to post on AOL message boards a series of fraudulent messages giving the false impression that Kenneth Zeran, an individual living in Seattle, was selling T-shirts bearing offensive slogans concerning the bombing of the federal building in Oklahoma City.[40] Zeran alleged that, as a result of these messages, which contained his first name and phone number, he received numerous abusive and threatening phone calls.[41] He claimed AOL was negligent because once he notified it of the problem, AOL allegedly did not remove the

---

38. *See, e.g.*, Does 1–30 v. Franco Productions, No. 99 C 7885, 2000 WL 816779 at *4 (N.D. Ill. June 22, 2000) (holding that web hosting activities fall within scope of Section 230 immunity); Marczeski v. Law, 122 F. Supp. 2d 315, 327 (D. Conn. 2000) (Section 230 bars defamation claim against host of chat room); *Stoner v. eBay*, 56 U.S.P.Q.2d 1852, 2000 WL 1705637 (Cal. Super. Nov. 1, 2000) (applying Section 230 to web site provider of online auction service); Sabbato v. Hardy, No. 1999-CV-02909 (Ohio Ct. of Common Pleas Feb. 22, 2000), *rev'd on other grounds*, No. 2000CA00136, 2000 Ohio App. LEXIS 6154 (Ohio Ct. App. Dec. 18, 2000).

Two cases have posed the question of whether section 230 applies to public libraries that offer Internet access to their patrons. In *Mainstream Loudoun v. Board of Trustees of the Loudoun County Library*, 2 F. Supp. 2d 783 (E.D. Va. 1998), a public library invoked section 230 against a constitutional challenge to its policy of utilizing screening software to block access to certain sites on the Internet containing allegedly objectionable material, such as obscenity. The court noted that the definition of interactive computer service includes "a service or system that provides access to the Internet [that is] offered by libraries or educational institutions," but concluded that the immunity was inapplicable because section 230 "was not enacted to insulate government regulation of Internet speech from judicial review." *Id.* at 789–90. Conversely, a California state court has ruled that section 230 does immunize a public library against a suit trying to force the library to engage in filtering of objectionable material. *See* Kathleen R. v. City of Livermore and Does 1–10, 104 Cal. Rptr. 2d 772, 776–79 (Ct. App. 2001).

39. Truelove v. Mensa Int'l, Ltd., No. 97-3463 (D. Md. June 15, 1999).

40. *Zeran*, 129 F.3d at 329.

41. *Id.*

messages quickly enough and did not prevent similar messages from being subsequently posted.[42] AOL—while prepared to prove that it rapidly removed the messages—invoked section 230 and moved for judgment on the pleadings on the ground that it was immune from suit.

The Fourth Circuit unanimously concluded that Zeran's suit did, in fact, seek to treat AOL as the "publisher or speaker" of third-party content, from three distinct perspectives.[43] First, Zeran's suit tried to put the service provider in the same legal position as the person who actually posted the bogus advertisements—that is, the person who clearly was a "publisher or speaker" of the content.[44] As the Fourth Circuit explained, Zeran's suit "cast [AOL] in the same position as the party who originally posted the offensive messages," thereby treating AOL as the "publisher or speaker" of the messages.[45] Whether by substituting the service provider as the defendant for the real creator and publisher of the content (as occurred in *Zeran*) or simply by adding the service provider as a defendant along with the actual creator and publisher, a suit against a service provider for third-party content treats the provider as the "publisher" of the content by placing it in the same legal jeopardy as the actual publisher.

Second, the Fourth Circuit found that Zeran's suit sought to treat AOL as the publisher of third-party content because the suit was premised on the proposition that AOL is obligated to perform functions that traditional publishers, such as publishers of newspapers and magazines, quintessentially perform. "[L]awsuits seeking to hold a service provider liable for its exercise of a publisher's editorial functions—such as deciding whether to publish, withdraw, postpone or alter content—are barred" under section 230.[46] Thus, imposing liability for a service provider's alleged failure to take steps such as screening content in advance or removing information upon notification that it was allegedly erroneous would "impose liability on [the service provider] for assuming the role for which [section] 230 specifically proscribes liability—the publisher role."[47]

Third, the Fourth Circuit concluded that Zeran's suit sought to treat AOL as a publisher or speaker of third-party content because his basic claim sounded in defamation—a tort whose key elements include "publication" of the content at issue. Indeed, the *Restatement (Second) of Torts* specifically refers to the perpetrator of a defamation tort as "the publisher" of the content at issue.[48] As the *Zeran* court explained, "[b]ecause the publication of a statement is a necessary

---

42. *Id.* at 330, 332.

43. *See id.* at 331–33.

44. As the U.S. Supreme Court recognized, each individual who communicates through an online service is a "publisher or speaker" in his or her own right: "Any person or organization with a computer connected to the Internet can 'publish' information." *Reno*, 521 U.S. at 853.

45. *Zeran*, 129 F.3d at 333.

46. *Id.* at 330.

47. *Id.* at 332–33.

48. RESTATEMENT (SECOND) OF TORTS § 558 (1977) (essential elements of any defamation action include "fault amounting to at least negligence on the part of the *publisher*") (emphasis added).

element in a defamation action, only one who publishes can be subject to this form of tort liability."[49] Under this line of reasoning, the protections of section 230 should also readily extend to any other type of tort action in which the plaintiff must show as an element of the tort that the defendant published information.[50]

But section 230's immunity is not restricted simply to torts for which publication is a required element. The plaintiff in *Zeran*, for example, framed his claim as one for simple negligence (based upon AOL's alleged failure to remove and screen for the postings containing his phone number). The court in *Zeran* squarely held that a plaintiff cannot escape the bar of section 230 by pleading a "negligence claim" that, at bottom, is nothing more than a defamation claim in recast form: "Although [plaintiff] attempts to artfully plead his claims as ones of negligence, they are indistinguishable from a garden variety defamation action."[51] More generally, courts routinely reject attempts by creative plaintiffs to evade the many protections the law affords to defamation defendants by merely repackaging defamation claims in the guise of other torts.[52]

The scope of the "publisher or speaker" element of section 230(c)(1) is further illustrated by *Doe v. America Online, Inc.*, where the Florida Supreme Court affirmed the trial court's holding that the provision applied not only to a negligence claim, but also to allegations that AOL violated state pornography statutes. In *Doe*, the plaintiff alleged that AOL negligently permitted one of its subscribers to disseminate in AOL chat rooms advertisements for a videotape depicting the subscriber having sex with the plaintiff, who was a minor.[53] The plaintiff claimed that AOL was negligent for allegedly failing to monitor and screen the speech in its chat rooms and that it was liable in tort for allegedly violating two state statutes that established criminal penalties for certain conduct involving the sale or distribution of obscene materials.[54] Both in the trial court and on appeal, the Florida courts held the suit was barred because plaintiff sought to treat AOL as a publisher or speaker of the subscriber's content. In particular, the court concluded the suit put AOL in the same shoes as the

---

49. *Zeran*, 129 F.3d at 332; *see also Blumenthal*, 992 F. Supp. at 50–51; *Ben Ezra*, 206 F.3d at 986.

50. For example, because a basic element of the tort of invasion of privacy for placing an individual in a false light is that the defendant must have "publicized" the information at issue, a service provider cannot be liable for this tort in connection with third-party information. *See* RESTATEMENT (SECOND) OF TORTS § 652E (1977) (false light invasion of privacy action requires showing that defendant gave "publicity" to allegedly harmful information).

51. *Zeran*, 129 F.3d at 332. Similarly, in *Aquino v. Electriciti, Inc.*, 26 Media L. Rep. (BNA) 1032 (Cal. Super. Ct. Sept. 23, 1997), the court found that section 230 immunized an interactive service provider from liability for torts such as negligence, breach of contract and intentional infliction of emotional distress arising from the provider's distribution of material posted by an anonymous third party accusing the plaintiffs of engaging in various crimes.

52. *See, e.g.*, Hustler Magazine, Inc. v. Falwell, 485 U.S. 46, 56–57 (1988) (plaintiff cannot circumvent First Amendment defenses to defamation action by pleading claim for another tort); Dworkin v. Hustler Magazine, Inc., 668 F. Supp. 1408, 1420 (C.D. Cal. 1987) ("Without such a rule, virtually any defective defamation claim . . . could be revived by pleading it as one for [another tort]."), *aff'd*, 867 F.2d 1188 (9th Cir.), *cert. denied*, 493 U.S. 812 (1989).

53. Doe v. America Online, Inc., No. SC94355, 2001 WL 228446 at *1 (Fla. Mar. 8, 2001).

54. *Id.*

subscriber who published his statements and attempted to impose upon AOL the quintessential duties of a publisher.[55]

The *Zeran* and *Doe* courts' application of section 230 immunity to a wide range of torts is consistent with the statute's purpose. Section 230 was enacted to eliminate liability for third-party "objectionable or inappropriate online material" of all sorts, whether it be "trafficking in obscenity" or "harassment by means of computer."[56] Thus, as long as the other elements of section 230 are satisfied, "[b]y its plain language, [section] 230 creates a federal immunity to *any cause of action* that would make service providers liable for information originating with a third-party user of the service."[57]

A final issue concerning the meaning of the "publisher or speaker" element of section 230(c)(1) concerns the distinction between "publishers" and "distributors." This distinction has been in play in the context of section 230 in large measure because of the prominence of the categories "publisher" and "distributor" in the pre-section-230 case law. In *Cubby*, the court granted summary judgment in part because it classified CompuServe as a "distributor"— the same status as bookstores, newsstands and libraries. These entities may be held liable for harmful information originated by third parties only if they had specific knowledge of the content and its harmful nature.[58] In essence, *Cubby* recognized that providers of interactive computer services, as mere distributors of information transmitted by third parties, enjoy an extra level of First Amendment protection that requires a special threshold showing before they can legally be treated as publishers of such information.

Plaintiffs in some of the early section 230 cases argued that because the statute uses the term "publisher," but not "distributor," the statute does not immunize service providers from the types of liability to which mere distributors may be subject. The plaintiff in *Zeran* raised precisely this argument, and the Fourth Circuit rejected it:

> Zeran contends that the term "distributor" carries a legally distinct meaning from the term "publisher." Accordingly, he asserts that Congress's use of only the term "publisher" in [section] 230 indicates a purpose to immunize service providers only from publisher liability. He argues that distributors are left unprotected by [section] 230 and, therefore, that his suit should be permitted to proceed against AOL. We disagree. Assuming arguendo that Zeran has satisfied the requirements for imposition of distributor liability, *this theory of liability is merely a subset, or a species, of publisher liability, and is therefore also foreclosed by [section] 230.*[59]

---

55. *See id.* at *5–*6.

56. *See* 47 U.S.C. §§ 230(b)(4), 230(b)(5), 230(c)(2)(A) (2000).

57. *Zeran*, 129 F.3d at 330 (emphasis added).

58. *Cubby*, 776 F. Supp. at 139–41.

59. *Zeran*, 129 F.3d at 331–32 (emphasis added); *see also Blumenthal*, 992 F. Supp. at 52 ("Any attempt to distinguish between 'publisher' liability and notice-based 'distributor' liability and to argue that [s]ection 230 was only intended to immunize the former would be unavailing. Congress made no distinction between publishers and distributors in providing immunity from liability."); *Doe*, 1997 WL 374223, at *3.

In other words, according to the Fourth Circuit, a lawsuit that seeks to hold a distributor liable for third-party content is, in reality, simply a suit that treats the distributor as a "publisher" of that content in contravention of section 230.

C. Information "Provided by Another Information Content Provider"

The final requirement for applicability of immunity under section 230(c)(1) is that the information be "provided by another information content provider." The statute expressly defines an information content provider as "any person or entity that is *responsible, in whole or in part, for the creation or development of information* provided through the Internet or any other interactive computer service."[60] This element probably is most clearly satisfied in cases such as *Zeran* and *Doe*, in which the allegedly tortious information was posted by a subscriber to an interactive service. The subscriber clearly "provided" the content and was "another information content provider"—the subscriber was distinct from AOL (that is, "another") and he or she was responsible for the creation or development of the information. Conversely, this element probably is not satisfied when the allegedly tortious information is created and developed entirely by an employee of the interactive computer service acting within the scope of his duties.

(1) Content Provided by Third-Party Contractors

A question that sparked greater controversy was whether section 230 extends to cases where the third party who originates the content is an independent contractor whom the online service pays to provide the content. This issue was posed directly in the *Blumenthal* case, which arose out of an allegedly defamatory story that was published by Internet columnist Matt Drudge and concerned Sidney Blumenthal, a well-known former journalist and White House aide.[61] The story contained the following allegation:

> The DRUDGE REPORT has learned that top GOP operatives who feel there is a double-standard of only reporting Republican shame believe they are holding an ace card: New White House recruit Sidney Blumenthal has a spousal abuse past that has been effectively covered up.[62]

The story further stated that an anonymous White House source labeled the allegation "pure fiction" and that Drudge's attempts to reach Blumenthal for comment had been unsuccessful.[63] Within hours of publication, counsel for

---

60. 47 U.S.C. § 230(e)(3) (2000) (emphasis added).
61. *Blumenthal*, 992 F. Supp. at 46.
62. *Id.*
63. *Id.*

Blumenthal and his wife informed Drudge by letter that the story was false, and Drudge promptly withdrew the story and issued a retraction.[64]

Drudge published the Blumenthal story in an edition of his *Drudge Report*, a popular electronic publication that contains topical reports relating to (among other things) celebrities, news and events in the fields of politics and entertainment. Drudge is the sole creator, author and publisher of all stories in the *Drudge Report*, including the Blumenthal story; he posted the *Drudge Report* for free on his own web site and transmitted it via e-mail (again at no charge) to thousands of subscribers.[65] Most people who accessed or received the Blumenthal story did so through these two media.

The edition of the *Drudge Report* containing the Blumenthal story was also available through AOL's service. Drudge and AOL had entered a licensing agreement under which Drudge posted new editions of his publication to a designated area on the AOL service, in exchange for a royalty payment of $3,000 per month.[66] The agreement called for Drudge to provide and license to AOL the very same content of the *Drudge Report* that he continues to send to his e-mail subscribers and publish on his web site.[67] The license agreement left all responsibility for generating the content of the *Drudge Report* exclusively to Drudge; he was responsible for providing and editing the *Drudge Report* as it appeared on the AOL service, subject only to AOL's reserved right to remove content it reasonably determined violated the standard terms governing all content posted on AOL.[68] Consistent with the terms of this license agreement, no one at AOL played any role—supervisory or otherwise—in creating or writing the Blumenthal story.[69]

Blumenthal and his wife filed suit against Drudge and AOL in the U.S. District Court for the District of Columbia, claiming defamation and invasion of privacy. AOL was named as a defendant, on the theory that it "jointly and severally published" (along with Drudge) the allegedly tortious material. AOL moved for summary judgment on the basis of section 230(c)(1). The Blumenthals sought to avoid the immunity provision on the ground that AOL allegedly was "responsible" (at least in part) for the "creation or development" of the story at issue and that the story therefore was not "provided by another information content provider."

The Blumenthals first argued that AOL was not entitled to immunity because of its alleged editorial authority over the version of the *Drudge Report* available through the AOL service, particularly its limited contractual right to remove or change objectionable content. But the court specifically rejected the suggestion that AOL's retention of a contractual right to review and remove or

---

64. *Id.* at 48.
65. *Id.* at 47, 50.
66. *Id.*
67. *Id.*
68. *Id.*
69. *Id.* at 50.

require changes to objectionable content supplied by a third party deprived AOL of section 230 immunity.[70] Indeed, as discussed above, one of the primary purposes of section 230 was to overrule the holding of *Stratton Oakmont* that an interactive service could be subject to liability for third-party content on the ground that it sought to retain and exercise editorial control to regulate objectionable content.[71] As the Fourth Circuit explained earlier in *Zeran*, "Congress enacted [section] 230 to remove . . . disincentives to self[-]regulation" and expressly sought to avoid a regime in which "computer service providers who regulated the dissemination of offensive material on their services risked subjecting themselves to liability."[72]

Of course, editorial control might encompass more than simply the retention and exercise of the right to remove objectionable content. The undisputed facts in *Blumenthal* clearly demonstrated that AOL had no editorial involvement whatsoever in the *Drudge Report*.[73] No court has yet confronted a case in which the service provider actually makes substantive changes to content otherwise provided by a third party, although at least two courts have in dicta suggested that immunity may not apply in such circumstances.[74] Nonetheless, there is room to argue that section 230 immunity should still be available. For example, the statutory definition of "information content provider" explicitly recognizes the possibility that any given unit of "information" may be provided by more than one "information content provider."[75] As a result, information may still be "provided by another information content provider"—and immunity therefore still available under section 230(c)(1)—even when the information also has been provided "in part" by the interactive service provider that claims immunity. Moreover, the statutory objective of encouraging service providers to self-regulate the content available on their systems arguably would be undermined if the service provider must forfeit immunity whenever it actually edits and changes content (at least when those changes do not themselves create new tortious content).

In addition to arguing that AOL's alleged editorial authority deprived it of section 230 immunity, the Blumenthals alleged that the nature of the business relationship between AOL and Drudge meant that Drudge's story about Sidney Blumenthal was not "information provided by another information content provider." In particular, they argued that because AOL contracted with Drudge

---

70. *Id.* at 51–52.

71. Section 230's separate Good Samaritan provision, section 230(c)(2), also manifests Congress's intent to remove disincentives to the exercise of editorial control: it expressly prohibits holding a service provider liable "on account of" good-faith action "to restrict . . . availability of material that the provider . . . considers to be . . . objectionable. . . ." 47 U.S.C. § 230(c)(2) (2000).

72. *Zeran*, 129 F.3d at 331.

73. *See Blumenthal*, 992 F. Supp. at 50.

74. *Ben Ezra*, 206 F.3d at 985 n.4; Zeran v. America Online, Inc., 958 F. Supp. 1124, 1133 n.20 (E.D. Va. 1997).

75. *See* 47 U.S.C. § 230(f)(3) (2000) ("The term 'information content provider' means any person or entity that is responsible, in whole or *in part*, for the creation or development of information provided through the Internet or any other interactive computer service.") (emphasis added).

to provide content in exchange for a royalty fee, along with other aspects of their business relationship, AOL was vicariously responsible for the creation and development of the *Drudge Report* simply by virtue of its relationship with Drudge.[76] But the district court in *Blumenthal* also rejected this argument.

Over several hundred years, the common law has yielded sophisticated and well-entrenched doctrines requiring a special type of relationship—specifically, an employer/employee or principal/agent relationship—before one party can be held generally liable (or responsible) for specific acts of another party in which the first party had no direct role.[77] In *Blumenthal*, the undisputed evidence overwhelmingly established that Drudge was neither an employee nor agent of AOL, and the court thus easily rejected on factual grounds the contention that AOL was responsible for the *Drudge Report* on the basis of the AOL/Drudge relationship.

The issue of when information is "provided by another information content provider" also arose in the *BEW* case. The plaintiff BEW claimed that AOL was liable for damages purportedly caused by alleged errors in stock quote information concerning the plaintiff's stock that was available through AOL's service. AOL filed a motion for summary judgment on the ground that it was immune under section 230 because the stock quotation information in question was jointly provided by a third-party stock quote vendor under a contract with AOL (S&P ComStock, Inc.) and the vendor's designated supplier of certain necessary computer software (Townsend Analytics, Ltd.). In support of its motion, AOL submitted undisputed evidence that "ComStock and Townsend alone created the stock information at issue" and that AOL did not revise or change the information.[78]

Nevertheless, BEW argued on the basis of various facts that AOL should be deemed an additional "information content provider" of the allegedly erroneous stock quote information and that AOL had therefore forfeited the protection of section 230. First, BEW claimed that AOL was responsible in part for the development of the stock quote information because it (1) informed ComStock and/or Townsend when AOL learned (usually from its subscribers) of any suspected errors, (2) provided further information that might help in diagnosing those errors and (3) communicated with ComStock and/or Townsend about the status of any fixes for those errors. The Tenth Circuit Court of Appeals rejected BEW's contention, holding that "such communications simply do not constitute the development or creation of the stock quotation information."[79] Indeed, as with *Blumenthal*, making AOL liable on the basis of such

---

76. *See Blumenthal*, 992 F. Supp. at 51–52.
77. *Black's Law Dictionary* defines "vicarious liability" as "[t]he imposition of liability on one person for the actionable conduct of another, *based solely on a relationship between the two persons.*" BLACK'S LAW DICTIONARY 1566 (6th ed. 1990) (emphasis added). It identifies only two relationships—employer/employee and principal/agent—that support vicarious liability.
78. *BEW*, 206 F.3d at 986.
79. *Id.* at 985.

communications would have turned section 230 on its head by penalizing AOL for its self-regulatory efforts.

BEW also argued that AOL was an information content provider because it occasionally deleted stock quote information for a particular security when it learned the information might be erroneous, with the result that information for the security was unavailable to AOL subscribers until ComStock and Townsend provided new information for that security. Again, however, the Tenth Circuit rejected that contention, concluding that "[b]y deleting the symbols, [AOL] simply made the data unavailable and did not develop or create the stock quotation information displayed."[80]

More generally, BEW claimed that AOL must have been an information content provider because its hardware and software were involved in delivering the stock quote information provided by ComStock and Townsend to AOL subscribers.[81] BEW pointed to no evidence that AOL's hardware or software actually changed the content of the stock quote information in any way. In the absence of such evidence, BEW's argument had to fail as a matter of law: an interactive computer service could not serve as a conduit of third-party content without its hardware and software playing a role in making the content available to its subscribers. Accordingly, accepting BEW's argument would have rendered section 230 meaningless. The Tenth Circuit rejected all of BEW's arguments and affirmed the grant of summary judgment in favor of AOL.

(2) Employee and Agency Relationships

Notwithstanding the broad holdings of both *Blumenthal* and *BEW*, the issue of when, if ever, the nature of the relationship between a service provider and a third-party content provider might render section 230 immunity inapplicable has not been fully resolved in the courts. For example, no court has yet decided whether a nonemployee agency relationship would be sufficient to deprive a service provider of immunity based upon a theory of vicarious liability. A good argument may be made that immunity should be available even in that setting. After all, "to hold someone vicariously liable literally means to impute to them certain actions of *another person*."[82] In the absence of a definitive court ruling to this effect, however, it may be safer from a liability standpoint for a service provider to structure its relationships with third-party content providers so that the third parties are nonagent independent contractors—not employees or agents.

The sine qua non of both an employee and agency relationship is the right to control the means and manner of the putative employee/agent's performance.[83] Significantly, efforts to monitor and control the *results* of a contractual

---

80. *Id.* at 986.
81. *See id.* at 985.
82. Hunt v. Marchetti, 824 F.2d 916, 919 (11th Cir. 1987) (emphasis added); *see also* BLACK'S LAW DICTIONARY 1566 (6th ed. 1990) (defining "vicarious liability" as "[t]he imposition of liability on one person for the actionable conduct of *another*," as in holding principal responsible for torts of agent) (emphasis added).
83. *See, e.g.,* Community for Creative Non-Violence v. Reid, 490 U.S. 730, 751 (1989).

relationship are not the relevant form of control; the central inquiry is whether the alleged employer/principal controls the "means and manner" of the performance by "regulat[ing] the actual activities undertaken by the [putative] employee in the course of his occupation."[84] Thus, mere editorial control over the final product generally is not sufficient to create an employee or agency relationship.[85] The types of factors that can make a difference—either because they help establish the requisite control or because they are otherwise indicia of an employee or agency relationship—include (1) whether the two parties have consented to create such a relationship (which might be evidenced by language in the contract), (2) the extent to which the alleged employer/principal has the right to control attributes such as the third party's hours or who, if anyone, it hires and (3) whether the relationship is such that the purported agent/employee has a fiduciary obligation to the service provider.[86]

In sum, though it is clear that certain types of editorial control and relationships do not deprive a provider of immunity, a number of undecided issues remain about when information is "provided by another information content provider." And those open issues are by nature fact-specific and may not lend themselves to easy generalization. As a result, ensuring the availability of section 230 immunity requires careful advance thought by the service provider in structuring its relationships with third-party content providers.

iv. Litigating Section 230 Immunity

One of the significant advantages of section 230 immunity is that it usually can be established as a threshold defense to litigate before other issues are raised in a case. Depending upon the allegations in the complaint, the defense often can be raised in a motion to dismiss or for judgment on the pleadings, as it was in *Zeran* and *Doe*. In other contexts, when facts outside the complaint are relevant to the immunity issue (for example, to demonstrate the absence of an employer/ employee relationship between the service provider and the content provider), the more appropriate vehicle might be a summary judgment motion, as occurred in *Blumenthal* and *BEW*. The ease of raising this defense is often further enhanced by the existence of one or more of the prerequisites for immunity— they are sometimes so clear that the plaintiff cannot reasonably contest them.

---

84. Local 777, Democratic Union Org. Comm. v. NLRB, 603 F.2d 862, 873–75 (D.C. Cir. 1978); C.C. Eastern, Inc. v. NLRB, 60 F.3d 855, 858 (D.C. Cir. 1995).

85. *See, e.g.*, Chaiken v. VV Publ'g Corp., 119 F.3d 1018, 1034 (2d Cir. 1997) (freelance reporter not employee of newspaper even though newspaper edited his stories before they were published); Nelson v. Globe Int'l, Inc., 626 F. Supp. 969, 978 (S.D.N.Y. 1986) (newspaper that selected article topic and then edited resulting article lacked sufficient control over author's performance to make author an employee); *Cubby*, 776 F. Supp. at 143 (right to remove content not sufficient control to create agency relationship).

86. *See generally* RESTATEMENT (SECOND) OF AGENCY §§ 1, 220 (1958); *Community for Creative Non-Violence*, 490 U.S. at 751.

In *Zeran*, for example, the plaintiff conceded both that AOL was a provider of an "interactive computer service" and that the messages were "information provided by another information content provider." Similarly, in *Blumenthal* and *BEW*, the plaintiffs did not contest that AOL was an interactive computer service provider or that they sought to treat AOL as a "publisher or speaker."

Another important benefit of section 230 immunity is that it may be used as a basis to stay discovery on all other facets of the case until the immunity issue is resolved. In the *BEW* case, AOL successfully moved to have discovery generally stayed pending resolution of its section 230 defense. At approximately the same time as it filed its summary judgment motion under section 230, AOL filed a separate motion seeking to stay all discovery (except to the extent that plaintiff could demonstrate discovery was necessary on issues relating to the section 230 motion) until its summary judgment motion was resolved. The court granted AOL's motion. It reasoned that section 230 immunity is analogous to qualified immunity afforded government officials performing discretionary functions, in that both forms of immunity protect against not only the imposition of liability, but also the burdens of litigation, including discovery.[87] The court in *Blumenthal* similarly stayed discovery pending resolution of the section 230 immunity issue.

Thus, section 230 immunity, as construed by the courts, is more than simply another defense in a defendant's arsenal. Instead, section 230 can be a broad, threshold shield against not only liability, but also the burdens and costs of litigation.

2. Potential Criminal Liability for Third-Party Content

An interactive service provider's risks are not limited to civil liability for torts or infringement. Criminal liability also lurks as a possibility. In at least one case, a computer bulletin board operator was prosecuted for what was apparently third-party content.[88] But the magnitude and scope of risk remain uncertain. As discussed below, section 230 provides some guidance regarding interactive service providers' criminal liability, at least on the state side. But there is no definitive law in the United States concerning whether or when to hold an interactive service provider criminally liable for third-party material. Despite the resulting uncertainty, some general principles of liability can be discerned.

Like any means of communication, the Internet creates opportunities for its users to commit criminal acts. Any crime that involves a communication can be committed through the Internet, and other crimes can be facilitated by

---

87. 26 Media L. Rep. (BNA) 2211, 2213 (D.N.M. July 16, 1998).
88. United States v. Thomas, 74 F.3d 701 (6th Cir.), *cert. denied*, 519 U.S. 820 (1996).

communications on the Internet. An analysis of an interactive service provider's potential criminal liability should begin with a clear understanding of the relationship between a third party's content and the crime. Sometimes a communication or content itself is criminal; other times a communication becomes criminal when combined with separate circumstances or a separate malicious intent; and still other times content is not criminal, but a communication is used to commit or bring about a criminal act.

Those relationships inform whether and how section 230, the various criminal statutes, and the First Amendment should apply to interactive service providers. If holding an interactive service provider liable would treat that provider as a publisher or distributor, then section 230 should provide immunity from *state* criminal laws, as it does from state and federal civil laws. Section 230, however, appears to provide no such immunity from *federal* criminal laws. But most federal criminal statutes have scienter requirements that generally preclude interactive service provider liability for content of which the service provider is not aware. Underlying such scienter requirements is a basic First Amendment protection. At least when an interactive service provider acts as a distributor of third-party information, the First Amendment generally protects the service provider from criminal liability unless that service provider has knowledge of the content of the third party's material.

i. Section 230's Effect on Criminal Liability

Although no court apparently has yet been called upon to apply section 230 in the context of a criminal prosecution, on its face it appears to immunize interactive service providers from liability under state criminal laws (as long as each of the three elements of the immunity are met). Section 230 does not appear to apply to federal criminal prosecutions, however, and its applicability to private civil actions under a federal criminal law has not been resolved.

A. Section 230 and State Criminal Laws

(1) Criminal Liability

On its face, section 230's protection appears to extend to liability under state criminal laws. Section 230(e)(3) states that "[n]o cause of action may be brought and no liability may be imposed under *any* State or local law that is inconsistent with this section."[89] This provision does not distinguish between state civil and criminal laws. In contrast, as discussed below, section 230 ex-

---

89. 47 U.S.C. § 230(e)(3) (2000) (emphasis added).

plicitly exempts from its reach "the enforcement of any ... *Federal* criminal statute."[90] The statute also lists several other exceptions, all unrelated to state criminal laws.[91] Thus, the statutory construction canon *expressio unius est exclusio alterius*—which generally provides that when Congress expressly enumerates certain exceptions or exclusions from a statute, the statute should apply to all cases not specifically excluded[92]—also suggests applying section 230 to state criminal statutes. Such a reading comports with section 230's purposes.[93] If fear of being held civilly liable for third-party content would chill free speech and create disincentives for screening offensive material, the disincentives created by fear of criminal liability arising from a multitude of differing statutes in fifty states would likely be even greater.

(2) Civil Liability Based upon State Criminal Statutes

Even if a court were to disagree with the foregoing analysis and permit an interactive service provider to be held criminally liable under state statutes, section 230 should at the very least preclude civil actions arising from state criminal statutes. The Florida Supreme Court did just that in *Doe v. America Online, Inc.*[94] *Doe* was a suit brought by a minor's mother who claimed AOL violated the Florida Computer Pornography and Child Exploitation Act of 1986, a criminal statute, by allegedly allowing a third party to use an AOL chat room to arrange the sale of a videotape containing sexually explicit pornographic images of her minor child.[95] She asserted that AOL's alleged violation of the criminal statute constituted negligence per se.[96] The Florida courts, however, held that section 230 immunized AOL from liability for these claims, because holding AOL liable would treat it as the "publisher or speaker" of the third-party advertising content.[97]

B. Section 230 and Federal Criminal Statutes

Unlike in the realm of state criminal law, section 230(e)(1) carves out an apparent exception for the enforcement of federal criminal laws. It states, "Nothing in this section shall be construed to *impair the enforcement* of section 223 or 231 of this title, chapter 71 (relating to obscenity) or 110 (relating to sexual exploitation of children) of Title 18, or *any other Federal criminal statute.*"[98] The statute's preamble also states that "[i]t is the policy of the United

---

90. *Id.* § 230(e)(1) (emphasis added).

91. *See id.* § 230(e).

92. Norman J. Singer, Sutherland Statutory Construction § 47.23, at 217 (5th ed. 1992).

93. These are discussed in detail in Section 4.1.1 of this chapter.

94. *See* Doe v. America Online, Inc., No. SC94355, 2001 WL 228446 (Fla. Mar. 8, 2001).

95. *Id.* at *1.

96. *Id.*

97. *See id.* at *4–*6.

98. 47 U.S.C. § 230(e)(1) (2000) (emphasis added). Section 223(d) prohibits sending or displaying offensive material to persons under eighteen. Section 231 is intended to restrict minors' access to commercially distributed materials that would be harmful to them.

States ... to ensure vigorous enforcement of Federal criminal laws to deter and punish trafficking in obscenity, stalking, and harassment by means of computer."[99]

(1) Federal Criminal Prosecutions

Section 230(e)(1)'s language begs the question of what it means to "impair the enforcement of" a federal criminal statute. Presumably, applying section 230 to immunize an interactive service provider from criminal prosecution under a federal criminal statute constitutes "impair[ing] the enforcement" of that statute. To be sure, exempting federal criminal prosecution from the ambit of section 230 appears to run counter to the purposes of section 230. If by monitoring and blocking some objectionable content, an interactive service provider risks having gained knowledge of criminal activity and thus being potentially liable under a federal criminal statute, then there remains a strong incentive not to screen or block material at all. Nevertheless, it appears Congress balanced its policy of encouraging self-regulation against the competing policy of ensuring "vigorous enforcement of Federal criminal laws." The limitation of this exception to *federal* criminal statutes may be the flip side of that balance: perhaps Congress recognized that in contrast to the multiplicity of varying state criminal statutes governing crimes that can be committed over the Internet, the universe of federal criminal laws is relatively limited, and the standards imposed by federal criminal laws are uniform and subject to Congress's control. In addition, and as discussed below, Congress has often provided interactive service providers special defenses and protections in some of the federal criminal statutes that are most likely to apply to them.

(2) Civil Liability under Federal Criminal Statutes

Although section 230 is fairly clear that it does not immunize interactive service providers against prosecution under federal criminal laws, the applicability of section 230 to a private cause of action based upon a federal criminal statute has yet to be determined. As courts resolve this untested issue, they must confront whether section 230 would "impair the *enforcement of any Federal criminal statute*" if it allowed interactive service providers to avoid private actions that are based upon criminal statutes. Or, stated another way, courts must decide whether Congress intended that plaintiffs be allowed to circumvent section 230's protections by framing their private causes of action as based upon federal criminal statutes rather than upon other statutory or common-law theories.

Violating a federal criminal statute can give rise to civil liability in three ways. First, state courts or legislatures can incorporate a standard of conduct established by a federal criminal law into a private state law cause of action. The most common example is a negligence per se action that incorporates a

---

99. *Id.* § 230(b)(5).

standard of conduct from a federal criminal statute. In such cases, interactive service providers may be able to make a persuasive argument that a plaintiff is "enforcing" the state law, rather than the federal criminal statute that supplies the standard the state law incorporates, and that applying section 230 therefore would not impair enforcement of a federal criminal statute. Second, in very narrow circumstances that involve issues of "uniquely federal concern," federal courts can fashion private civil actions as matters of federal common law, and use a criminal statute as a standard for liability.[100] Again, interactive service providers have strong arguments that in such cases, the federal criminal statute is not being "enforced." Third and finally, Congress can expressly—or by implication—create a civil cause of action in the context of a statute also providing for criminal penalties.[101] A service provider may have several arguments that immunity applies to such an action: (1) at least when the civil cause of action is designed simply to compensate the victim for an injury, such an action may not constitute "enforc[ing] a federal criminal statute," (2) the term "enforcement" may refer only to actions by prosecutors seeking to impose criminal penalties or (3) a provision providing civil remedies, even if located within a broader statute that also prescribes criminal penalties, may not be a "criminal statute." Courts have not yet had occasion to assess the merits of these arguments.

ii. Scienter Requirements and Other Protections for Interactive Service Providers

Perhaps partly as a result of underlying constitutional concerns (see Section 5.2.2.iii below), Congress has generally been careful in federal criminal statutes most likely to apply to interactive computer service providers to circumscribe their potential liability for third-party content by, for example, imposing potential liability only when providers know of the criminal content. A brief look at the particular federal criminal statutes Congress mentioned in section 230(e)(1) illustrates the types of protections that may be available to interactive computer service providers.

---

100. *See generally* Northwest Airlines, Inc. v. Transp. Workers Union of Am., 451 U.S. 77, 90–91 (1981) (cause of action may become part of federal common law "through the exercise of judicial power to fashion appropriate remedies for unlawful conduct"); Note, *Implying Civil Remedies from Federal Regulatory Statutes*, 77 HARV. L. REV. 285, 286 (1963) (this theory "regards the statute as declaring wrongful certain behavior, from which the court itself then creates a new cause of action").

101. *See, e.g.*, Burke v. Compania Mexicana de Aviacion, 433 F.2d 1031 (9th Cir. 1970) (implying private civil action from federal statue with criminal penalty); Fitzgerald v. Pan Am. World Airways, Inc., 229 F.2d 499 (2d Cir. 1956) (private right of action implied from prohibition that was only expressly enforceable by administrative proceeding or criminal action); Reitmeister v. Reitmeister, 162 F.2d 691 (2d Cir. 1947) (private right of action implied from prohibition against intercepting and divulging telephone messages, even though act was expressly enforceable only by criminal penalty).

A. Statutes Concerning Online Obscenity and Child Pornography

The first two federal criminal statutes enumerated in section 230(e)—sections 223 and 231—have been partially blocked by the courts on First Amendment grounds and at present apply only to unprotected speech such as obscenity and child pornography.[102] These statutes exemplify the breadth of protection from liability that Congress may give interactive computer services, even when section 230 immunity does not apply. Both statutes—like most other federal criminal statutes—contain scienter requirements that often would not be satisfied in the context of third-party material. Section 223, in relevant part, proscribes "knowingly" using an interactive computer service to send or make available to a person under eighteen a communication that depicts sexual activities in patently offensive terms.[103] Similarly, section 231 prohibits a person from "knowingly and with knowledge of the character of the material" making a commercial communication over the World Wide Web that (1) is available to minors and is obscene or (2)(a) appeals to the prurient interest, (b) offensively depicts sexual acts or lewd exhibitions of sex organs and (c) taken as a whole, lacks serious literary, artistic, political or scientific value for minors."[104]

In addition to these scienter requirements, sections 223 and 231 explicitly exempt entities whose only involvement in the dissemination of obscene or otherwise proscribed material is to make it accessible by providing services such as Internet access or storage. Section 223(d), for example, states that:

> [n]o person shall be held to have violated subsection (a) or (d) of this section solely for providing access or connection to or from a facility, system, or network not under that person's control, including transmission, downloading, intermediate storage, access software, or other related capabilities that are incidental to providing such access or connection that does not include the creation of the content of the communication.[105]

The Conference Report explained the purpose of this provision as follows:

> This provision is designed to target the criminal penalties of new sections 223(a) and (d) at content providers who violate this section and persons who conspire with such content providers, rather than entities who simply offer general access to the Internet and other online content. The conferees intend that this defense be construed broadly to avoid impairing the growth of online communications through a regime of vicarious liability.[106]

Section 231 similarly provides that a person shall not be considered to make any proscribed communications to the extent that the person is "engaged in

---

102. ACLU v. Reno, 521 U.S. 844 (1997); ACLU v. Reno, 31 F. Supp. 2d 473, 499 (E.D. Pa. 1999).
103. 47 U.S.C. § 223(d)(1) (1999).
104. *Id.* §§ 231(a)(1), 231(e)(6).
105. *Id.* § 223(e)(1).
106. H.R. Conf. Rep. No. 104–58, at 74 (1996).

the business of providing an Internet access service," "engaged in the business of providing an Internet information location tool," or "similarly engaged in the transmission, storage, retrieval, hosting, formatting, or translation . . . of a communication made by another, without selection or alteration of the content of the communication, except that such person's deletion" is not "selection or alteration" if done consistently with section 230.[107] Presumably, this last exception refers to the protection in section 230 for "any action taken in good faith to restrict access to or availability of material" that is obscene, lewd or "otherwise objectionable."[108]

B. General Federal Obscenity Statutes

In addition to sections 223 and 231, the exceptions clause of section 230 expressly excludes the general federal obscenity statutes[109] from the ambit of section 230's protections. The general anti-obscenity provisions that could affect interactive service providers include (1) section 1462, which in relevant part forbids knowingly bringing into the United States or knowingly using an interactive computer service to carry or receive in interstate commerce "obscene, lewd, lascivious, or filthy" materials,[110] (2) section 1465, which in relevant part forbids knowingly transporting in interstate commerce or using an interactive computer service to sell or distribute "obscene, lewd, lascivious, or filthy" materials[111] and (3) section 1470, added in 1998, which forbids knowingly transferring or attempting to transfer obscene matter to a person younger than sixteen, while knowing that person is younger than sixteen.[112]

Although these statutes contain no explicit, special protections for interactive computer service providers akin to those in sections 223 and 231, their scienter requirements are likely to limit the situations in which service providers may be liable. An interactive service provider conceivably could be prosecuted under sections 1462 and 1465 for knowingly using its service to carry obscene materials or otherwise knowingly importing or transmitting obscene materials, but only if the provider has knowledge of the contents of the material. In addition, a violation of section 1465 requires that an interactive service provider have the purpose of selling or distributing obscenity. To violate section 1470, an interactive service provider must know the character of the third-party content, and must know the recipient of the content is under sixteen.[113]

---

107. 47 U.S.C. §§ 231(b)(2)–(4) (1999).
108. *Id.* § 230(c)(2)(A).
109. 18 U.S.C. ch. 71 (1999).
110. 18 U.S.C. § 1462 (1999).
111. *Id.* § 1465.
112. *Id.* § 1470.
113. Although in many situations service providers do not know the ages of their users, that is not, of course, always true. The Children's Online Privacy Protection Act, 15 U.S.C. § 6501 *et seq.*, is premised upon the idea that at least some service providers do know they are dealing with children.

The operation of these statutes in the context of online content is illustrated by *United States v. Thomas*,[114] in which operators of a computer bulletin board were successfully prosecuted under sections 1462 and 1465. In *Thomas*, the operators of the bulletin board purchased sexually explicit magazines from adult bookstores, scanned them into the computer and made them available for downloading by subscribers to the operators' bulletin board.[115] Under the facts of the case, there was no question that—even if the images were created by third parties—the service operators had sufficient knowledge of the contents and nature of the material to satisfy the statutory requirements.

But in some sense, the *Thomas* case represents the exception—it was clearly the intent of the service provider there to disseminate obscene and other unlawful material. Most service providers will not have such intent and often will not be in a position to know that such material is being disseminated over their systems. Thus, even absent section 230 immunity, an interactive service provider is unlikely to be subject to liability under federal obscenity statutes for third-party content, except in relatively limited circumstances. If an interactive service provider does become aware of the nature of obscene material being posted or communicated through its service, however, the potential for criminal liability could arise, and the service provider must assess what action (removing the material, for example) it must take to avoid such liability.

Like federal obscenity laws, federal criminal laws enacted to prevent children from being sexually exploited—the final category of statutes explicitly mentioned as outside the scope of section 230—may also impose criminally enforceable duties upon interactive service providers in connection with third-party content. The provisions pertinent to interactive service providers include (1) section 2251, which in relevant part forbids a person from knowingly publishing or causing to be published any notice or advertisement seeking—or offering to produce or traffic in—visual depictions of minors engaging in sexually explicit acts,[116] (2) section 2252, which in relevant part prohibits knowingly transporting or receiving, "by any means including by computer," a visual depiction involving a minor engaging in sexually explicit conduct[117] and (3) section 2252A, which in relevant part prohibits knowingly transporting, receiving or distributing, by any means, including by computer, child pornography.[118] Each of these criminal provisions includes as an element that publication, transport or distribution of the solicitation or child pornography be "knowing."[119] Therefore, criminal laws impose upon interactive service providers no enforce-

---

114. United States v. Thomas, 74 F.3d 701 (6th Cir.), *cert. denied*, 519 U.S. 820 (1996).

115. *Id.* at 705.

116. 18 U.S.C. § 2251(c) (1999).

117. *Id.* § 2252(a).

118. *Id.* § 2252A(a). "Child pornography" is defined to include visual depictions of minors engaging in sexually explicit conduct, and visual depictions that appear, or are advertised, to be of minors engaging in sexually explicit conduct. *Id.* § 2256(8).

119. In *United States v. X-Citement Video, Inc.*, 513 U.S. 64 (1994), the U.S. Supreme Court held that despite the natural grammatical reading of section 2252, its "knowingly" requirement extended "both to the sexually explicit nature of the material and to the age of the performers." *Id.* at 78.

able duty to remove child pornography unless they learn someone is using their services to solicit, send or distribute the offending material. Of course, if a service provider does obtain such knowledge, it must determine what action to take to avoid potential liability (for example, terminating the account of the person using the service to transmit the offending material). In some circumstances, a service provider also has a duty to report to law enforcement when it obtains knowledge that its service is being used in connection with child pornography.[120]

Of course, federal crimes are not limited to obscenity, child pornography and other sexually oriented content. Yet, in most cases, federal crimes include as an element a requirement that the perpetrator knowingly commit the prohibited act. Although negligence and strict-liability-based crimes do exist, it is unlikely that one will give rise to a situation in which an interactive service provider becomes criminally liable for third-party communications. If that situation were to arise, however, an interactive service provider should be able to resort to the protections that the First Amendment provides to distributors of information.

iii. First Amendment Protection

As this discussion makes apparent, the threat of an interactive service provider facing criminal liability in the United States for third-party content is relatively limited: Section 230 appears to foreclose liability under state criminal laws, and most applicable federal criminal statutes at a minimum contain the type of knowledge or other scienter requirements that will be inapplicable to interactive service providers in most instances, given the practical impediments to gaining the requisite level of awareness concerning any particular transmission among the vast content available online. But even absent these statutory protections, the First Amendment circumscribes interactive service providers' exposure to criminal liability for third-party content. In particular, interactive service providers should be classified as "distributors" of information, much like bookstores and libraries, and accordingly should be free from liability absent a showing of actual knowledge (or, arguably, some lesser level of scienter) concerning the allegedly illegal third-party content.

Courts generally provide distributors of third-party information—such as libraries and bookstores—additional First Amendment protection beyond that accorded to other types of publishers, such as newspapers. Courts are likely to view interactive service providers as distributors of third-party content, though the issue is not free from doubt. The case most directly discussing this matter is *Cubby, Inc. v. CompuServe Inc.*[121] In *Cubby*, a New York federal district court

---

120. 42 U.S.C. § 13032 (2000).
121. Cubby, Inc. v. CompuServe, Inc., 776 F. Supp. 135 (S.D.N.Y. 1991).

decided the interactive service provider CompuServe was "in essence an elec-tronic, for-profit library" that generally may not be held liable for harmful material that might be among the vast quantities of information it makes avail-able. As the court explained:

> CompuServe has no more editorial control over such a publication than does a public library, bookstore, or newsstand, and it would be no more feasible for CompuServe to examine every publication it carries for potentially defamatory statements than it would be for other distributors to do so. . . . A computerized database is the functional equivalent of a more traditional news vendor, and the inconsistent application of a lower standard of liability to an electronic news distributor such as CompuServe than that which is applied to a public library, bookstore, or newsstand would impose an undue burden on the free flow of information.[122]

Thus, the *Cubby* court quite clearly came down on the side of treating interactive computer services as distributors of third-party information entitled to heightened First Amendment protection.

Nevertheless, in *Stratton Oakmont, Inc. v. Prodigy Services Co.*,[123] a New York state court distinguished *Cubby* and held that on the particular facts of that case, the interactive service provider Prodigy was not a distributor and therefore was not entitled to any special protection. The court acknowledged that "[c]omputer bulletin boards should generally be regarded in the same context as bookstores, libraries, and network affiliates," but it held that Prodigy was not a distributor because it decided to exercise editorial control over its bulletin boards. The court noted as follows:

> First, Prodigy held itself out to the public and its members as controlling the content of its computer bulletin boards. Second, Prodigy implemented this con-trol through its automatic software screening program, and the Guidelines which Board Leaders are required to enforce. By actively utilizing technology and manpower to delete notes from its computer bulletin boards on the basis of offensiveness and "bad taste," for example, Prodigy is clearly making deci-sions as to content . . . and such decisions constitute editorial control. That such control is not complete and is enforced both as early as the notes arrive and as late as a complaint is made, does not minimize or eviscerate the simple fact that Prodigy has uniquely arrogated to itself the role of determining what is proper for its members to post and read on its bulletin boards.[124]

As discussed in Section 5.2.1, Congress overruled the result of *Stratton Oak-mont* by enacting section 230, in part because the holding seemed to create the perverse incentive for service providers not to screen their services for illegal and otherwise offensive content.

---

122. *Id.* at 140.
123. Stratton Oakmont, Inc. v. Prodigy Servs., Inc., 1995 WL 323710 (N.Y. Sup. Ct. May 24, 1995).
124. *Id.* at *4.

Of course, Congress's enactment does not necessarily control how a court would classify an interactive service provider for *constitutional* purposes. But the *Stratton Oakmont* classification has yet to find sympathy in other courts. Indeed, the New York courts themselves overruled *Stratton Oakmont* on grounds apart from section 230. In *Lunney v. Prodigy Services Co.*,[125] the highest court of New York rejected the *Stratton Oakmont* holding on common-law principles. In particular, the court relied upon an earlier case giving telephone companies a common-law immunity from liability for third-party content they transmit.[126] The case on which *Lunney* relied, *Anderson v. New York Telephone Co.*,[127] held that a telephone company, unlike a telegraph company, is not a publisher of third-party content.[128] In addition, the lower court dissent that the *Anderson* court adopted stated that, even if a telephone company were the equivalent of a publisher, it would be protected by a qualified common-law immunity from defamation that New York courts had extended to telegraph companies.[129] *Lunney*, in turn, held that "we are unwilling to deny Prodigy the common-law qualified privilege accorded to telephone and telegraph companies" and concluded that "Prodigy was not a publisher" of messages on its electronic bulletin boards.[130]

Assuming interactive service providers are distributors, they are entitled to special First Amendment protection. In particular, a distributor generally cannot be held liable for third-party content unless it has the requisite scienter regarding the nature and character of the content. In *Smith v. California*,[131] the U.S. Supreme Court invalidated an obscenity statute that allowed a bookseller to be prosecuted even if that bookseller did not have knowledge of the contents of the offensive material, on the ground that such a rule would force the bookseller to make a dramatic reduction in the books sold in his shop. The Court explained that:

> [by]y dispensing with any requirement of knowledge of the contents of the book on the part of the seller, the ordinance tends to impose a severe limitation on the public's access to constitutionally protected matter. For if the bookseller is criminally liable without knowledge of the contents, and the ordinance fulfills its purpose, he will tend to restrict the books he sells to those he has inspected. . . . "Every bookseller would be placed under an obligation to make himself aware of the contents of every book in his shop. It would be altogether unreasonable to demand so near an approach to omniscience." . . . If the contents of bookshops and periodical stands were restricted to material of which their proprietors had made an inspection, they might be depleted indeed.[132]

---

125. Lunney v. Prodigy Servs. Co., 701 N.Y.S.2d 684, 687 (1999).
126. *Id.* at 686–87.
127. Anderson v. New York Tel. Co., 320 N.E.2d 647 (N.Y. 1974).
128. *See id.* at 648–49.
129. *See* Anderson v. New York Tel. Co., 345 N.Y.S.2d 740, 750 (Sup. Ct. App. Div. 1973) (Witmer, J., dissenting).
130. *Lunney*, 701 N.Y.S.2d at 686–87.
131. Smith v. California, 361 U.S. 147 (1959).
132. *Id.* at 153.

Smith's position applies equally to interactive service providers.

What is not clear, however, is the precise mental state a distributor must have before the First Amendment will permit criminal liability to attach based upon third-party content. The First Amendment does not require that an interactive service provider know the third-party material actually meets the formal legal standard for what is obscene, or otherwise violates the law. Rather, as the U.S. Supreme Court explained in *Hamling v. United States*,[133] to hold a distributor liable, "[i]t is constitutionally sufficient that the prosecution show that a defendant had knowledge of the contents of the materials he distributed, and that he knew the character and nature of the materials."[134] Thus, if an interactive service provider has knowledge of the character and nature of third-party content—whether or not it knows the material is technically unlawful—*Smith* would not prevent a court from holding the service provider liable for that material.

Moreover, even "knowledge" may not be required. The Court in *Smith* was careful to explain it was not deciding "what sort of mental element is requisite to a constitutionally permissible prosecution of a bookseller for carrying an obscene book in stock."[135] Since *Smith*, the minimum mental state required has remained unclear. As one commentator recently observed, "[i]n consistently reaffirming the rule of *Smith*—that strict liability with regard to the obscenity of material is unconstitutional—the Court has not identified the minimum mental state needed to pass constitutional muster."[136] In *Mishkin v. New York*,[137] the Supreme Court held that the following "weak knowledge"[138] definition of scienter—which the New York Court of Appeals had read into an obscenity statute—"fully meets the demands of the Constitution": "[O]nly those who are in some manner aware of the character of the material they attempt to distribute should be punished. It is not innocent but calculated purveyance of filth which is exorcised. . . ."[139] And in *Osborne v. Ohio*,[140] the Supreme Court allowed punishment for child pornography if the purveyor has a reckless mental state.[141]

Whether a distributor can be punished when it merely has "reason to know" the nature of the content distributed is much less clear. One source of this confusion is the U.S. Supreme Court's decision in *Ginsburg v. New York*.[142] In *Ginsburg*, the Court upheld a New York statute that prohibited "knowingly" selling obscene materials to minors. The defendant challenged the statute's

---

133. Hamling v. United States, 418 U.S. 87 (1974).
134. *Id.* at 123.
135. *Smith*, 361 U.S. at 154.
136. Allen C. Michaels, *Constitutional Innocence*, 112 Harv. L. Rev. 828, 870 (1999).
137. Mishkin v. New York, 383 U.S. 502 (1966).
138. Michaels, *supra* note 136, at 870.
139. *Mishkin*, 383 U.S. at 510 (quoting definition of scienter read into New York anti-obscenity statute by New York Court of Appeals in *People v. Finkelstein*, 174 N.E.2d 470, 471 (N.Y. 1961)).
140. Osborne v. Ohio, 495 U.S. 103 (1990).
141. *See id.* at 115 (stating punishment for mental state of recklessness "plainly satisfies the requirement . . . that prohibitions on child pornography include some element of scienter").
142. Ginsburg v. New York, 390 U.S. 629 (1968).

scienter requirement because it defined "knowingly" to include "reason to know" or "a belief or ground for belief which warrants further inspection or inquiry of both: (i) the character and content of any material . . . which is reasonably susceptible of examination by the defendant, and (ii) the age of the minor."[143] The Supreme Court rejected the defendant's challenge, but in doing so did not approve a "reason to know" standard. Instead, the Court interpreted the statute prohibiting distribution of obscene material to minors as incorporating the same scienter definition as it approved in *Mishkin*.[144] The Court thus found it unnecessary to define further "what sort of mental element is requisite to a constitutionally permissible prosecution."[145]

Despite the fact that *Ginsburg* inferred a knowledge requirement into the New York statute, some lower courts have interpreted *Ginsburg* as approving a "reason to know" standard.[146] Though it did not rely upon *Ginsburg*, *Cubby* also stated that "the appropriate standard of liability to be applied to CompuServe is whether it knew or *had reason to know* of the allegedly defamatory . . . statements."[147] There is substantial doubt, however, whether such a watered-down version of the scienter requirement passes constitutional muster.

In sum, interactive service providers should be able to assert the same First Amendment protections as traditional information distributors. But the scope of this protection is unclear. Although knowledge of the "character and nature of the [third-party] materials" and even recklessness is sufficient, it remains unclear whether the First Amendment permits holding a distributor criminally liable for third-party content if it only had "reason to know" the character of that content.

3. Service Provider Liability for Copyright Infringement by Third-Party Content

One legal arena that has been the subject of some of the most intense discussions after the spread of the Internet and other online media has been whether, and when, online service providers should be liable for copyright infringement in connection with third-party material carried over—or available on—their systems. As discussed in Chapter 3, under traditional copyright law, service providers are potentially liable for direct, contributory and/or vicarious infringe-

---

143. *Id.* at 643–44.
144. *See id.* Michaels observed that "[t]his holding would seem to limit application of the New York statute to those with some degree of knowledge." Michaels, *supra* note 136, at 870 n.225 (citing *Hamling*, 418 U.S. at 123).
145. *See Ginsburg*, 390 U.S. at 644–45 (quoting *Smith*, 361 U.S. at 154).
146. *See, e.g.*, Newman v. Conover, 313 F. Supp. 623 (N.D. Tex. 1970); St. John v. North Carolina Parole Comm'n, 764 F. Supp. 403 (W.D.N.C. 1991).
147. *Cubby*, 776 F. Supp. at 140–41 (emphasis added).

ment, and courts have begun to develop law on the circumstances in which such liability attaches. Not surprisingly, service providers have long argued that such liability is unreasonable, particularly because many activities in which they engage (from caching to hosting) naturally involve copying third-party content, but they have no practical way of screening such material for copyright infringement.

In 1998, Congress at least partially heeded the call of service providers when it enacted the Digital Millennium Copyright Act (DMCA).[148] DMCA includes "safe harbors" that insulate "service providers" from liability for monetary relief for copyright infringement by third-party content in connection with four of the more common functions provided online: (1) acting as a conduit for electronic communications, (2) automatic system caching or mirroring, (3) hosting or otherwise storing information at a user's request and (4) providing information location tools such as a search engine. These safe harbors are independent and not mutually exclusive. For example, a service provider may meet the prerequisites for two of the safe harbors (and therefore be immune from liability in connection with those two functions), but fail to satisfy the conditions of a third safe harbor (and therefore be potentially subject to liability in connection with that third function).[149] If a service provider does fail to satisfy the prerequisites for one of these safe harbors, preexisting copyright law governs its potential liability.

The four safe harbors immunize service providers from liability for monetary relief and, in most circumstances, injunctive or other equitable relief for copyright infringement. It is important to note that the statutory safe harbors do not extend beyond copyright infringement. For example, a service provider may not rely upon these safe harbors as a defense against a claim that the provider violated 17 U.S.C. § 1201(a), which prohibits the circumvention of products and technologies designed to protect copyrights.[150] Moreover, even for copyright infringement claims, a court may order a service provider whose activities fall within a safe harbor to (1) terminate the account of a subscriber or account holder using the service to engage in infringing activity and (2) refrain from providing access, by taking reasonable steps specified in the court order, to a specific online location outside the United States.[151]

The safe harbors apply to persons or entities that fit within the definition of a "service provider" in 17 U.S.C. § 512(k). To qualify as a "service provider" for purposes of the "conduit" safe harbor, a company must be

---

148. The DMCA includes a number of separate measures; the portion discussed herein is Title II of the DMCA, designated as the Online Copyright Infringement Liability Limitation Act, Pub. L. No. 105–304, 112 Stat. 2860, 2877 (1998).

149. 17 U.S.C. § 512(n) (2000); A&M Records, Inc. v. Napster, Inc., 54 U.S.P.Q.2d 1746, 2000 WL 573136 (N.D. Cal. May 12, 2000), *aff'd in part and rev'd in part*, 239 F.3d 1004 (9th Cir. 2001).

150. *See* Universal City Studios, Inc. v. Reimerdes, 82 F. Supp. 2d 211, 217 & n.17 (S.D.N.Y. 2000).

151. 17 U.S.C. § 512(j)(1)(B) (2000).

an entity offering the transmission, routing, or providing of connections for digital online communications, between or among points specified by a user, of material of the user's choosing, without modification to the content of the material as sent or received.

17 U.S.C. § 512(k)(1)(A).[152]

For the remainder of the safe harbors, a "service provider" is more broadly defined as any "provider of online services or network access, or the operator of facilities therefor," including services that provide the conduit function discussed above. 17 U.S.C. § 512(k)(1)(B). Under current case law there is some discrepancy concerning the scope of "online services" that qualifies an entity as a "service provider." On the one hand, in a case discussed in further detail below, the Ninth Circuit apparently considered it to be a "significant" question whether Napster, Inc. provided "online services" that would qualify it as a service provider.[153] On the other hand, the Fourth Circuit understood "online services" to be entitled to a significantly broader construction.[154] In addition, the DMCA imposes two threshold requirements for safe-harbor eligibility. First, the service provider must not interfere with reasonable, industry-standard technical measures used to identify or protect copyrighted materials (as long as such measures do not impose "substantial costs . . . or substantial burdens" on the provider).[155] Second, a provider must have "adopted and reasonably implemented" a policy providing for termination of a subscriber who is a "repeat infringer," and inform subscribers of this policy.[156] This second requirement, at least, may pose a more substantial hurdle than it first appears. In *A&M Records, Inc. v. Napster, Inc.*,[157] the district court found there were genuine issues of material fact concerning whether a provider "reasonably implemented" its termination policy, when the provider blocked the password of an infringing user but did not block the user's IP address (allowing the user to register using a new name and password).[158]

Assuming a service provider satisfies these two threshold requirements, it may be entitled to immunity for copyright infringement by third-party content

---

152. According to the legislative history, this definition is derived from the definition of "telecommunications" in 47 U.S.C. § 153(48) and is meant to refer only to the act of carrying digital information over "digital or analog networks." S. Rep. No. 105–190 at 54 (1998); *see also* H.R. Rep. No. 105–551 Pt. 2 at 63 (1998). The function described by this definition is the act of providing connectivity. *See* S. Rep. No. 105–190 at 54 (stating that "hosting a World Wide Web site does not fall within" this definition, but "providing connectivity" for such a site does fall within this definition); H.R. Rep. No. 105–551 Pt. 2 at 63 (same).

153. *See* A&M Records, Inc. v. Napster, Inc., 239 F.3d 1004, 1025 (9th Cir. 2001). Somewhat confusingly, the *Napster* court phrased the issue as whether Napster was a service provider "as defined by 17 U.S.C. § 512(d)," which presumably incorporates by reference the applicable definition in 17 U.S.C. § 512(k)(1)(B).

154. *See* ALS Scan, Inc. v. RemarQ Communities, Inc., 2001 WL 98364 at *4 (4th Cir. Feb. 6, 2001). *ALS* involved a service provider that connected subscribers with Usenet newsgroups, through which copyrighted photographs were being copied by, and distributed among, members.

155. *Id.* §§ 512(i)(1)(B), 512(i)(2).

156. *Id.* § 512(i)(1)(A).

157. A&M Records, Inc. v. Napster, Inc., 2000 WL 573136 (N.D. Cal. May 12, 2000).

158. *Id.* at *9–*10.

under one of the four safe harbors. Each safe harbor requires the service provider to satisfy certain conditions.

i. Transitory Digital Network Communications

The first safe harbor applies when a service provider acts as a conduit for infringing material; more specifically, when a service provider is engaged in "transmitting, routing, or providing connections for material through a system or network controlled or operated by or for a service provider," as well as the "intermediate and transient storage" associated with such transmission.[159] This safe harbor applies only if a third party initiates or directs the transmission and selects both the material to be transmitted and its recipients.[160] Conversely, the safe harbor does not apply if the service provider stores a copy of the material for longer than reasonably necessary for transmission, or modifies the material's content during transmission.[161]

To date, only one case has construed the meaning of this safe harbor. In *A&M Records, Inc. v. Napster, Inc.*,[162] plaintiff record companies sued Napster for alleged contributory and vicarious copyright infringement. Napster operates a web site that enables users to exchange MP3 music files that provide the user with unauthorized copies of songs copyrighted by the companies. After downloading Napster's MusicShare software (provided without charge), a user can access the Napster system from her computer. The user can elect to share MP3 files with other users of the system. Napster's server maintains an index and directory of all MP3 files that its users have collectively chosen to make available. A user can enter the name of a song or artist in a search page of the MusicShare program to locate a list of matching files. If the user selects a file to download, the Napster server facilitates a connection between the user requesting the file and the user offering it, by obtaining the offering user's IP address and providing that address to the requesting user's software. The server then initiates the downloading of the file without any further action by either user. The file itself is then transmitted over the Internet without passing through Napster's server.[163]

Napster claimed its activities were entitled to the conduit safe harbor. The plaintiffs disagreed, arguing that the MP3 files are not "transmit[ted] ... *through* a system or network controlled or operated" by Napster: the MP3 files reside on the users' computers and are transmitted between them through the public Internet.[164] Napster countered that the MusicShare browser software re-

---

159. 17 U.S.C. § 512(a) (2000).
160. *Id.*
161. *Id.*
162. A&M Records, Inc. v. Napster, Inc., 2000 WL 573136 (N.D. Cal. May 12, 2000), *aff'd in part and rev'd in part*, 239 F. 3d 1004 (9th Cir. 2001).
163. *Id.* at *1–*2.
164. *Id.* at *4.

siding on each user's computer was part of Napster's system. The District Court for the Northern District of California rejected Napster's argument. It held that even assuming Napster's characterization was correct, the transmission of the files did *not* occur "through a system or network controlled" by Napster because it simply occurred over the public Internet; at most, the court concluded, the transmission went *between* parts of Napster's system, not *through* it.[165]

The district court further concluded that Napster did not "provid[e] connections through a system or network" controlled by it. The court held that although Napster's system supplies the information necessary to establish a connection between the two users, "the connection itself occurs through the Internet."[166] In other words, although Napster may serve as a "conduit" for the address information that makes the connection possible, it is not a conduit for the connection itself.[167] On appeal, the Ninth Circuit did not directly review the district court's analysis of § 512(a), holding only that plaintiffs had "raise[d] serious questions regarding Napster's ability to obtain shelter under § 512." [168]

The lower court *Napster* decision—assuming other courts follow it—has the potential to limit the scope of the conduit safe harbor significantly. Read broadly, it might even suggest that any transmission that travels at least in part over the public Internet does not fall within the ambit of the safe harbor. Alternatively, the decision may be limited only to communications that do not at any point transit over the service provider's servers or other facilities. Like the statute itself, the decision leaves open many questions that will be answered only as more cases are litigated.

ii. System Caching

This safe harbor applies to the "intermediate and temporary storage of material on a system or network controlled or operated by or for the service provider," or what is known as *caching* or *mirroring*.[169] The safe harbor is limited to material that is (1) made available online by a third party, such as the original web site, (2) transmitted by that third party through the service provider's system to someone requesting the material and (3) stored only temporarily and automatically for the purpose of making the material available for requests by other subscribers or users of the service provider's system.[170] For example, if a user of a service such as Earthlink enters the Uniform Resource Locator (URL) of a site to call up that web site, Earthlink may automatically and temporarily

---

165. *Id.* at *7–*8.
166. *Id.*
167. *Id.*
168. *See* A&M Records, Inc. v. Napster, Inc., 239 F.3d 1004, 1025 (9th Cir. 2001).
169. 17 U.S.C. § 512(b) (2000).
170. *Id.* § 512(b)(1).

store the contents of that site on its system so it can make the contents available to another Earthlink subscriber that subsequently requests the same site. To qualify for this safe harbor, a service provider must:

1. leave the cached content unmodified,
2. comply with the rules specified by the original site governing refreshing, reloading or otherwise updating material, as long as these rules are consistent with generally accepted industry standards and are not used by the original site to prevent or unreasonably impair caching,
3. not interfere with technology that records and relays information about the use of the material (such as measuring the number of "hits" on a particular web site), as long as that technology does not significantly interfere with the provider's own system or caching and is consistent with general industry standards,
4. limit access to cached material to subscribers meeting substantially the same conditions that are required to access the material directly on the original site (for example, registering, subscriber or payment of a fee) and
5. promptly remove or disable access to cached material upon receiving notification of claimed infringement from a copyright owner, when the notification states the material has been removed or disabled from the original site, or a court has ordered such removal or disablement.[171]

Generally, most caching activities used by service providers today should qualify for protection under this safe harbor.

iii. Information Residing on a Service Provider's System or Network at the Direction of Users

This safe harbor applies when a service provider stores material on its system or network at the direction of the user, such as in connection with the provision of web hosting services.[172] To qualify for this safe harbor, a service provider may not receive any financial benefit directly attributable to the infringing activity (as opposed to a flat rated subscription fee for its service), if it has the right and ability to control the infringing activity.[173] The service provider also must expeditiously remove or disable access to material if it gains actual knowledge that the material (or an activity using the material) is infringing, or becomes aware of facts and circumstances that make infringement apparent.[174]

---

171. *Id.* § 512(b)(2).
172. *Id.* § 512(c).
173. *Id.* § 512(c)(1).
174. *Id.*

This safe harbor also requires service providers to abide by a relatively complex notice and takedown (and counternotification) procedure for situations in which a person provides notice that material being stored at a user's behest infringes upon a copyright owned by the person providing notice. A service provider must designate an agent for receiving such notice and provide to users—somewhere on its web site or service—contact information for that agent.[175] The statute has detailed requirements for the information an effective notification of alleged infringement must contain, including the identity of the copyrighted work allegedly being infringed and the allegedly infringing material.[176] In *ALS Scan, Inc. v. RemarQ Communities, Inc.*,[177] the Fourth Circuit construed compliance with the notice provision generously. In *ALS*, the plaintiff was a company that created and distributed "adult" photographs. The defendant was an Internet service provider that connected subscribers to a variety of newsgroups, including two that used the ALS name—"alt.als" and "alt.binaries.pictures.erotica.als." Plaintiff's notice asserted that these newsgroups were "created for the sole purpose of violating our Federally filed Copyrights and Tradename."[178] Defendant refused to block access to these newsgroups but advised that it would eliminate individually-identified infringing items from the newsgroups. The court held that plaintiff's notice substantially complied by (1) identifying sites created for the sole purpose of publishing plaintiff's copyrighted works; (2) asserting that virtually all the images at the sites were its copyrighted material; and (3) referring defendant to two URLs where defendant could find pictures of plaintiff's models and obtain plaintiff's copyright information.[179]

Upon receipt of a notice substantially complying with the statutory requirements, the service provider must expeditiously remove the allegedly infringing material to remain within the safe harbor; alternatively, a service provider may choose to ignore the notice because, for example, it believes the subscriber's activities constitute "fair use," but this would deprive the service provider of the safe-harbor protection, and the notice itself may increase the service provider's exposure to liability for contributory infringement.[180]

Upon removing the material that is the subject of this kind of notice, the service provider—to insulate itself from potential liability to the subscriber or user that initially directed the provider to store the removed material—must take reasonable steps to notify the affected subscriber promptly.[181] The subscriber, in turn, may make a counternotification to the service provider, stating

175. *Id.* § 512(c)(2).
176. *Id.* § 512(c)(3).
177. 2001 WL 98364 (4th Cir. Feb. 6, 2001).
178. *Id.* at *1.
179. *Id.* at *7.
180. 17 U.S.C. § 512(c)(1)(C). The statute further provides that when a notice does not meet the statutory requirements, the notice generally may not be considered in evaluating whether the service provider had reason to know the material was infringing and therefore had an independent duty to remove the material. *Id.* § 512(c)(3)(B).
181. *Id.* § 512(g).

under penalty of perjury that the subscriber has a good-faith belief that the material was removed as a result of a mistake or misidentification.[182] If a service provider receives such a counternotification that meets the statutory requirements, it must then provide a copy of that counternotification to the person who originally claimed the material was infringing.[183] That person may then file a legal action seeking a court order prohibiting the subscriber from engaging in infringing activity related to the removed material.[184] If, however, the service provider does not receive notice of such an action, it must, within ten to fourteen business days after receiving the counternotice, replace the removed material.[185]

iv. Information Location Tools

This safe harbor applies to a service provider when it refers or links users to an online location containing infringing material, such as through a hypertext link, a search engine or some other index or pointer.[186] A service provider must satisfy the same conditions as delineated above in connection with storing information at a user's behest: (1) a provider must not have knowledge that the material is infringing or of facts making such infringement apparent, (2) not receive financial benefits directly attributable to the infringing material if the provider has the right and ability to exercise control over the material and (3) remove (and restore) allegedly infringing material in accordance with the same notice and counternotice regime.[187]

4. Conclusion

The DMCA regime is clearly quite complex and detailed and leaves many questions to be answered by courts that interpret it in the coming years. It is interesting to note the contrast between this statute and section 230, discussed earlier in connection with other forms of liability for third-party content. Section 230 provides almost blanket immunity from liability for third-party content (with, of course, a few exceptions such as enforcement of federal criminal statutes and intellectual property). In particular, as construed by the courts, section 230 immunity applies even when the service provider has notice or otherwise knows

---

182. *Id.*
183. *Id.*
184. *Id.*
185. *Id.*
186. *Id.* § 512(d).
187. *Id.*

that particular content is unlawful. In contrast, DMCA imposes detailed procedures and requirements that a service provider must satisfy to take advantage of its safe harbors. Moreover, in direct contrast to section 230, at least three DMCA safe harbors do not apply once the service provider has notice or other reason to believe that the third-party material is infringing. Congress may well have had policy reasons for this difference; for example, copyright violations may be a sufficiently circumscribed category, when compared with more open-ended torts such as defamation and infliction of emotional distress, so there is less threat of suppression of speech as a result of spurious claims that particular content is illegal. In any case, unlike section 230, service providers that wish to take advantage of the DMCA safe harbors should carefully study the statute and adopt policies and procedures consistent with its requirements.

§ 4.2 Third-Party Content Liability in Europe

1. EU Legal Framework

There are currently fifteen Member States of the European Union (EU).[188] Various EU Member States[189] have adopted or proposed legislation to make host service providers liable for content hosted on their servers only when they (1) can reasonably be expected to be aware that the content is prima facie illegal or (2) fail to take reasonable measures to remove such content, once it has been brought to their attention. Thus, once a host service provider becomes aware of the prima facie illegality of the content hosted on its server, in principle, the legislation in those Member States requires that the host service provider take steps to remove the content. Some rules go beyond this and require access providers to restrict access to other sites containing illegal content.

It is the intent of the European Community (EC)[190] to provide minimum legal standards for e-commerce and related technologies, while at the same time not encumber the development of e-commerce by placing excessive legal burdens on Internet service providers regarding content liability. Only an EU-level

---

188. These are Austria, Belgium, Denmark, Finland, France, Germany, Greece, Ireland, Italy, Luxembourg, The Netherlands, Portugal, Spain, Sweden and the United Kingdom.

189. Austria, France, Germany and the United Kingdom, for example.

190. Although the EU provides a common "shelter" for cooperation of its Member States, it is still the EC (formerly EEC) that passes the relevant pieces of legislation and undertakes nearly all other relevant legal actions.

legal framework on content liability will induce the Member States to modify or clarify their national laws to facilitate the activities of Internet service providers by creating a balance between potential exposure to third-party content liability on the one hand, and avoidance of inappropriate censoring of third-party content (by the Internet service providers) on the other hand.

A great number of different national laws—related to areas such as contracts, torts, unfair competition and consumer protection—currently govern business activities in the Member States. It is clearly the responsibility of Member States to ensure the application of existing laws regarding content liability on the Internet, including intellectual property laws, criminal laws and laws relating to the protection of minors. Of course, while the criminal laws of a particular country may forbid certain content under threat of criminal prosecution, the global nature of the Internet means the author, content provider and Internet service provider may all be outside the jurisdiction of national law enforcers. For effective enforcement, therefore, the Member States must define certain minimum common standards in their criminal legislation.

2. The Measures of the EC

In 1996, the European Parliament determined that liability of Internet service providers should be regulated at the international level.[191] It called upon the European Commission (Commission) to submit proposals for a common regulation of liability for Internet content.

On January 25, 1999, the European Parliament and the European Council of Member States (Council) adopted an action plan for promoting safer use of the Internet by combating illegal and harmful content on global networks.[192] The action plan covers a period of four years, from January 1, 1999, to December 31, 2002, and has the objective of promoting safer use of the Internet and encouraging, at the European level, an environment favorable to the development of the Internet industry. The responsibility for prosecuting and punishing those responsible for illegal content remains with the national law enforcement authorities.

Only with the E-commerce Directive, *Certain Legal Aspects of Information Society Services, in particular Electronic Commerce, in the Internal Market* (E-commerce Directive)[193] and the draft *Directive for the Harmonization of Cer-*

---

191. Resolution of 24 April 1997 on the Commission Communication on Illegal and Harmful Content on the Internet, 1997 O.J. (C 150) 38.

192. Decision No. 2761999EC of the European Parliament and of the Council of 25 January 1999 Adopting a Multiannual Community Action Plan on Promoting Safer Use of the Internet by Combating Illegal and Harmful Content on Global Networks, 1999 O.J. (L 033) 1–11.

193. Directive 2000/31/CE of the European Parliament and of the Council of 8 June 2000 on Certain Legal Aspects of Information Society Services, in particular Electronic Commerce, in the Internal Market, 2000 O.J. (L 178) 1–16.

tain Aspects of Copyright Law and Related Rights in the Information Society (Copyright Directive)[194] has the EC taken a decisive step toward a common regulation of this new medium. Both directives are intended to provide a new and common foundation within the Internal Market for the core areas of the new media environment, including the Internet.

The directives share similar elements.[195] They are technology-neutral; that is, they are not specific to a particular technology and thus should not become outdated, despite the rapid development of Internet technologies.[196] The directives are not directly applicable EC law; they must first be implemented by the Member States. Thus, the directives do not set forth detailed rules, but rather, enjoin the Member States from imposing certain restrictive regulations in their national laws. Also, both directives are intended to promote competition in the Internal Market, and their aim is to create minimum standards and legal certainty in the Member States.

i. The E-Commerce Directive

The E-commerce Directive applies only to providers of Information Society Services[197] (ISS) established within the EU. Member States have eighteen months to implement the E-commerce Directive into their national laws following its publication in the Official Journal of the European Communities.[198]

The E-commerce Directive is aimed at ensuring that ISS providers (1) benefit from the Internal Market principles of free movement of services and free-

---

194. Directive 2001/29/EC of the European Parliament and of the Council of 22 May 2001 on the Harmonization of Certain Aspects of Copyright and Related Rights in the Information Society, 2001 O.J. (L 167) 10–19.

195. To stay within the scope of this chapter, Section 4.2 focuses upon the parts of these directives that relate to Internet content liability. Note, however, that the scope of the directives is much broader, given that the commercial use of new media also affects other areas of law.

196. The E-commerce Directive covers all Information Society Services, both business-to-business and business-to-consumer, and services provided free of charge to the recipient (for example, funded by advertising or sponsorship revenue), and services allowing online electronic transactions, such as interactive teleshopping and online shopping malls. Examples of sectors and activities covered include online newspapers, online databases, online financial services, online professional services (such as lawyers, doctors, accountants and estate agents), online entertainment services (such as video on demand), online direct marketing and advertising, and services providing access to the World Wide Web.

197. Information Society Service means any service normally provided for remuneration, at a distance, by electronic means, and at the individual request of a recipient of services. At "a distance" means that the service is provided without the parties being simultaneously present. "By electronic means" means that the service is sent initially and received at its destination by means of electronic equipment for the processing (including digital compression) and storage of data, and is entirely transmitted, conveyed and received by wire, radio, optical means or other electromagnetic means. "At the individual request of a recipient of services" means that the service is provided through the transmission of data on individual request. The E-commerce Directive does not apply to radio or television broadcasting services, which are covered by Article 1(a) of Directive 89552EEC.

198. 2000 O.J. (L 178) 1–16.

dom of establishment and (2) can operate throughout the EU if they comply with the laws in their home Member States.[199]

A. Country-of-Origin Principle

Article 3.1 of the E-commerce Directive establishes the *Country-of-Origin Principle,* by determining that each Member State will ensure that the ISS provided by a service provider established in the Member State's territory will comply with the Member State's applicable national provisions that fall within the Coordinated Field (that is, EC legislation that coordinates Members' laws).

Article 2(c) of the E-commerce Directive defines an "established service provider" as a person or an entity who effectively pursues an economic activity through a fixed establishment for an indefinite period. This definition, in combination with Article 3.1, is therefore relevant in determining which national law applies to the service provider, and is designed to remove legal uncertainty by ensuring that a service provider does not elude regulation, given that the service provider is subject to the laws applicable in the Member State where it is established.

It is important to note that under the E-commerce Directive, the location of the ISS technical facilities (for example, the location of web sites or servers or mailboxes of the service provider) is not taken into consideration. Rather, the location where the actual business activity is conducted (usually where the registered office of the ISS provider is located) determines the country in which such service provider is "established" for purposes of the E-commerce Directive.

Instead of fully harmonizing the different national laws, the Country-of-Origin Principle provides that an ISS provider must comply only with the national laws of the country in which the service provider's business is established. The Country-of-Origin Principle reflects acknowledgement that a full harmonization process would not cope with the need for urgent measures to create the legal certainty that enhances e-commerce activities. As a desired side effect, the Country-of-Origin Principle should enable small and medium-sized enterprises to reduce the legal costs of the ISS providers, as they are not forced to ensure their activities are in line with the differing legal provisions of fifteen different Member States.

Impact on the Applicability of National Laws

Currently, it is difficult to perceive the effects the Country-of-Origin Principle will have on the conflict-of-law rules in the Member States, and vice versa.

---

199. The E-commerce Directive establishes specific harmonized rules only when strictly necessary to ensure that businesses and citizens can supply and receive ISS throughout the EU, regardless of frontiers. These areas include, inter alia, a definition of where operators are established, transparency obligations for operators, transparency requirements for commercial communications, conclusion and validity of electronic contracts, liability of Internet intermediaries, online dispute settlement and the role of national authorities. In other areas, the E-commerce Directive builds upon existing EU instruments that provide for harmonization or mutual recognition of national laws.

The conflict-of-law rules of each Member State determine which national law applies to cross-border agreements and other commercial and noncommercial activities, such as the provision of content through a web site that is, at least potentially, subject to more than one jurisdiction. Article 1(4) of the E-commerce Directive clarifies that it does not modify the national conflict-of-law rules. Therefore, it appears that under the new rules, companies doing business in several EU Member States may still need to comply with several different national laws if the conflict-of-law rules of the EU Member State in which they are established provide that certain foreign laws apply to foreign transactions, sales or other e-commerce activities. Therefore, it is predictable, for example, that the national laws on consumer protection issues, including related unfair competition practices, are not completely set aside by the Country-of-Origin Principle.

As mentioned, the E-commerce Directive provides that the Country-of-Origin Principle applies only if the service provider has an establishment within a Member State; the Country-of-Origin Principle requires a minimum of harmonization among jurisdictions, which cannot be assumed on a global level.

(1) Inherent Limitations

The Country-of-Origin Principle applies only to certain regulated areas that fall under the so-called Coordinated Field—that is, the field of EC legislation expressly intended to coordinate the Member States' laws relevant to the ISS (for example, the E-commerce Directive, the Data Protection Directive[200] and the Copyright Directive).

The legal framework provided by the Coordinated Field sets forth the requirements for the specific online activity as such—that is, it sets forth only the requirements that address the starting and conducting of the ISS (including quality and content). The Coordinated Field does not include the legal requirements applying to goods per se or their delivery, or the performance of services by other than electronic means.[201] These requirements are therefore subject to the applicable laws of the country in which the ISS are offered, regardless of whether a foreign or EU service provider offers them.

(2) Copyright Law

There are further exceptions to the Country-of-Origin Principle. In certain regulatory contexts, local laws apply regardless of whether the ISS are performed by a domestic or foreign service provider, or whether the law pertains to the Coordinated Field. These exceptions, listed in Article 3(3) of the E-commerce

---

200. Directive 95/46/EC of the European Parliament and of the Council of 24 October 1995 on the Protection of Individuals with regard to the Processing of Personal Data and the Free Movement of Such Data, 1995 O.J. (L 281) 31–50.

201. More specifically, the Coordinated Field does not cover requirements regarding safety regulations, labeling obligations, product liability or similar legal requirements.

Directive, include local laws governing copyrights and related proprietary rights, such as proprietary semiconductor rights, proprietary rights to databases and industrial property rights.[202] For these areas of the law, the creation of a common legal framework within the Member States is a goal of utmost importance. The Copyright Directive, discussed in Section 5.3.2.iii, is an additional step toward reaching this goal.

(3) Individual Protective Measures in Member States

On a case-by-case basis, Member States will be allowed under the E-commerce Directive to impose restrictions upon ISS supplied from another Member State if necessary to protect the public interest, on grounds such as the following: protection of minors; combating prejudice on grounds of race, sex, religion or nationality, including offenses to human dignity concerning individual persons; public health or security, including the protection of national security and defense interests; and consumer protection, including the protection of investors. In these cases, Member States are allowed to enact suitable measures on their own initiative, without being hindered by the Country-of-Origin Principle.

Such restrictions must be proportionate to their stated objective, however. Moreover, with the exception of cases of urgency or court actions (including preliminary proceedings and criminal investigations), the restrictions can be imposed only after the Member State where the service provider is established has been asked to take adequate measures and failed to do so, and the intention to impose restrictions has been notified to the Commission and to the Member State where the service provider is established. In cases of urgency or court actions, the Commission and the Member State of the service provider must be notified, as soon as possible, of the reasons for the restrictions (and the urgency). When the Commission considers the proposed or actual restrictions unjustified, Member States will be required to refrain from imposing them or must immediately cease them.

According to rulings of the European Court of Justice previous to the E-commerce Directive, the commercial activities of a company established in another Member State may be prohibited if such company relocates its establishment for the sole purpose of evading legal restrictions imposed by a Member State.[203] At this stage, it is difficult to predict whether such earlier case law is completely overruled by the Country-of-Origin Principle.

---

202. The exceptions contained in the Annex of Article 3(3) include local laws governing the spending of electronic money; direct insurance; contracting parties' ability to choose which law will govern their transactions; contractual obligations concerning consumer contracts; formality requirements regarding contracts establishing or transferring rights to real property, provided that the Member State in which the real property is located has prescribed such formality requirements; and whether unsolicited commercial communication by electronic mail or comparable individual communication is permitted.

203. TV 10 SACommissariaat voor de Media, ECJ Judgement of 05/10/1994, 1994 E.C.R. 1–4795.

(4) Relevance of the Brussels Convention and Lugano Convention

In connection with the exceptions to the Country-of-Origin Principle contained in the E-commerce Directive, it is worth mentioning the proposed amendments to the Brussels Convention and Lugano Convention.[204] These conventions regulate the jurisdiction of local courts as forums for legal actions and enforcers of judgments in the commercial areas. The draft revisions of these conventions proposed by the Commission provide that the local courts in a consumer's country of origin would generally have jurisdiction over disputes arising out of—or in connection with—consumer contracts. These proposed amendments, if enacted, would cause a portion of the area governed by the laws of the service provider's country of origin (such as direct solicitations of consumers and offers to consumers via the Internet, and related unfair competition practices) to be reallocated to the courts of the consumer's country of residence.

ii. Content Liability

The liability of service providers for unlawful content is governed by Articles 12 through 15 of the E-commerce Directive; those articles classify service providers depending upon the types of ISS being offered, and set forth the legal requirements for liability.

In light of the broad definition of ISS, any service provider that does no more than grant access to the Internet is potentially liable for unlawful third-party content. Given the critical role that service providers play in electronic commercial communications—crucial for further development of the European Internal Market—there is a real need to limit the liability of service providers for unlawful content, while defining duties that protect the Internet from the dispersion of unlawful content.

A. The Concept of "Mere Conduit"

To eliminate existing legal uncertainties and to avoid divergent approaches between Member States, Article 12 of the E-commerce Directive establishes an exemption from liability for those service providers that play a passive role as "mere conduits" for unlawful content from third parties.[205]

---

204. Council Regulation (EC) No. 44/2001 of 22 December 2000 on Jurisdiction of Courts and the Recognition and Enforcement of Judgments in Civil and Commercial Matters, 2001 O.J. (L 012) 1–23.

205. According to Article 12 of the E-commerce Directive, a service provider is not liable for the information transmitted, provided the service provider (1) does not initiate the transmission, (2) does not select

Article 12's mere-conduit exemption implies that a service provider renders to users not more than routing services and does refrain from any (other) form of direct communication of contents with users of such services. Article 12(1) therefore grants an exemption from liability for unlawful contents related to the provision of access to a communication network, and acts of transmission of information in which the service provider plays a passive role as a conduit of information for third parties. (The unlawful contents include those arising, for example, from copyright piracy, unfair competition practices, and criminally sanctioned and harmful contents of a racial, sexual and discriminatory nature, under the national laws of the Member States.)

Pursuant to Article 12(2), the acts of transmission and provision of access "include the automatic, intermediate and transient storage of the information transmitted in so far as this takes place for the sole purpose of carrying out the transmission in the communication network, and provided that the information is not stored for any period longer than is reasonably necessary for the transmission."[206]

Article 12(3) specifies that the above provisions do not prejudice the possibility of a court or administrative body, pursuant to the applicable legislation of the Member States, requiring that the service provider terminate or prevent an infringement related to unlawful contents.

B. The Concept of Caching

Article 13 regulates the responsibility of service providers who provide temporary storage of third-party content for quick access by other customers (known as caching). Article 13(1) grants an exemption from liability for illegal contents related to acts of transmission of information in which the service provider performs an "automatic, intermediate and temporary storage of that information . . . for the sole purpose of making more efficient the information's onward transmission to other recipients of the service upon their request,"[207] provided the service provider (1) does not modify the information, (2) complies with conditions regarding access to the information, (3) complies with rules regarding the updating of the information, (4) does not interfere with the lawful use of technology to obtain data on the use of the information and (5) acts expeditiously to remove or disable access to the information it has stored upon

---

the receiver of the transmission and (3) does not select or modify the information contained in the transmission.

206. *See supra* note 193, Art. 12(2).

207. *Id.* Art. 13(1). The definition of "recipient of a service" covers all types of usage of ISS, both by persons who provide information on open networks such as the Internet, and by persons who seek information on the Internet for private or professional reasons (Cons. 20 of the E-Commerce Directive).

having obtained "actual knowledge of the fact that the information at the initial source of the transmission has been removed from the network, or access to it has been disabled, or that a court or an administrative authority has ordered such removal or disablement."[208]

Article 13(2) specifies that the above provisions do not prejudice the possibility of a court or administrative body, pursuant to the applicable legislation of the Member States, requiring that the service provider terminate or prevent an infringement related to unlawful contents.

C. The Concept of Hosting

Article 14 concerns hosting—that is, the liability of service providers that do more than just temporarily store third-party content. Article 14(1) grants an exemption from liability for a third party's illegal content stored by a service provider, provided the service provider (1) "does not have actual knowledge of illegal activity or information and, as regards claims for damages, is not aware of facts or circumstances from which the illegal activity or information is apparent,"[209] or (2) "upon obtaining such knowledge or awareness, acts expeditiously to remove or to disable access to the information."[210] Article 14(2) specifies that this provision shall not apply when the server is operated under the authority or control of the service provider.

In addition, Article 14(3) clarifies that the above provisions do not prejudice the ability of a court or administrative body, pursuant to the applicable legislation of the Member States, to require the service provider to terminate or prevent an infringement related to unlawful content, nor do the above provisions prejudice the possibility of the Member States creating "procedures governing the removal or disabling of access information."[211]

D. No Monitoring Duties

Articles 12, 13 and 14 provide that under Article 15(1), service providers have no monitoring duties regarding information they transmit or store, nor do they have any general obligation to seek facts or circumstances indicating illegal content. A service provider is exempt from liability if it complies with applicable industry standards and promptly informs the competent public authorities upon learning of illegal content, thus preventing further dissemination of such illegal content. To the extent a service provider does not comply with

208. *Id.*
209. *Id.* Art. 14(1).
210. *Id.*
211. *Id.* Art. 14(3).

these requirements, it becomes subject to the liability laws of the Member State in which it is established.

E. Content Liability for Hyperlinks

It is difficult to determine where the law stands regarding liability for third-party content that a service provider makes available by way of hyperlinks. Article 21(2) of the E-commerce Directive provides that the liability of service providers in connection with hyperlinks, as well as the procedures for giving notice on and subsequent removal of unlawful content, together with the attribution of liability following such removal of content, shall be reviewed by the Commission in a report to the European Parliament, the Council and the Economic and Social Committee, three years after the E-commerce Directive becomes effective, and every two years thereafter. The report is to encompass technical and economic developments, rulings of the courts of the Member States and proposals for amendment of the E-commerce Directive.

iii. Copyright Directive

The Copyright Directive expressly states that it, in connection with copyright and related rights, supplements those provisions in the E-commerce Directive that address liability for activities in the network environment, including liability for unlawful content arising from acts in other areas such as defamation, misleading advertising or infringement of trademarks.[212] In other words, the Copyright Directive addresses aspects of content liability that are directly related to the lawful copying, transmission and other uses of copyright protected content on the Internet.

The Internet and, in general, the technical evolution, have made possible new forms of reproduction, such as acquiring printed works via scanner, or downloading and uploading digitized, copyright protected material. The Copyright Directive considers these new forms of reproduction when it establishes a clear EU-level framework of rules on the liability of intermediaries for copyright and related rights infringements. The Copyright Directive clearly identifies the works protected and the holders of copyright and related rights (rightholders).[213]

---

212. Cons. 16 of the Copyright Directive.

213. The Copyright Directive seeks to provide a harmonized and appropriate legal framework in the Internal Market for copyright and related rights in the Information Society. In particular, it seeks to harmonize the reproduction, communication, availability and distribution of works.

The Copyright Directive aims to achieve the correct balance between the interests of rightholders on the one hand, and those of other parties on the other hand (such as service providers, end users, consumers in general, equipment manufacturers, libraries, archives, educational and cultural establishments, and other beneficiaries of exceptions to rights in the Member States). In particular, the directive takes into account the possibilities offered by new technologies.

A. Reproduction Rights

Article 2 of the Copyright Directive calls upon Member States to provide authors with exclusive rights to authorize or prohibit "direct or indirect, temporary or permanent reproduction by any means and in any form, in whole or in part," of their works.[214]

Direct reproduction means the act of directly reproducing a work or other subject matters on identical or similar media. Indirect reproduction means reproduction that occurs, for example, in more than one phase (such as the recording of a sound that has occurred by phonogram). According to Article 2 of the Copyright Directive, temporary reproduction includes any kind of copying of a protected work onto the RAM of a computer (such as a display on a computer monitor). Permanent reproductions include the downloading of such work on hard disks or other data carriers.

Certain acts of copying protected works would therefore be lawful without prior authorization of the rightholder, under the following circumstances: (1) access to the site is conditioned upon payment of a fee, (2) visualization of the site necessarily entails copying information or (3) the nature of the work requires copying (for example, freeware and shareware must be downloaded in users' computers to be used).

B. Right of Communication to the Public

Article 3(1) of the Copyright Directive calls upon Member States to provide authors with exclusive rights to authorize or prohibit "any communication to the public of originals and copies of their works, by wire or wireless means, including the making available to the public of their works in such a way that members of the public may access them from a place and at a time individually chosen by them."[215] This is a clear reference to the Internet, where access is interactive and on demand.

---

214. *See supra* note 194, Art. 2.
215. *Id.* Art. 3(1).

Therefore, uploading—that is, introducing an intellectual property work into the network via a server—constitutes prohibited use of the work and thus must be authorized by the rightholder, regardless of whether such activity is conducted without the intention of making a profit. If the rightholder does not grant an authorization, the transaction or activity is illegal even if a legitimate user (such as a purchaser of the work) conducts the transaction or activity. In such cases, the principle of exhaustion (which applies to the right of distribution—see following discussion of Article 4) does not apply.

C. Distribution Right

Article 4(1) of the Copyright Directive calls upon Member States to provide authors—in connection with originals and any copies of their works—with exclusive rights to any form of distribution to the public. The distribution right will be exhausted within the EU only when the first sale or other transfer of ownership within the EU is made by the rightholder or with the rightholder's consent.

D. Exceptions to the Above Rights

The Copyright Directive lists exceptions to the above rights. Article 5(1) provides that the "temporary acts of reproduction referred to in Article 2, which are transient or incidental [and] an integral and essential part of a technological process, and whose sole purpose is to enable (a) a transmission in a network between parties by an intermediary, or (b) a lawful use of a work or other subject matter to be made, and which have no independent economic significance," shall be exempted from the rights granted under Article 2.[216] This is a mandatory exception required by all Member States, and is clearly applicable to certain Internet communications.

The other exceptions are optional for the Member States and may apply in specific cases that do not unreasonably prejudice the legitimate interests of the rightholders, and do not conflict with a normal exploitation of the work or other subject matter by their Rightholders. These exceptions may apply to reproduction for the following uses, for example: private use, use by noncommercial end users, use for the purpose of illustration in teaching and scientific research, use for the benefit of people with disabilities, specific acts of reproduction made by libraries for archiving or conservation purposes, or recordings of broadcasts made by social institutions.[217] In principle, rightholders are entitled to receive fair compensation in some of these cases.

---

216. *Id.* Art. 5.
217. These exceptions are similar to the "fair use" limitations provided under 17 U.S.C. § 107.

CHAPTER **5**

Regulation

Contents

Regulation

Chapter 5 addresses regulation of the Internet, including both criminal and noncriminal behavior. Chapter 5 focuses primarily upon U.S. law, given its wide scope and depth. The reader should be aware that many foreign jurisdictions either apply existing law or have developed new regulations applicable to the online context.

Section 5.1, written by Lawrence M. Hertz, analyzes U.S. laws and regulations that apply when advertising online. Hertz emphasizes Federal Trade Commission rules issued in both the online and offline contexts. Hertz briefly addresses state regulations in this area and discusses codes that have been developed by private industry, such as those published by the Better Business Bureau.

Section 5.2 of this chapter, written by Denis T. Rice, addresses securities regulations, particularly the sale of online securities. Rice describes applicable state and federal regulations and then discusses specific initiatives the Securities and Exchange Commission has pursued in the online context to prevent abuses, including its expectations concerning disclosures over the Internet. He closes with a discussion of state blue-sky initiatives regarding cybersecurities.

Thomas P. Vartanian authored Section 5.3 of this chapter. He addresses U.S. regulations applicable in the context of online banking. He begins his segment with a discussion of how the Internet is revolutionizing the way banks conduct business and then discusses existing banking regulations applicable to the Internet and how several of these laws and regulations overlap. He closes with a thorough analysis of federal agencies claiming jurisdiction and the rules they have issued.

Section 5.4, authored by Jennifer Gray, focuses upon antitrust regulation in the context of the Internet. Gray discusses how existing federal antitrust laws are particularly well suited for the Internet, especially given that the Internet has no geographic boundaries and is therefore ripe for abuse. She analyzes how certain practices on the Internet, such as restrictions on sales and advertising as well as exclusive dealing arrangements, may be prohibited under some circumstances. Gray also provides guidance on how business-to-business exchanges can stay clear of potential antitrust violations.

Peter J. Allen, in Section 5.5, discusses U.S. customs and export rules applicable to Internet commerce. Allen discusses the basis for U.S. jurisdiction in these areas by a variety of U.S. agencies. For each agency, he discusses the applicable prohibitions, license requirements and available exemptions. He closes his segment with useful advice on how to structure an e-business model to ensure compliance with the applicable regulations.

Finally, Section 5.6 explores consumer protection issues on the Internet in the context of self-regulation. Section 5.6.1, authored by Martin Saad, discusses how the OECD Guidelines set forth basic consumer protections and contemplate self-regulation by businesses as a major tool for implementing such protections. Section 5.6.2, authored by Elizabeth Blumenfeld, outlines how the BBB Code allows companies who participate and abide by its terms to place a seal of reliability on their web sites to boost consumers' confidence when accessing and using those sites.

§ 5.1 Advertising

Advertising on the Internet is subject to regulation from a variety of sources, including federal and state regulatory agencies, and private sector bodies. These sources, however, have not developed a separate body of law to deal specifically with this new and revolutionary medium. Instead, they have applied largely traditional law and regulation to protect consumers from misleading, deceptive and fraudulent advertising practices. Where practical differences from traditional media and technological factors have made clarification or modification necessary, these bodies have gradually modified their regulations. This section will discuss the major respects by which traditional advertising regulations have been adapted to meet the peculiarities of the Internet.

1. Federal Regulation

i. Federal Trade Commission

A. Background

The principal federal agency with jurisdiction over advertising generally is the Federal Trade Commission (the "Commission"). The principal federal statute used by the Commission to regulate advertising generally is the Federal Trade Commission Act (the "FTC Act").

Section 5 of the FTC Act prohibits all "unfair or deceptive acts or practices in or affecting commerce."[1] Section 12 of the FTC Act states that the dissemi-

---

1. 15 U.S.C. § 45(a)(1)(2001). Section 5 also prohibits "unfair methods of competition in or affecting commerce." This power, however, is part of its mission to enforce antitrust laws and is beyond the scope of this section.

nation of "false advertisements" (defined by the FTC Act as an advertisement that is misleading "in a material respect"[2]) relating to food, drugs, devices, services, or cosmetics constitutes one form of "unfair or deceptive act or practice."[3] Section 5 authorizes the Commission to issue cease and desist orders against those engaging in any such acts.[4] The FTC Act does not authorize anyone other than the Commission to enforce its provisions.

The Commission has issued three key policy statements under Section 5 of the FTC Act. Two of these policy statements articulate and summarize its positions on the "deception" and "unfairness" elements of a cause of action under Section 5. The third policy statement focuses on the concept of "substantiation" and on how the lack of substantiation for advertising claims impacts upon both elements.

An act or practice is "deceptive" if it involves a material "representation, omission or practice that is likely to mislead the consumer acting reasonably in the circumstances, to the consumer's detriment."[5] The Commission has considered information material when it is important to a consumer's decision whether to buy or use a product such as when it involves purpose, safety, efficacy, or cost, of the product or service, or its durability, performance, warranties or quality.[6] When representations or sales practices are targeted to any specific audience such as children, the elderly, or the terminally ill, the Commission evaluates the effect of the practice on a reasonable member of that group rather than the effect on consumers as a whole.[7]

An act or practice is "unfair" if it causes or is likely to cause "substantial injury to consumers" (such as monetary loss or unwarranted health or safety risks), which is "not reasonably avoidable by consumers themselves" and not "outweighed by countervailing benefits to consumers or to competition."[8]

An objective statement in an advertisement is deceptive and unfair if not substantiated.[9] Prior to disseminating an advertisement, all express or implied objective claims within it must have at least the advertised level of substantiation (e.g., nine out of ten doctors recommend, studies show, etc.). Absent an express or implied level of support, all claims must have at least a "reasonable level of support."[10] The type of evidence necessary to provide a "reasonable level of sup-

---

2. 15 U.S.C. § 55(a)(2001).

3. 15 U.S.C. § 52(b)(2001).

4. 15 U.S.C. § 45(b)(2001).

5. *See FTC Policy Statement on Deception, appended to Cliffdale Associates, Inc.*, 103 F.T.C. 110, 174 (1984), <http://www.ftc.gov/bcp/policystmt/ad-decept.htm> (last visited June 1, 2001) [hereinafter *Deception Policy Statement*].

6. *Id.*

7. *Id.*

8. 15 U.S.C. § 45(n)(2001). *See FTC Policy Statement on Unfairness, appended to International Harvester Co.*, 104 F.T.C. 949, 1070 (1984), <http://www.ftc.gov/bcp/policystmt/ad-unfair.htm> (last visited June 1, 2001) [hereinafter *Unfairness Policy Statement*].

9. *See FTC Policy Statement on Advertising Substantiation, appended to Thompson Medical Co.*, 104 F.T.C. 648, 839 (1984), *aff'd*, 791 F.2d 189 (D.C. Cir. 1986), *cert. denied*, 479 U.S. 1087 (1987), <http://www.ftc.gov/bcp/guides/ad3subst.htm> (last visited June 1, 2001) [hereinafter *Substantiation Policy Statement*].

10. *Id.*

port" depends upon several factors including "the type of claim [e.g., safety or health related], the product [e.g., food, drug or potentially hazardous product], the consequences of a false claim [e.g., injury to person or property], the benefits of a truthful claim, the cost of developing substantiation for the claim, and the amount of substantiation experts in the field believe is reasonable."[11]

The FTC Act empowers the Commission to issue rules ("Rules") and guides ("Guides") regarding "unfair or deceptive acts or practices in or affecting commerce."[12] Rules define specific acts and practices that the Commission has determined to be unfair or deceptive. Guides are administrative interpretations that provide examples and directions on how to avoid unfair or deceptive acts or practices.

The Commission has issued numerous Rules and eighteen Guides[13] addressing advertising claims made about products or services in specific industries. Among the most significant Guides and Rules are the *Mail or Telephone Order Merchandise Rule* (relating to requirements for product shipment claims, time periods within which products must be shipped and refund rights that must be offered to consumers when products are not shipped on time)[14]; *Guides for the Advertising of Warranties and Guarantees* (relating to the pre-sale availability of written warranty terms and certain pre-conditions for use of the phrases "satisfaction guaranteed," "money-back guaranty" and "free trial offer")[15]; *Guide Concerning Use of the Word "Free" and Similar Representations* (relating to certain limitations on the ability to use "free," "half-price," "2-for-1" and similar phrases in advertisements)[16]; and the *Guides Against Deceptive Pricing* (relating to certain limitations on how advertisers may refer to former prices, competitors' prices and manufacturers' suggested retail prices).[17]

B. Applicability of Traditional Law to Internet Advertising Generally

The FTC Act's prohibition in Section 5 addresses "deceptive acts and practices" generally without reference to a particular medium of dissemination. Accordingly, the Commission takes the position that its role in protecting consumers "encompasses advertising, marketing and sales online . . . [and is not limited] to those activities in print, television, telephone and radio."[18]

---

11. *Id.*; *Pfizer, Inc.*, FTC Dkt. 8819 [1970–73 Transfer Binder] Trade Reg. Rep. (CCH) ¶ 20,056 (July 11, 1972).

12. 15 U.S.C. § 57a (2001).

13. *See generally* 16 C.F.R. pt. 17–703 (2001).

14. 16 C.F.R. pt. 435 (2001).

15. 16 C.F.R. pt. 239 (2001).

16. 16 C.F.R. pt. 251 (2001).

17. 16 C.F.R. pt. 233 (2001).

18. *Dot Com Disclosures: Information About Online Advertising* (May 2000), <http://www.ftc.gov/bcp/conline/pubs/buspubs/dotcom/index.html> (last visited June 1, 2001) [hereinafter *Dot Com Disclosures*].

Rules and Guides, for the most part, address claims about products and services without reference to a particular medium of dissemination.[19] The Commission has concluded that "the plain language . . . [of these] rules and guides applies to claims made on the Internet."[20] In some instances, the Commission has amended a Rule or Guide to clarify its applicability to the Internet.[21] Rarely will a Rule or Guide not apply to the Internet. This would occur only if "its scope is . . . limited by how claims are communicated to consumers, how advertising is disseminated, or where commercial activities occur."[22]

C. "Clear and Conspicuous Disclosures" in Online Advertisements

Rules and Guides require that certain types of disclosures accompany various claims. Disclosures may be required for any of three reasons: (1) to prevent claims from being misleading or deceptive such as when an endorsed result is not typical of the result consumers might generally expect from a product or service,[23] (2) to ensure that consumers receive certain material terms in a transaction such as the terms of a warranty or how the consumer can obtain a free copy of such information,[24] or (3) for public policy reasons such as the disclosure of energy efficiency ratings on appliances to promote energy conservation.[25]

The terms of these Rules and Guides generally mandate that the required disclosures be set forth in a "clear and conspicuous" or "clear and prominent" manner, which are viewed synonymously by the Commission.[26] Some of the unique features of online advertising such as scrolling and hyperlinking, however, have raised questions as to whether a disclosure could be viewed as "clear and conspicuous" if a user could view the disclosure only by scrolling down the page or following a hypertext link. In May 2000, the Commission issued a staff working paper entitled *Dot Com Disclosures: Information About Online Advertising*[27] that focuses on how required disclosures can be presented "clearly

---

19. *Id.*
20. *Id.*
21. The Commission, for example, amended the *Mail or Telephone Order Merchandise Rule* to include "direct or indirect use of the telephone to order merchandise" thereby covering Internet purchases. 60 Fed. Reg. 56949 (1995) (codified at 16 C.F.R. § 435.2(b) (2001)); *The FTC's First Five Years Protecting Consumers Online* (December 1999) at n. 29, <http://www.ftc.gov/os/1999/9912/fiveyearreport.pdf> (last visited June 1, 2001) [hereinafter *FTC Five-Year Report*].
22. *Dot Com Disclosures, supra* note 18, at n. 8.
23. *See, e.g., Guides Concerning Use of Endorsements and Testimonials in Advertising*, 16 C.F.R. pt. 255, cited in *Dot Com Disclosures, supra* note 18, at n. 15.
24. *See, e.g., Guides for the Advertising of Warranties and Guarantees*, 16 C.F.R. pt. 239, cited in *Dot Com Disclosures, supra* note 18, at n. 16.
25. *See, e.g., Rule Concerning Disclosures Regarding Energy Consumption and Water Use of Certain Home Appliances and Other Products Required Under the Energy Policy and Conservation Act*, 16 C.F.R. pt. 305, cited in *Dot Com Disclosures, supra* note 18, at n. 17.
26. *Dot Com Disclosures, supra* note 18, at n. 8.
27. *Dot Com Disclosures, supra* note 18.

and conspicuously" in online advertisements. In recognition of the reality that there can be no set formula for a clear and conspicuous disclosure given the variety of types of online advertisements, the Commission's working paper recognized a six-part test.

To determine whether an online disclosure is "clear and conspicuous," the Commission will consider (1) the placement of the required disclosure and its proximity to the claim; (2) the prominence of the required disclosure; (3) the presence of distracting features within the advertisement; (4) the need for the repetition of the required disclosure due to the length of the advertisement; (5) the adequacy of volume, cadence and duration of any audio disclosure; and (6) the understandability of the language of the disclosure.

(1) Proximity and Placement of Disclosure to Ad

Where possible (and always in the case of cost, health and safety informa- tion[28]), disclosures should be placed on the same screen as the claim "next to the information, product or service to which it relates."[29] Where scrolling is necessary to view a disclosure, text prompts indicating the subject matter of the disclosure and importance of the information that consumers will find should be used, and the claim and related disclosure should not be separated by ex- cessive blank space or unrelated text or graphics.[30] Less critical disclosures, particularly when lengthy, may be hyperlinked to claims but (1) the hyperlink should clearly and obviously convey "the importance, nature and relevance of the information it leads to"; (2) hyperlink styles (e.g., text or graphics, format, color, etc.) should be used consistently throughout the site to signal the avail- ability of additional hyperlinked disclosures; (3) the hyperlink should be adja- cent to the triggering claim, easily noticeable, and not separated by other text, graphics, blank space or intervening hyperlinks; and (4) the hyperlink should take consumers directly to the disclosure on the click-through page which should be free of "distracting visual factors, extraneous information and 'click- away' opportunities.[31]

Consumer viewing behavior should be monitored to help evaluate whether the particular technique of disclosure selected (e.g., hyperlink, pop-up window, interstitial page, frame, scrolling marquee or other new tool) is an effective method of disclosure and appropriate adjustments should be made or an al- ternative method of disclosure should be selected where evidence indicates that consumers are not viewing a disclosure.[32]

Disclosures should be displayed prior to purchase, but disclosures should not be made solely on the order page.[33]

---

28. *Id.* § III.C.1.b.
29. *Id.* § III.C.1.a.
30. *Id.*
31. *Id.* § III.C.1.b.
32. *Id.* § III.C.1.c.
33. *Id.* § III.C.1.d.

Where banner advertisements are interactive and permit consumers to consummate a purchase without clicking through to a web page, all disclosures must be included within the banner itself. Where the banner is not interactive, a determination to place the required disclosures on the web site to which the banner is linked should be made only after considering "how important the information is to prevent deception, how much information needs to be disclosed, the burden of disclosing it in the banner ad, how much information the consumer may absorb from the ad, and how effective the disclosure would be if it was made on the Web site."[34]

(2) Prominence of Required Disclosures

Disclosures should be at least as large in type size as the claim to which they relate and they should appear in a color that contrasts with the color of the background against which they appear to avoid the possibility that the disclosures are likely to be missed.[35]

(3) Distracting Features within Ads

Elements such as graphics, sound, text or even hyperlinks should not undermine the prominence of a disclosure to the point that it results in consumers failing to notice, read or listen to such disclosures.[36]

(4) Repetition

Disclosures may need to be repeated on complex web sites (that consumers may access at different points causing disclosures to be missed) or on web sites where claims are repeated on various pages.[37]

(5) Multimedia Messages

Where online advertisements contain audio claims requiring disclosures, such disclosures should be in a volume and cadence (evaluated in relation to the rest of the message including the claims) sufficient for a reasonable consumer to hear and understand them.[38] Visual disclosures in online advertisements should appear for a duration sufficient for consumers to "notice, read and understand them."[39]

(6) Understandable Language

Advertisements should use clear language and syntax and avoid legalese and technical jargon when making required disclosures.[40]

---

34. *Id.* § III.C.1.e.
35. *Id.* § III.C.2.
36. *Id.* § III.C.3.
37. *Id.* § III.C.4.
38. *Id.* § III.C.5.
39. *Id.*
40. *Id.* § III.C.6.

D. Scope of the Terms "Written," "Writing" and "Printed" in Rules and Guides

While the Commission has periodically amended a few of its Rules and Guides to clarify or confirm how they apply in the online context,[41] the Commission's working paper *Dot Com Disclosures* indicates its general position that an "Internet ad that uses visual text is the equivalent of a 'written' ad" and that Rules and Guides that apply to "writings" and "written" and "printed" matter generally will apply to visual text displayed on the Internet.[42]

E. Using E-Mail to Comply with Notice Requirements of Rules and Guides

Where Advertisers want to use e-mail to comply with the various notice requirements contained in the Rules and Guides, they should take affirmative steps to ensure that consumers understand and expect to receive notices by this method, and any such notices or information should be provided in a form that consumers can retain either by saving or printing.[43]

F. Liability of Web Site Designers for Unfair and Deceptive Advertisements

Web site designers may be surprised to learn that the Commission expects them to review the information used by advertisers to substantiate ad claims made on their web sites.[44] This is an extension of a long-standing legal requirement that "ad agencies have a reasonable basis for advertising claims before they are disseminated."[45] The Commission now warns that web site designers "may not simply rely on an advertiser's assurances that the claims are substantiated."[46] In determining the issue of liability, the Commission has stated that

---

41. For example, the Commission amended certain definitions appearing in the *Rules and Regulations Under the Textile Fiber Products Identification Act* including "mail order catalog" and "mail order promotional material" to include materials that are disseminated to ultimate consumers "by electronic means." 63 Fed. Reg. 7518 (1998) (codified at 16 C.F.R. § 303.1 (2001)). Moreover, the Commission amended the provisions governing the use of terms in written advertisements that imply the presence of a particular fiber to include "advertisements disseminated through the Internet and similar electronic media." 63 Fed. Reg. 7523 (1998) (codified at 16 C.F.R. § 303.40 (2001)).

42. *Id.* § IV.A.1.

43. *Id.* § IV.A.2.

44. *Advertising and Marketing on the Internet: The Rules of the Road* (September 2000), <http://www.ftc.gov/bcp/conline/pubs/buspubs/ruleroad.htm> (last visited June 1, 2001) [hereinafter *Rules of the Road*].

45. *Substantiation Policy Statement, supra* note 9; *Standard Oil Co.*, 84 F.T.C. 1401, 1475 (1974), *aff'd and modified* 577 F. 2d 653 (9th Cir. 1978). An ad agency cannot ignore obvious shortcomings in an advertiser's substantiation. *Bristol Myers Co.*, 102 F.T.C. 21, 364 (1983).

46. *Rules of the Road, supra* note 44.

it will look at "the extent of . . .[the designer's] participation in the preparation of the challenged ad" and whether the designer "*knew or should have known* that the ad included false or deceptive claims."[47]

G. Enforcement Efforts

Between September 1994 and March 2001, the Commission has used its authority to initiate over 170 Internet-related enforcement actions.[48] Most of these actions involved traditional scams translated into the online context such as pyramid and credit repair schemes, sham investments and business opportunities, phony health care products and cures, and auctions in which sellers fail to deliver merchandise.[49] Some of these enforcement actions involved new technology-based scams such as modem hijacking (silently reconnecting consumers from their local Internet service provider to another provider at costly international telephone rates), web site hijacking (diverting consumers to look-alike sites), and web cramming (billing consumers' credit cards for unauthorized Internet services).[50] The Commission, however, has instituted an increasing number of these actions against national advertisers to confirm the applicability of traditional advertising law (including its Rules and Guides) to online marketing.[51]

In addition to instituting enforcement actions and obtaining consent decrees against violators of advertising laws, since 1996 the Commission has participated in over twenty-five Internet "surf" days with other United States and foreign agencies, identifying an estimated four thousand commercial web sites making apparently false or misleading claims.[52] Typically, it preserves the potentially offending web pages as potential evidence and e-mails messages to the operators of these sites explaining why the Commission believes that the sites may violate the law. Follow-up site visits determine whether corrective action has been taken or whether enforcement action is necessary. Depending upon the category of offense analyzed, the Commission has found that twenty to seventy percent of the sites that receive a warning remove the offending claim or take down their site entirely.[53]

---

47. *Id.* (emphasis added).

48. *Commission Enforcement Actions Involving the Internet and Online Services* (May 2001), <http://www.ftc.gov/opa/1999/9912/cases-internet.pdf> (last visited June 1, 2001) [hereinafter *FTC Internet Cases*].

49. *FTC Five-Year Report, supra* note 21.

50. *Id.*

51. *See, e.g., U.S. v. Federated Department Stores, Inc.*, FTC File No. 0023114 (D. Del.) (final consent Aug. 2000), <http://www.ftc.gov/os/2000/07/macysconsent.htm> (last visited June 1, 2001) (involving failure to comply with the Mail or Telephone Order Merchandise Rule); *Dell Computer Corporation*, Docket No. C-3888 (final consent Aug. 6, 1999) and *Micron Electronics, Inc.*, Docket No. C-3888 (final consent Aug. 6, 1999) (both involving failure to disclose clearly and conspicuously material leasing terms in their Internet advertising); *Geocities*, Docket No. C-3849 (final consent Feb. 12, 1999) (involving misrepresentation of the purpose for which personal identifying information was being collected).

52. *Combating Internet Fraud and Deception* (May 2001), http://www.ftc.gov/bcp/internet/cases-netsum.pdf (last visited June 1, 2001) [hereinafter *Fraud and Deception*].

53. *Id.*

Surf days have focused thus far on a variety of scams including two surf days each for illegal pyramid and credit repair schemes, sham investments and business opportunities, and phony health care products and cures (including one surf day devoted solely to lice treatment products).[54] Surf days also have focused on various aspects of traditional advertising law including compliance with the Textile Fiber Products Identification Act, the Wool Products Labeling Act, and Guides for the Use of Environmental Marketing Claims, as well as two surf days each focusing on compliance with adult and children's privacy requirements and the Guides for the Jewelry, Precious Metals, and Pewter Industries.[55]

H. Penalties

Advertisers that fail to comply with required standards face cease and desist orders,[56] federal district court injunctions,[57] and civil penalties of up to $11,000 per violation of any rule or cease and desist order regarding unfair or deceptive acts or practices "with actual knowledge or knowledge fairly implied on the basis of objective circumstances that such act is unfair or deceptive."[58] Additionally, the Commission may initiate civil actions on behalf of consumers seeking "rescission or reformation of contracts, the refund of money or return of property, the payment of damages, and public notification respecting the rule violation or the unfair or deceptive act or practice."[59]

In a few short years of prosecutions against Internet defendants, the Commission has obtained eight multimillion dollar judgments in cases seeking redress for consumer injuries including one judgment of $40 million in redress for unauthorized Internet services charged to consumers.[60] Other significant judgments include one awarding $900,000 in civil penalties against the world's leading manufacturer of portable data storage products—the largest civil pen-

---

54. *Id.*

55. *Id.*

56. 15 U.S.C. §45(b) (2001).

57. 15 U.S.C. §53(b) (2001).

58. 15 U.S.C. §45(m)(1)(A) (2001).

59. 15 U.S.C. §57b(a)(1) & (b) (2001).

60. *J.K. Publications, Inc., et al.,* Docket No. CV-990004 ABC (AJWx) (C.D. Cal. filed Jan. 5, 1999)($40 million in redress for unauthorized Internet services). Other multimillion dollar judgments for consumer redress in Internet-related actions include: *Intellicom Services, Inc.,* Action No. 97–4572 (Mcx) (C.D. Cal. filed June 3, 1997) (awarding $24 million in redress to 11 individual victims of fraudulent scheme promising enormous profits); *FutureNet et al.,* Civil Action 98–1113GHK (AIJx) (C.D. Cal. filed Feb. 17, 1998) (awarding up to $21 million in redress to victims of illegal pyramid scheme); *American Urological Clinic, et al.,* Civil No. 1:98-CV-2199 (JOS) (N.D. Ga. filed August 6, 1998) (awarding $18.5 in redress to victims of deceptive health claims); *Fortuna Alliance L.L.C., et al.,* Civ. No. C96–799M (W.D. Wash. filed May 23, 1996) (awarding $5.5 million in refunds to 15,622 victims of pyramid investment scheme); *JewelWay International, Inc.,* Action No. CV97–383 TUC JMR (D. Ariz. filed June 24, 1997) (awarding $5 million in redress to 150,000 victims of pyramid scheme); *Audiotex Connections, Inc.,* CV-97–0726 (E.D.N.Y. filed Feb. 13, 1997) (awarding $2.14 million in redress to 27,000 victims of modem hijacking); *Nia Cano, et al.,* Civil No. 97–7947-CAS (AJWx) (C.D. Cal. filed Oct. 29, 1997) (awarding $2 million in redress to victims of a pyramid scheme).

alty ever obtained for non-fraudulent violations of the Mail or Telephone Order Merchandise Rule.[61]

ii. Securities and Exchange Commission

The Securities and Exchange Commission ("SEC") has been equally aggressive in its Internet enforcement efforts. The SEC has conducted five nationwide Internet fraud sweeps bringing to two hundred the total number of Internet cases filed by the SEC to date.[62]

Typically, the actions brought by the SEC involve violations of Section 10(b) of the Securities Exchange Act of 1934 which makes it unlawful to use or employ, "in connection with the purchase or sale of any security [whether or not such security is registered on a national securities exchange] . . . any manipulative or deceptive device or contrivance [through any means or instrumentality of interstate commerce] in contravention of such rules and regulations as the Commission may prescribe."[63] The Rule most commonly violated in the SEC's Internet actions is Rule 10b-5 which makes it unlawful in connection with the purchase or sale of any security "to make any untrue statement of a material fact or to omit to state a material fact necessary in order to make the statements made, in the light of the circumstances under which they were made, not misleading."[64]

The actions brought by the SEC involve the use of various online means, including "spam" e-mails, electronic newsletters, websites, hyperlinks, message board postings and other Internet media to spread false or misleading information designed to drive up the price of the stock of targeted companies in order to sell such stock at a quick profit. The false or misleading information is of three general types: (1) false or misleading information relating to the performance or prospects of the company touted,[65] (2) failure of the information disseminators to disclose that they were compensated by the company or an affiliate to tout the company's stock,[66] or (3) failure of the information disseminators to disclose that they own securities of the company touted.[67]

---

61. *U.S. v. Iomega Corp.*, Civil Action No. 1:98CV00141C (D. Utah, complaint and consent filed Dec. 9, 1998).

62. *SEC Charges 23 Companies and Individuals in Cases Involving a Broad Spectrum of Internet Securities Fraud* (March 1, 2001), <http://www.sec.gov/news/press/2001–24.txt> (last visited June 1, 2001) [hereinafter *SEC Internet Crackdown*]. Documents relating to the SEC's Internet-related litigations are available on the SEC's web site under *Internet-Related Litigation and Administrative Proceedings Announcements*, <http://www.sec.gov/divisions/enforce/internetenforce/litreleases.shtml> (last visited June 1, 2001) and *Archived Internet-Related Litigation and Administrative Proceedings Announcements*, <http://www.sec.gov/divisions/enforce/internetenforce/internetlitrelold.shtml> (last visited June 1, 2001) [hereinafter, collectively, *SEC Internet Cases*].

63. Securities and Exchange Act of 1934, §10(b), 15 U.S.C. §78j(b)(2001).

64. 17 C.F.R. § 240.10b-5 (2001).

65. *See, e.g., SEC v. Chidwhite Enterprises, Inc., et al.*, Civil Action No A01-CV-131 (W.D. Texas, Austin Division, complaint filed Feb. 28, 2001) (false promises of imminent public offering); *SEC v. Pinkmonkey.com,*

iii. United States Department of Transportation

The United States Department of Transportation ("DOT") has been somewhat less active in its efforts to enforce advertising laws in the Internet context. DOT actions are predicated on a statute similar to Section 5 of the FTC Act in that it prohibits "unfair or deceptive practices or unfair methods of competition."[68]

The regulations promulgated under this statute define various activities as "unfair or deceptive practices."[69] The regulation that has seen the most enforcement in the Internet context controls price advertising and provides that "any advertising or solicitation by a direct air carrier, indirect air carrier, or an agent of either, for passenger air transportation, a tour . . . or a tour component . . . that states a price for such air transportation, tour, or tour component [is considered] to be an unfair or deceptive practice, unless the price stated is the entire price to be paid by the customer to the air carrier, or agent, for such air transportation, tour, or tour component."[70] In one of the earliest Internet-related actions brought by the DOT, Virgin Atlantic Airways was assessed $14,000 in civil penalties because one of its Internet advertisements listed a fare that was not available at the advertised price and another advertised fare did not include $38.91 in unspecified "taxes."[71]

iv. Other Federal Agencies

Other federal agencies have authority to exercise jurisdiction over specified categories of advertising but few have yet committed significant resources to Internet enforcement activities. Among these agencies are the Food and Drug Administration ("FDA"), and the Bureau of Alcohol, Tobacco and Firearms ("BATF").

The FDA has jurisdiction over the marketing of food, drugs, cosmetics and medical devices. Regulations pertaining to prescription drug advertising require

---

Inc., et al., Civil Action No. H-01-9711 (NFA) (S.D. Tex., Houston Division, complaint and consent filed Feb. 28, 2001) (false financial projections).

66. *See, e.g., SEC v. Internet Solutions for Business, Inc, et al.,* Civil Action No. CDS-01-0225 (DH) (D. Nev., complaint filed Feb. 28, 2001) (analyst received 12,500 shares in undisclosed compensation).

67. *See, e.g., SEC v. Jesse Hogan,* Civ. Action No. 00 C 5637 (N.D. Ill. Sept. 14, 2000) (caused investors to suffer almost $1 million in losses through "pump and dump" manipulation of five thinly traded stocks).

68. 49 U.S.C. §41712 (2001).

69. *See, e.g.,* 14 C.F.R. 399.80 (2001) (relating to unfair or deceptive acts or practices of ticket agents).

70. 14 C.F.R. §399.84 (2001).

71. *In re Virgin Atlantic Airways, Ltd.,* <http://dms.dot.gov/general/orders/19954qtr/951137.html> (last visited June 1, 2001).

the inclusion of information relating to side effects, contraindications and effectiveness.[72] The FDA has generally limited its involvement with food products to those implying a nutritional benefit[73] and those making claims relating to low calorie content and low sodium or dietetic benefits.[74] The BATF has issued extensive regulations relating to the advertisement of beer, wine and distilled beverages.[75]

2. State and Local Regulation

All fifty states have their own laws and regulations governing advertising. Each state has adopted its own version of the Federal Trade Commission Act which are known as "little" or "baby" FTC Acts.[76] The typical statute authorizes a state official or agency (typically the state's Attorney General) to conduct investigations of unfair or deceptive acts or practices[77] and obtain injunctions.[78] The statutes adopted in some jurisdictions authorize the official or agency to seek civil penalties[79] and/or restitution[80] on behalf of consumers. Unlike the comparable federal legislation, however, some of these statutes provide consumers with private rights of action.[81]

States have supplemented their baby FTC Acts with additional advertising laws that frequently are the product of local pressure groups addressing particular abuses. As a result, even a list of the titles of the various state advertising laws requires more than two hundred pages in a leading treatise on advertising law.[82]

In addition to the Federal and state advertising laws, various localities have enacted their own advertising regulations.[83]

States are increasingly using their authority to bring Internet-related enforcement actions against those involved in traditional scams,[84] as well as those

---

72. 21 C.F.R. pt. 302 (2001).

73. 21 C.F.R. § 101.9 (2001).

74. 21 C.F.R. § 105.66 (2001).

75. 27 C.F.R. pt. 4, 5 and 7 (2001).

76. *See, e.g.,* N.Y. Gen. Bus. Law §§ 349 *et seq.*; Cal. Bus. & Prof. Code §§ 17200 *et seq.*

77. *See, e.g.,* N.Y. Gen. Bus. Law § 349(b); Cal. Bus. & Prof. Code § 17204.

78. *See, e.g.,* N.Y. Gen. Bus. Law § 349(b); Cal. Bus. & Prof. Code § 17203.

79. *See, e.g.,* N.Y. Gen. Bus. Law § 349-c (authorizing civil penalties for consumer frauds committed against elderly persons); Cal. Bus. & Prof. Code §§ 17206, 17206.1, 17207.

80. *See, e.g.,* N.Y. Gen. Bus. Law § 349(b); Cal. Bus. & Prof. Code § 17203.

81. *See, e.g.,* N.Y. Gen. Bus. Law § 349(h).

82. George Eric Rosden & Peter E. Rosden, The Law of Advertising §16.02 (1990).

83. *See, e.g.,* N.Y. Cty. Admin. Code. § 20–708 (requiring conspicuous display of "total selling price exclusive of tax").

84. *See, e.g., New York v. Lipsitz—Internet Spam Scam Judgment* (July 15, 1997) <http://www.oag.state.ny.us/internet/litigation/lebedeff.html> (last visited June 1, 2001) (court granted injunctive relief and ordered restitution against respondent who violated New York State consumer protection laws by failing

large national advertisers that have allegedly breached traditional state advertising laws.[85]

3. Private Advertising Codes

The Council of Better Business Bureaus offers the most important private forum for the resolution of advertising disputes generally. The Council has promulgated the Code of Advertising of the Council of Better Business Bureaus (the "Code").[86] It supplements the Code with the regularly updated publication *Do's and Don'ts in Advertising*, which provides detailed guides for advertising in fourteen different industries.

The National Advertising Division of the Council of Better Business Bureaus (the "NAD") is responsible for implementing the Code and has handled over 3,500 cases during the past three decades.[87] The NAD confines its activities largely to examining the truth and accuracy of national advertising and the substantiation of claims. The NAD can institute proceedings on its own or as a result of complaints by competitors or consumers. NAD proceedings generally are completed within three months. The sole sanctions imposed by the NAD are directions to modify advertisements determined to be untruthful or inaccurate and the publication of its decisions in its national newsletter and various trade publications. Adverse rulings by the NAD are appealable to the National Advertising Review Board (the "NARB"). While compliance with rulings of the NAD and NARB is voluntary, it is generally widespread since failure to comply will result in referral of the matter to the Federal Trade Commission.

BBBOnLine, a wholly-owned subsidiary of the Council of Better Business Bureaus, has promulgated a Code of Online Business Practices (the "Online Code") designed to guide ethical "business to customer" conduct in electronic commerce.[88] Five basic principles guide the Online Code: (1) truthful and accurate communications in online advertising, marketing and use of technology, (2) accurate disclosure about the business, the goods or services available for sale, and the transaction itself, (3) adoption of appropriate practices to treat customer information with care, (4) adoption of customer satisfaction policies,

---

to deliver goods ordered over the Internet and falsely advertising attentive nature of its customer service through fictitious testimonials disseminated over the Internet).

85. *See, e.g., Comp-USA Settlement Requires Disclosure For Internet Sales* (Apr. 16, 2001), <http://www.oag.state.ny.us/press/2001/apr/apr16a_01.html> (last visited June 1, 2001) (settlement with New York State required company to modify Internet advertisement to eliminate need for consumers to click through multiple web page links in order to locate disclosures describing conditions to rebate offer).

86. *BBB Code of Advertising,* <http://www.bbb.org/advertising/adcode.asp> (last visited June 1, 2001).

87. Robert Pitofsky, Self-Regulation and Antitrust, Remarks at the D.C. Bar Association Symposium (Feb. 18, 1998).

88. *Code of Online Business Practices,* <http://www.bbbonline.org/code/code.asp> (last visited June 1, 2001).

and (5) use of special care when dealing with children under the age of thirteen.[89]

The Children's Advertising Review Unit ("CARU") of the Council of Better Business Bureaus was established to promote responsible child-directed advertising. It has promulgated seven basic Principles and a series of interpretive Guidelines that apply to advertising to children across all media. These Guidelines, the "Self-Regulatory Guidelines for Children's Advertising" relate to (1) product presentation and claims, (2) sales pressure techniques, (3) disclosures and disclaimers, (4) comparative claims, (5) the use of program or editorial characters to promote products, and (6) premiums, promotions and sweepstakes directed at children. CARU has promulgated additional guidelines highlighting issues unique to Internet and online advertising to children.[90] Its "Guidelines for Interactive Electronic Media" relate to (1) the specifics of making an online sale to children, including (a) informing children when they are being targeted for a sale, (b) notices requiring parental permission to consummate a sale, and (c) mechanisms for canceling the online purchase, (2) the collection of data from children, and (3) hyperlinking to third-party web sites that do not comply with CARU's Guidelines.[91]

The Electronic Retailing Association also has promulgated guidelines specifically directed at online advertising and requires association members to subscribe to these Ten Commandments of Electronic Retailing.[92] The guidelines deal with, among other things, truthful advertising, the presentation of disclosures that qualify claims, as well as substantiation, endorsements, warranties, and order fulfillment.

4. Private Litigation

The other general federal prohibition of misleading advertising (in addition to Section 5 of the FTC Act) is found in Section 43(a) of the Lanham Act.[93] Subsection (1)(a) prohibits "any false or misleading description. . .or representation of fact, which is likely to cause confusion. . . as to the origin, sponsorship or approval of. . .[one person's] goods, services or commercial activities by another person."[94] Subsection 1(b) prohibits "any false or misleading description. . .or representation of fact. . .in commercial advertising or promotion

---

89. *Id.*

90. *Self-Regulatory Guidelines for Children's Advertising,* <http://www.caru.org/carusubpgs/guidepg.asp> (last visited June 1, 2001).

91. *Id.*

92. *Ten Commandments of Electronic Retailing,* <http://www.retailing.org/regulatory/commandments.htm> (last visited June 1, 2001).

93. 15 U.S.C. §1125(a)(2001).

94. 15 U.S.C. §1125(a)(1)(2001).

[which] misrepresents the nature, characteristics, qualities or geographic origin of his or her or another person's goods, services or commercial activities."[95] Unlike Section 5 of the FTC Act, enforcement is not restricted to the Commission; a claim can be brought by "any person who believes that he or she is likely to be damaged."[96]

Where the Commission declines to bring suit under Section 5, competitors are likely to bring suit under Section 43(a) or under the state statutes providing private rights of action.[97]

§ 5.2 Securities

1. The Securities Regulatory Structure

i. Federal Regulation

Issuance of new securities in the United States is governed primarily by the Securities Act of 1933 (Securities Act),[98] which requires publicly offered securities to be registered with the Securities and Exchange Commission (SEC), absent an exemption. Trading in already-issued securities is primarily governed by the Securities Exchange Act of 1934 (Exchange Act).[99] The Exchange Act generally requires those engaged in the securities business as broker-dealers, and national securities exchanges, to be registered with SEC. Narrower in their coverage are the Investment Advisers Act of 1940 (Advisers Act),[100] which regulates investment advisers having $25 million or more under management or advising mutual funds, and the Investment Company Act of 1940 (1940 Act),[101] which governs both open-end and closed-end investment companies (mutual funds) that offer their securities to the public.

---

95. 15 U.S.C. §1125(a)(2)(2001).

96. *Id.*

97. *See supra* section 5.1.2.

98. 15 U.S.C. §§ 77a *et seq.* (1994 & Supp. III 1997).

99. *Id.* §§ 78a *et seq.* Though both acts address securities fraud, the Securities Act focuses upon securities issuance while the Exchange Act more broadly addresses both issuance and after-market trading.

100. *Id.* §§ 80b-1 *et seq.* The Advisers Act also covers an investment adviser, regardless of size, who is not regulated by the state where the adviser's principal place of business is located. *Id.* § 80b-3a(a)(1).

101. *Id.* §§ 80a-1 *et seq.*

ii. State Regulation

The states cannot regulate the issuance of securities listed—or authorized for listing—on the New York or American Stock Exchanges, or included—or qualified for inclusion—in the Nasdaq National Market System.[102] Nor can the states regulate those security issuances that are exempt from Securities Act registration by virtue of being private placements, including those made in reliance upon SEC Rule 506 in Regulation D.[103] The states still have authority to regulate most other kinds of exempt small offerings, particularly those made under SEC Rules 504 and 505,[104] as well as broker-dealers within their jurisdictions.

2. SEC Initiatives to Address Cybersecurities

i. Information Communicated Electronically: SEC Interpretations

Beginning in 1995, SEC has by rule and interpretive release sought to mesh all the above acts—as well as the regulatory framework built up around them—with the new world of electronic networks. Four interpretive releases and one concept release constitute SEC's principal guides regarding delivery of information on securities by electronic means.[105] In 1998, SEC also published an interpretive release on the application of U.S. federal securities laws to offshore electronic offerings and sales of securities and investment services by means of web sites.[106]

The Securities Act requires that the issuance of securities to the public be accompanied by disclosure of specified types of material information to potential investors. This has traditionally been accomplished by the print medium.

---

102. *Id.* § 77r(b)(4)(D) (added by the National Securities Markets Improvement Act of 1996 (NSMIA), section 102(a)).

103. Section 102(a) of NSMIA preempted regulation over securities issued under exemptions promulgated pursuant to section 4(2) of the Securities Act (the exemption for private offerings); *see* 15 U.S.C. § 77r(a) (1994 & Supp. III 1997).

104. Rules 504 and 505 are both exemptions based upon the SEC's authority under section 3(b) of the Securities Act to adopt conditional exemptions for offerings not exceeding $5 million.

105. The interpretive releases include Use of Electronic Media for Delivery Purposes, SEC Release No. 33-7233, 34-36345 (Oct. 6, 1995) [hereinafter Release 33-7233], SEC Release No. 33-7234, 34-36346 (Oct. 6, 1995), Use of Electronic Media by Broker-Dealers, Transfer Agents, and Investment Advisers for Delivery of Information; Additional Examples under the Securities Act of 1933, SEC Release No. 33-7288 (May 9, 1996) [hereinafter Release 33-7288] (setting forth criteria to be used in determining whether information transmitted electronically by broker-dealers, transfer agents and investment advisers can be deemed equivalent to the same information when transmitted by paper), and Use of Electronic Media, SEC Release No. 33-7856 (Apr. 28, 2000) [hereinafter Release 33-7856].

106. Use of Internet Web Sites to Offer Securities, Solicit Securities Transactions or Advertise Investment Services Offshore, SEC Release No. 33-7516, 34-39779, IA-1710, IC-23071 (Mar. 23, 1998) [hereinafter Release 33-7516].

Analogizing electronic distribution of information to the print medium, SEC views information distributed electronically as satisfying federal securities laws "if such distribution results in the delivery to the intended recipients of substantially equivalent information as these recipients would have had if the information were delivered to them in paper form."[107] SEC requires an investor's informed consent to receipt of information through the Internet (unlike information transmitted in paper form), and such consent is revocable at any reasonable time before electronic delivery of a particular document has actually commenced.[108]

When information is electronically delivered, investors must receive adequate and timely notice and have effective access to the information, and there must be reasonable assurance that the information has been delivered. Thus, merely posting a document on a web site does not constitute adequate notice, absent evidence of actual delivery to the investor.[109]

SEC requires that investors have access to disclosures "comparable" to postal mail and also have the opportunity to retain the information or have ongoing access equivalent to personal retention.[110] Moreover, once a document is posted on the Internet or made available through an online service, it should remain accessible for as long as any delivery requirement under SEC rules applies. Thus, if a preliminary prospectus is posted on a web site, it should be updated "to the same degree as paper."[111] SEC requires issuers to make paper versions of their documents available when there is computer incompatibility or computer system failure, or when consent to receive documents electronically is revoked by the investor.[112]

Issuers should have reasonable assurance, akin to that found in postal mail, that electronic delivery of information will actually occur. The delivery requirements can be satisfied by the investor's informed consent to receive information through an electronic medium, such as the Web, coupled with proper notice of access.[113] Sufficient evidence of delivery can also include (1) an electronic mail return receipt or confirmation that a document has been accessed, downloaded or printed, (2) the investor's receipt of transmission by fax, (3) the investor's

---

107. Release 33-7233, *supra* note 105, § II.A.

108. *Id.* at ex. 5. Consent may be given telephonically and may generally cover all documents of any issuers obtained through a given intermediary, and documents can be delivered in PDF format. *See* Release 33-7856, *supra* note 105, § II.A.

109. Release 33-7233, *supra* note 105, § II.B. Actual delivery can be accomplished by separately sending a letter or postcard by an Internet directed message (e-mail). If an investor consents to electronic delivery of the final prospectus for a public offering by means of a web site, but does not provide an electronic mail address, the issuer may post its final prospectus on the site and mail the investor a notice of the location of the prospectus on the Web, along with the paper confirmation of the sale. *Id.* at ex. 10.

110. *Id.* at n.22.

111. *Id.* at n.26.

112. *Id.* § II.B. FTC permits an offering to be limited entirely to persons that consent to receive a prospectus electronically, but if it is not so limited, a paper version of the prospectus must be given to broker-dealers to be made available to investors who do not have online access. In addition, SEC Rule 174 requires that an issuer in a public offering make paper versions available to after-market purchasers.

113. Release 33-7233, *supra* note 105, § II.C.

accessing a required document by hyperlink and (4) the investor's use of forms or other materials that are available only by accessing the document online.[114]

Proof of receipt of e-mail can be achieved in much the same way as proof of receipt of a registered letter, which the recipient signs upon delivery. The e-mail recipient can hit a reply button upon receipt of an electronic document, evidencing that receipt occurred.[115] Open-end mutual funds, which are engaged in continuous offers to sell and repurchase shares, are subject to the same SEC guidelines applicable to other issues in offerings.[116]

ii. Public Offerings

Apart from liberalized notice, access and delivery requirements, a securities offering in cyberspace remains generally subject to the regulatory scheme that predates the advent of the Internet. The Internet introduces issues unique to the medium, however, such as the effect of information posted on an issuer's own web site. Before a registration statement is filed, the issuer must take pains to avoid "conditioning the market" with online bullish statements and projections. After a registration statement becomes effective, the web site containing the final version of the prospectus can be hyperlinked to other sales literature.[117] The issuer or underwriter can mail sales literature to persons for whom delivery of the prospectus via the web site was effective, as long as notice of the availability of the final prospectus and its web site location accompanies or precedes the sales literature.[118] To give the investor the opportunity to access the final prospectus online, the issuer or broker can post sales materials with prominent hyperlinks to the prospectus embedded at the top of the first page of each page of the sales materials.[119]

Almost every company that has issued or contemplates issuing its securities to the public has a homepage somewhere on the World Wide Web, containing news and information about the company and its products. This also may contain links to current SEC filings, analysts' reports on the company's secu-

---

114. *Id.*

115. *See Compliance Navigator: Electronic Delivery of Prospectuses,* 7 INTERNET COMPLIANCE ALERT 7 (Apr. 6, 1998).

116. *See supra* text accompanying notes 105–114 (discussion of Release 33-7233). In addition, the regulatory arm of the National Association of Securities Dealers, NASD Regulation (NASDR), has special advertising rules applicable to mutual funds.

117. Release 33-7233, *supra* note 105, at ques. 19.

118. *Id.* at ex. 17. The notice of the location of the web site should be in forepart and clearly highlighted. Supplemental sales literature that must be accompanied or preceded by a prospectus can be made available if, before or at the time of delivery, a statutory prospectus is made available. *See* 17 C.F.R. § 230.134b (1992).

119. Release 33-7233, *supra* note 105, at ques. 35. Another approach is to place two different hyperlinks on a web page, with one linking to the prospectus and the other to the sales materials, both clearly identified and in close proximity. *Id.* at ques. 14, 15. In Release No. 33-7856, the SEC discusses how a link may or may not fall into the same electronic delivery "envelope" as a prospectus. *See* Release 33-7856, *supra* note 105, § II.A.4.

rities, news stories about the company and other third-party information. Whether third-party information will be attributed to a company issuing securities depends upon whether the issuer has involved itself in the preparation of the information (the *entanglement theory*) or has approved the information explicitly or implicitly (the *adoption theory*).[120]

Underwritten public offerings are traditionally preceded by a *road show*. The road show involves presentations made by the issuer and its underwriters to large investors, institutions and analysts. It is conducted during the period that starts when a registration statement is filed with SEC and ends when the registration becomes effective. In such presentations, the issuer's management and the underwriters explain the issuer's business and industry, as well as the offerings, and respond to questions. Through several no-action letters, SEC has allowed road shows to be legally conducted on the Internet.[121]

A direct public offering (DPO) differs from an underwriting, in that the issuer offers its own securities directly to investors on what is effectively a "best-efforts" basis. DPOs long preceded the Internet, but only a relatively small number were made. The Internet stimulates DPOs, because it allows for instant communication with tens of millions of potential investors.[122] DPOs have led to the creation of a new type of financial intermediary, namely the web site designed to develop databases of potential investors in new stock offerings, which can be linked on site to new DPOs. To avoid registering as a broker-dealer, the database operator must charge only a flat fee (not contingent upon success of the offering) to issuers for providing the web site that facilitates the issuer's online securities offering.[123] Moreover, the service should be provided only to issuers under registered offerings or those under exemptions provided for smaller offerings by SEC's Regulation A or Rule 504, not for securities privately offered pursuant to SEC Regulation D (see SEC Rules 505 and 506). Among a host of other conditions, there can be no *hot links* between the web

---

120. *Id.* § II.B.1.

121. Net Roadshow, Inc., SEC No-Action Letter, [1997 Transfer Binder] Fed. Sec. L. Rep. (CCH) ¶ 77,367 (Sept. 8, 1997); Bloomberg, L.P., SEC No-Action Letter, [1998 Transfer Binder] Fed. Sec. L. Rep. (CCH) ¶ 77,427–77,446 (Dec. 1, 1997); Charles Schwab & Co., Inc., SEC No-Action Letter, [1999–2000 Transfer Binder] Fed. Sec. L. Rep. (CCH) ¶ 77,632–77,650 (Nov. 15, 1999; clarified Feb. 9, 2000) (audience for road shows broadened to include more affluent IPO retail customers).

122. DPOs on the Web have generally (1) registered with the SEC using Form SB-2, (2) used an exemption from registration called SEC Regulation A, which exempts from registration offerings that do not exceed $5 million or (3) used SEC Rule 504, which exempts offerings directly by issuers (but not resales) of less than $1 million. Securities issued pursuant to the rule must be sold only to accredited investors as restricted securities, unless they have been qualified in at least one blue-sky jurisdiction that requires furnishing of an offering circular to prospective purchasers.

123. Internet Capital Corp., SEC No-Action Letter, [1998 Transfer Binder] Fed. Sec. L. Rep. (CCH) ¶ 77,473–77,445 (Dec. 18, 1997; revised Dec. 24, 1997). Under this no-action position, the web site can support a grouping of individual corporate bulletin board areas or "corporate listings." An individual logged on to the site could elect to visit any corporate bulletin board area where a tombstone, preliminary offering document or final offering document can be viewed regarding a specific company. Each issuer's bulletin board area should remain autonomous and operate separately from all other corporate areas, with offerings and information pertaining solely to that specific issuer being displayed in its bulletin board area.

site and any other corporate marketing information or a corporation's home-page.[124]

iii. Nonpublic Offerings

Using the World Wide Web for private placements exempt from Securities Act registration stems from a pre-Internet SEC policy that sanctioned the use of SEC's Regulation D private offering exemption, by prequalification of groups of accredited investors who would respond to extensive solicitations by furnishing extensive financial data.[125] In the Internet context, SEC's position is that prequalification of a number of accredited investors on a web site who are electronically notified in a secured, password-protected manner of subsequent private offerings does not involve a "general solicitation." At least for registered broker-dealers, this allows the building of investor databanks for private offerings made under SEC Regulation D.[126]

iv. Secondary Trading of Securities

The impact of the Internet on trading markets has been far more dramatic than on the issuance of securities. Starting from zero in 1995, online equity trading by individuals had jumped to 20% at year-end 1998, and would become an expected 49% at year-end 2000.[127] At the same time, the Internet has helped spawn a proliferation of new electronic trading systems, opening system membership to individuals as well as institutions. Institutional investors used extranet systems to support closed trading systems among themselves since the 1970s,[128] but the opening of similar "membership" trading to broader groups resulted in these alternative systems accounting, by 1999, for almost 25% of stock transactions by individual investors.[129] In April 1999, new SEC rules took

---

124. *See id. See also* the discussion of blue-sky safe harbors for web offerings at notes 136–137, *infra,* and accompanying text.

125. *See, e.g.,* H.B. Shaine & Co., Inc., SEC No-Action Letter, 1987 WL 107907 (S.E.C. May 1, 1987).

126. IPOnet, SEC No-Action Letter, [1996–97 Transfer Binder] Fed. Sec. L. Rep. (CCH) ¶ 77,252 (July 26, 1996); Angel Capital Electronic Network, SEC No-Action Letter, [1997 Transfer Binder] Fed. Sec. L. Rep. (CCH) ¶ 77,305 (Oct. 25, 1996); Lamp Technologies, Inc., SEC No-Action Letter, [1997 Transfer Binder] Fed. Sec. L. Rep. (CCH) ¶ 77,359 (May 29, 1997). The application of these no-action interpretations to third-party service providers who are not registered as broker-dealers was questioned in Release 33-7856.

127. L. N. Spiro, *Merrill's E-Battle,* Bus. Wk., Nov. 15, 1999, at 256, 258.

128. The pioneer was Instinet, which introduced a closed networked computer system in which a group of institutional members (such as mutual funds and investment brokers) could trade large blocks of securities electronically among themselves, thereby avoiding brokers in the middle. Operating outside the established stock exchanges, Instinet does not use the World Wide Web; instead, its members use the more limited electronic linking system of the extranet.

129. G. Morgenson, *Sailing into Murky Waters,* N.Y. Times, Feb. 28, 1999, at BU-2, BU-10. (Island reported 2.5 billion shares traded in 1998, while Archipelago reported 650 million).

effect, which sought to respond to these changes. The rules govern electronic networks and other screen-based alternative trading systems (ATSs), and include a controversial provision requiring larger-volume ATSs, such as Instinet, to display their institutional orders publicly.[130] The ATS rules—too complex to cover in this section—effectively allow an ATS to choose between registering as an exchange or as a broker-dealer.

v. SEC Jurisdiction over Cybersecurities

In April 1998, SEC issued an interpretive release on the application of federal securities laws to offshore Internet offers, securities transactions and advertising of investment services, seeking to "clarify when the posting of offering or solicitation materials" on web sites would not be deemed activity taking place in the United States for purposes of federal securities laws.[131]

SEC generally does not consider an offshore Internet offer made by a non-U.S. offeror as targeted at the United States; hence such offer is not subject to registration with SEC if (1) the web site includes a prominent disclaimer making clear that the offer is directed only to countries *other than* the United States and (2) the web site offeror implements procedures that are "reasonably designed to guard against sales to U.S. persons in the offshore offering."[132]

There are several ways to guard against sales to U.S. persons. For example, the offeror could determine the buyer's residence by obtaining the purchaser's mailing address or telephone number (including area code) before the sale. If the offshore party received indications that the purchaser was a U.S. resident (U.S. taxpayer identification number or payment drawn on a U.S. bank, for example), then the party might be on notice that additional steps would need to be taken to verify that a U.S. resident was not involved.[133]

When a U.S. issuer makes the offshore offering, stricter measures are required because U.S. residents can more readily obtain access to the offer. Accordingly, SEC requires a U.S. issuer to implement password procedures, under which access to the Internet offer is limited to persons who can obtain a password to the web site by demonstrating they are not U.S. citizens.[134]

SEC does not apply exchange registration requirements to a foreign exchange that sponsors its own web site, generally advertising its quotes or allowing orders to be directed through the web site, as long as it takes steps reasonably designed to prevent U.S. persons from directing orders through the site to the

---

130. Regulation of Exchange and Alternative Trading Systems, SEC Release No. 33-40,760 (Dec. 8, 1998).
131. Release 33-7516, *supra* note 106, at pt. I. The Release addressed when postings on web sites would be considered targeted at the United States; it did not address inherently "targeting" types of communications such as e-mail.
132. *Id.*
133. *Id.* at pt. III.B.
134. *Id.* at pt. IV.B.

exchange. Regardless of precautions taken by the issuer, SEC views solicitations as subject to federal securities laws if their content appears targeted at U.S. persons. For instance, SEC cited offshore offers that emphasized the investor's ability to avoid U.S. taxes on the investment.[135]

3. State Blue-Sky Initiatives Addressing Cybersecurities

If a nonexempt offering of securities is made "in" a given state, the state's blue-sky laws generally apply.[136] Mere posting of an offering on the World Wide Web, without more, however, constitutes insufficient evidence that the offer is specifically "directed" to persons in every state. Recognizing the practicalities of Internet offerings, the North American Securities Administrators Association (NASAA) adopted a model rule under which states will generally not attempt to assert jurisdiction over an offering if (1) the web site contains a disclaimer stating that no offers or sales are being made to any resident of that state, (2) the site excludes such residents from access to the purchasing screens and (3) no sales are, in fact, made to residents of that state.[137] As of early 2000, thirty-eight states had adopted a version of the NASAA safe harbor, by statute, regulation, interpretation or no-action letter.[138] Commonly, the disclaimer is contained in a page linked to the homepage of the offering.

In 1997, NASAA also adopted a policy exempting from the definition of "transacting business" within a state—for purposes of sections 201(a) and 201(c) of the Uniform Securities Act—the following communications by out-of-state broker-dealers, investment advisers, agents and representatives: those that involve generalized information about products and services, when it is clearly stated that the person may transact business in the state only if first registered or otherwise exempted, when the person does not attempt to effect transactions in securities or render personalized investment advice, and when the person uses specified legends and "firewalls" against directed communications.

---

135. *Id.* at pt. III.B.
136. Joseph Long, Blue Sky Law § 3.04(2), at 3–24 to 3–27 (rev. ed. 1997).
137. The *Model NASAA Interpretive Order and Resolution* is posted at NASAA's official web site, <http://www.nasaa.orgblueskyguidelinesinternetadv.html>.
138. *See* 1 Blue Sky L. Rep. (CCH) ¶ 6481 (June 2001).

§ 5.3 Banking

1. Introduction

i. Outside Market Forces

Banks and savings associations were the dominant providers of financial services to both individuals and businesses until the late 1970s, when the combination of unprecedented double-digit inflation and interest rates, product innovations of nondepository institution competitors and deregulatory government policies began to loosen the grip that banks had on the financial services sector. During the past two decades, these factors have led to a dramatic shift in the relative market positions of depository institutions and nondepository institutions across a wide range of financial services.[139]

Banks have lost much of the advantage they once enjoyed in connection with obtaining and retaining the financial services business of both individuals and businesses. Changes in transaction costs represent one of the major factors influencing this loss. Transaction costs, especially search costs, have traditionally attracted customers to use one financial institution (typically a depository institution) for multiple financial products and services, thereby allowing banks to cross-subsidize these activities in an attempt to maximize overall profits. The Internet and other nongeographically limited marketing and distribution methods can significantly reduce the search costs for an individual or business interested in comparing costs or returns associated with a single activity—such as obtaining a loan or establishing an investment relationship—offered by a variety of financial institutions. To capture these benefits, individuals and

---

139. *See* JOSEPH NOCERA, A PIECE OF THE ACTION: HOW THE MIDDLE CLASS JOINED THE MONEY CLASS (1994) (excellent discussion of how options for obtaining financial services, particularly for consumers, have changed and expanded over past three decades); PHILLIP L. ZWEIG, WRISTON (1995) (discussion of evolution of Citibank, a leading institution in terms of serving businesses and consumers, as well as in developing technology for banking and financial services applications).

Banks have argued that because of their heavily regulated status, they are often placed at a competitive disadvantage with nondepository entities. For example, banks cite the obligations imposed upon them under the Community Reinvestment Act, which do not apply to nondepository entities that directly compete with banks, such as money market mutual funds. *Community Reinvestment Act: Hearings Before the Subcomm. on Financial Institutions and Consumer Credit of the House Comm. on Banking and Financial Services*, 104th Cong. 62 (1995) (statement of James M. Culberson, Jr., American Bankers Association). Banks have also argued that the prohibition on paying interest on demand accounts held by most commercial organizations places them at a significant disadvantage in attracting and retaining such customers, as compared with competitors who are not subject to such limitations on the transaction-capable instruments they offer. *See ABA May Ask Congress to Expand MMDAs*, BANKING POL'Y REP., Aug. 4, 1997, at 4; Jaret Seiberg, *Fed Rebuffs ABA on NOW Accounts for Business*, AM. BANKER, July 17, 1997, at 11. Some members of Congress are beginning to agree. Several bills are pending in the Senate and House that would do away with the prohibition on interest-bearing commercial demand accounts. *See* Michele Heller, *Bill for Interest-Bearing Biz Checking*, AM. BANKER, Feb. 5, 2001, at 5; Finance Subcommittees Approve Banking Legislation, NAT'L J. CONGRESS DAILY, Mar. 22, 2001.

businesses become tempted to unbundle their relationships with a particular institution and seek the most cost-effective provider of each portion of their investment and loan relationships.

The principal exception to this significant erosion of bank dominance in the provision of financial services products is in the payment systems arena. If electronic banking develops in a way that ultimately erodes the banking industry's dominance in this arena, it could pose a fundamental threat to the future of the banking industry. Although there are exceptions (such as travelers' checks and money orders), banks and other depository institutions dominate—to an overwhelming degree—the movement of funds through the economy and payment systems. Some new electronic banking applications, such as stored-value cards and electronic money, create the potential for nonbanks to gain entry to payment systems in ways not previously envisioned, either by current payment systems participants or by existing laws and regulations. For example, nonbank entities—such as transit systems and universities—already serve as stored-value issuers.

Some nonbanks are likely to view the introduction of electronic banking as an opportunity to break into an emerging market that should not automatically be "off limits" to nonbanks. Questions regarding the types of entities that should be permitted to issue stored-value instruments, and the requirements that should be imposed upon various types of issuers, will be debated at both the federal and state levels.[140]

ii. A New Model: The "Internet Bank"

Those arguing that technology will have a relatively size-neutral impact contend that focusing upon asset size overlooks the true implication of interactive financial technology. The question they pose is whether new technology offers the opportunity to design a new type of bank—an Internet bank—that, regardless of size, could attain the level of success of current brick-and-mortar banks. Using the Internet as its advertising vehicle and as its principal method of serving customers, an Internet bank is fundamentally different from the de novo model that starts with a main office and seeks customers from its local community. In the new model, size and geography become incidental rather than critical. Marketing efforts become nationwide, perhaps targeting special niche markets that the bank intends to serve. Such an institution would avoid the substantial costs associated with establishing and growing a branch network.

Traditionally, a bank relies upon a local presence, as well as customer confidence and trust in its reputation, to attract business. In the electronic envi-

---

140. *See* Thomas P. Vartanian & Robert H. Ledig, *The Business of Banking in the Age of the Internet: Fortress or Prison*, Banking Pol'y Rep., Mar. 4, 1996, at 6.

ronment, however, a geographically remote bank can operate a web site that is as impressive and user-friendly as a site maintained by a local bank. Bank use of the Internet may, therefore, result in a dramatic change in the manner in which financial institutions compete for customers, with traditional methods becoming less significant.

Several start-up institutions have embarked upon an Internet bank strategy. Most prominent among these is Security First Network Bank, fsb (SFNB). The web site for this institution, which began serving customers on the Internet on October 18, 1995, describes the positive features of the small town in Kentucky where it is "located," for it acknowledges that few, if any, of its customers are likely to ever visit the bank in person.[141]

Some of the questions that will be faced by new bank organizers, or existing small banks considering this strategy, include the following:

- Will customers be willing to establish a full-service relationship with a bank that does not have an office within driving distance?
- Can an Internet-based bank be successful if it only attracts customers for specific individual products or services, rather than a full-service relationship?
- Will such an institution lose customers to locally based institutions as they begin to offer the same types of online services as the Internet-based bank?
- What are the likely demographic profiles of individual and business customers of the bank?
- How will the cost and revenue structures of a start-up Internet-based bank compare with those of a locally oriented small institution, a medium-size institution or a large institution?

It is not clear whether a de novo Internet bank strategy will prove to be a viable means of operation. The impact of pioneer institutions—which will be closely watched by other banks and industry analysts—could far outweigh their size. If a large institution concludes that it can reach the customers it wants to serve in neighboring states, or more distant regions of the United States, it may be able to do so by using electronic financial technology for a fraction of the cost associated with the interstate acquisition of an existing institution. Moreover, organizations that once were inclined toward a strategy of operating banks or branches throughout the United States must reconsider the relative costs and

---

141. SFNB, a federal savings bank wholly owned by Cardinal Bancshares, Inc. (Cardinal), a Kentucky-based bank holding company, is often cited as the first Internet-only banking institution. *See* Kelley Holland & Amy Cortese, *The Future of Money*, Bus. Wk., June 12, 1995, at 74. Since opening the bank in 1995, Cardinal has expanded its activities to providing software and data processing services to other banking institutions through its Five Paces Software, Inc. subsidiary. *See* Cardinal Bancshares, Inc., 82 Fed. Res. Bull. 674 (July 1996) (FRB order approving Cardinal's application to permit SFNB to acquire Five Paces' software business). In 1997, Cardinal announced plans to sell SFNB. *See* Tim Clark, *First Online Bank's Final Withdrawal*, News.com, Nov. 6, 1997, *available at* <http://news.cnet.com/news/0,10000-1003-200-323799,00html> (visited June 25, 2001).

benefits associated with such an approach. The possibility of a viable online banking strategy that does not depend upon in-person contact with the bank accentuates the importance of critically analyzing the viability of a branch-based strategy.

iii. Overlapping Legislative and Regulatory Regimes

Depository institutions in the United States are subject to the overlapping jurisdiction of federal and state laws, to varying degrees depending upon an institution's charter. In its operations, an institution must be cognizant of these laws and relevant federal preemption principles. Depending upon whether a depository institution is chartered as a federal or state institution, state corporate law principles may be fully or partially applicable to the institution's corporate governance. Federal and state banking regulators oversee banking activities of these organizations and related matters. The federal bank regulatory agencies formally act in concert, issuing joint policy statements through the Federal Financial Institutions Examination Council, an organization through which they coordinate matters relating to examination policy.

iv. Gramm-Leach-Bliley Act

A. Overview

The Gramm-Leach-Bliley Act (GBL Act) increased the range of activities in which a bank and bank holding company (BHC) may engage.[142] Among other things, it (1) repealed parts of the Banking Act of 1993, known as the Glass-Steagall Act, to allow bank and securities company affiliations, (2) repealed parts of the Bank Holding Company Act of 1956 (BHCA) to permit bank and insurance company affiliations and (3) established a new type of holding company, the financial holding company (FHC), which is allowed to own banks as subsidiaries, and own other subsidiaries that engage in all other financial activities, including those that the financial subsidiaries of banks cannot enter directly.

B. Bank Holding Companies and Financial Holding Companies

Activities—and the ownership of companies engaged in activities—that were permissible before the GLB Act remain permissible for BHCs that remain

---

142. Gramm-Leach-Bliley Act, Pub. L. No. 106-102, 113 Stat. 1338 (1999).

BHCs. These include activities that the Board of Governors of the Federal Reserve Board (FRB) approved under Regulation Y's "laundry list," as well as activities approved by FRB orders.

The GLB Act permits BHCs that meet certain requirements to qualify as FHCs and thereby engage in—and own entities engaged in—"financial activities." To qualify as and become an FHC, a BHC must comply with three provisions. First, all of its subsidiary depository institutions must be well-capitalized and well-managed.[143] Second, the BHC must file both a declaration with FRB that it elects to become an FHC, and a certification that it meets the well-capitalized and well-managed requirements. Third, each of the BHC's depository institutions must have at least a "satisfactory" Community Reinvestment Act (CRA) rating as of its most recent examination.[144] FHCs may engage in any activity that is financial in nature, incidental to such financial activity or complementary to a financial activity. It is the responsibility of FRB, with the concurrence of the Department of the Treasury (Treasury), to determine which activities are financial or incidental.

(1) Financial Activities

The statute defines financial activities broadly. It includes (1) bank lending and investment functions, (2) insurance underwriting, (3) financial, investment or advisory services and (4) underwriting and dealing in, as well as making markets in, securities. The definition of financial activities also includes activities that, before enactment of the GLB Act, FRB determined to be permissible for BHCs, by FRB order or Regulations Y or K.

(2) Incidental Activities

Incidental activities are those that FRB, with Treasury's concurrence, determines—by regulation or order—to be incidental to financial activities. Trea-

---

143. The new law provides that for purposes of applying the capital and management standards required to achieve FHC status, FRB will apply to foreign banks operating a branch or agency in the United States— or owning or controlling a commercial lending company in the United States—comparable capital and management standards, taking into account the principle of national treatment and equality of competitive opportunity.

If an FHC fails to comply with the well-capitalized or well-managed requirements within the allowed time (or any extension granted by FRB), FRB may require that the FHC divest itself of any of its depository institutions or, at the election of the FHC, cease to engage in any activities conducted by the FHC or its subsidiaries (other than a depository institution or its subsidiary) that are not permissible for a BHC that has not elected to become, and qualified as, an FHC. The divestiture remedy gives the FHC the choice of reverting to its earlier status as a BHC by divesting certain activities, or divesting its depository subsidiaries and retaining all other activities.

144. When a BHC has acquired a depository institution within the twelve-month period before submitting its declaration to become an FHC, and such depository institution has less than a satisfactory CRA rating, such adverse rating may be disregarded for twelve months following the acquisition if the BHC has submitted a remedial plan to the appropriate federal bank regulatory agency and the agency has approved such plan. There is no ongoing requirement that an FHC maintain a satisfactory CRA rating for all of its depository institution subsidiaries to maintain its own status as an FHC.

sury may also ask FRB to determine that an activity is a financial activity, or is incidental to a financial activity.

(3) Complementary Activities

Activities that are complementary to financial activities must be determined on a case-by-case basis by FRB, which must find that the proposed activity does not pose a substantial risk to the safety or soundness of depository institutions or the financial system generally. FRB is not obligated to consult with Treasury to determine complementary activities.

(4) Standard

In determining whether an activity is financial in nature or incidental to a financial activity, the statute directs FRB to take into account (1) the purposes of the GLB Act, (2) changes and reasonably expected changes in the marketplace, (3) changes and reasonably expected changes in technology for delivering financial services and (4) whether such activity is necessary to allow an FHC to compete effectively in the United States, to deliver services efficiently by technological means and to offer customers services by available and emerging technologies.

2. Perspective of the Comptroller of the Currency

i. National Bank Data Processing and Electronic Services

The long-standing and consistent position of the Office of the Comptroller of the Currency (OCC) regarding electronic banking has been to allow banks to employ new technologies in providing existing or emerging customer services that fall within the services historically associated with the business of banking, as broadly construed by the Comptroller. OCC's opinions and decisions regarding certain data processing activities and services as "incidental to banking" and therefore proper for national banks highlight a number of general principles that emerge from OCC's application of OCC's data processing rule. Banks may use their excess data processing capacity to provide services incidental to permissible banking services, sell their excess data processing capacity to nonfinancial institutions when that excess capacity was acquired in good faith to serve the bank's own needs, provide data processing services to other financial institutions, sell by-products of their data processing activities, such as software programs, when they are incidental to data processing, and share technology platforms used in customer service operations with other service providers.[145]

---

145. 12 C.F.R. § 7.3500 (1996).

ii. The 1996 Electronic Means and Facilities Rule

On February 9, 1996, OCC adopted a final rule to amend and recodify its interpretive rulings.[146] In its proposal to the final rule, OCC asked for comments regarding the language discussing the authority of national banks to sell excess capacity of data processing equipment and technology.[147] In the final rule, OCC responded to commentators' concerns regarding the language, "legitimate excess capacity," but instead opted for a "good-faith" standard.[148] Finally, OCC noted that the express language of the final rule—that sales of excess capacity are appropriate for a bank to optimize use of the bank's resources—parallels the standard applied by OCC in cases involving sales to nonbank users.[149] OCC's ruling provides as follows:

> A national bank may perform, provide or deliver through electronic means and facilities any activity, function, product or service that it is otherwise authorized to perform, provide, or deliver. A national bank may also, in order to optimize the use of the bank's resources, market and sell to third parties electronic capacities acquired or developed by the bank in good faith for banking purposes.[150]

The 1996 Electronic Means and Facilities Rule embraces the specific rulings and opinions examined earlier in this section, and sets the stage for future OCC rulings related to electronic banking and commerce. As illustrated by a number of recent OCC decisions, the regulatory approach for analyzing national banks' involvement in electronic banking and commerce is not limited to the Electronic Means and Facilities Rule. The following section examines a variety of issues that have arisen during the last several years, among them the issue of banks providing access to, and offering services over, the Internet. It also examines the authority of national banks to engage in electronic banking and commerce based upon the bank's status as a finder or correspondent banker.

iii. Internet-Based Services

OCC has addressed a series of novel requests by national banks to engage in Internet-related services. These include authorizing a national bank to use the

---

146. Interpretive Rulings, 61 Fed. Reg. 4,849 (1996) (to be codified at 12 C.F.R. pts. 7, 31) [hereinafter Electronic Means and Facilities Rule].
147. Interpretive Rulings, 60 Fed. Reg. 11,924, 11,927 (proposed Mar. 3, 1995) (to be codified at 12 C.F.R. pts. 7, 31).
148. Electronic Means and Facilities Rule, 61 Fed. Reg. at 4,853–54.
149. *Id.* at 4,854 (citing Letter from Peter Liebesman, Assistant Director, Legal Advisory Services Division (July 24, 1987) (unpublished) and cases cited therein, Wingert v. First Nat'l Bank of Hagerstown, Md., 175 F. 739 (4th Cir. 1909), *aff'd*, 223 U.S. 670 (1912); Brown v. Schleier, 118 F. 981 (8th Cir. 1902), *aff'd*, 194 U.S. 18 (1904)).
150. 12 C.F.R. § 7.1019 (2001).

"platform" of "smart phones"—which were already providing customers with banking and other financial services—to provide other data processing and communication services.[151] The bank sought to make its platform available to its correspondent financial institutions, which would, in turn, make banking services available to their customers. It also intended to enhance the package by allowing other service and information providers to access the platform. Finally, the national bank intended to offer the platform to other financial institutions as a gateway for financial settlement services. OCC found each of these ancillary uses incidental to banking, falling squarely within the area of traditional correspondent services.

Another interpretation permitted a bank to offer, through a wholly owned operating subsidiary, an information and payments exchange between insurance underwriters on the one hand, and general insurance agencies and their individual agents on the other.[152] Other interpretive rulings include the following:

- Granting a request by a group of banks to dispense public transportation tickets, event and attraction tickets, gift certificates, prepaid phone cards and similar products—such as promotional materials and debit/credit cards—through their network ATMs.
- Confirming that, as a service incidental to providing home banking via the Internet, a national bank operating a subsidiary is permitted to provide Internet access to the bank's customers and to persons who are not customers of the bank.[153]
- Allowing a national bank to establish a subsidiary to design, build and operate a system of toll plazas pursuant to a contract with a consortium of public authorities.[154]
- Permitting a national bank to provide computer networking services to other financial institutions.[155]
- Permitting twelve national banks to engage—with IBM and certain other financial institutions—in a joint venture to provide home banking and other financial services to the customers of the participating banks.[156]

---

151. OCC Interpretive Letter No. 611, [1992–1993 Transfer Binder] Fed. Banking L. Rep. (CCH) ¶ 83,449, at 71,572 (Nov. 23, 1992).

152. OCC Interpretive Letter No. 653, [1994–1995 Transfer Binder] Fed. Banking L. Rep. (CCH) ¶ 83,601, at 71,801 (Dec. 22, 1994).

153. Apollo Trust is a state-chartered bank. It sought OCC's opinion in connection with its request for Federal Deposit Insurance Corporation (FDIC) approval under 12 U.S.C. § 1831a(d) to establish a wholly owned subsidiary. That statutory section provides that a subsidiary of an insured state-chartered bank may not engage as principal in any type of activity that is not permissible for a subsidiary of a national bank, unless FDIC determines that the activity poses no risk to the insurance fund and the bank meets applicable capital standards.

154. OCC Interpretive Letter No. 731, [1995–1996 Transfer Binder] Fed. Banking L. Rep. (CCH) ¶ 81–048, at 90,339 (July 1, 1996).

155. OCC Interpretive Letter No. 754, [1996–1997 Transfer Binder] Fed. Banking L. Rep. (CCH) ¶ 81–118, at 90,268 (Nov. 6, 1996).

156. Letter from Julie L. Williams, Chief Counsel, OOC, to Gerald P. Hurst, Assoc. Gen'l Counsel, NationsBank Corp., Conditional Approval No. 221 (Dec. 4, 1996). IntegrionSM was formed in September 1996 as a limited liability company owned and operated by IBM, ABN AMRO North America, Bank One, Bank of America, Barnett Bank, Comerica, First Bank Systems, First Chicago NBD, Fleet Financial Group,

- Permitting four national banks (Wells Fargo Bank, N.A., Michigan National Bank, First National Bank of Chicago and Texas Commerce Bank) to each establish an operating subsidiary that would participate as an owner of a minority interest in each of two limited liability companies (LLCs).[157]
- Permitting banks to operate automated loan machines (ALMs) without regard to state geographic restrictions under the National Bank Act.[158]
- Permitting a bank's investment in a minority interest in an LLC that would act as agent in the placement of funds in certificates of deposit issued by foreign banks through traditional means of service, as well as through an Internet site linked to the bank's own Internet site.[159]
- Approving an application by a national bank to operate an Internet-based auto sales operation to enable consumers to locate specific models of used cars offered for sale.
- Approving an application by a national bank to establish an operating subsidiary to act as a certification authority and repository for certificates used to verify digital signatures.[160]

iv. Operating Subsidiaries of National Banks

On November 18, 1996, the Comptroller issued a final rule, effective December 31, 1996, substantially revising OCC's entire corporate activities rules, including the operating subsidiary regulation.[161] Most notable from the perspective of the increasing trend toward computer- and Internet-based products and delivery systems, the revised operating subsidiary rule held out the prospect for national bank operating subsidiaries to engage in activities not authorized for their par-

---

Key Corp., Mellon Bank, Michigan National Bank, NationsBank, PNC Bank, Royal Banc of Canada and Washington Mutual, Inc. *See* Jennifer Kingson Bloom & Drew Clark, *Major Banks, IBM Launch Network for PC Banking*, Am. Banker, Sept. 10, 1996, at 1. Thereafter, in 1997, First Union National Bank and Citibank joined Integrion. *See* Erich Luening, Integrion Gets Financial Boost (Sept. 26, 1997), <http://news.cnet.com/news/0-1007-200-322493.html> (visited June 19, 2001); First Union Joins Integrion Financial Network, First Union News Release (Sept. 25, 1997), <http://personalfinance.firstunion.com/pf/corp/0,2898,4_9,00.html> (visited June 15, 2001).

157. OCC Corporate Decision, Conditional Approval No. 220, at 2 n.4 (Dec. 2, 1996).

158. OCC Interpretive Letter No. 772, [1996–1997 Transfer Binder] Fed. Banking L. Rep. (CCH) ¶ 81–136, at 90,323 (Mar. 6, 1997).

159. The bank was chartered under the laws of the District of Columbia and, as such, was subject to the jurisdiction of OCC as its primary federal regulator. OCC Interpretive Letter No. 778, [1997 Transfer Binder] Fed. Banking L. Rep. (CCH) ¶ 81–205, at 90,210 (Mar. 20, 1997).

160. *See* Letter from Julie L. Williams, Chief Counsel, OCC, to Stanley F. Farrar, Esq. (Jan. 12, 1998), *available at* <http://www.occ.treas.govftprelease98–4.txt>. Zions Bank and DST must submit a description of their information and back-office systems to OCC for approval, as well as notify all third-party software/hardware vendors of OCC's regulatory authority. *See id.* at 20.

161. Rules, Policies, and Procedures for Corporate Activities, 61 Fed. Reg. 60,342, 60,348 (1996) (to be codified at 12 C.F.R. pt. 5).

ent banks, and for national banks to control less than eighty percent of their operating subsidiaries' voting securities.[162] In the regulation, OCC also provided for operating subsidiaries to be established as LLCs.[163]

v. Financial Subsidiaries

Section 121 of the GLB Act authorized national banks to invest in a new type of subsidiary, other than an operating subsidiary. As defined, a financial subsidiary is a company controlled by one or more insured depository institutions other than a subsidiary that is engaged solely in activities in which national banks may engage directly (under the same terms and conditions that govern the conduct of these activities by national banks) or a subsidiary that a national bank is specifically authorized to control under federal law. Under section 121, a financial subsidiary may engage in activities that are financial in nature, or in activities that are incidental to financial activities in which national banks may not engage, if the bank and subsidiary meet certain requirements and comply with stated safeguards. National banks may continue to use operating subsidiaries to engage in those activities that are part of, or incidental to, the business of banking. In March 2000, OCC amended its regulations to implement section 121, made conforming changes to its operating subsidiary rule and made corresponding changes to its equity investment regulations.[164]

vi. OCC Authorizes National Banks to Invest in Operating Subsidiaries for Identity Certification and Electronic Bill Presentment

Two decisions by OCC reflect its continuing commitment to allow national banks to be active participants in the evolving marketplace for electronic commerce and electronic financial services.

A. Citibank

On March 5, 1999, OCC approved Citibank's operating subsidiary application to engage in electronic bill payment and presentment services over the Internet.[165] Citibank and MSFDC (a joint venture between Microsoft Corpo-

---

162. 12 C.F.R. §§ 5.34(e)(1), (2) (2001).
163. *Id.* § 5.34(e)(2).
164. Financial Subsidiaries and Operating Subsidiaries, 65 Fed. Reg. 12,905 (2000) (to be codified at 12 C.F.R. pt. 5).
165. *See* OCC Conditional Approval No. 304 (Apr. 1999).

ration and First Data Corporation) agreed to form a joint venture to offer electronic bill payment and presentment services over the Internet. Electronic bill presentment allows sellers and service providers to make bills accessible through a customer's desktop computer.

B. Bank of America National Trust and Savings Association

On January 15, 1999, OCC approved an operating subsidiary application submitted on behalf of Bank of America National Trust and Savings Association, San Francisco, California, and Citibank, N.A., New York, New York, to own a minority interest in an LLC engaging in research and development activities in connection with the anticipated establishment of an identity certification service.[166] The applicant banks, as well as ABN AMRO N.V., Bankers Trust Company, Barclays Bank PLC, Bayerische Hypo-und and Verinsbank AG, The Chase Manhattan Bank, and Deutsche Bank AG, filed to invest in the Global Trust Organization (GTO) to provide digital certification services. GTO was subsequently renamed Identrus.

OCC has also issued a bulletin on digital certification activities and the operating standards and security procedures it expects national banks to adopt.[167]

vii. Minority Interest Investments

Over the last decade, OCC has developed a set of requirements for national banks wishing to acquire minority ownership interests in business entities. These minority investments have evolved into an important method by which banks may align themselves with other banks and nonbanks to develop important electronic technologies used in providing competitive financial services.

OCC Interpretive Letter No. 697 sets forth the following standards for banks wishing to have their operating subsidiaries participate in ventures as minority interest holders:[168] the business of the venture must be part of, or incidental to, the business of banking,[169] the bank must be able to prevent the venture from engaging in activities that do not meet the foregoing standard,[170]

---

166. *See* OCC Conditional Approval No. 301 (Feb. 1999).

167. *See* Certification Authority Systems, OCC Bull. 99-20 (May 4, 1999).

168. OCC Interpretive Letter No. 697, [1995–1996 Transfer Binder] Fed. Banking L. Rep. (CCH) ¶ 81–012, at 90,241 (Nov. 15, 1995) [hereinafter OCC Interpretive Letter No. 697].

169. *Id.* at 90,244 (citing OCC Interpretive Letter No. 380, [1988–1989 Transfer Binder] Fed. Banking L. Rep. (CCH) ¶ 85,604, at 77,909, 77,913 n.8 (Dec. 29, 1986); Letter from Robert B. Serino, Deputy Chief Counsel (Nov. 9, 1992) (unpublished); Letter from John E. Shockey, Deputy Chief Counsel (June 7, 1976) (unpublished)).

170. OCC Interpretive Letter No. 697, *supra* note 168 (citing OCC Interpretive Letter No. 625, [1993–1994 Transfer Binder] Fed. Banking L. Rep. (CCH) ¶ 83,507, at 71,617 (July 1, 1993); Letter from Peter Liebesman, Assistant Director, Legal Advisory Services Division (Jan. 26, 1981, Jan. 4, 1983) (unpublished)).

the bank's loss exposure must be limited, as a legal and accounting matter, and the bank must not have open-ended liability for the obligations of the enterprise,[171] and the investment must be convenient or useful to the bank in carrying out its business and not a mere passive investment unrelated to that bank's banking business.[172]

viii. Virtual Banks

A. OCC Grants Charter to a "Virtual Bank"

On August 20, 1997, OCC granted preliminary approval for a national bank charter to CompuBank, a Houston-based institution.[173] CompuBank planned to offer a variety of traditional and electronic banking services, such as checking and savings deposit products, ATM services and electronic bill payment, over the telephone or through a customer's personal computer. CompuBank conducted its banking business from a single location—a "call center"—that provided phone and computer dial-up connections for its customers.[174]

B. NextCard, National Association

On May 8, 1999, OCC authorized NextCard, Inc. (NCI) to open a new Internet credit card national bank.[175] NCI, formerly called Internet Access Financial Corporation, launched the NextCard VISA card in December 1997. It is marketed to consumers exclusively through its web site and can be used for both online and offline purchases. NextCard also offers several product and service enhancements specifically designed for the Internet-enabled consumer. These include a customized application process, Internet-based account management and online shopping enhancements.

---

171. OCC Interpretive Letter No. 697, *supra* note 168, at 90,245 (citing Merchants Nat'l Bank v. Wehrmann, 202 U.S. 295 (1906); OCC Interpretive Letter No. 289, [1983–1984 Transfer Binder] Fed. Banking L. Rep. (CCH) ¶ 85,453, at 77,616 (May 15, 1984)).

172. OCC Interpretive Letter No. 697, *supra* note 168, at 90,245–46 (citing OCC Interpretive Letter No. 543, [1990–1991 Transfer Binder] Fed. Banking L. Rep. (CCH) ¶ 83,255, at 71,336 (Feb. 13, 1991); OCC Interpretive Letter No. 554, [1991–1992 Transfer Binder] Fed. Banking L. Rep. (CCH) ¶ 83,301, at 71,401 (May 7, 1990); OCC Interpretive Letter No. 427, [1988–1989 Transfer Binder] Fed. Banking L. Rep. (CCH) ¶ 85,651 (May 9, 1988); OCC Interpretive Letter No. 421, [1988–1989 Transfer Binder] Fed. Banking L. Rep. (CCH) ¶ 85,645, at 78,018 (Mar. 14, 1988); Letter from Robert B. Serino, Deputy Chief Counsel (Nov. 9, 1992) (unpublished); Letter from James M. Kane, Central District Counsel (June 8, 1988); Letter from John E. Shockey, Deputy Chief Counsel (Dec. 19, 1975)).

173. Decision of the Office of the Comptroller of the Currency on the Application to Charter CompuBank, National Association, Houston, Texas (Aug. 20, 1997).

174. CompuBank has since sold its deposit accounts to Net Bank, Inc. *See In Brief: CompuBank Selling Accounts to NetBank*, AM. BANKER, Mar. 30, 2001, at 20.

175. OCC Conditional Approval No. 312 (May 1999).

C. CIBC National Bank

On July 9, 1999, OCC approved an application filed by Canadian Imperial Bank of Commerce, Toronto, Ontario, Canada, to charter a new full-service national bank, CIBC National Bank.[176] Though the bank is headquartered in Maitland, Orange County, Florida, it does not have any traditional banking offices, but rather delivers products and services to its customers through a variety of electronic delivery channels. Customers can conduct banking transactions through ATMs, through the Internet via a transactional web site and through the bank's toll-free customer service line. Customers can also access all these delivery channels at kiosks located on the premises of retail store partners.[177]

D. AeroBank.com

On January 29, 2000, OCC approved an application filed by a group of organizers to charter a new full-service national bank to be called AeroBank.com, National Association.[178] The organizers established a BHC, AeroBancorp.com Corporation. AeroBank and AeroFund Financial Inc., an existing accounts-receivable factoring company owned by one of the organizers, are subsidiaries of the BHC.

AeroBank does not have traditional offices; rather, it delivers banking products and services to its customers electronically. Customers can conduct bank transactions through ATMs, through the Internet with a transactional web site and through AeroBank's toll-free customer service line. AeroBank offers a full array of traditional banking products and services to small and medium-sized businesses by focusing on relationship banking with business development officers in the field, credit analysts at a central location and customer service agents at a telephone call center. A principal component of AeroBank's strategy is to establish alliances with third parties of interest to small and medium-sized businesses.

ix. Standards for Virtual Banks

The standards for OCC authorization of virtual institutions are becoming more clearly delineated. Under its corporate activities regulations, OCC considers whether the proposed bank has organizers who are aware of, and understand, national banking laws and regulations; has competent management, including

---

176. OCC Conditional Approval No. 313 (July 1999).
177. *Branching Out to New Forms of Banking*, DISTRIBUTION MGMT. BRIEFING, May 22, 2001, at 8.
178. OCC Conditional Approval No. 347 (Jan. 2000).

the board of directors, with ability and experience relevant to the types of services to be provided; has capitalization that is sufficient to support the projected volume and type of business; can reasonably be expected to achieve and maintain profitability; and will be operated in a safe and sound manner.

OCC's review of safety and soundness focuses upon a number of technology-related issues. For example, OCC confirms the adequacy of procedures during the preopening examination, with particular emphasis on areas of technology risk management and customer privacy. OCC reviews the bank's policies, procedures and controls for ensuring customer privacy and compliance with consumer protection laws and regulations. This review includes confirmation that adequate policies have been implemented. OCC also expects the bank's policies and procedures to comply with guidance issued by OCC and the Federal Financial Institutions Examination Council in connection with customer privacy, consumer protection and electronic banking.[179]

Of some significance to Internet banks is the regulatory evaluation of the process of outsourcing activities that the bank would otherwise perform for itself. This often implicates the requirements of the Bank Service Companies Act (BSCA).[180] Certain services performed for the bank by third parties are subject to OCC examination and regulation. New Internet banks are expected to notify potential vendors, in writing, of OCC's examination and regulatory jurisdiction.

Last, under CRA and its implementing regulations, OCC must consider a proposed insured national bank's description of how it will meet its CRA objectives. The requirement that a bank help meet the credit needs of its assessment area(s) through its lending activities, qualified investments and available services raises particularly interesting questions when the bank has no physical offices. In the case of the CIBC National Bank, the business plan's focus upon ATMs and supermarket kiosks made the identification of a "physical" market possible.

3. FRB's Perspective on Electronic Financial Products and Services

i. Bank Holding Company Activities

The regulations governing BHCs focus particularly upon FRB's actions regarding electronic banking and commerce activities of BHCs and state member

---

179. *See* Guidance on Electronic Financial Services and Customer Compliance, OCC Bull. No. 98-31 (1998); Technology Risk Management: PC Banking, OCC Bull. No. 98-38 (1998); Fair Credit Reporting Act, OCC Advisory Letter No. 99-3 (1999).

180. 12 U.S.C. §§ 1861–1867 (1994) & Supp. V 1999).

banks. The regulations address the following: (1) FRB's rules regarding joint ventures and minority interest investments in connection with nonbanking activities, (2) FRB's supervisory role, (3) whether and how electronic financial products and services implicate the consumer protection requirements set forth in the Electronic Fund Transfer Act (EFTA) and FRB's Regulation E and (4) FRB's 1997 Stored-Value Report.

A. Internet Banking Services

FRB approved the acquisition of Five Paces Software, Inc. (Five Paces) by Cardinal Bancshares, Inc. in 1996. Five Paces' nationwide operation involved providing data processing and transmission activities related to banking and financial services available over the Internet.[181] Because Five Paces conducted all its activities in connection with transactions for accounts maintained at depository institutions, the activities fell squarely within the financial, banking or economic information contemplated by Regulation Y.[182]

B. PC-Based Personal Financial Software

Does the development and creation of financially oriented software constitute (1) the manufacturing of a separate nonbanking product, (2) the production of a product that is closely related to the business of banking or (3) a distribution vehicle that facilitates banking and, therefore, may be considered closely related to it? FRB addressed this question in February 1996, when it approved an application by the Royal Bank of Canada (Royal Bank) to acquire twenty percent of the voting shares of MECA Software, L.L.C. (MECA). MECA, a software development firm, is owned jointly by subsidiaries of NationsBank and Bank of America, and is engaged in data processing activities related to its PC-based personal finance program, Managing Your Money.[183] MECA's software products enable customers to pay bills, reconcile checking account registers, access checking and savings account statements, transfer funds between accounts, receive stock quotations and conduct tax and financial planning.[184] Because MECA was primarily involved in the processing of financial, economic and banking data contemplated under the data processing provisions of Regulation Y, FRB considered this portion of MECA's activities to be "closely related to banking" under section 4(c)(8) of BHCA.[185]

---

181. Cardinal Bancshares, Inc., 82 Fed. Res. Bull. 674 (July 1996).
182. *Id.* at 675.
183. Royal Bank of Canada, 82 Fed. Res. Bull. 363, 364 (Apr. 1996).
184. *Id.* at 364 n.3.
185. 12 U.S.C. § 1843(c)(8) (Supp. V 1999).

Just over a year after the Royal Bank order, FRB dramatically shifted its approach in this area. Rather than requiring a showing that nonfinancial data processing activity did not represent a significant aspect of the data processing entity's activities, FRB shifted to a broad regulatory safe harbor for nonfinancial data processing. Under the amended data processing regulation promulgated in 1997, an entity's revenues from nonfinancial data processing services can be up to thirty percent of total data processing revenues.[186]

C. Providing Billing Services

In February 1996, FRB approved the application of Compagnie Financiere de Paribas (Paribas) to engage de novo (through a network of several foreign subsidiaries) in providing customer account billing services or software, or both, to digital mobile phone network operators (operators) throughout the United States.[187] The Paribas U.S. subsidiary planned to provide an integrated software program for account billing features. The computer software and hardware would be separate and distinct from the software and hardware running the telephone operating and switching system.[188] The software's principal function would be to collect data necessary to prepare and transmit bills on behalf of operators to their customers.

D. Dispensing Alternative Media

In 1996, a group of BHCs sought FRB approval for their jointly owned subsidiary to engage in certain data processing activities that would allow ATMs to dispense alternative media.[189]

E. Integrion Financial Network

In December 1996, FRB approved the participation of BHCs in the Integrion Financial Network (Integrion).[190] Integrion is currently owned and operated by

---

186. Bank Holding Companies and Change in Bank Control (Regulation Y), 62 Fed. Reg. 9,290, 9,338 (1997) (to be codified at 12 C.F.R. § 225.28(b)(14)(ii) [hereinafter Regulation Y]). In promulgating the regulation, FRB noted in the preamble that "this [thirty-percent] basket would not include revenue derived from the use of excess capacity or the sale of general purpose hardware that is currently permitted in accordance with [FRB's] regulation and policies governing those activities." *Id.* at 9,304 n.5.

187. Compagnie Financiere de Paribas, 82 Fed. Res. Bull. 348 (Apr. 1996).

188. *Id.* The Paribas subsidiary's product prepared customer billing information based upon customer call information provided by the operators, including time and duration of the call, terms of the customer's service contract and account balances. In addition, the software performed general accounts receivable and payable functions.

189. Banc One Corp., 82 Fed. Res. Bull. 848 (Sept. 1996). *See* OCC Interpretive Letter No. 718 [1995–1996 Transfer Binder] Fed. Banking L. Rep. (CCH) ¶ 81–033, at 90,299, 90,301 (Mar. 14, 1996).

190. Royal Bank of Canada, 83 Fed. Res. Bull. 135 (Feb. 1997).

its eighteen "owner" banks, in conjunction with their information technology partner, IBM.[191] It planned to offer interactive banking and financial and electronic commerce services to consumers and businesses, including data processing and transmission services, as well as Internet access.[192] FRB did not find providing Internet access to be a separate activity subject to approval.[193]

ii. Changes to Rule on Permissible Data Processing Activities

The data processing regulation promulgated by FRB in 1997 reflects two major changes—and one minor change—from its predecessor.[194] FRB increased the amount that the cost of hardware may represent, when it is provided as part of a packaged offering of software and hardware, from ten percent to thirty percent. This change enhances the ability of BHCs to compete with nonbanking companies that sell packaged systems, including hardware, representing a turnkey solution to clients' needs. FRB also removed the requirement that data processing services and facilities be designed, marketed and operated for processing and transmitting only financial, banking or economic data. FRB offered two reasons for the change.[195] First, the restriction was inhibiting the ability of BHCs to compete with other providers, who often combine financial and nonfinancial products. Second, strict limitations have hindered the ability of BHCs to recruit qualified employees whose expertise and interests include both financial and nonfinancial matters.[196] In addition, FRB eliminated the requirement that data processing services be rendered pursuant to a written contract.[197]

iii. Minority Interest Investment as an Activity

When BHCs make minority interest investments or participate in joint ventures in connection with permissible nonbank activities, FRB often imposes condi-

---

191. *Id.* at 156. *See also supra* note 156. With more than 60 million consumer accounts, these banking institutions claimed to have a customer base of more than half the total consumer accounts in North America. *See* Louis Gerstner, Chief Executive Officer, IBM, Remarks at Integrion Press Conference (Sept. 9, 1996) <http://www.ibm.com/lvg/integrion. phtml> (visited June 15, 2001).

192. *See* Thomas P. Vartanian, et al., *Integrion Financial Network: A New Stage for Electronic Banking,* ELECTRONIC BANKING L. & COM. REP., Oct. 1996, at 6 (further discussing scope of services to be provided by IntegrionSM network, and implications for electronic banking).

193. This continues a trend that has been embraced by various federal bank regulatory agencies; for example, OCC views the Internet as a means of distributing a financial product rather than a separate financial product in and of itself. *See* OCC Interpretive Letter No. 742, [1996–1997 Transfer Binder] Fed. Banking L. Rep. (CCH) ¶ 81–106, at 90,215 (Aug. 19, 1996).

194. Before the 1997 amendments, the regulation was found at 12 C.F.R. § 225.25(b)(7) (1997).

195. Regulation Y, 62 Fed. Reg. at 9, 304.

196. For the same reasons, FRB allowed up to thirty percent of management consulting revenues to be derived from providing advisory services other than in connection with financial, accounting and similar matters. *Id.*

197. State statutes based upon the Statute of Frauds may still require written contracts in many cases.

tions to ensure that the enterprise in which the BHC is investing does not involve itself in activities that are not permissible for BHCs.[198]

FRB now requires that in all joint venture applications, each BHC make two commitments.[199] The applicant, the joint venture company and the co-venturer must commit that they do not conduct—or anticipate conducting—any activities or relationships that would cause the applicant, its affiliates or the joint venture company to be engaged in any of the activities of the co-venturer or its affiliates (other than the joint venture company). The joint venture would also be treated as an affiliate.

iv. FRB's Proposals and Interim Rules Regarding Electronic Disclosures and Documentation

A. 1996 Electronic Fund Transfers Proposal

In the context of home banking and other financial services, the Electronic Fund Transfers (EFT) Proposal responded to financial institution inquiries regarding the circumstances under which written disclosures, such as initial disclosures under section 205.7 and periodic statements under section 205.9, may be provided to consumers by electronic means.[200] The EFT Proposal defined an "electronic communication" as an "electronically transmitted text message between a financial institution and a consumer's home computer or other electronic device possessed by the consumer."[201] The EFT Proposal, however, would limit "electronic communications" to those that can be displayed as visual text, such as on a computer monitor or screen phone.[202] Recognizing that electronic documents that are produced, stored or communicated by computer are generally considered to be "in writing," FRB proposed that Regulation E be amended to allow electronic communication to satisfy the written-communication requirements of Regulation E, subject to a consumer's right to receive paper-based information upon request within one year.[203]

B. 1998 Interim Rule and Disclosure Proposals

Following a review of public comments, the FRB issued an interim rule under Regulation E.[204] At the same time, FRB published proposals under Regula-

---

198. Cardinal Bancshares, Inc., 80 Fed. Res. Bull. 447 (May 1994); Credit Commercial de France, S.A. & Berliner Handels-und Frankfurter Bank, 81 Fed. Res. Bull. 390 (Feb. 1995).

199. Joint Venture Proposals Pursuant to Regulation Y: Guidance Regarding Issues, and Criteria for Delegation, SR 96–39 (Dec. 26, 1996).

200. Electronic Fund Transfers (Regulation E), 61 Fed. Reg. 19,696, 19,704–05 (proposed May 2, 1996) (to be codified at 12 C.F.R. pt. 205) [hereinafter EFT Proposal].

201. *Id.* at 19,696.

202. *Id.*

203. *Id.* at 19,697.

204. Regulation E, 63 Fed. Reg. 14,528 (1998) (to be codified at 12 C.F.R. § 205.4(c)).

tion DD (Truth in Savings),[205] Regulation M (Consumer Leasing),[206] Regulation Z (Truth in Lending)[207] and Regulation B (Equal Credit Opportunity).[208] The interim rule and the proposals were similar to the May 1996 proposal, except they did not require financial institutions to provide paper copies of disclosures to a consumer upon request if the consumer previously agreed to receive disclosures electronically.

C. 1999 Interim Rule under Regulation DD and Modified Disclosure Proposals

The FRB published modified and more detailed proposals in September 1999.[209] The FRB also approved an interim rule to permit the electronic delivery of periodic statements of account activity under Regulation DD.[210] Like the 1998 proposals, the modified proposals would authorize the electronic delivery of disclosures required under Regulations B, E, M, Z and DD. To provide disclosures electronically, however, financial institutions and others would have to provide consumers with a standard disclosure that describes information that could be sent electronically and specifies whether the information is available in paper form; identifies the address or location at which the information will be provided and, if at a location other than the consumer's electronic address, specifies the length of time the information will be available and how long it will be available after that period; specifies any technical requirements needed to receive and retain information, and enables consumers to confirm their computers meet the technical requirements; and provides a way for consumers to agree to receive information electronically and identifies a contact at the institution if consumers experience difficulties or have questions.

D. 2001 Interim Rules

Pursuant to the Electronic Signatures in Global and National Commerce Act (E-Sign Act) and in response to consumer comments, the FR adopted interim rules to establish uniform standards on the electronic delivery of dis-

---

205. Regulation DD (Truth in Savings), 63 Fed. Reg. 14,533 (proposed Mar. 25, 1998) .

206. Regulation M (Consumer Leasing), 63 Fed. Reg. 14,539 (proposed Mar. 25, 1998) (to be codified at 12 C.F.R. pt. 213).

207. Regulation Z (Truth in Lending) 63 Fed. Reg. 14,548 (proposed Mar. 25, 1998) (to be codified at 12 C.F.R. pt. 226).

208. Regulation B (Equal Credit Opportunity), 63 Fed. Reg. 14,552 (proposed Mar. 25, 1998) (to be codified at 12 C.F.R. pt. 202).

209. Electronic Fund Transfers, 64 Fed. Reg. 49,699 (proposed Sept. 14, 1999). FRB subsequently extended the public comment period to March 3, 2000. *See* Equal Credit Opportunity, Electronic Fund Transfers, Consumer Leasing, Truth in Lending, Truth in Savings, 64 Fed. Reg. 69,963 (notice Dec. 15, 1999) (to be codified at 12 C.F.R. pt. 230).

210. Truth in Savings, 64 Fed. Reg. 49,846 (1999).

closures required by law.[211] The interim rules cover consumer disclosures required by five consumer protection laws and their implementing regulations: Regulations B (Equal Credit Protection Act), E (Electronic Fund Transfers), M (Consumer Leasing), Z (Truth in Lending) and DD (Truth in Savings).[212]

Under the interim rules, financial institutions, creditors, lessors and others may deliver disclosures electronically only if they obtain a consumer's electronic affirmative consent. Disclosures may be sent by electronic mail (e-mail) to an electronic address designated by the consumer or the disclosures may be made available at another location, such as an Internet web site. If the disclosures are not sent by e-mail, consumers must receive a notice alerting them to the availability of the disclosures. Disclosures posted on a web site must be available for at least ninety days. Disclosures must be provided before a consumer opens an account; enters into a contract for electronic fund transfer services (or before the first transfer); enters into a lease for personal property in an amount not exceeding $25,000 for a term of more than four months (such as an automobile lease), or submits an application for credit. If an e-mail disclosure is returned undelivered, an institution must make a good faith attempt to redeliver the e-mail using the address information available in their files.[213]

v. Computer Network Payment Products

Finally, as part of its EFT Proposal, FRB also noted the increasing interest in systems that would allow for payments to be made over computer networks, including the Internet. FRB requested comment on how Internet and other computer network payment products should be treated for purposes of Regulation E.[214] Noting the differences in various proposed network payment systems, FRB concluded that "the same principles should apply to network payment products as to stored value card products in analyzing coverage under Regulation E."[215] FRB noted that some of these network payment products involve online access to consumer accounts at financial institutions and, accordingly, would be fully subject to Regulation E. On the other hand, FRB commented that other products may involve various procedures for authorizing and conducting transactions, and may or may not be subject to Regulation E.

---

211. Electronic Signatures in Global and National Commerce Act, Pub. L. No. 106–229, 114 Stat. 464 (2000).

212. Equal Credit Opportunity, 66 Fed. Reg. 17,779 (Apr. 4, 2001) (to be codified at 12 C.F.R. pt. 202); Electronic Fund Transfers, 66 Fed. Reg. 17,786 (Apr. 4, 2001) (to be codified at 12 C.F.R. pt. 205); Truth in Savings, 66 Fed. Reg. 17,795 (Apr. 4, 2001) (to be codified at 12 C.F.R. pt. 230).

213. The interim rules are at <http://www.federalreserve.gov/boarddocs/press/boardacts/2001/20010329/default.htm>.

214. EFT Proposal, 61 Fed. Reg. at 19,703.

215. *Id.*

vi. Federal Preemption of State EFT Laws

The federal Electronic Funds Transfer Act (EFTA)[216] provides that it does not annul, alter or affect similar state EFT laws, unless they are inconsistent with EFTA. In any event, such state laws are preempted only to the extent of such inconsistency.[217] In addition, EFTA grants FRB the authority to exempt by regulation any class of EFTs within any state if FRB determines the state laws provide consumer protections that are substantially similar to those provided under EFTA and Regulation E.[218] According to FRB's official staff commentary, a state law that is inconsistent may be preempted even if FRB has not yet issued a formal determination.[219]

4. The Federal Deposit Insurance Corporation's Perspective on Electronic Financial Products and Services

The Federal Deposit Insurance Corporation (FDIC) is best known for its role as the provider of deposit insurance for the nation's banks and savings associations. In that capacity, FDIC ultimately deals with all types of depository institutions—national banks, state member banks, state nonmember banks, and federal and state savings associations.

FDIC, as a result of its role as insurer, has greater experience in analyzing the causes of depository institution failures than any of the other federal bank regulatory agencies. Because of this presumed expertise, FDIC has increasingly been given the responsibility for guarding the financial system against risks that are likely to expose institutions to failure. Electronic banking and commerce will reconfigure the spectrum of risks to which banks must be sensitive.

---

216. 15 U.S.C. §§ 1693–1693r (1994).
217. Section 1693q provides as follows:
   This subchapter does not annul, alter, or affect the laws of any State relating to electronic fund transfers, except to the extent that those laws are inconsistent with the provisions of this subchapter, and then only to the extent of the inconsistency. A State law is not inconsistent with this subchapter if the protection such law affords any consumer is greater than the protection afforded by this subchapter. The Board shall ... determine whether a State requirement is inconsistent or affords greater protection. If the Board determines that a State requirement is inconsistent, financial institutions shall incur no liability under the law of that State for a good faith failure to comply with that law, notwithstanding that such determination is subsequently amended, rescinded, or determined by judicial or other authority to be invalid for any reason. This subchapter does not extend the applicability of any such law to any class of persons or transactions to which it would not otherwise apply.
15 U.S.C. § 1693q (1994).
218. *Id.* § 1693r.
219. 12 C.F.R. pt. 205, supp. I § 205.12(b) (2001).

i. Deposit Insurance for Stored-Value Products

Increasingly, insured depository institutions use technology to offer customers new retail payment products, including a variety of stored-value products. These emerging forms of electronic value raise a range of issues regarding the interpretation and application of the Federal Deposit Insurance Act (FDIA)[220] and FDIC's regulations thereunder.[221] At a basic level, whether the value underlying stored-value products fits within the statutory definition of "deposit" must be determined.[222] This depends upon a number of factors, including the following: (1) the type and design of the card, computer or other architecture used and (2) the availability and adequacy of the card or other storage device to store sufficient information to identify an account, an account holder and the nature of any fiduciary or deposit relationship between the stored-value holder and the issuer of the stored-value obligation.[223] Whether deposit insurance covers the new forms of electronic payment is an important consideration in the design of such products. It can also have a significant impact upon depositors and other purchasers and issuers of stored-value products, and ultimately upon the entire financial system.

ii. General Counsel's Opinion No. 8

FDIC, in its General Counsel's Opinion No. 8 (SVC Opinion), addressed and clarified whether federal deposit insurance applies to unpaid balances maintained on a stored-value card (SVC) or other electronic payment system before the use of the funds by consumers.[224] Issued on July 16, 1996, the SVC Opinion constituted FDIC's first official, formal regulatory action regarding stored-value

---

220. 12 U.S.C.A. §§ 1811–1835a (West 2001).

221. 12 C.F.R. §§ 303–69 (2001). *See also* General Counsel's Opinion No. 8; Stored Value Cards, 61 Fed. Reg. 40,490 (1996) [hereinafter SVC Opinion]; Task Force on Stored-Value Cards, Am. Bankers Ass'n, *A Commercial Lawyer's Take on the Electronic Purse: An Analysis of Commercial Law Issues Associated with Stored-Value Cards and Electronic Money*, 52 Bus. Law. 653 (Feb. 1997) (describing stored-value products and analyzing how existing commercial laws might apply to their use).

222. 12 U.S.C. § 1813(l) (1994 & Supp. V 1999).

223. Sharon P. Sivertsen, *Legal and Regulatory Issues in Stored-Value Card Technologies*, Electronic Banking L. & Com. Rep., May 1996, at 9–10.

224. SVC Opinion, *supra* note 221. This question has been addressed by a number of commentators. *See, e.g.*, Sivertsen, *supra* note 223; Thomas P. Vartanian, *Key Question for Emerging Systems: Where Is the Money?*, Am. Banker—Future Banking, June 17, 1996, at 6A. *See also* Thomas P. Vartanian, Statement before FDIC concerning Stored-Value Cards and Electronic Payment Systems (Sept. 12, 1996), *available at* <http://www.ffhsj.com>. There are advantages and disadvantages to having FDIC deposit insurance coverage for stored-value or other retail payment products. For example, the bank issuer of an insured SVC could use FDIC coverage as a marketing tool, allowing its products to be promoted as government insured. Covering stored-value products with FDIC insurance, however, would add to an institution's deposit base and thus increase the insurance premium paid to FDIC. Treating the funds as deposits would also eliminate the stored-value "float" income the bank issuer intends to receive from the funds held against future consumer purchases, because FDIC-insured balances would be maintained in consumer accounts, rather than the bank's

products.[225] Specifically, the SVC Opinion described FDIC's legal position on whether, and under what circumstances, the funds underlying SVCs may be considered "deposits" under FDIA[226] and therefore qualify for deposit insurance coverage and assessment.

The SVC Opinion identifies four types of stored-value systems:[227]

- Bank Primary—Customer Account Systems
- Bank Primary—Reserve Systems
- Bank Secondary—Advance Systems
- Bank Secondary—Preacquisition Systems

It divides SVCs into two basic types—primary, in which the bank holds the funds underlying the electronic value directly, and secondary, in which a third party (likely the issuer) holds the funds underlying the electronic value represented by the SVC.

5. The Office of Thrift Supervision's Perspective on Electronic Financial Products and Services

The stated mission of the Office of Thrift Supervision (OTS) is to "effectively and efficiently supervise thrift institutions to maintain the safety and soundness of institutions and to ensure the viability of the industry"[228] by creating a regulatory framework flexible enough to accommodate change without sacrificing safety and soundness.[229] This section summarizes the actions OTS has taken—in the form of regulations and supervisory guidance in connection with specific applications—to address electronic banking issues.

---

own account. *See FDIC Decides to Look before it Leaps on Covering Stored-Value Cards*, BANK NETWORK NEWS, July 26, 1996, at 3.

225. On the same day, FDIC issued a notice of public hearings and request for comment on the issues contained in the SVC Opinion. *See* Stored-Value Cards and Other Electronic Payment Systems, 61 Fed. Reg. 40,494 (notice Aug. 2, 1996). FDIC previously issued opinions on two related topics—deposit insurance for funds held by a company that provides payment services for Internet purchases, and the status of such a company as a "deposit broker" under section 29 of FDIA (12 U.S.C. § 1831f(f)(1994)). *See* Interpretive Letter from Jeffrey M. Kopchik on Internet payments (Oct. 20, 1995); Interpretive Letter from Joseph A. DiNuzzo on sponsoring company as a "deposit broker" under FDIA (Oct. 20, 1995). *See also* Thomas P. Vartanian, David L. Ansell and Robert H. Ledig, *FDIC Issues First Opinions on Internet Deposit Insurance Issues*, 21ST CENTURY BANKING ALERT® No. 96-2-12, Feb. 12, 1996, *available at* <http://www.ffhsj.combancmailbanc page.htm>.

226. *See* 12 U.S.C. §§ 1813(l)(1)–1813(l)(5) (1994 & Supp. V 1999).

227. SVC Opinion, 61 Fed. Reg. at 40,490.

228. Office of Thrift Supervision—OTS Mission and Functions, *available at* <http://www.ots .treas.gov> (visited June 17, 1997).

229. *Id.*

i. OTS Internet Banks

On May 8, 1995, OTS conditionally approved Security First Network Bank, FSB (SFNB) as the first Internet bank.[230] SFNB enabled potential customers nationwide the opportunity to visit SFNB's web site, to open deposit accounts and then to view account information and engage in transactions. To satisfy OTS safety and soundness concerns, SFNB—before opening for business—had to obtain independent tests of the functionality and security of its operations.

OTS approved a second Internet bank, Atlanta Internet Bank (AIB), on July 11, 1997.[231] In approving the establishment of AIB, OTS set conditions similar to those for approving SFNB. OTS required an independent security review and an AIB attestation that the computer system "does not allow unauthorized or undetected access to customer accounts, with reasonable certainty," by August 31, 1997.[232] Further, OTS required that AIB comply with the OTS Statement on Retail Online Personal Computer Banking.[233]

Thereafter, the OTS approved an application from the Principal Mutual Life Insurance Company to create a federal Internet thrift.[234] The OTS imposed similar conditions on Principal as it had on prior Internet thrift approvals.

ii. OTS Regulatory Actions

A. Electronic Operations

To meet its goal of creating a flexible regulatory framework, OTS undertook a comprehensive review of its regulations in 1995. As part of that review, OTS started addressing the impact of its regulations on electronic banking activities. On April 2, 1997, OTS published an advance notice of a proposed rule regarding the adequacy of OTS regulations governing electronic banking (Electronic Banking Notice).[235] In that notice, OTS recognized that although entirely new regulations might be more appropriate than simple updates, it intended to focus primarily upon updating three regulations currently affecting electronic opera-

---

230. *See Kentucky Thrift Given Authority to Offer Services over Internet,* OTS News Release 95-33 (May 10, 1995); Approval of Purchase of Assets and Assumption of Liabilities, OTS Order No. 95-88 (May 8, 1995).

231. *OTS Approves Internet Bank to Provide Range of Services,* News Release 97-44 (July 14, 1997); Approval of Holding Company Acquisition and Purchase of Assets and Assumption of Liabilities, OTS Order No. 97-66 (July 11, 1997) [hereinafter OTS Order No. 97-66].

232. OTS Order No. 97-66, *supra* note 231, at 3.

233. *Id.*

234. OTS Gives Approval to Create Thrift Institution, OTS Press Release 97-80 (Nov. 14, 1997).

235. Deposits and Electronic Banking, 62 Fed. Reg. 15,626 (advanced notice Apr. 2, 1997) (to be codified at 12 C.F.R. pts. 545, 556, 557, 561, 563 and 563g) [hereinafter Deposits and Electronic Banking].

tions directly: remote service units (RSUs),[236] home banking services[237] and data processing.[238] After reviewing the comments on the Electronic Banking Notice, OTS published a notice of proposed rule making (Electronic Operations Proposal) to eliminate the existing regulations and replace them with a single new subpart that would focus upon electronic operations.[239] In further response to comments received, OTS published a supplemental notice for public comment on a proposal to require prior notice to OTS before a transactional web site is established.[240] OTS subsequently adopted a final rule in November 1998 that incorporated the same principles and supervisory concerns of both the Electronic Banking Proposal and the supplemental proposal.[241]

(1) Electronic Banking Notice

In the Electronic Banking Notice, OTS identified three existing regulations that affect a federal savings association's ability to engage in electronic activities. The first two regulations govern the type of facility that such an institution can use to deliver services—RSUs and home banking services. The third regulation established parameters for permissible federal savings association data processing activities.[242] The Electronic Banking Notice divided the discussion into sections concerning facilities, permissible activities and other issues, a format reflecting the current regulatory framework.

(2) Facilities

Facilities through which a federal savings association may deliver services to customers include home offices, branches, agency offices, data processing or administrative offices, RSUs[243] and home banking.[244] In the Electronic Banking Notice, OTS questioned whether an automated loan machine (ALM)—which permits a customer to apply for a consumer loan up to a specific limit by entering certain information by keypad into a machine resembling an ATM—should be considered a branch or an RSU. The issue is significant because different rules govern the establishment of branches and RSUs. Branches are subject to application requirements, while RSUs are not. In 1981, the Federal Home Loan Bank Board replaced the enumerated activities permissible for RSUs with a statement that RSUs could not be used to establish loan accounts.[245]

---

236. 12 C.F.R. § 545.141 (1998).

237. *Id.* § 545.142 (1998).

238. *Id.* § 545.138 (1998).

239. Electronic Operations, 62 Fed. Reg. 51,817 (proposed Oct. 3, 1997) (to be codified at 12 C.F.R. § 545.92, pt. 550).

240. Electronic Operations, 63 Fed. Reg. 43,327 (proposed Aug. 13, 1998) (to be codified at 12 C.F.R. pt. 555).

241. Electronic Operations, 63 Fed. Reg. 65,673 (1998) (to be codified at 12 C.F.R. § 545.92, pt. 555, § 559.3) [hereinafter Electronic Operations Rule].

242. 12 C.F.R. § 545.138 (1998).

243. *Id.* § 545.141 (1998). An RSU is an information-processing device not on the premises of a federal savings association.

244. *Id.* § 545.142 (1998).

245. Deposits and Electronic Banking, 62 Fed. Reg. at 15,631. *See* Debit Cards, Remote Service Unit Amendments, 46 Fed. Reg. 8,438, 8,440 (1981); 12 C.F.R. § 545.141(b) (1998).

OTS questioned whether it should broaden the definition of RSU to include ALMs, and then adjust other facility definitions accordingly.[246] OTS is also considering whether a full range of banking services may be offered under the home banking services regulation.[247] When the regulation was drafted, home banking was defined to include only the "transfer of funds or financial information" and "the performance of other transactions initiated by the customer."[248] Accordingly, OTS raised the question of whether this definition is broad enough to cover the opening of new accounts or the processing of credit applications using electronic banking systems.

(3) Data Processing

OTS issued its data processing regulation when it interpreted data processing to mean the performance of nondiscretionary functions, such as maintenance of bookkeeping or accounting records.[249] Data processing technology now is capable of making risk-based decisions; for example, ALMs process loan applications. OTS indicated that it intends its regulations to reflect and accommodate such changes. In addition, OTS is reconsidering the necessity of restricting thrifts in the sales or marketing of services, software and excess data processing capacity. OTS noted that OCC afforded national banks broader authority to sell electronic services, products and excess capacity than OTS afforded federal savings associations.[250] OTS sought comment on whether it should provide similarly broad authority.

Although OTS adopted the final rule substantially as proposed, it clarified that management must identify and mitigate potential risks and establish prudent controls, in addition to implementing security measures designed to ensure secure operations.[251]

iii. Internet Access Provided by a Federal Savings Bank

In April 1997, OTS granted a savings bank permission to provide Internet access to customers and noncustomers through a subsidiary.[252] OTS found the au-

---

246. Deposits and Electronic Banking, 62 Fed. Reg. at 15,631.

247. *Id.* at 15,632.

248. Data Processing Activities of Federal Associations, Home Banking Services, 48 Fed. Reg. 7,428, 7,431 (1983) (to be codified at 12 C.F.R. § 545.138).

249. Deposits and Electronic Banking, 62 Fed. Reg. at 15,632.

250. *Id. See, e.g.,* OCC Interpretive Letter No. 611, [1992–1993 Transfer Binder] Fed. Banking L. Rep. (CCH) ¶ 83,449, at 71,572 (Nov. 23, 1992); OCC Interpretive Letter No. 742, [1996–1997 Transfer Binder] Fed. Banking L. Rep. (CCH) ¶ 81–106, at 90,215 (Aug. 19, 1996). *See also* OCC Interpretive Letter No. 196, [1981–1982 Transfer Binder] Fed. Banking L. Rep. (CCH) ¶ 85,277, at 77,415 (May 18, 1981); OCC Interpretive Letter No. 284, [1983–1984 Transfer Binder] Fed. Banking L. Rep. (CCH) ¶ 85,448, at 77,610 (Mar. 26, 1984); OCC Interpretive Letter No. 419, [1988–1989 Transfer Binder] Fed. Banking L. Rep. (CCH) ¶ 85,643, at 78,013 (Feb. 16, 1988).

251. Electronic Operations Rule, 62 Fed. Reg. at 65,677.

252. Letter from Dwight C. Smith, III, Deputy Chief Counsel (Apr. 14, 1997). OTS conditioned the approval upon the noncustomer accounts being part of a safe and sound implementation strategy approved

thority for providing these services in its home banking services regulation[253] and data processing regulation.[254]

iv. OTS Guidance on Retail Online PC Banking

On June 23, 1997, OTS issued to savings associations a statement of guidance on retail online personal computer banking (PC Banking Guidelines).[255] In a cover memorandum issued with the statement, OTS emphasized the importance of risk analysis and the implementation of appropriate risk controls.[256]

The PC Banking Guidelines define PC banking and emphasize the importance of planning, testing and monitoring PC banking activities "as part of the system development methodology and the risk management process."[257] They also focus upon the strategic, legal/regulatory and operational risks inherent in offering PC banking to customers. In discussing these risk areas, OTS explores traditional risks, as well as those unique to PC banking. In assessing the strategic risks of implementing PC banking, OTS recommends that financial institutions develop business plans that justify the programs, make sufficient resources available to support the programs, decide whether to outsource certain functions or perform them in-house and stay abreast of technological developments.[258]

§ 5.4 Antitrust[259]

1. Introduction

Antitrust principles permeate nearly every aspect of doing business on the Internet, from restrictions on distribution and advertising policies, to the formation of joint ventures and strategic alliances and the merger and acquisition of Internet companies. The antitrust laws, which have as their essential goal the

---

by the appropriate regional OTS office. *See also* OCC Interpretive Letter No. 742, [1996–1997 Transfer Binder] Fed. Banking L. Rep. (CCH) ¶ 81–106, at 90,215 (Aug. 19, 1996).

253. *See* 12 C.F.R. § 545.142 (1998).

254. *See id.* § 545.138 (1998).

255. *OTS Issues Guidance to Thrifts on Retail On-Line PC Banking, Statement on Retail On-Line PC Banking,* OTS News Release 97–39 (June 23, 1997) [hereinafter *PC Banking Guidelines*].

256. Memorandum from John Downey to Chief Executive Officers on OTS Statement on Retail On-Line PC Banking, CEO Letter No. 70 (June 23, 1997).

257. *PC Banking Guidelines, supra* note 255, at 8.

258. *Id.* at 2.

259. For more on antitrust issues, see section 3.3.12.

protection of competitive markets, are often said to apply equally well to any industry or market. To a certain extent, however, the Internet presents a unique market environment. The Internet is unbounded by geography. Wherever located, marketplace participants are all essentially located "just across street" from their suppliers, distributors and competitors. Communications occur with tremendous ease—business-to-business (B2B) marketplaces, bulletin boards and chat rooms all provide facilities for communication and trade. The proximity of online marketplace participants has significant implications for antitrust.

Another unique characteristic of Internet markets is their tendency to exhibit what are referred to as *network effects*, meaning that the value of the marketplace to each user increases as others use the marketplace. Network effects create tremendous efficiencies for users of a network, but may also cause marketplaces to grow rapidly, possibly leading to the growth of anticompetitive market power.

Despite these unique characteristics, the emergence of e-commerce is not likely to cause a substantial shift in antitrust analysis, and, in many ways, transacting business over the Internet raises few new antitrust issues (though it may raise a number of traditional concerns). Undoubtedly, the courts and federal agencies charged with enforcement of antitrust laws will, over the next several years, articulate how the unique characteristics of the Internet affect traditional antitrust analysis; Section 6.4 of this book, however, describes the basic principles that apply in evaluating antitrust and e-commerce issues.

2. Sources of Antitrust Law

i. The Sherman Act

The Sherman Act is the principle statute regulating competition law within the United States.[260] Section 1 of the Sherman Act prohibits agreements among two or more persons or companies to restrain trade in any product or service. The U.S. Supreme Court long ago determined that the Sherman Act prohibits only those contracts or agreements that restrain trade unreasonably. Court have, over the years, defined the types of agreements that are unreasonable. Some agreements are deemed so inherently anticompetitive that they are per se unlawful. Per se unlawful conduct includes price fixing, agreements among competitors to restrict output, allocations of markets among competitors, concerted boycotts among competitors and resale price maintenance.[261] Agreements not chal-

---

260. 15 U.S.C. § 1 (1994).

261. The Sherman Act is enforced principally by the Department of Justice, and violations may be prosecuted both civilly and criminally. Certain violations of the Sherman Act are considered a felony for which an individual may be imprisoned for up to three years and fined. The government typically reserves felony prosecutions for hard-core violations such as price fixing, bid rigging or market allocation schemes.

lenged as per se illegal are analyzed under the *rule of reason*. The central question under a rule-of-reason analysis is whether the relevant agreement harms competition by increasing the parties' ability or incentive to raise prices above—or reduce output, quality, service or innovation below—what would likely prevail in the absence of the relevant agreement.[262]

Section 1 of the Sherman Act requires some agreement or understanding between two or more companies, although a tacit understanding suffices. For example, a meeting of competitors in which one (or more) provides information designed to influence the business strategy of the others can be evidence of an unlawful agreement to restrain trade. Even the appearance of collusion can provide a sufficient basis for an adverse jury verdict under section 1.

Agreements between or among competitors, and agreements between or among other members of a supply chain, are all susceptible to section 1 scrutiny, although agreements among competitors by far raise the greatest concerns. Accordingly, competitors are generally advised to avoid sharing any information concerning prices, credit terms, other terms and conditions of sale, cost information, upcoming bids, sales territories or any other subjects related to the marketing of competitive products or services.

Section 1 also prohibits any agreement among competitors to allocate customers or potential customers, whether the allocation is by territory, customer or customer classification. Agreements to sell exclusively or primarily particular product lines or avoid product innovation are also illegal. Arrangements by which two or more competitors refuse—or threaten to refuse—to do business with customers, suppliers or a competitor may result in a violation, particularly when the boycotters possess market power or control an element essential to effective competition.

Section 2 of the Sherman Act forbids monopolizing—or attempting to monopolize—the market for any product or service in any area of the country.[263] Though section 2 maybe violated by a combination of companies, it differs from section 1 in that it can also be violated by a single company or entity acting alone, when that entity so dominates a market that it has the power on its own to raise prices above competitive levels or to exclude competitors from the relevant market. As section 2 has been interpreted, it is not necessarily illegal for a company to have a monopoly or to try to achieve a monopoly position.

It normally treats other violations as civil offenses punishable by fines and injunctions. Violations of the Sherman Act may also be prosecuted civilly by private parties, and treble damage penalties may be awarded in private actions.

262. The rule-of-reason analysis begins with an examination of the nature and business purpose of the collaboration, the extent of the parties' market power and various other factors that affect the parties' incentives to continue to compete aggressively. If the agencies find that an agreement is reasonably necessary to achieve the stated efficiencies, they will then balance the likelihood and magnitude of cognizable efficiencies against the likely anticompetitive harms to determine the agreement's overall actual or likely effect on competition in the relevant market. If the overall effect of the arrangement is anticompetitive, the agencies will most likely challenge the agreement as unlawful, whereas if on balance the arrangement is procompetitive, the agencies are unlikely to challenge the collaboration.

263. 15 U.S.C. § 2 (1994).

Section 2 is violated only if the company tries to maintain or acquire a monopoly position through exclusionary or predatory conduct. Accordingly, entities with market power are well advised to avoid tactics that could be viewed as designed to exclude or injure present or potential competitors, and entities should avoid taking actions that cannot be justified by sound business considerations. Claims of monopolization or attempted monopolization are evaluated under the rule of reason.

ii. The Clayton Act

The Clayton Act[264] specifically addresses issues of market power. Section 7 of the Clayton Act prohibits stock or asset acquisitions that may substantially lessen competition. Section 7 is most often invoked when the acquired company is a competitor, but the acquisition of a customer, supplier or potential competitor may be challenged if there were a harmful effect on competition. Section 7A of the Clayton Act, called the Hart-Scott-Rodino Act, requires the prior notification of large mergers to both FTC and the Department of Justice (DOJ). FTC and DOJ share jurisdiction over enforcement of the Clayton Act.

iii. The FTC Act

The FTC Act[265] outlaws unfair methods of competition and unfair or deceptive acts or practices. The FTC Act allows FTC to enjoin potentially anticompetitive conduct before it can ripen into a violation of other antitrust laws. Unfair trade practices include, among other things, (1) making false or deceptive statements about a company's products, business practices, financial status or reliability, (2) misrepresenting the price, composition, effectiveness, quality or other characteristics of a product and (3) passing off one's products as those of another manufacturer.

iv. The Robinson-Patman Act

The Robinson-Patman Act[266] prohibits a seller, under certain circumstances, from discriminating in the price of a product between two competing custom-

---

264. 15 U.S.C. §§ 12 *et seq.*
265. 15 U.S.C. §§ 4 *et seq.*
266. 15 U.S.C. §§ 13–13(b).

ers, or favoring one competing customer over another in the granting of promotional services, facilities or allowances.

3. Online Advertising, Sales and Distribution

Manufacturers' attempts to control the terms and conditions on which their products are advertised, sold or distributed are subject to scrutiny under both Section 1 and Section 2 of the Sherman Act. As a general matter, manufacturers and suppliers have broad latitude in directing the terms on which their products are sold by their distributors and retailers, especially when restrictions are designed to promote brand or product competitiveness. Certain restrictions that impair competition, however, may violate the antitrust laws. Accordingly, manufacturers' or suppliers' policies concerning Internet sales, and attempts to control Internet sales practices, should be formulated with the antitrust laws in mind.

i. Restricting Internet Sales

Manufacturers are generally free to limit the number of retailers authorized to sell their products in particular territories to certain classes of customers or by certain methods of distribution.[267] Thus, courts generally allow manufacturers to appoint different retailers to different channels or limit them to specific methods of distribution, such as catalog or in-store sales.[268] By analogy, a manufacturer has discretion to determine whether sales are made over the Internet, and by whom. A manufacturer may ban all Internet sales or reserve all Internet sales to itself or to selected retailers. Manufacturers are also generally free to limit the products a retailer sells, withhold particular product lines from certain dealers[269] and prevent unauthorized sellers from selling their products.[270] Accordingly, manufacturers are free to limit the array of products sold or distributed over the Internet, or sold by any particular reseller via the Internet.

---

267. *See, e.g.,* Credit Chequers Info. Servs., Inc. v. CBA, Inc., 1999–1 Trade Cas. (CCH) ¶ 72,518 (S.D.N.Y 1999) (motion to dismiss granted when data supplier refused to continue dealing with reseller that began distributing on Internet: "a supplier's restriction of its sales to those resellers who meet its specifications is not a per se restraint of trade"); Electronics Communications Corp. v. Toshiba Am. Consumer Prods., Inc., 129 F.3d 240 (2d Cir. 1997) (exclusive distributorship); Westman Comm'n Co. v. Hobart Int'l, Inc., 796 F.2d 1216 (10th Cir. 1986) (limited distributorships), *cert. denied,* 486 U.S. 1005 (1988).

268. *See, e.g.,* Parkway Gallery Furniture, Inc. v. Kittinger Pennsylvania House Group, Inc., 878 F.2d 801, 802 (4th Cir. 1989) (prohibiting dealers from soliciting or selling furniture by mail or telephone order to customers residing outside specified sales area).

269. *See* Purdy Mobile Homes, Inc. v. Champion Home Builders Co., 594 F.2d 1313 (9th Cir. 1979) (withholding particular product lines from particular dealers).

270. Karsten Mfg. Corp. v. Oshman's Sporting Goods, Inc., 869 F. Supp. 778 (D. Ariz. 1994).

Though manufacturers and other suppliers are free to restrict or limit Internet sales in a variety of ways, restrictions regarding Internet sales should be expressly set forth in dealer or distributorship agreements. If a dealer believes it has been afforded the right to engage in Internet sales under existing arrangements or pursuant to broad distribution clauses, it may claim that any subsequent restrictions amount to a material breach of the dealership arrangement or state dealership laws. Moreover, sudden changes in policy may competitively disadvantage some dealers at the expense of others, or constitute unfair trade practices, creating litigation risks.[271]

ii. Exclusive Distribution and Dealing Restrictions

An exclusive distribution arrangement typically provides a distributor with the right to be the sole outlet for a manufacturer's products or services within a given geographic area, or to use a particular mode of distribution. It is a vertical restriction on the manufacturer, prohibiting it from establishing its own competing sales outlet or selling to other distributors located within the area. Exclusive dealing arrangements require a buyer to purchase products or services for a period of time exclusively from one supplier. Exclusive distributorships and exclusive dealing foreclose competitors of the manufacturer and distributor from dealing in certain goods for the period of exclusivity.

Exclusive distribution and exclusive dealing arrangements may be unlawful if they have the effect of foreclosing a significant number of distributors or resellers from dealing in competitors' products. Accordingly, a manufacturer who wishes to grant an Internet distributor an exclusive arrangement should consider the degree of market foreclosure that will attend the exclusivity.

iii. Restrictions on Internet Advertising and Pricing

Manufacturers may exercise significant control over the advertising and promotion of their products by their distributors and retailers. Manufacturers may, for example, control the appearance of retail stores, the nature of displays, the size of inventories and the use of their own trademarks.[272] Within traditional

---

271. The nation's largest organization of independent computer resellers, ACII, recently filed a complaint with FTC alleging that two computer and peripheral manufacturers suddenly cut off the resellers' access to products that had been available through a major wholesaler, in favor of Internet resellers. In one instance, Taiwan-based Acer Company allegedly required Ingram Micro to halt sales of Acer's Travelmate 505DX notebook to independent computer dealers and resellers. Ingram Micro informed the resellers that the product would now be made available only to Internet resellers. ACII alleges that a similar change in distribution policy by Samsung Electronics caused Ingram Micro to halt sales of Samsung's products to independent resellers, while sales to Internet resellers were unaffected. The complaint alleges that such practices favor "e-tailers" and national chain stores at the expense of full-service resellers, and constitute unfair trade practices.

272. *See* Winn v. Edna Hibel Corp., 858 F.2d 1517, 1520 (11th Cir. 1988); Garment Dist., Inc. v. Belk Stores Servs., Inc., 799 F.2d 905, 910–11 (4th Cir. 1986).

channels of distribution, a manufacturer has very broad rights to determine the terms on which its products are sold.[273] For the most part, manufacturers have similarly broad latitude to control advertising and promotion of their products and services on the Internet. Although manufacturers are free to dictate the way in which products are advertised or marketed, they are not free to set resale prices. A manufacturer may not set the actual or minimum prices at which its products are sold by distributors or retailers, or require that its distributors or retailers obtain its consent regarding resale prices.[274] Such conduct could be found to constitute resale price maintenance, which is per se unlawful under Section 1 of the Sherman Act. Manufacturers are permitted, however, to set suggested retail prices and adopt policies against certain types of retailers' price advertising.[275] Since the Supreme Court's 1997 decision in *State Oil v. Kahn*,[276] manufacturers are generally permitted to agree with retailers on the maximum prices that retailers may charge, as long as the reseller at all times retains discretion to set the actual sale price.

Manufacturers should proceed with caution before making cooperative advertising funds dependent upon compliance with "suggested retail prices." For the past several years, the antitrust enforcement agencies have taken the position that manufacturers could make cooperative advertising funds dependent upon compliance with minimum suggested retail prices. The FTC appears to have reversed its position on cooperative advertising, however, and has taken enforcement action against companies that condition significant cooperative advertising upon compliance with suggested minimum resale prices.[277]

The line between "suggested" and actual prices may not be clear in connection with Internet retailing. On the Internet, an advertised price often

---

273. In *Credit Chequers Information Services, Inc. v CBA, Inc.*, 1999–1 Trade Cas. (CCH) ¶ 72,518 (S.D.N.Y. 1999), plaintiff Credit Chequers Information Services, Inc., a reseller of credit information, brought suit against Experian Information Solutions, Inc., Equifax, Inc. and Credit Bureau Associates for cutting off access to the credit information they supplied to Credit Chequers, allegedly because it made the information available over the Internet. CBA purchased credit reports from the three major suppliers of credit information and compiled the information into a "triple-merge" report. CBA resold triple-merge reports to the plaintiff, which in turn resold the information on the Internet. Within weeks of each other, Equifax and Experian cut off CBA's access to their credit reports. The plaintiff filed suit against Experian, Equifax and CBA, alleging that suspension by both Equifax and Experian constituted a concerted refusal to deal. On the defendants' motion to dismiss, the court found that the plaintiff had not put forth any evidence of an agreement between Equifax and Experian and that the restriction had not resulted in antitrust injury. The court dismissed the complaint for failure to state a claim because, under *Continental T.V. v. GTE Sylvania*, 433 U.S. 36 (1977), the suppliers of information were free to determine the mode of distribution through which their products would be sold.

274. Business Elecs. Corp. v. Sharp Elecs. Corp., 485 U.S. 717 (1988).

275. *See, e.g.*, Holabird Sports Discounters v. Tennis Tutor, Inc., 993 F.2d 228 (4th Cir.) (not for publication) (manufacturer unilaterally prohibited dealer advertising for less than suggested retail price), *cert. denied*, 510 U.S. 868 (1993).

276. State Oil v. Kahn, 522 U.S. 3 (1997).

277. *See* Consent Decree, FTC v. Sony Music, et al., 65 Fed. Reg. 31,319 (May 17, 2000). FTC alleged in its charges against the five largest distributors of recorded music that the companies required retailers to advertise CDs at or above the minimum advertised prices set by the record company, in exchange for cooperative advertising payments. The restrictions applied to all advertising, including television, radio, newspapers, and signs and banners within the retailers' own stores. Under the policies, the large music retailers would lose millions of dollars per year if they failed to follow the restrictions.

becomes the actual selling price, because a sale may be effected by simply click-ing on the advertised price. When the advertised prices are the equivalent of in-store price stickers, an Internet site's adherence to minimum advertised prices in exchange for cooperative advertising funding could be viewed as the equivalent of resale price maintenance. Manufacturers should ensure that at all times, their Internet dealers retain discretion to set prices at which goods may be purchased through them over the Internet.

iv. Dual Distribution on the Internet

A manufacturer is generally free to compete with its distributors or retailers in the wholesale or retail markets for its products. When a manufacturer distrib-utes its products both through its own efforts and through the use of distrib-utors or retailers, the arrangement is referred to as *dual distribution*. Most courts hold that in dual distribution arrangements, the relationship between the man-ufacturer and its distributors remains primarily one of supplier and distributor, and thus the sort of nonprice restrictions described in the foregoing sections are still permitted, even though such restrictions might not be permissible if the companies were simply competitors.

Given the ease with which a manufacturer may be able to engage in com-petitive retail sales with its dealers via the Internet, however, courts may not continue to characterize dual-distribution arrangements as predominantly ver-tical. Depending upon the circumstances, a court could determine that the competitive (horizontal) characteristics of a dual distribution relationship out-weigh the vertical ones. The characterization of the dual distribution relation-ship as vertical or horizontal is significant, as the lawfulness of a manufacturer's restrictions frequently turns upon that determination by a court. Accordingly, the ease with which a manufacturer may be able to compare and coordinate prices with its dealers via the Internet could render a manufacturer's nonprice restrictions on its Internet dealers unlawful. For example, when a distributor sells its products through a dual distribution system, using both independent retailers and its own retail efforts, including Internet sales, a pricing policy whereby the distributor's attempt to control the retail prices charged by its Internet distributors to customers may well be unlawful, given the direct com-petitive aspects of their relationship.[278] Manufacturers should proceed with caution when imposing restrictions on Internet distributors where dual distri-bution occurs.[279]

---

278. *See* Interphoto Corp. v. Minolta Corp., 295 F. Supp. 711, 718 n.2 (S.D.N.Y.), *aff'd*, 417 F.2d 621 (2d Cir. 1969).

279. Though dual-distribution arrangements are generally viewed leniently under the Sherman Act, state laws tend to produce more skeptical views. In 1985, the National Association of Attorneys General (NAAG) adopted, and amended most recently in 1995, guidelines for vertical restraints that reflect an inclination to challenge vertical price-fixing agreements, and an inclination to challenge dual-distribution restrictions as horizontal in some contexts.

v. Competitor Boycotts against Internet Sales

Courts generally interpret Section 1 of the Sherman Act to forbid competitors from agreeing not to deal with other economic actors. Such conduct is often referred to as a *group boycott* or *concerted refusal to deal.* Unlawful group boycotts may arise in a number of ways related to the Internet. These include agreements among manufacturers to refuse to sell to Internet resellers, or agreements among dealers to attempt to induce manufacturers or other parties not to deal with Internet sellers.[280] Courts sometimes classify such group boycotts as per se violations of Section 1 of the Sherman Act, although other courts recognize that some concerted refusals to deal should be examined under the rule of reason. Regardless of the standard applied, any concerted action that has the effect of restricting a competitor's access to a "supply, facility or market necessary to enable the boycotted firm to compete" is very likely unlawful.[281] Because ideas for coordinated activity, such as group boycotts, frequently arise within the context of trade associations, it is important that trade association activity be carefully monitored to avoid the risk of Section 1 violations.

4. Internet Joint Ventures and Other Collaborations[282]

Alliances are critical to doing business on the Internet. Even the relatively simple migration or expansion of a traditional brick-and-mortar business to the Internet requires alliances with software developers, web hosting companies, content providers and the like. Both formal and informal alliances must be scrutinized for potential anticompetitive effects under both Section 1 and Section 2 of the Sherman Act.

At one end of the spectrum, simple alliances among noncompetitors—such as a technology development alliance between an Internet company and a software provider—are likely to raise few antitrust concerns, although even agree-

---

280. FTC recently settled charges it brought against a group of twenty-five Chrysler dealers for engaging an unlawful boycott. FTC alleged that dealers were losing sales to another dealer that sold over the Internet at lower prices. To combat this new form of competition, the full-price dealers allegedly established the Fair Allocation System (FAS) and threatened to refuse to sell certain Chrysler models and limit the warranty service they would provide particular customers unless Chrysler limited the allocation of vehicles to the Internet seller. FTC charged that the agreement to boycott Chrysler violated section 5 of the FTC Act, and would have harmed competition and consumers by reducing competition among automobile dealers and depriving consumers of local access to particular models and warranty work. *See generally* David A. Balto, *Emerging Issues in Electronic Commerce*, 10 Cyberspace Lawyer, Jan. 2000, at 8. ("Traditional retailers afraid of losing sales to a competitor selling over the Internet similarly might pressure manufacturers to deny products to the Internet seller by threatening a boycott. This is not a difficult antitrust issue. There can be no competitive justification for retailers collectively attempting to choke off this new form of competition.").

281. *See* Northwest Wholesale Stationers, Inc. v. Pacific Stationery & Printing Co., 472 U.S. 284, 294 (1985).

282. For more information on joint ventures, see section 3.3.

ments among noncompetitors should be analyzed for the competitive effect of any ancillary restraints. If a party to the alliance holds a dominant or unique position in the market, exclusivity requirements or noncompete clauses could raise antitrust concerns if the effect of the restriction is to "lock up" a significant portion of the market.

At the other end of the spectrum, alliances, joint ventures and other arrangements among or involving competitors should be scrutinized for their likely effect on competition within the relevant market and may give rise to antitrust concerns. Agreements among competitors have long been subject to intense antitrust scrutiny, given their potential to harm competition within the market in which the competitors do business. The arrangement itself—as well as any restrictions or restraints ancillary to the arrangement—should be scrutinized in view of both Section 1 and Section 2 of the Sherman Act, as well as the Clayton Act. An alliance may be unlawful if the very fact of the agreement (or the ancillary restraint) unreasonably restrains trade, in contravention of Section 1, or if the agreement consolidates market powers in a way that affects competition, giving rise to concerns under Section 2 or the Clayton Act.

In April 2000, the FTC and DOJ jointly issued Antitrust Guidelines for Collaborations among Competitors[283] (Competitor Collaboration Guidelines), which set forth the approach of FTC and DOJ to analyzing collaborations involving competitors and determining when such collaborations are likely to have anticompetitive effects on the markets in which the collaborators compete. The Competitor Collaboration Guidelines do not carry the weight of law, but are advisory in nature. Nevertheless, they should be consulted in structuring any competitor collaboration and in evaluating the likelihood that a collaboration could be challenged as unlawful.

The Competitor Collaboration Guidelines define a competitor collaboration as "a set of one or more agreements, other than merger agreements, between or among competitors to engage in economic activity, and the economic activity resulting therefrom."[284] Competitor collaborations may involve one or more business activities, such as research and development, production, marketing, distribution, sales or purchasing. Pursuant to the Competitor Collaboration Guidelines, the FTC and DOJ review most competitor collaborations under the rule of reason, by examining the nature and business purpose of the collaboration, the extent of the parties' market power and various other factors. If this analysis shows no potential for anticompetitive harm, FTC and DOJ end the inquiry. If the investigation indicates potential anticompetitive harm, the agencies still examine the procompetitive benefits of the agreement—namely, whether "the relevant agreement is reasonably necessary to achieve procompetitive benefits that likely would offset anticompetitive harms."[285]

---

283. U.S. Dep't Justice & Fed. Trade Comm'n, Antitrust Guidelines for Collaborations among Competitors (2000) [hereinafter Competitor Collaboration Guidelines].
284. *Id.*
285. *Id.*

To credit claimed efficiencies fully, FTC and DOJ require that such efficiencies be both "verifiable" and "potentially procompetitive."[286] Efficiency claims that are vague or speculative or otherwise cannot be verified by reasonable means are not credited. Moreover, if the collaborators could achieve the same or similar efficiencies by practical, significantly less restrictive means, the agreement may be deemed not reasonably necessary to achieve those efficiencies.

Although much of the discussion below refers to online "market places," it is not intended to apply only to business-to-business electronic exchanges. Many, if not most, of the same issues apply to private electronic exchanges or intranets that connect a limited number of members along a supply chain.

i. Antitrust Risks Presented by Online Collaborations

Internet collaborations, such as B2B marketplaces, carry the potential to create tremendous efficiencies. By bringing buyers or sellers (or in the case of many B2B marketplaces, both buyers and sellers) together into a single online forum, the transaction of business through Internet marketplaces or hubs can reduce procurement costs, facilitate the exchange of information, provide buyers with greater choice and streamline sales and purchasing for businesses and consumers alike. For all these reasons, among others, the Internet has unleashed new markets and made many existing markets more competitive.

One of the most procompetitive aspects of online marketplaces is their ability to provide real-time pricing information to the market. Online marketplaces and certain other online collaborations provide buyers with easy access to information about the price, quality and availability of products. They may provide sellers with information about market demand. Some online marketplaces allow the buy or sell side to see bids or offers on one or both sides of a transaction, while others allow participants to view the prices and volumes at which other participants have consummated sales or transactions. In theory, this greater price transparency should reduce the costs that buyers and sellers would otherwise expend negotiating with each other, and should force firms to bid more aggressively with one another, bringing prices to their most competitive levels.

On the other hand, by eliminating uncertainty and making transactions more transparent, real-time electronic price communications may also enhance coordinated interaction among either rival buyers or rival sellers, particularly in concentrated industries. Buyers or sellers can more easily engage in collusion when their prices and price movements are easily observable by their competitors. For example, sellers could agree to price at the same level and then use the electronic medium to signal price changes to one another, or to monitor competitors' adherence to collusive pricing levels.

---

286. *Id.*

On the buy side, if a B2B marketplace allows participants to view bids and offers of identifiable buyers on the exchange, and if most or all of the competitors in an industry buy on the exchange, the B2B marketplace theoretically could convey information that facilitates coordination among buyers. Access to information about a competitor's purchase of supplies could also raise antitrust concerns, particularly when they constitute a significant portion of the value of the competitor's finished goods.

For these reasons, antitrust enforcement agencies have expressed concern that the Internet could be used as a vehicle for anticompetitive coordination among competitors. Even informal collaboration or communications via the Internet—through Internet mail, chat rooms, bulletin message boards and the like—could provide means through which sensitive information is shared among competitors. Because the exchange of competitively sensitive information may change companies' incentives and foundation to compete, antitrust enforcement authorities may view certain information exchanges, such as exchanges of price or cost information, as violating Section 1 of the Sherman Act. Not all information exchanges are unlawful, but those whose likely purpose or effect is to reduce or harm competition could be held unlawful. Companies generally are well advised to refrain from communicating with competitors about any competitively sensitive information.

ii. Minimizing Anticompetitive Information Exchanges

In reviewing online collaborations, FTC and DOJ consider the extent to which firewalls have been created or other protections adopted to limit competitors' access to bids, offers, transaction terms and any other competitively sensitive business information. To the extent possible, online marketplaces should be structured so that buyers bid confidentially and the terms of consummated transactions are not disclosed. Information should be limited to those with a legitimate need to know it. Venturers can employ a number of technology-based solutions to ensure that members of an exchange do not have access to competitors' sensitive pricing information.

In addition to the risk that transaction information is exchanged online, the process of collaborating to organize and oversee an online marketplace may create a risk that sensitive business information will be shared offline as well. Particularly when participants in the marketplace own and operate the marketplace, the process of collaborating entails meetings, communications and the sharing of some proprietary information among the participants. If, as noted above, a company has information about the costs of its competitors' supply purchases or other strategic information, it could theoretically establish its rivals' cost structures, thereby reducing its own incentive to compete on price. The sharing of information about competitively sensitive variables such as costs, output or strategic planning may very well be viewed as anticompetitive.

Firewalls to protect against the offline sharing of competitively sensitive information are needed to prevent such "spillover" of confidential information. Strict limitations should be placed upon the types of information shared among competitors. Safeguards to prevent spillover of competitively sensitive information may take the form of detailed restrictions about discussions in which competitors may engage and decision-making activities in which they may participate. When the competitors are involved in management of the online collaboration, guidelines restricting the type of management decisions in which the competitors may participate are advisable.

iii. Size of the Online Collaboration

Online marketplaces often exhibit *network effects*, in which the value of any product increases as others use the same product. These effects can be found in an "actual" network such as a telephone or fax network, or in a "virtual" network such as computer software, which becomes more valuable as more people use it and more software developers create compatible programs. Networks can be highly efficient, bringing many users together to create economic products and markets where none previously existed. The very existence of the network, however, may promote dominance by one firm once the network achieves a critical mass of users. Thus, while networks may enhance efficiency and innovation and contribute to rapid growth in high-tech industries, they may also bolster economic forces that create and sustain market dominance.

For these reasons, federal antitrust enforcement agencies may scrutinize online marketplaces involving participants that constitute a large share of the relevant market. The antitrust concern is that a single dominant marketplace, unconstrained by any competing marketplace, may be able to extract large fees for use of the marketplace, collude about prices charged for goods sold on the marketplace or otherwise set rules for doing business that have unfair consequences for some of the marketplace's members or for consumers. It is important to note, however, that the size of a marketplace does not normally give rise to liability under the antitrust laws—it is only the unreasonable use of market power, such as restrictions on access or extraction of high access fees, that can result in liability.

Marketplace size is also important when the collaboration involves the pooling of purchasing power. Online marketplaces may provide a means by which buyers of similar products can pool their purchasing needs to obtain goods at lower cost through volume discounts or reduced transaction costs. The Competitor Collaboration Guidelines recognize that joint buying is often procompetitive because it can provide economies of scale and promote efficiencies in the purchasing, warehousing and distribution of inputs. Joint buying may be anticompetitive, however, when the purchasers acquire sufficient market power to drive the price of goods or services below competitive levels. The ability of a company or coalition of companies to dictate purchase prices is known as *monopsony power.*[287]

Factors considered when determining whether monopsony power could be an issue include the following: (1) whether the participating buyers constitute a large portion of the purchasers of a given product, (2) whether the structure or operation of the online marketplace allows those buyers to make joint purchasing decisions through which they can force their suppliers to sell at prices below those that would prevail if the individual buyers were bidding against one another for the product and (3) whether, even if the buyers do not aggregate their purchases, they have agreed to a "toll" that suppliers must pay to gain access to the marketplace. The online cooperative purchasing arrangement should be structured to insulate each member of the buying group from the purchasing needs and transactions of the other members, and allow members the freedom to make purchases outside the venture.

iv. Membership Policies

Online marketplaces may serve a variety of user groups, including suppliers, buyers, data vendors, service providers and the general public, all of whom have varying business objectives. One of the initial operational issues with which B2B marketplaces must grapple is whether access to the marketplace will be open or closed, or exist somewhere along a continuum between those positions. Business-to-consumer marketplaces generally allow access to the general public, while B2B marketplaces generally limit access to members, who are usually limited to bona fide industry participants. In some B2B marketplace formats, members must be reviewed and approved by the marketplace. Criteria for membership might include whether the applicant is financially sound and creditworthy, and whether appropriate regulatory controls exist in connection with the applicant.

Though rules designed to foster the integrity of the marketplace and ensure efficient operation should raise no antitrust issues, other rules may have significant competitive impact. It may be important to consider the potential size of a marketplace when establishing marketplace membership criteria, such as capital or credit requirements. Independently owned and managed exchanges should not face significant antitrust exposure on the basis of access-limiting rules. While individual proprietors are generally free to make unilateral decisions, networks that are controlled, owned or managed by participants should ensure that rules limiting access do not effectively preclude competitors from

---

287. The Statement 7A U.S. Department of Justice and Federal Trade Commission Statement of Antitrust Enforcement Policy in Health Care (1996) suggest that if members of a joint purchasing pool constitute less than thirty-five percent of the buy-side market, they fall within an antitrust safe harbor.

competing in the relevant industry. If a site develops such a significant presence that access to the facility is critical to competing, denial of access may become a competitive problem. An antitrust violation could be found if a supplier is denied access to an online marketplace and thus suffers a significant impediment to its ability to distribute its products, or if an online collaboration controls so much of the purchasing for a particular product that a manufacturer that is denied access becomes unable to obtain supplies at the favorable prices enjoyed by its competitors.

v. Exclusivity

Membership rules at times require that members use that marketplace exclusively to transact business. As long as the marketplace is small, exclusivity restrictions should not raise antitrust concerns and, indeed, may further the important goal of enabling the marketplace to build sufficient volume to achieve its procompetitive potential. If a marketplace consists of large industry members or includes most industry participants, exclusivity restrictions may reduce the likelihood that competing exchanges will develop. The likely competitive effects of exclusivity provisions are highly fact sensitive, but should be considered within the context of access rules and the characteristics of the particular market.

vi. Marketplace Rules

Online marketplaces may establish rules for the operation of the marketplace. Antitrust enforcement agencies have cautioned that standardization of certain transaction terms and conditions could be anticompetitive.[288] For example, agreement on industry standard credit terms have, in other contexts, been held unlawful.

The marketplace may also need to establish a price for the services it offers. When the exchange is an independent entity, there should be little antitrust concern with establishing a fee for the services the marketplace provides. Even when the exchange is owned and managed by a group of competitors, the marketplace—as a legitimate business venture—is free to set a fee for its ser-

---

288. Catalano, Inc. v. Target Sales, Inc., 446 U.S. 643 (1980) (per curiam). In *Catalano*, the Supreme Court held that a conspiracy among competing wholesalers to standardize credit terms offered to a purchaser was per se illegal. And, several years ago, DOJ levied severe sanctions upon a large group of Nasdaq market-makers who allegedly adhered to a quoting convention by which they would bid only in even-eighth increments. The government charged that the effect of their agreement was to inflate the "inside spread" of certain stocks quoted on Nasdaq, increasing prices to consumers and profits to market-makers.

vices, unless the fee is so large that it effectively harms competing sellers or precludes them from accessing the marketplace. The exchange should not, however, be involved in regulating prices between its participants for exchange-related activities. Other activities or operating rules could raise antitrust concerns as well, such as buyers allocating separate auctions on which to bid or separate customers to whom they will provide service.

5. Online Information Exchanges among Competitors

Even outside the context of competitor collaborations, online exchanges of information through bulletin and message boards, chat rooms and company web sites could cause antitrust concerns, even for unwitting information exchanges. Various industries are the subject of significant discussion on message boards, in which employees trade comments about financial aspects of firms, including, but not limited to, salaries and compensation for employees. Trade associations may establish chat rooms or online communication forums that easily provide a vehicle for anticompetitive information exchanges. Such communications could raise antitrust concerns, depending upon the effect of the information exchange. It is also recognized, particularly in the context of trade associations, that antitrust liability can attach for knowingly providing a forum where price fixing or other unlawful antitrust activity takes place.[289] It is unlikely that sporadic exchanges of information by employees would support a section 1 claim, because there is unlikely to be an overall effect on competition. Nevertheless, companies are well advised to monitor potential anticompetitive information exchanges by employees over the Internet.

6. Mergers and Acquisitions

Consolidations of Internet companies will be analyzed by the federal agencies charged with approving proposed mergers in accordance with section 7 of the Clayton Act and the Horizontal Merger Guidelines.[290] The guidelines set forth an analysis for evaluating proposed or potential mergers, which involves determining the market likely to be affected by the consolidation and estimating the market power of the consolidated entity within that market. Determination of the relevant market includes considering the products or services provided by

289. Internet service providers should be immune from antitrust liability, however. *See, e.g.,* Lonney v. Prodigy Servs., 94 N.Y.2d 242, 250 (1999).
290. U.S Dep't Justice & Fed. Trade Comm'n, Horizontal Merger Guidelines (1992).

the merging entities, as well as reasonable substitutes. The critical issue for consolidation of Internet companies is likely to be whether Internet sales or services constitutes a unique product market, or whether such business activity is part of a larger product or service market that includes sales through other distribution mechanisms. Clearly, whether market definition is limited to Internet sales or services will have significant ramifications for estimating market power likely to result from an Internet collaboration.

§ 5.5 Trade

1. Imports

i. Introduction

The rapid growth of electronic commerce has not been lost upon the policymakers and regulatory bodies that govern international trade. Global e-commerce has been at the top of the discussion agenda for many such governmental bodies.[291] Despite (or perhaps because of) this focus, however, customs authorities in most jurisdictions have made few changes in their laws to address electronic imports. There appears to be a general consensus that products purchased over the Web and imported in tangible form are subject to traditional trade rules relating to imports of goods, while those transferred in digital form over the Web are beyond the reach of customs. The hands-off treatment of international electronic trade has been abetted to a great extent by a decision made by the World Trade Organization (WTO) member states to continue their practice of not imposing customs duties on electronic transmissions.[292]

This is not necessarily the end of the discussion on electronic imports. If books, software, sound recordings and video are classified as services rather than goods, they will be subject to the General Agreement on Trade in Services (GATS). This question of classification is important because GATS does not accord the same level of protection from trade restraints as WTO trade-in-goods rules. Thus it is foreseeable that some digital imports will be traded as goods under protection of the liberal trade-in-goods treaty provisions, while

---

291. *See, e.g.,* WTO Council for Trade in Goods, *Work Programme on Electronic Commerce*, G/C/W/158 (July 26, 1996).

292. WTO Ministerial Conference, *Declaration on Global Electronic Commerce*, WT/MIN/DEC/2 (May 25, 1998).

others may be susceptible to trade restraints on services as countenanced by the GATS rules.

ii. Customs Authority

The U.S. Customs Service (Customs) administers laws governing the entry of merchandise into the customs territory of the United States.[293] When merchandise is physically transferred to the United States from abroad, all the normal customs requirements apply. When imports consist of streams of data transmitted over the Internet, however, they are largely excluded from application of the customs rules.

All merchandise imported into the United States is subject to entry requirements, such as customs declarations and other filings, unless expressly exempted.[294] "Merchandise" is broadly defined to include goods of every description,[295] and Customs has determined that the transmission from a foreign country of software code constitutes an importation of "goods" that falls within Customs' jurisdiction.[296] Thus it can be inferred that most data transferred into the United States would be considered imported goods. Under the Harmonized Tariff Schedules of the United States (HTSUS), the general rule is that all imported goods are designated as either subject to duty or exempt.[297] Based upon General Note 16 of HTSUS, which exempts from duty goods entered via electronic transmissions, Customs has ruled that imports via the Internet are not subject to duty.[298] The Customs regulations similarly provide that goods imported by telecommunications transmissions are exempt from the requirement that importers formally enter the goods by submitting import declarations and supporting information.[299] Thus, Customs has adopted the position that merchandise imported in electronic form is free to pass into the United States without being subject to duty or required to be declared.

iii. Taxation

It is common for customs authorities to have responsibility for collecting taxes, as well as customs duties, on imports. For example, in countries that apply

---

293. The primary body of administrative law for which Customs is responsible is found in the U.S. Customs Regulations, 19 C.F.R. pts. 4 through 192.
294. 19 C.F.R. § 141.4(a) (1999).
295. 19 U.S.C. § 1401(c) (1999).
296. Customs Letter Ruling HR 114459 (Sept. 17, 1998).
297. Harmonized Tariff Schedules of the United States [hereinafter HTSUS], General Note 1 (2000).
298. Customs Letter Ruling HR 114459 (Sept. 17, 1998).
299. 19 C.F.R. § 141.4(b)(1) (1999).

imported goods consumption taxes, such as Value Added Tax (VAT), customs authorities typically collect these levies. The basis for assessing consumption taxes is the import declaration made by the importer. As in the case of import duties, there is a distinction between goods physically imported and those electronically transferred. Taxation will continue in its current form for physical imports. For electronic imports, customs authorities will be unable to collect taxes unless the importer submits a declaration covering its import shipments, an act that importers generally are not obligated to perform. For this reason, it is questionable whether customs authorities will play a role in the collection of import taxes related to electronic import transactions.

The virtual, borderless character of e-commerce requires taxing authorities to devise different systems for capturing revenue generated by digital business transactions. These might include introducing new consumption tax registration requirements or obligating the seller to collect the tax and make remittances to the country where the buyer is located. The weakness of such schemes is that they rely upon taxpayers to comply voluntarily—never an ideal model for maximizing collections. Further, this level of complexity may drive businesses to bypass the rules and run their sales organizations through offshore tax havens.

The United States does not levy any consumption-type taxes on imports. Customs consequently is not in the business of collecting such taxes for the Internal Revenue Service. If an import tax scheme were imposed, however, the U.S. government would face the same challenges with which jurisdictions seeking to collect import VAT and similar taxes are now wrestling. These challenges would include promoting exporter compliance, enforcing collections and potential flight to tax havens.

iv. International Issues

The global trading system has for years relied upon the internationally agreed-upon trading rules laid down by the General Agreement on Tariffs and Trade (GATT), and later WTO, to reduce barriers to trade and increase market access for goods. GATT signatories agreed to apply the lowest tariff rates to imports from all countries, make sharp reductions in duty rates, and make the rules enforceable by establishing a dispute resolution process.

Perhaps the most significant international development in the area of e-commerce import regulation is the agreement of WTO members not to impose customs duties on electronic transmissions.[300] The resolve of WTO to keep

---

300. WTO Ministerial Conference, *Declaration on Global Electronic Commerce*, WT/MIN/DEC/2 (May 25, 1998).

the Internet a tariff-free zone is obvious; less clear is whether other, nontariff barriers to trade might arise. A primary issue is determining which WTO rules will apply to products delivered in digital form.

Although Customs continues to treat digitally imported products as goods, there is an emerging international consensus that they should instead be considered services. This distinction is not merely academic. Under WTO rules, trade in goods is protected from national barriers to entry by agreement of WTO members. Under the rules established by GATT, signatories are obliged to bind their tariff rates (meaning the rates can never be increased), provide essentially all imports most-favored-nation (MFN) treatment (meaning there is no discrimination among other members) and accord national treatment to imports (meaning there is no discrimination in favor of national sellers). These commitments to open trade are nearly absolute and are credited in large part with the rapid expansion of international trade over the past three decades.

Services, on the other hand, fall within the ambit of GATS, the first set of multilateral, legally enforceable rules covering international trade in services. Although GATS is based upon the GATT trade-in-goods framework, it allows for significant derogations from GATT principles. In contrast with the GATT approach of requiring members' unconditional commitments, each GATS signatory is permitted to make specific and limited market-opening commitments on service sectors and activities within those sectors. For example, a member could make a market-access commitment by allowing foreign Application Service Providers (ASPs) to operate, but the member could limit the number of licenses it issues to foreign ASPs (a market-access limitation), or impose a limitation upon the scope of services provided by foreign ASPs while imposing none on domestic ASPs (an exception to national treatment). WTO members have also availed themselves of the option to except themselves from the MFN principle by giving more favorable treatment to particular countries. These exceptions are temporary, however, and can be exercised only once.

The concern, then, is not that governments will attempt to use tariffs to influence digital trade, but that they may formulate restrictions based upon the less-robust principles of GATS. It is possible that the market-access exceptions permitted by GATS will be used as trade policy tools to limit or tax the transmission of digitized products. To some extent, this concept is taken into account in GATS itself. For instance, in connection with internationally traded services, the GATS financial services annex accords governments the right to take steps deemed necessary to protect investors, depositors and insurance policyholders, and to ensure the integrity and stability of their financial systems. Although it is difficult to argue against these particular goals as a matter of policy, the pertinent issue may be whether governments can resist the temptation to use the latitude afforded by GATS to protect national interests.

2. Exports

i. Introduction

The United States casts a wide net in regulating the export of articles and technology that, for a variety of policy reasons, the government deems should not be provided to certain foreign destinations and persons without its prior authorization. Exports are regulated by a number of agencies, each administering its own rules. Section 6.5.2 discusses the primary export controls affecting e-commerce: the Export Administration Regulations of the Department of Commerce, the International Traffic in Arms Regulations of the Department of State, and the embargo regulations of the Treasury Department's Office of Foreign Assets Controls.

This discussion addresses how the regulatory scheme affects both electronic exports (such as software transmitted internationally over the Web) and e-commerce transactions in which physical articles are exported across national borders. Regardless of the mode of export, the common thread that runs through these regulations is that electronic exports are controlled on the basis of the character of the product or data, rather than the form in which they are exported. Thus, if export of certain data in hard copy or by fax requires an export license, transmitting those data to a controlled destination by e-mail or permitting a controlled person to download the data from a private web site will also require a license. By the same token, posting a document to a free public bulletin board on the Web will exempt from export controls the information contained in the document, just as if it were a hard copy made publicly available by being placed in a library.

Section 6.5.2 examines what the different agencies regulate, what constitutes an export, how licensing requirements are applied and what steps exporters involved in electronic commerce should take to maintain compliance with the crazy quilt of regulations that blankets exports from the United States.

ii. Commerce Department Controls

The Department of Commerce controls the export and reexport of certain items—including goods, software, technology and encryption—under the Export Administration Regulations (EAR).[301] For an item to be considered subject to EAR, it must be in the United States, of U.S. origin, made from a combination of U.S. and foreign-origin software or technology or made outside the United

---

301. 15 C.F.R. §§ 730–74 (1999).

States by the direct use of U.S. software or technology.[302] Controlled items are organized according to their respective functions and listed under entries on the Commerce Control List (CCL).[303] Controlled activities consist of:

1. exports from the United States and reexports,[304]
2. involvement of U.S. persons in providing foreign-origin items or in supporting transactions that could contribute to the proliferation of weapons of mass destruction,[305]
3. releases of software and technology to foreign nationals[306] and
4. electronic transmission outside the United States and posting to the Internet without limitation on foreign access.

The above analysis applies generally to all controlled exports, including software and technical data, but because the rules differ for nonencryption items and encryption items, they are treated separately.

A. What Does Commerce Consider an Export?

(1) Nonencryption Products and Data

Controlled articles, including software and technical data, are considered exported when actually transported or transmitted electronically outside the United States or released to a foreign national in the United States.[307] In addition, software and technology are exported when released in a foreign country.[308] Reexports consist of the transport or transmission of items from one foreign country to another, or the release of software or technology to a foreign national outside the United States.[309] Technology and software are considered exported by means of "release" when provided to foreign nationals by visual inspection, oral description or application of technical skills.[310] Releases to foreign nationals wherever located are "deemed" exports of controlled items to the home country of those persons.[311]

---

302. *Id.* § 734.3(a). As used in EAR, "software" includes both source code and object code, unless specifically noted. Technology consists of information for the development, production or use of other articles, or to activities subject to EAR, and takes the form of "technical data or "technical assistance." *Id.* § 772. Technical data includes designs, specifications, instructions and manuals. Technical assistance includes training, consulting and working knowledge, and may involve the transfer of technical data.
303. *Id.* § 774, supp. 1.
304. *Id.* § 734.2(b).
305. *Id.* §§ 734.5(a), 744.2–744.4, 744.6.
306. *Id.* § 734.2(b).
307. *Id.* § 734.2(b)(1).
308. *Id.* § 734.2(b)(2)(i).
309. *Id.* § 734.2(b)(4).
310. *Id.* § 734.2(b)(3).
311. Foreign nationals are persons not lawfully admitted to permanent residence status in the United States, except for individuals protected under the Naturalization Act (8 U.S.C. § 1324b(a)(3) (1999); 15 C.F.R. § 734.2(b)(2)(ii) (1999)).

(2) Encryption Items

EAR controls exports of encryption products, software[312] and technology[313] designated as encryption items (EI) under CCL. Encryption items (other than software) are considered exported when actually transported or transmitted outside the United States or released to a foreign national in the United States.[314] Encryption technology is also considered exported when released outside the United States[315] and "deemed" exported when released to a foreign national.[316] For encryption source code and object code software, "export" is defined as shipment, transfer or transmission out of the United States, or a transfer of such software to an embassy or affiliate of a foreign country.[317] The "deemed" export rule does not apply to encryption software.[318]

Persons selling, posting and transmitting items subject to EAR must understand what the agency considers to be an export, to be certain their e-commerce compliance programs cover all the activities proscribed by the Department of Commerce. This same rule applies to the regulations of each of the other administrative authorities discussed in this section.

B. Licensing

Commodities, software and technology subject to EAR may require licensing before they can be exported. Commerce licensing determinations are based upon how the item is classified under CCL[319] and the other provisions of EAR.[320] Items on CCL are controlled for a variety of reasons, such as national security and weapons proliferation, as well as compliance with embargoes.[321] These controlled items thus require licensing if exported to countries specified in EAR.[322] Exporters must also obtain licenses when they "know" an export will assist weapons proliferation,[323] or that a violation of EAR has occurred or is about to occur.[324] Such knowledge may be imputed to an exporter if certain "red flags" indicating possible problems are present. One such red flag is an Internet address code showing a communication originates from an embargoed destina-

---

312. Controlled encryption software is that designed or modified for the production, development or use of equipment otherwise controlled for security reasons. *See* 15 C.F.R. § 774, supp. 2 (1999).

313. Controlled technology includes data for the development, use or production of a controlled encryption product or software and assistance in training or service relating to such items. *Id.*

314. 15 C.F.R. § 734.2(b)(1) (1999).

315. *Id.* § 734.2(b)(2).

316. *Id.* § 734.2(b)(1).

317. *Id.* § 734.2(b)(9)(i).

318. *Id.*

319. *Id.* § 774, supp. 1.

320. *See id.* §§ 736, 738, 740, 746, 764.

321. *Id.* § 746.

322. *Id.* § 736.2(b)(1).

323. *Id.* § 736.2(b)(5).

324. *Id.* § 736.2(b)(1).

tion.[325] Finally, EAR prohibits exports to persons named in its "denied person"[326] and "entity"[327] lists. These various provisions of EAR give rise to the need for exporters to "screen" each proposed export transaction to determine whether a license or other authorization is required and, in some cases, whether the export will be permitted at all.

Special rules apply to the export of encryption items. A person exporting any controlled encryption commodity, software or technology must first apply for a license or license exception.[328] As part of this process, the exporter submits the item for a one-time technical review by the Commerce Department to determine whether it qualifies as a "retail" product that can be exported to all end users.[329] Failure to obtain a retail classification may result in restrictions on export of the products to government end users.[330] Exporters transmitting encryption products may also be subject to postexport reporting requirements.[331] Further, technical assistance and data incorporating encryption remain in all cases subject to licensing requirements, except when transmitted to a U.S. subsidiary.[332]

C. Exemptions from License Requirements

Though a number of factors may exempt a particular transfer or release from license requirements, three are noteworthy here. The first is that license exceptions—permission to export license-free—may apply, depending upon the circumstances of a given transaction.[333] Second, if no Department of Commerce license is required, it is still necessary to determine whether export controls administered by other federal agencies apply, because EAR does not cover items subject to the exclusive jurisdiction of another agency.[334] The third is that certain software and technology may be freely exported if considered "publicly available."[335]

The exclusion for publicly available items has particular relevance for controlled information that is transmitted electronically or posted to the Web. Software and data are considered published, and thus not subject to EAR, when

---

325. *Id.* § 732, supp. 1.

326. *Id.* § 764, supp. 2.

327. *Id.* § 744, supp. 4.

328. *See* 15 C.F.R. § 742.15, 65 Fed. Reg. 62,608 (2000); § 742, supp. 6, 65 Fed. Reg. 62,608 (2000).

329. *Id.* (with the exception of Cuba, North Korea, Iran, Iraq, Libya, Sudan and Syria).

330. This restriction, and the requirement for the preexportation technical review, have been lifted for exports to the European Union, Australia, Norway, the Czech Republic, Hungary, Poland, Japan, New Zealand and Switzerland. *See* 65 Fed. Reg. 62,600 (2000).

331. *See* 15 C.F.R. § 740.17(e), 65 Fed. Reg. 62,607 (2000).

332. *Id.* § 740.17(a)(1), 65 Fed. Reg. 62,605 (2000).

333. License exceptions are listed in 15 C.F.R. § 740.

334. *See* 15 C.F.R. § 734.3(b) (1999).

335. *Id.* §§ 734.3(b)(3)(I), 734.7–734.11.

made available for general distribution either for free or at a nominal cost, such as by placing them on electronic bulletin boards.[336] EAR provides that the export of data posted to the Web is not subject to control when:

1. information is uploaded to an electronic bulletin board by a person that is the owner or originator of the information,
2. that person does not charge a fee to the bulletin board administrator or the subscribers of the bulletin board and
3. the bulletin board is available for subscription to any subscriber in a given community, regardless of the cost of subscription.[337]

In these circumstances, the information is publicly available and therefore not subject to EAR, even if it is not elsewhere published or available in a library. The determinative facts are that subscribers are charged only for the costs of distribution, and the provider of the information is not compensated for the inherent value of the data.[338] This treatment is applicable to both nonencryption items and encryption technology and source code eligible for license exceptions ENC or TSU.

EAR does not extend the publicly available exception to other encryption software controlled under CCL Export Control Classification Number 5D002.[339] EAR makes special provision, however, for situations where such encryption software is placed in locations (including electronic bulletin boards, Internet file transfer protocol and web sites) outside the United States or accessible electronically from outside the United States.[340] Placing this encryption source code in these locations constitutes an export, unless specified precautions are taken to prevent unauthorized transfers of the code.[341] The mandatory precautions include the following:

1. an access control system that checks the address of every system outside the United States or Canada requesting or receiving a transfer, and verifies that such system does not have a domain name or Internet address of a foreign government end user,
2. an access control system that notifies every requesting or receiving party that the encryption software cannot be transferred outside the United States without government authorization and

---

336. *Id.* § 734.7(b). EAR also provides that in connection with software, if the source code version of a program is publicly available, the object code or machine-readable compilation is also considered publicly available. *Id.* § 734, supp. 1, ques. G(1).

337. *Id.* § 734, supp. 1, ques. I(3).

338. *Id.*

339. 15 C.F.R. §§ 734.2(b)(9)(ii), 65 Fed. Reg. 2,496 (2000); 15 C.F.R. § 734.7(c) (1999).

340. *See* 15 C.F.R. § 734.2(b)(9)(ii), 65 Fed. Reg. 2,496 (2000).

341. *Id.* Source code that is eligible for export under license exception TSU or ENC is not subject to this requirement. *Id.* (citing 15 C.F.R. §§ 740.13(e), 65 Fed. Reg. 62,605 (2000); 740.17(a)(5)(i), 65 Fed. Reg. 62,606 (2000).

3. an affirmative acknowledgment by every requesting or receiving party that the software is not intended for a government end user, is subject to EAR and may not be exported without government authorization.[342]

Taken together, these exceptions to EAR licensing requirements provide opportunities for items exported both by traditional methods of transportation and by cybertransmission. The key for exporters is to perform complete technical analyses of their products and the regulations to ensure their items are eligible for exportation without a license.

iii. State Department Controls

The State Department, by its Office of Defense Trade Controls (ODTC), regulates the export, reexport and retransfer of defense articles and furnishing of defense services, including technical data and software, under the International Traffic in Arms Regulations (ITAR).[343] ITAR identifies defense articles under twenty-one categories in the U.S. munitions list.[344] Defense services include furnishing technical data controlled under ITAR to foreign persons—whether or not in the United States.[345] Technical data are defined as information required for the design, development, assembly, production, repair, manufacture, operation, testing, maintenance or modification of defense articles, as well as software directly related to defense articles.[346] Defense articles and services are controlled because they are designed or adapted for military applications and are functionally different from related articles and services used by civilians.[347] Any person in the United States who engages in the manufacture or export of defense articles or furnishes defense services must register with ODTC.[348]

A. What Does State Consider an Export?

The ITAR definition of export includes not only sending items outside the United States, but also disclosing defense articles or defense technical data to foreign persons, whether in the United States or abroad.[349] Exports also occur

---

342. 15 C.F.R. § 734.2(b)(9)(iii), 65 Fed. Reg. 2,496 (2000). Acknowledgments may be made in electronic form, provided they are adequate to assure the parties' legal undertakings in a manner similar to written acknowledgments. *Id.* § 734.2(b)(9)(iii)(C).
343. 22 C.F.R. §§ 120–30 (1998).
344. *See id.* § 121.
345. *Id.* § 120.9.
346. *Id.* § 120.10.
347. *See id.* § 120.3.
348. *Id.* § 122.1.
349. *Id.* §§ 120.17(a)(1), 120.17(a)(3), 120.17(a)(4).

when a person performs a defense service on behalf of a foreign person, whether in the United States or abroad.[350] Because defense services include providing assistance—such as training—in connection with a defense article,[351] helping a foreign person design, manufacture or use a defense article is licensable under ITAR even if no technical data are disclosed.[352] Thus, a defense item or service is considered exported if it is transmitted electronically outside the United States or to a foreign person, wherever located.

B. Licensing

With limited exceptions, every exportation of a defense article[353] or defense technical data[354] requires an ODTC license or regulatory exemption. Only U.S. persons or foreign government entities in the United States may be granted a license.[355] Foreign persons may, however, apply for authorization to reexport or retransfer defense articles.[356] The exportation of defense services requires ODTC authorization in the form of a manufacturing license or technical assistance agreement.[357] ODTC maintains a policy of denying export applications for defense articles and defense services for exports to certain countries.[358] This policy also applies to countries against which the United States maintains arms embargoes.[359] Finally, ODTC imposes controls in defense items in support of United Nations arms embargoes[360] and Commerce Department terrorism controls.[361]

C. Exemptions from License Requirements

Some narrow exemptions from licensing requirements apply to defense articles, services and technical data. Exemptions for defense articles include those applicable to shipments to Canada,[362] reexports to NATO countries and the governments of Japan and Australia[363] and items exported for exhibit at a public exhibition, trade show or air show.[364] Exemptions for defense technical data

---

350. *Id.* § 120.17(5).
351. *Id.* § 120.9.
352. *Compare* 22 C.F.R. § 120.9(a)(1) (1998), *with* 22 C.F.R. § 120.9(a)(2) (1998).
353. 22 C.F.R. § 123.1 (1998).
354. *Id.* § 125.2(a).
355. *Id.* § 120.1(c).
356. *Id.* § 123.9(c).
357. *Id.* § 124.1.
358. At the time of writing, these countries were Armenia, Azerbaijan, Belarus, Cuba, Iran, Iraq, Libya, North Korea, Syria, Tajikistan, Ukraine and Vietnam. *Id.* § 126.1(a).
359. These countries include Burma, People's Republic of China, Haiti, Liberia, Rwanda, Somalia, Sudan and Zaire. *Id.*
360. *Id.* §§ 126.1(c), 126.1(f).
361. *Id.* § 126.1(d).
362. *Id.* § 126.5.
363. *Id.* § 123.9(e).
364. *Id.* § 123.16(b)(5).

include those for copies of technical data previously authorized for export,[365] basic operations, maintenance and training information relating to a defense article,[366] and transfers by U.S. corporations to U.S. persons employed abroad by those corporations or the U.S. government.[367] Defense services are subject to exemption from the requirement of a technical assistance agreement in connection with basic operation and maintenance of defense articles by the exporter.[368]

Of particular relevance to electronic data transmissions is an express exclusion for general scientific, mathematical or engineering principles,[369] and information in the public domain.[370] Data transmitted or posted to the Web are exempt from ITAR controls if it falls into one of these categories. To be eligible for the exemption as information in the public domain, the data may be:

1. published and generally accessible or available to the public through various means, including sales at newsstands and bookstores,[371] unrestricted subscriptions,[372] libraries accessible by the public,[373] distribution at open meetings[374] and patent filings,[375]
2. information approved for release by competent government agencies[376] or
3. fundamental research in science and engineering of the type ordinarily published and shared within the scientific community.[377]

Unlike their EAR counterparts, the public domain provisions of ITAR do not address electronic availability of data and thus, there is no express language covering information posted on publicly accessible electronic bulletin boards or web sites. It seems reasonable, nonetheless, to infer that such postings should be eligible for the public domain exclusion in the same manner as data in public libraries or other open sources.

iv. Treasury Controls

The Treasury Department's Office of Foreign Assets Control (OFAC) currently administers embargoes and economic sanctions against foreign countries to

---

365. *Id.* § 125.4(b)(4).
366. *Id.* § 125.4(b)(5).
367. *Id.* § 125.4(b)(9).
368. *Id.* § 126.2(a). This exception is very narrowly construed by ODTC.
369. *Id.* § 120.10(a)(5).
370. *Id.* § 120.11(a).
371. *Id.* § 120.11(a)(1).
372. *Id.* § 120.11(a)(2).
373. *Id.* § 120.11(a)(4).
374. *Id.* § 120.11(a)(6).
375. *Id.* § 120.11(a)(5).
376. *Id.* § 120.11(a)(7).
377. *Id.* § 120.11(a)(8).

address U.S. national security interests and foreign and economic policies.[378] The terms of the embargoes and sanctions are administered under different parts of the Code of Federal Regulations, and each is different from the others. OFAC exercises its authority primarily by prohibiting or regulating trade and financial transactions involving certain foreign countries, organizations or individuals. These sanctions may take the form of (1) restrictions on access to U.S. goods, services or technology, (2) prohibitions on investments and (3) assets freezes. OFAC sanctions focus upon the nature of the activity, the foreign end use and the end user. It is necessary to seek authorization from OFAC before engaging in any activity subject to the agency's sanctions.

A. What Does the Treasury Department Regulate?

Although OFAC regulates a variety of activities under its sanctions authority, this discussion is limited to trade and commercial embargoes, the areas most relevant to the conduct of e-commerce. The embargoes generally prohibit direct and indirect exports of goods, technology and services to the subject nations. Each embargo differs in affected activities and the manner in which sanctions are applied to persons subject to U.S. jurisdiction. A brief summary of OFAC trade embargoes follows:

- *Cuba*: The embargo prohibits commercial and trade transactions between persons subject to U.S. jurisdiction (including U.S.-owned or controlled overseas subsidiaries) and Cuba and its nationals.[379]
- *North Korea*: Prohibitions on commercial and trade transactions have been liberalized to permit certain exports between persons subject to U.S. jurisdiction and North Korea and its nations,[380] but these activities remain subject to technology controls imposed under EAR.[381]
- *Iran, Iraq, Libya and Sudan*: The embargoes prohibit commercial and import or export transactions between U.S. persons (but not foreign subsidiaries of U.S. companies) and the embargoed countries and their nationals.[382]
- *Afghanistan*: The embargo prohibits import or export transactions between U.S. persons and companies and the Taliban and any territory of Afghanistan controlled by the Taliban.[383]

---

378. 31 C.F.R. §§ 500–97 (1997); Exec. Order No. 13,129, 64 Fed. Reg. 6,759 (1999) (Taliban embargo).
379. 31 C.F.R. § 515.201(b) (1997).
380. 65 Fed. Reg. 38,165 (2000) (to be codified at 31 C.F.R. pts. 500.533, 500.586).
381. *See* 65 Fed. Reg. 38,151 (2000) (to be codified at 15 C.F.R. pt. 742.19).
382. 31 C.F.R. § 560.204 (1997) (Iran); *Id.* §§ 575.205, 575.411 (Iraq); *Id.* §§ 550.202, 550.409 (Libya); *Id.* § 538.205 (Sudan); Exec. Order No. 13,088, § 2(a), as added by Exec. Order No. 13,121, § 1(b), 64 Fed. Reg. 24,021 (1999) (Yugoslavia). OFAC also prohibits any transactions by U.S. persons or involving U.S. property with former Serbian leader Slobodan Milosevic, his family and close associates, and those convicted of war crimes relating to the conflict in the Federal Republic of Yugoslavia (Serbia, Kosovo and Montenegro). Exec. Order No. 13,192, 66 Fed. Reg. 7,379 (2001).
383. Exec. Order No. 13,129, 64 Fed. Reg. 36,759 (1999).

- *Angola*: The embargo prohibits export of certain articles by U.S. persons—or from the United States—to agents and instrumentalities of the National Union for the Total Independence of Angola.[384]

In addition, OFAC maintains lists of persons and companies located throughout the world that function (whether as representatives, agents, intermediaries or "fronts") as extensions of embargoed governments.[385] Dealings with these "Specially Designated Nationals" are subject to the same restrictions as the embargoed governments. Further, OFAC administers sanctions programs against individuals and entities that are not country-specific.[386] All transactions or activities considered "exports" under OFAC regulations should be screened against these lists to ensure compliance.

B. Licensing

The transactions and activities listed in OFAC regulations—whether involving listed countries, individuals or entities—are prohibited unless specifically authorized by license or other approval by OFAC.[387] Certain activities, however, are eligible for export under blanket approvals or "general licenses" listed in the regulations.[388] Exporters may also seek authorization for transactions not covered by general licenses by applying to OFAC.[389] Exporters must be cognizant that certain exports may be subject to EAR or ITAR in addition to OFAC controls.[390]

C. Exemptions from Licensing Requirements

OFAC regulations contain limited exemptions from certain embargoes for activities such as personal communications, travel and journalism. The exemption most relevant to e-commerce transactions is for information and informational materials. The principal statutes underlying OFAC regulations, the Trading with the Enemy Act[391] and the International Emergency Economic Powers Act,[392] exempt exports of information or informational materials from OFAC sanctions, whether or not commercial in nature and regardless of format or medium of transmission.[393] Information and informational materials include

---

384. 31 C.F.R. § 590.201 (1997).
385. These lists appear as appendices to the various sections of Chapter V of OFAC regulations.
386. Programs include the Foreign Terrorist Organizations, Specifically Designated Narcotics Traffickers and Specially Designated Terrorists.
387. 31 C.F.R. § 500.201(a) (1997).
388. See, e.g., id. §§ 500–79.
389. Id. § 500.801(b).
390. See, e.g., 15 C.F.R. § 746.1 (1999) (EAR embargoes).
391. 50 U.S.C. app. § 5(b) (2000).
392. 50 U.S.C. §§ 1701–06 (2000).
393. 50 U.S.C. app. § 5(b)(4) (2000) (TWEA); 50 U.S.C. § 1702(b)(3) (2000) (IEEPA).

publications, photographs, records, tapes, compact disks, CD-ROMS, newswire feeds and other data flows. This definition is broad enough to cover electronic transmissions and postings to the Web. The exemption for information and informational materials has been implemented in certain—but not all—OFAC sanctions programs.[394] This exemption is subject to certain "carve-outs" that prohibit the following:

- Transactions related to (1) information and informational material not fully created and in existence at the time of the transaction or (2) business consulting services[395]
- Transactions incident to the exportation of goods, software and technology controlled under EAR or related to the export of apparatus for the transmission of such controlled articles[396]

Further, the exempted informational data are defined to exclude items controlled by the Department of Commerce for national security, nonproliferation or antiterrorism purposes.[397] Taken together, these limitations disqualify for the exemption much technology-related data, but prudent e-businesses may nonetheless find that the laws provide worthwhile relief for commercial information posted or transmitted over the Internet.

v. International Issues

Many national governments regulate exports, and each nation's export laws are unique. Consequently, persons who export tangible goods from—or who electronically transmit data and are subject to the jurisdiction of—a country that maintains export controls must analyze whether they are in compliance with those export laws. The consequence is that export compliance, particularly in the global, e-commerce context, can be an extremely complicated task.

The one unifying factor in the global export control scheme is the Wassenaar Arrangement on Export Controls for Conventional Arms and Dual-Use Goods and Technologies (Wassenaar Arrangement), a multilateral arrangement covering both conventional weapons and so-called dual-use goods and technologies. The Wassenaar Arrangement is intended to contribute to global security and stability by promoting transparency and responsibility on the part of mem-

---

394. The exemption for information and informational materials is in effect under the following OFAC sanctions programs: Cuba (31 C.F.R. § 515.206(a)), Iran (31 C.F.R. § 560.210(c)), North Korea (31 C.F.R. § 500.206(a)) and Sudan (31 C.F.R. § 538.211(b)(1)).
395. *See* 31 C.F.R. § 515.206(a)(2) (1997) (Cuba); *id.* § 500.206(c) (North Korea); *id.* § 538.211(b)(2) (Sudan).
396. *See id.* § 515.206(a)(3) (Cuba); *id.* §§ 560.210(c)(3), 560.210(c)(4) (Iran); *id.* § 500.206(d) (North Korea); *id.* § 583.211(b)(3) (Sudan).
397. 50 U.S.C. app. § 5(b)(4) (2000) (TWEA); 50 U.S.C. § 1702(b)(3) (2000) (IEEPA).

bers in regulating transfers of controlled commodities from their respective territories. National governments implement the Wassenaar Arrangement controls by incorporating the Wassenaar provisions into their national laws. For instance, the U.S. Department of Commerce implements the Wassenaar Arrangement dual-use provisions under the national security controls in EAR, and the U.S. State Department incorporates Wassenaar controls for conventional arms in ITAR.

Although this incorporation of Wassenaar principles into national laws does result in regulatory commonality, the effect is limited, as countries are free to adopt additional and more stringent measures. Because most Wassenaar Arrangement provisions are subsumed in national laws, they are not readily identifiable to many exporters. The Wassenaar Arrangement nonetheless contributes to the regulatory scheme by imposing, for instance, periodic reporting requirements that place a direct burden on persons exporting goods and technologies covered by the multilateral program.

3. Designing a Compliant E-Commerce Model

The need for maintaining an effective export compliance process for e-commerce transactions perhaps runs contrary to the popular notion that Internet businesses have successfully slipped the regulatory tethers that bound (and constricted) traditional forms of commerce. If anything, the Internet raises new challenges for those who deal in controlled items and technology. This is because the Web is an open market where "sellers" may know nothing about their "customers" and transactions can be completed invisibly and in seconds. For instance, the person making available certain controlled goods, software or technology for purchase or perusal may have no contact with the person acquiring or accessing these items, and may not even be aware that such access or acquisition has taken place or that an export has occurred. This lack of human oversight presents opportunities to expand markets and commercial efficiencies, as well as risks that "untended" web site storefronts and postings may give rise to impermissible exports. Following is a summary of elements that should be considered in developing an e-commerce compliance program, and a discussion of the most common contexts in which such program elements may need to be deployed.

i. Elements of Compliant E-Business Model

Below is a description of the compliance steps that should be considered before making any controlled articles available on the Web or other electronic network; the description is based upon the export rules administered by the Departments of Commerce, State and Treasury. Given the complexity of the regulations and the multitude of products and activities that may raise compliance issues, it is difficult to do more than generalize about the scope of requirements that might apply to any particular e-commerce transaction. These guidelines accordingly should be viewed as minimum requirements.

A. Technical Review

The first step is to analyze the items that will be made available to determine whether they are controlled and, if so, under what circumstances. This will answer questions about whether and how to offer the items, when government approvals are required and the measures needed to prevent unlawful exports. The analysis will also determine the logic of the order management process and/or the site access controls to be employed. The technical review sets the stage for defining the elements of any export compliance program.

B. Screening

This process is directed toward those persons who would purchase or otherwise access the controlled items. Screening may be necessary for persons accessing the site externally, and for organization employees and agents who may gain access to the site. External screening would include checking the names of online purchasers against the various entity lists maintained by the government agencies, and screening Internet addresses for red flags such as codes indicating embargoed destinations. To expedite order processing, this screening should be automated. When the screen turns up a "hit," the site can refuse to process an order or not permit a download. Internal screening would include ensuring that foreign nationals employed by an organization do not improperly obtain access to controlled data maintained on a private network.

C. Blocking

Access to the site by particular persons or from certain destinations may be blocked. This can be achieved by (1) password-protecting the site, (2) using an automated process that denies access to the site from Internet addresses containing the code for a controlled country and (3) employing an order process that does not permit shipments to blocked destinations. At a minimum, the blocked destinations should include the countries subject to OFAC embargoes, plus Syria (to cover EAR prohibitions). Releases of data to embargoed countries should be permitted only if it is first ascertained that all such information is eligible for export as being publicly available, and/or is exempt information under OFAC rules.

D. Acknowledgments/Records

The site should incorporate a statement explaining that the controlled items are subject to the export laws and must not be put to any impermissible end uses. Persons purchasing the items should be required to acknowledge the statement. Records of the transactions, including the acknowledgments, should be retained in case of government enforcement actions.

ii. Application to E-Business Scenarios

There are two basic scenarios in which e-commerce activities may be affected by the export control rules. The first is when orders are placed electronically but products are physically exported, and the second is when both the requests for—and the delivery or transfer of—the products take place electronically. Related to these scenarios is the operation of a private computer network and maintenance of electronic data accessible to employees and others. This latter scenario has implications for the "deemed export" rule under EAR, as well as ITAR defense controls and OFAC embargo programs.

A. Electronic Order/Physical Delivery Model

In this first scenario, customers order controlled items by means of the Internet or the Web for physical delivery outside the country where the items are located at the time of the request—essentially a traditional export distribution model with an electronic front end. In a physical delivery model, it is necessary to perform a full technical review of the products to be offered. The focus of the review will be to determine applicable controls, and the circumstances requiring licenses or creating eligibility for exemptions from such requirements (for example, because the product is not subject to EAR or consists of publicly available data). The technical review should make possible a decision whether, or to what extent, it will be feasible to offer the products on the web site. If the applicable regulations would render e-commerce in the products impractical, the vendor may decide to use its web site purely as a promotional tool or as a means of connecting potential customers with sales representatives, with order processing done offline.

If the technical review indicates the products are subject to controls, but it is feasible to design a compliant e-commerce model, it will be necessary to code or flag the products so the order management system is prompted to run the proper screening scripts. All orders should be screened against the denied parties and other specially designated entity lists, as well as for impermissible export destinations. If the items are subject to EAR, the screening process should also check for red flags contained in the information provided by the person placing the order. These warning signs consist of indications the export could be used in proliferation activities or other violations.

The order process should also include blocking devices to prevent shipments to prohibited destinations. This can be achieved most effectively by omitting these countries from the fields where customers enter shipping and billing information. Finally, the vendor should require the customer to scroll through an export compliance statement and click on an "accept" button as a condition of placing orders.

B. Electronic Order/Electronic Delivery Model

Similar to the physical delivery model is one where the customer orders the product from a web site and the product is delivered by electronic transmission. Common examples of products currently available by this means include books, music, videos and software. In the electronic delivery model, the considerations are essentially the same as when the goods are delivered physically. The vendor must perform a technical review and implement an effective order screening process before offering any controlled items on the web site. The screening of transactions may be accomplished through the online order administration system. An additional challenge in this context is designing an order process that performs screening in real time, so the customer does not experience lengthy delays in order processing and delivery. Unlike the physical delivery model, where the customer does not expect to receive the product instantaneously (thus providing the vendor additional time to complete the screening process out of the customer's sight), the electronic delivery model may need an order administration process that can clear or block an order while the customer waits.

C. Web Downloading and Posting

Vendors commonly provide customers, on a subscription basis, access to online software patches or upgrades and technical data and services. The customer downloads this data after accessing the site by means of a password or other identifier assigned by the vendor. Because the downloads occur without the placement of an order or the provision of sufficient information for the vendor to perform effective export compliance screening, the vendor must prescreen the customer before approving the customer's access to the site. An additional consideration is whether to permit the customer to access the site from any remote computer. If this type of unrestricted access is permitted, the vendor faces the additional complexity of having only such information as is available from the customer's IP address to use in the screening process (that is, there will be no other means to determine whether the person accessing the site is, in fact, the registered—and screened—customer). When the information received in the course of the download transaction is deemed insufficient to perform effective screening, the vendor may consider it prudent to not offer certain data by this means. The downloading scenario requires a technical review of the data and screening (perhaps at more than one juncture), and exporters may want to include both acknowledgments and blocking processes as well.

When data are posted to web sites or bulletin boards accessible to the general public, the export compliance concerns may be diminished if the data are exempt from controls under one or more of the exceptions for publicly available information. Note that these exceptions have limited applicability to encryption software. As in all cases involving controlled data, however, the person posting the information is under an obligation to prohibit unlimited access by foreigners. Thus, a person posting controlled data is responsible under the export regulations to maintain restrictions on access by, for instance, persons and entities in certain embargoed destinations. This restriction might be implemented by screening and blocking IP addresses indicating the person seeking access is located in an embargoed nation. Web posting scenarios require a technical review of the data and some screening and/or blocking.

D. Postings on Private Networks

The presence of controlled data commonly found on companies' internal networks raises the issue of deemed exports or transfers to foreign nationals who are employees. Here, the challenge is not to screen persons unknown to the company from improper access, but to limit access by certain of the company's own workers. This can be a difficult task because the data may be necessary to perform job responsibilities and may be widely available via the network. Much of this information tends to be proprietary and thus does not qualify for exemption from export controls on the basis of public availability. The task for employers is to determine where on the network (or elsewhere) the controlled data resides and whether any foreign nationals have job responsibilities that potentially require access to the data. Having performed this analysis, the employer must either obtain licenses for any foreign nationals or cordon off this data from the foreign nationals (such as by means of password protection, network firewalls or tactical job assignments). Companies may also consider export law issues in their hiring practices—companies can avoid placing foreign nationals in positions where they will be exposed to controlled data, and they can explain in the terms of employment that eligibility for particular assignments is subject to applicable law. Posting to internal networks requires a technical review, manual screening of employees and possibly some form of blocking to prevent foreign nationals' access to data.

§ 5.6 Consumer Protection through Self-Regulation

The exact meaning of self-regulation can vary—for purposes of this section, the "self" in self-regulation should not be limited to industry. Rather, "the basic premise of self-regulation is continuous improvement to meet the needs of the particular business in the most efficient manner (with 'needs' encompassing company growth and consumer demand as well as the prevention and detection of unlawful or liability-producing conduct)."[398] Or, as the Council of Better Business Bureaus has stated, self-regulation "should be considered as a process driven by the enlightened self-interest of industry, supported in key ways by government to the ultimate benefit of consumers."[399] Thus, self-regulation has three participants: industry, government and consumers. And, when it is effective, self-regulation can prevent the enactment of sweeping direct governmental regulation that can "strangle innovation and discourage competition. [T]he synergistic relationship of meaningful industry standards and effective and supportive government actions will result in public confidence that will, in turn, positively reinforce industry's willingness to continue to develop meaningful standards."[400]

Two of the leading self-regulatory[401] initiatives in the area of consumer protection—the Organization for Economic Cooperation and Development Guidelines for Consumer Protection (OECD Guidelines), and the Better Business Bureaus/BBBOnLine Code of Online Business Practices (BBB Code)—are discussed below.

---

398. Observations on the State of Self-Regulation of the Internet, Presented at the Internet Law and Policy Forum (Oct. 1998), *available at* <http://www.ilpf.org/selfreg/whitepaper.htm>.

399. COUNCIL BETTER BUS. BUREAUS, PROTECTING CONSUMERS IN CROSS-BORDER TRANSACTIONS: A COMPREHENSIVE MODEL FOR ALTERNATIVE DISPUTE RESOLUTION 2 (2000).

400. *Id.* at 3.

401. Some refer to OECD's efforts as co-regulation, rather than self-regulation. For example, Erkki Liikanen, Member of the European Commission Responsible for Enterprise and the Information Society, stated as follows:

> The Commission backs self-regulation as a flexible, efficient and cost-effective alternative to regulation in many areas—achieving the same results without the delays of a time-consuming law-making process. Of course, certain conditions must be met. Self-regulation must be in conformity with, and backed by, law. It must be enforceable and verifiable. Until recently, regulation and self-regulation were often seen as diametrically opposed. Pressures from the new economy have changed that—leading to a high degree of consensus on this pragmatic approach. A major development in this respect is the concept of 'cooperative approach to governance'—or 'co-regulation.' Co-regulation takes self-regulation one step further. Beyond the mere coexistence of regulation and self-regulation, it implies the sharing of responsibilities between public and private partners.

Erkki Liikanen, *Is there a Third Way for the Internet in Europe?*, Global Internet Summit, Barcelona, Spain, May 22, 2000, *available at* <http://europa.eu.int/comm/information_society/speeches/liikanen/barcelona/index_en.htm>.

1. OECD Guidelines for Consumer Protection

i. Introduction

Recognizing the inherently international nature of electronic commerce, the Organization for Economic Cooperation and Development (OECD) has been active in advocating a global approach to consumer protection in the electronic marketplace.[402] According to OECD, "[d]isparate national policies may impede the growth of electronic commerce, and as such, these consumer protection issues may be addressed most effectively through international consultation and co-operation."[403]

OECD's most recent efforts to reach international consensus regarding on-line consumer protection culminated in Guidelines for Consumer Protection in the Context of Electronic Commerce (OECD Guidelines).[404] The OECD Guidelines have been formally recommended to the Member States by the OECD Council. They are designed as a framework for governments, businesses and consumer advocates to use in developing policies and regulations that limit fraudulent, misleading and unfair commercial conduct online, and that help build and maintain consumer confidence in e-commerce.

The OECD Guidelines contemplate self-regulation by businesses as a major tool for implementing a global cooperative effort to inform and protect consumers. One of the three underlying purposes of the OECD Guidelines is to assist "[b]usiness associations, consumer groups and self-regulatory bodies, by providing guidance as to the core characteristics of effective consumer protection that should be considered in reviewing, formulating, and implementing self-regulatory schemes in the context of electronic commerce. . . ."[405] To provide such guidance, the OECD Guidelines outline basic information disclosures and fair practices that businesses should follow—and that consumers should expect—when conducting transactions online.

---

402. OECD is an intergovernmental organization that provides a forum for governments to discuss economic and social policy in an effort to promote economic growth, trade and development. The organization, which works on a consensus basis, comprises twenty-nine member countries: Australia, Austria, Belgium, Canada, Czech Republic, Denmark, Finland, France, Germany, Greece, Hungary, Iceland, Ireland, Italy, Japan, Korea, Luxembourg, Mexico, the Netherlands, New Zealand, Norway, Poland, Portugal, Spain, Sweden, Switzerland, Turkey, the United Kingdom and the United States.

403. *Recommendation of the OECD Council Concerning Guidelines for Consumer Protection in the Context of Electronic Commerce*, at 1 (Dec. 9, 1999) [hereinafter *Council Recommendation*]; *see also* <http://www.oecd.org/dsti/sti/it/consumer/>.

404. *See OECD Guidelines for Consumer Protection in the Context of Electronic Commerce* (Dec. 9, 1999), annex to Council Recommendation, *supra* note 403 [hereinafter *OECD Guidelines*]; *see also* <http://www.oecd.org/dsti/sti/it/consumer/>.

405. *Council Recommendation, supra* note 403, at 1–2. *See also* <http://www.oecd.org/dsti/sti/it/consumer/>.

ii. The OECD Guidelines

The OECD Guidelines are designed to provide practical guidance to governments, businesses and consumers in arriving at methods of protecting consumers in the electronic marketplace. They reflect eighteen months of effort by the OECD Committee on Consumer Policy, working in collaboration with business and consumer representatives. The OECD Council approved the OECD Guidelines and formally recommended them to all member countries. Although the OECD Guidelines are nonbinding, the member countries will likely use and implement them, considering that representatives of those countries drafted and approved the document.

At base, the OECD Guidelines seek to provide consumers with at least as much protection as they are afforded in traditional commercial contexts. They address basic aspects of business-to-consumer e-commerce and, for the most part, reflect existing legal protections available to consumers in more traditional forms of commerce. Recognizing, however, that the unique aspects of e-commerce may create unfamiliar commercial situations for consumers, the OECD Guidelines note the increasing importance of informing consumers about their rights and obligations when conducting online transactions.

According to OECD, legitimate businesses will benefit from better-informed consumers, as those consumers will become more comfortable and confident in conducting transactions online, and more capable of detecting fraudulent and misleading offerings. OECD notes that one of the most common online consumer shopping experiences consists of buyers using the Internet to research products and services, and then turning to more traditional methods—such as phone, fax or retail outlets—to complete the transaction.

The OECD Guidelines are separated into four main parts: scope, general principles, implementation and global cooperation. A brief analysis of each part follows.

A. Scope

The OECD Guidelines apply only to business-to-consumer transactions; they do not apply to business-to-business transactions.

B. General Principles

(1) Level of Protection

Generally, the OECD Guidelines seek to offer consumers the same protections offered in the brick-and-mortar commercial context. According to the OECD Guidelines, "[c]onsumers who participate in electronic commerce should be afforded transparent and effective consumer protection that is not less than the level of protection afforded in other forms of commerce."[406] The OECD Guidelines urge governments, businesses, consumers and consumer advocacy groups to work together to achieve this level of protection, and to determine whether any additional protections are necessary in the online context. Although not necessarily additional protections, some traditional protections must be "reconfigured" to fit the unique characteristics of the online environment.

(2) Fair Business Practices

The OECD Guidelines ask that businesses engaged in e-commerce "pay due regard to the interests of consumers and act in accordance with fair business, advertising and marketing practices."[407] Those practices include the following:

- Refrain from making any representation or omission—or engaging in any practice—that is likely to be deceptive, misleading, fraudulent or unfair.
- Present information about the business and its goods and services in a clear, conspicuous, accurate and easily accessible manner.
- Comply with any representations made regarding policies or practices relating to transactions with consumers.
- Take into account the global nature of e-commerce and consider the various regulatory schemes in the targeted markets.
- Refrain from exploiting methods of e-commerce to hide the business's identity or to avoid compliance with regulatory schemes.
- Develop and implement easy and effective methods of allowing consumers to choose whether to receive unsolicited e-mail, and respect any indication from consumers that they do not want to receive unsolicited e-mail.
- Take special care in advertising and marketing directed to children, the elderly, and others who may not have the capacity to understand fully the information presented to them and/or the e-commerce methods utilized.

(3) Online Disclosures

Although seemingly obvious, companies operating in the electronic environment often forget to include basic identifying information, information about their products and services, and information about the terms and conditions of sale. As a result, the OECD Guidelines require online disclosures to be "easily accessible," and sufficient to allow a consumer to communicate with a company and make an informed decision regarding the purchase of a product or service before a transaction is consummated.

The OECD Guidelines ask that a business engaged in e-commerce make its identity—including the company's name, geographic and electronic addresses,

---

406. *OECD Guidelines, supra* note 404, at 4.
407. *Id.*

and telephone number—available in an accurate, clear and easily accessible manner. The information should allow for (1) prompt, easy and effective communication with the business, (2) the service of legal process and (3) the location of the business and its principals for purposes of law enforcement and regulatory officials.

The OECD Guidelines also ask that a business provide information regarding the products and services it offers in e-commerce. The information should be given in a manner that makes it possible for a consumer to maintain an adequate record of the information, and should be sufficient to enable a consumer to make an informed decision about whether to enter a transaction.

In connection with the transaction itself, the OECD Guidelines ask that a business provide information regarding the terms, conditions and costs associated with a transaction, so that a consumer can make an informed decision about whether to enter the transaction. The information should be provided in a clear, accurate and easily accessible manner, and, when applicable, should include the following:

- an itemization of total costs;
- notice of any other applicable costs that are not collected by the business itself or included in the total cost itemization (such as taxes);
- terms of delivery and performance;
- terms, conditions and methods of payment;
- restrictions and conditions of purchase, such as parental approval, geographic or time restrictions;
- instructions for proper use, including safety and health warnings;
- information relating to after-sale service;
- details and conditions relating to withdrawal, termination, return, exchange, cancellation and refund policies; and
- available warranties and guarantees.

Because of the international nature of e-commerce, the OECD Guidelines also ask that a business note the applicable currency and refer to all costs in that currency.

(4) Confirmation Process

To avoid any ambiguity, the OECD Guidelines ask that *before* any purchase is concluded, a business identify "precisely" the goods or services the consumer has expressed an interest in purchasing, give the consumer an opportunity to identify and correct any errors in the goods or services selected or information provided, and allow the consumer to modify or cancel the order. Following the purchase, a business should also give the consumer a complete and accurate record of the transaction. This is equivalent to what takes place at a cash register in a brick-and-mortar store—the clerk rings up each item for purchase and offers the consumer a total price, at which time the consumer has the opportunity to cancel the entire transaction or remove certain items from the selected basket of goods.

(5) Payment

The OECD Guidelines direct businesses to use easy and secure payment mechanisms, and to offer information regarding the level of security provided by those mechanisms. They also suggest limitations of liability for unauthorized or fraudulent use of payment systems, to build consumer confidence in conducting transactions online. The OECD Guidelines do not specify the types of technology that must be used to ensure secure payment.

(6) Dispute Resolution

The OECD Guidelines recognize the difficulties inherent in cross-border, e-commerce transactions, and they encourage governments to review their existing frameworks to determine whether such frameworks provide sufficient protection for consumers. Until an inexpensive, effective and efficient global mechanism for seeking redress in a cross-border transaction is devised, however, the most effective mechanism appears to be alternative dispute resolution. It specifically encouraged "the participation of consumer representatives in the development of self-regulatory mechanisms that contain specific, substantive rules for dispute resolution and compliance mechanisms."[408] To that end, the OECD Guidelines direct businesses to provide consumers with meaningful access to fair and timely alternative dispute resolution and redress without undue cost and burden. Perhaps more than any other area, the OECD Guidelines view this as a circumstance in which self-regulation is necessary and appropriate.

(7) Privacy

OECD long ago issued independent Guidelines Governing the Transborder Flow of Personal Data (1980), and it also issued a Ministerial Declaration on the Protection of Privacy on Global Networks (1998).[409] The OECD Guidelines ask that those conducting business in the electronic context consult and abide by those documents.[410]

(8) Education and Awareness

Lastly, the OECD Guidelines ask governments, businesses, and consumer groups "to work together to educate consumers about electronic commerce, to foster informed decision making by consumers participating in electronic commerce, and to increase business and consumer awareness of the consumer protection framework that applies to their online activities."[411] The end goal of this

---

408. *See OECD Guidelines, supra* note 404, at 7.

409. *See OECD Guidelines Governing the Transborder Flow of Personal Data* (1980), and *OECD Ministerial Declaration on the Protection of Privacy on Global Networks* (1998), *available at* <http://www.oecd.org/dsti/sti/it/secur/>.

410. *See infra* Chapter 7 for a discussion of privacy issues.

411. *OECD Guidelines, supra* note 404, at 8.

and the other general principles is to increase consumers' awareness of their rights and obligations, so they are more confident in conducting online transactions.

C. Implementation

Neither the OECD Council's Recommendation nor the OECD Guidelines are binding upon Member States or companies that operate within their borders. Rather, the OECD Council formally communicates and recommends that the respective Member States adopt the relevant sections of the OECD Guidelines. The individual Member States must act within their respective borders to implement the OECD Guidelines or any part(s) thereof. OECD envisions the process as nationwide endeavors by governments, industries and citizens of the Member States, whether by public or private means. In essence, the OECD Guidelines provide the basic set of expectations for consumer protection online, but it is up to the individual Member States' governments, businesses, consumers and consumer advocates to coordinate efforts to effectuate those consumer protections.

In making its recommendations, OECD acknowledged the effective self-regulatory efforts already undertaken by the private sector, and encouraged continued private sector leadership. It also asked the private sector to continue its leadership in the development of technology as a tool to protect and empower consumers.

D. Global Cooperation

To provide effective consumer protection on a global basis, the OECD Guidelines advise member countries to facilitate international communication and cooperation to combat fraudulent, misleading and unfair commercial conduct. The OECD Guidelines suggest cooperation among governments, businesses and consumer groups on an international level to achieve enhanced confidence, predictability and protection for consumers.

2. BBB Code of Online Business Practices

i. Introduction

The Better Business Bureau (BBB) and its online subsidiary, BBB*OnLine*, issued a Code of Online Business Practices (BBB Code)[412] to guide ethical business-

---

412. *See Do's & Don'ts in Advertising*, § 13, 265 Council of Better Business Bureaus, Inc. 2001, *available at* <http://www.bbbonline.org>.

to-customer conduct in global e-commerce.[413] Online companies that participate in the BBB's Reliability Seal Program are required to comply with these
guidelines.[414] The guidelines are voluntary for those not in the program. The
BBB Code encourages those businesses that want to promote their commitment
to the BBB Code's requirements to become participants in the BBBOnLine
Reliability Program.[415] Qualifying participants are issued a seal that serves as a
visual cue to prospective customers that the business intends to comply with
the program requirements.[416]

ii. The BBB Code

The BBB Code describes itself as containing practical, performance-based
guidelines for online businesses, rather than as dictating methods for achieving
the goals, which could interfere with particular business models.[417] The stated
purpose behind this methodology is two-fold: First, BBB recognizes that a business will know how the guidelines should be reached within its own business
model. Second, BBB did not want to dictate specific methods for achieving the
goals for fear that evolving technology would quickly outdate any specific methods required, thus rendering the BBB Code obsolete and limiting a business's
ability to foster innovative means to meet the guidelines.

The BBB Code also states what it is not. It is not a code for business-to-
business transactions.[418] It does not purport to specify which laws of a particular
country apply to a particular online transaction or advertising dispute.[419] In
fact, the BBB Code completely sidesteps the entire issue of jurisdiction in the
global online context, and instead offers language similar to that found within
the OECD Guidelines.[420] The BBB Code does advise online businesses to make

---

413. The BBB Code was developed using an open process. BBBOnLine posted three drafts of the BBB
Code online and solicited online comments, and held three regional meetings open to the public to discuss
the proposed provisions and obtain recommendations. Individuals, government officials and staffers, industry
representatives and consumer organizations contributed more than a thousand suggestions and comments
during this open process. *See* <http://www.bbbonline.org/businesses/code/index.htm>.

414. The Reliability Program's mission is to help web users find reliable and trustworthy businesses
online, as well as to enable reliable businesses to identify themselves as such, through voluntary self-regulatory
programs that help avoid government regulation of the Internet. *See* <http://www.bbbonline.org/businesses/
reliability/index.html>. A qualifying company receives a seal to post on its web site, which allows web
shoppers to check BBB information on the company and be assured the company is reliable. The requirements
to participate in the Reliability Program include (1) becoming a member of the appropriate local Better
Business Bureau, (2) having a satisfactory complaint-handling record with the BBB, (3) agreeing to participate
in the BBB's advertising self-regulation program, (4) responding promptly to all consumer complaints and
(5) agreeing to dispute resolution, at the consumer's request, for unresolved disputes involving consumer
products or services advertised or promoted online. *See* <http://www.bbbonline.org/businesses/reliability/
standards.html>.

415. *See* <http://www.bbbonline.org/businesses/code/code.htm>.

416. *Id.*

417. *See* <http://www.bbbonline.org/businesses/code/index.htm>.

418. The scope is similar to that found in the OECD Guidelines.

419. *See* <http://www.bbbonline.org/businesses/code/index.htm>.

420. *See* <http://www.oecd.org/dsti/sti/it/consumer/prod/CPGuidelines_final.pdf>.

their own determinations concerning whether their business practices comply with applicable laws, but without specifying what those laws might be.[421]

The BBB Code is not static. BBB indicates it will review the BBB Code and update it as needed to keep it current with developing technology, new business models and customer needs.[422]

Finally, the BBB Code is not meant to cover all business-to-consumer interactions on the Internet.[423] It narrows the scope of applicability by providing definitions of the two types of businesses it does cover: online advertisers and online merchants. The BBB Code defines an online advertiser as a person or entity that promotes its own goods or services on the Internet, and defines an online merchant as a person or entity that offers goods and services online and accepts online orders. The BBB Code then notes that an entity could act as an online advertiser or merchant in certain situations and not others, which indicates the BBB Code may apply only in certain situations. The BBB Code also notes that all online merchants are also online advertisers, so that merchants must adhere to all provisions of the BBB Code.[424]

The BBB Code[425] is based upon five principles: Truthful and Accurate Communications, Disclosure, Information Practices and Security, Customer Satisfaction, and Protecting Children.[426] The summaries of the principles are followed by a more detailed discussion of each.[427]

- *Principle I: Truthful and Accurate Communications.* Online advertisers should not engage in deceptive or misleading practices in connection with any aspect of electronic commerce, including advertising, marketing or use of technology.
- *Principle II: Disclosure.* Online merchants should disclose to their customers and prospective customers information about their businesses, the goods or services available for purchase online and the transactions themselves.
- *Principle III: Information Practices and Security.* Online advertisers should adopt information practices that treat customers' personal information with care. They should (1) post and adhere to privacy policies based upon fair information principles, (2) take appropriate measures to provide ad-

---

421. *See* <http://www.bbbonline.org/businesses/code/index.htm>.
422. *Id.*
423. *Id.*
424. *Id.*
425. Although the BBB Code and OECD Guidelines cover much of the same territory and have the same ultimate goal of protecting consumers, they were written for two fundamentally different audiences. The BBB Code is written for individual companies engaged in e-commerce and is very specific about particular practices. The OECD Guidelines, in contrast, are written as a broad outline to guide individual OECD member governments in crafting appropriate implementing legislation.
426. *See* <http://www.bbbonline.org/businesses/code/code.htm>.
427. The full text of the principles, along with supporting details, explanations and examples, may be found at <http://www.bbbonline.com/code/principle.asp>.

equate security and (3) respect customers' preferences regarding unsolicited e-mail.

- *Principle IV: Customer Satisfaction.* Online merchants should seek to ensure customer satisfaction by honoring their representations, answering questions and resolving customer disputes in a timely and responsive manner.
- *Principle V: Protecting Children.* If online advertisers target children under the age of thirteen, they should take special care to protect them by recognizing children's developing cognitive abilities.

A. Principle I: Truthful and Accurate Communications

The first principle of the BBB Code states, "Online advertisers should not engage in deceptive or misleading trade practices with regard to any aspect of electronic commerce, including advertising, marketing, or in their use of technology."[428]

In its supporting details, the BBB Code requires advertisers to adhere to the BBB's Code of Advertising,[429] which, among other things, requires advertisers to engage in truthful advertising, refrain from making deceptive or misleading representations or omissions of material facts, and possess reasonable substantiation before making claims.[430]

The BBB Code also requires online advertisers to cooperate with industry self-regulatory programs that provide means for resolving advertising disputes.[431] Examples of such programs include the National Advertising Review Council in the United States[432] and the European Advertising Standards Alliance in Europe.[433]

Noting that Internet technology allows advertisers to describe their products and services in innovative ways, the BBB Code requires online advertisers to use the technology to promote customers' knowledge of the offerings and not use it to mislead customers.[434] Examples include advertisers (1) using hyperlinks to embellish information about goods and services, but not using them to change the meaning of any material claims substantially, (2) using search terms or mechanisms that fairly reflect site content and (3) ensuring that third-party "seals" for self-regulatory or ethical standard programs are functional, so customers can verify membership in—and the scope of—the programs. The BBB

---

428. *See* <http://www.bbbonline.org/businesses/code/principle1.htm>.

429. *See* <http://www.bbb.org/advertising/adcode.asp>.

430. *See* <http://www.bbbonline.org/businesses/code/principle1.htm>.

431. *Id.*

432. *See* <http://www.bbb.org/advertising/>.

433. *See* <http://www.easa-alliance.org/>.

434. *See* <http://www.bbbonline.org/businesses/code/principle1.htm>.

Code also prohibits the use of technology that deceptively interferes with browsers, computers or appliances that customers use to access the Internet. The example offered relates to an advertiser who deceptively disables the back button of a customer's browser to prevent the customer from exiting the site.[435]

B. Principle II: Disclosure

The second principle of the BBB Code states, "Online merchants should disclose to their customers and prospective customers information about the business, the goods or services available for purchase online, and the transaction itself."[436]

The BBB Code requires that all information be clear and accurate, as well as easy to find and understand. Additionally, a customer should be able to retain a copy of material information by printing or storing it. If the information relates to the goods or services, or to the online transaction itself, it should be available before the consummation of the transaction, to help the customer make an informed purchasing decision.[437]

The BBB Code mandates that a merchant disclose specific contact information about itself, including its legal name, the name under which it conducts business, a principle physical address, an online method of contact, a point of contact and a telephone number.[438] It also requires a merchant that registers for an Internet domain name to do so accurately, using the appropriate top-level domain for the type of business registered.[439] The BBB Code explains that these disclosure requirements are appropriate for e-commerce—online merchants should not "hide" in cyberspace because anonymity, often considered a benefit of the Internet community, is inappropriate in connection with online transactions.[440] Just as a business needs to know whose credit card to charge for a transaction, a customer needs to know the business with which she is dealing.

Similarly, the BBB Code requires online merchants to provide information about goods or services available online that is sufficient to allow customers to make informed choices about whether they want to purchase such goods or services.[441] Because online customers cannot touch and examine products as they can in the offline world, online merchants should ensure they provide material information that customers would be able to see if they were buying the products offline.[442]

---

435. *See* <http://www.bbbonline.org/businesses/code/sample10.html>.

436. *See* <http://www.bbbonline.org/businesses/code/principle2.htm>.

437. *Id.*

438. The BBB Code does state, however, that if a merchant's operations would be disrupted by the requirement to provide a phone number (due to size and resources), then that merchant must at least have a working listed phone number instead. *Id.*

439. *Id.*

440. *See* <http://www.bbbonline.org/businesses/code/sample14.html>.

441. *See* <http://www.bbbonline.org/businesses/code/principle2.htm>.

442. *See* <http://www.bbbonline.org/businesses/code/sample15.html>.

The BBB Code requires online merchants to provide information about the transactions themselves, sufficient to allow customers to make informed choices about whether to engage in such transactions.[443] Specifically, the BBB Code requires online merchants to provide information about the terms of the transactions (including return or refund policies), product availability and shipping information (including when products are temporarily unavailable), and prices and customer costs (including prices, shipping and handling charges and expected taxes).[444]

The BBB Code also requires an online merchant, before completing a transaction, to provide a summary of information about the transaction, the selected payment method and the option to cancel or affirmatively complete the transaction.[445] Providing the opportunity to cancel before transactions are consummated is an important means by which online merchants can ease wary customers into shopping online. An online merchant must also provide a customer with the option of receiving a confirmation of the transaction after the transaction has been completed.[446] This confirmation should include a line-item statement of the order, prices and known charges, contact information (so the customer can obtain order updates) and the anticipated date of shipment.

C. Principle III: Information Practices and Security

The third principle of the BBB Code states, "Online advertisers should adopt information practices that treat customers' personal information with care. They should post and adhere to a privacy policy based on fair information principles, take appropriate measures to provide adequate security, and respect customers' preferences regarding unsolicited e-mail."[447]

The BBB Code requires the privacy policy to be open and transparent, and to meet generally accepted fair information principles. These principles include notice, choice, security, enforcement and redress. The policy should be easy to find and understand, and be available before—or when—the customer discloses any personally identifiable information.[448]

The BBB Code requires online advertisers to provide appropriate security for the type of information collected, maintained or transferred to third parties, and to use industry-standard levels of encryption, authentication, security and integrity. Online advertisers must also take reasonable steps to require third parties involved in fulfilling transactions to maintain adequate security.[449]

---

443. *See* <http://www.bbbonline.org/businesses/code/principle2.htm>.
444. *Id.*
445. *Id.*
446. *Id.*
447. *See* <http://www.bbbonline.org/businesses/code/principle3.htm>.
448. *Id.*
449. *Id.*

Online advertisers must accurately describe their unsolicited e-mail practices and, if involved in such marketing, provide customers with an online means to "opt out" of future solicitations. This information must be available on web sites, as well as in any marketing e-mails. Online advertisers that send unsolicited e-mails must subscribe to bona fide e-mail suppression lists.[450]

D. Principle IV: Customer Satisfaction

The fourth principle of the BBB Code states, "Online merchants should seek to ensure that their customers are satisfied by honoring their representations, answering questions, and resolving customer complaints and disputes in a timely and responsive manner."[451]

In connection with answering questions, the BBB Code notes it is insufficient for an online merchant simply to provide an e-mail address, if questions sent to that address are not promptly answered and/or are answered out of context.[452]

Under the BBB Code, an online merchant must not only provide an easy-to-find and understandable notice of how a customer can contact the business to resolve complaints or disputes related to a transaction, it must also have an effective and easy-to-use internal mechanism for addressing complaints and correcting errors.[453] The BBB Code offers fair exchange or return policies as examples of effective internal mechanisms that could be made available to customers.

The BBB Code goes one step further. It mandates that should the internal mechanism fail to resolve a customer's complaint, the online merchant must provide either a money-back guarantee or third-party dispute resolution as a means by which the customer can seek redress.[454] If the merchant chooses to provide third-party dispute resolution, it must use a trusted third party that offers impartial, accessible and timely arbitration that is either free or at least not disproportionate to the value of the goods or services in dispute. The merchant should also provide easy-to-find contact information about the third party and a link to any third-party sites used for such purposes.

E. Principle V: Protecting Children

The fifth and last principle of the BBB Code states, "If online advertisers target children under the age of 13, they should take special care to protect children by recognizing their developing cognitive abilities."[455]

---

450. *Id.*
451. *See* <http://www.bbbonline.org/businesses/code/principle4.htm>.
452. *See* <http://www.bbbonline.org/businesses/code/sample17.html>.
453. *See* <http://www.bbbonline.org/businesses/code/principle4.htm>.
454. *Id.*
455. *See* <http://www.bbbonline.org/businesses/code/principle5.htm>.

The BBB Code requires online advertisers that target children through age twelve to adhere to the Children's Advertising Review Unit's Guidelines for Interactive Electronic Media.[456] These guidelines have been harmonized with the Federal Trade Commission's final rule implementing the Children's Online Privacy Protection Act of 1998.[457]

For example, if a site offers a child the opportunity to place an online order, the ordering instructions must clearly and prominently state that a child must have a parent's permission to order, and there should be a clear mechanism after the order is placed that allows the child or parent to cancel the order.[458] Additionally, if a site intends to share personal information about the child with third parties, the advertiser must first obtain verifiable parental consent.[459]

456. *Id.*
457. *See* <http://www.bbb.org/advertising/caruguId.asp#media>.
458. *Id.*
459. *Id.*

Taxation

Contents

Taxation

One of the most important challenges facing companies engaged in electronic commerce transactions is determining how these transactions should be treated for tax purposes. Most tax rules were written without e-commerce in mind. Nevertheless, in most cases, tax authorities and taxpayers should be able to apply existing rules and concepts to e-commerce without undue difficulty or uncertainty.

The U.S. and global tax communities have been discussing the taxation of e-commerce for several years, and they continue to do so. In some cases, tax authorities have issued new rules addressing certain types of e-commerce. Tax authorities and international organizations have also issued a number of discussion papers on e-commerce, which have played a role in shaping the tax community's thinking on these issues and may indicate the direction that future changes in the law will take. Chapter 6 discusses these and other issues relating to the taxation of e-commerce.

Taylor S. Reid and Lance C. Martin have written sections 6.1 through 6.3 of this chapter. Section 6.1 of this chapter highlights some of the most significant authorities, papers and commentaries that have been released on the taxation of e-commerce in recent years. Section 6.2 covers U.S. federal income taxation of e-commerce, highlighting significant authorities and issues in this area. Many of the most difficult issues involve cross-border transactions. Accordingly, Section 6.3 covers the international taxation of e-commerce, with a focus on how tax treaties may alter the tax consequences that would otherwise result under U.S. federal income tax law. Section 6.4, authored by J. Pat Powers and Bartley B. Baer, covers the U.S. state and local taxation of e-commerce. Finally, Jan S. Snel addresses in Section 6.5 the taxation of e-commerce under consumption tax regimes, which is perhaps the most pressing e-commerce tax issue in European countries and is, therefore, of particular significance to taxpayers doing business abroad.

§ 6.1 Taxation of E-Commerce

1. United States

i. Software Revenue Characterization Regulations

In late 1996, the U.S. Treasury Department (Treasury) issued proposed regulations on the classification of transfers of computer programs.[1] These regulations
were finalized—with additional examples and clarifications—in September
1998.[2] Although these regulations do not apply to digitized products other than
software, their underlying principles may nevertheless be helpful in determining
the tax consequences of such digitized products. These regulations are discussed
in more detail below.

ii. Treasury Discussion Paper on Taxation of E-Commerce

In November 1996, Treasury published a discussion paper on the taxation of
electronic commerce.[3] The guiding principle in the Treasury discussion paper
is neutrality, which would argue against the imposition of new or additional
taxes on electronic transactions and would require that the U.S. tax system treat
similar income equally, regardless of whether it is earned through electronic
means or through existing channels of commerce. Treasury also identified three
major issue areas:

1. identification of the country or countries having jurisdiction to tax income from e-commerce;
2. classification of the income from transactions in digitized information;
   and
3. administration and compliance challenges in an increasingly digital
   environment.

---

1. Prop. Treas. Reg. § 1.861–18, 61 Fed. Reg. 58152 (Nov. 13, 1996). All section references are to the U.S. Internal Revenue Code of 1986, as amended, and the regulations thereunder, unless otherwise specified.
2. Treasury Dec. 8785, 1998-42 I.R.O. 5 (Oct. 2, 1998).
3. OFFICE TAX POLICY, DEP'T TREASURY, SELECTED TAX POLICY IMPLICATIONS OF GLOBAL ELECTRONIC COMMERCE (Nov. 1996).

2. Organization for Economic Cooperation and Development

The Organization for Economic Cooperation and Development (OECD) has also been very active in formulating tax policy for e-commerce. The OECD includes most of the world's developed countries and provides governments a setting in which to discuss and develop economic and social policy. It plays a significant role in the development of international consensus on tax issues, particularly through its Model Convention on Income Taxes for the Prevention of Dual Taxation, and the corresponding official commentary.[4]

i. OECD Ministerial Meetings

The OECD has held several ministerial meetings in recent years to address the taxation of cross-border e-commerce. The OECD convened its first discussion of e-commerce tax issues with the business community in Turku, Finland in November 1997. Since then, the OECD held similar meetings in Ottawa in 1998 and in Paris in 1999. In connection with these meetings, the OECD issued a proposed *framework conditions* document.[5] The framework conditions identify the general tax principles that should be applied to e-commerce, as well as the principal areas for further work. The document notes that the following widely accepted general tax principles should apply to the taxation of e-commerce:

- Neutrality;
- Efficiency;
- Certainty and simplicity;
- Effectiveness and fairness; and
- Flexibility.

Four major areas were identified for further work:

- Improving taxpayer service;
- Tax administration;
- Consumption taxes; and
- International taxation norms.

---

4. This refers to this and other conventions on income taxes for the prevention of dual taxation as tax treaties.
5. OECD Comm. Fiscal Affairs, Electronic Commerce: A Discussion Paper on Taxation Issues (Oct. 10, 1998).

ii. Technical Advisory Groups

In January 1999, the OECD formed five technical advisory groups (TAGs) to address the issues identified in the framework conditions document. TAGs were formed in the areas of income characterization, business profits/permanent establishment, consumption tax, professional data assessment and technology. In addition to representatives of OECD member countries, representatives of non-OECD countries and members of the business community participate in these TAGs. TAGs have made recommendations on some issues but continue their work on other issues. Some of the most significant recommendations to date relate to revenue characterization and permanent establishment issues and are discussed below in section 6.3.

iii. Modifications to OECD Model Tax Treaty Commentary

The OECD Model Tax Treaty serves as the basis, or at least the starting point, for many of the bilateral tax treaties negotiated between countries. The OECD commentary on its Model Tax Treaty serves as a basis, albeit nonbinding, for interpreting actual tax treaties with provisions similar to those in the OECD Model Tax Treaty. In recent years, the OECD revised the commentary on article 12 (royalties) to address the characterization of payments for computer software and to the commentary on article 5 (permanent establishment) to address the application of the permanent establishment standard to electronic commerce. These provisions are discussed in more detail below.

3. Other Countries

Tax authorities in other countries, including Australia, Canada and the United Kingdom, have also contributed to the discussion of e-commerce taxation. Australian tax authorities published a report that examined the e-commerce environment and made recommendations on how Australia's existing taxes could be properly administered in this new environment.[6] Canada published an advisory report on the potential impact of e-commerce on Canada's tax admin-

---

6. AUSTRALIAN TAXATION OFFICE ELEC. COMMERCE PROJECT TEAM, TAX AND THE INTERNET (Aug. 1997) (discussion report on challenges of e-commerce for tax administration).

istration.[7] U.K. tax authorities published a paper summarizing changes to U.K. tax policy and tax administration resulting from the rapid worldwide growth in e-commerce.[8]

§ 6.2 U.S. Federal Income Taxation of E-Commerce

1. Overview of U.S. Federal Income Taxation

The United States taxes its citizens and residents on their worldwide taxable income from whatever source derived.[9] For both individuals and corporations, the U.S. income tax is imposed at graduated rates on a taxpayer's net taxable income (that is, gross income less allowable deductions). The United States also imposes this net-basis, graduated-rate income tax on the taxable income of nonresident alien individuals and foreign corporations that is effectively connected with the conduct of a trade or business within the United States.[10]

The United States imposes an income tax at a flat rate of thirty percent (unless reduced or eliminated under a tax treaty) on certain items of gross income of nonresident alien individuals and foreign corporations from U.S. sources that are not effectively connected with the conduct of a trade or business within the United States.[11] This gross-basis, flat-rate tax is commonly referred to as withholding tax because the payor of the income is required to withhold the appropriate amount of tax at the time of payment and remit such amount to the Internal Revenue Service (IRS) before transferring the remaining amount to the payee.[12] Income subject to this withholding tax includes dividends, interest, rents, royalties and similar items. The United States does not tax income of nonresident alien individuals and foreign corporations that is from foreign sources and not effectively connected with the conduct of a trade or business within the United States.

7. THE MINISTER OF NATIONAL REVENUE'S ADVISORY COMMITTEE ON ELECTRONIC COMMERCE, ELEC. COMMERCE & CANADA'S TAX ADMIN., (Apr. 1998) (advisory report does not represent official position of Revenue Canada).

8. U.K. INLAND REVENUE & H.M. CUSTOMS AND EXCISE, PAPER ON THE TAXATION OF ELECTRONIC COMMERCE (Nov. 26, 1999).

9. I.R.C. §§ 1, 11, 61–63 (2000).

10. *Id.* §§ 871(b), 882.

11. *Id.* §§ 871(a), 881.

12. *Id.* §§ 1441, 1442.

U.S. taxpayers can generally elect to claim foreign taxes paid or accrued as a credit against their U.S. tax liability, rather than simply as a deduction in computing such liability.[13] A taxpayer's foreign tax credit for a taxable year is limited, however, to the amount of its U.S. tax, multiplied by the ratio of foreign source taxable income to total taxable income.[14] Thus, the amount of a taxpayer's income that is from foreign sources is a key factor in determining the taxpayer's ability to utilize foreign taxes as credits.

2. Income Characterization

Before a transaction's tax consequences can be determined, its character must be determined. That is, a label must be placed on a transaction—and on the resulting income or expense—to know which tax rules apply. For example, the United States imposes withholding tax only upon certain enumerated types of income in certain situations.[15] The type of income that arises from a transaction must be known to determine whether the income is potentially subject to withholding tax. The United States also has different rules on where income is considered to arise (that is, its source) depending upon the type of income involved.[16] For example, if a transaction gives rise to royalty income, it is potentially subject to U.S. withholding tax, and the income is sourced to the place where the licensed intellectual property is used. If the transaction is treated instead as a sale of inventory, then U.S. withholding tax should not apply, and the income is sourced—at least in part—according to the place where title to the property passes. The determination of character and source also affects the availability of foreign tax credits, the applicability of the antideferral rules of subpart F and the choice of transfer pricing rules applied to related party transactions (discussed below).

i. Transfer of Software and Other Digitized Information—Licensing, Selling and Leasing

A. Licensing and Selling of Copyright Rights

Under U.S. tax regulations finalized in 1998 on the characterization and sourcing of transfers of computer programs, the legal form of a transfer of

---

13. *Id.* §§ 901 *et seq.*
14. *Id.* § 904. The calculation of the section 904 limitation is considerably more complicated than this simple formula suggests due to issues such as separate limitation categories and look-through rules.
15. *See id.* §§ 871(a), 881.
16. *See id.* §§ 861–65.

computer programs is not determinative of its characterization for U.S. federal income tax purposes.[17] These regulations draw a distinction between transfers of copyright rights and transfers of copyrighted articles. Royalty treatment arises only if there is a partial transfer of a copyright right that does not constitute an alienation of the entire copyright right. Under these regulations, if a recipient receives more than a de minimis right to (1) make copies of a computer program for distribution to the public, (2) prepare derivative computer programs based upon a copyrighted computer program, (3) publicly perform a computer program or (4) publicly display a computer program, the recipient is treated as receiving a copyright right. Otherwise, the recipient is treated as receiving a copy of the computer program (referred to as a "copyrighted article").[18]

Under the regulations, a transfer of a copyright right is treated as either a license or a sale. If less than all substantial rights to a copyright right are conveyed, the transfer is treated as a license of the copyright right. If all substantial rights to a copyright right are conveyed, it is treated as a sale or exchange of the copyright right.

Although these regulations apply only to computer programs, the principles underlying them—especially the distinction between transactions in products and transactions in rights—nevertheless seem equally appropriate for other types of digitized products. Under these principles, income from the transfer of any digitized product should not be treated as royalty income unless the transaction involves the partial transfer of intellectual property rights.

B. Selling and Leasing of Copyrighted Articles

Under the U.S. software characterization regulations, a recipient of a computer program is treated as receiving a copyrighted article if the recipient (1) does not acquire more than a de minimis amount of the four copyright rights identified under the regulations and (2) does not receive more than a de minimis amount of programming services or know-how related to the computer program. The determination of whether a transfer of a copyrighted article is a sale or a lease is based upon whether, taking into account all facts and circumstances, the benefits and burdens of ownership have been transferred.[19] If they have, the transfer is treated as a sale of the copyrighted article. Otherwise, the transfer is treated as a lease of the copyrighted article.

---

17. *See* Treas. Reg. § 1.861–18 (1998). For ease of reading, this chapter often refers to "U.S. federal income tax" matters simply as "U.S. tax" or "tax" matters.

18. The regulations also provide that certain transactions constitute the provision of services relating to the development or modification of a computer program or the provision of know-how.

19. Treas. Reg. § 1.861–18(f)(2) (1998).

C. Electronic Delivery

The U.S. software characterization regulations provide that the means of transmission do not determine a transaction's characterization.[20] As an illustration, the regulations contain an example in which a transaction is characterized as the sale of a copyrighted article even though the software is transmitted electronically rather than through a physical medium such as a disk.[21] By analogy, it seems appropriate that the means of transmission for other e-commerce transactions should not control their characterization for tax purposes.

ii. Services

A. Rendition of Services versus Sale of Goods

When a vendor both transfers property to—and performs services for—a customer as part of a single transaction, it is often necessary to determine whether the income from the transaction should be characterized as income from the sale of goods or from the rendition of services. Existing tax authority on this point, which arose outside the e-commerce context, should provide guidance for making this distinction in e-commerce transactions. The term "property" should include electronic data such as software, digitized music or video images, and other forms of digital information and content.

Generally speaking, if a customer owns the property after the transaction, but ownership was not transferred from the vendor to the customer, then the transaction should be treated as a services transaction. For example, if the customer engages the vendor to create an item of property that the customer will own from the moment of its creation, no property will have been transferred from the vendor to the customer and the transaction should be characterized as the provision of services.[22]

If the vendor does transfer ownership of property to the customer, the transaction should still be characterized as a services transaction if the predominant nature of the transaction is the provision of services. This would be the case, for example, when the property itself has little intrinsic value and the vendor creates value through the exercise of its particular talents and skills to create a unique result for this customer.[23]

Providing consulting or other professional services online is an example of an electronic commerce transaction that should typically result in services in-

---

20. *Id.* § 1.861–18(g)(2).

21. *Id.* § 1.861–18(h), ex. 2.

22. *See* Boulez v. Commissioner, 83 T.C. 584 (1984).

23. *See* Guy F. Atkinson Co. of California and Subsidiaries v. Commissioner, 82 T.C. 275 (1984) (discussing whether income from constructing dam should be income from services or from sale of goods for

come. In these transactions, the customer often does not receive any form of property. If the customer does receive property, such as a report, it was probably created specifically for that customer and arguably was owned by the customer from the moment of its creation. In contrast, if the customer receives a valuable report or other property that was not created specifically for that customer (such as an investment report or other high-value proprietary information sold to multiple customers), the transaction could give rise to income from the sale of goods, even if the customer obtained the report electronically from a vendor engaged in the business of providing advice or other services in that area.

B. Rendition of Services versus Leasing

When a customer receives both a temporary interest in property and the performance of services from a vendor in a single transaction, it is often necessary to determine whether the income from the transaction should be characterized as rental income or services income.

The largest body of authority in U.S. tax law that addresses the distinction between service contracts and leases deals with the application of the investment credit regime as it existed before the 1990s.[24] Despite the fact that this authority developed in response to the need for guidance on the availability of investment credits when property is provided to tax-exempt entities, the distinction drawn in these authorities between service contracts and leases was not intended to be limited to that narrow context and has been applied in other contexts.[25] These authorities identified several nonexclusive factors indicating the existence of a lease rather than a services contract, including the following:

- the service recipient is in physical possession of the property;
- the service recipient controls the property;
- the service recipient has a significant economic or possessory interest in the property;
- the service provider does not bear any risk of substantially diminished receipts or substantially increased expenditures if there is nonperformance under the contract;

---

purposes of former Western Hemisphere Trade Corporation deduction). *See also* Rev. Rul. 86-155, 1986-2 C.B. 134 (discussing whether income from constructing oil drilling platform should be income from sale of goods or income from services for purposes of subpart F of Internal Revenue Code).

24. *See* I.R.C. § 7701(e) (2000); *see also* Smith v. Commissioner, 57 T.C.M. (CCH) 826 (1989); Priv. Ltr. Rul. 98-14-021 (Dec. 23, 1997); Priv. Ltr. Rul. 98-14-018 (Dec. 23, 1997); Priv. Ltr. Rul. 91-42-002 (July 19, 1991); Priv. Ltr. Rul. 89-18-012 (Jan. 24, 1989); Priv. Ltr. Rul. 87-18-016 (Jan. 23, 1987); Priv. Ltr. Rul. 86-04-066 (Oct. 30, 1985).

25. *See* I.R.C. § 7701(e) (2000); S. REP. No. 98-169 (1984); JOINT COMM. ON TAXATION, 98TH CONG., EXPLANATION OF THE DEFICIT REDUCTION ACT OF 1984 (Comm. Print 1984); Rev. Rul. 72-49, 1972-1 C.B. 125; Tech. Adv. Mem. 84-10-010 (Nov. 21, 1983); Tech. Adv. Mem. 82-23-009 (Feb. 23, 1982); Priv. Ltr. Rul. 82-13-048 (Dec. 31, 1981); Tech. Adv. Mem. 81-34-026 (May 20, 1981).

- the service provider does not use the property concurrently to provide significant services to entities unrelated to the service recipient; and
- the total contract price does not substantially exceed the rental value of the property for the contract period.

Other factors include whether the service provider had the right to remove property from service and replace it with comparable property, whether the property was a component of an integrated operation in which the taxpayer had other responsibilities, and whether the fee earned by the service provider is based upon the passage of time or the number of procedures performed.

It seems appropriate to apply these factors in the context of electronic commerce to distinguish services transactions from leases. For example, a limited-duration license to use software or other digitized products should typically result in rental income. The customer usually has possession and control of the digitized product, operates the product, has exclusive use of the product for a significant period of time and pays a fee based upon the passage of time. In contrast, a license for a single online use of a software program or other digitized product arguably should result in services income. The customer lacks possession and control of the digitized product, has the product for a single use rather than for a specific amount of time and pays a fee based upon usage rather than the passage of time, which is not related to the fair rental value of the product.

In many contexts, application service provider transactions should also give rise to services income. In a typical transaction, the service provider uses the software to provide services to customers, maintains the software as needed, owns the equipment on which the software is loaded, provides access to many customers to the same equipment and has the right to update and replace the software at will. The customer does not have possession or control of the software or equipment, accesses the software concurrently with other customers and may pay a fee based upon the volume of transactions processed by the software.

Likewise, data warehousing transactions should generally be treated as services transactions. The vendor uses computer equipment to provide data hosting services to customers, owns and maintains the equipment on which the data is stored, provides access to many customers to the same equipment and has the right to remove and replace equipment at will. The customer does not have possession or control of the equipment and uses the equipment concurrently with other customers.

C. Online Advertising Revenue

At present, much of the revenue derived from e-commerce is not derived from transactions with end users but from online advertising by third parties. The little guidance that exists on advertising revenue suggests that online advertising revenue should generally be characterized as income from services. Authorities that have at least indirectly addressed the characterization of advertising revenue suggest it is earned in exchange for the act of publishing or broadcasting advertisements for public consumption.[26] Under this line of analysis, advertising revenue should be income received for the rendition of services; that is, the service of disseminating a customer's ads to a particular audience. It seems appropriate to apply the same analysis to online advertising, as well as to similar electronic marketing or merchandising services such as online shopping sites and sales referrals.

D. Computer Programming Services

As discussed, the IRS has issued regulations on one type of service in the electronic commerce context: computer programming services. Under these software characterization regulations, the IRS may treat a transaction involving the transfer of a newly developed or modified computer program as a provision of services, rather than the sale of a copyrighted article. The intent of the parties, as evidenced by their written agreements and conduct, determines the treatment of the transaction.[27] The regulations identify two main factors as evidence of intent: who owns the copyright to the software and who bears the risk of development. For example, when the author of the software retains the copyright, and therefore the right to sell other copies of the software to other parties, the transaction is a sale, not a provision of services. On the other hand, if the person who receives the software must pay the developer even if the software does not work, the transaction represents the provision of services. In the United States, copyright automatically vests in the author of a work unless the parties agree otherwise.[28] Therefore, parties who want their transaction to constitute the provision of services should normally enter a written agreement in which the developer assigns the copyright in the software to the customer.

These regulations are designed to distinguish the provision of computer programming services from the transfer of computer programs, and, by analogy, it seems appropriate to apply the principles underlying these provisions to a nonsoftware context where it is unclear whether digitized products are being created as a service or are simply being transferred. These regulations, however, do not address characterization issues arising in connection with nonprogramming services such as consulting, training or technical support.

---

26. *See* Piedras Negras Broadcasting Co. v. Commissioner, 43 B.T.A. 297 (1941), *nonacq.*, 1941-1 C.B. 18, *aff'd*, 127 F.2d 260 (5th Cir. 1942). *See also* Korfund Co. v. Commissioner, 1 T.C. 1180 (1943); Priv. Ltr. Rul. 62-03-055590A (Mar. 5, 1962).
27. Treas. Reg. § 1.861–18(d) (1998).
28. 17 U.S.C. § 201 (2000).

E. Predominant-Character Rule

As is evident from the preceding discussion, many transactions in digital content exhibit both property and services characteristics. A general issue that arises is whether income from such a transaction should be classified according to the predominant character of the transaction, or should instead be allocated between property and services components. These issues are not new to e-commerce. For example, some amount of labor goes into the manufacture or preparation for sale of nearly all tangible items, but sales of those items are characterized strictly as transactions in goods, not services. Similarly, the provision of a memorandum containing legal advice to a client is treated as a transaction in services, even though the paper on which the memorandum appears is actually "sold" to the client as part of the transaction.

Existing law suggests that a predominant-character rule is generally appropriate for determining an integrated transaction's characterization for tax purposes.[29] For example, under such a rule, software maintenance contracts that bundle updates together with technical support services arguably should be characterized in accordance with their predominant nature as either a sale of additional software product or the provision of services. When the taxpayer's own commercial practice divides a mixed transaction into its component parts (for example, a software vendor that separately invoices for the update/upgrade and technical support elements of software maintenance), however, an allocation rule may be appropriate. In the case of computer programming services covered by the software characterization regulations, de minimis components of a transaction should be ignored.

iii. Know-How

The U.S. software characterization regulations also provide that a transaction involving computer programs can be treated as the provision of know-how. The regulations define the provision of know-how fairly narrowly: a transaction (1) in which information considered property subject to trade secret protection relating to computer programming techniques is furnished in a cross-border transaction under conditions preventing unauthorized disclosure and (2) for which the parties specifically contracted.[30]

---

29. *See* Guy F. Atkinson Co. of California v. Commissioner, 82 T.C. 275 (1984) (construction of dam); Rev. Rul. 86-155, 1982-2 C.B. 134 (construction of oil drilling platform); Treas. Reg. § 1.954-1(e)(3) (as amended in 1999) (providing for predominant-character rule under subpart F of Internal Revenue Code when portions of income from single transaction are of different categories and cannot be segregated from one another). *Cf.* Rev. Rul. 64-56, 1964-1 C.B. 133 (transfer of property in exchange for stock is tax free pursuant to section 351 even if some services provided in connection with transfer, as long as services "are merely ancillary and subsidiary to the property transfer").

30. Treas. Reg. § 1.861-18(e) (1998).

iv. Mixed Transactions

Under the U.S. software characterization regulations, transactions involving more than one of the four enumerated categories (that is, transfer of a copyright right, transfer of a copyrighted article, provision of services and provision of know-how) are treated as separate transactions, except that de minimis components are disregarded.[31] For example, when the transaction includes the transfer of a copyright right (such as the right to copy for distribution to the public) and a copy of the copyrighted article (such as a disk) containing the code to be copied, the transfer of the copyrighted article is ignored as a de minimis component.[32] Similarly, de minimis transfers of copyright rights, services and know-how are ignored.

3. Source of Income

The source of an item of income for tax purposes can have a number of tax consequences. For example, the source of income may affect which country has jurisdiction to impose tax upon that income, as well as a taxpayer's ability to use foreign taxes it has paid or accrued as credits against U.S. tax. The Internal Revenue Code (IRC) prescribes different sourcing rules for different categories of income (for example, sales income, services income, rents and royalties); therefore, determining the proper tax characterization of an item of income is the first step in determining its source.[33] Applying existing source rules to e-commerce transactions should be fairly straightforward in many circumstances but could raise issues for transactions such as the rendition of services or electronic delivery of digitized products.

i. Source of Income from Sales of Personal Property

Income from the sale of personal property other than inventory is generally sourced in the country in which the seller resides.[34] Such a rule, which is based upon the seller's residence, can be easily applied to e-commerce, even when the transaction giving rise to the income occurs electronically.

---

31. *Id.* § 1.861-18(b)(2).
32. *Id.* §§ 1.861-18(c)(1)(i), 1.861-18(h), exs. 5, 6.
33. Note that the IRC sources an item of income as either within or without the United States, rather than to a particular country.
34. *See* I.R.C. § 865(a) (2000).

Income from the sale of inventory is generally sourced where title and risk of loss pass.[35] Such a rule can be applied without difficulty to personal property that is sold electronically (such as over the Internet) but delivered by traditional, nonelectronic means. When inventory in the form of digitized information is delivered electronically, however, the "location" of the passage of title and risk of loss may not be meaningful commercial concepts. Nevertheless, at least insofar as the electronic transfer of software is concerned, the traditional rules still apply.[36] The preamble to the software characterization regulations explains that electronic transfer is generally not accompanied by the usual indicia of title transfer, but in many cases where source is governed by the title passage rule, the parties should be able to agree upon where title passes.[37] In the case of digitized products other than software, to which the software characterization regulations do not apply, it nevertheless seems appropriate to apply a similar focus upon contractual arrangements in determining title passage.

ii. Source of Income from Use of Property—Royalties and Rents

Rents and royalties are generally sourced to the location where the taxpayer uses the property.[38] The place where intellectual property is "used" is normally defined as the place where the licensee is entitled to use—and is legally protected in using—the intellectual property rights.[39]

The fact that property is delivered electronically, or that the arrangement for its use is made via electronic means, does not by itself affect the location of its use. In a software leasing transaction, for example, the place of use should be the location of the computer on which the software is installed. In the case of a license of content to a web site, however, it may prove difficult to establish all the places where the web site operator uses the content provider's copyright, because the content is broadcast to viewers around the world.

---

35. *See id.* §§ 861(a)(6), 862(a)(6); Treas. Reg. § 1.861-7(c) (1957).

36. In discussing the proper sourcing of income from the sale of copyrighted articles, the software characterization regulations refer to the traditional title passage rules for inventory property. Treas. Reg. § 1.861-18(f)(2) (1998).

37. 63 Fed. Reg. 52,971, 52,973 (1998).

38. I.R.C. §§ 861(a)(4), 862(a)(4) (2000).

39. Rev. Rul. 84-78, 1984-1 C.B. 173 (foreign copyright); Rev. Rul. 80-362, 1980-2 C.B. 208 (U.S. patent); Rev. Rul. 75-254, 1975-1 C.B. 243 (U.S. trademark); Rev. Rul. 72-232, 1972-1 C.B. 276 (foreign copyright); Rev. Rul. 68-443, 1968-2 C.B. 304 (foreign trademark); Tech. Adv. Mem. 64-021-25640A (Feb. 12, 1964) (foreign trademark).

iii. Source of Income from Rendition of Services

Income from the rendition of services is generally sourced where the services are performed.[40] Application of this rule is straightforward when, at the time services are rendered, the service provider is physically located at the same place as the consumer of the services. When services are provided remotely via electronic means, however, the locality where services are "performed" may not always be clear.

Generally speaking, the place where the service provider is located when it performs the activities for which the customer is paying should govern the source of that income. The place where the consumer of those services is located should be immaterial to the analysis. Courts that delve into the principles underlying the sourcing of services focus upon where the value that generates income is created.[41] In some cases, determining the location of a service provider should be straightforward. For example, when a doctor renders services to a remotely located patient via the Internet, it seems clear that the place where the doctor is physically located is where the service provider is, and is thus the source of the services income. Issues may arise, however, when an enterprise undertakes a variety of activities in a variety of places, all of which are related in some way to the ultimate provision of services to customers. For example, a company may have research personnel in one location, operations personnel in another location, administrative personnel in yet a third location and sales personnel spread over the world. It is not always clear which activities should be relevant to determining source.

When services are provided (at least in part) through a computer server or other passive means, determining where the service provider is considered to provide its services may be especially difficult. For example, when a company provides advertising services on its web site, the location of the server is arguably the place where the income should be sourced because the server transmits the web site. If, however, activities other than those performed by the server add value to the services the customer purchases, the location where such other activities take place should also be relevant in the sourcing analysis.[42]

Another issue is whether activities performed by an enterprise's agents or contractors, rather than its employees, are relevant to the sourcing analysis

---

40. I.R.C. §§ 861(a)(3), 862(a)(3) (2000).

41. *See Piedras Negras*, 43 B.T.A. at 309 (quoting 4 PAUL & MERTENS, LAW OF FEDERAL INCOME TAXATION 350 ("[The source of income] is not a place, it is an activity or property.... Thus, if an [item of] income [is to] be taxed [in the United States], ... the property or activities out of which the income issues or is derived must be situated within the jurisdiction so that the source of the income may be said to have a situs in this country."). *See also* Howkins v. Commissioner, 49 T.C. 689, 694 (1968) ("Congress thought of the 'source' of an item of income in terms of the place where the income was 'produced.'").

42. *See* Piedras Negras Broadcasting Co. v. Commissioner, 43 B.T.A. 297 (1941), *nonacq.*, 1941-1 C.B. 18, *aff'd*, 127 F.2d 260 (5th Cir. 1942) (holding that income from broadcast of advertising targeted to U.S. listeners from Mexican radio station was foreign source income based not only upon location of radio transmitter, but also upon location of other activities that contributed to generation of advertising income, such as acquisition and production of nonadvertising broadcast content).

when such activities are "inputs" to the services provided by the enterprise. For example, a web site operator might outsource all or part of certain functions to software developers, content providers, hosting service providers or communications service providers. By analogy to case law developed outside the e-commerce context, the activities of an independent agent should not affect the sourcing of the principal's services income,[43] but the activities of a dependent agent may be relevant.[44]

Finally, if the activities giving rise to services income have multiple locations, it appears that under current law the source of that income must be allocated accordingly.[45] Such allocation might be administratively burdensome and, in some instances, seem not to make sense. For example, suppose an information service provider is located in France and provides services to French customers, but uses billing personnel located in the United States. Current law seems to require that some small portion of the income of the French office be treated as U.S. source. Circumstances such as these may become more common as developments in telecommunications make decentralization of functions easier. Despite the potential difficulties with allocations, however, there appears to be no predominant-character rule for sourcing. Nor does there appear to be a de minimis rule that would allow the billing services in the example to be disregarded. Activities that are not integral to the services consumed by the customer, however, may not be relevant to a sourcing analysis.[46]

4. Jurisdiction to Tax—U.S. Trade or Business

The United States taxes the income of nonresident aliens and foreign corporations—income that is effectively connected with the conduct of a trade or business within the United States—in the same manner it taxes the income of U.S. citizens and residents (that is, at graduated rates on net income).[47] The purpose of the "U.S. trade or business" concept is to define when a nonresident has established a U.S. presence sufficient to warrant direct taxation of business profits here. How the IRS and courts will apply this standard in the e-commerce

---

43. *See, e.g.,* Perkins v. Commissioner, 40 T.C. 330 (1963), *acq.* 1964-1 (part I) C.B. 5; Le Beau Tours Inter-America, Inc. v. United States, 415 F. Supp. 48 (S.D.N.Y.), *aff'd,* 547 F.2d 9 (2d Cir. 1976); Miller v. Commissioner, 73 T.C.M. (CCH) 2319 (1997).

44. *See, e.g.,* Helvering v. Boekman, 107 F.2d 388 (2d Cir. 1939).

45. *See, e.g.,* Tipton and Kalmbach, Inc. v. United States, 480 F.2d 1118 (10th Cir. 1973) (holding that taxpayer's services income had to be allocated between U.S. and foreign sources); I.R.C. § 863(b) (2000) (making reference to "income derived from sources partly within and partly without the United States").

46. *See* Treas. Reg. § 1.864-4(b)(1)(i) (as amended in 1996) (indicating that allocation of compensation for services performed within and without United States should be based upon all facts and circumstances); *Piedras Negras,* 43 B.T.A. at 307 (declining to consider, in determining source of taxpayer's advertising revenue, those activities that consisted of sorting mail received by advertisers and dividing proceeds of remittances received); *but see* Tipton and Kalmbach, Inc. v. United States, 480 F.2d 1118 (10th Cir. 1973).

47. I.R.C. §§ 871(b), 882 (2000).

context is an unsettled issue. For example, whether a foreign corporation that sells and delivers electronic goods or services to U.S. customers through the Internet—without employees, agents or other physical presence in the United States—is conducting a trade or business within the United States is not entirely clear under existing law, especially when such sales are substantial and occur regularly. The "U.S. trade or business" standard is supplanted by the "permanent establishment" standard when the nonresident is a resident of a U.S. tax treaty partner. Similar jurisdictional issues are discussed further in that context below.

5. Subpart F Consequences

As a general rule, U.S. shareholders of foreign corporations are not subject to U.S. tax on the foreign corporations' earnings until such earnings are distributed to shareholders as dividends. Subpart F of the IRC creates a significant exception: where a foreign corporation is more than 50% owned by U. S. shareholders, each of whom owns at least 10% of the foreign corporation, such U.S. shareholders are currently taxable on income of the foreign corporation that falls within certain categories.[48] The categories of income identified in subpart F for immediate inclusion in U.S. shareholders' income are certain types of passive investment income and other "portable" income that could easily be shifted to low-tax jurisdictions, thereby deferring tax on the income until its ultimate repatriation to the United States.

Analyzing the consequences of e-commerce transactions under subpart F can be challenging. For example, characterizing income can be difficult in e-commerce, but it is a key issue under subpart F because only certain categories of income are subpart F income. Also, a foreign corporation's income from products it manufactures is generally excluded from subpart F income, but whether the activities performed to produce digital products constitute manufacturing is not always clear. As another example, certain exceptions to subpart F income depend on whether property is used in the foreign corporation's country of incorporation, but determining where property is used can be difficult in the e-commerce context.

6. Transfer Pricing Issues

When related parties do business with each other, the prices they charge are subject to scrutiny under a fairly well-developed set of transfer pricing rules,

---

48. *See id.* §§ 951-64.

the purpose of which is to prevent artificial shifting of income through manipulation of intercompany pricing. U.S. transfer pricing rules are based upon the arm's-length standard.[49] That is, pricing between related entities is evaluated in accordance with the way *unrelated* parties transacting business at arm's length would structure their uncontrolled transactions. Most transfer pricing norms in the international tax arena are also based upon the arm's-length standard.[50]

The character of the income determines the transfer pricing rules that apply to a given transaction. A services agreement might be priced on the basis of a recovery of costs plus a fixed percentage markup on those costs. Meanwhile, a distributor might be expected to purchase goods at a specified discount off the resale price, and a licensor of intellectual property would earn a percentage royalty on sales of products incorporating its intellectual property rights. In any given case, the cost-plus markup, resale margin or royalty depends upon all the facts and circumstances. In principle, each party to a transaction should receive a financial return consistent with the functions performed and risks assumed by that party. Generally speaking, the most reliable measure of an arm's-length price is found by looking at a comparable uncontrolled transaction. Because these are hard to come by, taxpayers must often rely upon other methods as well.

E-commerce transactions are likely to pose some unique challenges for transfer pricing. Many emerging e-commerce business models exhibit a tendency to disaggregate and decentralize commercial and economic functions and risks. This makes it particularly difficult to assign functions and risks to particular legal entities.

§ 6.3 International Taxation of E-Commerce

1. Overview of International Taxation and Tax Treaties

Because tax rules vary from country to country, taxpayers operating in more than one country can find two or more countries claiming tax jurisdiction

---

49. *See id.* § 482, and regulations thereunder.

50. *See, e.g.,* OECD Model Tax Treaty of 1992 (as amended), art. 9 Tax Treaties (CCH) ¶ 191 [hereinafter OECD Model Tax Treaty]. This is in contrast to the formula methodologies adopted in most states within the United States. In the international arena, the significance of transfer pricing is heightened by the fact that any adjustment to the income of an enterprise in one jurisdiction, if not accompanied by a corresponding adjustment in another jurisdiction, may result in double taxation.

over the same item of income. The United States has entered into a large number of bilateral tax treaties, the purpose of which is to avoid such double taxation of income. Though each bilateral tax treaty must be analyzed according to its own terms, following are some generalizations about typical treaty provisions.

Tax treaties operate to avoid or reduce double taxation in a number of ways. First, when certain passive income (such as dividends, interest and royalties) is subject to withholding tax at source, the source country agrees to reduce its rate of withholding tax, sometimes to as low as zero percent. Second, the source country agrees not to tax the normal business profits of an enterprise that is resident in the other treaty country, unless the income is attributable to a "permanent establishment" of the enterprise in the source country. Third, when the source country does impose tax upon the income of a resident of the other treaty country, the country of residence usually agrees to provide a mechanism under its domestic law for avoiding double taxation (a role the foreign tax credit regime serves in the United States). Finally, if after applying all three principles the income is still subject to double taxation, the tax treaty typically provides procedures for taxpayers to request that the taxing authorities in each country seek agreement on the treatment of income subject to double taxation.

2. Income Characterization

As under U.S. tax law, determining the character of an e-commerce transaction is a critical first step in analyzing a treaty's effect on the transaction's tax consequences. The relevant categories under a tax treaty, however, differ somewhat from the relevant categories for various U.S. tax purposes. Most treaties contain specific provisions for items such as business profits, interest, dividends, royalties, income from immovable property, income from activities of artists and sportspersons, income from personal services, and profits from the operation of ships or aircraft in international traffic. Some of the most important categories related to e-commerce are discussed below.

i. Business Profits

A treaty typically provides that a taxpayer's business profits are taxable only in the taxpayer's country of residence, except to the extent attributable to a permanent establishment of the taxpayer in the other country. Thus, for example, income of a U.S. resident or citizen that constitutes business profits is not taxed by a foreign treaty partner, even if such income arises from sources within that foreign country, unless the taxpayer has a permanent establishment in the foreign country, and then only to the extent attributable to such permanent establishment. In contrast, the foreign country could impose withholding tax (subject to any reduction or elimination under the treaty) upon income that falls within a treaty category other than business profits, if such income is sourced to the foreign country, regardless of whether the U.S. taxpayer has a permanent establishment in the foreign country.

Business profits are typically defined simply as the profits of an enterprise, with deductions for expenses associated with a permanent establishment allowed in computing them. An item of income described in a treaty category other than business profits generally does not constitute business profits, except to the extent attributable to a permanent establishment.

Certain categories of income relevant for U.S. tax purposes may not be relevant in the treaty context because they are lumped together as business profits. For example, income from the sale of goods, the leasing of personal property and the rendition of services is generally regarded as business profits under a tax treaty, and therefore the distinction between these categories of income is generally irrelevant for tax treaty purposes. Some bilateral tax treaties, however, contain special provisions that distinguish between sales and services, or between sales and leases.

ii. Royalties

A. Foreign Tax Law

A number of foreign countries have not adopted the U.S. approach to the tax characterization of transfers of digitized products, such as software. The U.S. software characterization regulations provide that the legal form of a transfer of a computer program does not determine its characterization for U.S. tax purposes; the regulations draw a basic distinction between transfers of copyright rights and transfers of copyrighted articles. Royalty income arises only if there is a partial transfer of a copyright right that does not constitute an alienation of the entire copyright right. In contrast, some countries take a more formalistic approach, and may characterize income from the transfer of digitized products as royalty income, even if in substance no license of intellectual property occurs.

B. Tax Treaty Provisions

Most U.S. tax treaties specifically enumerate royalties as a separate category of income. Royalty income is therefore subject to source-based taxation even if the taxpayer earning the income does not have a permanent establishment in the source country, except when the treaty eliminates withholding tax on royalties or when the royalty income is attributable to a permanent establishment and is therefore taxable as business profits.

Although definitions vary from treaty to treaty, royalties are typically defined as "payments of any kind received as a consideration for the use of, or the right to use, any copyright of literary, artistic or scientific work including cinematograph films, any patent, trademark, design or model, plan, secret formula or process, or for information concerning industrial, commercial or scientific experience."[51] Under this definition, payments for digitized products arguably should not constitute royalties unless they are in exchange for the right to use intellectual property rights or for know-how.

In 1998, the OECD revised its commentary on article 12 (royalties) of the OECD Model Tax Treaty, concerning the treatment of software payments. Consistent with the U.S. software characterization regulations, the OEDC took the position that a payment for software will be treated as a royalty only when it is consideration for a partial grant of copyright rights.[52] The TAG on Treaty Characterization of Electronic Commerce Payments had recommended that the commentary on article 12 (royalties) be further revised to state that similar principles should apply to transfers of digitized products other than software (e.g., images, sounds or text) and that under such principles a purchaser's electronic download of a digitized product should not result in royalty income where the purchaser does not receive the right to use copyright rights.[53]

iii. Payments for the Use of Industrial, Commercial or Scientific Equipment

Some tax treaties, contrary to the current OECD Model Treaty, define royalties to include payments for the use—or the right to use—industrial, commercial or scientific equipment (or similar language).[54] Under such treaties, certain items of income that would be treated as business profits in the absence of such a royalty clause might arguably be treated as royalties. For example, income received from a customer in exchange for licensing software to the customer for a limited duration should not constitute a royalty under the current OECD Model Treaty and should instead constitute business profits. In a treaty that

---

51. *Id.* art. 12(2).

52. OECD Model Tax Treaty, *supra* note 50, Commentary on Article 12 (Royalties) (1998).

53. OECD Technical Advisory Group on Treaty Characterisation of Electronic Commerce Payments, Tax Treaty Characterisation Issues Arising from E-Commerce: Report to Working Party No. 1 of the OECD Committee on Fiscal Affairs 5 (Feb. 1, 2001), *available at* <http://www.bmck.com/ecommerce/final TAG IC.pdf>.

54. The United States is a party to several such treaties, such as those between the United States and Estonia, Greece, India, Indonesia, Kazakhstan, Latvia, Lithuania, Mexico, New Zealand, Portugal, Spain, Tunisia, Turkey and Venezuela. *See also* United Nations Model Tax Treaty of 1980, Art. 12, Tax Treaties (CCH) ¶ 206.12; OECD Model Tax Treaty of 1977, Art. 12, Tax Treaties (CCH) ¶ 201.12.

includes payments for the use of industrial, commercial or scientific equipment as royalties, however, such income arguably might constitute a royalty. The TAG on Treaty Characterization of Electronic Commerce Payments concluded that payments for limited-duration use of software or other digital products should not be considered payments for the use or the right to use industrial, commercial or scientific equipment.[55] Similarly, the TAG concluded that in application hosting, data warehousing and similar e-commerce transactions, the use of hardware is merely ancillary to a services transaction, and the payments are not for the use of industrial, commercial or scientific equipment.[56]

iv. Technical Fees

Some tax treaties also contain an enumerated income category for "technical fees" (or a similar term), which are typically defined as payments of any kind to any person, other than to an employee of the person making the payments, in consideration for any service of a technical, managerial or consultancy nature.[57] Under such treaties, certain items of income that would be treated as business profits in the absence of such a provision might instead be treated as technical fees. For example, income received from a customer in exchange for online customer support could arguably be considered "service of a technical, managerial or consultancy nature" and therefore qualify as technical fees. The TAG on Treaty Characterization of Electronic Commerce Payments concluded that a technical fees provision should generally be interpreted narrowly, however, and noted that merely delivering a service via technological means does not make the service technical.[58]

---

55. OECD Technical Advisory Group on Treaty Characterisation of Electronic Commerce Payments, Tax Treaty Characterisation Issues Arising from E-Commerce: Report to Working Party No. 1 of the OECD Committee on Fiscal Affairs 12 (Feb. 1, 2001).

56. *Id.* at 13.

57. *See, e.g.,* Albania-Malaysia Tax Treaty, Tax Treaty, Jan. 24, 1994, Alb.-Malay., 96 T.N.I. 190-50. In some treaties, technical fees are included as royalties rather than as a separate category of income. The United States generally has not entered tax treaties that contain such a "technical fees" clause, and is a party to no tax treaties that define technical fees so broadly. The United States has entered only a few tax treaties with any type of technical fees provision, and in each case the scope of the relevant term is significantly more limited than the definition recited in the text. *See* Tax Treaty, Sept. 12, 1989, U.S.-India, S. Treaty Doc. No. 101-5; Tax Treaty, Aug. 1, 1977, U.S.-Morocco, T.I.A.S. No. 10194; Tax Treaty, June 17, 1985, U.S.-Tunisia, S. Treaty Doc. No. 99-13.

58. OECD Technical Advisory Group on Treaty Characterisation of Electronic Commerce Payments, Tax Treaty Characterisation Issues Arising from E-Commerce: Report to Working Party No. 1 of the OECD Committee on Fiscal Affairs 14 (Feb. 1, 2001).

3. Permanent Establishment

i. General Principles

A tax treaty typically provides that business profits are taxable only in the taxpayer's country of residence (or citizenship, in the case of the United States), except to the extent attributable to a permanent establishment of the taxpayer in the other country. Under this concept of a "permanent establishment," one treaty partner relinquishes its jurisdiction to tax the business profits of residents of the other treaty partner unless local activities rise to a certain threshold—that is, unless they amount to a permanent establishment. Thus, the purpose of the concept is to define when a nonresident has established a presence sufficient to warrant direct taxation of business profits there.

Tax treaties generally define a permanent establishment as a "fixed place of business"—including an office, a branch, a factory or a similar physical location—through which the business of an enterprise is wholly or partly conducted.[59] Most treaties, however, explicitly exempt certain preparatory or auxiliary activities from the definition of permanent establishment, even if those activities are conducted through a fixed place of business. For example, storage of merchandise, delivery of merchandise and maintenance of a fixed place of business to collect information, supply information or advertise, are generally labeled "preparatory or auxiliary" activities and do not give rise to a permanent establishment. Treaties usually explain the circumstances under which the activities of an agent give rise to a permanent establishment of the principal. Generally, a nonresident does not have a permanent establishment as a result of the activities of an agent, unless the agent is a dependent agent with authority to conclude contracts in the name of the nonresident principal.

ii. Application of Permanent Establishment Rules to E-Commerce Transactions

Under traditional principles, a taxpayer generally does not have a permanent establishment in a given jurisdiction unless it has a fixed physical presence or a dependent agent with contract-concluding authority in that jurisdiction. It is well settled that arrangements to contact customers via remote telecommunications (such as telephone, television or mail), even if supported by local advertising, do not give rise to a permanent establishment. The mere fact that an entrepreneur penetrates a market through electronic advertising, solicitation

---

59. *See, e.g.*, OECD Model Tax Treaty, *supra* note 50, art. 5.

and contracting, or the mere presence of customers in a particular jurisdiction, generally does not provide taxing authority to the market jurisdiction.

Consequently, one would expect that the mere visibility of a web site in a jurisdiction would not give rise to a permanent establishment. In fact, recent revisions to OECD's commentary on article 5 (permanent establishment) of the OECD Model Tax Treaty take the position that access to a web site from a particular jurisdiction should not, without more, create a permanent establishment for the business that owns and maintains the site.[60]

Whether the presence of a computer server in a particular jurisdiction, without more, might constitute a permanent establishment is still the subject of some debate. The recently revised article 5 commentary concludes that it is possible for a computer server to be a "fixed place of business," and that it is possible for the business of an enterprise to be conducted through a server without some amount of human intervention.[61] A number of countries, however, including the United Kingdom and Hong Kong, disagree with this conclusion.[62]

§ 6.4 U.S. State and Local Taxation of E-Commerce

1. Introduction

Electronic commerce raises several important state tax issues, many of which are analogous to federal and international issues. For example, questions about permanent establishment or engaging in a U.S. trade or business are replaced with questions of "nexus" for state tax purposes. Questions about the source and characterization of income remain key considerations in the state context. Various overlays of constitutional law and federalism also frame these state issues. Moreover, Congress has weighed in by passing legislation affecting states' ability to tax e-commerce. In 1998, the federal government enacted the Internet Tax Freedom Act, which imposes a moratorium upon new state taxes on the

---

60. *See* OECD Committee on Fiscal Affairs, Clarification on the Application of the Permanent Establishment Definition in E-Commerce: Changes to the Commentary on Art. 5 (Dec. 22, 2000), *available at* <http://www.bmck.com/ecommerce/tax/changes to Commentary on Article 5.pdf>.

61. *Id.*

62. Press Release, United Kingdom Inland Revenue, Electronic Commerce: Tax Status of Web Sites and Servers (April 11, 2000), *available at* <http://www.inlandrevenue.gov.uk/e-commerce/ecom15.htm>; Inland Revenue Department Hong Kong, Departmental Interpretation & Practice Notes No. 39: Profits Tax Treatment of Electronic Commerce (July 2001), *available at* <http://www.info.gov.hk/ird/ipn/ipn39.pdf>.

Internet, but grandfathers all state and local taxes "generally imposed and actually enforced prior to October 1, 1998." The act also established a nineteen-member Advisory Commission on Electronic Commerce to conduct a study of e-commerce and related issues and submit findings to Congress. The Advisory Commission met several times and presented its report to Congress in April 2000.

It is fair to say that e-commerce tax issues have stimulated at least as much commentary and speculation at the state level as they have at the federal level. As might be expected, states have not adopted uniform policy and the approaches taken by the different states are, so to speak, all over the map.

2. Importance of Nexus Concept to Taxation of E-Commerce

Perhaps the most important state tax issue affecting electronic commerce currently is the concept of *nexus*, which concerns whether a state can impose an income tax upon a remote seller, or require the remote seller to collect use or sales taxes in connection with sales to customers in the state. The nexus issue is of particular significance for online sellers, because the very nature of the Internet allows them to conduct business with customers in other states without any direct physical connections. Physical connections with a state traditionally have been the basis for asserting taxing jurisdiction.

i. Constitutional Limitations

The nexus issue concerns the limits on a state's power to tax persons outside the state. Under the U.S. Constitution, states have an implicit taxing power. This power is subject, however, to limits imposed by the Constitution, and by Congress when validly exercising its constitutional authority.

As discussed below, the principal limit imposed by the U.S. Constitution in a jurisdictional context is the "substantial-nexus" requirement of the Commerce Clause. This requires that a taxpayer have physical presence in a state for purposes of sales and use taxes, and possibly taxes based upon net income as well.

A. Commerce Clause and Due Process Clause Limitations

To withstand a constitutional challenge to an assertion of taxing jurisdiction, a state tax must satisfy tests under both the Commerce Clause and the Due Process Clause of the Constitution. This requirement is true for income as well as transactional taxes, such as sales and use taxes, although the considerations raised by e-commerce in the context of state income taxes may differ from those raised in the context of sales and use taxes.

(1) Commerce Clause

The Commerce Clause of the U.S. Constitution prohibits states from imposing any tax that interferes with interstate commerce, and reserves to Congress the power to regulate commerce among the states and with foreign countries.[63] To survive a Commerce Clause challenge, a state tax must satisfy the four-part test from *Complete Auto Transit, Inc. v. Brady*:[64]

1. the taxable activity must have a substantial nexus with the taxing state,
2. the tax must be fairly apportioned,
3. the tax may not discriminate against interstate commerce and
4. the tax must be fairly related to the services provided by the state.

In the context of whether an out-of-state company is subject to a state sales or use tax (for example, whether it is required to collect use tax on sales made via the Internet outside the taxing state), the issue normally raised is the substantial-nexus prong of the *Complete Auto Transit* test. The law is now clear that substantial nexus requires some physical presence in the taxing state, at least for sales and use tax purposes.

Specifically, the U.S. Supreme Court, in *Quill Corp. v. North Dakota*,[65] addressed whether North Dakota could require an out-of-state mail-order company to collect and pay use tax on goods sold to North Dakota customers when the company had no stores, offices, sales people or significant property in North Dakota. In determining whether there was a substantial nexus between the out-of-state company and North Dakota, the *Quill* court drew a bright line between:

1. out-of-state mail-order sellers who do no more than communicate with in-state customers by mail or common carrier as part of general interstate business and
2. those with retail outlets, solicitors or property within the taxing state (that is, some sort of physical presence).

Quill confirmed the existence of a safe harbor under the Commerce Clause: a state may not constitutionally require an out-of-state taxpayer to collect use tax when such taxpayer has no contacts in the state other than through mail or common carrier.[66]

---

63. U.S. CONST. art. 1, § 8, cl. 3.
64. Complete Auto Transit, Inc. v. Brady, 430 U.S. 274 (1977).
65. Quill Corp. v. North Dakota, 504 U.S. 298 (1992).
66. *Id.*; National Bellas Hess, Inc. v. Department of Revenue of State of Ill., 386 U.S. 753 (1967).

If significant physical presence exists, however, courts are quick to hold that a substantial nexus exists. The U.S. Supreme Court ruled that the following types of presence or activities rise to the level of substantial nexus:

- Sales arranged by local agents in the taxing state,[67]
- Mail-order seller maintains local retail stores or offices in the taxing state,[68] and
- Seller has ten independent contractors conducting continuous, local, in-state solicitation and forwards resulting orders out of state for shipment.[69]

Finally, Congress has power under the Commerce Clause to pass legislation enabling states to require out-of-state companies to collect use tax, regardless of whether a substantial nexus exists between the company and a taxing state. Over the years, members of Congress have introduced legislation to this effect several times, but they have failed to win passage. Many of these efforts were in the context of traditional mail-order sales. It is expected that similar legislation aimed at online sellers will be introduced in the future.

(2) Due Process Clause

Under the Due Process Clause of the U.S. Constitution, a state cannot impose a tax unless there is some minimum connection between that state and the person, property or transaction the state seeks to tax. In *Quill*, the U.S. Supreme Court stated that the minimum-contacts requirement under the Due Process Clause is met when a company merely concludes sales within a state, because the company has "fair warning" that its activities may be subject to tax by that state.[70] Thus, *Quill* appears to remove the Due Process Clause as a potential barrier to state taxation of out-of-state sales by Internet-based sellers to in-state purchasers, because any tax that satisfies the Commerce Clause's nexus requirement should not run afoul of the Due Process Clause's minimum-contacts requirement.

B. Attributional-Nexus Concept

An important, related issue concerns the extent to which the activities of an online company's agents or affiliates can be attributed to the company in creating nexus in a state. Initially, states asserted an attributional-nexus theory in the context of agents performing solicitation activities inside a state on behalf of an out-of-state seller. The Supreme Court agreed that solicitation performed by third parties on behalf of a seller can trigger nexus.[71] States have tried to

---

67. Felt & Tarrant Mfg. Co. v. Gallagher, 306 U.S. 62 (1939).

68. Nelson v. Sears, Roebuck & Co., 312 U.S. 359 (1941); National Geographic Soc'y v. California Bd. of Equalization, 430 U.S. 551, n. 7 (1977).

69. Scripto, Inc. v. Carson, 362 U.S. 207 (1960).

70. *Quill*, 504 U.S. at 308.

71. Scripto, Inc. v. Carson, 362 U.S. 207 (1960); Tyler Pipe Indus. Inc. v. Washington Dep't Revenue, 483 U.S. 232 (1987).

extend the boundaries of agency nexus and assert that the mere in-state presence of affiliates, who perform similar business activities as the remote seller, causes the remote seller to have nexus. The courts, however, consistently reject the notion that nexus can be created for an out-of-state seller solely by having a related entity engaged in substantially similar business activities in the state.[72]

That being said, difficult issues arise for companies selling online and seeking to avoid agency nexus, particularly in the context of traditional retailers establishing separate online companies that use some of the benefits of a physical retail network (that is, so-called *clicks-and-mortar companies*). For instance, these retailers prefer—for good business reasons—to allow customers buying from their online stores to return purchases to their local retail stores. Although case law suggests that returns of goods sold by a remote seller to an in-state affiliate does not trigger nexus for the remote seller, this is an area of law that will no doubt witness further litigation.[73]

C. Application of Constitutional Limitations to Sales and Use Taxes

Forty-five states and the District of Columbia impose sales tax upon sales of tangible goods occurring within their states (and, in some cases, on certain services). In addition, certain municipalities, like New York City, also impose a sales tax. Although sales taxes are generally imposed upon the purchaser of goods, states impose a withholding obligation upon the seller to collect and pay over the sales tax receipts withheld from sales occurring in the state. The so-called "dormant" or "negative" Commerce Clause of the U.S. Constitution prevents states from taxing interstate commerce, and thereby restricts states to taxing sales that are deemed to occur within their borders.[74] To determine the interstate character of a sale, states generally look to the transfer of title, possession or both.[75]

To prevent state residents from avoiding sales tax by purchasing goods outside their state, every state that imposes a sales tax also imposes a corresponding use tax on property purchased out of state. By taxing the use of goods (which

---

72. *See, e.g.,* Current, Inc. v. State Bd. of Equalization, 29 Cal. Rptr. 2d 407 (Cal. Ct. App. 1994).

73. *See, e.g.,* Bloomingdale's by Mail, Ltd. v. Pennsylvania Dep't Revenue, 567 A.2d 773 (Pa. 1989); SFA Folio Collection, Inc. v. Bannon, 585 A.2d 666 (Conn. 1991). This precise issue was raised in a case involving Borders Online recently argued before the California Board of Equalization, SC OHA 97-639364, California Board of Equalization, July 10, 2001. *See* Tax Analysts Doc. No. DOC2001-19729, 2001577 140-10.

74. McLeod v. J.E. Dilworth Co. et al., 322 U.S. 327 (1944) (Sales tax may not be imposed upon sales to residents of state by nonresident when orders accepted outside state, goods shipped from outside state, and title passes outside state; fact that use tax may be constitutionally applied is irrelevant).

75. This has become a very difficult issue in traditional, nonelectronic commerce, and promises to become even more complex with sales of digitized products. *See, e.g.,* VSA, Inc. v. Faulkner, 485 S.E.2d 348 (N.C. 1997) (state could not impose sales tax upon sale to nonresident corporation when sale occurred outside state, despite fact that products drop-shipped to nonresident's customer within taxing state).

occurs within the state) rather than the sale (which may occur outside the state), the use tax serves as a constitutional backstop to the imposition of sales tax. To prevent the double taxation that would arise in situations where a sales tax is imposed upon an out-of-state sale, states generally allow taxpayers to credit the amount of sales taxes they paid against their use tax liability.

Theoretically, states are owed use tax on transactions not subject to sales tax and, therefore, it might be argued that states should be indifferent to whether tangible property is purchased in local retail stores or electronically over the Web from remote online sellers. If a state resident purchases goods over the Internet from an out-of-state seller that has no contacts with the state, and the resident uses those goods within the state, the state can impose a use tax upon the purchased goods even though the state may be constitutionally prohibited from imposing a sales tax upon the sale. This theory works well, however, only if the seller collects and remits the use tax. If the seller is not required to collect the use tax, it is up to the purchaser to pay the tax to the state. In practice, self-assessment of use tax is uncommon. Moreover, the states have not developed a cost-effective method of collecting use taxes on a wide variety of products subject to the tax.[76]

Therefore, to preserve their sales and use tax collections, states have strong incentive to assert their taxing jurisdiction over out-of-state sellers. To do so successfully, however, they must satisfy the relevant constitutional principles. The threshold issue is whether the merchant's nexus with the taxing jurisdiction is sufficiently substantial to satisfy the physical-presence threshold of *Quill*. When the merchant is an out-of-state taxpayer whose only contact with a state is through the Internet, the merchant should fall within *Quill*'s safe harbor, and the merchant should not be subject to sales or use tax in that state because it does not have any physical presence. States aggressively pursue agency nexus and other attributional-nexus arguments, however, in attempts to assert use tax nexus over out-of-state sellers.

In some states, tax authorities or legislatures have adopted specific clarifications of the application of sales and use taxes to various aspects of e-commerce. For example, in California, retailers that accept orders through a telecommunications network and have no other presence in California are not required to collect California sales or use tax, as long as the retailer does not directly or indirectly own the network and the network provides primarily on-line communication services rather than electronic display of—and taking of orders for—products.[77]

---

76. Use tax on cars, for example, may generally be collected when the car is registered with the state's department of motor vehicles. Items of lesser value (such as household appliances and furniture) are not registered, and therefore state residents are left to remit use tax on their own initiative.

77. CAL. REV. & TAX. CODE § 6203(j) (West 2001).

D. Application of Constitutional Limitations to Income and Franchise Taxes

As discussed, the U.S. Supreme Court in *Quill* stated that some form of physical presence in a state is required for such state to impose sales or use taxes. Under *Quill*, this constitutional limitation on state tax authorities does not expressly apply to taxation based upon net income. Whether a future U.S. Supreme Court decision holds that some physical presence is required to impose income tax remains to be seen.

The lack of Supreme Court guidance has not stopped states from asserting that physical presence is not required to assert income tax nexus. In 1993, the South Carolina Supreme Court ruled in *Geoffrey, Inc. v. South Carolina Tax Commission* that a Delaware holding company was subject to South Carolina's income tax when the company merely licensed intangible property rights to a licensee in South Carolina and had no physical presence in the state.[78] The Court sidestepped *Quill*'s physical-presence requirement by interpreting it as limited to sales and use tax. The court concluded that by merely licensing intangibles for use in South Carolina, the company had the requisite nexus for Commerce Clause purposes and income tax could properly be imposed.

Taking the *Geoffrey* theory to its extreme, almost any material economic penetration into a state could trigger income tax nexus. Merchants selling goods via the Internet would have nexus wherever the Internet reaches—that is, all fifty states and the District of Columbia. Many believe that such an expansive reach is not permitted by the Commerce Clause without enabling federal legislation. Interestingly, this expansive view may not even survive a challenge under the Due Process Clause.

States' assertions of the *Geoffrey* theory can be expected to play out in the courts for a number of years, possibly culminating in a U.S. Supreme Court decision. Although many states initially indicated an intention to push this theory, they largely have been unsuccessful in the state courts. Courts in Tennessee, Maryland, Alabama and New York have thus far rejected the *Geoffrey* theory.[79]

---

78. Geoffrey, Inc. v. South Carolina Tax Comm'n, 437 S.E.2d 13 (S.C. 1993).

79. J.C. Penney Nat'l Bank v. Johnson, Comm'r of Revenue, State of Tennessee, 19 S.W.3d 831 (Tenn. Ct. App. 1999); Petition of Toys 'R' Us-NYTEX, Inc., TAT(H) 93-1039 (GC) New York City Tax Appeals Tribunal (Aug. 4, 1999) CCH New York State Tax Rptr. ¶ 600-377; SYL, Inc. v. Comptroller of Treasury, C-99-002389AA, Cir. Ct. for Baltimore City, Mar. 17, 2000, CCH Maryland State Tax Rptr. ¶ 201-610; Crown Cork & Seal (Delaware) Inc. v. Comptroller of Treasury, No. 24-C-99-002388AA, Cir. Ct. for Baltimore City, Mar. 17, 2000, CCH Maryland State Tax Rptr. ¶ 201-609; Cerro Copper Prods., Inc. v. Alabama Dep't Revenue, F. 94-444 (Ala. Admin. Law Div. Dec. 11, 1995) CCH Alabama State Tax Rptr. ¶ 200-517; 9.4% Manufactured Hous. Contract Pass-Through Certificate Series 1989A v. Alabama, Admin. Law Docket 95-162 (Ala. Admin. Law Div. Dec. 11, 1995).

ii. Federal Limitations on Nexus—Public Law 86-272

In one area of potential state jurisdiction to impose income tax, Congress acted to restrict states from taxing certain types of businesses. Although this legislation was adopted long before anyone thought of e-commerce, it restricts states from imposing income tax upon online merchants meeting the requirements set forth in the law. Public Law 86–272,[80] enacted in 1959, prohibits states from assessing corporate income tax upon out-of-state corporations that limit themselves merely to soliciting orders for sales of tangible personal property, when orders are approved and filled outside the state. As a result, merchants that sell tangible goods via the Internet and meet the requirements of Public Law 86–272 would escape state income tax nexus in states where their customers are located (assuming they did not have any other, nonsolicitation contacts with the states). Public Law 86–272 does not, however, apply to taxpayers that sell services, intangible property or real estate. As a result, if an online company selling software, music and other categories of products changes its delivery method from sales via CD-ROMs and other tangible media to delivery via electronic transmission or download, it may transform itself from an exempt company without nexus (under the protection of Public Law 86–272) into a company with nexus (outside the protection of that safe harbor, assuming it has other connections with the states to which it makes sales).

3. E-Commerce Transactions Subject to Sales and Use Taxes—Which Transactions Are Taxable?

Whether products are sold in tangible form or transmitted electronically can affect liability for collection and remittance of sales and use taxes. Traditionally, many states have imposed their sales and use taxes only upon the sale or purchase of tangible personal property. Other transactions, including services and sales (or licenses) of intangible property, are not subject to tax under the traditional approach. Some states expressly exempt the sale of products that are delivered through electronic transmission. Even if there were no express exemption under state law, to the extent that a state applies its sales tax only to transfers of tangible personal property, the sale or license of a packaged software program or similar product should not be a taxable transaction if the program were transferred by remote telecommunications from the seller's place of business to the purchaser's computer, and the purchaser did not obtain possession of any tangible personal property (such as storage media) in the transaction. As a result, a shift in delivery method for software, music and many other

---

80. 15 U.S.C. § 351 (2000).

categories of products—from a tangible medium like CD-ROM to electronic transmission or download—may transform a taxable transaction into an exempt transaction in many states.

It is not possible to avoid the imposition of sales and use taxes upon the transfer of digitized products via the Internet or other electronic means in every state, particularly in the case of software. Several state statutes tax the sale of software expressly and do not distinguish between software delivered via tangible medium and other means. Some states do not have an express provision concerning software, but interpret state law to allow taxation of software regardless of delivery method. A small number of states tax all gross receipts. Undoubtedly, further developments will occur as states consider extending the special rules they have developed regarding software to other products that lend themselves to electronic delivery, such as music.

4. Income Tax Issues Related to E-Commerce—How Are Revenues Sourced?

Assuming an online company is subject to tax in a particular state, it is necessary to determine how much of the company's income is taxable in that state. If the company is taxable in more than one state, the normal approach is to apportion income from business operations to the various states where the company does business, on the basis of the states' apportionment formulas. These formulas tend to be mechanical, although companies often attempt to manipulate their apportionment factors to minimize the amount of income taxable in given states. Some online businesses may be particularly well suited to use certain established planning techniques to minimize state income taxes.

Multistate businesses must calculate the portion of their income subject to state taxation by apportioning it in accordance with formulas established by state statute. Traditionally, most states have applied a three-factor formula, consisting of equally weighted property, payroll and sales factors. More recently, states have adopted double-weighted sales factors and some have gone to a single factor based upon sales, to benefit in-state businesses. For example, the numerator of each factor would be the total dollar amount of property within the state, and the denominator of each factor would be the total dollar amount of property in every state.

Many states require "unitary" businesses to report on a combined basis instead of a separate-company basis, which means that members of a unitary group must take into account their combined income. Likewise, combined income is apportioned using the group members' combined apportionment factors. Generally, in combined-reporting states, the income and apportionment factors of unitary affiliates that do not have nexus with the state can be taken into account to determine the amount of income of the unitary group that is taxable in the state. A few states, including California, extend the unitary business principle to both foreign and domestic affiliates, although water's-edge reporting generally is available to limit the unitary group to a large extent, in most cases, to domestic entities.

State income tax liability may be reduced by minimizing the apportionment factors sourced or located in the state. E-commerce transactions may offer interesting opportunities to minimize apportionment factors in certain states, particularly the sales factor, which in turn could significantly reduce taxation in those states. For instance, an online business may be structured so that business operations are conducted in, and orders are fulfilled from, certain tax-beneficial states. In the case of sales of tangible personal property, the ideal state for operations and fulfillment would be either a state that does not impose an income tax or a state that does not have a so-called *throwback rule* for purposes of the sales factor. Generally, sales of tangible personal property are sourced in the states to which the goods are shipped. A throwback rule means that sales of goods shipped *from* a state are sourced in that state if the seller does not have nexus in the state to which the goods are shipped. If a state does not have a throwback rule, sales of goods shipped from such a state would not be sourced in either the destination state (assuming the seller does not have nexus) or the state from where the goods are shipped, resulting in "nowhere" sales.

In the case of all other transactions not involving the sale of tangible personal property, most states source receipts for purposes of the sales factor to the state where the "income-producing activities" that generated the receipts occur. If those activities occur in more than one state, the receipts are sourced to the state where the greater portion of the "costs of performance" of those activities is incurred. States and taxpayers have long struggled to apply these rules, and there is surprisingly little guidance in the way of regulations and case law. In particular, few authorities define income-producing activities. Nevertheless, online transactions could possibly be restructured—with relatively modest effort—to cause the relevant income-producing activities and costs of performance to occur in low-tax states. Though achieving this result requires careful planning, it serves to illustrate the potential for e-commerce businesses.

5. Federal Influence on State Taxation of E-Commerce

i. Internet Tax Freedom Act

A. Key Elements of Internet Tax Freedom Act

The Internet Tax Freedom Act (ITFA) was originally introduced in March 1997 by Representative Chris Cox, a Republican from California, and Senator Ron Wyden, a Democrat from Oregon, to place a moratorium on new taxes on electronic commerce and to direct federal officials to work with state and local officials to develop a coordinated national policy for taxing electronic commerce. After nineteen months of debate and five revisions of the senate bill, President Clinton signed the legislation on October 21, 1998. The bill that finally became law imposes a three-year moratorium upon state and local taxes on Internet access, multiple taxes on e-commerce and discriminatory taxes on e-commerce.[81] To satisfy the states' interest in protecting their revenue bases, ITFA grandfathers state and local taxes "generally imposed and actually enforced prior to October 1, 1998," and protects existing tax liabilities.

Contrary to popular misconception, ITFA does not ban state taxes on transactions over the Internet. Sales and use taxes still apply to the sale and purchase of goods over the Internet under existing standards.

B. Internet Access Taxation

The prohibition against taxes on Internet access forbids states from taxing charges for a "service that enables users to access content, information, electronic mail or other services over the Internet." The prohibition does not, however, apply to any tax that was "generally imposed and actually enforced prior to October 1, 1998." A tax is considered to have been generally imposed and actually enforced if, before October 1, 1998, the tax was authorized by statute and either the Internet access provider had reason to know the taxing authority interpreted its statute as applying to Internet access providers, or the state generally collected taxes on Internet access charges. States such as Connecticut, Iowa, Nebraska, North Dakota, Ohio, South Carolina, South Dakota, Tennessee, Texas and Wisconsin taxed Internet access charges before October 1, 1998, and may continue to do so under ITFA. Thus, the effect of ITFA is that it bars *new* state and local taxes on Internet access.

The prohibition against new Internet access taxes does not apply to taxation of telecommunications services. Excluding telecommunications services creates a problem when, for example, a traditional telephone company bundles telephone services and Internet access services for sale to end users. In the area of sales and use taxes, states generally take the position that when taxable and nontaxable items are bundled together in one charge, the entire transaction is subject to taxation. For competitive reasons, the vendor may not want to state the charges for Internet access and telecommunications services separately. In this situation, it is not clear whether states would be allowed to impose the tax upon the entire transaction. A federal law generally trumps contrary state law, but the federal law grandfathers existing taxes on Internet access. Arguably, the states can point to their consistent stance that bundled transactions have always been taxable.

---

81. 112 Stat. 2681, 2681-719, §§ 101100-1104 (1998).

C. Bar against Discriminatory or Multiple Taxes

ITFA bars discriminatory taxes on electronic commerce, which is broadly defined as "any transaction conducted over the Internet or through Internet access comprising the sale, lease, license, offer, or delivery of property, goods, services or information."[82] Discriminatory taxation of e-commerce, as discriminatory treatment is commonly understood, would mean that e-commerce is singled out for more burdensome treatment as compared with other types of commercial transactions. There appear to be no taxes at the state level that explicitly discriminate against e-commerce transactions.

ITFA also bars multiple taxes on e-commerce. A multiple tax is "any tax that is imposed by one state on the same or essentially the same electronic commerce that is also subject to another tax imposed by another state ... (whether or not at the same rate or on the same basis), without a credit (for example, a resale exemption certificate) for taxes paid in other jurisdictions."[83] Sales or use taxes imposed concurrently by a state and its political subdivisions are not deemed multiple taxes. Although the objective of preventing multiple taxation is laudable, ITFA leaves room for controversy when it vaguely bars multiple taxation of "essentially the same electronic commerce." In addition, the implication is that multiple taxation can occur even though the taxes may have different rates or bases. There has been little guidance regarding how this section should apply.

ii. Advisory Commission on E-Commerce

ITFA established a nineteen-member Advisory Commission on Electronic Commerce to conduct a study of federal, state, local and international taxation of Internet transactions and Internet access. The Advisory Commission on Electronic Commerce was required to submit its report to Congress within eighteen months of enactment (by April 21, 2000).

The commission met for the first time on June 21 and 22, 1999, in Williamsburg, Virginia. The group heard opening statements from commission members and testimony from various tax experts, but took no action other than approving a subcommittee report on funding. The second meeting, held on September 14 and 15, 1999, in New York City, was much like the first except the commission called for interested parties to submit proposals regarding a simplified tax system. Thirty-seven proposals from various groups and individuals were received before the third meeting, held on December 14 and 15, 1999, in San Francisco. At that meeting, the commission heard more testimony from

---

82. *Id.* § 1104(3).
83. *Id.* § 1104(6).

tax experts and other interested parties regarding whether e-commerce should be treated differently than commerce involving traditional brick-and-mortar businesses. The commission took no action that moved it closer to finalizing the report due to Congress in April 2000.

The fourth and final meeting took place in Dallas on March 20 and 21, 2000. Despite months spent examining e-commerce and how to tax it, members of the commission were unable to reach agreement on any of the more important topics they discussed. The commission's nineteen members divided into three separate interest groups—the federal government (federal caucus), state and local governments (state caucus) and representatives of the e-commerce industry and telecommunications carriers (business caucus). On one side of the debate were members of state and local governments who feel strongly about state sovereignty and increasing states' powers to impose sales tax collection obligations upon remote sellers. On the other side were members of the business community who want to limit such powers and make the Internet a duty-free zone.

The commission's mandate was to sift through various issues involved with taxation of e-commerce and Internet access, and to issue a report to Congress setting forth formal recommendations. By statute, formal recommendations required the support of at least two-thirds of the commissioners. Although this supermajority was reached on some minor issues, the commission failed to get the two-thirds approval on many matters before it. With the support of the chairperson, however, the commission included in its report certain proposals from the business caucus that were supported by a simple majority. This procedural tactic was strongly contested by those opposed to the majority—principally from the state caucus—who argued that there was no congressional authority for submitting any recommendation other than one supported by the required supermajority.

The commission issued its final report to Congress on April 12, 2000, reflecting the outcome of the Dallas meeting. Among the recommendations set forth in the majority report, two proposals elicited the strongest objections from the state caucus: (1) clarification that certain activities within a state will not create sufficient nexus to impose collection obligations upon remote sellers and (2) proposed tax exemptions for digital products and their conventional counterparts.

The report provides that certain factors, by themselves, should not create a nexus between a seller and state sufficient to permit a state to impose sales tax collection obligations upon the seller. These nexus "carve-outs" included the following:

- The presence of a seller's customers in a state;
- A seller's affiliation with another taxpayer that has physical presence in that state;
- The performance of repair or warranty services related to property sold by a seller that does not otherwise have physical presence in that state; and

- A contractual relationship between a seller and another party located within that state, which permits goods or products purchased through the seller's web site or catalog to be returned to the other party's physical location within that state.

The principal argument made by the state caucus in opposition to these limitations was that it would be unfair to small local businesses for their online competitors to avoid nexus by operating in states through affiliated, yet legally distinct, brick-and-mortar companies. A more general criticism made by the state caucus was that the proposals "try to define nexus in terms that are focused on physical presence in a state, when the world of electronic commerce is increasingly borderless, digital and intangible."[84]

The majority proposal would also impose a five-year prohibition on taxing sales of digitized goods or products (such as downloaded software) and preempt the taxation of "functionally equivalent" goods sold via traditional means. The majority supported this proposal by noting that it advances tax neutrality by treating conventional movies, tapes, CDs, magazines, newspapers and boxed software the same as new digital forms of such items. The minority's response to this position was that true neutrality would require that "sales taxes be collected on all items sold over the Internet and by catalog just as those taxes are collected in local stores."[85]

Aside from these two proposals, the majority report recommends that the current moratorium against new Internet taxes be extended by five years, and that the three-percent federal telecommunications tax be eliminated.

iii. Congressional Responses to Advisory Commission Report

In the wake of the majority report of the Advisory Commission on Electronic Commerce, members of Congress have introduced numerous pieces of legislation affecting state taxation of e-commerce. Many of the bills follow some or all of the recommendations of the report. At least one bill seeks to incorporate each of the recommendations related to sales and use taxes, including the limitations on nexus and exemptions of certain digitized products (and their traditional, tangible counterparts) from sales and use taxes. It is too early to predict whether any of this proposed legislation will become law.

---

84. Internet Tax Reform and Reduction Act of 2000: Hearing on H.R. 4267 Before the House Comm. on the Judiciary Subcomm. on Commercial and Administrative Law, 106th Cong. (May 17, 2000) (prepared testimony of Gene N. Lebrun, Member, Advisory Commission on Electronic Commerce).
    85. *Id.*

§ 6.5 Consumption Tax

1. Introduction

Consumption tax is levied upon the supply of goods and services. Although many countries have a consumption tax, the following discussion focuses upon consumption tax within the European Union (EU). Consumption tax in the EU is more commonly referred to as Value Added Tax, or VAT. The tax is levied at each stage of the chain of supply as a percentage of the price. For example, if a paper manufacturer sells paper at a price of EUR 100 to a retailer, and the rate of VAT is 10%, the paper manufacturer is obliged to charge EUR 110 for its paper. If the retailer then resells the paper at a price of EUR 200 to a consumer, the retailer is obliged to charge the consumer EUR 220 for the paper.

The idea behind VAT is that only consumption should be taxed. Therefore, only the last stage in the chain of supply (that is, the consumer) should bear the economic cost of VAT. Because each stage in the chain of supply is obliged to charge VAT, a refund mechanism is necessary to ensure that only the ultimate consumer actually bears VAT on the total value of the supply. In the above example, this means that the manufacturer will charge EUR 10 of VAT on top of its sale price to the retailer, and will actually receive this amount and pay it to the tax authorities. The retailer, however, will only pay EUR 10 to the tax authorities despite having collected EUR 20 in VAT from the consumer. The EUR 10 that the retailer paid to the manufacturer is considered "refundable" or "deductible input VAT" and is credited against the EUR 20 in VAT collected on the sale from the retailer to the consumer, thereby reducing the amount of tax the retailer must remit to the tax authorities to EUR 10 (20 minus the EUR 10 of VAT the retailer already paid to the manufacturer). The consumer, as the last stage in the chain of supply, has paid both amounts of VAT. He actually paid EUR 220 (including 2 times EUR 10 of VAT) for the paper and cannot get a refund.

The European VAT system could have been relatively easy to comprehend and uniform throughout the EU if not for the current EU VAT regulations (particularly the Sixth EU Directive), which resulted from compromises between many EU Member States. This has created a situation in which all EU Member States are allowed to deviate to a certain extent from VAT directives. Nevertheless, the rules in cross-border situations for the place (that is, country) where a supply is subject to VAT are generally the same throughout the entire EU. If one EU Member State is allowed to levy VAT upon the supply of a good or service, the other Member States should not be allowed to levy VAT upon that exact same supply. A specific system for determining the place of taxation for goods and services has been established to ensure the VAT system works neutrally in the internal EU market. To avoid distortion in competition in e-commerce transactions, the European Commission issued a proposed directive to change the current VAT system for those types of transactions. The proposed directive deals specifically with distortions in international competition that exist under the current system in the context of e-commerce.

2. Proposed VAT Directive on E-Commerce

The proposal to change the EU VAT regime for e-commerce operators was launched by the European Commission on June 7, 2000.[86] The proposal is part of a long line of legislative changes that have recently taken place in the EU regarding e-commerce. The European Commission already issued a directive that deals with the legal (civil law) aspects of electronic trade in the internal European market. This directive addresses issues such as determining the place where operators are established, guidelines for commercial communication over the Internet, the legal validity of agreements concluded on the Internet, consumer protection and the liability of Internet agents and intermediaries. The European Commission also issued a directive regarding the conditions under which electronic signatures may be considered legally valid.

The proposed directive on the value-added taxation of e-commerce seems to follow the EU Member States' guidelines and discussions of previous years on this topic. The proposal makes an important distinction between direct and indirect e-commerce. Indirect e-commerce concerns electronic ordering—and the subsequent physical delivery—of goods (for example, ordering CDs over the Internet that are subsequently physically supplied). Direct e-commerce concerns electronic ordering and electronic delivery of the ordered product or service. Because the EU VAT regime follows the flow of goods, indirect e-commerce that still involves physical delivery of goods would not impose new problems. It is direct e-commerce—involving the supply of "virtual goods"—that raises many problems from a VAT perspective. The proposed directive focuses upon this type of e-commerce.

3. Basic Principles for a New VAT System for Direct E-Commerce

In the explanatory memorandum to the proposal, the European Commission states that three main principles form the basis for a new VAT regime for direct e-commerce:

---

86. Commission Proposal for a Council Directive Amending Directive 77/388 EEC as Regards the Value Added Tax Arrangements Applicable to Certain Services Supplied by Electronic Means, 2000 O.J. (C 337 E) 63.

1. No new taxes should be considered regarding direct e-commerce.
2. For VAT purposes, electronic deliveries should not be considered goods, but rather, services.
3. The consumption of such services within the borders of the EU should also be taxable within the EU.

The European Commission stated in a June 1999 working paper that a new VAT regime for direct e-commerce should be clear and consistent (providing legal certainty), simple (keeping the burdens of compliance to a minimum), neutral and nondiscriminatory. International cooperation would be necessary to prevent distortions in competition between e-commerce companies inside and outside the EU.

Under the neutrality principle, the current proposal attempts to eliminate the unfair competition currently existing between EU and non-EU operators. At the moment, many online deliveries provided to consumers are subject to VAT at the place of origin (that is, the country where the online service operator is located). In practice, that means that non-EU companies can provide online deliveries to consumers in the EU without charging VAT, while EU providers of online deliveries must charge VAT to both EU and non-EU consumers. The European Commission stated that this type of distortion should be avoided and that the EU VAT system should ensure that online services, supplied for consumption in the EU, should be taxed within the EU, while online services provided for consumption outside the EU should not be taxed within the EU.

The European Commission proposes to reach this goal by obliging operators of online supplies for consumption in the EU to register in one of the EU Member States, where the operator would account for and deduct VAT for all its EU supplies. Cross-border online supplies made to business customers will be subject to VAT under a "reverse-charge" mechanism, under which the recipient of the service (the EU-based customer) accounts for and remits the VAT due on the service fee. The non-EU service provider will not charge EU VAT in that situation.

Consequently, a different VAT regime will apply to services provided to private customers and those provided to business customers. All non-EU online operators should be aware of their customers' characteristics. Under the proposal, an online operator must make a taxing decision for every sale it makes to an EU customer. EU customers that cannot be recognized as businesses should be charged EU VAT. To charge VAT to this type of customer, the proposal would require the non-EU online operator to register in one of the EU Member States. (An exemption for registration would exist for companies with online revenues under EUR 100,000.) Registration and invoicing would be done in accordance with VAT regulations for that particular Member State. Obviously, the EU Member States with a lower VAT rate will be likely candidates for such a "single point of registration." Currently, the VAT rate in the EU varies from 15% (Luxembourg) to 25% (Sweden and Denmark).

The idea of a single point of registration for a non-EU online operator has been proposed to meet the requirement of simplicity for non-EU e-commerce operators. The alternative would be to apply VAT regulations to each EU Member State where the online operator's product is consumed. Though this is not desirable from a business perspective, the suggestion for a single point of registration is strongly opposed by EU Member States with high VAT rates (such as Sweden and Denmark). Not only will those countries lose the battle for new tax revenues, retail businesses competing with online suppliers in EU Member States with a high VAT rate will also lose business. Therefore, some of the main objectives of the proposed VAT directive (neutrality and nondiscrimination) will not be completely fulfilled.

It has been suggested that the application of an equal VAT rate to all e-commerce transactions would restore neutrality if this rate also applied to retailers competing with online operators. Although the European Commission indicated it would develop such a proposal, it seems to be planning to lower VAT rates only for online supplies. This would not solve the retailers' competitive disadvantage. The differences in VAT rates between EU Member States will also be too high to bring all VAT rates to the same level.

Because the Council of EU Ministers still must agree upon the content of the new proposal to tax direct e-commerce in the EU, the discussion of how VAT should be levied upon direct e-commerce transactions will continue. From a U.S. perspective, it is seen as problematic that U.S. businesses with no physical presence in the EU would be required to act as EU tax collectors. Furthermore, it has been suggested that enforcement of this proposed regime for non-EU businesses may not be so easy. The success of ideas such as a single point of registration will depend upon the willingness of operators to comply with such regulations. Despite opposition to the proposed VAT directive, the European Commission at this time does not seem willing to give in.

Information Practices

Contents

Information Practices

Chapter 7 addresses information practices as they relate to the Internet. First, David Bender and Adam Chernichaw discuss the state of U.S. law regarding privacy in section 7.1. They open with a general discussion of privacy concepts and then address the U.S. approach to privacy and the tension that exists between protecting free-market Internet commerce and the rights of individuals to limit distribution of personal information. The authors evaluate existing legislation regarding Internet privacy at both state and federal levels.

Section 7.2 of this chapter, authored by Barbara S. Wellbery, discusses European philosophy toward privacy and how it differs dramatically from the U.S. approach. Wellbery offers a succinct review of U.S. law, including self-regulatory privacy initiatives. She then reviews European legislation, including the European Union Privacy Directive and national implementations that have occurred. Wellbery evaluates the efforts of the United States and the European Union to reach a compromise on privacy through a safe harbor. She closes with guidance on the likely outcome of these ongoing negotiations.

Finally, section 7.3 deals with encryption and anonymity, and is authored by Daniel J. Greenwood. Greenwood discusses how encryption and anonymity can be used as tools to obtain security and privacy on the Internet. He addresses when anonymity can be appropriate, such as when used as a means of providing security in banking and securities markets, and when it is inappropriate, such as when used to avoid accountability to another party when a duty is owed. He closes with a discussion of various types of encryption and how they can be used appropriately in different contexts.

§ 7.1 Privacy Issues in the United States

As we enter the twenty-first century, the innovative technology that gives rise to burgeoning advances in communications and computing also threatens to expose to the world more of our private lives and conduct than we might like. The Internet is unprecedented in its capacity as a learning and research tool. It allows people from around the world instantaneous access to materials; retrieval of these materials in the past would have required time-consuming, expensive trips to libraries or other information repositories. The Internet also provides convenient, instant and inexpensive access to personal information that many individuals do not want proliferated. Technological advances now allow for the widespread and efficient collection and storage of information on individuals without their knowledge or consent. This is often done to streamline business transactions or governmental procedures. The ability to retrieve personal information, however, "conflicts with the need to protect the privacy of the individuals who are subjects of the information." [1] Loss of control over what was once considered an individual's private business has fueled "loss of personal privacy" concerns among the citizenry of the United States and other nations.[2]

One type of privacy right likely to be infringed in an online environment is the common-law "right to be let alone" (closely connected, in the case of government intrusion upon privacy rights, with violations of the Fourth Amendment to the Constitution). This right was originally recognized in a renowned 1890 law review article by Samuel Warren and Louis Brandeis, and has been generally accepted by courts in the United States as proscribing intrusion into an individual's private activities.[3] Although the Supreme Court has never ruled upon whether monitoring e-mail or collecting personal information over the Internet is actually an invasion of privacy, as long ago as 1977 in *Whalen v. Roe* [4] it recognized that "the accumulation of vast amounts of personal information in computerized databases or other massive government files" is a threat to privacy.[5]

Section 7.1 of this chapter focuses upon collecting, monitoring and using private information and the concerns associated with such practices in the United States. It provides a background for the current debate about the protection of privacy rights in an online environment, both in and out of the workplace, and analyzes the current state of privacy protection and recent initiatives to enhance or diminish privacy rights.

1. Collection of Information on Internet Users

Imagine that the next time you purchase a wallet it contains—unbeknownst to you—a computer chip that can be remotely scanned at any time to report your location to a central database. Database users know exactly who you are because you purchased the wallet with your credit card and, as the wallet was being

---

1. James V. Vergahi, Fundamentals of Computer-High Technology Law 240 (1991).
2. *See, e.g., It's Time for Rules in Wonderland*, Bus. Wk., Mar. 20, 2000, at 83, 84.
3. Samuel D. Warren & Louis D. Brandeis, *The Right to Privacy*, 4 Harv. L. Rev. 193 (1890).
4. Whalen v. Roe, 429 U.S. 589 (1977).
5. *Id.* at 605. *See also* Raphael Winick, *Searches and Seizures of Computers and Computer Data*, 8 Harv. J.L. & Tech. 75, 76 (1994) ("Americans' growing reliance on computers has vastly increased the potential for the government to use electronic surveillance to intrude into its citizens' private lives.") (cited in Scott A. Sundstrom, *You've Got Mail! (And the Government Knows It): Applying the Fourth Amendment to Workplace E-mail Monitoring*, 73 N.Y.U. L. Rev. 2064, 2065 (Dec. 1998)).

scanned over what you believed was a magnet to disable the store's antitheft device, it was actually coordinating your billing information with the embedded computer chip. Scanners for these chips are hidden at the entrances to every store and airport, mounted on tollbooths and traffic lights, and placed in hotels, restaurants and even certain sections of libraries and stores where items of a "controversial" nature are located. Soon after you purchase your wallet, you start receiving "junk mail" related to items you recently purchased or in which you expressed interest. Because targeted advertising has long been in use, you might not notice. You start receiving "cold calls" from car dealerships pitching their vehicles. (You were in the market for one recently and visited some dealerships.) You would probably think that, for some reason, the automotive sales industry was becoming more aggressive. Out of the blue, you receive a visit from police officers because you were recently in the vicinity of a crime (unbeknownst to you) and they wanted to check whether you saw anything suspicious. How did they know you were there? You get a call from your home security company reminding you to turn on your alarm the next time you travel and saying, "We hope you enjoyed the Cape; it's beautiful this time of year, isn't it?"

This scenario may seem far-fetched, but through our increased use of—and reliance upon—the Internet, we are moving closer to the involuntary loss of what we heretofore have considered our private realm. When we are on the Internet, we should suspect that the advertisements and other materials being "pushed" onto our screens are there because of the prior browsing behavior attributed to our computers. Thus, we need to be concerned that our surfing habits are being collected and stored, possibly for use or sale to the highest bidder. Should banners promoting a "right to life" web site or a magazine like *High Times* lead us to suspect that our teenage children are contemplating abortion or drug use?[6] Certain advertisements could lead to all sorts of suspicion that could eviscerate any sense of privacy or anonymity that people should expect when searching for information or just acting as a result of curiosity. Furthermore, would we want to be harangued by calls and materials from special interest groups (or worse, be subject to hate mail or death threats) because the owner of some web site that tracked our surfing behavior decided to sell that information over an online auction site? Should our web-surfing activities to be available to cybercops[7] or to prosecutors who could use such records against us in court?[8] The potential for abuse of technology is relatively

---

6. *Cf.* Austin Bunn, *One or Two Things I'd Rather You Didn't Know About Me*, N.Y. Times Mag., Apr. 30, 2000, at 52, 53.

7. For example, the Office of National Drug Control Policy admitted to implanting software on the computers of visitors to its web site to track such visitors' activities on the Internet. Amy Harmon, *Living Riskier Electronically*, N.Y. Times, June 25, 2000, at 4–1. Also, civil liberties groups have grown concerned over the FBI's "Carnivore" surveillance system, which can search and intercept online communications of individuals not suspected of crime. White House Proposes Regulating Cyberspace Surveillance, <http://www.ipnetwork.com> (July 18, 2000).

8. *Cf.* Jeffrey Rosen, *The Eroded Self*, N.Y. Times Mag., Apr. 30, 2000, at 46, 66.

clear and may have a chilling effect on our desire to learn or seek information. Given the association and behavioral implications that may be drawn from such conduct, people may be less likely to surf web sites containing materials generally considered personal or private or advocating political beliefs that may not be generally accepted if there is risk that such activity could become public information.

On the flip side, of course, is the fact that a basic component of the Internet economy is the ability to conduct efficient and effective targeting of advertisements and other information to users who may have expressed interest in such items. Web sites generate revenue through advertising, although some believe that a strong correlation between online advertising and online purchasing has not yet been established. Nonetheless, the marketing philosophy has been that the more advertising that can be viewed by the targeted audience, the more revenue can be generated by each advertisement. Internet companies provide targeted advertising by soliciting information from users (either expressly through various prompts, or by tracking user surfing habits through the placement of encoded "cookies" on user hard drives) and then directing advertisements to those users that the companies believe, based upon the information profiles collected, would be interested in those ads. Companies also sell and exchange user profiles. Revenue generation through efficient advertising and profile exchange, it is argued, keeps the cost of doing business down and consequently ensures that web sites do not need to charge their users for services and content. Further, law enforcement officials argue that they should be able to use whatever technology is at their disposal to root out threats to security from terrorists, drug dealers and international crime syndicates. Current technology allows them to do that, in part, by monitoring and intercepting online communication.[9]

One aspect of the debate regarding Internet privacy stems from pieces of data innocuously termed *cookies.* Cookies are pieces of information deposited on a user's hard drive by some web sites the user visits.[10] The web site that places a cookie later uses it to identify the user when she returns to that particular site so she can avoid completing form information each time.[11] Cookies can also be used to track a user's movements around the Internet.[12] A perfect example of how privacy rights are implicated through use of cookies is DoubleClick, Inc.'s Dynamic Advertising Reporting and Targeting (DART) technology and the problems DoubleClick experienced in the evolution of the use of that technology.

Through use of its DART technology, DoubleClick, Inc.,[13] captures data about a user's online behavior and uses the data to develop a profile of the

---

9. *See* Harmon, *supra* note 7.

10. *It's Time for Rules in Wonderland, supra* note 2, at 92.

11. Lori Eichelberger, M.L.I.S., *The Cookie Controversy* (last reviewed May 1, 2001), *at* <http://www.cookiecentral.com/ccstory/>.

12. *It's Time for Rules in Wonderland, supra* note 2, at 92.

13. DoubleClick, Inc., is a leading provider of global Internet advertising. DoubleClick centralizes planning, execution, control, tracking and reporting for online media campaigns.

individual, which identifies the user's preferences so the user can be targeted with appropriate online advertisements.[14] DoubleClick assigns a user a unique identifying number the first time the user is "served" an advertisement on a web site belonging to DoubleClick's network of web sites.[15] This identifier is contained within a cookie that is placed on a user's hard drive without the user's consent. When that user subsequently visits another web site that is part of DoubleClick's network, DoubleClick reads the numerical address uniquely associated with that site, thereby storing information identifying sites that particular user visited. DoubleClick can thereby send the user advertisements based upon what the user unsuspectingly indicated as an interest by way of the surfing profile.[16]

So long as this tracking was done "anonymously," no one seemed to take much notice. DoubleClick's acquisition of Abacus Direct (a compiler of consumer information for the direct-marketing industry), however, aroused the suspicions of various online consumer watchdog organizations. They were concerned that the speed of data collection and transfer—possible by virtue of the new technological environment that is the Internet—would invite abuse and invade the privacy of individuals at unprecedented speed and to an unprecedented extent. DoubleClick announced it would be assembling a database that coupled personal information (such as names, e-mail addresses and regular addresses) it had by virtue of the Abacus acquisition with anonymous surfing information it compiled through DART.[17] Various watchdog organizations then sounded the alarm that DoubleClick would be able to "stalk" users around the Internet and attach an individual's name and other personal information to surfing habits. This raised the ire of certain individuals who did not, without their consent, want personal information collected and compiled into a centralized database for nearly instantaneous retrieval or sale to third parties. DoubleClick was soon the target of numerous class-action lawsuits based upon claims that ranged from violations of the right to privacy to the tort of trespass (because cookies were put on a user's hard drive without consent).[18]

As part of its response to these lawsuits (and to inquiries by the Federal Trade Commission and various states' attorneys general), DoubleClick announced it would appoint a privacy board, hire a chief privacy officer and allow users to "opt out" of the Abacus-DART combination by visiting a certain page on DoubleClick's web site.[19] The reaction to this was subdued. The watchdog

---

14. Will Rodger, *Activists Charge DoubleClick Double Cross: Web Users Have Lost Privacy with the Drop of a Cookie, They Say,* USA TODAY, Jan. 25, 2000, *available at* <http://www.usatoday.com/life/cyber/tech/cth211.htm>.

15. *See* Report of [DoubleClick's] Independent Accountants (June 7, 2000), *available at* <http://www.doubleclick.net/us/lives/price-waterhouse.asp>.

16. Eichelberger, *supra* note 11.

17. Rodger, *supra* note 14.

18. Hariett Judnick filed an invasion-of-privacy lawsuit in the Superior Court of Marin County, California, seeking class-action status. She alleged that DoubleClick misled the public by announcing it did not collect personal information and identifying data but nonetheless proceeded to use computer technology to identify Internet users and record their activities online while obtaining personal and confidential information.

19. *Crisis Control @ DoubleClick: FTC, Michigan & NY; Stock Takes Hit,* Privacytimes.com, Feb. 18, 2000, *available at* <http://www.privacytimes.com/New/Webstories/doubleclick_priv_2_23.htm>.

groups were critical of these changes because most Internet users do not know they are being tracked by DoubleClick or realize when they are on a web site subject to DoubleClick tracking. These organizations further noted that most users who visit web sites on the DoubleClick network have never visited DoubleClick's web site. DoubleClick's assurances that it would send billions of banner ads notifying users that they had the opportunity to opt out did nothing to decrease the flow of class-action suits against DoubleClick. Eventually, DoubleClick relented and issued a press release stating that until there were enforceable government and/or industry standards addressing the use of personal information gathered via the Internet, it would not couple Abacus-generated information with DART-generated information.[20] Recently, one such class action suit was dismissed by the U.S. District Court for the Southern District of New York on the grounds that DoubleClick's conduct did not violate the federal statutes as plaintiff charged.[21] Unless it is reversed on appeal, one of the most important implications of the decision seems to be that the Electronic Communications Privacy Act (discussed *infra*) and the Federal Wiretap Act, federal statutes specifically designed for the electronic age, do not prohibit the use of cookies, at least the way DoubleClick uses them. It remains to be seen whether, in light of the dismissal, DoubleClick will change the way it uses collected personal information.

For years, many have recognized the potential for advancing technology to lead to abuse of individuals' privacy rights. The DoubleClick matter galvanized public opinion on the issue, which in turn led to the current policy debate. A variety of public figures are actively addressing privacy rights by supporting bills and initiatives to restrict the ability of private organizations to gather and use personal information.[22]

2. Industry Self-Regulation

The Internet industry in the United States has favored self-regulation to address privacy concerns, although it has chosen not to implement an industrywide mechanism for protecting online privacy rights. This lack of effective self-regulation can be illustrated by the ability of companies with posted privacy policies to change those policies with retroactive effect. Further, customers can never

---

20. Ben Hammer, *DoubleClick Beats a Retreat on Data Privacy*, Industry Standard, Mar. 6, 2000, *available at* <http://www.thestandard.com/article/display/0,1151,12596,00.html?nl = dnt>.

21. In re DoubleClick Inc., S.D.N.Y., No. 00 Civ. 0641 (NRB), Mar. 28, 2001.

22. Alex Keto, *Clinton Warns Net Industry to Set Standards for Privacy*, Wall St. J. Interactive Ed., Mar. 3, 2000, *available at* <http://interactive.wsj.com/articles/SB952127598514787472.htm>. (President Clinton addressing technology industry: "I hope that all of you will work with us and work together among yourselves to maximize the possibilities of an open Internet by securing Americans' fundamental right to privacy."). Note that, at the same time, law enforcement agencies are attempting to give themselves far more ability to encroach upon the privacy rights of individuals on the Internet—often with the support of the same politicians who want to legislate restrictions on corporate America's ability to do the same. *See* William Safire, *Consenting Adults*, N.Y. Times, May 1, 2000, at A23.

be sure that companies with posted privacy policies will actually follow those policies (as there is no express threat to discourage companies from breaching their own policies).

The two standards most frequently discussed in connection with collecting, marketing and using information from Internet users are the *opt-in* and *opt-out standards*. The opt-in standard requires the express affirmative consent of the user before an Internet company can exchange a user profile created on its web site with other Internet companies.[23] The opt-out standard has often been called a "lazy alternative" to the opt-in standard (which may be the reason, in part, for industry preference for the opt-out standard). Opting out requires the user to give express instructions to the Internet company not to exchange with other Internet companies personal information collected from the user via the company's web site. Without such express instructions, the opt-out standard assumes the user consents to the exchange. The problem with the opt-out standard, however, is that many users do not carefully consider the ramifications of the choice; some do not even notice the opt-out option (sometimes because they fail to read a web site's terms of service carefully, and other times because the opt-out feature is not prominently placed on relevant web pages).[24] Thus, many users unsuspectingly give Internet companies permission to collect and exchange information via the companies' web sites.

In late July 2000, the Federal Trade Commission (FTC) and a group of Internet advertising companies (including DoubleClick) agreed upon a set of standards under which information may be collected on Internet users.[25] The standards provide for:

1. certain disclosure requirements on data collection practices;
2. the ability for Internet users to opt out;
3. an opt-in requirement before the linking of anonymous information with "personally identifiable data"; and
4. an independent enforcement mechanism.[26]

Further, a group of major Internet companies and the World Wide Web Consortium developed the Platform for Privacy Preferences (P3P) initiative partly to complement industry self-regulation by permitting users to select privacy preferences that would control which web sites a user's browser would access. The P3P technology reads the privacy policy of each accessed web site and determines whether that policy complies with the user's preselected pref-

---

23. The opt-in standard has been effectively resisted by the Internet industry based upon industry assertions that it would drastically limit the ability to collect, use and market personal information and would "cripple the use of online profiling and cause advertising revenues to plummet." Jeffrey Rosen, *The Eroded Self,* N.Y. Times Mag., Apr. 30, 2000, at 46.
   24. *See id.*
   25. David Stout, *Advertising,* N.Y. Times, July 28, 2000, at C6.
   26. *Id.*

erences. Critics of P3P have stated that the technology is a tool that would potentially allow companies to avoid complying with new privacy protection laws, and that it may lull Internet users into having a false sense of security when surfing the Internet.[27]

It has yet to be seen how these efforts at self-regulation will be implemented and enforced, and what impact, if any, they will have upon current efforts to pass privacy legislation. In early May 2001, however, National Security Council Director Richard Clarke warned private industry representatives that if they do not get active in promoting customer data protection, Congress will step in with legislation, a move he said that no one in private industry should desire.[28]

3. Employer Monitoring of Employee Online Communications

An August 25, 1999, Gallup poll reported that 58% of U.S. employees have access to a computer at work and 38% have access to the Internet. Another Gallup poll found that 90% of large businesses use e-mail and that an estimated 40 million workers correspond via e-mail.[30] The proliferation of e-mail and Internet use at work raises employers' concerns that their employees' actions may expose them to legal liability[31] and that distribution of e-mail messages with attached files might disrupt e-mail servers or permit third parties to "hack" into these systems. This has led some employers to install software to help monitor employee e-mail and Internet activity.[32] Monitoring for attached files so large that they may crash an e-mail server may be a relatively benign reason for monitoring employee e-mail. But once an employer opens such a Pandora's box by monitoring and reading employee e-mail, the potential for abuse and implications for privacy arise.

It is currently estimated that 66% of U.S. companies are engaged in at least one form of worker surveillance. It is open season on monitoring e-mail and

---

27. Jeri Clausing, *New Technology Is Aimed at Increasing Web Privacy*, N.Y. Times, June 22, 2000, at C6.

28. <http://www.newsbytes.com/news/01/165781.html>.

30. Sundstrom, *supra* note 5. The actual numbers of workers using e-mail is probably much higher than the statistics provided, due to the rapid proliferation of technology in the workplace and given that the polls cited were taken one and two years ago, respectively.

31. *See, e.g.*, Kevin J. Baum, *E-mail in the Workplace and the Right of Privacy*, 42 Vill. L. Rev. 1011, 1014 (1997) ("[E]-mail communications can be discoverable evidence during a civil or criminal proceeding against an employer [and] the contents of workplace e-mail may be the primary reason an employer is being sued. For example, in the first reported case in which e-mail was the basis for an employment discrimination claim, two employees filed a racial discrimination lawsuit against their employer . . . after they received racially offensive material via e-mail from coworkers . . . because the messages created a 'hostile work environment.' ").

32. Lisa Gaernsey, *You've Got Inappropriate Mail: Monitoring of Office E-mail Is Increasing*, N.Y. Times, Apr. 5, 2000, at C1. Additional reasons employers monitor employees in the workplace are "to monitor 'employee performance-productivity, quality of work, . . . customer satisfaction' [and] employee misconduct [and] to protect employee safety and health." Baum, *supra* note 30, at 1017 (citing *Employers Stepping up Monitoring in Workplace* (CNN television broadcast, Sept. 1, 1996)).

Internet use in the workplace,[34] with estimates of 54% of employers monitoring employee Internet use and 38% monitoring employee e-mail.[35] No laws exist to either safeguard the privacy of employees or establish guidelines employers must observe to monitor their employees' online activities.[36] Existing legislation is proving insufficient to guard against the monitoring of e-mail and other online transmissions.

For example, in *United States v. Simons*,[37] the Fourth Circuit expressly held that, for government employees, there is no expectation of privacy in the contents of a workplace computer or in the details of a government employee's Internet use. In this case, involving the receipt and possession of child pornography by an employee of a division of the Central Intelligence Agency (CIA), the illegal activity was discovered by a government contractor during routine examination of the CIA's firewall. The contractor noticed an unusual amount of activity relating to a sexually explicit web site and was able to trace it to the defendant's computer workstation. Without the employee's knowledge, CIA investigators copied files from the employee's hard drive and eventually removed the hard drive and replaced it with a copy. The FBI then obtained a search warrant and copied the defendant's hard drive and various files, documents and correspondence. After he was indicted, the defendant moved to suppress evidence obtained during the initial searches on the grounds that it was obtained without a warrant or proper justification. The Fourth Circuit denied the defendant's motion. The court's decision was partly based upon the fact that the bureau for which the defendant worked had an Internet use policy that described permitted and prohibited uses of the bureau's computer system, and also notified employees there would be audits to monitor Internet use. The court held that even if the defendant believed the files he was downloading were private, such belief "was not objectively reasonable after [the bureau] notified him that it would be overseeing his Internet use."[38]

Consistent with the Fourth Circuit opinion in *Simon*, the Notice of Electronic Monitoring Act, a bill pending before Congress, would mandate notification of employer monitoring. A similar bill was passed by the California State Legislature but was vetoed by the state's governor in October, 1999. Although these proposed laws would impose a burden upon employers to notify employees of their monitoring policies, they would do little to safeguard com-

---

34. *See* Baum, *supra* note 30, at 1017 (citing Eryn Brown, *The Myth of E-Mail Privacy*, FORTUNE, Feb. 3, 1997, at 66 ("Never expect privacy for e-mail sent through a company system.")).

35. Kathleen O'Brien, *Maybe They Should Just Send in a Camera Crew*, N.Y. TIMES, May 3, 2000, at G1. Jarrod J. White, Commentary, *E-mail@work.com: Employer Monitoring of Employee Email*, 48 ALA. L. REV. 1079, 1099 (1997).

36. In fact, in the early 1990s, Congress failed to adopt two pieces of legislation that would have set basic limitations on employer monitoring of employee e-mail. White, *supra* note 35. This may change some of the issues raised in the current privacy debate.

37. United States v. Simons, 206 F.3d 392 (4th Cir. 2000).

38. *Id.*

munications that many people would expect to fall within the penumbra of protected privacy.

In instances outside the workplace, courts have implied that the general right of privacy applies to users of e-mail services.[39] Courts have been reluctant, however, to attribute such right to a workplace environment. In a case involving the common-law right to privacy, the court in *Smyth v. Pillsbury Co.*[40] dismissed the plaintiff's claim for violation of his right to privacy after he was fired for inappropriate content contained in an e-mail message he sent. The court held that (1) the plaintiff could not have reasonably expected that the e-mail messages he was sending from his office were private, (2) even if he could reasonably expect privacy in connection with e-mail sent over his employer's system, the defendant's "interception" of the e-mail was not highly "offensive" because it was not invasive to the plaintiff's person or personal effects and did not require him to disclose personal information and (3) the defendant's interests in keeping inappropriate, unprofessional comments out of the workplace outweighed any of the plaintiff's privacy interests. It is interesting to note that even though Pillsbury, the defendant, had implemented a policy to assure its employees that management would not monitor employee e-mails, the plaintiff sent the inappropriate message to his supervisor and thereby likely waived any right that could otherwise have been derived from his employer's policy regarding management. ("Once plaintiff communicated the alleged unprofessional comments to a second person (his supervisor) . . . any reasonable expectation of privacy was lost.")[41] Because management was the intended recipient of the e-mail, there was no breach of company policy regarding monitoring of employee e-mail.[42]

It seems that the current judicial trend is against extending the penumbra of privacy to the workplace (whether public or private), and that recognition of any such rights will therefore require legislation.

4. Existing Legislation

Currently, the law is a patchwork of federal and state legislation that addresses various aspects of collecting and distributing information about individuals.[43] Whether existing legislation will be held applicable to the online environment or whether new, Internet-specific legislation will be implemented has yet to be

---

39. *See, e.g.,* McVeigh v. Cohen, 996 F. Supp. 59 (D.D.C. 1998).

40. Smyth v. Pillsbury Co., 914 F. Supp. 97 (E.D. Pa. 1996).

41. *Id.* at 101.

42. Even if the court found the company was in breach of its own policy, the two other grounds upon which its decision was based would likely have been sufficient justification for the employer's conduct.

43. Jonathan P. Cody, Comment, *Protecting Privacy Over the Internet: Has the Time Come to Abandon Self-Regulation?* 48 Cath. U. L. Rev. 1183, 1199 (1999).

seen. Existing legislation, although potentially applicable to certain forms of Internet and online communication, tends to carve out specific types of communications or industries and, therefore, no one piece of legislation (or even a collection of existing legislation) can be deemed blanket protection for individual privacy rights online.[44]

For example, the Cable Communications Policy Act of 1984 (CCPA)[45] governs the disclosure, collection and use of personal, identifiable customer information by cable television service providers.[46] CCPA requires cable companies to notify consumers annually about the use of their personal information and the purpose for which it is collected.[47] The importance of CCPA to Internet privacy increases as more people access the Internet through cable modems.[48] It remains to be seen whether courts will apply CCPA to violations of individual privacy rights online; if at all, it would likely apply *only* to users who obtain Internet access from cable television service providers.

Courts will likely defer applying CCPA to the Internet, perhaps in anticipation of comprehensive legislation delineating online privacy rights. One court did exactly that, in *United States v. Kennedy.*[49] This was a criminal case involving a computer user who received child pornography over the Internet. The Internet service provider over whose service some of the pornographic material was transferred, divulged to the government the identity of the computer user suspected of receiving such pornography. The court came very close to being forced to decide the issue of whether CCPA applies to Internet situations. The court determined that, although CCPA may have been violated, it did not include suppression as a remedy. Thus, the court had no need to—and did not—decide whether CCPA applies to Internet providers. A recent amendment to CCPA, however, was intended to "reflect the evolution of cable to include interactive services such as game channels and information services made available to subscribers by the cable operator, as well as enhanced services."[50]

More recent legislation, which addresses the specific (and some would argue more pressing) issue of collecting data and building user profiles about children, is the Children's Online Privacy Protection Act of 1998 (COPPA). COPPA di-

---

44. For example, note the history of the Video Privacy Protection Act of 1988 (VPPA), 18 U.S.C. §§ 2710, 2711 (1994), which prohibits disclosure of a customer's videotape or any other audiovisual rental records without the customer's consent or court approval (the one exception being that disclosures may be authorized when incident to the ordinary course of business, such as providing customer information to a debt collection agency). Enactment of VPPA is widely credited as a result of events related to the confirmation hearings of Judge Robert Bork. A journalist looking to uncover skeletons that would seem contrary to Bork's standing as an archconservative obtained rental records from the video store frequented by Bork. News reports implied the records reflected rentals of adult movies, notwithstanding the fact that they did not. It seems Congress panicked, perhaps fearing similar information could be obtained for any of its members (which could be used against such member in campaigns or otherwise). VPPA was enacted shortly thereafter.

45. 47 U.S.C. § 551 (1994).

46. *See id.*

47. *See id.* at § 551(a)(1)(A).

48. *See* Cody, *supra* note 41, at 1201 (1999).

49. United States v. Kennedy, 81 F. Supp. 2d 1103 (D. Kan. 2000).

50. *See* H.R. Conf. Rep. No. 104–458, at 169 (1996), *reprinted in* 1996 U.S.C.C.A.N. 124, 182.

rects the FTC to prescribe regulations requiring commercial web site operators to follow fair information practices in connection with the collection and use of personal information from children under age sixteen, including regulations for obtaining verifiable parental consent for the collection, use or disclosure of personal information from children under the age of thirteen.

COPPA is the first piece of Internet-related opt-in legislation enacted by Congress. Of course, it cannot be deemed opt-in for the specific Internet user (the child) because it is not the user, but the user's parents, who are given the choice of whether to allow data about the user to be collected. Indeed, the act's title may be a misnomer—the act does not attribute any right of privacy to the users and may instead violate the privacy rights of the users it purports to protect. COPPA requires web sites seeking information on children to inform parents and guardians about which web sites their minor children have been visiting. As between children and their parents or guardians, COPPA by its nature implies that children have no expectation of privacy. COPPA may have a chilling effect on minors researching information over the Internet (particularly information they do not want their parents or guardians to know they are viewing). Notwithstanding the foregoing, COPPA may well be found unconstitutional on First Amendment grounds[52] because, among other things, of the breadth of the community standard used in the antipornography provisions of the statute. (For example, how could a web site simultaneously meet multiple international community standards?)

On November 12, 1999, the Financial Services Modernization Act, more commonly known as the Gramm-Leach-Bliley Act (the "GLBA") became law. The GLBA made far-reaching changes in the law regarding financial institutions and contains an extensive title dealing with privacy.[53] Of particular significance are sections 6802 through 6807, which contain a number of restrictions, requirements and exceptions to be implemented by those institutions falling within the purview of the GLBA.[54] Further, the GLBA also provides for criminal penalties against those who violate its provisions.[55]

A number of federal agencies are identified in the statute, and directed to establish privacy standards relating to administrative, technical and physical safeguards against security and confidentiality breaches, and unauthorized use of or access to the protected information. The Federal Bank Regulatory Agencies[56] issued rules to ensure compliance with the GLBA.[57] The rules became effective November 13, 2000, and compliance was required as of July 1, 2001.

---

52. *See, e.g.,* ACLU v. Reno, No. 95–1324, 2000 WL 801186, *2 (3d C.S. June 22, 2000); ACLU v. Reno, 31 F. Supp. 2d 473, 498, 499 (E.D. Pa. 1999).

53. The privacy title is codified at 15 U.S.C. §§ 6801 *et seq.*

54. *See* 15 U.S.C. §§ 6802–07.

55. *See* 15 U.S.C. §§ 6821–23.

56. These agencies are the Office of the Comptroller of the Currency, the Federal Reserve Board, the Federal Deposit Insurance Corporation, and the Office of Thrift Supervision.

57. For a discussion of these rules, *see generally,* C. Mitchell, *Privacy and Gramm-Leach-Bliley's Financial Services Modernization,* 223 N.Y.L.J. 1 (Apr. 19, 2000); C. Mitchell, *Final Privacy Rule Under Gramm-Leach-Bliley: Changes, Recpetion,* 224 N.Y.L.J. 1 (July 19, 2000).

The Federal Trade Commission (FTC) has also promulgated rules to comply with the GLBA, published as 16 CFR § 313.[58] In summarizing its detailed rules, the FTC states that its rules require a financial institution to provide notice to customers about privacy policies and practices, to describe the conditions under which a financial institution may disclose nonpublic personal information about consumers to nonaffiliated third parties.[59] Finally, as an aid to those subject to its regulations, the Federal Deposit Insurance Corporation has released a "Financial Institution Letters" document (the "FIL") setting forth its views on the requirements of the GLBA.

By 2001, with the GLBA enacted and theregulations of both the Federal Bank Regulatory Agencies and the FTC issued, the interests of financial institutions have turned to maintaining a semblance of order in the various privacy tenets that control their activities. In particular, they are concerned that the various States might enact a myriad of related laws, thereby creating a multitude of additional—and possibly inconsistent—requirements. In the words of one industry executive: "We will embark on a proactive effort to preempt state law rather than experience death by 1,000 different privacy laws."[60]

The Electronic Communications Privacy Act of 1986 (ECPA) prevents the disclosure, interception or unauthorized access of private electronic communications by the government, individuals or third parties.[61] Any party that commits a "knowing or intentional" violation is subject to a civil cause of action. Specifically, ECPA prohibits unauthorized access to stored electronic communications, which includes voice mail and e-mail. There are three exceptions to this rule: "(1) disclosures that are authorized by the sender or the receiver of the message; (2) disclosures that are necessary for the efficient operation of the communications system; and (3) disclosures to the government."[62] If the government is requesting the information, the customer must be notified before disclosure.

In one case, the Navy's actions very likely violated ECPA when information about a Navy officer's sexual orientation was obtained from an Internet service provider.[63] ECPA allows the government to obtain information from an online service provider if the government first obtains a warrant or gives notice to the online subscriber.[64] In this case, neither step was taken before the government solicited information about the user from the service provider. Although the court did not fully decide the ECPA issue, other courts will likely address it in the near future.

---

58. 65 Fed. Reg. 33646 (May 24, 2000).

59. 16 CFR § 313.1.

60. Statement of Steve Bartlett, president of the Financial Services Roundtable, quoted in *Privacy Issues, Tax Reforms Lead Financial Services Industry Into 21st Century*, PRIVACY L. ADVISER (Feb. 7, 2001), at 450.

61. *See* 18 U.S.C. §§ 2510–22, 2701–09, 3121–27 (1994 & Supp. III 1997).

62. *See* KENT D. STUCKEY, INTERNET AND ONLINE LAW § 5.02[5] (2000).

63. *See* McVeigh v. Cohen, 983 F. Supp. 215 (D.C. 1998).

64. *See* 18 U.S.C.A. §§ 2703(b)(1)(A), 2703(b)(1)(B), 2703(c)(1)(B) (West 2000).

In another case involving ECPA, the plaintiff placed a sexually explicit message on an Internet message board and falsely identified the author of the message as her new husband's ex-wife.[65] When the ex-wife discovered the message, she had her brother contact the Internet service provider (AOL) for the identity of the person who posted the message, which AOL did not release until subpoenaed by the ex-wife. The plaintiff then sued AOL for violation of ECPA. The court held that ECPA authorized the disclosure, made pursuant to a subpoena by a private individual. Specifically, "a provider of electronic communication service or remote computing service may disclose a record or other information pertaining to a subscriber to or customer of such service . . . to any person other than a governmental entity."[66] Thus, ECPA did not protect the plaintiff from having her identity disclosed by her Internet provider.

ECPA is the "only federal statute that arguably applies to e-mail monitoring by employers."[67] Courts have been reluctant, however, to find that ECPA applies in employer/employee relationships, and the act itself has a number of loopholes that severely limit any applicability it may have to such relationships. Generally speaking, e-mail is not "intercepted" in the same manner as a telephone conversation (e-mail is broken up and sent in "packets," with packets often traveling over different routes to get to the intended recipient), and thus may be difficult to intercept in the traditional sense. Instead, e-mail is generally monitored from a server that stores copies of the outgoing messages or the hard drives on the employees' terminals. Thus, the interception provisions of ECPA would generally not apply to employee e-mail monitoring. The other provision of the act arguably applicable to the monitoring of employee e-mail prohibits intentional "access without authorization to a facility through which an electronic communication service is provided."[68] Such provisions do not, however, apply to conduct (1) authorized "by the person or entity providing a wire or electronic communications service" and, therefore, arguably do not apply to employers who maintain the e-mail service or (2) authorized "by a user of that service with respect to a communication of or intended for that user," which authorization might be expressly given or arguably implied in the case of an employer/employee relationship by virtue of the employee using the system provided by the employer.[69]

The Fair Credit Reporting Act (FCRA) controls the collection and disclosure of personal information in the credit reporting industry.[70] FCRA sets forth procedures for disclosing personal information without the subject's consent.

---

65. *See* Jessup-Morgan v. America Online, Inc., 20 F. Supp. 2d 1105 (E.D. Mich. 1998).
66. *See* 18 U.S.C.A. § 2703(c)(1)(A) (West 2000).
67. Sundstrom, *supra* note 5, at 2071.
68. 18 U.S.C.A. § 2701(a)(1) (West 2000).
69. *Id.* at 2701(c)(1) (cited in Baum, *supra* note 30, at 1024 ("One commentator has noted that 'it may reasonably be contended that employers have the right to search in-house E-mail under [ECPA] because such communications, if limited to exchanges of employer information, may constitute the employer's property, which the employer retains the right to supervise.' " James Baird et al., Public Employee Privacy: A Legal and Practical Guide to Issues Affecting the Workplace 60 (1995))).
70. *See* 15 U.S.C. § 1681 (1994 & Supp. III 1997).

FCRA requires credit agencies to take reasonable steps to ensure the accuracy of the information and establishes dispute resolution procedures for situations where consumers believe their personal identifiable information is not accurately reported.[71] FCRA covers credit reporting activities on the Internet.[72] A consumer brought an action under FRCA alleging that a reporting agency improperly released from her files information relating to a credit application by an impostor.[73] The court held that the credit disclosure did not violate FCRA because the credit agency made the disclosure to a person it reasonably thought was authorized to have access to it.

The Health Insurance Portability and Accountability Act of 1996 (HIPAA)[74] is an extensive piece of legislation that calls for the implementation of privacy regulations relating to health care information. The final privacy regulations became effective on April 14, 2001, and compliance with the regulations is required by April 14, 2003.[75] HIPAA regulations include standards for the following:

- electronic transactions involving health care information;
- national health care provider identifier, national employer identifier and national health plan identifier;
- security and electronic signatures;
- privacy and patient confidentiality;
- electronic claims attachments; and
- enforcement.

The Privacy Act of 1974 focuses upon government conduct pertaining to the collection and use of personal information.[76] This act affords protection to government-held personal information. The Privacy Act limits federal agencies' collection of personal information for government records to information that is relevant and necessary to a mandated agency purpose. Further, agencies must ensure that the information is accurate and that security procedures are in place. The act defines records as "any item, collection, or grouping of information about an individual that is maintained by an agency including, but not limited to, his education, financial transactions, medical history and criminal or employment history and that contains his name, . . . or other identifying particular assigned to the individual. . . ." Information that does not fall within this relatively narrow definition is not covered by the Privacy Act.[77]

---

71. *See id.*

72. *See* 15 U.S.C. § 1681a(d)(1) (Supp. III 1997).

73. *See* Andrews v. Trans Union Corp., 7 F. Supp. 2d 1056 (C.D. Cal. 1998).

74. Pub. L. No. 104-191, 110 Stat. 1936 (Aug. 21, 1996).

75. Although small health plans have until April 14, 2004, to comply. *Health Privacy Project, Summary of HIPPA Privacy Regulation,* at <http://www.healthprivacy.org/usr_doc/final_summit_summary2.pdf>.

76. 5 U.S.C. § 552a (1994 & Supp. III 1997).

77. *See* HENRY H. PERRITT, JR., LAW AND THE INFORMATION SUPERHIGHWAY: PRIVACY, ACCESS, INTELLECTUAL PROPERTY, COMMERCE, LIABILITY § 3.16, at 121 (1996).

The Communications Assistance for Law Enforcement Act (CALEA), passed in 1994,[78] was enacted to allow the government to continue intercepting communications involving advanced technologies by requiring telephone companies to restructure digital telephony to facilitate government interception.[79] CALEA requires telecommunications carriers to ensure their systems contain sufficient capability and capacity to permit law enforcement to conduct electronic surveillance.[80] Law enforcement personnel must still obtain search warrants to conduct wiretaps. Since the enactment of CALEA, the FBI has tried to use it as the basis of expanding surveillance features in the U.S. telecommunications systems.[81] Their attempts have been met with mixed results.[82]

The Escrow Encryption Standard (Clipper Chip) was developed by the National Security Agency to facilitate electronic surveillance by government agents through the interception of communications by suspected criminals. The Clipper Chip was initially a proposal that would require domestic encryption devices to be accessible to law enforcement by means of a special password or "key" that would, on a uniform basis, allow for the decryption of encrypted messages. Such a key would be analogous to the government requiring everybody in the construction industry to install bugs in the walls of residences to facilitate government spying. After the computer industry and public interest groups rallied against the Clipper Chip, the government retracted its original plan and submitted new proposals that would apply to the export of encryption keys.[83] Recently, there has been a reversal of government policy regarding export encryption technology. The government relaxed a number of its previously existing export controls related to such technologies.[84] Given this reversal, the original Clipper Chip debate may be moot.[85] The term *Clipper Chip* is now commonly used to describe the continuing effort by the U.S. government to monitor individuals' electronic communications and Internet use.

Each piece of the above-described privacy legislation may apply to an online environment. Relying upon the existing patchwork of legislation to protect individual privacy rights online, however, risks inconsistent results. Individuals may be deemed to have privacy rights in some circumstances but not in others, even when the medium for communication is the same. For example, individuals using cable modems to access the Internet may have certain privacy rights under CCPA, whereas users with DSL lines making the same use of the Internet

---

78. Wireless Telecommunications Bureau, Communications Assistance for Law Enforcement Act (CALEA), <http://www.fcc.gov/wtb/csinfo/calea.html>.

79. *Telecom Associations File Briefs Challenging FCC's CALEA Order*, 3 TELECOMM. INDUS. LITIG. REP. 5 (2000).

80. *See* 47 U.S.C.A. §§ 1001–21 (West Supp. 2000).

81. Jerry Berman & Deirdre Mulligan, *The Internet and the Law: Privacy in the Digital Age: Work in Progress*, 23 NOVA L. REV. 549, 562 (1999).

82. *Id.*

83. Webopedia, *at* <http://www.webopedia.internet.com>.

84. Dep't of Commerce, Draft of Encryption Regulations, 15 C.F.R. §§ 734, 740, 742, 772, 774 (Jan. 14, 2000), *available at* <http://www.cdt.org/crypto/admin>.

85. *Cf.* Harmon, *supra* note 7 (regarding "Carnivore").

may be deemed to have none. This inherent inequity in existing legislation suggests the need for new, comprehensive legislation to define whether online privacy rights exist and, if so, exactly how they should be defined.

5. Pending Legislation

There is a large volume of legislation pending before Congress that addresses current privacy concerns. The following are brief summaries of a sampling of such bills.

The Consumer Internet Privacy Enhancement Act would make it unlawful for a commercial website operator to collect personal information from online users of a website. The operator of a website must first provide both notice and opportunity for online users to limit the use and disclosure of their personal information collected online. Violations of the act would be considered an "unfair or deceptive act or practice in affecting commerce," thus falling under the jurisdiction of the FTC and other federal and state agencies. Violators would be subject to civil penalties of $22,000 for wach violation, with a maximum aggregate of penalties not to exceed $500,000 for a related series of violations.[86]

The Online Privacy Protection Act of 2001 would require the FTC to prescribe regulations protecting the privacy of personal information collected from, and about, individual Internet users who are not covered by the Children's Online Privacy Protection Act of 1998.[87]

The Consumer Online Privacy and Disclosure Act would make it unlawful for the operator of a website or online service provider to collect, use, or disclose personal information concerning an individual, over the age of thirteen, in a manner that violates regulations to be prescribed by the FTC. The Act prohibits any website or Internet Service Provider (ISP) from: (1) correlating ISP address information with personal information, absent a pre-existing business relationship; (2) allowing a third party to attach a persistant cookie (Internet activity tracker) as a means of developing a personal profile on an individual, without allowing the individual to opt-out of such attachment; or (3) selling transactional information as a means to satisfy creditors.[88]

The Social Security On-line Privacy Protection Act would prohibit an interactive computer service from disclosing to a third party an individual's social security number, or related personal information, without the individual's prior informed written consent.[89]

Under the Controlling the Assault of Non-Solicited Pornography and Marketing Act of 2001 it would be prohibited for those who send unsolicited com-

---

86. *See* H.R. 237, 107th Cong. (2000).
87. *See* H.R. 89, 107th Cong. (2000).
88. *See* H.R. 347, 107th Cong. (2000).
89. *See* H.R. 91, 107th Cong. (2000).

mercial electronic mail to disguise the source of their messages. Further, consumers would be given the opportunity to stop future transmission of a sender's unsolicited commercial electronic mail.[90]

The Unsolicited Commercial Electronic Mail Act of 2001 would amend the federal criminal code to provide criminal penalties for intentionally initiating the transmission of unsolicited commercial electronic mail to a protected computer in the United States with the knowledge that the domain name, or other initiator identifying information, is false or inaccurate. It would also be prohibited to send commercial electronic mail unless the message contains a valid electronic mail address, conspicuously displayed, to which a recipient may send notice of a desire to no longer receive messages.[91]

The Electronic Privacy Protection Act would prohibit the making, importation, exportation, distribution, sale, offer for sale, installation, or use of an information collection device without proper labeling or notice and consent.[92]

6. Conclusion

Protection of individual privacy on the Internet is in its infancy. The vast majority of the U.S. citizenry has only recently awakened to the potential for abuse resulting from the "e-world." The move is toward specific legislation addressing Internet privacy issues, as existing legislation does not suit the online environment and corresponding expectations. Particularly in the workplace, boundaries are not set between the private and nonprivate—it seems that so long as employer conduct is not outrageously unreasonable, there will be no prohibition on employer monitoring of employee e-mail and Internet use (although eventually employers may need to comply with notification procedures before monitoring employees). The near future will likely see the government setting limits and boundaries on intrusions into individual privacy online.

---

90. *See* S. 630, 107th Cong. (2000).
91. *See* H.R. 95, 107th Cong. (2000).
92. *See* H.R. 112, 107th Cong. (2000).

§ 7.2 Bridging the Difference: The Safe Harbor and Privacy in the European Union and United States

1. Introduction

Today's technologies allow information to be collected, compiled, analyzed and delivered around the world more quickly and inexpensively than ever before. Where it was once difficult, time consuming and expensive to obtain and compile information, it is now often available with a few simple clicks of a computer mouse. This increased access to information facilitates personal and political expression, as well as commerce, education and health care.

Information technologies are transforming the face of global commerce. World trade involving information technologies and related services and products (computer software, movies, sound recordings, databases and financial services, to name just a few) has grown rapidly in the past decade and now accounts for over $120 billion of U.S. exports alone.[93] We are said to live in an "Information Economy."

Consumers benefit from increased access to information. They surf the Internet seeking all kinds of information. Thinking about buying a house? You can shop for it on the Internet. Information is available about neighborhoods, prices and schools; you can even take a virtual tour of the house while online.

Companies, too, benefit. They can create new markets as the Internet allows them to reach potential customers easily and cheaply. Increased access to information about customers can reduce marketing and inventory costs and allow better target advertising. As a result, consumer information has become a "hot" commodity.

Not surprisingly, then, there is a growing demand for all kinds of information. The great promise of the Information Age is, however, also its greatest threat. The increased market for personal information, coupled with the ability to collect and compile it easily, have led to an enormous increase in the amount of information collected about individuals as they conduct commercial transactions and cruise the Net. Banks and credit card companies maintain information on financial records, payment histories, shopping locations and purchasing trends. Supermarkets and other retail stores track consumer purchases using checkout scanners. As individuals peruse various sites on the Internet, mouse clicks can be tracked with so-called cookies. Profiles can be compiled not only of what people buy, but what they read, their health concerns

---

93. U.S. Dep't Commerce, Digital Economy 2000 53 (June 2000).

and perhaps their political and sexual preferences as well. Thus, information technology increases risks to privacy exponentially.

Moreover, privacy issues are complicated by the fact that so much information is used on a global basis. Multinational companies may ship all their personnel data to one location for purposes of record keeping, benefits and payroll; credit card companies may do the same with bankcard information for billing purposes. Credit and insurance markets increasingly operate on a global basis and may require the transfer of information about individuals across borders to evaluate their creditworthiness or insurance risks. The inherently global nature of the Internet further complicates the matter. Citizens of one country may easily visit web sites in other countries, transferring personal information across borders as they visit. Laws, which generally are limited by nations' borders, may have little effect in a medium without borders.

Many nations share concerns about how the expansion of electronic networks affects privacy. The United States and the European Union (EU) are both addressing these concerns but in markedly different ways. Section 7.2 of this chapter examines EU and U.S. approaches to privacy—their differences and similarities, the disruptions in global commerce the differences could cause and one solution that has been developed for bridging those differences.

2. The European Approach to Privacy Protection

Although the United States and EU generally agree upon the underlying principle that individuals should have the opportunity to control the ways their personal information is used, they employ very different means to achieve that goal. The EU's approach to privacy grows out of Europe's history and legal traditions. In Europe, protection of information privacy is viewed as a fundamental human right. The emphasis given it arises partly from intrusions into privacy that were at the root of certain World War II abuses. Europe also has a tradition of prospective, comprehensive lawmaking that seeks to guard against future harms, particularly where social issues are concerned.

The EU began examining the impact of technology on society more than fifteen years ago. The inquiry culminated in the adoption of a directive in July 1995, specifically addressing information privacy issues. The Council Directive on the Protection of Individuals With Regard to the Processing of Personal Data and On the Free Movement of Such Data (the Directive) took effect in October 1998.[94] Member States were required to bring into force laws, regulations and administrative provisions to comply with the Directive by its effective date. Last

---

94. Directive 95/46/EC of the European Parliament and of the Council of 24 October 1995 on the protection of individuals with regard to the processing of personal data and on the free movement of such data, 1995 O.J. (L 281) 0031–0050 [hereinafter Directive].

year, the European Commission announced its intention to take five of the fifteen Member States to court for failing to implement measures within the deadline established by the Directive; two of those Member States are expected to implement legislation this year.[95]

A quick review of its terms makes clear that, consistent with European tradition, the Directive takes an overarching, highly regulatory and inclusive approach to privacy issues. It has two basic objectives: to protect individuals in connection with the processing of personal information (defined as information relating to an identified or identifiable natural person) and to ensure the free movement of personal information within the EU through the coordination of national laws.[96]

The scope of the Directive is extraordinarily broad. It applies to all processing of data—online and offline, manual as well as automatic—and all organizations holding personal data. It excludes from its reach only data used "in the course of purely personal or household activity."[97] The Directive establishes strict guidelines for the processing of personal information. "Processing" includes any operations involving personal information, except perhaps its mere transmission.[98] For example, copying information or putting it in a file is viewed as processing it. The substantive aspects of the Directive's privacy protections are based upon the Guidelines on the Protection of Privacy and Transborder Flows of Personal Data, adopted by the Organization for Economic Cooperation and Development (OECD) in 1980.[99]

i. Components of the Directive

A. Data Quality

The Directive requires that all personal information be processed fairly and lawfully so that, for example, an individual knows his personal information is being collected and knows its proposed uses. Furthermore, the use of personal information must be limited to the purpose first identified and to other compatible uses, and no more information may be collected than is required to satisfy the purpose for which it is collected. In other words, if a person provides information to obtain telephone service, the information should not be used to target that person for information about vacation trips, nor should information relevant to a customer's interests in vacation trips be required to get telephone service. Information must be kept accurate and up to date.[100]

---

95. *See* <http://europa.eu.int/comm/internal_market/en/dataprot/news/2K-10.htm>.
96. Directive, *supra* note 94, art. 1.
97. *Id.* art. 3.
98. *Id.* art. 2.
99. Guidelines on the Protection of Privacy and Transborder Flows of Personal Information, Organisation for Economic Cooperation and Development (1980).
100. Directive, *supra* note 94, art. 6.

B. Legitimate Data Processing

The Directive sets forth rules for "legitimate" data processing. In general, this requires obtaining consent from individuals (data subjects) before their information is processed, unless specific exemptions apply.[101] In addition, certain information must be provided to data subjects when their personal information is processed, such as whether they have rights to see the data, correct any information that is inaccurate or know who will receive the data.[102]

C. Sensitive Data

Sensitive data—such as that pertaining to racial or ethnic origins, political or religious beliefs, or health or sex life—may not be processed at all unless such processing comes within limited exceptions.[103]

D. Security

The Directive requires that "appropriate technical and organizational measures to protect data" against destruction, loss, alteration or unauthorized disclosure or access be taken.[104]

E. Data Controllers

The Directive mandates that those processing data fulfill very specific requirements. They must appoint a "data controller" responsible for all data processing who must register with government authorities and notify those authorities before processing any data.[105] Notification must, at a minimum, include the purpose of the processing, a description of the data subjects, the recipients or categories of recipients to whom the data might be disclosed, proposed transfers to third countries and a general description that would allow a preliminary assessment of whether requirements for security of processing have been met.

F. Government Data Protection Authorities

The Directive also mandates a government authority to oversee data processing activities. Each Member State must establish an independent public

---

101. *Id.* art. 7.
102. *Id.* art. 10, art. 12.
103. *Id.* art. 8.
104. *Id.* art. 17.
105. *Id.* art. 18, art. 19.

authority to supervise the protection of personal data. These "Data Protection Commissions" must have the power to investigate data processing activities and monitor application of the Directive and to intervene in the processing and order blocking, erasure or destruction of data as well as ban its processing. They must also be authorized to hear and resolve complaints from data subjects and issue regular public reports on their activities.[106]

G. Transfers of Data outside the EU

Most important from the U.S. perspective, the Directive requires that Member States enact laws prohibiting the transfer of personal data to non-EU countries that fail to ensure an "adequate level of [privacy] protection."[107] When the level of protection is deemed inadequate, Member States are required to take measures to prevent any transfer of data to the third country. Member States and their Data Protection Commissions must inform each other when they believe a third country does not ensure an adequate level of protection.

ii. What Constitutes Adequacy under the Directive?

The aspect of the Directive that raises major questions for the United States and other non-EU countries is the issue of what constitutes an adequate level of protection. The Directive provides some guidance on how adequacy is to be determined. For example, it states that the adequacy of the protection offered by the recipient country shall be assessed in light of all the circumstances surrounding a data transfer, including the following:[108]

- the nature of the data;
- the purpose and duration of the proposed processing operation;
- the country of origin or the country of final destination;
- the rules of law in force in the destination country; and
- the professional rules and security measures that apply within the recipient country.

Although there seems to be general consensus that adequacy means something less than equivalence, the Directive leaves unspecified the substantive rules that, in fact, constitute adequacy as well as the procedural means for achieving it.

---

106. *Id.* art. 28.
107. *Id.* art. 25.
108. *Id.*

In June 1997, the European Commission's Working Party on the Protection of Individuals with Regard to the Processing of Personal Data (Working Party) released a discussion paper entitled *First Orientations on Transfers of Personal Data to Third Countries—Possible Ways Forward in Assessing Adequacy.*[109] The Working Party paper identifies two criteria essential to a finding of adequacy: the core substantive rules and the enforcement mechanisms. The substantive rules identified in the paper closely track the Directive's requirements and include the following:

1. Information must be processed for a particular purpose and used only to the extent its use is not incompatible with the purpose of its collection;
2. Information must be accurate and up to date, and not excessive in relationship to the purposes for which it is collected;
3. Individuals must be provided with information about the purpose of the collection;
4. Organizational and technical measures must be taken to keep the data secure;
5. Data subjects must be able to obtain copies of all data and have a right to rectification if they are inaccurate, and must have the right to oppose processing; and
6. Transfers to third countries must be restricted unless they provide an adequate level of protection.

The enforcement mechanisms must provide a good level of compliance, support and help to individual data subjects, as well as appropriate redress. The Working Party paper also recognizes that legislation is not necessary for adequate privacy protection so long as these goals are accomplished through other means.

In *Transfers of Personal Data to Third Countries: Applying Articles 25 and 26 of the EU Data Protection Directive*, a more recent report issued in July 1998, the Working Party elaborated further on the criteria necessary for a self-regulatory regime to be considered adequate.[110] First, it reiterated that the substantive rules and enforcement mechanisms identified in its July 1997 report must be met. The self-regulatory regime must also be binding for all companies or institutions to which personal data are transferred and provide for adequate safeguards if data are passed on to nonmembers. In addition, the privacy regime must be transparent and have mechanisms that effectively ensure a good level of compliance. Individuals must be ensured certain rights, such as easy access

---

109. First Orientations on Transfers of Personal Data to Third Countries—Possible Ways Forward in Assessing Adequacy, Working Party on the Protection of Individuals with Regard to the Processing of Personal Data, DG XV D 5020/97 (June 1997).
110. Transfers of Personal Data to Third Countries: Applying Articles 25 and 26 of the EU Data Protection Directive, Working Party on the Protection of Individuals with Regard to the Processing of Personal Data, DG XV D/5025/98 (July 1998).

to an impartial and independent body that can hear complaints, adjudicate breaches of the code and provide a remedy and compensation. Finally, there must be a guarantee of appropriate redress in cases of noncompliance.

Neither paper issued by the Working Party, however, provides guidance on how or when an "adequate" privacy law or program in a third country might differ from the requirements of the Directive. The nature of "adequacy" under the Directive would remain unclear until there were specific examples to examine and the EU made "adequacy" findings.

3. The U.S. Approach to Privacy Protection[111]

Legal and historical traditions have evolved quite differently in the United States than in Europe, and the United States takes a different approach to privacy issues. The U.S. legal tradition, rooted in concerns about governmental excesses, has led to a preference for decentralized authority, a reluctance to regulate the private sector absent demonstrated need, and generally a greater concern about government excess than private sector excess. And, although the U.S. Constitution establishes certain privacy protections for individuals, such as the right to be free from warrantless searches, it does not explicitly protect *information* privacy, nor has any such constitutional right been inferred. In addition, a fundamental tenet of American democracy—the First Amendment to the U.S. Constitution—requires a balance between the privacy rights of individuals and the benefits that stem from the free flow of information within and across U.S. borders.

Accordingly, when the United States adopted a comprehensive privacy law—the Privacy Act of 1974—it governed only the federal government's use of citizens' personal information. Other federal privacy protection statutes apply to specific government agencies or information, such as income tax and census data. Comprehensive privacy protections affecting private sector data use, however, have not been adopted by either the federal government or state governments. (Some state constitutions—such as those of California, Florida and Hawaii—explicitly set forth a right to information privacy without specifying any rights relating directly to information privacy.)

Generally, the information privacy laws that govern the private sector in the United States were adopted because of specific instances of abuse, perceived market failure or the involvement of particularly sensitive groups and/or information. Also, due to a concern that a "one size fits all" legislative approach would lack the necessary precision to avoid interfering with the benefits of the free flow of information, the adoption of sector-specific privacy legislation is limited. As a result, a number of statutes cover the collection and use of personal information in specific contexts, such as information about children, information collected by telephone and cable companies and credit bureaus, and

---

111. For more on privacy issues, see section 7.1.

financial, video rental and drivers' license information. A brief review of three of these statutes makes clear that privacy statutes in the United States take different approaches and impose different schemes for protecting privacy, depending upon the circumstances.

i. Fair Credit Reporting Act

Congress enacted the Fair Credit Reporting Act (FCRA) in 1970 to deal with widespread concerns about incorrect and widely disseminated consumer credit reports.[112] FCRA governs disclosure of consumer credit information by credit bureaus. It starts with the premise that widespread availability of correct credit information to parties with a real need for the information benefits the U.S. economy. It provides consumers with a limited right to consent to the use of their personal information.

FCRA imposes strict regulations regarding the use and accuracy of credit information. It limits the disclosure of credit information to businesses with a legitimate need for it, and provides certain rights to consumers when credit information is used to deny them an important benefit. To help ensure accuracy, FCRA requires that consumers have access to information maintained about them, and sets forth fairly prescriptive rules governing how access must be provided. The act also requires that recipients of credit reports be identified, prohibits the reporting of obsolete information, and provides a correction process for inaccurate or incomplete information. And, if a consumer is denied credit for personal, family or household purposes, or is denied employment and the denial is based upon information in a consumer report, the entity receiving the report is required to notify the consumer and identify the credit bureau that furnished the report. FCRA allocates enforcement responsibilities among a number of federal agencies (primarily FTC).

ii. Children's Online Privacy Protection Act

In October 1998, Congress passed the Children's Online Privacy Protection Act (COPPA).[113] The law applies to operators of commercial web sites and online services that collect or maintain information from web site or service visitors and users. COPPA prohibits the collection of information from children under the age of thirteen without verifiable parental consent. It also provides for a safe harbor from privacy liability when companies adhere to a self-regulatory program approved by FTC. FTC, which was charged with enforcing regulations under the statute, issued implementing rules in April 2000.

---

112. *See* 15 U.S.C. §§ 1681–1681u (1999).
113. *See* 15 U.S.C. §§ 6501–6506 (1999).

These rules set forth criteria for web site operators and online services when they target children or have actual knowledge that the persons from whom they seek information are children. The rules require notice of the personally identifiable information being collected, how it will be used and whether it will be disclosed. Subject to certain exceptions, web sites must notify parents when they plan to collect information from their children, and obtain parental consent before the information is collected, used or disclosed. Conditions for more than reasonably necessary information may not be placed upon a child's participation in online activities. In addition, parents must be allowed to review information collected from their children, have it deleted and prohibit further collection. Finally, companies must implement procedures to protect the confidentiality, security and integrity of personal information collected from children.

iii. Financial Modernization Act

More recently, in November 1999, President Clinton signed into law the Financial Modernization Act.[114] The act's primary purpose was to overhaul U.S. laws governing the financial services industry, but the legislation also increased the level of financial privacy protections afforded consumers. The law requires financial institutions to disclose their privacy polices initially and annually, allowing consumers to make informed choices about privacy protection. Financial institutions must also inform consumers if they intend to share or sell consumers' financial data, either within the corporate family or to third parties. Consumers are entitled to choice if a financial institution plans to share information with unaffiliated third parties, subject to certain exceptions. Enforcement is allocated among FTC, state insurance authorities and federal functional regulators (such as the Office of the Comptroller of the Currency, the Securities and Exchange Commission, and the Federal Reserve Board). The legislation directs these agencies to prescribe regulations necessary for implementation. Regulations have been finalized for all federal regulators. Businesses must be in full compliance by July 2001.

iv. Self-Regulatory Privacy Initiatives

Without broad, multisector privacy laws, information privacy protection in the United States has largely relied upon voluntary adoption of self-regulatory

---

114. Gramm-Leach-Bliley Act, Pub. L. No. 106-102, 113 Stat. 1338, codified in scattered sections of 12 U.S.C. and 15 U.S.C. (1999).

codes of conduct by industry. These codes take as their point of departure the Guidelines on the Protection of Privacy and Transborder Flows of Personal Data, which were adopted by OECD as the basis for the European Directive on Data Protection. As long ago as 1983, 183 U.S. companies endorsed those guidelines. The U.S. government has also repeatedly endorsed them, most recently in October 1998, when the Clinton administration reiterated endorsement of the guidelines as part of the Ministerial Declaration on the Protection of Privacy on Global Networks issued at the Ottawa Ministerial Conference.

Recent years have witnessed growing concern about whether information privacy in the United States is sufficiently protected. This concern has led to enactment of additional sector-specific legislation. It has not, however, resulted in any significant movement toward a European-type regulatory approach or law. Rather, the emphasis has been upon adoption and implementation of more effective self-regulatory regimes to protect privacy (self-regulation with "teeth").

Thus, when in 1997 the Clinton administration released *A Framework for Global Electronic Commerce*,[115] which examined the policy issues raised by the development of electronic commerce, it noted the growing concerns about information privacy and recognized that, unless they were addressed, e-commerce would not develop to its full potential. The report specifically recognized the high value Americans place upon privacy, and recommended private-sector efforts and technological solutions to protect privacy. The report also identified several factors suggesting that comprehensive legislation could harm the development of e-commerce. The lack of national borders on the Internet has heightened interest in self-regulation and technological solutions to problems generally, and to privacy concerns specifically. On the Internet, national laws are difficult—if not impossible—to enforce. In addition, because the Internet and e-commerce are still rapidly evolving, any legislated approach is at best likely to be outdated as soon as it is adopted, and at worst likely to stifle further development of these media. The report takes the view that when it comes to fixing the problem, government should be the last—not first—resort. Accordingly, when the report was issued, the Secretary of Commerce and Director of the Office of Management and Budget were directed to encourage private industry and privacy advocacy groups to develop and adopt effective codes of conduct, industry-developed rules and/or technological solutions to protect privacy on the Internet.

Subsequent annual reports on e-commerce issued by the Clinton administration confirmed the administration's preference for self-regulatory solutions to privacy protection. At the same time, the Clinton administration continued to recognize that sector-specific privacy legislation might be appropriate in certain areas, such as when the information is considered highly sensitive, as is the case with children's and financial information. The Clinton administration also

---

115. A Framework for Global Electronic Commerce, July 1, 1997, *available at* <http://www.ecommerce.gov/framewrk.htm>.

repeatedly cautioned that if industry did not produce adequate privacy policies, government action would be needed to safeguard legitimate privacy interests.

Since issuance of the Clinton administration's landmark e-commerce report in 1997, industry has undertaken concerted efforts to create effective privacy protection via self-regulation. More than eighty of the largest companies doing business on the Internet and twenty-three business organizations that represent thousands of other companies formed the Online Privacy Alliance (OPA) to promote privacy online. OPA developed *Guidelines for Effective Privacy Policies*, which outline protections for individually identifiable information in online and e-commerce environments. OPA also produced guidelines for effective enforcement of these policies.

Organizations such as BBB*OnLine*, TRUSTe and CPA WebTrust have been formed to provide independent third-party enforcement regimes that promote compliance with information practice codes. The Council of Better Business Bureaus, a nonprofit, well-regarded organization that helps resolve consumer complaints, established BBB*OnLine* as a privacy program for online businesses. Businesses joining the program may display a seal or trust mark to notify consumers that their web sites follow fair information practices, but only after they adopt privacy policies that comport with the program's principles and complete an assessment indicating they have implemented those policies. Members must also submit to monitoring and review by BBB*OnLine* and agree to participate in a consumer complaint resolution system. The other enforcement programs include similar requirements, and allow the display of seals or trust marks to notify consumers. Nearly two thousand sites carry a privacy seal from a trusted third party and more than a thousand additional sites have applied for a seal from third-party enforcement services.

In what is perhaps a uniquely American approach, the enforcement of self-regulatory programs is backed up by FTC (and other federal and state agency) enforcement. Section 5 of the FTC Act prohibits "unfair or deceptive acts or practices" in or affecting commerce.[116] Deceptive practices have been defined to include representations, omissions or practices that are likely to mislead reasonable consumers in a material fashion. FTC has repeatedly used its equitable powers under section 5 to enforce the provisions of privacy (and other self-regulatory) policies, even when companies have voluntarily adopted those policies. Consequently, when a company adopts a privacy policy, it is akin to adopting a privacy law for that particular company.

The FTC Act provides FTC with authority to seek injunctive relief against future violations of the statute, as well as to provide redress for injured consumers.[117] FTC can obtain substantial penalties when its orders are violated. The authority of FTC and other federal and state agencies to control unfair and deceptive practices, and their willingness to use it to enforce self-regulatory

---

116. *See* 15 U.S.C. § 45 (2000).
117. *Id.* § 45(a)(l).

policies, helps ensure the effectiveness of self-regulation in the United States. All fifty states plus the District of Columbia, Guam, Puerto Rico and the U.S. Virgin Islands have enacted laws similar to the FTC Act to prevent unfair or deceptive acts. Their attorneys general enforce these laws, adding additional resources to government enforcement of self-regulation.

Evidence now exists to show that the decentralized, self-regulatory approach to privacy issues can be an effective means of protecting personal information in a globally networked environment. A 1999 FTC survey involving a random sample of web sites found that the number of privacy policies rose from 14% in 1998 to 88%, and that 100% of the most popular group of web sites had privacy policies.[118] Though only 8% of the random sample had privacy seals from one of the independent third-party enforcement groups, 45% of the most popular group did.[119] Other surveys show that self-regulation is working and that businesses are taking effective steps to establish and post privacy policies. For example, a Jupiter Communications study determined that 70% of U.S. web sites that collect information post privacy policies linked to their home-pages.[120]

At the same time, there have been increasing demands for privacy legislation in the United States. In May 2000, FTC called for legislation to protect privacy online based upon its most recent report, which identified problems of "free riders" and poor-quality privacy policies.[121] According to the report, the number of web sites disclosing information practices had increased, but the quality of these practices fell short. In addition, the report noted that although the creation of the self-regulatory enforcement programs has been a positive development, the number of participants in these groups has been relatively small. In part because these enforcement programs have not been widely implemented, FTC concluded that such efforts alone are not sufficient to ensure adequate protection of consumer privacy online.

Several members of Congress have also introduced privacy legislation in Congress to protect privacy, particularly in the areas of online privacy, electronic surveillance and medical and financial record-keeping. Although many of these bills are given little chance of passage, at a minimum they indicate impatience with the pace of adoption and dissatisfaction with the quality of private sector codes of conduct. For example, in the first few months of this year alone, there have been at least eighteen bills proposing privacy legislation. These have ranged from the basic requirements that disclosure must be provided with an opportunity to prohibit further interaction to more stringent bills requiring affirmative consent in advance to collect and disclose personally identifiable

---

118. Privacy Online: Fair Information Practices in the Electronic Marketplace, A Report to Congress, Federal Trade Commission (May 2000), at 10.

119. *Id.* at 20.

120. Neglecting Consumers' Privacy Concerns Will Limit Revenue Opportunities, Jupiter Communications, Nov. 1999.

121. Privacy Online: Fair Information Practices in the Electronic Marketplace, A Report to Congress, Federal Trade Commission (May 2000).

information. Some industry officials are, for the first time, urging Congress to pass limited privacy laws. They are concerned that the lack of federal standards will lead to a confusing patchwork of state regulations.

For its part, the Clinton Administration saw substantial progress being made by the private sector, although it too believed more needs to be done and more quickly. The new Administration, however, has yet to articulate its policies in this area and whether it will also encourage adoption by industry of effective privacy policies and technological solutions.

Although privacy policies in the United States are evolving, this much is clear: the United States is committed to ensuring personal privacy through a variety of means that reflect its deeply rooted tradition of enhancing the free flow of information and avoiding unnecessary government intervention in private affairs. The United States relies upon private sector, self-regulatory efforts—backed up by government enforcement—to ensure that companies implement their privacy policies. The government becomes involved only when it determines individuals' privacy rights are not otherwise sufficiently protected. The U.S. approach to privacy relies upon an amalgam of laws, codes of conduct and technology to provide effective privacy protection.

Given U.S legal traditions and history, and the advantages of a self-regulatory approach to privacy in an information economy, the United States is unlikely at this time to abandon self-regulation. And even if the United States were to adopt privacy legislation in new and different situations, it is highly unlikely it would adopt the type of overarching, comprehensive, highly regulatory and centralized approach of the EU.

4. Safe Harbor

Neither the EU nor the United States appears likely to change its approach to privacy protection in any significant way. Given these long-standing differences, many U.S. organizations were concerned about the impact of the "adequacy" standard on personal data transfers from the European Community to the United States. Many feared an across-the-board interruption in data flows, which could affect as much as $120 billion in trade each year, interfere with multinational companies' abilities to pay and manage employees, and disrupt routine activities conducted by investment bankers, accountants, pharmaceutical companies and travel companies. Others dismissed fears of a complete interruption in data flows as unlikely, noting that it would be potentially devastating for both economies.

The more likely situation—limited data flow interruptions involving one industry sector or perhaps one company—posed similar dangers, however, because it was feared they could easily evolve into a trade war, depending upon U.S. reactions and European counterreactions. Just the threat of action by European authorities left U.S. companies with a great deal of uncertainty. Also, ad hoc approaches available to satisfy the Directive's "adequacy" standard threatened to be expensive and time consuming, and were thus suitable for larger companies only.

Against the backdrop of these different privacy approaches and the serious consequences that could flow from them, the United States and EU accepted the difficult challenge of bridging the differences in their respective approaches to privacy. Toward that end, in March 1998, the U.S. Department of Commerce initiated a high-level, informal dialogue with the European Commission Directorate for Internal Markets to ensure the continued free flow of data. From the start, both sides recognized that any interruption in transborder data transfers could have a serious impact upon commerce between the EU and United States, and that they thus needed to begin with an acceptance of their differences and develop ways to bridge those differences. At the outset, the two sides agreed upon twin goals—to maintain data flows between the United States and EU and to retain high standards of privacy protection—and worked to identify common ground upon which to build a solution. The dialogue revealed much common ground between the two sides on what constitutes effective privacy protection. Both the European and U.S. approaches, despite their differences, are based upon the 1980 OECD Privacy Guidelines.

In late 1998, the dialogue led to the proposal of a safe harbor for U.S. companies that adhere to the so-called safe-harbor framework, which encompasses the safe-harbor principles and frequently asked questions (FAQs). U.S. companies adhering to the framework will be judged adequate, and data flows to them from Europe will continue. The safe-harbor principles more closely reflect the U.S. approach to privacy, but at the same time would meet the EU Directive's requirements. The FAQs were developed to provide further guidance to U.S. companies and to elaborate upon how various issues, such as enforcement, will work. Both the principles and FAQs were developed in close consultation with the European Commission and the U.S. public, and both are considered integral to an "adequacy" determination. Drafts of documents were posted for U.S. public comment fours times during the two-year negotiation, and U.S. negotiators held numerous meetings with consumer advocacy and industry groups to obtain their views on the draft documents.

The dialogue also led to a standstill between the United States and the EU in late 1998. The EU made a political commitment to not interrupt data flows while the dialogue proceeded in good faith. On March 14, 2000, the U.S. Department of Commerce and the European Commission announced they had reached a tentative conclusion to the safe-harbor dialogue. At the same time, the two sides agreed to continue their discussions pertaining to the financial services sector, given the recent passage of the Financial Modernization Act and the fact that the regulations had not yet been issued. On May 31, 2000, the EU Member States voted unanimously to approve the safe-harbor arrangement.[122]

---

122. *See* Safe Harbor Privacy Principles (2000), *available at* <http://www.export.gov/safeharbor>.

The safe harbor provides a number of benefits to U.S. firms. Most important, it provides predictability and continuity for U.S. companies that receive personal information from Europe. All fifteen Member States will be bound by the European Commission's finding of adequacy. The safe harbor streamlines the Directive's bureaucratic burdens, by creating one privacy regime applicable to U.S. companies, rather than fifteen. It also eliminates the need for prior approval to begin data transfers to the United States, or makes such approval automatic. The safe harbor offers a simpler and less expensive means of complying with the adequacy requirements of the Directive, which should benefit all U.S. companies, particularly small and medium-sized enterprises.

An organization's decision to enter the safe harbor is entirely voluntary. An organization that decides to participate in the safe harbor, however, must publicly declare in its published privacy policy statement that it adheres to the safe harbor and then it must do so. To continue to be assured of safe-harbor benefits, an organization must self-certify annually to the Department of Commerce, in writing, that it adheres to the safe harbor's requirements. The Department of Commerce maintains a list of all organizations that file self-certification letters and makes both the list and self-certification letters publicly available.

i. Safe-Harbor Requirements

Organizations must follow seven privacy principles and the FAQs to comply with the safe harbor.[123] The principles require the following:

- Notice
- Choice
- Onward transfer restrictions
- Access
- Security
- Data integrity
- Enforcement

A. Notice

Organizations must notify individuals about the purposes for which they collect and use information about the individuals. An organization must provide information about (1) how individuals can contact the organization with

---

123. The Safe Harbor Principles, Frequently Asked Questions and Answers, as well as other safe harbor documents, *available at* <http://www.export.gov/safeharbor>.

any inquiries or complaints, (2) the types of third parties to which the organization discloses information and (3) the choices and means the organization offers for limiting use and disclosure of the information.

B. Choice

An organization must give an individual the opportunity to choose whether personal information may be disclosed to a third party or used for a purpose incompatible with that for which it was originally collected or subsequently authorized by the individual (opt out). For sensitive information, affirmative or explicit choice must be given if the information is to be disclosed to a third party or used for a purpose other than the original purpose or the purpose subsequently authorized by the individual (opt in).

C. Onward Transfer Restrictions (Transfers to Third Parties)

An organization may transfer information to a third party that is acting as an agent[124] if the organization ensures the third party subscribes to the safe-harbor principles or is subject to the Directive or another adequacy finding. As an alternative, the organization can enter a written agreement with such third party, requiring that the third party provide at least the same level of privacy protection as is required by the relevant principles.

D. Access

Generally, an individual must be given access to personal information that an organization holds, and be able to correct, amend or delete that information when it is inaccurate. Exceptions to this general rule are permitted when the burden or expense of providing access would be disproportionate (unreasonable) to the risks to the individual's privacy, or when the rights of persons other than the individual would be violated.

E. Security

Organizations must take reasonable precautions to protect personal information from loss and misuse, and from unauthorized access, disclosure, alteration and destruction.

---

124. "It is not necessary to provide notice or choice when disclosure is made to a third party that is acting as an agent to perform task(s) on behalf of and under the instructions of the organization. The Onward Transfer Principle, on the other hand, does apply to such disclosures." Safe Harbor Principles (2000).

F. Data Integrity

Personal information must be relevant to the purpose for which it is to be used. An organization should take reasonable steps to ensure that data are reliable for their intended use, as well as accurate, complete and current.

G. Enforcement

Organizations must have readily available and affordable independent re-course mechanisms that allow each individual's complaints to be investigated and resolved, and damages awarded when applicable law or private sector initiatives so provide. In addition, the organization must establish procedures for verifying that the commitments companies make to adhere to the safe-harbor principles have been implemented. Finally, the organization must remedy problems arising out of a failure to comply with the principles. Sanctions must be sufficiently rigorous to ensure compliance.

The FAQs provide further guidance that clarifies and supplements the safe-harbor principles on issues such as access, publicly available information and public record information, as well as sector-specific guidance for information processing by medical, pharmaceutical, travel and accounting firms. They also address how human resources information will be handled under the safe harbor.

ii. Safe-Harbor Enforcement

Perhaps the most difficult difference to bridge in the safe-harbor dialogue was the issue of enforcement. Though the EU's Working Group had already determined in the abstract that self-regulation was a valid means to "adequacy," accepting the adequacy of a particular self-regulatory enforcement regime proved far more difficult. Adding to this difficulty was the complexity of the multilayered approach to enforcement in the United States, which relies upon self-regulation fortified by FTC enforcement, sector-specific laws and recourse to lawsuits.

Ultimately, an understanding was reached on an enforcement arrangement. In general, enforcement of the safe harbor will take place in the United States in accordance with U.S. law and will be conducted primarily by the private sector. The safe harbor provides for at least three different ways to satisfy the enforcement principle.[125] An organization can join a self-regulatory privacy program that adheres to the safe harbor's requirements. It can also

---

125. *See* Safe Harbor Privacy Principles (2000).

develop its own self-regulatory privacy policy that conforms to the safe harbor. And an organization can meet the safe-harbor requirements if it is subject to a statutory, regulatory, administrative or other body of law that effectively protects personal privacy.

As part of its safe-harbor obligations, an organization is required to make available a dispute resolution system that investigates and resolves individual complaints and disputes. The organization is also required to remedy problems arising out of a failure to comply with the principles. Sanctions must be severe enough to ensure compliance; they must include publicity for findings of non-compliance and deletion of data in certain circumstances. They may also include suspension from membership in a privacy program (and thus effectively from the safe harbor) and injunctive orders.

The dispute resolution, verification and remedy requirements can be satisfied in different ways. For example, an organization could comply with a private sector privacy seal program that incorporates and satisfies the safe-harbor principles. If, however, the seal program provides for dispute resolution and remedies but not verification, then the organization would need to satisfy the verification requirement in an alternative way. An organization can also satisfy the dispute resolution and remedy requirements through compliance with government supervisory authorities or by committing to cooperate with data protection authorities located in Europe.

When an organization relies upon self-regulation to ensure privacy protection under the safe harbor, there must be a U.S. agency (state or federal) with jurisdiction over the organization that will enforce the safe-harbor policies. The agency must be willing to take action under federal or state law prohibiting unfair and deceptive acts when the company fails to comply with the safe harbor or the organization is not eligible to join the safe harbor. The FTC, comparable U.S. government agencies and/or the states (depending upon the industry sector) will provide overarching government enforcement of the safe-harbor principles. An annex to the safe-harbor principles contains a list of U.S. enforcement agencies recognized by the European Commission. Third-party self-regulatory programs (such as BBBOnLine, TRUSTe, and WebTrust) are also subject to enforcement under unfair/deceptive practice statutes in many—if not most—instances, if they claim to be enforcing the safe-harbor framework for their safe-harbor members but do not.

iii. Failure to Comply with Safe-Harbor Requirements

If an organization persistently fails to comply with the safe-harbor requirements, it will no longer be entitled to benefit from the safe harbor.[126] Persistent

---

126. *See* Frequently Asked Question No. 11: Dispute Resolution and Enforcement.

failure to comply arises when an organization refuses to comply with a final determination by any self-regulatory or government body, or when such a body determines that an organization frequently fails to comply with the requirements, to the point where its claim to comply is no longer credible. In these cases, the organization must promptly notify the Department of Commerce of such facts. Failure to do so may be actionable under the False Statements Act (18 U.S.C. § 1001). The Department of Commerce will indicate on the public list it maintains of organizations self-certifying adherence to the safe-harbor requirements any notification it receives of persistent failure to comply, and will make clear which organizations are assured of safe-harbor benefits and which are not. An organization applying to participate in a self-regulatory body for the purposes of requalifying for the safe harbor must provide that body with full information about its prior participation in the safe harbor.

5. Conclusion

The safe-harbor arrangement has been called a major accomplishment for both the United States and the EU. It comes at a time when trade disagreements—rather than agreements—between the United States and Europe dominate the news. The framework has also been labeled a landmark accord for e-commerce. It bridges the different approaches of the United States and the EU in a way that protects EU citizens' privacy when information is transferred to the United States, maintains data flows, creates the necessary environment for e-commerce and provides predictability for U.S. companies. At the same time, the arrangement demonstrates EU recognition that a carefully constructed and well-implemented system of self-regulation, as advocated by the Clinton administration, can protect privacy. It is a creative and innovative vehicle—perhaps the first international framework to rely upon the private sector for its implementation. It thus can serve as a model in other contexts as we seek to ensure the development of a seamless global environment for electronic transactions.

The challenge in providing privacy protection in the Information Economy is to balance appropriately the free flow of information against an individual's right to privacy so we do not jeopardize the benefits these new information technologies promise or trench on the First Amendment. Whether the safe harbor will provide that balance remains to be seen. If the safe harbor is ultimately to be judged a success, sufficient numbers of companies will need to join it and consumers will need to feel comfortable with how their personal information is used and their ability to control its use.

§ 7.3 Anonymity and Encryption

1. Introduction

Section 7.3 of this chapter deals with information practices issues affecting Internet commerce.[127] Privacy lies at the core of these issues. Encryption and anonymity are two areas that relate directly to privacy and also to broader information practices issues.

The technologies implementing encryption can provide important tools to safeguard privacy and ensure the reliability of information practices. In a sense, privacy can be understood as the result of anonymity. That is, when one is anonymous, one has privacy. Authenticating a person by means of a user name, smart card or other form of digital identification restricts or precludes anonymity. Of course, one can use multiple identities (known as pseudonyms) and can employ other methods to create privacy. *Encryption* is a technology that scrambles digital information according to a code that allows authorized users to unscramble the data later. Encryption can be used to prevent others from perceiving what one is saying, doing or keeping electronically. This is another way to create a veil of privacy.

Although one's identity may be known (that is, one is not anonymous), one may still hold electronic documents and speech beyond the perception of others by using encryption. Anonymity and encryption can be used for some digital information, but not for other information, and they can be used in many interesting combinations. Anonymity and encryption are powerful tools for sculpting creative and tailored information practices and policies.

2. Anonymity and Pseudonymity

Anonymity is being unknown or unacknowledged. *Pseudonymity* is being identified by an assumed (often pen) name. The use of authentication technologies to establish the identity of a person is incompatible with anonymity because it prevents the person from being unknown. There are legal consequences to being anonymous and to being authenticated or identified.

Identifying every user on a network is not always necessary. Perhaps an anecdote will help illustrate this point. When I worked as a lawyer in the state government of Massachusetts, we implemented the first known public sector

---

127. This section was greatly enhanced by Jessica Natale, a third-year law student at Suffolk University Law School.

credit card payment applications online for citizens to use on the Internet. The application allowed users to renew a vehicle registration, order custom "vanity" license plates and pay tickets. An important part of the reason these transactions were chosen was precisely because they did not require authentication of the identity of the user. A driver's license or change-of-address transaction, on the other hand, would require such authentication.

There was, of course, a possibility that the "wrong" person might conduct one of these transactions. In other words, person A could log onto the site and, appearing to be person B, might attempt to conduct the transaction. My legal analysis of this scenario, under Massachusetts's law, was that person B would be guilty of providing a "gift" to person A. My personal analysis was that I hoped person B would quickly and routinely log on to pay my own tickets under any identity the person cared to assume. It is generally unwise as a business or technical matter to use more or different security than needed for a given application (it depletes resources, creates complexity and invites problems). It was primarily for these reasons that the Commonwealth of Massachusetts chose "unauthenticated" electronic transactions as its first e-business application.

i. Context Determines Desirability of Authentication or Anonymity

The foregoing story illustrates a relatively simple example of a business choice to assume no special authentication of a user for an e-commerce application. The legal, business, technical and policy aspects of authentication or anonymity are often far less simple than the decision to allow unauthenticated renewal of a car registration. For example, at their thorniest, the issues parallel the classic struggles between national or corporate security and individual liberty. The needs for security usually require authentication of individuals and their activities, whereas civil liberties—especially, but not exclusively, including privacy—often favor anonymity or pseudonymity.

More frequently, the question of anonymity and authentication arise in more mundane circumstances, such as merchants with web sites who seek to generate a commercial advantage by authenticating the identities of users based upon resale of the user's preferences to marketers. An individual user might find such authentication annoying (due to the additional screens, time and trouble of user name/password management), and the ensuing marketing communications may well be deemed meddlesome.

A more benign example of the use of authentication would involve the provider of interactive media who seeks to authenticate an individual user for the purpose of generating highly customized and personally relevant information and resources to that user. Such a user might desire this level of individual tailoring and thus tolerate the authentication procedure to access the service.

At best, authentication regimes are desired and required by both the user and the provider in the same way a bank account holder would probably not use an ATM machine unless adequate authentication (like a debit card and PIN) was required to prevent unauthorized users from withdrawing funds. More typically, authentication is simply required as a standard business risk control measure (as with employee log-in to company computer networks). At worst, authentication measures are undesired and/or unknown by the users (as when browser cookies identify the sites an Internet surfer visits, and when that user's personal information is later sold).

ii. When Anonymity Is Bad: Anonymity as Accountability Avoidance

There are some who believe that anonymity is little more than a method of avoiding responsibility for one's actions. Any number of laws, regulations and corporate policies require identification of people as a necessary part of a transaction. U.S. Supreme Court Justice Scalia, in a dissenting opinion that struck down a law prohibiting anonymous political pamphleting, made perhaps the clearest and most succinct case against anonymity. Scalia wrote that anonymity:

> facilitates wrong by eliminating accountability, which is ordinarily the very purpose of the anonymity. . . . [T]o strike down the Ohio law in its general application—and similar laws of 49 other States and the Federal Government—on the ground that all anonymous communication is in our society traditionally sacrosanct, seems to me a distortion of the past that will lead to a coarsening of the future. I respectfully dissent.[128]

There appears to be relevant research in the social sciences to confirm Justice Scalia's viewpoint. Evidently, anonymity and merging of one's self into a group has been correlated to an increase in coarse, and even brutal, behaviors. In an article presented at the Annual Conference of the European Institute for Computer Anti-Virus Research, Dr. Kabay of the International Computer Security Association put forth an impressive compilation of studies tending to show a link between anonymity and antisocial conduct. Dr. Kabay overviews the potential harms associated with anonymity in this way:

> In general, the findings are not encouraging for the future of cyberspace unless we can somehow avoid the known association of antisocial behaviour and anonymity. Early work on people in groups focused on anonymity as a root of the

---

128. McIntyre v. Ohio Elections Comm'n, 514 U.S. 334, 385 (1995) (Scalia, J., dissenting).

perceived frequency of antisocial behaviour (Le Bon, 1896). The anonymous members of a crowd show reduced inhibition of antisocial and reckless, impulsive behaviour. They are subject to increased irritability and suggestibility. One wonders if the well-known incidence of *flaming* (rude and largely *ad hominem* communications through e-mail and postings on the Usenet and other public areas) may be traceable to the same factors that influence crowd behaviour. Later social psychologists formulated a theory of deindividuation (Festinger et al., 1952) in which they proposed that one's personal sense of identity can be overwhelmed by the sense of belonging to a group. Zimbardo (1970) suggested that anonymity, diffusion of responsibility and arousal contributed to deindividuation and antisociality. He noted that deindividuated people display reduced inhibitions, reduced reliance on internal standards that normally qualify their behaviour, and little self-awareness. . . . Writers of computer viruses and others in the criminal computer underground may also focus so intensely on the challenge of defeating machines that they lose sight of their human victims. Criminal hackers have expressed themselves as attacking systems, not people. . . .[129]

Dr. Kabay also points to studies showing that people who are anonymous tend to behave dishonestly and are more likely to be violent toward others, and suggesting that the behavior of hackers acting as unidentified network users may in fact be "relatively normal people responding in predictable ways to the absence of stable identification and identity."[130]

iii. When Anonymity Is Good: Anonymity as a Core Value, Like Privacy

Set against the view that anonymous communication and conduct in an electronic environment are presumptively negative exists the widely held conviction that ensuring anonymous and pseudonymous transactions is one of the most pressing needs of our time. For example, the Privacy Commission—recently commissioned by FTC—reported that the United States is in urgent need of allowing anonymity for Internet transactions as a method of assuring privacy.[131] Roger Clarke, visiting fellow at the Department of Computer Science, Australian National University, put forward a crisp viewpoint in support

---

129. M. E. Kabay, Ph.D., Anonymity and Pseudonymity in Cyberspace: Deindividuation, Incivility and Lawlessness versus Freedom and Privacy, Paper Presented at the Annual Conference of the European Institute for Computer Anti-virus Research (EICAR), Munich, Germany (Mar. 16, 1998).

130. *Id.* at 3.1.2.

131. Federal Trade Comm'n, Advisory Comm. on Online Access and Security, Draft Advisory Committee Report (as of April 26, 2000) ("Maintaining the ability of individuals to be anonymous on the Internet is a critical component of privacy protection. Access systems should not require indentification in all instances." <http://www.ftc.gov/acoas/papers/draft_advisory_committee_report_body.htm>.

of assuring protection of the right to anonymity. In his paper, *Identified, Anonymous and Pseudonymous Transactions: The Spectrum of Choice*, Clarke argued that there are two critically important policy imperatives of the next hundred years:[132]

Policy Imperative 1:

- maximize the use of **anonymous transactions**, and **resist and reverse the conversion** of anonymous to identified transactions;
- maximize the use of **pseudonymous transactions**, where anonymity is not an effective option; and
- preclude **identified transactions** except when functionally necessary, or when meaningful, informed consent exists.

Policy Imperative 2:

- enable **multiple identities** for multiple roles;
- enable the **authentication of pseudonyms**;
- provide **legal, organizational and technical protections** against access to the link between a pseudonym and the person behind it;
- resist and reverse **multiple usage of identifiers**; and
- resist and reverse the **correlation of identifiers**.

The first of these imperatives would deny the increasingly common assumption by governments and corporations that individuals are to be subjected to authentication as a matter of course. The second would deny governments and corporations alike the ability to consolidate personal data through the use of common identifiers. It further stresses the central importance of pseudonymity as a primary means of achieving the necessary balance between the needs for privacy and for accountability.

iv. Applying Legal Precedents on Anonymity to Interactive Media Environments

Federal and state statutes, regulations and case law recognize various situations in which anonymity or pseudonymity is either protected or prohibited. The legal precedents discussed below can provide some guidance, directly or indirectly, to counsel, businesspersons and technologists who seek to understand

---

132. Roger Clarke, Identified, Anonymous and Pseudonymous Transactions: The Spectrum of Choice, Paper Prepared for Presentation at the User Identification & Privacy Protection Conference, Stockholm (June 14, 1999), *available at* <http://www.anu.edu.au/people/Roger.Clarke/DV/UIPP99.html>.

whether, how and how much anonymity may be desirable for any given electronic transaction or set of transactions.

The right to freedom of expression has also generated legal precedents protecting anonymity. For example, individuals may anonymously make political expressions relating to an election in the form of pamphlets.[133] Anonymous campaign literature is an important component to a free society because it assures all citizens the opportunity to add to the marketplace of ideas without fear of reprisal by employers or others. At election time in the future, will there be facilities or other technical functions that permit users of computer networks to express political ideas anonymously? On the other hand, it has also been held that requiring an identification badge is permissible for vendors selling periodicals on streets and in other public areas.[134] Such a badge or permit requirement makes sense as a matter of urban planning and assuring efficient traffic and pedestrian flows. This precedent also shows how a court may be less willing to grant anonymity for commercial sales and more likely for speech generally. However, the right of publishers, printers and distributors generally to maintain anonymity has been held to be an important part of press freedom.[135]

Perhaps the strongest case in support of anonymous speech is *Talley v. California*.[136] *Talley* explicitly establishes that the First Amendment right of freedom of speech includes the right to remain anonymous. In *Talley*, the U.S. Supreme Court reviewed a Los Angeles city ordinance prohibiting distribution of any handbill unless it had the name and address of the person who produced it and who caused it to be distributed were printed on the document. In the words of the court:

> Anonymous pamphlets, leaflets, brochures and even books have played an important role in the progress of mankind. Persecuted groups and sects from time to time throughout history have been able to criticize oppressive practices and laws either anonymously or not at all. . . . The old seditious libel cases in England show the lengths to which government had to go to find out who was responsible for books that were obnoxious to the rules. . . . Even the Federalist Papers, written in favor of the adoption of our Constitution, were published under fictitious names. It is plain that anonymity has sometimes been assumed for the most constructive purposes.[137]

This language reflects the importance given to anonymity be the judiciary. This point of view is not afforded only to verbal speech and ideas printed on paper. Rather, courts have been willing to apply protection of anonymity to encompass various media, including telephone answering machines.[138]

---

133. *See supra* note 128.
134. City of Manchester v. Leiby, 117 F.2d 661, *cert. denied,* 313 U.S. 562 (C.C.A. 1 N.H. 1941).
135. Bursey v. U.S., 466 F.2d 1059 (CA-9 Cal. 1972).
136. 362 U.S. 60 (1960).
137. *Id.* at 64–65.
138. U.S.C.A. CONST. Amend. VI-Jury Trials; State v. Baker, 621 N.E.2d 1347 (Ohio App. 1 Dist. 1993).

In the business world, the transfer of money out of a checking, savings or investment account is the best example of a transaction that requires, for business and legal reasons, authentication. As suggested earlier in this section, account holders and financial institutions alike share a desire to prevent unauthorized usage of a customer account. In response to this, and to avoid money laundering that is associated with anonymous or insufficiently identified bank account holders, financial institutions have developed "Know Your Customer" programs.[139] More formal "know your customer" rules[140] for financial institutions were proposed[141] to reduce, identify and prosecute illegal financial acts.[142] These proposed rules spawned vigorous criticism and debate[143] and were finally withdrawn.[144] Although one may assume that financial transfers by their very nature require individual authentication in all cases to protect the sensitivity and value of the transaction, there are in fact many applications for anonymous money (like cash). Similarly, as with any other transaction, a simple cost/benefit and risk analysis is required to determine the levels at which authentication may be needed.

Another federal agency that has embarked upon a "know your customer" initiative is the Bureau of Export Administration (BEX) of the U.S. Department of Commerce.[145] Certain provisions in the Export Administration Regulations (EAR) require an exporter to submit an individual validated license application if the exporter "knows" that an export that is otherwise exempt from the validated licensing requirements is for end-uses involving nuclear, chemical, and biological weapons (CBW), or related missile delivery systems, in named destinations listed in the regulations. The details of encryption export are dealt with elsewhere in this book, but in this context, it is interesting to point out that authentication (and not anonymity) is required for end-users. Beyond knowing the named identity of a buyer of certain goods, exporters must also know a great deal about exactly what uses to which the goods will be put and

---

139. More on these programs is available at <http://www.moneylaundering.com>.

140. Proposed to have been codified as 12 C.F.R., Part 326.

141. 63 Fed. Reg. 67524 (Dec. 7, 1998).

142. On December 7, 1998, the Comptroller of the Currency, the Office of Thrift Supervision, the Federal Reserve Board and the Federal Deposit Insurance Corporation published proposed "Know Your Customer" regulations. Ostensibly, these regulations would have required banks and thrift institutions to:

1. identify their customers;

2. determine the sources of funds for each customer;

3. determine the "normal and expected" transactions of each customer;

4. monitor each customer's account activity and measure it against historical patterns; and

5. report to the U.S. Treasury Department's Financial Crimes Enforcement Network (FinCEN) any transactions that are "suspicious" because they do not conform to historical patterns.

143. *See*, for example, the testimony of Solveig Singleton, Lawyer, The Cato Institute before the U.S. House of Representatives Committee on the Judiciary Subcommittee on Commercial and Administrative Law, at <http://www.cato.org/testimony/ct-ss030499.html>. *See also* the open letter by Lowell H. Becraft, Jr. to the Federal Deposit Insurance Corporation at <http://www.garynorth.com/y2k/detail_.cfm/3472>.

144. Press Release, by Representative Ron Paul, a libertarian-leaning member of Congress, lauding the withdrawal illustrated the vigor with which these rules were resisted, *available at* <http://www.house.gov/paul/press/press99/pr032399-kyc.htm>.

145. *See* <http://www.bxa.doc.gov/Enforcement/knowcust.htm>.

where the goods will end up. The BEX "Know Your Customer Guidance" gives a variety of circumstances for exporters to monitor and which may indicate an inappropriate end-use, end-user, or destination for their goods.[146]

Outside of the mercantile worlds of export and banking, the controversy between anonymity and authentication has generated no shortage of litigation. For example, numerous medical conditions involving social stigma or religious doctrine have raised legal claims for anonymity.[147] Individuals making requests for public information under the Freedom of Information Act are not entitled to learn the identity of confidential informants to the government.[148] It is typical for the law to protect the right of individuals to be anonymous with respect to these types of issues. Another situation in which the need for anonymity is frequently invoked involves police informants. In this situation, the law must balance the rights to a fair trial and to confront an accuser with the competing public policy need to encourage citizens to cooperate with police.[149] A creative precedent for handling this tension can be for a judge to interview the informer directly, and make the resulting information available to all parties, without revealing the identity of the informant.[150] One can imagine various ways to use a judge or other magistrate for this type of purpose in the context of electronic communications.

In the context of public trials, there are a series of cases which weigh the need for open and transparent courts versus the need to protect the privacy and other constitutional rights of certain parties to litigation. In these situations, a litigant may seek to proceed as John or Jane Doe, rather than identify themselves on the pleadings or other court documents, including situations protecting the identity of children, religious and racial minorities seeking to uphold their rights, and persons with medical and psychological disabilities.[151] The mere

---

146. *Id.*

147. W.G.A. v. Priority Pharmacy, Inc., 184 F.R.D. 616 (E.D.Mo.1999) (protecting litigants from public knowledge of AIDS status); Eilers v. Palmer, 575 F. Supp. 1259 (D.C.Minn.1984) (names of individuals supporting unorthodox religious views, need not be disclosed).

148. 5 U.S.C.A. § 552; New England Apple Council v. Donovan, 725 F.2d 139 (Mass. 1984); Lame v. U.S. Dept. of Justice, 654 F.2d 917 (CA-3 Pa. 1981); Cofield v. City of LaGrange, Ga., 913 F. Supp. 608 (D.D.C. 1996).

149. State v. Gamble, 631 So.2d 586 (La. App. 3d Cir. 1994); Roviaro v. U.S., 353 U.S. 53 (Ill. 1957); Westinghouse Elec. Corp. v. City of Burlington, 351 F.2d 762, *rem'd* 246 F. Supp. 839 (C.A.D.C. 1965); People v. Woolnough, 180 A.D.2d 837, *appeal denied* 596 N.E.2d 422 (1992); State v. Baker, 621 N.E.2d 1347 (Ohio App. Dist. 1993).

150. Rodriguez v. City of Springfield, 127 F.R.D. 426 (D.Mass.1989).

151. 42 U.S.C.A. §§ 12133, 2000c-6; Heather K. by Anita K. v. City of Mallard, Iowa, 887 F.Supp. 1249 (N.D. Iowa 1995); (protecting child's need for anonymity to avoid harassment and permanency of lawsuit's record, concerning child's action the Americans with Disabilities Act); Doe v. Covington County School Bd., M.D., 884 F. Supp. 462 (M.D.Ala. 1995) (protecting anonymity of children suing school officials based upon alleged sexual abuse by public school teacher); Doe v. Stegall, 653 F.2d 180, *rehearing denied*, 659 F.2d 1075 (CA-5 Miss. 1981) (protecting anonymity of litigants challenging prayer and bible reading in schools to avoid exposing litigants' personal beliefs and practices); Plaquemines Parish School Bd. v. U.S., 415 F.2d 817 (CA-5 La. 1969) (civil rights era African-American litigants entitled to proceed anonymously in segregation case); Doe v. Blue Cross & Blue Shield of Rhode Island, 794 F. Supp. 72 (D.R.I. 1992) (in case against insurer to recoup medical expenses for a sex change operation, litigant was entitled to proceed under fictitious name to avoid threat of economic harm resulting from stigma); Anonymous v. Legal Services Corp. of Puerto Rico, 932 F. Supp. 49 (D.P.R. 1996) (Americans with Disabilities Act suit against former employer involving mental illness of plaintiff entitled plaintiff to proceed anonymously).

claim of discrimination based upon gender, however, was not held to be sufficiently important to outweigh the broader interest in open trails.[152] Similarly, to preserve the right of financial privacy, certain proceeding before a federal Tax Court may be closed to the public.[153]

Children's identities are protected under the law well beyond the context of public trials, including in the electronic arena. For example, the Children's Online Privacy Protection Act and accompanying rules[154] prohibit unfair or deceptive acts or practices in connection with the collection, use, and/or disclosure of personal information from and about children on the Internet.

OSHA rules require particular responses by employers to reports of hazardous conditions in the workplace which require inspections (hence possible business disruption). Employers must permit employees to file these reports anonymously.[155] This is an example of the law finding that the general societal good of assuring safe workplaces requires protecting the anonymity of individuals. One can imagine analogous situation occurring on office networks and extra-nets, where employees file these or other societally important information anonymously. In these types of situations, it would not make sense to require full individual authentication of every employee on a business network at all times. Rather, under particular scenarios, there may even be a role for anonymous communication within the intranet of a corporation.

In the legal area of reproductive issues, there are several examples of legal rules protecting anonymity of individuals involved with the adoption and the abortion processes. Under the U.S. Code, the Attorney General of the United States must pay for up to two anonymous test for sexually transmitted diseases for victims of rape.[156] Understandably, the protection of anonymity given to victims of sexual assault are forcefully taken from perpetrators. The judiciary has upheld statutes for registration and community notification of convicted sex offenders.[157]

The Georgia Anti-Mask statute was not held to violate the right to freedom of association in litigation by members of the Ku Klux Klan.[158] The court found that the interests of Klan members in remaining anonymous while engaged in threatening mask-wearing behavior was counterbalanced by the general public interest in protecting citizens from violence and intimidation.

---

152. Luckett v. Beaudet, 21 F. Supp.2d 1029 (D. Minn. 1998).
153. 26 U.S.C.A. § 6110, 51 Rule 227.
154. 5 U.S.C. §§ 6501, *et seq.*; 16 C.F.R. Part 312.
155. Executive Order No. 12196 Occupational Safety And Health Programs For Federal Employees, Feb. 26, 1980, 45 F.R. 12769, as amended by Ex. Ord. No. 12223, June 30, 1980, 45 F.R. 45235; Ex. Ord. No. 12608, Sept. 9, 1987, 52 F.R. 34617; 5 U.S.C.A. § 7092, 1–201.
156. 42 U.S.C.A. § 10607.
157. Doe v. Poritz, 662 A.2d 367 (N.J. 1995); 36 A.L.R.5th 711; 42 U.S.C.A. § 14071.
158. State v. Miller, 398 S.E.2d 547 (Ga. 1990).

v. The Purpose of Legal Precedents on Anonymity

These examples of situations, in some cases, bear directly upon the set up of electronic transactions system. For example, the need to identify the citizenship and location of users who download certain encryption software applies directly to encryption companies. In other situations, the legal rules can be applied only by analogy. For example, it is possible that the legal precedent against the wearing of a mask for the purpose of intimidating another person could be interpreted to apply to the masking of an IP address with mal-intent. In general, the above listing is intended to point toward examples of circumstances where society has deemed identity or anonymity to be important. It is up to the bar and the rest of the information society to apply these principles to cyberspace over time.

3. Encryption and Authentication

This section is intended for readers who want a deeper understanding of encryption, how it works and business applications for its use. Encryption can be explained as:

> [t]he translation of data into a secret code. Encryption is the most effective way to achieve data security. To read an encrypted file, you must have access to a secret key or password that enables you to decrypt it. Unencrypted data is called plain text; encrypted data is referred to as cipher text. There are two main types of encryption: asymmetric encryption (also called public key encryption) and symmetric encryption.[159]

Encryption can be used to ensure that data remain confidential or secret by making it impossible for parties without the proper codes necessary to use decryption mechanisms to access the data. Much of the work of information practices is concerned with implementing methods to control access to data according to authorization. Encryption is the most important tool for restricting digital information for such purposes.

---

159. Although more technical definitions abound, this explanation is from the Webopedia, an online dictionary and search engine for computer and Internet technology. *See* <http://webopedia.internet.com/TERM/e/encryption.html>. This source defines cryptography, a closely related concept, as the "art of protecting information by transforming it (encrypting it) into an unreadable format, called cipher text. Only those who possess a secret key can decipher (or decrypt) the message into plain text. Encrypted messages can sometimes be broken by cryptanalysis, also called codebreaking, although modern cryptography techniques are virtually unbreakable. . . ."

i. Encryption for Authentication

Encryption can also be used to facilitate determination of the identity of a party for the purpose of establishing whether that party is authorized to access data. For example, if a particular web site requires a user name and password to access certain information or resources, then it is good practice to ensure the communications channel between the user and the system is encrypted when the password is transmitted. This is because the Internet is not a secure network, and it is possible for unauthorized persons to intercept the password and later impersonate the authorized user. This is, however, only one simple way that encryption can be used to facilitate the determination of identity. When combined with other technologies and appropriate business practices and models, it is possible to use *asymmetric encryption,* also known as *public key cryptography,* to create a digital signature that can provide a high degree of certainty about the identity of the signer. In this way, use of encryption can be tightly associated with the process of identification or with continued anonymity of an individual.

ii. Electronic Signatures

An *electronic signature* is:

> an electronic sound, symbol, or process, attached to or logically associated with a contract or other record and executed or adopted by a person with the intent to sign the record.[160]

There are many ways to create an electronic signature. These can range from simple methods, such as typing a name at the bottom of an e-mail message, to more complex and secure methods involving biometric technologies, such as a fingerprint or retinal scan. Other types of authentication methods used to create electronic signatures include magnetic stripe cards and PIN numbers, user names and passwords, public key cryptography, writing tablets with electronic pens, and even smart cards that generate a unique access code every few seconds. As technology advances, the list of viable alternatives is certain to grow.

Because there are so many ways to create electronic signatures, and because many of them do not resemble a holographic "autograph," some law reform efforts have adopted the term *authentication* rather than *signature.*[161] Currently, however, it is best practice to use the word *sign* to indicate something a user

---

160. This definition is from the state Uniform Electronic Transactions Act (UETA), *available at* <http://www.law.upenn.edu/bll/ulc/uecicta/uetast84.htm>, and has more recently been reflected in the federal law known as the Electronic Signatures in Global and National Commerce Act (E-SIGN), enacting Senate Bill 761 in the 106th Congress, Pub. L. No. 106-229, 15 U.S.C.A. § 7001.

161. The best example is the state Uniform Computer Information Transactions Act (UCITA), which provides as follows:

does to identify himself or to manifest assent, and the word *authenticate* to indicate something the receiver of a signature would do to validate that the signature is genuine. It can be said that one authenticates a signature when that signature is checked.

One of the most interesting and robust technologies being used and developed for authentication purposes is known as public key cryptography, which allows for a very high degree of reliability when implemented properly. A *digital signature* does not refer to the image of a signature in any way. Unlike an electronic signature, which is simply any symbol or process intended to be a signature, and a *digitized signature*, which refers to an electronic image of a signature, a digital signature is a term of art that refers to scrambling data to provide security and authentication. The term "electronic signature" is the overarching concept, and does not indicate any particular technology. The term "digital signature" is a term of art that denotes use of public key cryptography (though these terms are not infrequently used interchangeably in the popular media).

Although the technical details of public key cryptography are extremely complex and have limited utility to a broader audience, an understanding of the basic concepts is both accessible and useful. Due to the current interest in deploying large-scale public key systems, this technology will likely touch many areas of the economy. In fact, the growth of public key systems in many sectors of the economy suggests that a rudimentary knowledge of these concepts will serve lawyers well when legal questions arise as a result of this technology.[162]

iii. The Basics of Public Key Cryptography

Codes and cryptography are thousands of years old. Although cryptography became much more sophisticated in modern times, its core still depended upon the sender and the receiver knowing the same "secret key" to encode and then decode messages. To be secure, a secret-key coding system requires some method for distributing the secret key to intended users without it falling into the hands of other parties.

"Authenticate" means:

(A) to sign; or

(B) with the intent to sign a record, otherwise to execute or adopt an electronic symbol, sound, message, or process referring to, attached to, included in, or logically associated or linked with, that record.

Available at <http://www.law.upenn.edu/bll/ulc/ulc_frame.htm>. Note, however, that as of this writing, UCITA has been adopted in only two states and is viewed as highly controversial, while UETA has been adopted in more than twenty states. The term *electronic signature*, as reflected by UETA and under federal law, appears to be well established.

162. The following section on public key cryptography is borrowed and updated from an earlier published article co-authored by Daniel Greenwood. *See* Daniel J. Greenwood & Ray A. Campbell, *Electronic Commerce Legislation: From Written on Paper and Signed in Ink to Electronic Records and Online Authentication,* 53 Bus. Law. 307–38 (1997).

The nature of the Internet makes it poorly suited for a secret-key system because it is an "open" network in which messages may make several "stops" before arriving at their final destination. This creates a serious risk that a third party could intercept a secret key at some point along its routing, which would allow that party to read encoded messages or even send coded messages purporting to be from an authorized holder of the secret key. Physically delivering a secret key to every user by secure channels would be slow, expensive and unwieldy. Furthermore, physical distribution would effectively rule out serendipitous or one-time transactions between people and firms that have not previously exchanged secret keys. Although this property of public key cryptography is intriguing, current business models—especially business-to-business models—already use secure channels, which can be leveraged to swap authentication mechanisms (such as PINs and other secrets).

The cost of adopting a public key system may not be appropriate when other alternatives are suitable. More to the point, because most business channels do not rely upon or require serendipitous or one-time transactions, it is becoming obvious that this property of public key cryptography is a solution without a problem for most situations. In the future, as new business channels emerge, this property of public key cryptography may be more important to more people and businesses. For the moment, the costs of creating the infrastructure necessary for strangers to trust one another based upon a technology appears beyond reach. Rather, it will be necessary for business relationships to develop over time, whereby the risk is borne by responsible parties who not only facilitate stranger-to-stranger transactions but also stand behind them. Alliances, insurance, bonding, membership organizations and many other models are emerging. One thing seems clear: No matter how interesting a property of technology may be, technology alone is not sufficient to create trust and manage risk.

Public key cryptography eliminates the need for users to share a secret key, which makes it ideally suited for communications over "open" networks such as the Internet. Although the following illustration describes a complex process, the hardware and software that implement this technology shield the end user from these details. Moreover, end users have no need to concern themselves with the complicated background operations that make the system possible.

With a public key system, each user has software that generates two related keys, known as the *public key* and the *private key*. The fundamental characteristic of these key pairs is that the public key—and only that public key—can decrypt a message encrypted with its corresponding private key. Similarly, the private key—and only that private key—can decrypt a message encrypted with its corresponding public key. As such, these key pairs are analogous to secret decoder rings from cereal boxes, where each ring fits into its companion ring and no other.[163]

---

163. The math underlying public key cryptography is rather esoteric and beyond the scope of this chapter. In short, public key cryptography is based upon the fact that the only way to factor a large prime

Once Bob, a user, generates his public/private key pair with a computer, he keeps his private key very secure (protected by a password on his computer or, preferably, a smart card locked in a safe), but he makes his public key freely available by sending it to people or by posting it to a public key directory on the Internet. Then, if Alice, another user, wants to send Bob a private message, she can obtain Bob's public key and use it to encrypt the message. Because only Bob's private key can decrypt a message that has been encrypted with his public key, both Alice and Bob can be sure that only Bob can read the message. Thus, public key cryptography allows two people to send secure messages without exchanging a secret key through a secure channel. Only Bob's public key needs to be shared for Bob to receive completely secure messages.

This unique characteristic of public key cryptography also forms the basis for secure digital signatures. This process is illustrated in Figure 1. To generate a digital signature, Bob must first have a message (1) that he wants to sign and send to Alice. The message could be as simple as an e-mail message or as complicated as a lengthy contract. Bob runs his communication to Alice through one of several standard algorithms, known as a hash function (2), which performs a series of mathematical operations on the original message. The hash function produces a number called a message digest (3), which can be thought of as a fingerprint of the message, because any change in the message—no matter how slight—causes the hash function to produce a completely different message digest. Bob then encrypts the message digest with his private key (4). The message digest encrypted with Bob's private key forms the actual digital signature for the message.[164] Finally, Bob transmits both the digital signature and his original message to Alice (5). If Bob also wants to keep his

Figure 1.

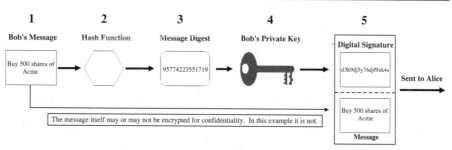

product (a very large number derived by multiplying two large prime numbers) is by having a computer calculate every possible combination of numbers to find the two component numbers. If the component numbers are large enough, solving the equation becomes "computationally intractable." The current generation of public key cryptosystems uses numbers so large that it could take extremely powerful computers years, and millions of dollars (or more), to crack a single public/private key pair.

164. The digital signature is created through two distinct steps: First, the message digest—created through the use of a hash function—ensures the integrity of the content of the intended communication. Second, the use of the private key to encrypt the message digest authenticates the identity of the person sending the message.

message to Alice confidential, he could encrypt the message using Alice's public key (not shown).

Upon receipt of the message, Alice's computer and software perform two separate operations to verify Bob's identity and to determine if the message was altered in transit, as shown in Figure 2. As a practical matter, it is not important which operation is performed first.[165] To verify Bob's identity, Alice's system takes Bob's digital signature (1) and uses Bob's public key (2) to decrypt the digital signature, which produces the message digest (3). If this operation is successful, Alice knows for a fact that Bob, who alone has access to his private key, must have sent the message.

To ensure that Bob's message was not altered in transit, Alice can run Bob's message (4) through the same hash function (5) that Bob used, which yields a message digest of Bob's message (6). Alice then compares the two message digests (7), and if they are the same, she knows for a fact that the message was not altered in transit.

Thus, public key cryptography allows people and businesses to exchange messages over open networks with a high degree of confidence that those messages are confidential (unable to be read by unauthorized persons), authentic (the sender's identity can be verified), and of high data integrity (the message cannot be altered without detection). This is a level of security far greater than that afforded by ink signatures.

Nothing said thus far, however, rules out the possibility that an impostor could generate a public/private key pair and then post the public key on the Internet, claiming it belongs to Bob. Unaware of the deception, Alice might then use this public key to send messages that the impostor, but not Bob, could read. The impostor could also use the falsely identified private key to digitally

Figure 2.

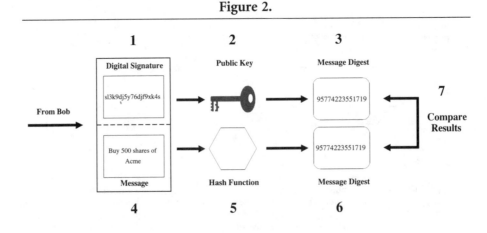

---

165. The two operations are performed upon separate documents: one upon the digital signature, an encrypted message digest, and the other upon the message itself. Although the results of both operations are compared against each other to obtain a true verification, it is irrelevant which operation is performed first.

sign messages that Alice would assume Bob sent, because they can be decoded using the public key, which Alice does not yet realize is fraudulent. To prevent this, parties relying upon digital signatures must have confidence that the public key that is on the Internet and which supposedly belongs to a certain person is, in fact, owned by that person.

One proposed approach to handle this practical problem has been to rely upon a trusted third party, known as a *certification authority* (CA), which binds the identity of a particular party to a particular public key and, by implication, a particular private key. What follows is an explanation of how some envision this trusted third-party CA model should operate.

CAs would bind the identity of a party to a public key by issuing a digital certificate. A digital certificate is a small electronic record that (1) identifies the CA issuing it, (2) identifies the subscriber, (3) contains the subscriber's public key and (4) is digitally signed with the CA's private key. The digital certificate can contain additional information, including a reliance limit or a reference to the CA's *certification practice statement*, which gives relying parties notice of the level of inquiry conducted by the CA before issuing the certificate.

To obtain a digital certificate, Bob presents the CA with a copy of his public key along with sufficient proof of his identity. For digital certificates that could be used for larger transactions, the CA might charge a higher fee and require greater proof of identity. Once satisfied with the identity of the subscriber, the CA issues the subscriber a digital certificate. When Bob wants to use his digital signature, he also transmits a copy of his digital certificate to Alice. In addition to the steps described above, when Alice's computer receives Bob's message, it also confirms with the CA identified in the digital certificate that Bob is who he purports to be and that his certificate has not expired or been revoked. If Bob learns or fears that his private key has been compromised, he notifies his CA of this fact so it can post that information to its *certificate revocation list* (CRL) or, perhaps, refer to an online check of a database using a certificate-checking protocol. All this activity takes place in the background, unseen and unnoticed by Alice, and happens in much the same way as occurs with online credit card validation systems.

iv. Different Models, Implementations and Approaches

There are many different models for using public key cryptography that do not assume or require a CA, including the implementations known as Pretty Good Privacy (PGP), which uses a "web of trust" wherein users vouch for each other (Abe knows Betty and Cathy and introduced them to each other). Another non-CA system is known as Account Authority Digital Signature (AADS), which simply binds a public key with a user account number. Banks and other institutions that primarily refer to user identities by account might find this system efficient and useful. Neither PGP nor AADS require certificates. Current certificate technologies (which rely upon the ISO standard X.509 version 3 digital certificates) are difficult to establish, manage, use and upgrade. The Commonwealth of Massachusetts published a detailed review of the experience of a five-state e-commerce pilot, in which certificates were used to identify individual buyers of supplies. Massachusetts, New York, Idaho, Texas and Utah participated in the pilot, known as the Multi-State Emall. Continued use of digital certificates and the trusted third-party CA model was not recommended.[166]

One of the major unanswered questions about the use of public key cryptography for digital signatures, and a major point of contention between advocates of different types of electronic signature laws, relates to the business model for CA services that will ultimately prevail in the marketplace. A Public Key Infrastructure (PKI) would need to evolve to support use of technology using a trusted third-party CA.[167] Although advances in technology will certainly create new possibilities not presently contemplated, the two primary business models currently vying for support are known as the *open PKI* and *closed PKI* models.

An open PKI model assumes that subscribers will obtain from CAs digital certificates that will securely link their identities to their public keys for all—or at least many—purposes. Thus, in an open PKI environment, a person could obtain a digital certificate and then use it to order goods online from various merchants, sign legally binding agreements or even file documents with a government entity. A subscriber could use its certificate for any transaction requiring a digital signature. In the closed PKI model, users would obtain different digital certificates for each community of interests with which they interact online. For example, a user could have one certificate for transactions with a bank, a different certificate for communications with an employer and yet another certificate for dealings with a health care provider.

The difference between the two models is significant. Under an open PKI model, a person's certificate could potentially be used to sign any document, which makes the consequences extremely severe if the user's private key is compromised. In a closed PKI model, on the other hand, the risks to the user and the CA from an improperly signed document are more limited due to the system's more narrowly defined scope. Furthermore, the members of a particular community within a closed PKI system may enter agreements that define the rights and responsibilities of the members, which would further reduce the risks and uncertainty in such a system.

The Multi-State Emall used a closed system in which all parties agreed by contract in advance to the same set of operating rules and conventions for using the technology. The use of operating rules—whereby multiple parties can join a secure and enforceable community of trade or other transactions—is becoming the norm. Like trading-partner agreements that supported Electronic Data

---

166. For the full report, see sections 8 and 9 of the *Emall Evaluation*, at <http://www.emall.isa.us/>.

167. The acronym PKI stands for Public Key Infrastructure, reflecting the fact that the use of digital signatures based upon public key cryptography requires an elaborate infrastructure (technical, business, policy and legal) to support its use.

Interchange, these newer sets of operating rules are becoming standard methods of managing risk and trust for transactions over the Internet.[168]

It is becoming clear, from a business perspective, that the most important question does not revolve around PKI, but around the business, legal, policy and cultural infrastructures upon which use of technology must rest. That is, public key technologies are best applied in a tailored manner to suit the needs of the business and practical requirements of parties. It is unreasonable to expect parties to contort their business relationships to meet an unnecessary and costly PKI, rather than simply purchase technologies that support and reflect their real business needs.

So-called digital signature laws, like statutes in Utah and Washington,[169] exist to support a PKI and trusted third-party CA. In the mid-1990s, there was considerable interest in enacting this type of law for the purpose of facilitating e-commerce. The consensus quickly swayed against these types of laws, however, because they enshrined a particular technology and business model into law and distorted the otherwise competitive marketplace for different technologies and approaches. Most states have opted to enact electronic signature statutes, and a majority of states have further harmonized laws around the Uniform Electronic Transactions Act.[170] This approach ensures that any technology parties choose can be sufficient to create a valid signature or record. Congress also reflected this policy in the Electronic Signatures in Global and National Commerce Act (E-SIGN), passed in 2000.[171]

v. Non-PKI Technology: The Importance of Maintaining Options

Although PKI assumes the use of a trusted third party, several implementations of public key technologies do not assume the same model. AADS and PGP are noncertificate implementations, and they do not require a trusted third party. The Simple Public Key Infrastructure (SPKI)[172] standard can also be used without a trusted third party. Finally, when all the parties who use a set of public key technologies sign contracts with one another or otherwise agree to a set of

---

168. The National Automated Clearinghouse Association published guidelines to assist parties in establishing rules to which they would contractually agree before relying upon digital certificates. *See* Certification Authority Ratings and Trust Guidelines (CARAT), *available at* <http://internetcouncil.nacha.org/Projects/CARAT_Final_011400.doc>.

169. UTAH CODE ANN. Ch. 4 § 46.

170. *See* <http://www.law.upenn.edu/bll/ulc/uetast84.htm>.

171. 15 U.S.C.A. § 7001. *See also* <http://www.mbc.com> for a good overview of the various laws enacted in this area.

172. *See* <http://www.ietf.org/html.charters/spki-charter.html>. It should be noted that standards such as SPKI are not widely implemented and do not have robust tool sets to aid users. Though PKI technologies are costly, it can be even more costly to tailor design tools. Non-public-key technologies often present the simplest and least expensive alternatives.

operating rules to define their rights and responsibilities, then no trusted third party is needed. Use of public key technologies within a single institution (such as between employees) would also obviate the need for a trusted third party.

In addition to various implementations of public key technologies, there are a number of non-public-key technologies that exist in order to achieve electronic authentication. Mainstream authentication technologies include Keberos, passwords and PINs (including one-time PINs), radius implementations, virtual private networks (to create secure sessions), smart cards, cards with information on magnetic strips, biometric technologies and challenges based upon knowledge (such as the maiden name of the user's mother). It can be said that all authentication technologies fall into at least one of three categories: something you know (like a password), something you have (like an ATM card) and something you are (like a fingerprint or retinal scan).

One very interesting technology is known as Signature Dynamics. It is a mechanism for the secure capture, management and verification of handwritten signatures by electronic means. PenOp[173] has been the most well-known company that implements Signature Dynamics. Signature Dynamics captures signatures simply and reliably, and enables them to be securely stored and safely transported between different systems. For evidentiary purposes, Signature Dynamics can verify the authenticity of a transaction upon which signatures were executed. Signature Dynamics can also verify the authenticity of the signature on the document with an accuracy and speed unparalleled in the paper domain. In so doing, this technology provides evidence that is relevant to regulatory and legal requirements for handwritten signatures.

For the signatory, Signature Dynamic's major attraction is the familiarity of submitting a normal handwritten signature—using a pen (or, for devices like a Palm Pilot, a stylus). For corporate users, the main benefit is the ability to complete business processes electronically, achieving major cost savings by reducing the need for paper. Signature Dynamics removes the need for passwords and PINs, public/private key pairs and certificates. The state of California was the first to recognize this technology in law. The Californian regulations on the use of digital signatures provide helpful definitions and contexts for this technology.[174]

---

173. PenOp recently acquired Communication Intelligence Corporation.
174. The California Digital Signature Regulations address Signature Dynamics as follows:

List of Acceptable Technologies
The technology known as "Signature Dynamics" is an acceptable technology for use by public entities in California, provided that the signature is created consistent with the provisions in Section 22003(b)(1)–(5).
1. Definitions—For the purposes of Section 22003(b), and unless the context expressly indicates otherwise:
A. "Handwriting Measurements" means the metrics of the shapes, speeds and/or other distinguishing features of a signature as the person writes it by hand with a pen or stylus on a flat surface.
B. "Signature Digest" is the resulting bit-string produced when a signature is tied to a document using Signature Dynamics.
C. "Expert" means a person with demonstrable skill and knowledge based on training and experience who would qualify as an expert pursuant to California Evidence Code § 720.

In addition to encryption and Signature Dynamics, *biometric technologies* can be used. Biometric technology can be defined generally as:

> the study of measurable biological characteristics. In computer security, bio-metrics refers to authentication techniques that rely on measurable physical characteristics that can be automatically checked. Examples include computer analysis of fingerprints or speech.[175]

Biometrics can be used to establish the identity of a given party and encryption should be used to secure a communications channel over which the biometric data flow, to prevent a so-called man in the middle attack. Such an attack would involve an unauthorized third party intercepting the data that reflect the biometric measure (such as the voice print or retinal scan) and copying the data to be used for later impersonation. Using encryption between the biometric measurement device (such as the fingerprint reader or facial recognition camera) and the end authentication database would help to defend against such an attack.

Although technologies such as biometrics may appear to defeat the cause of privacy and anonymity, there are situations in which authentication is necessary for confidentiality. For example, to ensure that only authorized individuals can access a person's medical records, a strong system of authentication and authorization must be implemented. The same biometric technologies that pose the ultimate threat to a person's privacy can be used to ensure privacy. This

---

D. "Signature Dynamics" means measuring the way a person writes his or her signature by hand on a flat surface and binding the measurements to a message through the use of cryptographic techniques.

2. California Government Code § 16.5 requires that a digital signature be "unique to the person using it." A signature digest produced by Signature Dynamics technology may be considered unique to the person using it, if:

A. the signature digest records the handwriting measurements of the person signing the document using Signature Dynamics technology, and

B. the signature digest is cryptographically bound to the handwriting measurements, and

C. after the signature digest has been bound to the handwriting measurements, it is computationally infeasible to separate the handwriting measurements and bind them to a different signature digest.

3. California Government Code § 16.5 requires that a digital signature be capable of verification. A signature digest produced by Signature Dynamics technology is capable of verification if:

A. the acceptor of the digitally signed message obtains the handwriting measurements for purposes of comparison, and

B. if signature verification is a required component of a transaction with a public entity, the handwriting measurements can allow an expert handwriting and document examiner to assess the authenticity of a signature.

4. California Government Code § 16.5 requires that a digital signature remain "under the sole control of the person using it." A signature digest is under the sole control of the person using it if:

A. the signature digest captures the handwriting measurements and cryptographically binds them to the message directed by the signer and to no other message, and

B. the signature digest makes it computationally infeasible for the handwriting measurements to be bound to any other message.

5. The signature digest produced by Signature Dynamics technology must be linked to the message in such a way that if the data in the message are changed, the signature digest is invalidated.

CAL. CODE REGS. tit. 2, § 22003(b).

175. *See* <http://webopedia.internet.com/TERM/b/biometrics.html>.

conundrum exists among all authentication technologies, but is most pronounced with biometric data, because such data literally and unambiguously are linked to particular persons.

There are many objections to biometric systems, but the most interesting critique is that once such an authentication device is compromised, it can be impossible to continue using the technology. Unlike passwords, which can be reissued once compromised, a person will quickly and permanently run out of fingers and other biometric data sources. A person's DNA (the ultimate biometric) can be compromised only once before irreparable harm occurs. Nonetheless, because biometric authentication is possibly the best source of individual identification, it is a good bet that this technology will continue to evolve and be ever more useful in business transactions.

vi. Determining Whether, Which and How Much Authentication Is Needed

It is important for lawyers to understand that various technologies and approaches exist to meet the authentication and confidentiality needs of organizations or other clients. It is not an overstatement to say that legal requirements drive the perceived need for most security and authentication technology purchases. Whether there is a statutory requirement for a signature, fear of liability for lack of authentication or any of a wide variety of other legal needs, it is the law that stands as the source of most technical requirements in this area. Ascertaining the legal and business requirements for a given transaction or set of transactions is a necessary prerequisite to providing counsel on the adequacy— or overkill—of any given proposed technology or application for authentication and encryption.

Before a lawyer can assess whether or how much technical authentication or encryption is needed for a given web site or other multimedia resource, a more fundamental analysis of security and authentication needs for an individual transaction must be undertaken. Basic judgments about security and authentication must be made by the lawyer and communicated to the technical and business persons responsible for implementing encryption and authentication processes. In determining whether a given security need exists, the lawyer should consider questions such as the following:

- How is this process implemented today in paper?
- Does it require a signature?
- Is there a statute or regulation that requires privacy or confidentiality or individual identification?
- Is this an area where there has been litigation or other disputes in the past? If so, what are the problems and how do they relate to the online system?

- How much financial or other legal liability exposure exists for the parties if there is a problem with this transaction?

The Security and Authentication Requirements matrix (Table 1) provides a general method for analyzing legal information security needs. This matrix is not intended as a complete solution but rather as a general model for approaching analysis of these issues.

The left column lists categories of transactions that clearly implicate different legal arenas. Across the right columns are security requirements broken into three levels: network, document and application. To make use of the matrix, a company would first determine which characteristics apply to its particular application. Then, reading across, the company would check off appropriate security requirements for each of the application characteristics that apply. It is important to note that application characteristics are separated to assist lawyers in targeting solutions to the specific part of the application where such solutions are required.

Security solutions can be costly, time consuming and resource intensive, and should therefore be matched closely to actual application needs. It is important to avoid requiring too little security, but it may be even more important to avoid heaping on too much security. Depending upon the costs, the liability, the benefits and the total risk picture, a company that opts for security overkill may actually harm its business interests. As noted earlier, in addition to the relatively high costs of information security technologies, end user burdens and other harms to timely, responsive and flexible service can significantly disadvantage an online business channel.

For any given type of transaction, there is a checklist of information security requirements that might apply. These are in three levels: network, document and application. Some security deals only with the flow or control of data moving over a network (including the Internet):

- *Confidentiality* means preventing interception and reading of the data flowing over the network.
- *Authentication for Access Control* means allowing only certain users access to certain areas or resources on a network.

The next level, document security, deals with the transactional data itself—the data that constitute the request for a purchase or the bid in an auction, for example. This data may need to be kept over time, secured or authenticated:

- *Data Privacy* relates to data in which a person or entity has a continuing legal interest or right. Medical records, proprietary information and financial data would usually require this type of security.
- *Receipt or Acknowledgment* relates to those instances when confirmation of transmission receipt is required for a given document or data set.
- *Authentication for Binding Intent* relates to data that form the basis of a contract or other document that is being assented to or "signed."

- *Data Integrity* relates to the need to show that the data originally sent have not been tampered with during a given period of time. This may require secure, digital, time-stamping services.

The last level, application, involves functions available within the application:

- *Authentication of Role or Authority for Specific Actions* relates to an individual user's ability to perform any given function within the application, such as approving data or setting user rights.

These categories overlap to some extent, but they form the basis for thinking about information security needs for a given application in a structured and solution-oriented manner.

Based upon the boxes checked in the matrix, a lawyer can assist business and technical persons in matching the security requirements with an available menu of technical security offerings. Such a menu would include smart cards, biometrics, public key cryptography, Signature Dynamics and other technologies offered by vendors. Based upon an analysis of costs, benefits and risks, the choice of technical offerings can be closely tailored to the actual application needs.

If the transaction involves the interstate sale of goods, then the rules of the federal E-SIGN legislation[176] would probably apply. If the transaction further involved a consumer who by law is entitled to receive notices relating to a sale (such as a vehicle recall or repossession notice), then special rules apply before that consumer can legally elect to receive such notices electronically. Similarly, if the transaction involves adult entertainment, then it is necessary to establish the age of the viewer. An assent—confirming age—may be part of the solution to this requirement. The list of transactions is purely to illustrate that the different issues raised depend upon the nature of the interaction, the parties and the applicable law.

A single matrix (at least on such a small piece of paper) is inadequate to convey the full, interconnected dynamics of a complex set of system security requirements. Depending upon the types of transactions to be facilitated, it may be desirable to modify a matrix to separate the interface and also individual electronic records (at the subdocument level), in addition to the network, documents and application. Examples of subdocument electronic records include data that come from more than one database to form a single screen of information. In addition, to ensure a truly secure and reliable system, one must add a layer of nontechnical features, such as appropriate audits or internal business controls. Legal rules affecting records retention and filings with governmental entities of records related to transactions will constitute another source of technical requirements.[177]

---

176. *See supra* note 160.

177. E-SIGN, while allowing for the use of electronic records, ensures that government records retention and filings authority remains. This law also enables the government to set technical requirements for "performance standards" affecting records retention, including accuracy and integrity.

Table 1—Security and Authentication Requirements

Transaction Type	Network Level		Document Level			Application Level
	Transmission Confidentiality	Authentication for Access Control	Data Privacy	Receipt or Acknowledgment	Authentication for Binding Intent	Data Integrity and Digital Time Stamping	Authentication of Role or Authority for Specific Actions
Interstate Commercial Transaction							
Public Bids							
Newspaper							
Adult Entertainment							
Real Estate							
Securities Transfer							

CHAPTER **8**

Jurisdiction

Contents

By Margaret Stewart

Jurisdiction*

Chapter 8, authored by Margaret Stewart, discusses jurisdiction in an online environment. Section 8.1 explores the circumstances under which an online defendant is subject to personal jurisdiction. Section 8.2 addresses the authority of a state to apply its own law to regulate conduct, contrasting U.S. and European treatment of this area. Finally, Section 8.3 discusses enforcement of a judgement rendered in another forum.

§ 8.1 Personal Jurisdiction

Issues of personal jurisdiction are resolved by different methods in common-law countries and civil-law countries. Thus, in the United States, jurisdictional principles are developed in case law and focus upon broad concepts applied to specific fact patterns. In the European Union and Japan, by contrast, the basic jurisdictional law is statutory and is frequently thought to be more predictable as a result.[1] In many instances, the results in both systems are the same. The fluidity of the common-law approach, however, does allow jurisdictional assertions by analogy and, therefore, has responded more directly to issues in the context of electronic commerce.

1. Classic Jurisdiction

Historically (and internationally) the jurisdictional inquiry has focused upon (1) where a defendant was personally served with process when the state was

---

* This chapter is an edited version of part of: Committee on Cyberspace Law, *Achieving Legal and Business Order in Cyberspace: A Report on Global Jurisdiction Issues Created by the Intranet*, 55 Bus. Law. 1801 (2000), sponsored by the American Bar Association's Section of Business Law, for which Ms. Stewart served as reporter.

1. The discomfort of many civil-law countries with the U.S. doctrine of *minimum contacts* is reflected in the current debate regarding article 9 of the Draft Convention on Jurisdiction and Foreign Judgments in Civil and Commercial Matters proposed by the Hague Conference on Private International Law (May 5, 1992) [hereinafter Hague Convention], which provides for jurisdiction over a defendant when it has a branch, agency or other establishment and the claim relates directly to the activities of that branch, agency or establishment. The U.S. delegation wishes also to provide for jurisdiction in a forum when the defendant has carried on related regular commercial activity in the absence of a permanent presence, a provision that many other delegations find troubling because of the definitional issue regarding "regular commercial activities."

thought to need physical control over her,[2] (2) where acts giving rise to or related to the claim brought against the defendant occurred when a state was exercising jurisdiction over a nonresident defendant not personally served in the state[3] and (3) where the defendant was a citizen when a state claimed the ability to assert jurisdiction over her on any claim.[4]

Even before the advent of the Internet, however, the United States recognized that jurisdiction might sometimes be properly asserted by a state in which no act had been undertaken by the defendant. If a defendant, for example, enters into a negotiated, long-term, valuable, supervised venture with a forum resident, disputes arising out of that relationship may be heard in the forum, even though the defendant never entered it.[5] Similarly, if a defendant intentionally causes an impact in the forum state (by writing a libelous article about a forum citizen, for instance), he may be called to account in the forum's courts.[6]

Electronic commerce does not negate any of these historical constructs. To the extent that people continue to occupy and act in real space, the jurisdictional implications of their conduct remain unchanged.[7]

The new issue confronting courts involves the jurisdictional significance of a new method of communicating, selling, buying and informing. In particular, courts are struggling to determine what kind and level of use of the Internet under what circumstances ought to subject an absent defendant to jurisdiction.

---

2. Pennoyer v. Neff, 95 U.S. 714 (1877).

3. Since 1945, when *International Shoe Co. v. Washington*, 326 U.S. 310 (1945), was decided, the United States has recognized that the constitutional demands of due process are met if a defendant has minimum contacts with a state, so that the assertion of jurisdiction comports with traditional notions of fair play and substantial justice. Such contacts exist only if the defendant has purposefully availed itself of the privilege of conducting activities in the state, thus invoking the benefits and protections of state law (*Hanson v. Denckla*, 357 U.S. 235 (1958)), and if the assertion of jurisdiction would be reasonable (*Asahi Metal Industry Co. v. Superior Court*, 480 U.S. 102 (1987)). The Convention on Jurisdiction and the Enforcement of Judgments in Civil and Commercial Matters, Sept. 30, 1968, 1978 O.J. (L 304) [hereinafter Brussels Convention] similarly permits the assertion of jurisdiction based upon where acts relevant to the claim took place. *Id.* § 2, art. 5.

4. Blackmer v. United States, 284 U.S. 421 (1932); Brussels Convention, *supra* note 3, tit. II, § 1, art. 2. Although the propriety of assertions of so-called general jurisdiction over noncitizen residents of a state is in dispute in the United States, the European Union clearly limits general jurisdiction to those domiciled—as opposed to resident—in the state. *Id.* tit. II, § 1, art. 5.

5. Burger King Corp. v. Rudzewicz, 471 U.S. 462 (1985) (claim was failure to pay monies owed Florida plaintiff, an obligation to be performed by defendant in Florida). The result under the Brussels Convention would have been the same, as it permits jurisdiction to be asserted over a defendant in "the place of performance of the obligation in question." *See* Brussels Convention, *supra* note 3, tit. II, § 2, art. 5.

6. Calder v. Jones, 465 U.S. 783 (1984). Again, the result under the Brussels Convention would have been the same, as it permits jurisdiction to be asserted over a defendant if conduct outside the forum resulted in tortious injury to the plaintiff within it. *See* Brussels Convention, *supra* note 3, § 2, art. 5.

7. The Internet equivalents of *Burger King* and *Calder* are *Compuserve, Inc. v. Patterson*, 89 F.3d 1257 (6th Cir. 1996), and *Panavision International, L.P. v. Toeppen*, 938 F. Supp. 616 (C.D. Cal. 1996), *aff'd*, 141 F.3d 1316 (9th Cir. 1998). *See also* Blumenthal v. Drudge and America Online, 992 F. Supp. 44 (D.C. 1998).

2. Jurisdiction and the Internet

The first reported decision involving the jurisdictional significance of an out-of-state web site accessible to forum residents, *Inset Systems, Inc. v. Instruction Set, Inc.*,[8] was wrongly decided and is now not widely followed, but it left its mark. The defendant, Instruction Set, Inc. (ISI), was a Massachusetts corporation with its principal place of business in Massachusetts. ISI provided computer technology and support to thousands of organizations throughout the world, but it did not have any employees or offices in Connecticut, nor did it conduct any business on a regular basis in that state. Inset argued, however, that jurisdiction could be obtained over ISI under Connecticut's long-arm statute because "ISI has repeatedly solicited business within Connecticut via its Internet advertisement and the availability of its toll-free number."[9] Although there was no evidence that anyone in Connecticut had actually viewed the web site, the court agreed, finding that a web site accessible in the state constituted purposeful activity by ISI there.[10]

Under this analysis, a company that simply maintains a web site could be subject to jurisdiction wherever the Internet is accessible—which encompasses most of the world. Nothing connected ISI to Connecticut beyond what also connected it to Chiapas, Mexico except the presence of the plaintiff in Connecticut, a fact unknown to ISI.

From a policy perspective, a defendant cannot be subject to universal jurisdiction merely as a result of maintaining a web site if the new technology is to be capable of meaningful use.[11] Something more must exist to satisfy the Supreme Court's requirement that a defendant invoke the benefits and protections of the forum. In the United States, the analytical framework supplied by *Zippo*

---

8. Inset Sys., Inc. v. Instruction Set, Inc., 937 F. Supp. 161 (D. Conn. 1996).

9. *Id.* at 164.

10. *Id.*

11. If each web site subjected its author to universal jurisdiction, many would forego use of the technology for fear of its secondary costs. If these costs were, in practice, nonexistent because judgments rendered by distant courts were not enforced by courts that could seize the person or assets of the defendant, an evolving and necessary system of internationally accepted jurisdictional principles would be undermined. One decision by the British Columbia Court of Appeals does leave the impression that a web site makes a foreign defendant's plea of lack of jurisdiction less likely to succeed; the site means the defendant has portrayed itself as an international actor. *See* Old N. Brewing Co. v. Newlands Servs. Inc. [1998], B.C.J., No. 2474, discussed at Arlan Gates, Paul Tackaberry & Adam Balinsky, *Canadian Law on Jurisdiction in Cyberspace*, *available at* <http://www.kentlaw.edu/cyberlaw/docs/foreign/>, at 3–4. The case itself, however, was simplistic and not dependent upon Internet advertising; it involved the purchase and installation of equipment in the forum by the defendant, as well as losses suffered there by the plaintiff. More troubling is another Canadian decision, *Alteen v. Informix*, [1998] N.J. No. 122, decided by the Newfoundland Supreme Court. Newfoundland investors sued a California company for misrepresentation; jurisdiction was upheld because investment information was available in Canada via the Internet, making Canadian investment foreseeable to the defendant. The site contained no disclaimer, but contact between the parties apparently did not take place in the forum. *See* Gates, at 4, 6. By comparison, if a defendant is already subject to an injunction precluding the use of an infringing mark in the United States, maintenance of a web site accessible in the United States is sufficient if other requirements are met to constitute contempt. *See* Versace, Inc. v. Gianni Versace, S.p.A., 87 F. Supp. 2d 281 (S.D.N.Y. 2000); Playboy Enters., Inc. v. Chuckleberry Publ'g, Inc., 939 F. Supp. 1032 (S.D.N.Y. 1996).

Manufacturing Co. v. Zippo Dot Com, Inc.[12] has become the one most frequently used by lower courts. The *Zippo* court held that whether jurisdiction can be properly asserted depends upon the nature and quality of the defendant's Internet commercial activity or Internet-related contacts:

> At one end of the spectrum are situations where a defendant clearly does business over the Internet. If the defendant enters into contracts with residents of a foreign jurisdiction that involve the knowing and repeated transmission of computer files over the Internet, personal jurisdiction is proper. At the opposite end are situations where a defendant has simply posted information on an Internet Web site which is accessible to users in foreign jurisdictions. A passive Web site that does little more than make information available to those who are interested in it is not grounds for the exercise [of] personal jurisdiction. The middle ground is occupied by interactive Web sites where a user can exchange information with the host computer. In these cases, the exercise of jurisdiction is determined by examining the level of interactivity and commercial nature of the exchange of information that occurs on the Web site.[13]

Under this view, jurisdiction cases fall somewhere on a "sliding scale" or "spectrum" where "the likelihood that personal jurisdiction can be constitutionally exercised is directly proportionate to the nature and quality of commercial activity that an entity conducts over the Internet."[14]

The *Zippo Dot Com* formulation was subsequently adopted[15] by the Ninth Circuit in *Cybersell, Inc. v. Cybersell, Inc.*,[16] which was the first circuit court case to evaluate whether jurisdiction could be obtained over a defendant, consistent with due process, based solely upon the defendant's operation of a passive web site. In *Cybersell, Inc.*, the Ninth Circuit held that jurisdiction could not be constitutionally asserted simply because an out-of-state defendant operated a passive web site accessible to residents of the forum state. The web site at issue displayed the name, logo and local (as opposed to toll-free)[17] telephone number of the defendant and included a link that invited visitors to submit their names to obtain additional information. A contrary result, the court noted, would

---

12. Zippo Mfg. Co. v. Zippo Dot Com, Inc., 952 F. Supp. 1119 (W.D. Pa. 1997).

13. *Id.* at 1124 (citations omitted). The court held that it had jurisdiction over the defendant because Zippo Dot Com had entered contracts with approximately 3,000 Pennsylvania residents and seven Pennsylvania Internet service providers and, therefore, was doing business in the state. *See* ABA SECTION OF PUB. UTIL., COMMUNICATIONS & TRANSP. LAW, 1999 ANNUAL REPORT 217–32 (1999) (arguing that *Zippo*'s three categories are being collapsed into two—passive and interactive).

14. *Zippo*, 952 F. Supp. at 1124.

15. The Ninth Circuit did not expressly state that it accepted the *Zippo Dot Com* court's analysis, but analyzed the facts before it in terms of the three categories outlined there and expressly quoted *Zippo Dot Com*'s analysis of interactive web sites.

16. Cybersell, Inc. v. Cybersell, Inc., 130 F.3d 414 (9th Cir. 1997).

17. The jurisdictional significance of maintaining a toll-free number is questionable. Given the number of different area codes that may exist within a single metropolitan area and the frequency with which people travel on business, it is not unusual for small businesses that operate primarily within a single state (or even county)—such as real estate brokers and mortgage bankers—to maintain toll-free numbers for the convenience of existing and potential clients.

mean that "every complaint arising out of alleged trademark infringement on the Internet would automatically result in personal jurisdiction wherever the plaintiff's principal place of business is located . . . [which] would not comport with traditional notions of what qualifies as purposeful activity invoking the benefits and protections of the forum state."[18]

Under the *Zippo Dot Com/Cybersell, Inc.* guidelines, specific jurisdiction may be found when, in addition to operating a passive web site, a defendant has other contacts with the forum or when its Internet presence allows for some level of commercial interactivity. Mere advertisement on the Web, without more, is insufficient to confer jurisdiction under this analysis.

Courts clearly are convinced that the nature of a defendant's web site is relevant to the jurisdictional issue, but the failure to articulate *why* it is relevant makes it difficult to determine where the jurisdictional line should be drawn in cases that fall between *Zippo*'s two extremes. A recent opinion by Chief Judge Harry Edwards of the D.C. Circuit Court of Appeals provides a glimmer of guidance. *GTE New Media Services, Inc. v. BellSouth Corp., et al.,*[19] involved the application of the District's long-arm statute, which required that, before asserting jurisdiction over a defendant whose activities outside the District caused harm to a plaintiff there, the defendant either regularly do or solicit business there, engage in another persistent course of conduct there or derive substantial revenue from goods used or consumed, or services rendered, there. The court was clear that merely because an interactive web site of the defendant was available to District residents the defendant was not, therefore, automatically subject to the District's jurisdiction. It is not the nature of the site per se that is critical. In certifying its jurisdictional decision for appeal, the district court in *GTE* noted that other cases basing jurisdiction upon an interactive site involved defendants with other contacts with the forum related to the cause of action.

To understand why interactivity is relevant, it is necessary to go back to basic jurisdictional theory. Jurisdiction is about chosen contacts between the defendant and the forum. This is the premise of *Worldwide Volkswagen v. Woodson.*[20] Of course, and as that case indicated, the seller of an automobile could reasonably foresee that the vehicle would be driven in a state other than the one in which it was sold and that, therefore, injury arising from its negligent preparation could occur elsewhere. The seller had no control over where the vehicle was taken by the owner, however, and thus no way to prevent his "contact" with the forum; therefore, there was no jurisdiction in the state where the accident occurred. In much the same way, the author of a passive web site has no way to control the forums to which she is "connected" by the user. Although the maintenance of an interactive site alone may express the author's willingness

---

18. *Cybersell*, 130 F.3d at 420.
19. GTE New Media Servs., Inc. v. BellSouth Corp., et al., 199 F.3d 1343 (D.C. Cir. 2000).
20. Worldwide Volkswagen v. Woodson, 444 U.S. 286 (1980).

to become connected to all forums in which the site is accessible (assuming it does not contain any disclaimers), it does not constitute that connection.[21] Nor, of course, does the mere accessing of the site by forum residents constitute that connection.[22] On the other hand, the site author of an interactive site who does business electronically knows—or can take reasonable steps to discover—the location of the party with whom she is interacting. Once the interactive site is engaged, the defendant can no longer argue persuasively that he did not choose to become connected to the forum of the other party. He may not have intended whatever consequences the plaintiff alleges flowed from that connection, but although that may defeat certain intentional claims against him (libel and trademark infringement, for example) it does not defeat the jurisdictional relevance of the connection.

Reliance, then, upon the interactive nature of the web site alone is misplaced. If an interactive site is not targeted to a specific forum,[23] courts should focus upon how the site is actually used. A nonpresent party's knowing and willing use of it to enter into dealings with persons or businesses in the forum demonstrates a chosen contact with the forum, provides the forum with an interest in the relationships thus created and makes it less likely that multiple forums with different applicable laws will attempt to regulate the site and assert jurisdiction over its author with respect to claims arising out of those relationships.

To date, apparently no other country has focused upon the degree of a site's interactivity in assessing jurisdiction. In part, this may reflect the relative lack of case law outside the United States dealing with e-commerce. But in part its irrelevance may be systemic; if the central issue is where acts occurred rather than what choices a defendant has made, interactivity would be relevant only in determining whether, for example, a transfer of digital property was "performed" at the seller's or buyer's terminal.[24]

---

21. This was the insight of the court in *Millennium Enterprises, Inc. v. Millennium Music LP*, 33 F. Supp. 2d 907 (D. Or. 1999), which refused to conflate the potential of doing business on an interactive site with citizens of the state with actually doing such business. *See also* Rothschild Berry Farm v. Serendipity Group LLC, 84 F. Supp. 2d 904 (S.D. Ohio 1999) (interactive site not utilized by forum residents insufficient to sustain assertion of personal jurisdiction in trademark infringement claim).

22. Following the *Inset* opinion, the court in *Maritz v. CyberGold, Inc.*, 947 F. Supp. 1328 (E.D. Mo. 1996), found relevant the number of "hits" on the defendant's site by forum residents. The case involved trademark infringement, so the number of Missouri residents who saw the site, and thus the injury to the plaintiff in Missouri, was important. There are problems with relying upon this case, however. First, there was no indication that the defendant intentionally sought to infringe the trademark, the issue another court found dispositive. *See* Bensusan Rest. Corp. v. King, 937 F. Supp. 295 (S.D.N.Y. 1996), *aff'd*, 126 F.3d 25 (2d Cir. 1997). Second, the numbers are unreliable and ultimately unhelpful. Not all addresses (which is how those who come to the site are identified) are geographically located, not all those who visit a site do so from their own address and not all addresses belong to different visitors. Finally, the number of visitors from a given forum, even if known, really does not say anything about the importance of that forum to the site sponsor. In *CyberGold*, the court was swayed by 131 hits from Missouri. The significance of the number is unclear.

23. If a site is so targeted, the forum may assert jurisdiction over its author and its content, pursuant to *Asahi* and *Calder*.

24. The difficulty in sensibly "locating" acts in cyberspace was at the center of one of the first seminal articles on jurisdictional issues in this new era. David R. Johnson & David G. Post, *Law and Borders—The Rise of Law in Cyberspace*, 48 Stan. L. Rev. 1367 (1996).

All the situations discussed thus far involve assertions of what is called *specific* or *special jurisdiction*. The contacts the defendant has with the forum or certain acts there are sufficient to permit jurisdiction to be asserted in connection with related claims, but are presumptively insufficient to permit jurisdiction to be asserted in connection with claims that have no relationship to those contacts or acts. *General jurisdiction*, on the other hand, describes jurisdictional assertions that are proper—no matter what claim is brought against the defendant—because of the extent and nature of the defendant's contacts with the forum.[25]

For the most part, courts agree that the maintenance of a web site outside the forum, even when coupled with sales in the forum, is insufficient to sustain an assertion of general jurisdiction.[26] Apparently, only one court has found an assertion of general jurisdiction over a nonresident defendant to be proper, based, in part, upon its Internet contacts with the forum. In *Mieczkowski v. Masco Corp.*,[27] a federal court in Texas asserted jurisdiction over a North Carolina manufacturer of children's beds, although the bed that allegedly caused the death of the plaintiff's son had been sold by the defendant to a third party in Washington, D.C., who thereafter sold it to the plaintiff in Virginia. The defendant, however, sold the same product to Texas residents and maintained a web site from which its products could be ordered. Although the plaintiff's claim clearly had nothing to do with those contacts, had an identical claim arisen from the sale of a bed to a Texas resident, the court's jurisdiction over that claim would have been unquestioned. Given that the burden of defending the plaintiff's suit was no different from the burden of defending a suit arising from the sale of a bed in Texas, which the defendant had already assumed, due process arguably was thus not offended by the assertion of general jurisdiction. In one sense, this is not "true" general jurisdiction, but a limited variety of it, justified by the similarity between the actual claim and the specific jurisdiction that could be asserted.[28]

In one other situation, jurisdiction may be asserted against a defendant who lacks contacts with the forum relevant to the claim. In 1990, a unanimous Supreme Court held that jurisdiction was proper when the defendant was personally served with process while in the forum (so-called *tag jurisdiction*).[29]

---

25. The easiest example is that of a state asserting jurisdiction over one of its own domiciliaries. If a domiciliary of Illinois contracts with a domiciliary of Indiana for the provision of services in California, the Indiana plaintiff could institute suit in California, where the services were to be performed, but for convenience might well prefer to bring suit closer to her home. Jurisdiction over the Illinois domiciliary in Indiana would not be proper because the defendant has no contacts with that forum and the contractual performance was not to occur there, but an assertion of jurisdiction by Illinois would be consistent with due process. Blackmer v. United States, 284 U.S. 421 (1932) (absent U.S. citizen is subject to jurisdiction of U.S. courts); Milliken v. Meyer, 311 U.S. 457 (1940) (absent state citizen is subject to exercise of personal jurisdiction by that state's courts); Brussels Convention, *supra* note 3, tit. II, § 1, art. 2. *See also* HITOSHI ODA, JAPANESE LAW 295 (2d ed. 1999).

26. *See* Digital Equip. v. Altavista Tech., 960 F. Supp. 456 (D. Mass. 1997).

27. Mieczkowski v. Masco Corp., 997 F. Supp. 782 (E.D. Texas 1998).

28. *See* Buckeye Boiler Co. v. Superior Court, 458 P.2d 57 (Cal. 1969).

29. Burnham v. Superior Court, 495 U.S. 604 (1990).

Technology does not change this basis of jurisdiction; the requirement is personal service on the real—not virtual—person of the defendant in the forum.

Under the Brussels Convention, tag jurisdiction is prohibited by article 3. That article itself, however, reveals that the national laws of many of the contracting states do permit its assertion.[30]

3. Contractual Choice of Forum

The complexities of the law of personal jurisdiction in cases involving e-commerce may, in some instances, be obviated by prior agreement between the parties, just as they have been historically. Such an agreement may simply express a party's consent to be sued in a specific forum (usually the home of the other party),[31] or it may identify the only forum in which litigation concerning the contract shall be filed.[32] In either instance, there may be difficulty regarding the validity of the agreement under the applicable law of contract, but if contractually valid, it governs the location of the litigation. That validity may be problematic, however.

Many contracts between consumers and vendors (both offline and online) are not negotiable and are drafted by the vendor. Consumer advocates and consumer protection agencies want to ensure that, to the extent online contracts are premised upon unequal bargaining power and pressure to buy (or violate fundamental public policy), provisions of these contracts can be overridden by local law.

Under U.S. law, *adhesion contracts* (unilaterally drafted form agreements) are enforceable absent a finding of unfairness or unconscionability. Both terms are susceptible to many meanings. "Unfairness" often means that the weaker party is not in a position to shop around for better terms, or that the weaker party is so bereft of bargaining power that he has no real choice. "Unconscionability" often means that terms are grossly unreasonable in light of the mores and business practices of the time. A finding that a given contract is a contract of adhesion is the beginning of the analysis, not the end, and courts try to distinguish enforceable adhesion contracts from unenforceable ones.

Such clauses are not enforced in European countries in business-to-consumer transactions unless they favor the consumer.[33] Australia also is more reluctant to enforce such clauses against consumers than it is when the objecting

---

30. *See generally* Kevin M. Clermont, *Jurisdictional Salvation and the Hague Treaty*, 85 Cornell L. Rev. 89, 91–95 (1999).
31. National Equip. Rental, Ltd. v. Szukhent, 375 U.S. 311 (1964).
32. Carnival Cruise Lines, Inc. v. Shute, 499 U.S. 585 (1991).
33. They are enforceable, however, in business-to-business contracts. Brussels Convention, *supra* note 3, art. 17.

party is a business, particularly in the international context when, absent such a clause, Australian consumer protection laws would apply.[34] Japan, on the other hand, will enforce such clauses unless they are "too unreasonable and contrary to public policy."[35]

The U.S. Supreme Court opinion upholding such a contractual clause, *Carnival Cruise Lines, Inc. v. Shute*,[36] involved Washington passengers on a cruise ship that departed from California. The contract (found on the back of the ticket) chose Florida as the exclusive location for litigation and was upheld.[37] Interestingly, however, the Court did not simply rely upon a prior case, *The M/S Bremen v. Zapata Off-Shore Co.*, which upheld such a clause in an international contract between two businesses.[38] Instead, it noted, but distinguished, *Bremen*'s recognition that "the serious inconvenience of the contractual forum to one or both of the parties might carry greater weight in determining the reasonableness of the forum clause."[39] Although the U.S. home forum of a seller may be presumptively reasonable in a dispute with a U.S. consumer (although in *Carnival Cruise Lines*, the reasonableness of Florida was enhanced because the accident that gave rise to the lawsuit occurred off the coast of Mexico), its reasonableness may not be as apparent if the consumer is domiciled abroad. Similarly, U.S. courts might be reluctant to find the choice of a foreign seller's home reasonable in a contract featuring a U.S. consumer. It is at least possible that, in the international context, the positions of the United States and other countries are not as far apart as they presume.

§ 8.2 Prescriptive Jurisdiction

1. Constitutional and Other Local Restraints

Prescriptive jurisdiction is the authority of a state to apply its own law to regulate conduct. Clearly, this is critical to the global nature of e-commerce, but it is

---

34. *See Comments-Australia*, submitted by Stephen Jacques Mallesons, at 3.58 *et seq.*, *available at* <http://www.kentlaw.edu/cyberlaw/docs/foreign/> [hereinafter Mallesons].

35. Joseph W.S. Davis, Dispute Resolution in Japan 197 (1996).

36. Carnival Cruise Lines, Inc. v. Shute, 499 U.S. 585 (1991).

37. Not surprisingly, "click-wrap" agreements—the online equivalent of ticket retention—are also upheld. *See* Lieschke v. RealNetworks Inc., 2000 U.S. Dist. LEXIS 1683 (N.D. Ill. Feb. 10, 2000); In re RealNetworks Inc. Privacy Litigation, 2000 U.S. Dist. LEXIS 6584 (N.D. Ill. May 11, 2000).

38. The M/S Bremen v. Zapata Off-Shore Co., 407 U.S. 1 (1972) (enforcing contractual choice of London Court of Justice in connection with suit between an American and a German company concerning towing of drilling rig from Louisiana to Italy).

39. *Id.* at 17.

particularly germane to industries such as banking and securities, which are highly regulated. When such jurisdiction exists, entities subject to that law are compelled to comply with it; failure to do so leads to litigation, enforcement or incarceration, which may involve a dispute about the jurisdiction itself.

Frequently, a court capable of asserting personal jurisdiction over a defendant can also properly apply local law to the dispute. There are situations, however, in which such conjunction does not exist, either because the basis of personal jurisdiction is unconnected to activities in the forum related to the claim or because another state has a manifestly greater interest in the dispute recognized by the forum.

In the United States, two constitutional provisions are frequently considered relevant to the question of whether a state may exercise prescriptive jurisdiction: the Due Process Clause[40] and the Full Faith and Credit Clause.[41] In fact, only the former restrains a state's choice to apply its own law. Full faith and credit requires the courts of one state to recognize and apply the substantive law of another state when the forum state has no law of its own to apply. It does not appear, as a matter of U.S. constitutional law, that either clause prohibits a state from preferring its own law to that of a sister state when the forum state has both prescriptive jurisdiction and substantive law to apply.[42] Any other reading would prevent a state from using its own law whenever that of another state could constitutionally apply—an irrational result that the Supreme Court has never required. If forum state law is not applicable, however, whether because its choice is constitutionally precluded by the Due Process Clause or because the law on its own terms is not applicable, the Full Faith and Credit Clause prevents a state from refusing to accept otherwise proper jurisdiction merely because the claim is to be decided under the law of another state.[43]

The restriction that due process imposes upon a state's assertion of prescriptive jurisdiction is easily met. There must be a reasonable connection between the state and the transaction.[44] Rarely is such a connection lacking; in

---

40. U.S. Const. amend. XIV, § 1 ("No State shall ... deprive any person of life, liberty, or property, without due process of law.").

41. U.S. Const. art. IV, § 1 ("Full Faith and Credit shall be given in each State to the public Acts, Records, and judicial Proceedings of every other State."). This clause is most familiar to U.S. lawyers because of its requirement that one state enforce a valid judgment of another state, but by its terms it also defines the recognition one state must give to another's laws.

42. The precepts of international law, according to section 403 of the *Restatement (Third) of Foreign Relations Law of the United States*, may require one state to abstain from applying its own law when another state has a stronger claim to the application of its law.

43. Hughes v. Fetter, 341 U.S. 609 (1951). This case neatly demonstrates the disjunction between subject matter jurisdiction and prescriptive jurisdiction, a line blurred by a majority of the Supreme Court in *Hartford Fire Insurance Co. v. California*, 509 U.S. 764 (1993). State courts are presumed to have subject matter jurisdiction over private transitory claims; federal courts have similar jurisdiction in diversity cases. Whether the state law of the state in which the court sits may be used does not affect the existence of that jurisdiction. If either a private or public nonfrivolous claim is brought in federal court because the plaintiff alleges it arises out of federal law, and the court determines that law is inapplicable, the case should be dismissed for failure to state a claim upon which relief may be granted.

44. Home Ins. Co. v. Dick, 281 U.S. 397 (1930). The case involved an attempt by Texas to use its statute of limitations in deciding an insurance claim between Mexican parties based upon a policy issued in Mexico covering a vessel in Mexican waters. The attempt was held to violate the defendant's right to due process by increasing its obligation to the plaintiff under a law that had no connection to the claim. (The plaintiff was

fact, the Supreme Court's jurisprudence related to this due process limitation is conspicuously undeveloped compared with its complex personal jurisdiction matrix.[45] In *Allstate Insurance Co. v. Hague*,[46] for example, Allstate insured a Wisconsin citizen killed in a Wisconsin car accident; the deceased's widow moved to Minnesota after the accident, was appointed there as his personal representative and sued there for a declaratory judgment of the defendant's liability on the policy, which had been issued in Wisconsin. Minnesota was permitted to apply Minnesota law to determine liability. Relevant contacts included the fact that the deceased had worked in Minnesota, Allstate was doing business in the state, its alleged obligation was to a current resident of Minnesota and Allstate could not legitimately have expected only Wisconsin law to apply to the policy (had the accident occurred outside Wisconsin, or had the deceased moved from Wisconsin before his death, another state's law could obviously have applied). Just why these contacts were relevant to anything other than the convenience of the plaintiff is unclear; in dissent, Justice Powell argued that to be sufficient, the contacts must form a link between the litigation and state policy.[47]

Given the wide variety of conduct over which a state may constitutionally exercise control, a state must frequently determine whether its law or that of another state applies. The doctrine used to make such a determination is known as *choice of law*. Choice-of-law rules, however, are themselves informed by international law restraints.

Although Story treated conflict of laws as a subject of international law (and today the subject is often referred to as private international law), it is local—or as international lawyers say, "municipal"—in an important respect. The choice-of-law rule that determines whether the substantive law of another sovereign applies to a particular controversy is the law of the forum. The analysis used depends upon the choice-of-law doctrine of the sovereign in which the court deciding the case sits. When two states may legitimately exercise prescriptive jurisdiction over the same transaction or conduct, and the contents of the laws emanating from the two sovereigns differ, a tribunal deciding a dispute related to the transaction or conduct must choose which law to apply. If another sovereign purports to apply its substantive law to aspects of a controversy, and that application exceeds the extent of prescriptive jurisdiction permitted by

---

a Texas citizen who had been assigned the claim against the insurance company.) *See also* Phillips Petroleum Co. v. Shutts, 472 U.S. 797 (1985).

45. The Supreme Court's apparent reluctance to impose meaningful restraints upon a state's assertion of prescriptive jurisdiction may contribute to the strictness with which it reviews assertions of personal jurisdiction. In *Hanson v. Denckla*, 357 U.S. 235 (1958), had the court of Florida been able to obtain jurisdiction over the Delaware trustee, it would have used Florida law to find that the trust agreement, entered by a then-citizen of Pennsylvania and the Delaware bank, was invalid under Florida law (it had been "republished" there when the grantor exercised her power of appointment under the trust agreement). Clearly, use of Florida law to determine the validity of an agreement entered in Delaware is not intuitively logical, but it is constitutional.

46. Allstate Ins. Co. v. Hague, 449 U.S. 302 (1981).

47. *Id.* at 334.

international law, a second sovereign is unlikely to recognize the first sovereign's decision as regulating the controversy.

Before turning to a discussion of those international restraints and their reflection in various doctrines, it must be noted that the terminology used in much conflict-of-laws writing can be confusing. Conflicts writers usually talk about the jurisdiction of "courts," and assess the relationship between "parties" and states. The practices of many lawyers, and many jurisdiction problems, involve not the regular courts, but administrative agencies, and not parties in the sense of corporations or individuals, but regulators. It is important to understand that all the analysis in this section relating to the jurisdiction of courts also applies to administrative agencies and that parties include agencies and government officers as well as private citizens and corporations.

2. The Restraint of International Law

Although the U.S. Supreme Court has never held that the Constitution precludes an assertion of jurisdiction in violation of international law,[48] it has long held that congressional legislation is presumed to be enacted in accordance with that law and will be interpreted in violation of it only if no other recourse is open to the court.[49] A second canon of statutory construction, reflecting an original principle of international law, is that congressional enactments are presumed to apply only to conduct undertaken within the territory of the United States.[50] Instances in which this second presumption are overcome exceed those in which the first is turned aside, presumably in large measure because international law itself has come to acknowledge the propriety of certain assertions of jurisdiction beyond the territory of the regulating sovereign.[51]

International law requires a basis for the exercise of prescriptive jurisdiction. The four currently acknowledged bases are set forth in section 402 of the *Restatement (Third) of Foreign Relations Law:* conduct within a nation's territory, nationality, effects within a nation's territory and protective jurisdiction (jurisdiction of any state to punish a limited number of offenses directed against the security or integrity of a state).[52] By far the most controversial basis of prescrip-

---

48. Similarly, the Australian constitution does not itself limit the extraterritorial reach of the Australian parliament, although Australia does use its principles of private international law to determine the law applicable to a dispute. *See* Mallesons, *supra* note 34, at 2.13, 2.18.

49. Murray v. Schooner Charming Betsy, 6 U.S. 64 (1804).

50. Foley Bros., Inc. v. Filardo, 336 U.S. 281 (1949).

51. The territoriality principle was the foundation of prescriptive jurisdiction, and expansions of the doctrine may be seen as exceptions to this basic principle. Thus, 170 years ago, Joseph Story in the first *Conflict of Laws* treatise, observed that the starting point for the subject is the territorial limits of law. Joseph A. Story, Conflict of Laws 8 (2d ed. 1883).

52. For a rare example of the latter basis, see *United States v. Bin Laden*, 92 F. Supp. 2d 189 (S.D.N.Y. 2000), which upheld the application of U.S. antiterrorism statutes to acts of foreign nationals committed abroad that resulted in the death of U.S. nationals (among others) and the destruction of U.S. property

tive jurisdiction is the effect that conduct undertaken outside a state has within the state asserting jurisdiction.[53] The *Restatement (Third) of Foreign Relations Law*, however, precludes assertion of jurisdiction on any basis if its exercise would be "unreasonable" and lists a nonexhaustive set of factors to be considered in reaching that conclusion.[54] This parallels the approach that first surfaced in *Lauritzen v. Larsen*,[55] and that was adopted by numerous lower courts following *Timberlane Lumber Co. v. Bank of America*.[56] The Supreme Court's most recent foray into the area, however, apparently rejects the notion that such a balancing test—which takes into account the interests of various nations in the litigation and very much resembles the domestic conflict-of-laws approach—is required.

In *Hartford Fire Insurance Co. v. California*,[57] the Sherman Act—previously held to apply to conduct that occurred outside the United States but was intended to, and did, produce substantial effects in the United States[58]—was held by the majority to apply to such conduct whether or not the interests of another country (in this instance, Britain, where the conduct occurred and where it was apparently in accordance with national policy) could be considered to outweigh those of the United States. Writing for five members of the Court, Justice Souter held that international comity would argue against the assertion of jurisdiction only when there was a "true conflict" between the laws of the relevant nations, and that such a conflict exists only if compliance with both laws is impossible.[59]

Of course, because an effect in the United States would quite clearly satisfy the constitutional requirements of due process, and because courts construing the extraterritorial reach of U.S. law are attempting to ascertain the intent of Congress (which is only presumed not to desire to violate international law),

---

(embassies). Section 404 of the *Restatement (Third) of Foreign Relations Law* also recognizes universal jurisdiction—the authority of any state to punish "certain offenses recognized by the community of nations as of universal concern, such as piracy, slave trade, attacks on or hijacking of aircraft, genocide, war crimes, and perhaps certain acts of terrorism."

    53. The basis is accepted in international law, even though its use in certain circumstances by the United States has been criticized. *See generally* John A. Trenor, *Jurisdiction and the Extraterritorial Application of Antitrust Laws after Hartford Fire*, 62 U. Chi. L. Rev. 1583, 1601 (1995).

    54.   (a) the needs of the interstate and international systems,

        (b) the relevant policies of the forum,

        (c) the relevant policies of other interested states and the relative interests of those states in the determination of the particular issue,

        (d) the protection of justified expectations,

        (e) the basic policies underlying the particular field of law,

        (f) certainty, predictability and uniformity of result, and

        (g) ease in the determination and application of the law to be applied.

Restatement (Third) of Foreign Relations Law § 403 (1987).

    55. Lauritzen v. Larsen, 345 U.S. 571 (1953).

    56. Timberlane Lumber Co. v. Bank of Am., 549 F.2d 597 (9th Cir. 1976).

    57. Hartford Fire Ins. Co. v. California, 509 U.S. 764 (1993).

    58. Matsushita Elec. Indus. Co. v. Zenith Radio Corp., 475 U.S. 574 (1986); United States v. Aluminum Co. of Am., 148 F.2d 416 (2d Cir. 1945).

    59. *Hartford,* 509 U.S. at 769. In dissent, Justice Scalia maintained that a conflict exists whenever states provide different substantive rules of decision, and that the majority misread section 403(3) of the *Restatement (Third) of Foreign Relations Law;* it does indeed command deference only when compliance with both laws is impossible, but it presupposes that the interest balancing mandated by section 403(2) has already taken place.

the fact that effects in the United States may be sufficient in the eyes of the court does not necessarily mean they satisfy international law. At least some support for this basis of jurisdiction can be found in Europe,[60] however, and the need for—as well as the wisdom of—interest balancing is debatable.

On the other hand, even though Congress could intend the broadest possible reach for U.S. law, it obviously need not. For example, Title VII of the Civil Rights Act of 1964[61] was interpreted by the Supreme Court not to extend its protection to U.S. employees employed abroad by U.S. employers,[62] although under the nationality principle such jurisdiction would clearly be proper. Similarly, although a nation clearly may regulate conduct that occurs in its territory, not all such conduct is, in fact, subject to U.S. law.[63]

When a court confronts a choice-of-law problem, it, in effect, asks itself, "Is this dispute within the prescriptive jurisdiction of more than one sovereign?" If it is, the court then asks if more than one jurisdiction has expressed the intent that its substantive law extend to the disputed transaction or conduct. If the answer is yes, the court returns to an assessment of the same kinds of interests considered in prescriptive jurisdiction analysis.

3. U.S. and European Approaches to Choice of Law

If more than one country can—consistent with domestic and international law—assert prescriptive jurisdiction, the choice between the laws is determined by the forum's choice-of-law doctrine. That doctrine has followed very different paths in the United States and Europe. In the United States, formal approaches exemplified by the law of the place of the wrong (lex loci delicti) for torts, the law of the place of contracting (lex contractu) for contracts and the law of the situs of property (lex sitae rei) for property disputes has largely been replaced by more flexible approaches that analyze contacts between the dispute and contending sovereigns, supplemented by an interest approach that examines the interests of competing sovereigns in having their own law applied to particular issues in controversy.[64] Thus, section 6 of the *Restatement (Second) of Conflict of Laws*, followed by most states, directs a court's attention, absent a

---

60. *See supra* note 52.

61. 42 U.S.C. § 2000e–2000e-17 (1972).

62. EEOC v. Arabian Am. Oil Co., 499 U.S. 244 (1991). The decision was overturned by the passage of an amendment to the Civil Rights Act. 42 U.S.C. § 2000e(f) (1991); Pub. L. No. 102–166, 105 Stat. 1071 (1991).

63. *See, e.g.*, Europe & Overseas Commodity Traders, S.A. v. Banque Paribas London, 147 F.3d 118 (2d Cir. 1998) (U.S. securities laws not applicable to sale of foreign securities made in Florida by foreign corporation to another foreign entity's president). For a discussion of the varying approaches of circuit courts to the reach of the securities laws, see *Kauthar SDN BHD v. Sternberg*, 149 F.3d 659 (7th Cir. 1998).

64. The formal U.S. approach is associated with the *Restatement (First) of Conflict of Laws* and Joseph Henry Beale, its reporter. The newer approach is identified with Brainerd Currie and the *Restatement (Second) of Conflict of Laws*.

statutory directive, to concerns similar to those found in section 403 of the *Restatement (Third) of Foreign Relations Law*.[65] There is much debate among U.S. conflict-of-laws scholars about what should be done to clarify a set of doctrines that are perceived as being unsatisfactory because they are so unpredictable. Europe—especially Germany—still adheres to a more formal approach that resembles in its basic rules the approach of the U.S. *Restatement (First) of Conflict of Laws*. So, too, does Japan, where the place of the relevant act, without consideration of "various nexuses," governs.[66] Thus, in tort cases, for example, the applicable law is that of the place where the facts giving rise to the claim arose, and in contract cases, absent party choice, the governing law is that of the place where the offer was dispatched.[67]

The differences between the U.S. approach and the European and Japanese approaches are more theoretical than real, however. In torts, for instance, the substantive law that is applied under modern contacts or interests analysis in the United States most often is the same law that would be applied under lex loci delicti. Moreover, during the era when lex loci delicti was the norm, a variety of avoidance mechanisms were used to make the formal rule more flexible, including characterization of some issues as procedural and therefore always subject to the law of the forum, as opposed to substantive and thus within the scope of the lex loci delicti rule. As another example, the doctrine of *renvoi* was used to change the outcome. Under the purportedly formal approaches, questions regularly arise about where the harm occurred for application of the tort choice-of-law rule.

4. The Internet and International Law

The interesting question, then, is whether characteristics of Internet transactions necessitate new approaches to choice of law, which have not been adopted

---

65. Compare section 403(a) of the *Restatement (Third) of Foreign Relations Law*, *supra* note 54, with the following section of the *Restatement (Second) of Conflict of Laws*:

> d. Needs of the interstate and international systems. Probably the most important function of choice-of-law rules is to make the interstate and international systems work well. Choice-of-law rules, among other things, should seek to further harmonious relations between states and to facilitate commercial intercourse between them. In formulating rules of choice of law, a state should have regard for the needs and policies of other states and of the community of states. Rules of choice of law formulated with regard for such needs and policies are likely to commend themselves to other states and to be adopted by these states. Adoption of the same choice-of-law rules by many states will further the needs of the interstate and international systems and likewise the values of certainty, predictability and uniformity of result.

RESTATEMENT (SECOND) OF CONFLICT OF LAWS § 6 cmt. (d) (1971).

66. ODA, *supra* note 25, at 443.

67. Tokushige Yoshimura, *Jurisdiction Research, available at* <http://www.kentlaw.edu/cyberlaw>.

under the pressure of earlier forms of commerce. The possibility of economic burdens arising from differing requirements imposed by multiple jurisdictions is not new with e-commerce on the Internet. The Internet does complicate matters, however, because the typical facts of a political or commercial transaction conducted through the Internet support competing inferences regarding the place and time of the transaction. (Where is a web page located? Where it is viewed on a client computer, or where the server transmitting the code is located? Is a transaction completed when the server transmits a web page, or when a client transmits the URL that automatically causes the page to be transmitted from a remote server?) Much of this difficulty is encompassed by the argument about which law should be applied to e-commerce disputes involving consumers—the law of the place of origin or the law of the place where the consumer is located.

It also can be argued that the Internet's inherently global reach justifies special efforts to reduce uncertainty concerning choice of law. Pre-Internet modes of doing business make it relatively easy to limit business to those states where the seller is willing to comply with the local law protecting consumers in that state. With the Internet, a seller must undertake extraordinary steps to limit the reach of its solicitation of customers and receipt of customer orders; the Internet does not naturally associate either sellers or buyers with physical places. Technology, however, may be used to redress the jurisdictional issues raised by the technological efficiencies and global reach of the Internet. The existence and continuing development of intelligent electronic agents— which can be deployed by sellers and purchasers to evaluate the relative product, price and jurisdictional terms of the potential relationship—provide a basis for a global standard, so long as the underlying legal "code" can be agreed upon.

It should be noted that choice of law and personal jurisdiction interact. Whether a court gets the chance to apply its own choice-of-law rule depends upon whether that court has personal jurisdiction. If it adjudicates the case and applies its choice-of-law rule, which rejects application of the substantive law of another sovereign and causes the substantive law of the forum sovereign to be applied, the efficacy of that decision depends upon whether the court had personal jurisdiction. If the judgment debtor (usually the defendant) has no assets within the forum sovereign state, the judgment must be enforced in a sovereign state where the judgment debtor does have assets. The court of that sovereign is entitled to reassess the question of personal jurisdiction in deciding whether to recognize—and then to enforce—the first judgment. If the court in the second sovereign determines that the first court lacked personal jurisdiction, the choice of law made by the first court is defeated.

§ 8.3 Enforcement Jurisdiction

Enforcement of a judgment generally can be had only in a forum in which assets belonging to the defendant can be found and, pursuant to a court order of that forum, seized by the executive arm of government and sold, with the proceeds given to the plaintiff in satisfaction of the judgment.[68] As jurisdiction is exercised more frequently over defendants not physically present in the state rendering the initial judgment, the need to involve other states in the enforcement of judgments increases.[69]

Enforcement of a judgment rendered by another forum requires its recognition by courts of the forum requested to enforce it. If the judgment is that of a U.S. state court, the Full Faith and Credit Clause of the Constitution[70] requires that it be recognized and enforced by the courts of all other states if it was rendered in accordance with due process (that is, if the court rendering it had personal jurisdiction over the defendant). A defendant who defaulted may argue to the court requested to enforce the judgment that the rendering court lacked such jurisdiction; if she so convinces the court, the judgment will not be enforced.[71] If, however, the defendant argued in the first forum that the court lacked personal jurisdiction, and the defendant lost, he may not relitigate the issue in the court from which enforcement is sought; his only recourse is to appeal the first court's decision in the courts of that forum.[72]

When the judgment for which recognition is sought has been rendered by a foreign court, its recognition depends upon local statutory law[73] or comity.[74] Basically, these sources of law require recognition unless the party opposing it

---

68. Exceptions to this include situations where regulatory agencies seek to enforce judgments issued or obtained against entities not currently in the forum through the prohibition of their activities in the forum.

69. Typically, although not necessarily, the forum asked to enforce a foreign judgment is the defendant's home state, where he is clearly subject to personal jurisdiction and where his assets are likely to be found. Other forums, however, in which his assets are located may also be asked to enforce the judgment. Jurisdiction there is satisfied because the property in the state constitutes a purposeful contact with it and the claim is, even after *Shaffer v. Heitner*, 433 U.S. 186 (1977), sufficiently related to the property to make an exercise of jurisdiction reasonable.

70. U.S. Const. art. IV, § 1.

71. Pennoyer v. Neff, 95 U.S. 714 (1877). If, however, she loses her jurisdictional argument, the judgment will be enforced; she may not litigate the merits of the claim underlying the default judgment.

72. Baldwin v. Iowa State Traveling Men's Ass'n, 283 U.S. 522 (1931).

73. *See, e.g.*, The Uniform Foreign Money Judgments Recognition Act, 13 U.L.A. 261 (1962) (adopted by about half the states).

74. *See* de law Mata v. American Life Ins. Co., 771 F. Supp. 1375 (D. Del. 1991). Canada also bases the recognition and enforcement of foreign judgments upon notions of comity, although it does require reciprocal recognition of valid Canadian judgments. *See* Old N. State Brewing Co. v. Newlands Servs. Inc. [1998] B.C.J., No. 2474. Of course, such recognition will be disallowed if the rendering court lacked jurisdiction in the opinion of the Canadian court. *See* Braintech, Inc. v. Kostiuk [1999] B.C.J., No. 622, discussed at Gates, *supra* note 11, at 4 (British Columbia Court of Appeals refused to enforce default Texas libel judgment in dispute between two British Columbia domiciliaries because presence of defamatory material on site accessible in

can show violations of procedural due process,[75] lack of personal jurisdiction by the rendering court[76] or, in rare instances, violations of public policy in the recognition state.[77]

Not all nations rely solely upon common or international law notions of comity to determine the circumstances under which judgments of foreign courts will be enforced. In Australia, for example, the common law permits recognition and enforcement of foreign money judgments if the defendant either resided in the forum whose courts render the judgment or submitted to that court's jurisdiction. Otherwise, final and conclusive foreign judgments are recognized and enforced pursuant to section 7 of the Foreign Judgments Act of 1991 (Cth), which specifies courts and countries covered by it and is dependent upon reciprocal recognition and enforcement of Australian judgments.[78]

National procedures required for recognition and enforcement of judgments vary widely, both in detail and complexity. Whether reciprocal recognition is required and what that requirement entails differ from country to country. Some countries will not recognize a default judgment, whereas others will.[79] One of the most beneficial potentials of the draft Hague Convention is its dual nature: judgments rendered by a contracting state in accordance with its jurisdictional rules are enforceable in all contracting states.[80]

Because in all instances enforcement of foreign judgments depends upon the existence of personal jurisdiction in the rendering state, agreement between nation-states in particular concerning what that jurisdiction necessitates is critical to effective judicial dispute resolution involving parties from different states.

Texas did not provide "real and substantial connection" between claim or defendant and Texas). Of course, the degree of procedural difficulty may vary widely, even if underlying principles are similar. Both Brazil and Columbia, for example, have quite elaborate statutory requirements for recognition. *See* Noronha Advogados, *A Brazilian Perspective* §§ 5.1.2, 5.4.1, *available at* <http://www.kentlaw.edu/cyberlaw/docs/foreign/>; Luisa Gamboa, *Colombian Comments*, *available at* <http://www.kentlaw.edu/cyberlaw/docs/foreign/>.

75. *See, e.g.*, Bridgeway Corp. v. Citibank, 201 F.3d 134 (2d Cir. 2000) (refusing to enforce final judgment of Supreme Court of Liberia rendered during period in which Liberian judicial system was described by U.S. State Department as corrupt and incompetent).

76. Although one state is bound by another's determination of its own jurisdiction, courts asked to enforce foreign judgments typically feel free to reconsider the existence of jurisdiction in the rendering state.

77. *See* Matusevitch v. Telnikoff, 877 F. Supp. 1 (D.D.C. 1995) (refusing to recognize and enforce British libel judgment because British libel law lacked constitutional protections applied in United States).

78. Mallesons, *supra* note 34, at 2.20 *et seq.*

79. *See generally* ENFORCEMENT OF FOREIGN JUDGMENTS (Dennis Campell ed., LLP Limited 1997).

80. Hague Convention, *supra* note 1.

Bibliography

Advertising

Better Business Bureau Code of Advertising, *at* <http://www.bbb.org/advertising/adcode.asp>.

Better Business Bureau Code of Online Business Practices, *at* <http://www.bbbonline.org/code/code.as>.

Federal Trade Commission, *at* <http://www.ftc.gov>.

Interactive Advertising Bureau, *at* <http://www.iab.net>.

Robert Pitofsky, Self-Regulation and Antitrust, Remarks at the D.C. Bar Association Symposium (Feb. 18, 1998).

GEORGE ERIC ROSDEN & PETER E. ROSDEN, THE LAW OF ADVERTISING (1990).

Internet-Related Litigation and Administrative Proceedings Announcements, Securities and Exchange Commission, *at* <http://www.sec.gov/divisions/enforce/internetenforce/litreleases.shtml>.

Archived Internet-Related Litigation and Administrative Proceedings Announcements, Securities and Exchange Commission, *at* <http://www.sec.gov/divisions/enforce/internetenforce/internetlitrelold.shtml>.

Anonymity and Encryption

Roger Clarke, Identified, Anonymous and Pseudonymous Transactions: The Spectrum of Choice, Presentation at the User Identification & Privacy Protection Conference, Stockholm (June 14–15, 1999), *available at* <http://www.anu.edu.au/people/Roger.Clarke/DV/UIPP99.html>.

Daniel J. Greenwood & Ray A. Campbell, *Electronic Commerce Legislation: From Written on Paper and Signed in Ink to Electronic Records and Online Authentication,* 53 BUS. LAW. 307 (1997).

M. E. Kabay, Ph.D., Anonymity and Pseudonymity in Cyberspace: Deindividuation, Incivility and Lawlessness Versus Freedom and Privacy, Paper Presented at the Annual Conference of the European Institute for Computer Anti-Virus Research (EICAR), Munich, Germany (March 1998).

Antitrust Regulation

David A. Balto, *Emerging Antitrust Issues in Electronic Commerce,* 19 J. OF PUBLIC POLICY & MARKETING 2 (2000).

Robert B. Bell & William F. Adkinson, Jr., *Antitrust Issues Raised by B2B Exchanges*, 15 ANTITRUST 18 (2000).

Dennis W. Carlton, *Practical Strategies for Doing Business on the Web: Economic Analysis of Antitrust Issues Raised by E-Commerce*, 1236 PLI/CORP 91 (March 2001).

Jeffery Church & Roger Ware, *Network Industries, Intellectual Property Rights and Competition Policy*, in COMPETITION POLICY AND INTELLECTUAL PROPERTY RIGHTS IN THE KNOWLEDGE-BASED ECONOMY (Robert D. Anderson & Nancy T. Gallinin eds., 1998).

Harry S. Davis, *Practical Strategies for Doing Business on the Web: To B2B or Not to B2B, That Is the Antitrust Question: An Introduction to Antitrust Issues for Companies That Do Business on the Web*, 1236 PLI/CORP 91 (March 2001).

Susan S. DeSanti, *Antitrust Law in the 21st Century: The Evolution of Electronic B2B Marketplaces*, SF63 ALI-ABA 201 (Sept. 14, 2000).

David H. Evans, *B2Bs—A Technical Perspective*, 15 ANTITRUST 45 (2000).

Joseph Farrell, Thoughts on Antitrust and Innovation, Address Before the National Economists' Club (Jan. 25, 2001), *available at* <http://www.usdoj.gov/atr/public/speeches/7402.htm>.

Federal Trade Commission Report: News Brief, *FTC Issues Report on B2B Electronic Marketplaces*, 8 ANDREWS ANTITRUST LITIG. REP. 11 (2000).

Alan Gahtan, *B2B Exchanges*, 5 CYBERSPACE LAWYER 2 (2000).

Richard Gilbert, *Symposium on Compatibility: Incentives and Market Structure*, 40 J. IND. ECON. 1 (1992).

Ilene Knable Gotts & Joseph G. Krauss, *Antitrust Review of New Economy Acquisitions*, 15 ANTITRUST 59 (2000).

Joel Klein, Rethinking Antitrust Policies for the New Economy, Address at the Haas/Berkeley New Economy Forum, Haas School of Business, University of California at Berkeley (May 9, 2000), *available at* <http://www.usdoj.gov/atr/public/speeches>.

Gail F. Levine & Hillary Greene, *Antitrust Guideposts for B2B Electronic Marketplaces*, 15 ANTITRUST 26 (2000).

Marc D. Machlin, *Sleeping with the Enemy? Antitrust Advice for Online Collaborators*, 16 PUB. UTIL. FORT. 38 (2000).

A. Douglas Melamed, Network Industries and Antitrust, Address Before the Federalist Society, The Eighteenth Annual Symposium on Law and Public Policy: Competition, Free Markets and the Law (April 10, 1999), *available at* <http://www.usdoj.gov/atr/public/speeches/2428.htm>.

Mark W. Merritt, Commentary, *E-Commerce and Antitrust: The Manufacturers' Perspective*, 20 ANDREWS CORP. OFF. & DIRECTORS LIAB. LITIG. REP. 14 (2000).

Joel M. Mitnick, *A Structural Approach to Analyzing Competition in B2B E-Commerce*, 15 ANTITRUST 31 (2000).

Robert Pitofsky, Electronic Commerce and Beyond: Challenges of the New Digital Age, Address Before The Federalist Society, The Eighteenth Annual Symposium on Law and Public Policy: Competition, Free Markets and the

Law (February 10, 2000) *available at* <http://ftc.gov/speeches/pitofsky/abaremarks.htm>.

Mark E. Plotkin, *E-Commerce Strategies for Success in the Digital Economy: Challenge and Opportunity: Electronic Business-to-Business Transactions and Markets*, 618 PLI/PAT 9 (Sept. 2000).

Jonathan M. Rich & Harry T. Robins, *Antitrust Consideration for Internet-Based Joint Ventures in the Financial Markets*, 10 WALLSTREETLAWYER.COM 1, (2001).

Daniel Rubinfeld, Competition, Innovation, and Antitrust Enforcement in Dynamic Network Industries, Address Before the Software Publishers Association (March 24, 1998).

CARL W. SHAPIRO & HAL R. VARIAN, INFORMATION RULES: A STRATEGIC GUIDE TO THE NETWORK ECONOMY (1999).

Robert A. Skitol, Antitrust Issues Confronting Collective Standard Setting in High-Technology Industries, Remarks Before the ABA Antitrust Section (February 25, 1999).

Richard M. Steuer, *To B2B or Not to B2B?*, 14 ANTITRUST 4 (2000).

Alan J. Weinschel, Representing the New Media Company 2001: E-Commerce Antitrust Issues, 631 PLI/PAT 691 (January 2001).

Banking Regulation

ABA May Ask Congress to Expand MMDAs, BANKING POL'Y REP., Aug. 4, 1997, at 4.

Tim Clark, *First Online Bank's Final Withdrawal*, NEWS.COM Nov. 6, 1997, *available at* <http://www.news.com/news/0,10000–1003–200–323799,00html> (visited June 25, 2001).

FDIC Decides to Look Before it Leaps on Covering Stored Value Cards, Bank Network News, July 26, 1996, at 3.

FDIC Issues First Opinions on Internet Deposit Insurance Issues, 21st Century Banking Alert® No. 96–2–12, Feb. 12, 1996, *available at* <http://www.ffhsj.com/bancmail/bancpage.htm>.

Finance Subcommittees Approve Banking Legislation, NAT'L J. CONGRESS DAILY, Mar. 22, 2001.

Kelley Holland & Amy Cortese, *The Future of Money*, BUS. WEEK, June 12, 1995, at 74.

JOSEPH NOCERA, A PIECE OF THE ACTION: HOW THE MIDDLE CLASS JOINED THE MONEY CLASS (1994).

Jaret Seiberg, *Fed Rebuffs ABA on NOW Accounts for Business*, AM. BANKER, July 17, 1997, at 11.

Sharon P. Sivertsen, *Legal and Regulatory Issues in Stored Value Card Technologies*, ELECTRONIC BANKING L. & COM. REP., May 1996, at 9–10.

Task Force on Stored-Value Cards, *A Commercial Lawyer's Take on the Electronic Purse: An Analysis of Commercial Law Issues Associated with Stored-Value Cards and Electronic Money*, 52 Bus. Law. 653 (Feb. 1997).

Thomas P. Vartanian, *Key Question for Emerging Systems: Where is the Money?*, Am. Banker—Future Banking, June 17, 1996, at 6A.

Thomas P. Vartanian, Statement before the Federal Deposit Insurance Corporation Concerning Stored Value Cards and Electronic Payment Systems (Sept. 12, 1996), *available at* <http://www.ffhsj.com>.

Thomas P. Vartanian & Robert H. Ledig, *The Business of Banking in the Age of the Internet: Fortress or Prison*, Banking Pol'y Rep., Mar. 4–18, 1996, at 6.

Thomas P. Vartanian, Robert H. Ledig & Edward B. Whittemore, *Integrion Financial Network: A New Stage for Electronic Banking*, Electronic Banking L. & Com. Rep., Oct. 1996, at 6.

Phillip L. Zweig, Wriston (1995).

Development/Linking Agreements

Kara Beal, *The Potential Liability of Linking on the Internet: An Examination*, 2 BYU L. Rev. 703 (1998).

G. Gervaise Davis, III, *Multimedia 1997: Protecting Your Client's Legal and Business Interests, Website and Multimedia Development Agreements*, 467 PLI/PAT 299 (Jan. 1997).

Rinaldo Del Gallo, III, *Who Owns the Web Site? The Ultimate Question When A Hiring Party Has A Falling-Out With the Web Site Designer*, 16 J. Marshall J. Computer & Info. L. 857 (Summer 1998).

Eric Goldman, *eCommerce: Strategies for Success in the Digital Economy: A Fresh Look At Web Development and Hosting Agreements*, 570 PLI/PAT 91 (Aug./Sept. 1999).

Julian S. Millstein, Jeffrey D. Newburger & Jeffrey P. Weingart, Doing Business On The Internet: Forms and Analysis (1999).

Brian T. Nash & Diane L. Liskowski, *Law and the Internet: Crafting Contracts for Your Web Site*, 19 Oct. Pa. Bar Ass'n. 21 (Sept.–Oct. 1997).

Matthew M. Neumeier, Brent E. Kidwell & Christine R. Weber, *Ecommerce: Strategies for Success in the Digital Economy 2000, E-Commerce "Storefront" Development & Hosting*, 588 PLI/PAT 237 (Jan. 2000).

Richard Raysman & Peter Brown, Computer Law: Drafting and Negotiating Forms and Agreements (1992).

Clarence H. Ridley, Peter C. Quittmeyer & John Matuszeski, Computer Software Agreements: Forms and Commentary (3d ed. 1999).

J.T. Westermeier, *Representing the New Media Company 1999: Web Developments and Web Hosting Agreements*, 545 PLI/PAT 477 (Jan. 1999).

Electronic Transactions

Directive 1999/93/EC of 13 December 1999 on a Community framework for electronic signatures, *available at* <http://europa.eu.int/comm/internal_market/en/media/sign/index.htm>.

Electronic Signatures in Global and National Commerce Act (E-SIGN), S. 761, Pub. L. No. 106–229, 15 U.S.C. §§ 7001 *et. seq.*, signed by President Clinton on June 30, 2000, and effective October 1, 2000.

Electronic Transaction Legislation (U.S. state and federal) and International Electronic Signature Legislation, *available at* <www.bakernet.com/ecommerce>.

Information Security Committee, Electronic Commerce Division, ABA Section of Science & Technology Law, *Digital Signature Guidelines* (Aug. 1996), *available at* <www.abanet.org/scitech/ec/isc/dsgfree.html>.

UNCITRAL Draft Guide to Enactment of the Model Law on Electronic Signatures (A/CN. 9/WG.IV/WP.88), *available at* <http://www.uncitral.org/english/sessions/wg_ec/wp-88e.pdf>.

UNCITRAL Model Law on Electronic Commerce with Guide to Enactment 1996, *available at* <www.un.or.at/uncitral/english/texts/electcom/ml-ec.htm>.

Uniform Electronic Transactions Act (UETA), approved by the National Conference of Commissioners on Uniform State Laws (NCCUSL) on July 23, 1999, *available at* <www.law.upenn.edu/bll/ulc/fnact99/1990s/ueta99.htm>. For an updated list of those states that have enacted UETA, see <www.bakernet.com/ecommerce/uetacomp.htm>.

Intellectual Property

J. Thomas McCarthy, McCarthy on Trademarks (1999).

Raymond T. Nimmer, The Law of Computer Technology (3d ed. 1998).

Raymond T. Nimmer & Patricia A. Krauthaus, *Information as Property: Databases and Commercial Property*, 1 Oxford J. Info. L. & Comp. Tech. 2 (1993).

David Nimmer & Melville Nimmer, Nimmer on Copyright (1990).

Michael O. Sutton, Patent Case Law Update, Paper Presented at the Texas State Bar Annual Meeting (July 11, 2000).

Joint Ventures

David E. Brown, Jr., Kathryn M. Cole & Joseph A. Smith, Jr., *Strategic Alliances: Why, How and What to Watch For*, 2 N.C. Banking Inst. 57 (April 1999).

Howard H. Chang, David S. Evans & Richard Schmalensee, *Some Economic Principles for Guiding Antitrust Policy Toward Joint Ventures*, 1998 Colum. Bus. L. Rev. 223 (1998).

Byron E. Fox & Eleanor M. Fox, Corporate Acquisitions and Merger (2000).

Richard D. Harrock & Stephen I. Glover, Negotiating and Structuring Joint Ventures & Strategic Alliances, Law Journal Seminars (1999).

Julian S. Millstein, Jeffrey D. Neuburger & Jeffrey P. Weingart, Doing Business on the Internet: Forms and Analysis (2000).

Richard Raysman, Edward A. Pisacreta, Kenneth A. Adler & Seth H. Ostrow, Intellectual Property Licensing: Forms and Analysis (2000).

Strategic Alliance Guide, Forbes Best of the Web (May 21, 2001).

Jurisdiction

Dan L. Burk, *Muddy Rules for Cyberspace*, 21 Cordozo L. Rev. 121 (1999).

Committee on Cyberspace Law, *Achieving Legal and Business Order in Cyberspace: A Report on Global Jurisdiction Issues Created by the Internet*, 55 Bus. Law. 1801 (2000).

Andrew E. Costa, *Minimum Contacts in Cyberspace: A Taxonomy of the Case Law*, 35 Hous. L. Rev. 453 (1998).

Developments in the Law—The Law of Cyberspace III. The Long Arm of Cyber-Reach, 112 Harv. L. Rev. 1610 (1999).

Developments in the Law—The Law of Cyberspace VI. Cyberspace Regulation and the Discourse of State Sovereignty, 112 Harv. L. Rev. 1680 (1999).

James E. Gaylord, *State Regulatory Jurisdiction and the Internet: Letting the Dormant Commerce Clause Lie*, 52 Vand. L. Rev. 1995 (1999).

Jack L. Goldsmith, *Against Cyberanarchy*, 54 U. Chi. L. Rev. 1199 (1998).

Mark S. Kende, *Lost in Cyberspace: The Judiciary's Distracted Application of Free Speech and Personal Jurisdiction Doctrines to the Internet*, 77 Or. L. Rev. 1125 (1998).

Timothy B. Nagy, *Personal Jurisdiction and Cyberspace: Establishing Precedent in a Borderless Era*, 6 CommLaw Conspectus 101 (1998).

Maureen A. O'Rourke, *Fencing Cyberspace: Drawing Borders in a Virtual World*, 82 Minn L. Rev. 609 (1998).

Veronica M. Sanchez, *Taking a Byte out of Minimum Contacts: A Reasonable Exercise of Personal Jurisdiction in Cyberspace Trademark Disputes*, 46 UCLA L. Rev. 1671 (1999).

Joseph Schmitt & Peter Nikolai, *Application of Personal Jurisdiction Principles to Electronic Commerce: A User's Guide*, 27 Wm. Mitchell L. Rev. 1571 (2001).

Russell D. Shurtz, *WWW.International_Shoe.com: Analyzing* Weber v. Jolly Hotels' *Paradigm for Personal Jurisdiction in Cyberspace*, 1998 B.Y.U. L. Rev. 1663 (1998).

Symposium of the Internet and Legal Theory, 73 Chi.-Kent L. Rev. 941 (1998).

Joel P. Trachtman, *Cyberspace, Sovereignty, Jurisdiction, and Modernism*, 3 Ind. J. Global Legal Studies 561 (1998).

Licensing Transactions

Warren E. Agin, Bankruptcy and Secured Lending in Cyberspace (2000).

Lorin Brennan, *Why Article 2 Cannot Apply to Software Transactions*, 38 Duq. L. Rev. 459 (2000).

Vern Countryman, *Executory Contracts in Bankruptcy, Part I*, 57 Minn. L. Rev. 439 (1973).

The Electronic Commerce and Law Report (BNA, Inc.), *available at* <http://www.bna.com>.

FAQs, Trademark and Domain Name Lawfinder, *available at* <http://www.high-tech.law.com/trademark/faq.html> (a good source of general information regarding trademarks and domain names).

Grant Gilmore, *On The Difficulties Of Codifying Commercial Law*, 57 Yale L. J. 1341 (1948).

Ingrid Michelsen Hillinger, *The Article 2 Merchant Rules: Karl Llewellyn's Attempt to Achieve The Good, The True, The Beautiful in Commercial Law*, 73 Geo. L.J. 1141 (1985).

Information regarding source code escrow, including sample clauses, may be found at <http://www.dsiescrow.com/index.html>.

Andrew M. Kaufman, *Technology Transfers and Insolvency—Some Practical Considerations*, 10 Computer Lawyer 21 (Sept. 1993).

J. Thomas McCarthy, McCarthy on Trademarks and Unfair Competition (3d. ed. 1996).

Robert Merges, *The End of Friction? Property Rights And Contract In the 'Newtonian' World of On-Line Commerce*, 12 Berkeley Tech. L.J. 115 (1997).

John H. Mutchler, *Circumvention of Copyright Protection Systems*, 10 Intell. Prop. Tdy. 12 (2000).

Raymond T. Nimmer, *Breaking Barriers: The Relation Between Contract And Intellectual Property Law*, 13 Berkeley Tech. L.J. 827 (1998).

Raymond T. Nimmer, *Images and Contract Law—What Law Applies to Transactions in Information*, 36 Hous. L. Rev. 1 (1999).

Maureen A. O'Rourke, *Copyright Preemption After the ProCD Case: A Market-Based Approach*, 12 Berkely Tech. L.J. 53 (1997).

Pamela Samuelson, *Intellectual Property and the Digital Economy: Why Anti-Circumvention Regulations Need to Be Revised*, 14 Berkeley Tech. L.J. 519 (1999).

Survey, *The Treatment of Intellectual Property Interests in Bankruptcy*, 4 J. BANKR
L. & PRAC. 437 (May/June 1995).

Trademark and Domain Name Lawfinder, *available at* <http://www.high-
tech.law.com/trademark> (a good starting point in accessing may of the
statutes and arbitration decisions on trademarks and domain names that
were cited in this section).

Online Landscape

Bill Barnes, *The XML Men: Saving the World from Evil Mutant Data*, SLATE,
August 23, 2000, *at* <http://slate.msn.com/webhead/00–08–22/webhead.
asp>.

Chip Bayers, *Capitalist Econstruction*, WIRED, Mar. 2000, *at* (http://www.
wired.com/wired/archive/8.03/markets.html).

TIM BERNERS-LEE, WEAVING THE WEB: THE ORIGINAL DESIGN AND ULTIMATE
DESTINY OF THE WORLD WIDE WEB BY ITS INVENTOR (1999).

Jon Bosak & Tim Bray, *XML and the Second Generation Web*, SCI. AM., May
1999, *at* <http://www.sciam.com/1999/0599issue/0599bosak.html>.

PHILIP EVANS & THOMAS S. WURSTER, BLOWN TO BITS: HOW THE NEW ECO-
NOMICS OF INFORMATION TRANSFORMS STRATEGY (1999).

David Lake, *The Web: Growing by 2 Million Pages a Day*, THE INDUSTRY STAN-
DARD, Feb. 28, 2000, *available at* <http://www.thestandard.com/research/
metrics/display/0,2799,12329,00.html>.

John Markoff, *Computer Scientists Are Poised for Revolution on a Tiny Scale*, N.Y.
TIMES, Nov. 1, 1999, *available at* <http://www.nytimes.com/library/tech/99/
11/biztech/articles/01nano.html>.

Thomas W. Malone & Robert J. Laubacher, T*he Dawn of the E-lance Economy*,
HARV. BUS. REV., Sept.-Oct. 1998, at 145.

Mark A. Reed & James M. Tour, *Computing With Molecules*, SCI. AM., June
2000, *available at* <http://www.scientificamerican.com/2000/0600issue/0600
reed.html>.

Howard Rheingold, *You Got the Power*, WIRED, Aug. 2000, *available at* <http://
www.wired.com/wired/current.html>.

Nathan Rosenberg, *The Impact of Technological Innovation: A Historical View*,
in THE POSITIVE SUM STRATEGY: HARNESSING TECHNOLOGY FOR ECONOMIC
GROWTH, (Ralph Landau and Nathan Rosenberg eds., 1986).

CARL SHAPIRO & HAL VARIAN, INFORMATION RULES: A STRATEGIC GUIDE TO
THE NETWORK ECONOMY (1998).

David Streitfeld, *The Web's Next Step: Unraveling Itself*, THE WASH. POST, July
18, 2000.

Jon William Toigo, *Avoiding a Data Crunch*, SCI. AM., May 2000, *available at*
<http://www.sciam.com/2000/0500issue/0500toig.html>.

Hal Varian, *The Internet Carries Profound Implications for Providers of Information*, N.Y. TIMES, July 27, 2000.

Hal Varian, *When Commerce Moves Online, Competition Can Work in Strange Ways*, N.Y. TIMES, Aug. 24, 2000.

Privacy

DAVID BENDER, COMPUTER LAW (1978, 2001).

Scott Blackmer, The European Union Data Protection Directive: A Compact Summary, Paper Provided for the Privacy and American Business Meeting on Mode Adate Protection Contracts and Laws, Washington D.C. (Feb. 1998).

FRED H. CATE, PRIVACY IN THE INFORMATION AGE (1997).

SIMSON GARFUNKEL, DATABASE NATION, THE DEATH OF PRIVACY IN THE 21ST CENTURY (2000).

ORGANIZATION FOR ECONOMIC COOPERATION AND DEVELOPMENT, GUIDELINES FOR THE PROTECTION OF PRIVACY AND TRANSBORDER DATA FLOWS OF PERSONAL DATA (Sept. 1980).

PRIVACY LAW ADVISER (Pike & Fischer, Sliver Spring, MD.).

PETER P. SWIRE & ROBERT E. LITAN, NONE OF YOUR BUSINESS: WORLD DATA FLOWS, ELECTRONIC COMMERCE, AND THE EUROPEAN PRIVACY DIRECTIVE (1998).

U.S. DEPT OF COMMERCE, NATIONAL TELECOMMUNICATIONS AND INFORMATION ADMINISTRATION, PRIVACY AND SELF-REGULATION IN THE INFORMATION AGE (1997).

Securities Regulation

Compliance Navigator: Electronic Delivery of Prospectuses, 7 INTERNET COMPLIANCE ALERT 7 (April 6, 1998).

JOSEPH LONG, BLUE SKY LAW (rev. ed. 1997).

G. Morgenson, *Sailing Into Murky Waters*, N.Y. TIMES, Feb.28, 1999, at BU-2, BU-10.

L.N. Spiro, *Merrill's E-Battle*, BUS. WK., Nov. 15, 1999, at 256, 258.

Self-Regulation

Better Business Bureau, *at* <http://www.bbbonline.org>.

European Advertising Standards Alliance, *at* <http://www.easa-alliance.org>.

Organization for Economic Cooperation and Development, *at* <http://www.oecd.org>.

Taxation

Selected Tax Policy Implications of Global Electronic Commerce, Department of the Treasury, Office of Tax Policy (November 1996).

Electronic Commerce: A Discussion Paper on Taxation Issues, a discussion paper prepared by the OECD Committee on Fiscal Affairs (October 10, 1998).

Tax and the Internet, Discussion report of the Australian Taxation Office Electronic Commerce Project Team on the challenges of electronic commerce for tax administration (August 1997).

Electronic Commerce and Canada's Tax Administration, A Report to the Minister of National Revenue from the Minister's Advisory Committee on Electronic Commerce (April 1998). This advisory report does not represent the official position of Revenue Canada.

U.K. Inland Revenue and H.M. Customs and Excise, Paper on the Taxation of Electronic Commerce (Nov. 26, 1999).

Revised Draft of Proposed Clarification of the Commentary on Article 5 of the OECD Model Tax Convention of Working Party No. 1 on Tax Conventions and Related Questions (March 3, 2000).

Third-Party Content Liability

Janet Kornblum, *Library Filtering Suit Dismissed*, Oct. 21, 1998, *available at* <http://www.news.com/News/Item/0,4,27818,00.html)>.

Allen C. Michaels, *Constitutional Innocence*, 112 HARV. L. REV. 828 (1999).

Note, *Implying Civil Remedies from Federal Regulatory Statutes*, 77 HARV. L. REV. 285 (1963).

NORMAN J. SINGER, SUTHERLAND STATUTORY CONSTRUCTION (5th ed. 1992).

Glossary

Above The Fold: An advertisement that is loaded onto a user's computer screen (viewed at 800 by 600 resolution) without the need to scroll in any direction.

Acknowledgment: Instances when confirmation of transmission receipt is required for a given document or data set.

Ad Broker Agreement: An agreement in which a third-party broker is retained by a site owner to design a strategic media plan for the site and negotiate for the purchase of advertising space at appropriate web sites.

Adhesion Contracts: Unilaterally drafted form agreements.

Adoption Theory: With respect to whether third-party information will be attributed to a company issuing securities, theory by which the issuer has approved the information explicitly or implicitly.

Advertising Agreement: An agreement in which the target site pays another site a fee to place a link in the form of an advertisement to the target site.

Advertising Network Agreement: An agreement in which an ad network agrees with each member to negotiate with advertisers to place advertisements at the sites of categories or groups of members of the network.

Affiliate Agreement: An agreement in which the target site allows other sites to link to it and pays linking sites a referral fee based upon customers who arrive at and conduct business on the target site.

Anonymity: To be unknown or unacknowledged.

Assuming the License: With respect to a software license in a bankruptcy case, keeping the license in effect.

Authenticate: Action by a receiver of a signature to validate that a signature is genuine.

Authentication for Access Control: Allowing only certain users access to certain areas or resources on a network.

Authentication for Binding Intent: Data that form the basis of a contract or other document that is being assented to or "signed."

Authentication of Role: A user's ability to perform any given function within the application, such as approving data or setting user rights.

Authenticity: The source or origin of a communication.

Authority for Specific Actions: See *Authentication of Role.*

Auto-Load Link: Link invoked automatically by the viewer's web browser when the linking page is displayed in the viewer's browser.

Automatic Refresh: A device that effectuates a timed rotation of advertisements.

Banner: A type of web advertisement.

Beta Software: Prereleased software to selected licensees or any licensee that requests access.

Biometric Technology: The study of measurable biological characteristics. Authentication techniques that rely on measurable physical characteristics that can be automatically checked (e.g., computer analysis of fingerprints or speech).

Branding: Identifying a product, service or company; increasing marketplace recognition of a trademark.

Browser: With respect to the World Wide Web, software enabling the viewing of web pages.

Bug: A software defect caused by an error in design or programming.

Buttons: A defined area of a computer screen that resembles a pushbutton and that triggers an action when clicked on by a user.

Buy/Sell Rights: With respect to a joint venture agreement, each venturer has the right—after a date certain—to set a price at which it would be willing to buy the other party's interest in the venture.

Caching: The intermediate and temporary storage of material on a system or network controlled or operated by or for the service provider.

Certification Authority: A trusted third party which binds the identity of a particular party to a particular public key and, by implication, a particular private key.

Certification Practice Statement: A statement by a certification authority giving relying parties notice of the level of inquiry conducted by the certification authority before issuing the certificate.

Clean Room: Process in which engineers without direct exposure to a software program are asked to duplicate its functions.

Click-Through(s):   The number of times that users click through the hyperlink connecting the advertisement to the advertiser's site.

Click-Through Agreements: A form agreement accepted by clicking on, for example, an "I accept" button.

Click-Wrap Agreement: An agreement in which the agreement is displayed in a separate window from which it cannot be downloaded or printed.

Clicks: See *Click-Through(s)*.

Clicks-And-Mortar Companies: Companies that sell online and seek to avoid agency nexus in the context of traditional retailers establishing separate online companies that use some of the benefits of a physical retail network.

Clipper Chip: The Escrow Encryption Standard developed by the National Security Agency to facilitate electronic surveillance by government agents through the interception of communications by suspected criminals.

Closed PKI: A business model where users obtain different digital certificates for each community of interests with which they interact online.

Co-Branding Agreement: An agreement in which one site (branded site) commissions another site (provider site) to create a co-branded web page bearing both the branded site brand as the dominant brand and the provider site's brand as the lesser brand.

Common Advertising Agreement: An agreement executed directly between the advertiser and the host site that will display its advertisement setting forth specific requirements regarding the advertisements to be delivered, the method or methods for calculating the advertising fee earned, and various representations, warranties, disclaimers, indemnities, termination rights and other rights and obligations of the parties.

Community Computing: See *Distributed Computing*.

Compiler: A software program that takes source code written by a programmer in a high-level language (such as C++) and translates it into object code, which, when linked with any necessary libraries or other modules, can then run as a stand-alone program.

Concerted Refusal to Deal: Agreement between competitors not to deal with other economic actors.

Confidentiality: Preventing interception and reading of the data flowing over a network.

Consent to Assumption: Contract provision in which a patent license allows assumption or retention in a bankruptcy proceeding.

Cookies: Pieces of information deposited on a user's hard drive by some web sites the user visits.

Copyright Management Information: The title, copyright notice, name of the author and other specified information.

Country-of-Origin Principle: Principle by which each Member State will ensure that the ISS provided by a service provider established in the Member State's territory will comply with the Member State's applicable national provisions that fall within the Coordinated Field.

Countryman Definition: With respect to determining whether a contract is executory, a standard in which a contract is so far unperformed that the failure of either to complete performance constitutes a material breach excusing the performance of the other.

Data Integrity: Data that has not been tampered with during a given period of time.

Data Privacy: Data in which a person or entity has a continuing legal interest or right.

Deep Links: Links to a remote page that is not the homepage of the target site, but rather a subpage within the interior of that site.

Digital Signature: A type of electronic signature created through the use of public key cryptography (i.e., scrambling data to provide security and authentication).

Digitized Signature: An electronic image of a signature.

Dilution: A lessening of the capacity of a famous mark to identify and distinguish goods or services.

Distributed Computing: Process by which computers are linked together to work on shared projects when they are not engaged in local tasks.

Domain Name: A unique string of letters that the domain registrar agrees—on a first-come, first-serve basis—to associate with a given IP address for a given length of time, thus enabling other participants on the Internet to find certain files that the operator of the server associates with the domain name.

Dual Distribution: When a manufacturer distributes its products both through its own efforts and through the use of distributors or retailers.

Electronic Agents: Software used independently to initiate an action or respond to electronic messages or performances without intervention by an individual at the time of the action, response or performance.

Electronic Data Interchange (EDI): The direct electronic exchange of information between computers; the data is formatted using standard protocols so that it can be interpreted and implemented directly by the receiving computer.

Electronic Form: A computer-based version of a paper form.

Electronic Record: A computer-based version of a paper record.

Electronic Signature: An electronic sound, symbol or process attached to or logically associated with a contract or other record and executed or adopted by a person with the intent to sign the record. Not associated with any particular technology.

Encryption: A technology that scrambles digital information according to a code that allows authorized users to unscramble the data later.

Entanglement Theory: With respect to whether third-party information will be attributed to a company issuing securities, theory by which the issuer has involved itself in the preparation of the information.

Executable Code: The machine language that a computer platform can read, which is produced by running object code through a program called a linker, assembler or loader.

Executory Contracts: A contract in which performance is due by both parties.

Fair Use Doctrine: An exception to the exclusivity of copyrights where the use of copyrighted material has a minor effect on the copyright owner and is far outweighed by general benefits for society.

Fiber-to-the-Curb: Broadband service provided to a neighborhood connection point or node by fiber optics.

Field-of-Use Restrictions: Restrictions that enable a licensor to maximize the amount of royalties because the licensor can arrange lower royalties for low-demand fields and higher royalties for high-demand fields.

Fingerprint: A message digest.

First Two Scrolls: An advertisement placed within the top 1,200 pixels of a user's computer screen.

First-Sale Rule: An exception to the exclusivity of copyrights where, with respect to an authorized sale of a work, the buyer at the first sale does not infringe the copyright if it subsequently resells the copy.

Flaming: Rude and largely ad hominem communications through e-mail and postings on the Usenet and other public areas.

Framing: A type of linking in which the linking page includes commands that cause the user's browser to divide the screen display into separate windows or frames. Used to create a border around the target page information.

Functional Analysis Approach: With respect to determining whether a contract is executory, a test that looks to the nature of the parties and goals of reorganization as well as whether acceptance or rejection will benefit the bankruptcy estate.

General Jurisdiction: Jurisdictional assertions that are proper no matter what claim is brought against the defendant because of the extent and nature of the defendant's contacts with the forum.

Group Boycott: See *Concerted Refusal to Deal*.

Homepage: (1) The web page automatically loaded when a user starts the web browser (which, in modern browsers, can be set by the user) or (2) the main or starting page of a web site.

Hot Link: A hypertext link from one web site to another. Users branch outward from a central text to other bodies of information, often third-party web sites. See also *Link*.

Hyperlinks: See *Hot Link*.

Impression: Access by a single Internet user of a data file containing an advertisement.

In-Line Link: See *Auto-Load Link*.

Integrity: The accuracy and completeness of a communication.

Interactive Service Providers: A company that provides users with dial-up or other access to the Internet, usually in exchange for a monthly service fee.

Interstitial Advertisement: A type of advertisement that appears while the page requested by the user is loading.

Invoke-to-Load Links: Links typically appearing either as highlighted text or as an image.

Link: A Uniform Resource Locator (URL) that is embedded in a web page.

Linked-To Page: A web site to which a link leads, as opposed to the web site that contains the link.

Linking Page: A web site that contains a link, as opposed to the web site to which the link leads.

Local Links: Links in one web page that refer to a document stored at the same web site as the originating page.

Maintenance: A licensor's postformation willingness or obligation to provide subsequent modifications or new releases of licensed software.

Material-Breach Test: See *Countryman Definition*.

Metadata: Data carrying descriptive tags.

Metatags: Identifiers that can influence Internet search engines to select a particular site given a particular search request.

Mirroring: See *Caching*.

Monopsony Power: The ability of a company or coalition of companies to dictate purchase prices.

Moore's Law: Law by which processor performance continues to double approximately every eighteen months.

Naked License: A license without control over trademark quality.

Navigate: The movement from one web page to another via links.

Network Effects: The increase in the value of the network to all its users, which occurs as the number of network participants increases.

No-Challenge Clause: Clause whereby the licensee agrees to refrain from challenging the validity of the patent.

No-Challenge Termination Clause: Clause authorizing the licensor to terminate the license if the licensee challenges the validity if the patent.

No-Competitive-Links Provision: A restriction that prevents the linking site from posting links of business entities that compete with the target site.

Nonrepudiation: The ability to hold a sender to his communication in the event of a dispute.

Object Code: The interim by-product of running source code through a translation program called a compiler.

Open PKI: A business model that assumes that a subscriber will obtain from a certification authority digital certificates that will securely link their identities to their public keys for all—or at least many—purposes.

Open Source: A movement to develop an alternative to commercial software using volunteer resources. The Linux operating system is an example of Open Source software.

Opt-In Standard: With respect to collecting, marketing and using information from Internet users, a standard that requires the express affirmative consent of the user before an Internet company can exchange a user profile created on its web site with other Internet companies.

Opt-Out Standard: With respect to collecting, marketing and using information from Internet users, a standard that requires the user to give express instructions to the Internet company not to exchange with other Internet companies personal information collected from the user via the company's web site.

Page Views: Similar to *Impressions* except that the advertiser is obligated to pay only where the full page containing the advertisement is fully loaded onto the user's computer.

Pixels: The smallest unit of display on a computer's display screen. Often used as a measurement of the size of a web page (for example, web sites will often state that they are "best viewed at 800 by 600 pixels").

Pop-Up Advertisement: See *Interstitial Advertisement.*

Prescriptive Jurisdiction: The authority of a state to apply its own law to regulated conduct.

Private Key: Key generated by software that can decrypt a message encrypted with its corresponding public key.

Pseudonymity: To be identified by an assumed (often pen) name.

Public Key: Key generated by software that can decrypt a message encrypted with its corresponding private key.

Published Information Content: Concept that merchantability warranties do not apply to public information.

Random Access Memory: A type of computer memory that does not store information after the computer is turned off.

Receipt: See *Acknowledgement.*

Received: Point in time when an electronic record enters an information processing system that the recipient has designated or uses for the purpose of receiving electronic records of the type sent and from which the recipient is able to retrieve the electronic record, and is in a form capable of being processed by that system.

Record: See *Electronic Record.*

Referring Site: The web site from which a user came (used in the context of following a hyperlink).

Rejecting the License: With respect to a software license in a bankruptcy case, terminating the license.

Remote Links: Links that refer to a web page that is stored at a web site other than the site where the linking document resides.

Request For Proposal: A formal document requesting a proposal to develop custom software or code.

Right of First Offer: With respect to a joint venture agreement, each participant is obligated to offer its co-venturers the first opportunity to purchase its equity interest.

Right of First Refusal: With respect to a joint venture agreement, an offer is made by an outside party before the transferring party becomes obligated to offer the equity to its co-venturers.

Road Show: A series of presentations made by the issuer and its underwriters to large investors, institutions and analysts during the period that starts when a registration statement is filed with the SEC and ends when the registration become effective.

Rule of Reason: Analysis to determine whether the relevant agreement harms competition by increasing the parties' ability or incentive to raise prices above— or reduce output, quality, service or innovation below—what would likely prevail in the absence of the relevant agreement.

Sales Representative Agreement: See *Advertising Network Agreement.*

Semantic Web: A Web of data with meaning in the sense that a computer program can learn enough about the data to process it.

Sent: A point in time when information enters an information processing system outside the control of the sender or enters a region of the information processing system designated or used by the recipient which is under the control of the recipient.

Servers: Computers or software used to support multiple users. For example, most commercial web sites are hosted on dedicated computers ("servers") running software that allow multiple users to access the web site at the same time ("server software").

Shrink-Wrap Agreement: A software license agreement included with retail software, called "shrink-wrap" because, historically, it appeared inside or on the shrink-wrapped box in which the software was sold. Because there is no opportunity for the retail purchaser to negotiate the terms of the shrink-wrap license, shrink-wrap licenses raise serious enforcability issues.

Sign: Action by a user to identify himself or to manifest assent.

Signature: See *Electronic Signature.*

Signature Dynamics: A biometrics-based technology.

Software: A set of instructions and procedures guiding the operation of a computing system or computing functions.

Source Code: One of three formulations of software typically subject to license involving high-level languages in which computer programmers write.

Special Jurisdiction: See *Specific Jurisdiction.*

Specific Jurisdiction: Situation in which the contacts the defendant has with the forum or certain acts there are sufficient to permit jurisdiction to be asserted in connection with related claims, but are presumptively insufficient to permit jurisdiction to be asserted in connection with claims that have no relationship to those contacts or acts.

Subpage: A web page within a web site that is not the home (or main) page of the site.

Tag Jurisdiction: Jurisdiction that is proper when the defendant is personally served with process while in the forum.

Target Page: See *Linked-To Page.*

Technical Support: A licensor's postformation willingness or obligation to answer technical questions regarding the licensed software and its use.

Text Link: A type of web advertisement that appears only as text, without any graphical banner or button.

Toolkits: Prewritten source code.

Traffic: The number of people visiting a web site.

Transaction: An action or set of actions relating to the conduct of business, consumer, or commerical affairs between two or more persons, including any of the following types of conduct: (A) the sale, lease, exchange, licensing, or other disposition of (i) personal property, including goods and intangibles, (ii) services, and (iii) any combination there of; and (B) the sale, lease, exchange, or other disposition of any interest in real property or any combination thereof.

Transformative Use: With respect to the Fair Use Doctrine, use of the expression of the original copyrighted material to create a new work that does not compete with the original but may reference it in innovative ways.

User Action Transactions: Transactions where the host site receives fixed payments for users who take a specified action such as completing a survey, requesting product information, or opening a customer account.

User Purchase Transactions: Transactions where the host site receives a percentage of the gross sales revenue realized by the advertiser when users click-through an advertisement and purchase products or services at the advertiser's site.

Web Site: An integrated collection of web pages posted on one server under the same domain name.

Web Site Forms: A way in which a web site operator offers goods or services for sale, which the customer orders by completing and transmitting an order form displayed on the screen.

Work of Authorship: A copyright granting an author certain exclusive rights.
World-Wide Web: Files or pages specially formatted using Hypertext Markup Language (HTML) and made available to the public via computers known as web servers.

Index to Topics

About the Authors

David Reiter is vice president and general counsel for 724 Solutions Inc. in Austin, Texas. His practice areas include software licensing, intellectual property, litigation, labor and employment, customs and trade, and international taxation. He is co-chair of the Internet Law Subcommittee of the American Bar Association's Section of Business Law. His other professional responsibilities include chair of the ACCA Houston International Law Committee. Mr. Reiter sits on both the UETA and UCITA Advisory Committees to the Texas Bar Association. He is a frequent speaker at seminars and conferences addressing issues in technology and Internet law. Mr. Reiter is a graduate of the University of Southern California (J.D. '93) and the University of Notre Dame (MA '89). He also holds an MBA from the University of Sheffield, UK, a Master of International Relations from the University of Southern California, and is admitted to the Texas Bar.

Elizabeth Blumenfeld is director of Policy and Business Strategy for BBB*OnLine*, Inc., the online subsidiary of the Council of Better Business Bureaus. Prior to joining BBB*OnLine*, Ms. Blumenfeld was deputy director for Legal and Brand Policy at America Online, Inc. She served as co-reporter for the American Bar Association's *Transnational Issues in Cyberspace: A Project on the Law Relating to Jurisdiction*. In this capacity, she helped direct and codify the ABA's multilateral effort to analyze jurisdictional problems that impact global electronic commerce. Additionally, Ms. Blumenfeld co-chairs the Internet Law Subcommittee of the Cyberspace Law Committee of the American Bar Association's Section of Business Law and is an advisory board member of BNA's *Electronic Information Policy and Law Report*. Ms. Blumenfeld graduated from Yale Law School and received her BA, junior Phi Beta Kappa, from The University of Chicago.

Mark Boulding is general counsel and executive vice president, Government and Regulatory Affairs, of Medscape. Mr. Boulding is a member of the Cyberspace Law Committee of the American Bar Association's Section of Business Law. Mr. Boulding co-founded the Internet Healthcare Coalition, a nonprofit organization dedicated to education, guidance and policymaking in the service of high-quality health care information on the Internet. He also participates as Medscape's representative on the Board of Directors of the Health Internet Ethics ("Hi-Ethics") group, which was created by the leading healthcare web sites to improve consumer confidence in Internet healthcare through self-regulatory systems. An honors graduate of Yale College, Mr. Boulding received his law degree *cum laude* from the University of Michigan.

Warren E. Agin is a founding member of Swiggart & Agin, LLC, a software and Internet boutique in Boston, Massachusetts. Mr. Agin's practice focuses in the areas of bankruptcy and insolvency law, corporate law, and computer and Internet law. He currently chairs the Electronic Transactions in Bankruptcy Subcommittee (within the Business Bankruptcy Committee) of the American Bar Association's Section of Business Law, and is vice-chair of the ABA's Joint Subcommittee on Electronic Financial Services. Mr. Agin has written and lectured extensively on the topics of bankruptcy and technology law, including presentations for the American Bar Association, National Business Institute and Practising Law Institute.

Peter J. Allen is director and senior counsel, Global Business Units, in the Law Department of Compaq Computer Corporation. His practice concentrates on the development, licensing and marketing of information technology products and solutions, with a special emphasis on e-commerce issues. He is co-chair of the Privacy in Commerce Task Force, Internet Privacy Subcommittee, of the American Bar Association's Cyberspace Law Committee. He graduated from New England College and Fordham University School of Law, where he served on the international law journal.

Bartley B. Baer is a partner in the Multistate Tax Services Group of Deloitte & Touche. Mr. Baer specializes in state and local tax planning and controversy resolution, and his practice emphasizes the management of California income tax and sales and use tax issues for multinational corporations. Mr. Baer is currently chair of the State and Local Tax Committee of the California State Bar Taxation Section and is a member of the American Bar Association. He graduated from Hastings College of Law, University of California in 1985. In addition, he earned an LL.M. in taxation from New York University School of Law in 1989.

Andrew R. Basile, Jr. is a partner and head of the Information Technology Practice Group in the San Francisco office of Cooley Godward LLP. His practice emphasizes transactional work relating to the Internet, information technology and intellectual property. He focuses his practice on emerging growth companies in the areas of electronic commerce, new media and information technology. He has also guest-lectured at Kellogg Business School and Northwestern University Law School. He is admitted to practice before the U.S. Patent and Trademark Office and has experience in patent prosecution and litigation. He earned his J.D., *cum laude*, from the University of Michigan in 1989 and his B.S. in electrical engineering and computer science from Princeton University in 1986.

David Bender is Of Counsel in the New York City office of White & Case LLP, where he specializes in litigation, transactional matters and counseling in the areas of intellectual property law and information technology law. He previously served as head of AT&T's IP Litigation Department, where he was responsible for all IP litigation brought by or against any Bell System company.

He is the immediate past president of the Computer Law Association. Mr. Bender holds an S.B. in applied math from Brown University, an LL.B. from the University of Pennsylvania, an LL.M. in patent law from George Washington University, and an S.J.D. (specializing in computer law) from George Washington University. In a previous life, Mr. Bender served as an engineer with Ford Aerospace and as a mathematician with Hughes Aircraft.

Patricia A. Buckley is a senior policy advisor in the Economics and Statistics Administration of the U.S. Department of Commerce working to standardize and resolve the definitional and measurement issues related to the shift to a digital economy and analyzing the domestic and international economic impacts of electronic commerce and electronic business processes. She earned a Ph.D. in economics from Georgetown University and her bachelor's degree from Clemson University.

Joann Nesta Burnett, an associate in the Ft. Lauderdale office of Becker & Poliakoff, is a commercial litigator concentrating her practice in the areas of technology law, noncompete litigation, real estate law and covenant enforcement actions. She earned her J.D. at Nova Southeastern University, where she served on the law review, and her bachelor's degree at the University of South Florida.

Patrick Carome is a partner of Wilmer, Cutler & Pickering. He is a member of the firm's General Litigation and Communications groups and specializes in litigation and other representation on behalf of communications and media companies. He formerly was a staff attorney for *The Washington Post* and staff counsel to the U.S. House of Representatives Select Committee to Investigate Covert Arms Transactions with Iran. He has served as chair of the American Bar Association's Committee on Government Information and Right to Privacy of the Administrative Law and Regulatory Practice Section and chair of the Steering Committee of the Administrative Law and Agency Practice Section of the District of Columbia Bar. Mr. Carome is a graduate of Harvard Law School and Boston College.

Adam Chernichaw is an associate in the New York office of White & Case. He represents institutional and start-up clients in the high-tech, Internet, telecommunications, media and fashion industries in technology transfer, strategic alliances, merger and acquisitions, software development, procurement and licensing, and day-to-day service and operational transactions. Mr. Chernichaw is a graduate of the Benjamin N. Cardozo School of Law, where he was an editor and published member of its law review, and the State University of New York at Albany.

David K. Daggett spent over ten years as a computer programmer, systems analyst and local area network engineer before entering the legal profession. As a Novell Certified Network Engineer, Mr. Daggett installed and maintained numerous personal computer networks. In addition, Mr. Daggett wrote and maintained the billing software for the nation's largest construction and temporary fencing rental firm. Wishing to broaden his expertise, Mr. Daggett entered Gonzaga University School of Law, from which he graduated first in his class. Today, Mr. Daggett is licensed to practice in Washington, Idaho and California and conducts an intellectual property and business practice with Preston Gates & Ellis LLP. Mr. Daggett is involved in the representation of clients in technical standards setting consortia, transactions involving licenses of intellectual property, and other multiparty agreements, as well as in insurance coverage disputes related to intellectual property.

Jeff C. Dodd is a partner at the Houston and Austin offices of Mayor, Day, Caldwell & Keeton, L.L.P., with extensive experience in the areas of intellectual property, technology, e-commerce, communications and corporate law. He is also an adjunct professor of law at the University of Houston Law Center, Intellectual Property and Information Law Program, and at the South Texas College of Law—Business Planning. Mr. Dodd is a member of several organizations, including the American Bar Association, Texas Bar Association and Houston Bar Association. Mr. Dodd earned both his bachelor's degree, *magna cum laude*, and juris doctor, *summa cum laude*, at the University of Houston.

Alexander Duisberg joined Baker & McKenzie in 1997 as an associate after earning law degrees at the University of Bonn and admittance to the German bar in 1996. Following over two years of IT and corporate practice in the Frankfurt office and sixteen months in the Italian offices at Rome and Milan, he is now a member of the team of IT lawyers at the Munich office of Baker & McKenzie.

John G. Flaim is a partner at the law firm of Baker & McKenzie. His practice encompasses patent litigation, patent prosecution and patent licensing matters in a wide variety of fields, including telecommunications, voice messaging, software and semiconductor fabrication processes. Mr. Flaim received his B.S. degree, *magna cum laude*, in electrical engineering from Manhattan College in 1989 and his J.D., with honors, from St. John's University School of Law in 1992.

Robert E. Freeman is a senior associate in the New York office of Brown Raysman Millstein Felder & Steiner, LLP, where he specializes in the areas of technology, new media, intellectual property and the Internet. Mr. Freeman is a graduate of Princeton University and the Georgetown University Law Center.

Jennifer L. Gray chairs the Antitrust Practice Group at Brown Raysman Millstein Felder & Steiner, LLP. She specializes in antitrust counseling and litigation and related areas such as corporate compliance. She speaks and writes frequently on topics concerning antitrust, e-commerce and intellectual property. Ms. Gray is vice-chair of the Corporate Counseling Committee of the Antitrust Section of the ABA and a member of the Committee on Antitrust and Trade Regulation of the Association of the City of the Bar of New York. Ms. Gray earned her bachelors degree at Douglass College and her law degree at Rutgers University School of Law—Newark, where she was notes and comments editor of the Rutgers Law Review.

Daniel J. Greenwood is a lecturer at MIT and is director of the MIT E-Commerce Architecture Project. He is also a practicing attorney specializing in information technology policy and e-contracts and has worked extensively in the public sector on legislation for e-signatures and online business transactions. Mr. Greenwood runs the e-commerce consultancy "civics.com" and serves on the boards of various Internet standards-making bodies.

Mark Grossman is a shareholder and chairs Becker & Poliakoff's Computer and E-Commerce Law Group. He is also the "Tech Law" columnist for the *Miami Herald*. He has been appointed a subject matter expert to Florida's Internet Task Force and is on the board of editors of *The Internet Newsletter*. Mr. Grossman lectures throughout the world; his recent appearances include presentations at COMDEX in Las Vegas, chairing the American Conference Institute's "Advanced Forum on Application Service Providers," the keynote address at the 20th Annual United States Department of Energy's Computer Security Conference, Georgetown University Law Center's Advanced Computer Law Institute, and speeches to the American Corporate Counsel Association, the keynote address at LegalTech, and numerous others. A graduate of the State University of New York at Stony Brook (B.A., with high honors, 1979) and Georgetown University Law Center (J.D., *cum laude*, 1982), Mr. Grossman is a member of the Florida Bar and is admitted to practice in the U.S. District Court, Southern District of Florida.

Michael W. Hauptman is an associate in the Information Technology practice group at the San Francisco office of Cooley Godward LLP. His practice focuses on a full range of intellectual property and technology-based transactions, including Internet and web transactions covering digital content licensing, e-commerce arrangements, co-marketing and sponsorship agreements; web development agreements; software and product licensing and development agreements; and general intellectual property counseling. He earned his J.D. from the New York University School of Law and a B.A. from the honors program in the Department of Government and Foreign Affairs at the University of Virginia.

Lawrence M. Hertz is a partner in the New York office of Hall Dickler Kent Goldstein & Wood, LLP, where he concentrates his practice in the areas of computer software, intellectual property and the Internet. He is a frequent lecturer and columnist on Internet-related topics and currently serves on the board of editors of *The E-Commerce Law Reports*, published by Glasser LegalWorks. He is a graduate of Hofstra University and New York University School of Law.

Truiken J. Heydn, from the office of Baker & McKenzie in Munich, Germany, concentrates on litigation in the areas of intellectual property and unfair competition law with a specific focus on the IT industry. She is admitted to the German Bar and is a member of the German Association for Industrial Property and Copyright Law (Deutsche Vereinigung für gewerblichen Rechtsschultz und

Urheberrecht e.V.) and of the German Association for Law and Information Technology (Deutsche Gesellschaft für Recht und Informatick e.V.). She is a graduate of the University of Regensburg, Germany, where she earned a Dr. jur.

Samir Jain is an attorney at Wilmer, Cutler & Pickering, where he practices in the Communications Practice Group with an emphasis on electronic commerce, the Internet and telecommunications. Mr. Jain has represented Internet service providers and other clients before federal and state courts concerning such issues as defamation, privacy, the First Amendment, electronic surveillance and telecommunications regulation, as well as counseling clients concerning a variety of Internet law matters, including online consumer protection. Mr. Jain served as a law clerk to Judge James Browning of the United States Court of Appeals for the Ninth Circuit. Mr. Jain is a graduate of Stanford University and Harvard Law School, where he was an editor of the *Harvard Law Review* and articles editor of the *Journal of Law and Technology*.

Lance C. Martin is an associate in the San Francisco/Palo Alto office of Baker & McKenzie and a member of the Tax Practice Group. Mr. Martin specializes in international tax planning. He is a member of the Taxation Section of the American Bar Association and the California State Bar Association. Mr. Martin received his J.D. form the University of California, Berkeley, Boalt Hall School of Law in 1998.

Elliot E. Maxwell is presently Senior Fellow for the Digital Economy and director of the Internet Policy Project for the Aspen Institute's Communications and Society Program. The Internet Policy Project addresses emerging legal and policy issues likely to affect the growth and development of the Internet. Prior to joining the Aspen Institute, he was special advisor to the U.S. Secretary of Commerce for the Digital Economy. In this position, he served as principal advisor on the Internet and electronic commerce to Secretary William Daley and Secretary Norman Mineta. He graduated from Brown University and Yale University Law School.

William McSpadden is a registered patent attorney in the Dallas office of Baker & McKenzie. Prior to attending law school, Mr. McSpadden studied electrical engineering at the University of Texas and worked as a semiconductor engineer at National Semiconductor. Mr. McSpadden's practice focuses on a variety of intellectual property issues, including patent prosecution, patent litigation and patent opinion work.

Amanda J. Mills is currently a student at Yale Law School. She has worked in the Office of the Secretary of the U.S. Department of Commerce and assisted Donna Hoffman of the Owen Graduate School of Management in her studies of disparate online access. She earned her B.A. from Vanderbilt University where she majored in Communication, Technology, and Public Policy.

Sabrina L. Montes is a policy analyst in the Economics and Statistics Administration of the U.S. Department of Commerce where she explores the economic and policy implications of the Internet and other emerging information technologies. She earned a masters degree in public policy from the University of Michigan and her bachelor's degree from the University of California at Davis.

Jeffrey Neuburger is a partner in the New York office of Brown Raysman Millstein Felder & Steiner, LLP, where he specializes in the areas of technology, new media and the Internet.

Raymond T. Nimmer is a Leonard Childs Professor of Law at the University of Houston Law Center and co-director of the Houston Intellectual Property and Information Law Program. Professor Nimmer is the reporter to the Drafting Committee on the Uniform Computer Information Tranactions Act, which addresses the licensing of computer information under state contract law. He also serves as a consultant to the Office of the Legal Advisor of the U.S. State Department. Mr. Nimmer is listed in *Who's Who in America* and *Who's Who in American Law*, as well as in the *International Who's Who of Internet Lawyers*.

J. Pat Powers is a partner in the San Francisco/Palo Alto office of Baker & McKenzie and currently serves as chairman of Baker & McKenzie's State and Local Tax Practice. He is a recognized innovator in tax planning and has created and developed many of the leading techniques used by multinationals to reduce their worldwide tax burden, such as use of factoring companies and use of foreign entities classifiable as partnerships for U.S. tax purposes. Mr. Powers earned a J.D. from the University of California, Berkeley, Boalt Hall School of Law in 1974. At Boalt, he served as an editor of the California Law Review. Upon graduation he was elected to Order of the Coif.

Taylor S. Reid is an associate in the San Francisco/Palo Alto office of Baker & McKenzie and a member of the firm's Tax Practice and E-Commerce Groups. He is a member of the American Bar Association, Section of Taxation and is admitted to practice law in California, Illinois and before the U.S. Tax Court. Mr. Reid received his J.D., *cum laude*, from Northwestern University School of Law in 1993, where he served as articles editor on the Northwestern Journal of International Law and Business.

Denis T. Rice, a founding member of Howard, Rice, has been listed in "Best Lawyers in America" both as a corporate lawyer and business litigator. Mr. Rice is chair of the Committee on Cyberspace Law of the California State Bar and of the ABA's subcommittees on Asia-Pacific Law and International Venture Capital, and vice-chair of the Committee on International Securities Transactions of the ABA's Section on International Law. He chaired the Working Group on Securities of the ABA Project on Jurisdiction in Cyberspace and is former vice-chair of the State Bar Business Law Section and chair of its Committee on the Administration of Justice. Mr. Rice has published two dozen articles and several books on Internet law and securities law. He is a graduate of Princeton University and Michigan Law School.

Martin L. Saad is an associate in the Washington, D.C. office of Venable, Baetjer, Howard & Civiletti. He concentrates his practice on intellectual property and competition law litigation. He earned his J.D. and undergraduate degree in economics at the University of Michigan.

Valerio Salce is an attorney in the Rome office of Baker & McKenzie where he is the co-coordinator of the IT/C Practice Group. Mr. Salce specializes in mergers and acquisitions, information technology, intellectual property and e-commerce law. He is admitted to practice in Italy and in New York. He received his law degree from La Sapienza University of Rome and earned an LL.M. from Georgetown University Law Center.

Thomas J. Smedinghoff is a partner with the law firm of Baker & McKenzie and North American coordinator of the firm's Electronic Commerce Law Practice. He was chair of the Illinois Commission on Electronic Commerce and Crime and author of the Illinois Electronic Commerce Security Act, 5 Ill. Comp. Stat. 175/5–1-5. Mr. Smedinghoff was the 1999–2000 chair of the American Bar Association's Section of Science & Technology Law and is the current chair of the American Bar Association's Electronic Commerce Division. He is a member of the U.S. delegation to the United Nations Commission on International Trade Law (UNCITRAL), through which he participates in the Working Group on Electronic Commerce that is drafting international electronic and digital signature legislation.

Jan S. Snel is an associate in the Amsterdam office of Baker & McKenzie and a member of the Tax Practice Group. His practice emphasizes international EU VAT and customs law, primarily on behalf of high-tech and e-commerce companies. Mr. Snel is an active member of the Dutch Bar Association, the Dutch Tax Advisers Bar Association, The Dutch Tax Scholar Association and speaks four languages. Mr. Snel graduated from the University of Nijmegen (Netherlands) Law School in 1994 and from the same in 1995 with a Notarial law degree. In 1998, Mr. Snel graduated from the University of Amsterdam Tax Law School.

Margaret G. Stewart is a professor of law at IIT Chicago-Kent College of law where she has taught since 1977. After graduating from Northwestern University School of Law in 1971, where she served as notes and comments editor of the Law Review, she was an associate with Willkie Farr & Gallagher in New York for three years before joining the faculty at the University of South Carolina Law Center prior to moving to Chicago-Kent. Professor Stewart teaches and publishes in the fields of civil procedure and constitutional law. Most recently, she served as the reporter for a project on transnational jurisdictional issues and the Internet sponsored by the Business Law Section of the American Bar Association.

William F. Swiggart is partner in Swiggart & Agin, LLC, and concentrates his practice in the representation of technology companies. Mr. Swiggart has served as general counsel and Secretary to Bitstream Inc., a Cambridge-based software company (BITS on NASDAQ), and as general counsel of ON Technology Corporation (ONTC on NASDAQ). He is author of numerous legal articles and addresses on topics of business and technology law.

Thomas P. Vartanian is a partner resident in Fried Frank's Washington, DC office and is the chairman of its Electronic Commerce and Technology Transactions Group. He is the former managing partner of the Washington, DC office and chairman of its Corporate Department (1987–1999). He joined the firm in 1983. Mr. Vartanian is a nationally known writer of numerous books and publications, lecturer, and radio and television commentator on electronic commerce and financial services issues. Mr. Vartanian is chair of the American Bar Association's Committee on Cyberspace Law.

Barbara Wellbery is a partner in the Washington office of Morrison & Foerster LLP. She was previously counselor to the Under Secretary for Electronic Commerce in the U.S. Department of Commerce. While there, she was the chief architect and a principal negotiator of the safe harbor privacy accord between the U.S. and the European Union.

Mary L. Williamson is a partner in the Technology and Intellectual Property department of Preston Gates & Ellis, where she practices in the areas of technology licensing, e-commerce and international transactions. She represents a variety of developers and distributors of software, telecommunications and other high technology products and services. Her practice includes advising clients on issues involving electronic commerce in both the national and international contexts. Ms. Williamson received her J.D. from Stanford Law School and holds an M.A. from the Johns Hopkins School of Advanced International Studies.

Mark Wittow is a partner in Preston Gates & Ellis LLP's Technology and Intellectual Property Department, where he focuses on transactions and litigation concerning the acquisition, development and distribution of computer technologies and online services and the licensing of intellectual property. His recent experience includes representation of Microsoft in its litigation with Sun Microsystems concerning the licensing of Java technology and of the Business Software Alliance in the *Mortenson v. Timberline* appeals concerning software licensing issues. He currently chairs the Copyright Subcommittee of the Computer Programs Committee of the Intellectual Property Law Section of the American Bar Association.